Also Available from McGraw-Hill

Schaum's Outline Series in Civil Engineering

Most outlines include basic theory, definitions, and hundreds of example problems solved in step-by-step detail, and supplementary problems with answers.

Related titles on the current list include:

Descriptive Geometry
Elementary Statics & Strength of Materials
Engineering Economics
Engineering Mechanics
Fluid Dynamics
Fluid Mechanics & Hydraulics
Introductory Surveying
Mathematical Handbook of Formulas & Tables
Mechanical Vibrations
Reinforced Concrete Design
Statics & Mechanics of Materials
Strength of Materials
Structural Analysis
Structural Steel Design (Load and Resistance Factor Method)
Theoretical Mechanics

Schaum's Solved Problems Books

Each title in this series is a complete and expert source of solved problems with solutions worked out in step-by-step detail.

Related titles on the current list include:

3000 Solved Problems in Calculus
2500 Solved Problems in Differential Equations
2500 Solved Problems in Fluid Mechanics & Hydraulics
3000 Solved Problems in Linear Algebra
2000 Solved Problems in Numerical Analysis
700 Solved Problems in Vector Mechanics for Engineers: Dynamics
800 Solved Problems in Vector Mechanics for Engineers: Statics

Available at most college bookstores, or for a complete list of titles and prices, write to: Schaum
          A Division of the McGraw-Hill Companies
          11 West 19th Street
          New York, NY 10011

CONSTRUCTION PLANNING, EQUIPMENT, AND METHODS

Fifth Edition

R. L. Peurifoy, P.E.
Late Consulting Engineer
Austin, Texas

W. B. Ledbetter, P.E.
Consulting Engineer
Pendleton, South Carolina

C. J. Schexnayder, P.E.
Eminent Scholar
Del E. Webb School of Construction
Arizona State University

The McGraw-Hill Companies, Inc.

New York   St. Louis   San Francisco   Auckland   Bogotá   Caracas   Lisbon
London   Madrid   Mexico City   Milan   Montreal   New Delhi
San Juan   Singapore   Sydney   Tokyo   Toronto

CONSTRUCTION PLANNING, EQUIPMENT, AND METHODS
International Editions 1996

4 5 6 7 8 9 0 CMO PMP 9 8

This book was set in Times Roman by Publication Services, Inc.
The editors were B. J. Clark and James W. Bradley;
the production supervisor was Leroy A. Young.
The cover was designed by Carla Bauer.

Library of Congress Cataloging-in-Publication Data

Peurifoy, R.L. (Robert Leroy), (date).
    Construction planning, equipment, and methods / R.L. Peurifoy.
  W.B. Ledbetter, C.J. Schexnayder.
    p.   cm.
    Includes bibliographical references and index.
    ISBN 0-07-049836-9
    1. Building.   I. Ledbetter, William Burt.   II. Schexnayder, Cliff J.
  III. Title.
  TH145.P45   1996
  624–dc20   95-10819

ABOUT THE AUTHORS

R.L. Peurifoy (1902–1995) was a retired Civil Engineering Professor and Consultant in the project management aspects of design and construction of engineered facilities. Refer to the Dedication (p. viii).

W.B. Ledbetter is a consultant in the quality performance management aspects of design and construction of engineered projects. Holding the doctorate degree in Civil Engineering, he has worked in private practice, industry, the government, and higher education for more than 30 years. He has held professorships at Texas A&M University and Clemson University. As the developer of the Quality Performance Management System for the Construction Industry Institute, Dr. Ledbetter guided its implementation by major owners, engineering firms, and construction companies in the United States, Canada, and Europe. He has developed practical engineering solutions in the fields of quality performance management, project management, engineering economy, and concrete construction, to name a few. He has published more than 60 technical publications, is a registered professional engineer, and holds memberships in the American Society of Civil Engineers (Fellow), American Society for Quality Control, and the National Society of Professional Engineers.

C.J. Schexnayder holds the Eminent Scholar position in the Del E. Webb School of Construction at Arizona State University. He received his Ph.D. in Civil Engineering from Purdue University. A construction engineer with over 30 years of practical experience, he has worked on major heavy/highway projects as a field engineer, estimator, and corporate Chief Engineer. He is a registered professional engineer in nine states and a member of the American Society for Engineering Education, the Transportation Research Board, and the American Society of Civil Engineers, having served as chairman of ASCE's Construction Division.

DEDICATION

R. L. Peurifoy held the bachelors and masters degrees in Civil Engineering, and he worked in industry, the government, and higher education for more than 40 years. He held professorships at Texas A&M University, Oklahoma State University, and the University of Santiago, Chile. One of the leading pioneers in project management, he established one of the first such educational programs at Texas A&M. His three books on construction have enjoyed worldwide use for more than 30 years. In recognition of his outstanding accomplishments, the American Society of Civil Engineers established the Robert L. Peurifoy Construction Research Award in 1985. Among his other honors and awards is the ASCE Construction Management Award in 1979.

He remained active throughout his life, providing leadership for this fifth edition. Along with this book. his legacy lives on through his two children, six grandchildren, and five great grandchildren.

W. B. Ledbetter

CONTENTS

PREFACE

[handwritten margin notes:]
- *government power.*
- *contractor*
- *workforce*
- *designer/architect*
- *other contributors*
- *owner*
- *reporter, tenant.*

The construction industry continues to progress through improvements in equipment, planning, and construction methods. This fifth edition follows in the tradition of the first four by providing the reader with the fundamentals and applications of many of these advances in a logical, simple, and concise format.

Significant changes have been made to this edition. The chapters on "Operational Analysis," "Foundation Grouting," and "Tunneling" have been dropped because they are specialized subjects requiring much more coverage than is possible in this text. Two new chapters have been added, "Cranes" and "Asphalt Mix Production and Placement." Cranes, which were covered in previous editions as part of "Excavation Equipment," have been expanded to include tower cranes and selected other important uses of this versatile piece of equipment. "Asphalt Mix Production and Placement" is included because asphalts are widely used in highways, roads, and streets. Each of the remaining chapters has undergone revision, ranging from simple clarification to major modifications, depending on the need to present the latest technology.

This book enjoys wide use as a reference book by the profession and as a college textbook. We have continued the practice of including liberal use of updated illustrations of equipment and methods. We have kept the use of examples throughout the text as they reinforce the concepts through practical application.

To enhance the value of the book as a college textbook, we have updated and expanded the problems at the close of each chapter. Together with the examples, they facilitate learning and give students the confidence that they can master the subjects being presented.

At the close of most chapters there are names and addresses of manufacturers of construction equipment illustrated and described in this book. We are deeply grateful to the many individuals and firms who have supplied information and illustrations. Two individuals are owed a particular debt of gratitude for their support and efforts. Mr. Pat Gleuso of Neil F. Lampson, Inc., contributed many ideas and a critical review of the chapter on "Cranes." Mr. R. R. Walker of Tidewater Construction Corporation drafted the revised chapter on "Piles and Pile-Driving Equipment" and assembled many of the figures included in the chapter. We would like to express our thanks for the many useful comments and suggestions provided by the following reviewers:

Laura Demsetz, University of California;
F. H. Griffis, Columbia University;
Donn Haucher, University of Kentucky; and
Raymond E. Levitt, Stanford University.

However, we take full responsibility for the material. Finally, we wish to acknowledge the comments and suggestions for improvement received from persons using the book. We solicit comments on this edition.

R. L. Peurifoy
W. B. Ledbetter
C. J. Schexnayder

LIST OF ABBREVIATIONS AND SYMBOLS

ACI	American Concrete Institute
AOA	Activity on arrow
AON	Activity on node
ASTM	American Society for Testing and Materials
AGC	Associated General Contractors of America, Inc.
bbl	barrel
bhp	brake horsepower
bm	bank measure, volume of earth prior to loosening
°*C*	Celsius temperature
cfm	cubic feet per minute
const	construction
cpm	cycles per minute
cps	cycles per second (hertz)
cu ft	cubic foot
cu m	cubic meter
cu yd	cubic yard
cwt	100 pounds
deg	degree
est	estimated
°*F*	Fahrenheit temperature
FOB	free on board
fpm	feet per minute
fps	feet per second
ft	foot
ft-lb	foot-pound
gal	gallon
gpm	gallons per minute

hp	horsepower
hr	hour
in.	inch
kW	kilowatt
lb	pound
lin ft	linear foot
M	1,000
m	meter
m³	cubic meter
max	maximum
M fbm	1,000 feet board measure of lumber
min	minute, minimum
mm	millimeter
mph	miles per hour
op	operation
PERT	Program evaluation review technique
plf	pounds per linear foot
psf	pounds per square foot
psi	pounds per square inch
rpm	revolutions per minute
sec	second
sq ft	square foot
sq in.	square inch
square	100 square feet of area
sq yd	square yard
std	standard
tph	tons per hour
wk	week
yd	yard
yr	year

CONSTRUCTION PLANNING, EQUIPMENT, AND METHODS

1

INTRODUCTION

THE PURPOSE OF THIS BOOK

All the parties involved in a construction project—owner, designer, supplier, constructor, and end user—strive for the same goal: a facility meeting the expectations of the owner and end user. Concepts expressed by the owner are turned into design drawings, specifications, and purchase orders by the designer. Materials and equipment are purchased and shipped to the construction site. *Construction* is the step in which the plans, specifications, materials, and permanent equipment are transformed by a constructor, usually called a *contractor,* into a finished facility.

Construction of engineered facilities requires the utilization of construction equipment. This book applies engineering fundamentals and analyses to the planning, selection, and utilization of construction equipment. Construction equipment planning and selection begin long before a constructor moves onto the construction site. Information is presented to assist the reader in understanding (1) the total construction process, from inception of the idea through construction and start up, and (2) how construction equipment should be selected and used to produce the intended quality in the most cost-effective manner.

THE CONSTRUCTION INDUSTRY

The construction industry in the United States is a $400 billion industry, with over one million constructors employing five million people. The industry is unique in several respects. First among the factors which make the construction industry unique is that constructors strive very hard to work themselves out of a job. The faster and better they perform, the sooner they will be looking for another project to build. The word *cyclic* takes on a much larger meaning in construction because work is often boom or bust, with many employees working for short durations at remote sites, being laid off

1

as projects are completed, traveling to another remote site, and working on a new, short-term project for a different constructor.

Second, the products of construction are usually one-of-a-kind facilities, individually designed and built. The construction labor force comes together at the start of the project and must be quickly indoctrinated in the specific project by the project management.

Third, construction is inherently a dangerous occupation, involving large and costly construction equipment. Even on a small project, expensive equipment is often employed and the value of this equipment may exceed the contract value.

The ability of a constructor to win contracts and to perform them at a profit is determined by two vital assets: people and construction equipment. This equipment often represents the constructor's primary capital investment. To be economically competitive, the equipment spread must be competitive—mechanically, technologically, and productively. Old equipment must be replaced with newer, safer, more reliable, and more productive equipment. The spread must be designed to perform in an optimum manner. This requires careful planning of the construction process so that people and machines work as a team to complete the facility at the least possible cost.

CONSTRUCTION CONTRACTS

An understanding of construction contracts is essential for the proper management of a construction project, and the engineer/architect contributes an important service in developing the contract. While the subject is exceedingly complex and beyond the scope of this book to cover in any significant detail, fundamental concepts and definitions are introduced. For more complete information on construction contracts the reader can refer to a number of excellent texts, some of which are cited at the end of this chapter.

Although there are many types of construction contracts, all of them must contain four attributes to be valid. First, there must be an *agreement* between the parties involved. Such an agreement involves *offer* (e.g., the signed bid by a constructor proposing to construct a project constitutes an offer) and *acceptance* (e.g., when the owner notifies the winning proposer). Second, there must be *consideration*. In the case of a construction contract, if a constructor promises to build an addition to a home without compensation and then changes his mind, he generally cannot be forced to build the addition because there was no *consideration* for his services. Third, there must be *capacity*. This means that both parties must be of sufficient age to enter into a contract and mentally aware of what they are doing. Finally, for a contract to be valid, it must be *legal*. Obviously, a contract between two parties in which one agrees to commit an illegal act cannot be enforced! Of the many types of construction contracts, generally most will fall into one or more of three general types: the lump-sum contract, the unit-price contract, and the cost-plus-fee contract.

Lump-sum contract. The terms of this contract provide that the owner will pay to the constructor an agreed-upon sum of money for the completion of a project conforming to a well-defined scope of work. If the contract is for construction, the scope should include complete plans and specifications furnished by the owner (or his agent, an engineer, or an architect). It is common practice for the owner to pay the constructor a portion of this money at specified intervals, such as monthly, with the amount of each payment depending on the value of the work completed during the prior period of time, or according to some other agreed-upon schedule of payments. Under the terms of this contract a constructor may earn a profit (if he prepared a good estimate and stayed within budget) or he may sustain a loss (if his actual costs exceed his estimate). This is the preferred type of contract for many construction services because the owner can obtain the benefits of competitive bidding and knows what the project will cost before he enters into a contract with a constructor. However, *effective* lump-sum contracts can *only* be obtained if well-defined scopes of work are prepared in advance, which requires very careful and complete planning and scheduling.

Unit-price contract. The terms of this type of contract provide that the owner will pay to the constructor an agreed-upon amount of money for each unit of work completed in a project. The units of work may be any items whose quantities can be determined. In a construction contract this may be cubic yards of earth, lineal feet of pipe, square yards of concrete pavement in-place, and so on. Payments are usually made by the owner to the constructor at specified intervals during the construction of the project, with the amount of each payment depending on work actually completed during the prior period of time. This type of contract also requires a complete scope of work and is the preferred type of contract when the actual final quantities are not known with certainty beforehand. For example, the exact amounts of soil and rock to be excavated may not be known until the constructor actually performs the excavation. The owner, by requiring this type of contract, obtains the benefits of competitive bidding without having constructors bidding higher to cover the unknown quantities involved. Under the terms of this contract the constructor may earn a profit or incur a loss, depending on the accuracy of his estimate per unit of work. The risk associated with quantities has been assumed by the owner.

Cost-plus-fee contract. The terms of this type of contract provide that the owner will reimburse the constructor for all costs specified to construct the project, including all labor costs, material costs, equipment usage costs, subcontractor costs, and job supervision costs. In addition, the owner agrees to pay the constructor an additional fee, which is essentially a management fee, and to reimburse the constructor for the costs incurred at both his head and field offices resulting from the execution of the project. Items which are usually included in the fee are such costs as rent, taxes, insurance, interest on borrowed money for the project, and main office supervision and control costs, to name a few. Finally, the fee will include some expected profit for the constructor as that is the primary reason for the constructor to be in business. Whether or not the constructor actually makes a profit depends only on how accurately he estimated his other costs which make up the remainder of the fee. Under this type of contract the constructor usually takes the least risk, and therefore has the least incentive to keep costs down. It is used primarily in situations where the scope of work cannot be well defined ahead of construction or when the state of the art for the particular project is not well known. To exercise some control and to give some incentive to the constructor to hold costs down, there are many variations to this type of contract, including cost-plus-a-percentage-of-cost, cost-plus-a-fixed-fee, and cost-plus-a-sliding-fee, all with guaranteed maximums or with incentives for holding down costs. These types of contracts are complicated, and the reader should examine specific references in this area for more information.

PERFORMANCE GUARANTEES

Constructors frequently are required to furnish a performance bond for each project. This bond, which is not to be confused with insurance, is a three-party instrument in which a bonding company (termed *surety*) guarantees (or bonds) to the owner that the project will be built by the constructor in accordance with the contract. If for any reason the constructor becomes unable or unwilling to complete the contract, the surety will take steps to engage another constructor to complete the contract or to take other steps as specified in the instrument. The cost of a performance bond will vary, depending on the size and risk of the contract and the reputation and expertise of the constructor. In general, constructors with good reputations who are constructing typical projects can obtain performance bonds for something less than 1% of the project cost.

CONSTRUCTOR SPECIALTIES

Constructors tend to specialize somewhat in various types of work. Although there are no clear-cut lines separating the many fields of construction, they may be divided into *residential*, *building-commercial*, *industrial*, *highway-heavy*, and *specialty*. Specialty constructors are numerous and include those involved with pipeline, power, transmission line, steel erection, railroad, offshore, pile driving, concrete pumping, to name a few. The reasons for specialization involve complexity and uniqueness. Few constructors are large enough to have the necessary expertise and sufficient inventory of expensive construction equipment to engage in all types of construction.

EQUIPMENT-INTENSIVE OPERATIONS AND RISKS

By the nature of the product, the constructor works under a unique set of production conditions which directly affect the selection of construction equipment. Whereas most manufacturing companies have a permanent factory where raw materials are transformed into permanent products in a repeating, assembly-line process, a construction company carries its factory to each job site. At each site the constructor erects a construction plant specifically designed for that project. While a manufacturer can "fine tune" his manufacturing process to eliminate waste and to increase productivity, the constructor has little opportunity for such fine tuning. Construction projects are completed too fast, and lessons learned from previous projects have limited applicability to future projects because of the one-of-a-kind nature of each construction project. Thus, there are significant risks involved in utilizing construction equipment, especially on those jobs requiring large equipment-resource investment. Such projects as earth and rock dam construction and canal work demand large concentrations of equipment. In addition, such work is usually bid on a unit-price basis and can be subject to large variations between estimated and actual quantities. Highway work, often the least profitable of all heavy construction projects, frequently requires an equipment commitment that is greater than the gross contract value. Such a situation forces a highway constructor into a continuing sequence of jobs in order to support his long-term equipment payments. In such circumstances a business condition of desperation can easily arise, pushing profit margins still lower. Furthermore, highway work is usually spread over several miles, making its control and management very difficult.

Airport construction is another heavy construction area which requires a large equipment spread. But perhaps the most volatile type of equipment-intensive work is pipeline construction. Those constructors who build the big cross-country lines must maintain equipment spreads that are capable of putting a mile or more of pipe in the ground each day. Because of the speed of pipeline work, they are hard pressed to keep current on job costs and overruns. All the aforementioned types of construction, because of their outdoor nature, share a critical dependence on the climate and the weather.

Additional risk factors facing constructors in equipment-intensive work include financing mechanisms, construction activity levels, labor regulations and agreements, and safety. Projects requiring two or more years to complete are not uncommon in the industry. Contract payment retention provisions allow owners to retain substantial dollar amounts, which constructors have already earned, for long periods of time. Although retainage is a receivable and shows as an asset on a constructor's books, it cannot be utilized for operation and growth and can cause serious cash flow problems. Many constructors consider cash flow to be the critical factor in any equipment decision.

Construction activity level is another risk factor which can seriously affect equipment decisions. Since a large portion of the construction activity in the equipment-intensive contracting areas is attributable to government-sponsored projects, control of the funds for such work provides the bureaucracy with a direct method of regulating the economy. During slow or stagnant times funds can be pumped into projects to stimulate the economy. During rapid-growth and inflationary times funds can be withheld and project starts can be delayed. By being in the direct chain of action used by the government to control *economic* cycles, a constructor can be affected no matter which way the cycle is moving.

During such economic swings a construction company with required long-term equipment payments may be forced to seek short-term work at severely reduced profit margins or, in some cases, with no profit at all. However, if such a financial policy is pursued past the short term, it will quickly make equipment decisions moot since the constructor will be broke!

Three other government-initiated actions which seriously affect the operating environment of the construction contractor are labor legislation/regulation, safety directives, and workmen's compensation insurance. In each of these areas there are a multitude of regulations which impact on a constructor's operations and that may directly influence equipment decisions. Legislative acts which exert direct pressure on equipment questions include the Davis-Bacon Act, which is concerned with wage rates; the Occupational Safety and Health Act, which specifies workplace safety requirements; and each state's requirement that employers pay compensation benefits to their employees for job-related injuries. Over one-half the dollar volume of work in the equipment-intensive fields of construction is subject to wage determinations under the Davis-Bacon

Act, and this strongly influences the labor costs incurred by constructors. The Occupational Safety and Health Act (OSHA), by its rollover protective structures mandate, substantially increased the cost of construction equipment. This particular regulation had a single-point-in-time effect on equipment decisions, much like that resulting from the introduction of new equipment technology. The possibility remains for additional safety requirements (e.g., sound attenuation), which will trigger other "step-jumps" in equipment cost. And finally, in many states workmen's compensation insurance costs have grown *significantly*, increasing construction costs and eroding profits on long-term projects which were contracted on a fixed-price basis.

CONSTRUCTION ECONOMICS AND THE DESIGNER

The cost of a project is determined by the requirements of the contract documents. Prior to completing the final design, the engineer should give careful consideration to the method and equipment which may be used to construct the project. Requirements which increase the cost without producing commensurate benefits should be eliminated. The decisions of the engineer should be based on a sound knowledge of the construction methods and equipment to be employed.

The budget for a project may be divided into six or more items: materials, labor, equipment, subcontracts, overhead, and profit/risk. The design engineer has a strong influence over the cost of these items. If the engineer specifies materials which must be transported over long distances, or specifies excessive testing, or does not allow substitution of equal-quality materials, the costs may be higher than necessary. Other costly engineering practices include requiring many one-of-a-kind items which cannot be mass-produced, using nonstandard materials or techniques when not required, and establishing standards of quality that are higher than necessary.

The following list indicates some methods which an engineer may use to reduce the costs of construction:

1. Design concrete structures with as many duplicate members as practical in order to permit the reuse of forms without rebuilding.
2. Simplify the design of the structure where possible.
3. Design for the use of cost-saving equipment and methods. For example, use prefabricated items as much as possible.
4. Eliminate unnecessary special construction requirements.
5. Design to minimize labor-intensive activities.
6. Specify a quality of workmanship that is consistent with required project quality.
7. Furnish adequate subsurface information where possible.
8. Refrain from requiring the constructor to assume the adequacy of design or the responsibility for information that should be furnished by the engineer or architect.
9. Use local materials when they are satisfactory.
10. Write simple, straightforward specifications which clearly state what is expected. Define either the results expected or the methods of accomplishing the desired results, but not both.

11. When possible, use standardized specifications which are familiar to the constructors.
12. Hold prebidding conferences with constructors in order to eliminate uncertainties.
13. Use inspectors who have sufficient judgment and experience to understand the project and to give them the authority to make decisions.

CONSTRUCTION ECONOMICS AND THE CONSTRUCTOR

Most construction contractors work within a unique market situation. The job plans and specifications, which are supplied by the owner, will dictate the sales conditions and product, but not the price. The vast majority of work in the construction industry is awarded on a bid basis, through either open or selective tender procedures. The constructor states his price after estimating the cost, including his overhead, evaluating the risk, and adding a desired profit. It is tacitly assumed that the winning constructor has been able to underbid his competitors because of a more efficient work plan, lower overhead costs, or a willingness to accept a lower profit.

Not infrequently, however, the range between the high and low bids is much greater than these factors would justify. The primary cause for this variance in bids is the constructor's inability to estimate costs accurately. Each construction project usually represents a custom-built situation which is subject to a new set of governing cost conditions, requiring atypical estimates. However, the largest portion of estimating variance is probably not caused by this but, rather, by a lack of accurate cost records. Many constructors have cost-reporting systems, but in numerous cases the systems fail to allocate expenses to the proper sources, and therefore cause false conclusions when used as the historical database for estimating future work.

A construction company owner will frequently use both contract volume and contract turnover to measure the strength of his firm. Contract volume refers to the total dollar value of awarded contracts which a firm has on its books *at any given time*. Contract turnover measures the dollar value of work that a firm completes during a specific *time interval*. Contract volume is a guide to the magnitude of resources that a firm has committed at any one time, as well as to possible profit if the work is completed as estimated. But contract volume fails to answer any timing questions. A constructor who, with the same contract volume as his competitors, is able to achieve a more rapid project completion, and therefore a higher capital turnover rate while maintaining his revenue-to-expense ratio, will be able to increase his firm's profits. Construction management's most effective procedure to maximize profit is to improve production and to increase contract turnover.

THE TIME VALUE OF MONEY

Today almost everyone is aware of the fact that money has a time value. One dollar today is worth more than $1 tomorrow. This fact is vividly reinforced when monthly charge bills are examined. Failure to pay the bill promptly results in an imposed additional charge. This added charge amounts to rent/risk on the money that is owed, termed *interest.* Interest, usually expressed as a percentage of the amount owed, becomes due and payable at the close of each period of time involved in the statement of the bill. For example, if $1,000.00 is borrowed at 14% interest, then $0.14 \times 1,000$, or $140.00, in interest is owed on the *principal* of $1,000.00 after one year. If the borrower pays back the total amount owed after one year, she will pay $1,140.00. If she does not pay back any of the amount owed after one year, then normally the interest owed, but not paid, is considered now to be additional principal, and thus the interest is *compounded.* Then after two years she will owe $1,140.00 + 0.14 \times 1,140.00$, or $1,299.60. If your credit is good and you have borrowed the $1,000.00 from the bank, the banker normally does not care whether you pay him $1,140.00 after one year or $1,299.60 after two years. To him, the three values ($1,000, $1,140, and $1,299.60) are *equivalent.* In other words, $1,000 today is equivalent to $1,140 one year from today, which is equivalent to $1,299.60 two years from today. While these three values are obviously not equal, they are *equivalent.* *Note that the concept of equivalence involves time and a specified rate of interest.* The three preceding values are only equivalent for an interest rate of 14%, and then only at the specified times. *Equivalence* means that one sum or series differs from another only by the accrued, accumulated interest at rate i for n periods of time.

Note that in the example the principal amount was multiplied by an interest rate to obtain the amount of interest due. To generalize this concept, we use the following symbols:

P = a present single amount of money
F = a future single amount of money, after n periods of time
i = the rate of interest per interest period (usually one year)
n = the number of periods of time (usually years)

Equations for single payments. To calculate the future value F of a single payment P after n periods at an interest rate i, we make the following calculation:

At the end of the first period: $F_1 = P + Pi$
At the end of the second period: $F_2 = P + Pi + (P + Pi)i = P(1 + i)^2$
At the end of the nth period: $F = P(1 + i)^n$

Or the future single amount of a present single amount is

$$F = P(1 + i)^n \tag{1-1}$$

Note that F is related to P by a factor which depends only on i and n. This factor, termed the *single payment compound amount factor* (SPCAF), makes F equivalent to P. This factor may be expressed in a functional form as

$$(1 + i)^n = \left(\frac{F}{P}, i, n\right)$$

and Eq. (1-1) can be expressed as

$$F = P\left(\frac{F}{P}, i, n\right) \tag{1-1a}$$

If a future amount F is given, the present amount P can be calculated by transposing the equation to

$$P = \frac{F}{(1 + i)^n} \tag{1-2}$$

or in functional form as

$$P = F\left(\frac{P}{F}, i, n\right) \tag{1-2a}$$

The factor $1/(1 + i)^n$ is known as the *present worth compound amount factor* (PWCAF). To compute either P or F, one only needs to solve Eq. (1-1) or Eq. (1-2). Tables of values for the two functions for typical values of i and n are given in Appendix A.

Example 1-1. A constructor wishes to set up a revolving line of credit at the bank to handle her cash flow during the construction of a project. She believes that she needs to borrow $12,000 with which to set up the account, and that she can obtain the money at 1.45% per month. If she pays back the loan and accumulated interest after 8 months, how much will she have to pay back?

To solve, use Eq. (1-1):

$$F = 12,000(1 + 0.0145)^8 = 12,000(1.122061)$$
$$= 13,464.73 = \$13,465$$

The amount of interest will be $1,465.

Example 1-2. A construction company wants to set aside enough money today in an interest-bearing account in order to have $100,000 five years from now for the purchase of a replacement piece of equipment. If the company can receive 8% interest on its investment, how much should be set aside now to accrue the $100,000 five years from now?

To solve, use Eq. (1-2):

$$P = \frac{100,000}{(1 + 0.08)^5} = \frac{100,000}{(1.46933)} = \$68,058.32 = \$68,060$$

An alternate solution is to use the tables in Appendix A. Here the functional form of the equation is used [Eq. (1-2a)]:

$$P = 100,000\left(\frac{P}{F}, 8, 5\right) = 100,000(0.6805832)$$
$$= \$68,058.32 = \$68,060$$

In the preceding examples and explanation equivalent single payments now and in the future were equated. Four parameters were involved: P, F, i, and n. *Given any three parameters, the fourth can easily be calculated.*

Formulas for a uniform series of payments. Often payments or receipts occur at regular intervals, and such uniform values can be handled by the use of additional functions. First, let us define another symbol:

A = uniform *end-of-period* payments or receipts continuing for a duration of n periods

If this uniform amount A is invested at the end of each period for n periods at a rate of interest i per period, then the total equivalent amount F at the end of the n periods will be

$$F = A[(1 + i)^{n-1} + (1 + i)^{n-2} + \cdots + (1 + i) + 1]$$

By multiplying both sides of the equation by $(1 + i)$ and by subtracting the result from the original equation, we obtain

$$Fi = A(1 + i)^n - 1$$

which can be rearranged to

$$F = A\left[\frac{(1 + i)^n - 1}{i}\right] \tag{1-3}$$

This relationship can also be expressed in functional form as

$$F = A\left(\frac{F}{A}, i, n\right) \tag{1-3a}$$

The relationship $[(1 + i)^n - 1]/i$ is sometimes known as the *uniform series, compound amount factor* (USCAF).

The relationship can be rearranged to yield

$$A = F\left[\frac{i}{(1 + i)^n - 1}\right] \tag{1-4}$$

which can be expressed in functional form as

$$A = F\left(\frac{A}{F}, i, n\right) \tag{1-4a}$$

The relationship $i/[(1 + i)^n - 1]$ is known as the *uniform series sinking fund factor* (USSFF) because it determines the uniform end-of-period investment A that must be made in order to provide an amount F at the end of n periods.

In order to determine the equivalent uniform periodic series required to replace a present value of P, simply substitute Eq. (1-1) for F into Eq. (1-4) and rearrange. The resulting equation is

$$P = A\left[\frac{(1 + i)^n - 1}{i(1 + i)^n}\right] \tag{1-5}$$

In functional form the equation is

$$P = A\left(\frac{P}{A}, i, n\right) \tag{1-5a}$$

This relationship is known as the *uniform series present worth factor* (USPWF).

By inverting Eq. (1-5), we can obtain the equivalent uniform series of end-of-period values A from a present value P. The resulting equation is

$$A = P\left[\frac{i(1 + i)^n}{(1 + i)^n - 1}\right] \tag{1-6}$$

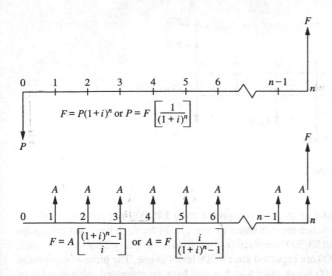

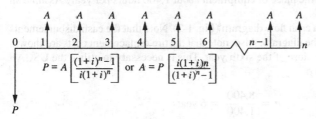

FIGURE 1-1
Cash flow diagrams.

In functional form the equation is

$$A = P\left(\frac{A}{P}, i, n\right) \tag{1-6a}$$

This relationship is often called the *uniform series capital recovery factor* (USCRF).

To aid in the calculations using these relationships, you can also find values for F/A, A/F, P/A, and A/P in Appendix A for typical values of i and n. For each relationship, knowing any three of the four parameters will allow you to calculate the fourth one.

As an aid to understanding the preceding six equivalence relationships, appropriate cash flow diagrams can be drawn. *Cash flow diagrams* are drawings where the horizontal line represents time and vertical arrows represent cash flows at specific times. The cash flow diagrams for each relationship are shown in Fig. 1-1. These relationships form the basis for many complicated engineering economy studies involving the time value of money, and there are many excellent texts specifically on the subject.

Most complicated engineering economy problems can be broken down into parts where the previous six relationships can be utilized. The following examples illustrate how this can be done.

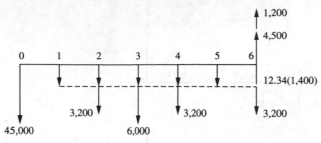

FIGURE 1-2
Cash flow diagram for Example 1-3.

Example 1-3. A piece of construction equipment costs $45,000 to purchase. Fuel, oil, grease, and minor maintenance are estimated to cost $12.34 for each hour that the equipment is used. The tires cost $3,200 to replace (estimated to occur every 2,800 hours of use), and major repairs of $6,000 are expected after 4,200 hours of use. The piece of equipment is expected to last for 8,400 hours, after which it will have an estimated salvage value of 10% of the purchase price. How much should the owner of the equipment charge, per hour of use, if he expects to use the piece of equipment about 1,400 hours per year? Assume an annual interest rate of 15%.

To solve, first draw a cash flow diagram (Fig. 1-2). Note that the cash disbursements are shown going down on the diagram. Also, note that the tire replacement costs are shown, and then subtracted, at the close of the sixth year. This is necessary to utilize the USCAF $(A/F, i, n)$ in calculating A_3.

$$n = \frac{8,400}{1,400} = 6 \text{ years}$$

$$A_1 = -45,000 \left(\frac{A}{P}, 15, 6 \right) = -45,000 \, (0.26424) = -11,890.80$$

$$A_2 = -12.34 \, (1,400) \qquad\qquad\qquad = -17,276.00^\dagger$$

$$A_3 = -3,200 \left(\frac{A}{F}, 15, 2 \right) = -3,200 \, (0.46512) = -1,488.38$$

Note that this is analogous to

$$-3,200 \left(\left(\frac{P}{F}, 15, 2 \right) + \left(\frac{P}{F}, 15, 4 \right) + \left(\frac{P}{F}, 15, 6 \right) \right) \left(\frac{A}{P}, 15, 6 \right)$$

$$A_4 = -6,000 \left(\frac{P}{F}, 15, 3 \right) \left(\frac{A}{P}, 15, 6 \right)$$

$$= -6,000 \, (0.65752)(0.26424) \qquad = \qquad 1,042.46$$

$$A_5 = +(4,500 + 3,200) \left(\frac{A}{F}, 15, 6 \right) = +7,700 \, (0.11424) \qquad = \qquad +879.65$$

$$A_T = \text{the total annual cost} \qquad\qquad\qquad = -\$30,817.99 = -\$30,820$$

†This neglects interest earned *within* a given year.

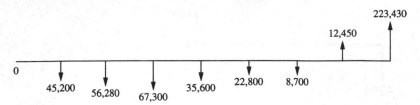

FIGURE 1-3
Cash flow diagram for Example 1-4.

The hourly cost will then be

$$\frac{30,817.99}{1,400} = \$22.01 \text{ per hour}$$

Example 1-4. A contractor calculates that she will have the following cash flow over-drafts on a construction project. These overdrafts are due to the delays in receiving progress payments from the owner and because retainage is being held by the owner until completion of the project. If the contractor's cost of money is 2% per month, how much total interest will she have to pay as a result of these cash flow overdrafts?

Month 1	−$45,200
Month 2	−56,280
Month 3	−67,300
Month 4	−35,600
Month 5	−22,800
Month 6	−8,700
Month 7	+12,450
Month 8	+223,430

The cash flow diagram for this problem is shown in Fig. 1-3. To solve, calculate the future worth (F) of the cash flow, as the total amount of money involved (excluding time value) equals zero:

$$F = -45,200\left(\frac{F}{P},2,7\right) - 56,280\left(\frac{F}{P},2,6\right) - 67,300\left(\frac{F}{P},2,5\right) - 35,600\left(\frac{F}{P},2,4\right)$$

$$- 22,800\left(\frac{F}{P},2,3\right) - 8,700\left(\frac{F}{P},2,2\right) + 12,450\left(\frac{F}{P},2,1\right) + 223,430$$

$$F = -45,200(1.1486) - 56,280(1.1261) - 67,300(1.1040) - 35,600(1.0824)$$
$$- 22,800(1.0612) - 8,700(1.0404) + 12,450(1.0200) + 223,430$$

$$F = -\$25,244$$

Note: This problem points out the potential significant costs of overdraft cash flows during construction, especially if interest rates are high. In this example 2% per month is equivalent to $(1 + .02)^{12} - 1$ or 26.8% per year. If the contractor could borrow money for 1% per month (12.7% per year), her total interest would reduce to $12,339.

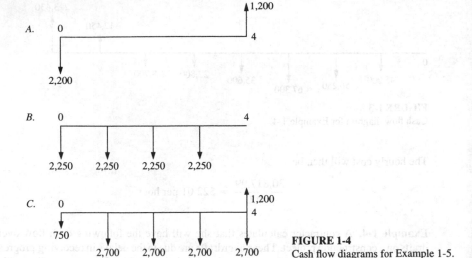

FIGURE 1-4
Cash flow diagrams for Example 1-5.

DISCOUNTED PRESENT WORTH ANALYSIS

Often in engineering economic studies, as well as in general financial analyses, a discounted present worth analysis is made of each alternative under consideration. This type of analysis involves calculating the *equivalent* present worth or present value of all the dollar amounts involved in the alternative to determine its present worth. This present worth is *discounted* at a predetermined rate of interest, often termed the *minimum attractive rate of return* (MARR or i^*). The MARR is usually equal to the current rate of interest for borrowed capital plus an additional rate for such factors as risk, uncertainty, and contingencies. The following example illustrates the use of discounted present worth to evaluate three mutually exclusive alternatives.

Example 1-5. The Ace-in-the-Hole Construction Company is considering three methods of acquiring company pickups for use by field engineers. The alternatives are:

A. Purchase the pickups for $7,200 each and sell after 4 years for an estimated $1,200 each.

B. Lease the pickups for 4 years for $2,250 per year paid in advance at the beginning of each year. The contractor pays all operating and maintenance costs on the pickups and the leasing company retains ownership.

C. Purchase the pickups on special time payments with $750 down now and $2,700 per year at the end of each year for 3 years. Assume the pickups will be sold after 4 years for $1,200 each.

If the contractor's MARR is 15%, which alternative should he choose? The cash flow diagrams for these three alternatives are given in Fig. 1-4. To solve, calculate the net present worth (NPW) of each alternative at 15% and select the least costly alternative:

$$\text{NPW}_A = -7,200 + 1,200 \left(\frac{P}{F}, 15, 4 \right) = -7,200 + 686.1 = -\$6,514$$

$$NPW_B = -2,250 - 2,250\left(\frac{P}{A}, 15, 3\right) = -2,250 - 5,137 = -\$7,387$$

$$NPW_C = -750 - 2,700\left(\frac{P}{A}, 15, 3\right) + 1,200\left(\frac{P}{F}, 15, 4\right) = -\$7,742$$

The least costly alternative is A.

The foregoing example was simplified in two respects. One, the amount of calculations required was quite small. Two, all three alternatives involved the same lives (4 years in the example). Problems involving more data and calculations are no different in approach from the example cited. But when alternatives involve different lives, the analysis becomes more difficult. Obviously, if you are comparing one alternative with a life of 5 years with an alternative with a life of 10 years, their respective discounted present worths are not directly comparable. How do you handle this situation? There are two approaches generally used. They are:

Approach 1. Truncate (cut off) the longer-lived alternative(s) to equal the shorter-lived alternative and assume a salvage value for the unused portion of the longer-lived alternative(s). Then make the comparison on the basis of equal lives.

Approach 2. Assume equal replacement conditions (costs and incomes) for each alternative and compute the discounted present worth on the basis of the least common multiple of lives for all alternatives.

The following example illustrates these two approaches.

Example 1-6. A contractor is considering the purchase of either a new track-type tractor for $73,570, which has a 6-year life with an estimated net annual income of $26,000 and a salvage value of $8,000, or a used track-type tractor for $24,680, with an estimated life of 3 years and no salvage value and an estimated net annual income of $12,000. If the contractor's MARR is 20%, which tractor, if any, should she choose?

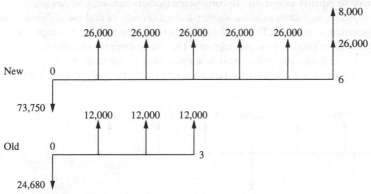

FIGURE 1-5
Cash flow diagrams for Example 1-6.

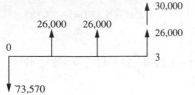

FIGURE 1-6
Cash flow diagram for Example 1-6.

The cash flow diagrams for these two alternatives are shown in Fig. 1-5. Note the unequal lives. In order to use approach 1, a suitable salvage value must be assumed for the new tractor after 3 years. For this example let us assume a 3-year salvage value for the new tractor of $30,000. Now the cash flow diagram for the new factor looks like that shown in Fig. 1-6. The discounted present worth of each alternative is

$$\text{NPW}_{\text{new}} = -73,570 + 26,000\left(\frac{P}{A}, 20, 3\right) + 30,000\left(\frac{P}{F}, 20, 3\right) = -\$1,443$$

$$\text{NPW}_{\text{old}} = -24,680 + 12,000\left(\frac{P}{A}, 20, 3\right) \qquad\qquad = +\$597$$

Using approach 1, purchasing the used tractor is the better alternative. Using approach 2, the cash flow diagram for the used tractor is shown in Fig. 1-7. The discounted present worths of the alternatives are

$$\text{NPW}_{\text{new}} = -73,570 + 26,000\left(\frac{P}{A}, 20, 6\right) + 8,000\left(\frac{P}{F}, 20, 6\right) = +\$15,570$$

$$\text{NPW}_{\text{old}} = -24,680 + 12,000\left(\frac{P}{A}, 20, 6\right) - 24,680\left(\frac{P}{F}, 20, 3\right) = +\$944$$

Using approach 2, purchasing the new tractor is the better alternative. Neither of the approaches discussed is entirely satisfactory, and they can yield different solutions (as shown in the example). Which solution, if either, is correct? The answer is "whichever one best fits the situation." To assume you can receive a high (or low) salvage value by selling a piece of equipment before the end of its useful life may be very erroneous. On the other hand, to assume an equal replacement cost for a used piece of equipment 3 years in the future may be equally erroneous. To complicate matters further, you can assume inflation (or deflation) on replacement of the shorter-lived alternatives and use different values for the replacement conditions. But in all approaches you are making assumptions and your results are only as good as your assumptions. The real answer is to use the most *reasonable* approach to each specific problem. It is a good idea to calculate both approaches. The differences provide a feeling for the risk associated with the assumptions used.

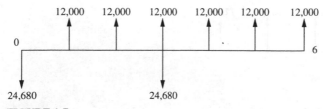

FIGURE 1-7
Cash flow diagram for Example 1-6.

RATE OF RETURN ANALYSIS

Often, the use of discounted present worth analysis raises more questions than it answers because the assumptions involved in its use are very visible to anyone reviewing the analysis. Interestingly, if the *rate of return* analysis is used, many people will accept the results without considering the assumptions involved, even though the resulting answer will be the same. There is something about knowing the anticipated *rate of return* of an investment that permits a decision to be made with more "perceived" confidence.

The *rate of return* of a proposed investment is that interest rate which makes the discounted present worth of the investment equal to zero. To calculate the *rate of return*, simply set up the equation and solve for i. The following example illustrates the procedure.

> **Example 1-6 (same example).** A contractor is considering the purchase of either a new track-type tractor for $73,570, which has a 6-year life with an estimated net annual income of $26,000 and a salvage value of $8,000, or a used track-type tractor for $24,680, with an estimated life of 3 years and no salvage value and an estimated net annual income of $12,000. Which tractor, if either, should she choose?
>
> The cash flow diagrams are given in Fig. 1-4 except that in this case no MARR is given. Note again the unequal lives. The resulting equations are
>
> $$\text{NPW}_{\text{new}} = -73,570 + 26,000\left(\frac{P}{A}, i, 6\right) = 0$$
>
> $$\left(\frac{P}{A}, i, 6\right) = \frac{73,570}{26,000} = 2.82962 = \frac{(1+i)^6 - 1}{i(1+i)^6}$$
>
> This equation can be solved directly if you have a calculator that will perform the necessary calculations, or you can use the interest tables, selecting values of $(P/A, i, 6)$ just higher and just lower than the value needed, and then interpolate to find the value of i which makes the equation equal to zero.
>
> The resulting value of i is
>
> $$i_{\text{new}} = 26.8\%$$
>
> $$\text{NPW}_{\text{old}} = -24,680 + 12,000\left(\frac{P}{A}, i, 3\right) = 0$$
>
> $$\left(\frac{P}{A}, i, 3\right) = \frac{24,680}{12,000} = 2.05667 = \frac{(1+i)^3 - 1}{i(1+i)^3}$$
>
> $$i_{\text{old}} = 21.5\%$$
>
> The use of this approach suffers from the same problem as the discounted present worth analysis in that it ignores the different lives of the two alternatives. In this case, while the rates of return for each alternative are correct, what happens during the *second* 3-year period using the old tractor? If equal replacement conditions are assumed, then the rate of return for the old tractor does not change and the conclusion reached is that the new tractor yields a higher rate of return.
>
> However, if we assume the salvage value of the new tractor is $30,000 after 3 years and compare the rates of return on the basis of 3-year lives, the resulting equation for the new tractor is

$$\text{NPW}_{\text{new}} = -73{,}570 + 26{,}000\left(\frac{P}{A}, i, 3\right) + 30{,}000\left(\frac{P}{F}, i, 3\right) = 0$$

This equation can be solved as before, and the result is

$$i_{\text{new}} = 18.9\%$$

Using the values for i of 21.5 and 18.8% for the old and the new tractor, respectively, you can see that the old tractor will yield a better rate of return. Again, the answer depends on the assumptions used. Note that a decision as to which tractor to purchase is still not made. The only thing you know is their respective rates of return. Before a decision can be reached, you must know your MARR. If we use the 3-year analysis period, and if the MARR is 20%, then the choice would be to purchase the used tractor. But if the minimum attractive rate of return is 30%, then the choice would be to choose *neither*! When you analyze alternatives involving positive rates of return, the *do-nothing* alternative is always a possibility.

If the previous example is analyzed further, a curious result can occur. If the MARR were 15%, which alternative should be selected? They both *exceed* the MARR. But since the old tractor yields a higher MARR, should it not be selected? To answer this question, determine each alternative's net present worth at 18%.

$$\text{NPW}_{\text{new}} = -73{,}570 + 26{,}000\left(\frac{P}{A}, 15, 3\right) + 30{,}000\left(\frac{P}{F}, 15, 3\right) = \$5{,}519$$

$$\text{NPW}_{\text{old}} = -24{,}680 + 12{,}000\left(\frac{P}{A}, 15, 3\right) = \$2{,}719$$

According to our NPW analysis, the new tractor yields a higher value *for a MARR of 15%*. How can this be? Intuitively, it would seem that the alternative with the higher rate of return would yield the higher NPW regardless of the assumed interest rate. That is not true! In this example there is a hidden consideration that strongly influences the result. Notice that the initial investments are *not the same*. We are looking at initial investments of $73,570 and $24,680. When we examine the rate of return of each of these alternatives, we have ignored their respective differences in initial cash flows. Therefore, we can obtain misleading results through such an analysis.

To handle unequal initial investments, *an incremental rate of return* (IROR) *analysis* is required. Essentially, the question that must be answered is: "For alternatives that have a satisfactory rate of return (ROR), what is the IROR of the difference in the cash flows of the alternatives?" To make this analysis, first arrange the alternatives in ascending order of initial cash flow. Then compare alternatives, two by two, alternatively rejecting the alternative with the lower IROR.

For our example of the two tractors the incremental cash flow diagram is given in Fig. 1-8. The cash flow equation is

$$\text{NPW}_{\text{new}-\text{old}} = -48{,}890 + 14{,}000\left(\frac{P}{A}, i, 6\right) + 24{,}680\left(\frac{P}{F}, i, 3\right) + 8{,}000\left(\frac{P}{F}, i, 6\right) = 0$$

Solving for i (IROR) yields

$$i = 30.9\%$$

Now the picture is clear. While the initial investment of $24,680 for the old tractor will yield a ROR of 21.5%, the incremental increase in initial investment of $48,890 (by purchasing the new tractor) will yield an IROR of 30.9%. Now that all the rates of return

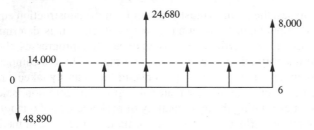

FIGURE 1-8
Incremental cash flow diagram for two tractors (Example 1-6).

are known, a decision can be reached *which is dependent on the MARR*. For a MARR of 20% the ROR of the new tractor is too low, and therefore the old tractor is chosen. For a MARR of 15% both alternatives exceed it and we have to examine the IROR. In this case the IROR is higher than the MARR, so we should choose the new tractor. Looking at the problem another way, for the MARR of 15% a $73,570 investment earning 18.9% is better than a $24,680 investment earning 21.5% if the incremental investment of $48,890 can only earn the MARR of 15%.

EQUIPMENT PLANNING AND ESTIMATING

Each piece of construction equipment is specifically designed by the manufacturer to perform certain mechanical operations. The task of the project planner/estimator is to match the right machine or combination of machines to the job at hand. The proof of how well the planner understands the project and coordinates the utilization of the company's equipment is in the bottom line when the contract is completed—profit or loss!

Considering individual tasks, the degree of performance is measured by matching machine production against machine cost. To estimate the equipment component of the project cost, we must first determine machine *productivity*. Productivity is governed by engineering fundamentals and management ability. Chapter 4 covers the principal engineering fundamentals which control machine productivity. Each level of productivity has a corresponding cost associated with the effort expended. The expenses that a firm experiences through machine ownership and use, and the method of analyzing such costs, are presented in Chap. 3. The remaining chapters describe the operational characteristics and present construction methods of major equipment types.

While each major type of equipment has different operational characteristics, it is not always obvious which machine is best for a particular task. After studying the plans and specifications, performing a quantity takeoff, and (if at all possible) visiting the project site, the planner must visualize how she can best employ the available equipment to accomplish the work. Is it less expensive to make an excavation with scrapers or to top-load trucks with a dragline? Both methods may yield the required end result, but which is the most economical method?

To answer that question, the planner develops an initial plan for employment of the scrapers and then calculates their production rate and the resulting cost. The same process is followed for the top-load operation. The type of equipment which has the lowest estimated total cost is selected for the job.

To perform such analyses, the planner must consider both the construction equipment and the methods of employment in relation to one another. If it is determined that different equipment and methods will be used as an excavation progresses, then it is necessary to divide the quantity takeoff calculations in a manner that is compatible with the proposed equipment layout. The person performing the quantity takeoff must calculate quantities based on groups of similar materials (granular, common, select). This is not just a question of estimating the total quantity of rock and a total quantity of soil to excavate. All factors which affect equipment performance and choice of method, such as water table, clay or sand seams, site dimensions, depth of cuts, and compaction specifications, must be considered in making the quantity takeoff.

The normal operating modes of particular machines are discussed in the chapters on equipment types. That presentation, though, should not blind the reader to other possible applications. The most successful construction companies are those which carefully study all possible approaches to the construction process of each individual project. No two projects are exactly alike; therefore, it is important that the engineering planner begin each new project with a completely open mind and review all possible options. Additionally, machines are constantly being improved and new equipment introduced. In 1920 a four-horse team and Fresno scraper could move an average of 4 cu yd (cubic yards) of earth per hour on a 400-ft haul. By 1939 crawler tractors and rubber-tired scrapers were moving 115 cu yd of earth per hour the same distance. Today bulldozers would be considered for such a short haul and, depending on their size, they can push 200–700 cu yd of earth per hour.

Heavy equipment is usually classified or identified by one of two methods: *functional* identification or *operational* identification. A bulldozer, used to push a stockpile of material, could be identified as a support machine for an aggregate production plant. A grouping could also include front-end loaders. The bulldozer could, however, be *functionally* classified as an excavator. In this book a combination of functional and operational groupings are utilized. The basic purpose is to explain to the reader the critical performance characteristics of a machine and then to describe that machine's most common applications.

The efforts of engineers and equipment manufacturers, striving to improve and develop new ideas constantly, push machine capabilities forward. As the array of useful equipment increases, the importance of careful planning and execution of construction projects increases. New machines allow greater economies. It is the job of the engineer to match equipment to project situations, and that is the central focus of this book.

PROBLEMS

1-1. Solve the following problems with the rate of interest equal to 9% compounded annually:

    (*a*) If $20,000 is invested today, what will be its value after 5 years? 10 years?

    (*b*) How long will it take for invested money to double in value?

    (*c*) If $1,500 is invested today, and an equal amount is invested each year for 6 years (seven payments), what will be the value after the last payment in 6 years? After 10 years?

    (*d*) If $140,000 is needed at the close of 5 years, what equal annual payment must be made starting today and ending at the close of 4 years (five payments)?

1-2. A friend offers to double your money in 6 years if you will invest in his venture. What annual rate of interest will you receive if you invest and your friend's prediction is correct? If it takes 9 years to double your money, what rate of interest will you receive?

1-3. A contractor is considering the following three alternatives:
A. Purchase a new microcomputer system for $5,017. The system is expected to last for 6 years with a salvage value of $1,000.
B. Lease a new microcomputer system for $1,400 per year, payable in advance. It should last 6 years.
C. Purchase a *used* microcomputer system for $2,720. It is expected to last 3 years with essentially no salvage value.
(*a*) For a MARR of 12%, which alternative should be selected?
(*b*) For a MARR of 15%, which alternative should be selected?
(*c*) What is the IROR between alternatives A and B?
Note: Assume equal replacement conditions for this problem.

1-4. Same as Prob. 1-3, except assume that for alternative B the new computer can be leased for $1,020 per year, payable in advance.

1-5. A large engineering company is considering the following three major capital investments (each investment is considered to have zero salvage value at the end of its life):
(*a*) Calculate the rate of return for each investment.
(*b*) For a MARR of 15%, which investment, if any, would you select? Why? (How do you handle the unequal lives?)

Investment	Initial capital required ($)	Estimated annual receipts ($)	Estimated annual disbursements ($)	Estimated life (years)
M	300,000	130,000	62,000	12
P	140,000	175,000	126,000	6
S	120,000	56,000	25,000	8

1-6. Discuss the importance of not ignoring the unequal lives in Prob. 1-5.

1-7. A house was purchased 5 years ago for $92,000. The terms were $18,400 down at the time of purchase and the remainder to be paid monthly at a monthly interest rate of 1.25% (an annual *nominal* rate of 15% and an annual *effective* interest rate of 16.075%) for a 20-year period.
(*a*) What are the monthly payments on the loan for principal and interest?
(*b*) Since loan rates are now much lower (around 9% nominal annual interest, or 0.75% per month), the owner decides to pay off the note today, just after his 60th monthly payment. In order for him to pay off the note in one lump sum today, what total amount of money would he have to pay (i.e., what is the balance due on the note today)?
(*c*) In part (*b*), if the owner pays off the loan by refinancing the home at 0.75% per month for 15 more years, and can obtain the entire amount he needs to refinance, what will be his new monthly payments?

1-8. The engineering estimate for the cost, installed, of a new Astro-Turf for the college football field is $378,000 and is guaranteed for 5 years. Another artificial turf, the MACHO-TURF, is advertised for $494,000, installed, and guaranteed to last 8 years. Neglecting salvage value, which turf should be selected:
(*a*) if the MARR is 12%?
(*b*) if the MARR is 20%?

REFERENCES

1. National Research Council, *Building for Tomorrow: Global Enterprise and the U.S. Construction Industry,* National Academy Press, Washington, DC, 1988.
2. Adrian, James J., *Business Practices for Construction Management,* American Elsevier, New York, 1976.
3. Maher, Richard Patrick, *Introduction to Construction Operations,* Wiley, New York, 1982.
4. Hildebrandt, Patrica M., *Economic Theory and the Construction Industry,* Macmillan, London, 1974.
5. Collier, Courtland A., and W. B. Ledbetter, *Engineering and Economic Cost Analysis,* 2d ed., Harper & Row, New York, 1988.

CHAPTER 2

THE PLANNING PROCESS FOR EQUIPMENT AND METHODS

GENERAL INFORMATION

This chapter deals with the planning process for equipment and methods that is necessary both prior to and during the actual construction of a project. Such planning is required for production achievement, cost control, commitment, consistency, communication, and coordination of the project and the parties involved in the project. This planning must clearly identify the work to be done and establish (1) the desired schedule, (2) realistic cost estimates, (3) quality objectives, and (4) the best contracting strategy.

Formal planning involves the following steps:

1. Analyze the project, establish the scope and feasibility, and specify the limitations involved:
   • Time
   • Money
   • Location (climate, work force, regulations)
   • Competition for resources
   • Coordination requirements

   The assumptions you make in your analysis should always be written down. A paper trail *must* be provided!

2. Divide the project down into specific and discrete activities. When performing this step, use a reasonable number of activities. Each activity must have an identifiable start and finish. For large projects, combine small activities into larger activities (hierarchical). This is known as "hammocking."

3. Estimate the time, resources, and cost required to perform each activity. Such estimates must be reasonable. This will provide an estimate of the types, quantities, and duration of construction plant and equipment. Neglect (for the time being) factors of weather and resource limitations. This helps prevent becoming too conservative.

4. Place activities in proper relation to each other with respect to their logic constraints. For example, activity P cannot begin until activity F is finished.

5. Portray the plan in the form of a network, which shows the interrelationships (logic constraints) between the activities (see next section). The plan at this stage does not consider actual dates.

6. Place activities in time sequence, noting which activities must be performed sequentially and which can be performed simultaneously. A bar chart is an excellent way of depicting this information.

7. Apply limitations of time, available resources, climate, and so on (assuming you know the start date). This will provide:
   - The times for delivery of materials and installed equipment
   - The classification and numbers of workers needed and the periods of time they will be needed

General sequencing and activity planning should be performed prior to bidding a project. Such planning will *always* reveal factors which significantly affect the cost and timing of the project. A necessary step in pricing the work is to analyze proposed methods and to establish durations so that both direct and indirect costs can be accurately estimated.

PROJECT NETWORK ANALYSIS (CPM)

This method of project planning involves the identification of specific activities, their durations, and their interrelationships. There are two types of networks in general use: (1) the activity-on-arrow (AOA) type, commonly called *arrow diagramming*, and (2) the activity-on-node (AON) type, commonly called *precedence diagramming*. Each of these types, both generally termed *critical path methods* (CPM), uses the same information in a slightly different form. The basic principles and limitations for these diagrams are that:

1. They portray the dependency relationships among activities (logic constraints).

2. All activities have a single duration and must have an identifiable beginning and end.

3. All activities preceding a given activity must be completed before the given activity can begin. (Advanced scheduling techniques can overcome this limitation.)

4. Basic networks do not indicate the time sequence of a project.

5. An activity may *not* be interrupted. This is a *major* limitation!

ACTIVITY-ON-ARROW DIAGRAMMING

To illustrate the process, use as an example the placement of a mobile home on a permanent site. Table 2-1 lists the activities, their probable durations, and precedence

TABLE 2-1
List of activities, durations, and precedences for a mobile home installation project

Activity		Events		Duration	Activities which	
Code	Description	From	To	(days)	Precede	Follow
A	Site layout	1	2	1	—	B, C
B	Slab excavation	2	3	4	A	D
C	Slab forms	3	5	1	B	G
D	Place blocks	2	4	1	A	E, F
E	Rough plumbing	4	6	2	C	H
F	Rough electrical	4	8	2	C	K
G	Place concrete	5	7	1	D	I, J
H	Place home	6	8	1	E	K
I	Remove forms	7	9	2	G	X
J	Cure concrete	7	10	7	G	L
K	Hookup home	8	11	4	F, H	L
L	Cleanup	10	11	2	J, K, X	—
X	Dummy	9	10	0	I	L

relationships. The units of time involved should be convenient for the degree of accuracy desired that is *consistent with keeping the level of detail reasonable*. Units such as days, weeks, and months are generally used. Once the units are selected, the usual practice is to use integer quantities only, rounding off all durations to the nearest integer value (some planners always choose the next higher integer value). In this example workdays are chosen. Note that each activity is identified by both a symbol and a numbering sequence which describes the from-to relationship for the activity. To express the interrelationships clearly among activities, the "from" node *must* be a lower number than the "to" node. In that way the direction of the arrow is clearly established. Figure 2-1 illustrates the AOA diagram for this example problem. Note that the figure depicts the construction sequence and interrelationships among the activities. The following terms are used in the construction of this type of diagram and its various parts.

> *Activity.* A specific job or task that has to be performed. Normally, time is required to complete an activity. For example, "cure concrete" is an activity in the preceding example.
>
> *Event.* The start or completion of an activity. It requires no time in itself and is usually indicated on the AOA diagram by a number enclosed in a circle. The event is sometimes referred to as a *node*.
>
> *Arrow.* A line drawn to represent each activity in a network, joining two events (the start and the finish of an activity). The arrow is usually designated by two numbers, one at the tail (the "from" event) and one at the head (the "to" event). To avoid confusion, the "from" number should *always* be less that the "to" number. Generally, the length of the arrow has no relation to the duration of the activity which it represents.

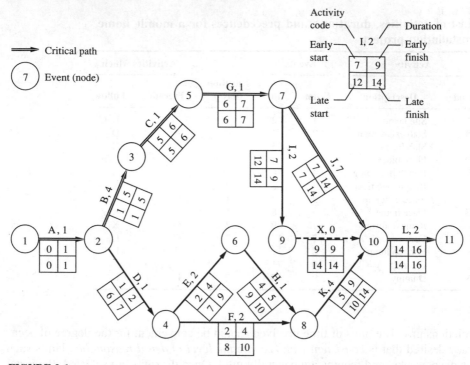

FIGURE 2-1
AOA diagram for mobile home installation project.

AOA network. This is the arrow diagram drawn to portray the proper relationships among the activities in a project. It is common practice to start time with zero and to start the first arrow or arrows at the left end of the network and to proceed to the right.

Dummy. This is an artificial activity, usually represented on the diagram by a dotted line, to describe the proper relationship among activities. For example, activity X in Fig. 2-1 is a dummy activity and indicates that activity L cannot start until both I and J are completed. It is included to avoid having two different activities possess the same from-to numbers. A dummy activity has zero duration.

Early start (ES). This is the earliest time that an activity can start.

Duration (D). The estimated time to perform an activity. For example, it is estimated that the concrete must be cured for 7 days.

Early finish (EF). This is the earliest time that an activity can be finished. It is equal to the early start time plus the duration of the activity: EF = ES + D.

Late start (LS). This is the latest time that an activity can be started without delaying the completion of the project: LS = LF − D.

Late finish (LF). This is the latest time that an activity can be finished without delaying the completion of a project: LF = LS + D.

Total float (TF). This is the amount of time that an activity may be delayed without delaying the completion of the project. It is equal to the difference between the late start and early start, or late finish and early finish: TF = LS − ES = LF − EF. In Fig. 2-1 the total float of activity I is 5 days (10 − 5).

Free float (FF). This is the time that the finish of an activity can be delayed without delaying the early start time of any following activity: FF = ES of following activity −EF of this activity.

Critical path. This is the *longest* interconnected path of activities through the network. Its length determines the overall duration of the project. All activities on the critical path have zero float times. A project may have more than one critical path.

Critical activity. This is an activity on the critical path. It has zero float time, that is, LS − ES = 0 and LF − EF = 0. Activities A, B, C, G, J, and L are critical activities and make up the critical path for the mobile home installation project shown in Fig. 2-1.

The uses of these terms and symbols are illustrated more fully in the examples which follow. Persons who wish more comprehensive information on this subject can find many excellent texts covering critical path networks.

Steps in critical path scheduling. To apply the critical path method (CPM) of scheduling the construction of a project, use the following steps:

1. Separate the project into discrete activities, each with a definite starting point and ending point.

2. Estimate the duration of each activity.

3. Determine the proper sequencing of each activity, including which activities must precede or follow other activities.

4. Draw an AOA network with the activities and events properly interconnected. Where necessary, include dummy activities to clarify the network and to avoid redundancy in activity event numbers.

5. Examine the network and optimize, if possible, to eliminate unnecessary dummy activities.

6. Assign numbers to all events, being sure that the "from" number is always less than the "to" number. This establishes the proper direction of the activities.

7. Make a forward pass and a backward pass through the network to establish early start, late start, early finish, and late finish times for all activities.

8. Determine the critical path, or paths, and critical activities.

9. Prepare a table listing all activities, their designations, durations, and ES, LS, EF, and LF times, and their total float. Their free float can also be listed, if desired.

To illustrate these steps, let us go through the preceding example of the placement of a mobile home on a permanent site. Steps 1, 2, and 3 are illustrated in Table 2-1. Note that each activity has a specific duration and the precedence relationship among all the activities is shown in the last two columns of the table. Of course, at this stage the node numbers would not be known, and those two columns would initially be left blank. The dummy activity would also be unknown until the network was constructed. Once this preliminary information is determined, the AOA diagram can be constructed (step 4). Figure 2-1 shows the completed AOA diagram with the dummy included. Remember that initially you might have several dummy activities which had to be included to avoid redundancy, but after optimizing the network (step 5), only one dummy activity would be needed in this case. Step 6 involves assigning numbers to all the events (nodes). Note that the "from" node is always less than the "to" node. Also, note that the numbers do not have to be consecutive and any sequence of numbers could be used.

Step 7 is a forward pass calculation. Normally, the first activity starts at time zero (rather than time 1). Starting at the left-hand side of the diagram with 0 as the ES time for activity A, add the duration to its ES to obtain its EF time (in this case, time 1 at node 2). Here the diagram splits, and two activities begin at node 2. Continuing the forward pass with activity B, we see that its ES is identical with the EF of its preceding activity (1 in this case). Adding the duration of B to its ES time yields its EF time of 5 (1 + 4). In a similar manner, you can progress through the network, calculating ES and EF times for all activities, until you reach activities K and L. Each of these activities has more than one activity preceding it with different EF times. Which one do you choose? The answer is to choose the preceding EF with the *longest* duration. Thus, for activity K its ES time is 5 (rather than 4) because it cannot start until activity H is completed at time 5. The fact that activity F could be finished at time 4 does not mean that activity K can start then, as activity H still has one more day before it is finished. Similarly, activity L cannot start until time 14. Adding the duration of 2 to the ES time of activity L yields an EF time of 16 days. As this is the last activity, you now know the duration of the project (16 days) and you have completed the forward pass. Next comes the backward pass.

On the last activity, the LF time will be set as either the contract duration or the EF time, depending on whether or not the planner wishes to show the total project float based on the contract duration or no float on the critical path(s). (Of course, if the contract duration is *earlier* than the EF time, the project has negative float—a situation that must be altered before beginning.) For this example let us assume that EF equals the LF time for the last activity. The LS time of the last activity is simply its LF time minus its duration (16 − 2), which yields an LS time of 14 for activity L. The LF time of all activities immediately preceding activity L must equal the LS time of activity L (day 14). Working backward, the LF and LS times for preceding activities can be determined until you come to activity G. It has two activities which immediately follow it (activities I and J) with different LS times. The LF time of activity G must be the *smaller* of the two following LS times (7 days rather than 12). In other words, for activity G *not* to delay either activity I or J, it cannot finish any later (LF) than time 7. In a similar manner, the remaining LF and LS times can easily be calculated until you are at the beginning of the network.

The next step is to determine the critical path. The critical path is defined as the *longest* interconnected path through the network. All activities on this path have the same ES and LS times (and similarly, they have the same EF and LF times). In the example problem the critical path is 1-2-3-5-7-10-11 and contains activities A, B, C, G, J, and L. The critical path is denoted by a double line in Fig. 2-1. Note that these activities have no "float" to their durations, which is a definition of a critical activity.

The final step, which is to calculate the floats (total and free) for all activities, can easily be calculated knowing each activity's ES, LS, EF, and LF times and the adjacent activity's times. Placing these values in a table completes step 9 and is illustrated in Table 2-2.

TABLE 2-2
List of activities, times, and floats for a mobile home installation project

Activity							
Code	Duration	ES	EF	LS	LF	TF	FF
A	1	0	1	0	1	0	0
B	4	1	5	1	5	0	0
C	1	5	6	5	6	0	0
D	1	1	2	6	7	5	0
E	2	2	4	7	9	5	0
F	2	2	4	8	10	6	1
G	1	6	7	6	7	0	0
H	1	4	5	· 9	10	5	0
I	2	7	9	12	14	5	0
J	7	7	14	7	14	0	0
K	4	5	9	10	14	5	5
L	2	14	16	14	16	0	0
X	0	9	9	14	14	5	0

ACTIVITY-ON-NODE DIAGRAMMING

One problem with the AOA diagram (arrow) is the necessity to include dummy activities. Such activities increase the length of the tables, enlarge the graph, and take time to calculate. They also increase the complexity of the network. Another type of project network can be used, called the *activity-on-node* (AON) diagram, or the precedence diagram, which overcomes these problems. In the AON diagram the activities are denoted by boxes, and arrows are used *only* to designate the interrelationship among activities. Figures 2-2(*a*) and (*b*) illustrate the differences between the AOA and AON diagrams.

Figure 2-3 is the AON (precedence) diagram for the mobile home installation project. Note the absence of dummy activities and the clear precedence relationship

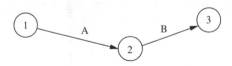

(*a*)　AOA diagram for two activities

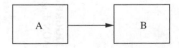

(*b*)　AON diagram for two activities

FIGURE 2-2
AOA and AON diagrams contrasted.

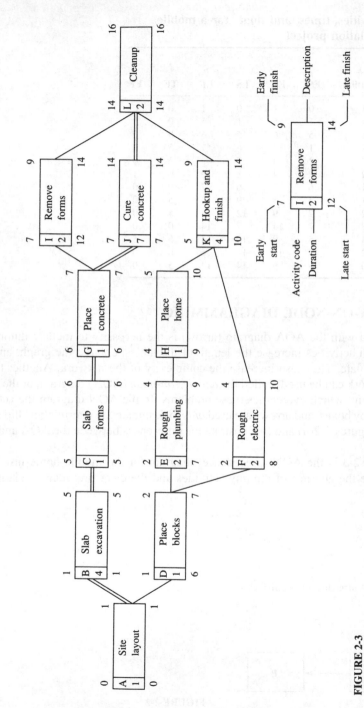

FIGURE 2-3
AON diagram for mobile home installation project.

among activities. In this figure neither the size of the box nor the length of the arrows denotes a time interval. The ES, LS, EF, and LF times, as well as the critical path, are clearly depicted in the figure. Calculation of these values and float times is identical to that described earlier for the AOA diagram.

To most users the AON diagram is simpler to draw, is easier to explain, and presents a clearer picture of the project than the arrow diagram. If that is the case, then why describe the arrow diagram at all? The fact is since arrow diagramming was developed first, it is still widely used. Both methods have their advocates, and the beginner needs to understand that both will be encountered in practice.

ADVANCED NETWORK ANALYSIS TECHNIQUES

To overcome some limitations of basic AOA and AON diagrams, we often use four lead-lag relationships (see Fig. 2-4). Note that:

1. These relationships have meaning for AON diagrams *only*.
2. The exact beginning and ending locations of the connecting lines on the diagram are very important. If boxes are used to portray the activities, the lead-lag relationships are very clear.
3. The value of n, which mathematically can be positive or negative, in real-life situations should *always* be a positive number (signifying a positive delay time).
4. Overlapping activities add confusion to networks, as the normal meanings of *float* are no longer valid.

Precedence diagram	Relationship	Definition
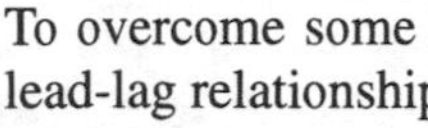 A —n→ B	FS = n	Finish to start. Activity B cannot start until n days after activity A is finished.
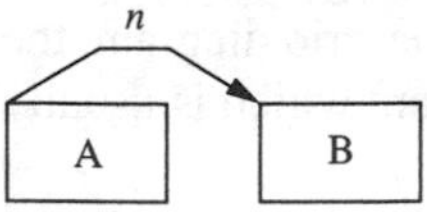 A n B	SS = n	Start to start. Activity B cannot start until n days after activity A is started.
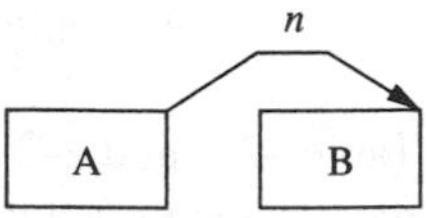 A n B	FF = n	Finish to finish. Activity B cannot finish until n days after activity A is finished.
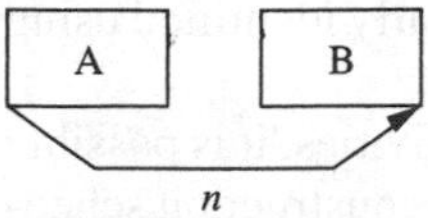 A B n	SF = n	Start to finish. Activity B cannot finish until n days after activity A is started.

FIGURE 2-4
Lag-lead relationships for AON (precedence) diagrams.

To illustrate the value of lags and leads, for the mobile home project, assume:

1. There must be a 1-day lag between the finish of "place concrete" (activity G) and the start of "remove forms" (activity I).
2. "Cleanup" (activity L) can occur concurrently with "cure concrete" (activity J).

One way to diagram this is to show a finish-to-start lag between activities G and I and a finish-to-finish relationship (lag of zero) between activities J and L, as shown in Fig. 2-5. Note that the project can now be finished in 14 days, 2 days less than before. But the forward and backward passes are more difficult to complete and some traditional definitions of *float* may no longer be valid. It is beyond the scope of this text to go into further detail concerning this technique. There are a number of excellent texts on scheduling which include detailed explanations.

THE TIME-GRID DIAGRAM

The arrow and precedence diagrams described thus far do not graphically portray durations of activities. Since diagrams deal with time, often it is helpful to indicate relative durations along the abscissa. This can be accomplished easily by drawing all arrows in the AOA diagram horizontally and scaling their lengths in accordance with their durations. This is illustrated in Fig. 2-6, which is the same diagram as that shown in Fig. 2-1 for the mobile home installation project. To gain the benefit of a time-scale, additional dummy activities had to be generated. These are the vertical lines on the diagram.

Because the float times are represented by broken horizontal lines whose lengths indicate time, it is relatively easy to determine the float time for any activity by inspecting the diagram. Because the arrows are drawn to a time-scale, it is possible to show the calendar dates for the activities, which the typical arrow (AOA) diagram does not show. Space in the time schedule is usually provided for work days only, but weekends and holidays can be easily included if desired.

Prior to drawing the time-grid diagram, steps 1, 2, 3, 4, and 7 appearing on pages 27–28 should be completed. Step 7 will indicate those activities lying on the critical path, that is, those with zero float time. Then, when drawing the time-grid diagram, the critical path can be drawn through or near the middle of the diagram, which is usually desirable.

If the name of each activity is written along its arrow and the dates are shown along the bottom of the diagram, the diagram can be a very useful reference during construction.

The diagram in Fig. 2-6 is based on the information listed in Tables 2-1 and 2-2. Note that the differences between the AOA and AON networks become insignificant when presented as a time-grid diagram. In fact, the time-grid diagram may be thought of as a fancy bar chart in which the precedence relationships are clearly identified using vertical broken lines.

Because the diagram shows a time relationship among the activities, it is possible by a visual examination to determine the desirability of shifting the construction schedules for some activities to obtain better distribution of materials, labor, or equipment, or for other reasons. In a similar manner, it is possible that altering the schedule for

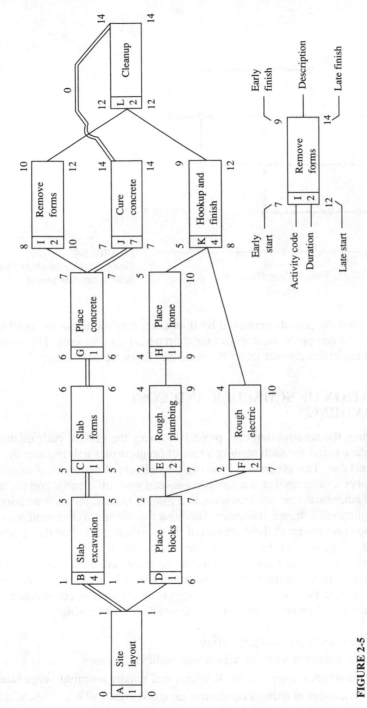

FIGURE 2-5
AON diagram for mobile home installation project with lags.

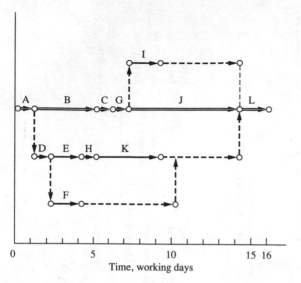

FIGURE 2-6
Time-grid diagram (AOA) for mobile home installation project.

0   5   10   15 16
Time, working days

activities, within the periods permitted by float time, may eliminate the need for providing additional equipment on a project for short periods of time only. The subject will be covered later in this chapter under the heading "Resource Scheduling."

INTEGRATION OF SCHEDULE AND COST FOR "CRASHING"

When planning the construction of a project by using the critical path method, it is usual practice to select for each activity a rate of progress that will produce the lowest practical direct cost. This progress is based on the delivery of materials, if required, the number of laborers available or the number who can work efficiently, and the number and types of equipment that are available, at a minimum cost, for each activity. After the network diagram is drawn, it is determined that the minimum time required to complete the project is the sum of the durations of those activities lying on the critical path. Such a construction plan is referred to as a *normal* program.

However, it may become desirable for some reason either to reduce or lengthen the total duration of the project. When the normal time is reduced, the project, or a portion of it, is said to be under a *crash* program. If a project is constructed under a crash program, it will be necessary to do some or all of the following:

1. Increase the rates of providing materials.
2. Increase the number of workers, which may reduce efficiency.
3. Assign the workers to overtime work, which will require premium wage rates.
4. Increase the number of units of equipment assigned to critical activities, which may require the rental of equipment that is not presently owned, or which may reduce the productivity per unit of equipment.

If some or all of these steps are adopted, there will usually be an increase in the direct cost of the activities involved in the crash program. Similarly, increasing the project duration will often also increase the direct cost of those.activities that are increased in duration, especially since equipment ownership costs generally accrue at a constant rate regardless of the productivity rate of the equipment.

Notice that thus far we have been addressing *direct* costs only (defined here as labor, equipment, materials, and the like directly and solely associated with the particular activities involved). The indirect costs—supervision at the job site, general overhead, job security, and so on—are generally provided as a direct function of project duration. The longer the duration of the project, the higher the indirect costs. An idealized cost schedule for both direct and indirect costs for a project is shown in Fig. 2-7.

If crashing is desired, in order to keep the total increase in cost to a minimum, we must select for crash operations those activities that will permit the desired reductions in construction time at the least total increase in cost. Because the duration of a project is determined by the activities lying on the critical path, the desired reduction in time should be attained by reducing the durations of one or more critical activities. In order to determine which critical activities to crash first, we will need to determine the *increase* in the cost per unit of time reduction associated with each of the critical activities, as well as near critical activities which may become critical as the project duration is reduced. This increase in cost, which is defined as the cost slope, may be expressed as dollars per day, dollars per week, or in other suitable units. While not strictly accurate, the cost slope for a given activity is usually considered to be a straight line with time.

Consider a project whose time-grid diagram is illustrated in Fig. 2-8. Assume that it is desired to reduce the total duration of this project from 36 to 32 working days with a minimum increase in project cost. Table 2-3 shows the duration and total direct cost for each critical activity under normal and crash programs, the possible reduction in duration, and the direct cost slope in dollars per day for reducing the duration of each activity. Because all other activities except Q and R have adequate float, their crash costs may be disregarded and they can be constructed under normal conditions.

An examination of Table 2-3 reveals that reductions in the following activities should be considered since they have the lowest cost slopes:

Activity	Possible reduction (days)	Direct cost slope ($ per day)
D	2	$116
H	2	106
P	2	95
Q	1	138

It appears that the desired reduction can be obtained from activities H and P at the least increase in total direct cost. However, Fig. 2-8 reveals that activity Q has only 1 day of float. If the duration of P is reduced only 1 day, there is no effect on Q. But if the duration of P is reduced 2 days, it will be necessary to reduce the duration of Q by

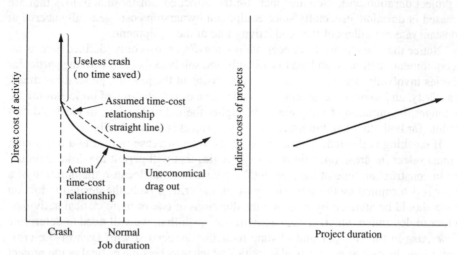

FIGURE 2-7
Costs associated with an idealized project.

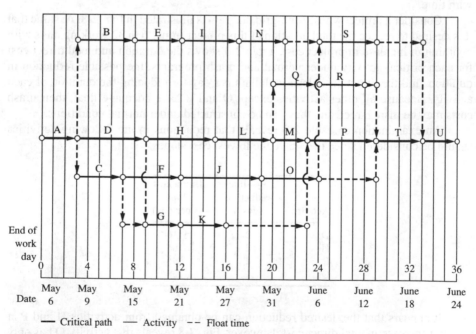

FIGURE 2-8
Example time-grid AOA diagram.

TABLE 2-3
Determining the cost slope for activities under a crash program

	Normal		Crash			
Activity	Duration (days)	Total direct cost	Duration (days)	Total direct cost	Possible reduction (days)	Direct cost slope (per day)
A	3	$ 876	2	$ 1,164	1	$288
D	6	16,454	4	16,686	2	116
H	6	14,231	4	14,443	2	106
L	5	8,592	4	8,744	1	152
M	3	6,490	3	6,490	0	0
P	6	18,670	4	18,860	2	95
T	4	12,836	3	13,264	1	428
U	3	944	2	1,168	1	224
Q	4	3,848	1	3,986	1	138
R	4	7,614	1	7,814	1	200

1 day, at an extra cost of $138, for a total cost for P and Q equal to $95 + $138 = $233. Thus, the reductions in durations for a minimum increase in direct cost should be

Reduce D 1 day at $116   = $116
Reduce H 2 days at $106   = $212
Reduce P 1 day at $95   = $95

    Total reduction of 4 days = $423 increase in direct cost

    Because the activity chain C, F, J, O, and S has a float of 4 days, the reduction (crashing) of 4 days in total project duration will cause this path to become an additional critical path.

    The previous example dealt with direct costs only, as these costs will increase as the project duration is crashed (shortened). The indirect costs, as shown in Fig. 2-7, will generally decrease as the project duration is crashed. Therefore, the overall increase in total project cost from selective crashing may be slightly less than the calculated increase in direct cost.

COMPUTERIZED SCHEDULING

There are a number of sophisticated, yet easy to use, computer software programs available in the areas of cost and schedule planning and control. Almost any issue of such publications as *Engineering News Record* or *Civil Engineering* will contain numerous advertisements from companies offering computer software programs in this area. Considering the savings in manpower; reduction in error; and increased capability to plan, control, and update schedules with a minimum of effort, these software programs have been shown to be quite cost-effective. But the planner first must develop the activity logic before turning to the computer to perform the calculations and to draw the diagram.

    The computer overcomes one of the major shortcomings to using the critical path method (CPM)—updating and revising the network schedule. While many companies recognize the value of *initially* preparing a CPM schedule before commencing with the construction of a complex project (and many owners insist on contractors providing such an initial plan), often the CPM schedule has then been "shelved" and not used again. The more easily updated bar charts are used to control the work. The reason for this was the large effort required to update the network periodically, especially if there were several hundred activities, all of which had to be changed manually when the schedule along the critical path changed. The computer has changed all that! It will update and produce a revised schedule almost instantaneously. Then it can prepare lists and diagrams of selected activities, in almost any desired form. Of particular value is a list of those activities which are behind schedule (with their revised ES, LS, EF, LF, and float—negative in this case) for any particular phase of the project.

The computer also allows the planner to play "what if" scenarios such as: "What happens to the schedule and cost if additional needed equipment is rented or leased?" or "What happens to the schedule and cost if critical delivery of major equipment items is delayed?"

RESOURCE SCHEDULING

If construction on a project is to proceed efficiently and as scheduled, it is necessary to know accurately the types and quantities of resources that will be needed and when they will be needed. Consider the mobile home installation project presented in Table 2-1 and Fig. 2-1. Let us assume that the following laborers are required for each activity:

Code	Description	Duration (days)	Number of laborers
A	Site layout	1	1
B	Slab excavation	4	4
C	Slab forms	1	4
D	Place blocks	1	3
E	Rough plumbing	2	2
F	Rough electrical	2	2
G	Place concrete	1	6
H	Place home	1	2
I	Remove forms	2	3
J	Cure concrete	7	1
K	Hookup	4	1
L	Cleanup	2	4

One way to look at resource scheduling is to construct a resource allocation chart for the ES and LS schedules. Figure 2-9 contains the ES time-grid diagram and resource allocation charts for both the ES and the LS schedules. Two things are immediately apparent from an examination of the charts. One is that the demand for laborers fluctuates from day to day, and if the LS schedule is followed, during day 7 a total of nine laborers will be needed. Further examination reveals that if the contractor desires to have as uniform a demand for laborers as practicable, he will follow a slightly altered schedule from the ES, probably delaying activity C for a few days, not doing any other activities at the same time as activity G, and thus getting by with a maximum of only six laborers during any given day. Another observation which can be made from this example is that

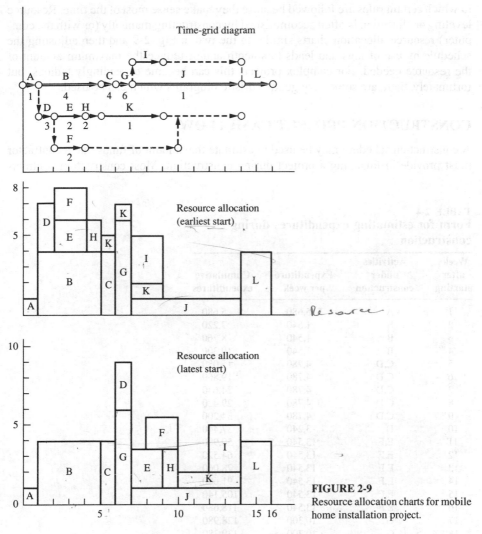

FIGURE 2-9
Resource allocation charts for mobile home installation project.

a number of possible schedules can be followed to allocate resources. Thus, resource scheduling can be very complex, especially if resources are limited (as they almost always are).

There are two types of resource scheduling problems. These are:

1. *Resource leveling.* This involves the scheduling of resources to smooth out the peaks and valleys in resource use within the constraint of project duration.
2. *Resource allocation.* This involves the allocation of available resources to project activities to determine the shortest project duration that is consistent with fixed resource limits.

Resource leveling and resource allocation programs have been written for projects, and they generally are of the *heuristic* type (which means simply *rule of thumb*) in which certain rules are followed because they make sense most of the time. Resource leveling or allocation is often accomplished by constructing manually (or with the computer) resource allocation charts similar to the two in Fig. 2-9 and then adjusting the schedule by use of lags and leads to smooth and/or reduce the maximum amount of the resource needed. For complex projects this can become exceedingly tedious, but fortunately, there are some very good heuristic programs which can be used.

CONSTRUCTION PROJECT CASH FLOW

A construction schedule may be used to estimate the amount of funds that a contractor must provide in financing a project during construction. Most construction contracts

TABLE 2-4
Form for estimating expenditures during construction

Weeks after starting	Activities under construction	Expenditure per week	Cumulative expenditures
1	A	$ 5,680	$ 5,680
2	B	1,540	7,220
3	B	1,540	8,760
4	B	1,540	10,300
5	C,D	4,780	15,080
6	C,D	4,780	19,860
7	C,D	4,780	24,640
8	C,D	4,780	29,420
9	C,D	4,780	34,200
10	D	3,240	37,440
11	E,F	13,540	50,980
12	E,F	13,540	64,520
13	E,F	13,540	78,060
14	E,F	13,540	91,600
15	E,F	13,540	105,140
16	E,F	13,540	118,680
17	G	10,300	128,980
18	G	10,300	139,280
19	G	10,300	149,580
20	G	10,300	159,880
21	G	10,300	170,180
22	G	10,300	180,480
23	H	55,500	235,980
24	H	55,500	291,480
25	H	55,500	346,980
26	H	55,500	402,480
27	H	55,500	457,980
28	H	55,500	513,480
29	H	55,500	568,980
30	H	55,500	624,480
31	I	1,200	625,680
32	J	1,860	627,540

specify that the owner will pay to the contractor a stated percentage of the value of work completed during each month. The payment for work completed during the previous month is made by a specified time in the following month. Upon completion of the project, the retained funds, often 10% of the contract value of the work, is paid to the contractor. An analysis of the construction schedule will yield the approximate expenditures and receipts through any desired date. If there is an excess of expenditures over receipts the contractor must provide financing from sources other than the owner.

The estimated expenditures are determined as illustrated in Table 2-4. The amounts shown are the costs of materials, equipment usage, labor, and general overhead.

Table 2-5 illustrates a form that may be used to estimate the receipts from the owner of the project. The prices received during construction are 90% of the contract prices for the respective items, assuming receipts for a given month are payable to the contractor by the 10th of the following month.

TABLE 2-5
Estimated receipts during construction

Month	Activities under construction	Weeks under construction	Units completed per week	Unit price received during construction	End-of-period receipts	Total period receipts	Cumulative receipts[†]
April	A	1.0	1	$ 0	$ 0	0	
	B	2.4	6	270.00	3,888	$ 3,888	$ 3,888
May	B,C	4.6	6	270.00	7,452		
	D	4.0	1	3,240.00	12,960		24,300
June	C	1.0	6	270.00	1,620		
	D	2.0	1	3,240.00	6,480		
	E	2.0	1	3,240.00	6,480		
	F	2.0	14,367	0.72	20,688	35,268	59,568
July	E	4.0	1	3,240.00	12,960		
	F	4.0	14,367	0.72	41,377		
	G	0.6	14,367	0.72	6,207	60,544	120,112
August	G	4.4	14,367	0.72	45,515	45,515	165,627
September	G	1.0	14,367	0.72	10,344		
	H	3.2	12,674	4.41	178,854	189,198	354,825
October	H	4.6	12,674	4.41	257,105	257,105	611,930
November	H	0.2	12,674	4.41	11,179		
	I	1.0	1	0.00	0		
	J	1.0	1	0.00	0	11,179	623,109
Amount retained							69,234
Total amount of contract							$692,343

† Amount payable by the 10th of the following month.

TABLE 2-6
Estimated expenditures and receipts during construction

Month	Activities under construction	Weeks under construction	Expenditures per week	Expenditures for month	Cumulative expenditures	Total receipts for month	Cumulative receipts[†]
April	A	1.0	$ 5,680	$ 5,680			
	B	2.4	1,540	3,696	$ 9,376	$ 3,888	$ 3,888
May	B,C	4.6	1,540	7,084			
	D	4.0	3,240	17,960	29,420	20,412	24,300
June	C	1.0	1,540	1,540			
	D,E	4.0	3,240	12,960			
	F	2.0	10,300	20,600	64,520	35,268	59,568
July	E	4.0	3,240	12,960			
	F,G	4.6	10,300	47,380	124,860	60,544	120,112
August	G	4.4	10,300	45,320	170,180	45,515	165,627
September	G	1.0	10,300	10,300			
	H	3.2	55,500	177,600	358,080	189,198	354,825
October	H	4.6	55,500	255,300	613,380	257,105	611,930
November	H	0.2	55,500	11,100			
	I	1.0	1,200	1,200			
	J	1.0	1,860	1,860	627,540	11,179	623,109
Amount retained							69,234
Total amount of contract							$692,343

[†] Amount payable by the 10th of the month.

Table 2-6 illustrates a form that may be used to determine the estimated expenditures and receipts for the end of each month during construction. At the end of July the estimated cumulative expenditures amount to $124,860. At this time the cumulative receipts, shown for the end of June and payable by the 10th of July, amount to $59,568. Thus, there is a difference of $124,860 − $59,568 = $65,292 which the contractor may have to provide from another source for 10 days.

The information presented will assist the contractor when she prices the job since the costs associated with financing the job are part of the total job costs. This information can also be used to plan activities in such a way as to minimize these financing costs (which is very important if the cost of borrowed money becomes high).

JOB LAYOUT

One of the tasks of the constructor when he estimates and plans the project is to prepare a job layout for the project. On this layout he will draw to scale the area available for offices; warehouses; storage of materials, equipment, and earth; and constructing forms and fabricating reinforcing steel. In preparing the job layout, the constructor should endeavor to arrange all areas to reduce the time consumed in carrying materials from storage areas to the project. Materials that are similar in use should be stored close together, where possible. The general office and warehouse should be located near the main entrance in order that persons visiting the project for business purposes will not have to travel around the construction areas to reach the office. This should reduce the danger of injuries to visitors and the confusion that frequently is associated with the presence of strangers around a project. If the general warehouse is near the entrance, it will facilitate the delivery of material to be stored in the warehouse. However, if a warehouse is needed to store heavy materials, such as machines that will be incorporated into the project, it may be desirable to consider using additional warehouses located nearer the project.

Figure 2-10 illustrates a job layout for a multistoried reinforced-concrete frame building. The constructor is fortunate in having adequate area for easy storage of all materials at the job site. This is not commonly the case for buildings erected in congested cities, where storage areas at the job site are limited or nonexistent. If area is not available at the job site, the constructor must obtain a storage area as near the site as possible or very carefully schedule and monitor all deliveries.

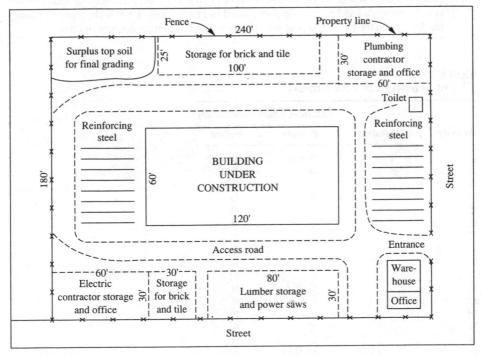

FIGURE 2-10
Job layout for multistoried reinforced-concrete building.

PROJECT CONTROL DURING CONSTRUCTION

At specified intervals, usually weekly or monthly, reports should be prepared showing the actual progress and costs on each activity during the appropriate time interval or through the effective date of the report. If the progress or costs on one or more activities or on the entire project is behind schedule or over budget, such information will be known early so that corrective steps can be taken.

PROBLEMS

2-1. Prepare an AON (arrow) diagram, showing ES, LS, EF, and LF times and the critical path, for a project involving the activities listed in Table 2-7.

2-2. Prepare an AON (arrow) diagram, showing ES, LS, EF, and LF times and the critical path, for a project involving the activities listed in Table 2-8.

2-3. Same as Prob. 2-1, except prepare a precedence diagram.

2-4. Same as Prob. 2-2, except prepare a precedence diagram.

2-5. Prepare a time-grid diagram for the project of Prob. 2-2, for which the durations are expressed in days. Assume a week of 5 days, with work to start on the first Monday in September of the current year. Show the calendar days for the starting and finishing of each activity, with no lost time as a result of weather or other causes.

2-6. Prepare a list of activities for the construction of a 20 ft wide by 40 ft long reinforced-concrete home swimming pool, 8 ft deep at one end and 3 ft deep at the other end. The site is to be excavated and a concrete pool placed in-ground, with a 5 ft wide concrete coping border around the pool. The pool is to be fenced and to contain outdoor lighting.

TABLE 2-7
List of activites for Problem 2-1

Activity	Duration	Activities which immediately	
		Precede	Follow
A	3	None	B, C
B	5	A	D, E
C	4	A	F, I
D	7	B	G
E	6	B	H
F	11	C	H
G	6	D	K
H	4	E, F	K
I	3	C	K, L
J	6	D	M
K	5	G, H, I	N
L	7	I	O
M	5	J	P
N	3	K	P
O	2	L	P
P	4	M, N, O	None

TABLE 2-8
List of activites for Problem 2-2

Activity	Duration	Activities which immediately	
		Precede	Follow
A	3	None	C
B	5	None	D, E
C	4	A	F, G, H
D	8	B	F, G, H
E	9	B	I
F	5	C, D	J, K, L, M
G	8	C, D	K, L, M
H	6	C, D	I
I	5	E, H	P
J	4	F	N
K	7	F, G	O
L	6	F, G	Q
M	7	F, G	P
N	4	J	R
O	8	K	R
P	4	I, M	R
Q	5	L	R
R	3	N, O, P, Q	None

2-7. For Prob. 2-6, assign precedence relationships to each activity and prepare an arrow diagram.

2-8. Same as Prob. 2-7, except prepare a precedence diagram.

2-9. (*a*) For the arrow diagram shown in Fig. 2-11, determine the ES, LS, EF, and LF times for each activity and indicate the critical path(s).

　　(*b*) For activity 30-60; what is the total float? What is the free float?

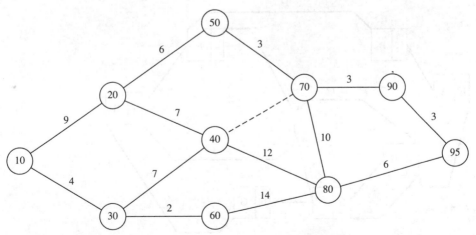

FIGURE 2-11
Arrow diagram for Prob. 2-9.

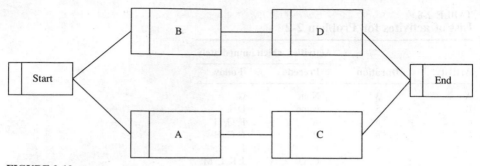

FIGURE 2-12
Precedence diagram for Prob. 2-10.

2-10. For the precedence diagram shown in Fig. 2-12, determine the optimal completion time. Indirect costs are $2,000 per day and there is a bonus of $500 per day for each day that the project is completed ahead of day 15. The following table lists the direct costs for the activities:

Activity	Normal duration/cost	Crash duration/cost
A	12 days/$12,000	6 days/$18,000
B	10 days/$20,000	5 days/$30,000
C	14 days/$20,000	6 days/$32,000
D	16 days/$40,000	6 days/$45,000

2-11. For the precedence diagram shown in Fig. 2-13, determine the ES, LS, EF, and LF times for each activity and indicate the critical path.

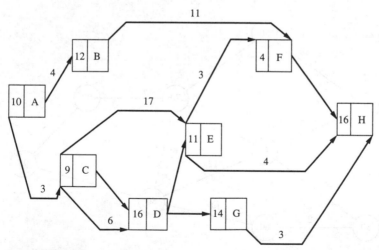

FIGURE 2-13
Precedence diagram for Prob. 2-11.

2-12. Prepare a precedence diagram for the construction of a concrete retaining wall 800 ft long. The wall is to be built in sections, each 100 ft in length, using forms eight times. Use appropriate lags and leads and estimate durations for each activity. Then calculate ES, LS, EF, and LF times and the critical path.

REFERENCES

1. Stevens, James D., *Techniques for Construction Network Scheduling,* McGraw-Hill, New York, 1990.
2. Moder, Joseph J., Cecil R. Phillips, and Edward W. Davis, *Project Management with CPM, PERT and Precedence Diagramming,* 3d ed., Van Nostrand Reinhold, New York, 1983.
3. *Construction Planning and Scheduling,* Associated General Contractors of America, Washington, DC, 1994.
4. Horsley, William F., *Means Scheduling Manual,* 3d ed., R. S. Means, Kingston, MA, 1991.
5. Willis, Edward M., *Scheduling Construction Projects,* Wiley, New York, 1986.

CHAPTER
3

EQUIPMENT COST

GENERAL INFORMATION

From the standpoint of cost, equipment costs rank second to labor cost in terms of uncertainty and in their effect on the outcome of the anticipated profit of a particular project. Thus, the accurate estimation of equipment cost is of primary importance to the successful constructor. There are three means by which a piece of equipment may be employed on a project:

1. Machines may be purchased by the constructor and thus become part of his equipment fleet. This usually results in the lowest hourly use charge, *provided the equipment is utilized most of the time.* Constructors spend many sleepless nights worrying about keeping their equipment fleet busy. The reason? Ownership costs accrue whether or not the equipment is working. In terms of company profit equipment utilization is often the most important factor.
2. Machines may be leased. This usually results in a higher use charge than owning a piece of equipment, but there is a lower risk involved than in owning because you only have to utilize the equipment for the duration of the lease.
3. Machines may be rented. Usually, renting results in the highest use charge, but the expense is justified when the use is for relatively short periods of time.

Constructors in a competitive environment want to utilize the most suitable equipment. They consider the money spent for equipment as an investment which is recovered with a profit as the equipment is utilized on projects. A constructor does not pay for a piece of equipment; the equipment must pay for itself by earning the constructor more money than it costs. Since owning a piece of equipment involves a major investment, constructors build up their fleets very carefully, choosing pieces which they think will be utilized often and that, through ownership, will give them a competitive advantage.

There is no best or standard piece of equipment for any particular job. Instead, frequently many different possibilities are available to perform any given task. A constructor can never afford to own all types and sizes of equipment that might be used for the kind of work he performs. Using the techniques described in this text, the constructor will often be able to determine what kind and size of equipment seem to be the most suitable for a given project; but this information alone will not necessarily justify the purchase of equipment. The constructor will generally try to use his own equipment first, whether or not it is the "optimum" piece. If the constructor does not have the equipment, or it is unavailable due to its being committed elsewhere, purchasing will be considered, along with other options (leasing and renting), and the *total* costs of each option will be compared. If the project is small, if the equipment cannot be easily sold upon completion of the work, if future needs for the equipment are deemed remote, then purchase normally will not be selected.

Costs associated with leasing and renting equipment are readily available from firms in the business of providing these services. Estimation is quite easy, usually involving only a telephone call to verify equipment availability and cost. The costs associated with owning a piece of equipment are much more complex. This chapter deals with the costs associated with owning and operating equipment.

EQUIPMENT TYPES

Equipment may be classified a number of ways. In this text equipment is classified according to the type of work it performs, as can be seen from the Contents. Another classification is *standard* and *special. Standard* generally applies to equipment which is commonly manufactured and available to prospective purchasers. In addition, standard equipment would have readily accessible spare parts—an important factor that is often overlooked. *Special* applies to equipment which has to be manufactured for a specific project or which does not have readily accessible spare parts. Examples of special equipment include tunnel-boring machines, large hauling units, and very large shovels (such as a 90-cu-yd shovel used to strip-mine coal). Regardless of the type of equipment, estimated costs of owning and operating equipment are calculated in the same manner.

THE COST OF CONSTRUCTION EQUIPMENT

OWNERSHIP COSTS

Ownership costs involve those costs which accrue whether or not the equipment is used. Ownership costs include a number of components. First, a great deal of money can be tied up in the purchase of a large piece of equipment. This money, if borrowed, costs money (interest). This money, if available as part of a company's reserve funds, is diverted from an interest-earning use, which deprives the company of interest income and thereby costs money. Therefore, the interest expense or the interest-income loss is part of the ownership costs. Second, the equipment loses value (it depreciates) and usually must be sold for less than what it cost when purchased. This loss in value is part of the ownership cost. Third, most major equipment is taxed as property—again, whether or not the equipment is utilized. Taxes are part of the ownership costs. Fourth, equipment usually must be insured against loss, which costs money. And fifth, equipment must be stored and these storage expenses are part of ownership costs.

Compounding the issue are the costs associated with major overhauls, modifications, and additions to the equipment. Such costs are sometimes considered to be ownership costs—other times they are considered to be operating costs.

All these costs make the accurate estimation of ownership costs very difficult. Carefully kept records for equipment previously used should give some information which may be used as a guide, but such historical records of *ownership* costs are of limited value. Conditions of equipment-use, equipment-technology, interest rates, and the like, change, thus diminishing the value of historical records.

There are several methods of estimating the probable ownership cost of equipment. While no method will yield the exact cost predictions, the following widely used method is relatively simple and will yield close approximations of the cost—provided correct assumptions are made. This method, using the time-value-of-money approach discussed in Chap. 1, involves the following steps:

1. Estimate the purchase price of the equipment that is delivered to the company. Then estimate the expected useful life and probable salvage value if it is sold at the end of its useful life (based on historical records or manufacturer's information).
2. Select an appropriate interest rate for money. Most companies take the current rate of interest for borrowing money and add to it a factor to account for the risk involved in the purchase of equipment, thus establishing a minimum rate of return (MARR). The MARR will always be higher than the current rate of interest on borrowed capital.
3. Estimate the average costs associated with taxes, insurance, and storage each year and convert these costs into an equivalent interest rate based on the value of the equipment at any given time.
4. Add these two interest rates together and use the time-value-of-money approach to estimate uniform annual ownership costs.

The following example illustrates the method.

Example 3-1. A piece of equipment is estimated to cost $67,000 new and to have a useful life of 7 years with a salvage value of $7,000. The company believes that a realistic MARR would be 12%. Taxes, insurance, and storage should amount to an additional 8%, which results in an overall cost of money of 12 + 8, or 20%.

The cash flow diagram for the purchase of this piece of equipment is shown in Fig. 3-1. The equivalent uniform annual ownership cost is

$$A = \$67{,}000 \left(\frac{A}{P}, 20, 7 \right) - \$7{,}000 \left(\frac{A}{F}, 20, 7 \right) = \$18{,}045$$

Note that the estimated ownership costs are expressed in uniform annual equivalents, which are then easy to manipulate. Also, note that these costs accrue, whether or not the equipment is used. To recover these costs, an appropriate amount must be charged for equipment usage. There are several methods for charging ownership costs.

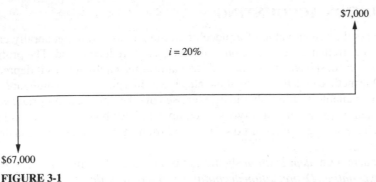

FIGURE 3-1
Cash flow diagram for Example 3-1.

One is to charge per hour of use, based on an expected use rate per year. For example, if the expected use rate is around 1,400 hours per year, then the ownership charge per hour will be

$$\text{Hourly ownership charge} = \frac{\$18,045}{1,400}$$

$$= \$12.89 \text{ per hour of use}$$

If the expected use rate is around 1,000 hours per year, then the ownership charge per hour will be

$$\text{Hourly ownership charge} = \frac{\$18,045}{1,000}$$

$$= \$18.05 \text{ per hour of use}$$

Another method is to charge the equipment on a daily, weekly, or monthly rate that it is available on the job, whether or not used. For example, if historical records indicate that this type of equipment is assigned to projects around 260 days per year, then the ownership charge per day of availability will be

$$\text{Daily ownership charge} = \frac{\$18,045}{260}$$

$$= \$69.40 \text{ per day of availability}$$

This method encourages the construction superintendent to utilize the equipment as much as possible when it is on-site. If he can utilize it 8 hours each day, his actual hourly charges will be

$$\$69.40/8 = \$8.675 \text{ per hour of use}$$

Remember, this method is only as valid as the underlying assumptions of interest rate and equipment use! Equipment owners are always very concerned about equipment use. If the owner of the equipment in the previous example charged $12.98 per hour of use (assuming 1,400 hours per year of use) and ended up with only 1,000 hours of use, he lost a considerable sum of money. With equipment rarely, if ever, utilized in the manner predicted when its initial charges are established, construction companies are very careful about purchasing equipment lest they will not be able to recover their ownership costs.

DEPRECIATION ACCOUNTING

Depreciation is the loss in value of a piece of equipment over time, generally caused by wear and tear from use, deterioration, obsolescence, or reduced need. The profitable equipment owner must have an estimate of the value of the equipment as it depreciates over time. One method of determining this value is to utilize the market value for similar equipment, if available. Caution should be exercised in selecting the appropriate *market value*. For example, most standard types of equipment have both wholesale and retail values, which are averages of reported sales to and from equipment dealers and depend on many factors.

The general term *depreciation* should not be confused with the specific term *depreciation accounting*. *Depreciation accounting* is the *systematic* allocation of the costs of a capital investment over some specific number of years. There are three reasons for calculating the depreciation accounting value (usually termed *book value*) of a piece of equipment. These are:

1. To provide the construction owner and project manager with an easily calculated *estimate* of the current market value of the equipment. To do this the method of depreciation accounting selected should approximate market value.
2. To provide a systematic method for allocating the depreciation portion of equipment ownership costs over a period of time and to a specific productivity rate. The method chosen should be simple and easily understood.
3. To allocate the depreciation portion of ownership costs in such a manner that the greatest tax benefits will accrue. Depreciation accounting for this purpose must follow strict legal governmental guidelines, which frequently change as new laws are enacted.

It is common to utilize at least two, and sometimes three, different depreciation accounting methods on a particular piece of equipment, reporting one value to the estimators for use on construction and another to the Internal Revenue Service to obtain the most favorable tax benefits.

To calculate the depreciation by any depreciation method, close estimates of the following items must be known:

1. The purchase price of the piece of equipment (termed P)
2. The economic life of the equipment (the optimum period of time to keep the equipment) or the *recovery* period allowed for income tax purposes (termed N)
3. The estimated resale value at the close of the economic life, known as the *salvage value* (termed F)

With these three items of information known or estimated, the depreciation can be calculated by using a number of methods which have been devised. The following three methods are the most commonly used:

1. Straight-line method
2. Sum-of-the-years method
3. Declining-balance method

Straight-line method of depreciation accounting. Straight-line (SL) depreciation is the easiest method to calculate and is probably the most widely used method in construction. The annual amount of depreciation D_m, for any year m, is a constant value, and thus the book value BV_m decreases at a uniform rate over the useful life of the equipment. The equations are

$$\text{Depreciation rate, } R_m = \frac{1}{N} \tag{3-1}$$

$$\text{Annual depreciation amount, } D_m = R_m(P - F) = \frac{P - F}{N} \tag{3-2}$$

$$\text{Book value at year } m, \ BV_m = P - mD_m \tag{3-3}$$

(*Note:* The value $P - F$ is often referred to as the *depreciable value* of the investment.) An example follows.

> **Example 3-2 (SL problem).** A piece of equipment is available for purchase for $12,000, has an estimated useful life of 5 years, and has an estimated salvage value of $2,000. Determine the depreciation and the book value for each of the 5 years using the SL method.
>
> $$R_m = \tfrac{1}{5} = 0.2$$
>
> $$D_m = 0.2(12,000 - 2,000) = \$2,000 \text{ per year}$$

The table of values is:

m	BV_{m-1}	D_m	BV_m
0	$ 0	$ 0	$12,000
1	12,000	2,000	10,000
2	10,000	2,000	8,000
3	8,000	2,000	6,000
4	6,000	2,000	4,000
5	4,000	2,000	2,000

Further, let us assume the equipment is expected to be used about 1,400 hours per year. The estimated hourly depreciation portion of the ownership cost of this piece of equipment is

$$\frac{\$2,000}{\$1,400} = \$1.428 = \$1.43 \text{ per hour}$$

Sum-of-the-years (SOY) method of depreciation accounting. This is an *accelerated* method (fast write-off), which is a term applied to accounting methods which permit rates of depreciation faster than straight line. The rate of depreciation is a factor times the depreciable value $(P - F)$. This factor is determined as follows:

1. The denominator of the factor is the sum of the digits including 1 through the last year in the life of the piece of equipment. Thus,

$$\text{SOY} = \frac{N(N + 1)}{2} \tag{3-4}$$

2. The depreciation rate R_m is

$$R_m = \frac{N - m + 1}{SOY} \tag{3-5}$$

3. The annual depreciation D_m for the mth year (at any age m) is

$$D_m = R_m(P - F) = \frac{N - m + 1}{SOY}(P - F) \tag{3-6}$$

4. The book value BV_m at the end of year m is

$$BV_m = P - (P - F)\left[\frac{m\left(N - \dfrac{m}{2} + 0.5\right)}{SOY}\right] \tag{3-7}$$

An example of the use of the method follows.

Example 3-3 (SOY method). Using the same values as given in Example 3-2, calculate the allowable depreciation and the book value for each of the 5 years using the SOY method.

$$SOY = 1 + 2 + 3 + 4 + 5 = 15 \qquad \text{or} \qquad = \frac{5(6)}{2} = 15$$

$$R_m = \frac{5 - m + 1}{15}$$

$$D_m = R_m \times (12{,}000 - 2{,}000) = \frac{(5 - m + 1)(10{,}000)}{15}$$

Pertinent data are tabulated in the following table:

Year	R_m	D_m	BV_m
0		$ 0	$12,000
1	$\frac{5}{15}$	3,333	8,667
2	$\frac{4}{15}$	2,667	6,000
3	$\frac{3}{15}$	2,000	4,000
4	$\frac{2}{15}$	1,333	2,667
5	$\frac{1}{15}$	667	2,000

Notice in this case the allowable depreciation each year is different, which makes calculations of hourly costs cumbersome as they would change each year. Similarly, calculations of depreciation costs per unit of work would also be cumbersome. Consequently, many companies use the straight-line method of depreciation accounting when calculating hourly or other unit costs to recover depreciation on the equipment.

Declining-balance methods. Declining-balance (DB) methods also are accelerated depreciation methods that provide for even larger portions of the cost of a piece of equipment to be written off in the early years. Interestingly, this method often more nearly approximates the actual loss in market value with time. Declining methods range from 1.25 times the current book value divided by the life to 2.00 times the current book value divided by the life (the latter is termed *double declining balance*). Note that although the estimated salvage value F is not included in the calculation, the book value *cannot* go below the salvage value. The following equations are necessary to use the declining-balance methods.

The symbol R is used for the depreciation rate for the declining-balance method of depreciation:

1. For 1.25 declining-balance (1.25DB) method, $R = 1.25/N$.
   For 1.50 declining-balance (1.5DB) method, $R = 1.50/N$.
   For 1.75 declining-balance (1.75DB) method, $R = 1.75/N$.
   For double-declining-balance (DDB) method, $R = 2.00/N$.

2. The allowable depreciation D_m for any year m and any depreciation rate R is

$$D_m = RP(1 - R)^{m-1} \quad \text{or} \quad D_m = (BV_{m-1})R \tag{3-8}$$

3. The book value for any year m is

$$BV_m = P(1 - R)^m \quad \text{or} \quad BV_m = BV_{m-1} - BV_m, \text{ provided that } BV_m \geq F \tag{3-9}$$

Since the book value can never go below the estimated salvage value, the DB method must be *forced* to intersect the value of F at time N. This may be accomplished by switching from the DB method to either the SOY method or the SL method. The following example illustrates this method of depreciation.

Example 3-4 (DDB method). For the same piece of equipment described in Example 3-3, calculate the allowable depreciation and the book value for each of the 5 years of its life.

$$R = \frac{2.0}{5} = 0.4$$

$$D_m = 0.4(BV_{m-1})$$

$$BV_m = BV_{m-1} - D_m$$

The results of the calculation are given in the following table:

Year	D_m	BV_m
0	0	12,000
1	$0.4 \times 12{,}000 = 4{,}800$	7,200
2	$0.4 \times 7{,}200 = 2{,}880$	4,320
3	$0.4 \times 4{,}320 = 1{,}728$	2,592
4	$0.4 \times 2{,}592 = 592$	2,000
5	0	2,000

Note that in year 4, the calculated depreciation using the DDB method resulted in a book value lower than the estimated salvage value. Therefore, the allowable depreciation was only $592, which in effect was a straight-line depreciation taken in year 4. Then in year 5, since all the depreciation had already been taken, the allowable depreciation would equal zero.

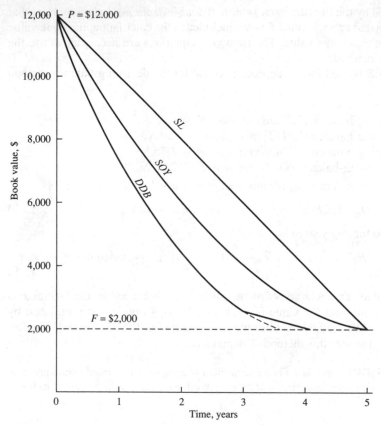

FIGURE 3-2
Allowable depreciation curves for three methods of depreciation.

The allowable depreciation for the example piece of equipment using each of the three methods is shown in Fig. 3-2.

OPERATING COSTS

Operating costs are those costs associated with the operation of a piece of equipment. In contrast to ownership costs, which generally accrue whether or not the equipment is actually being used, operating costs usually occur *only* when the equipment is being used. Operating costs include the fuel and lubrication costs, operator costs, and minor maintenance and repair costs. The other costs involved in equipment are major maintenance, major repair, and tires. These costs are sometimes included in the cost of ownership and sometimes in the cost of operating. Either way, they represent a significant cost category and should not be overlooked. Each of the operating costs is discussed in the following paragraphs.

Maintenance and repairs. The cost of maintenance and repairs will vary considerably with the type of equipment, the service to which it is assigned, and the care which it receives. If a bearing is greased and adjusted at frequent intervals, its life will be much longer than if it is neglected.

The annual cost of maintenance and repairs may be expressed as a percent of the annual cost of ownership or it may be expressed independently of ownership. In any event, it should be sufficient to cover the cost of keeping the equipment operating efficiently. The annual cost of maintenance and repairs for a power shovel may vary from 80 to 120% of the annual cost of ownership, with 100% a fair average value. The annual cost for certain types of rock-crushing equipment may be much higher, whereas for an electric motor it will be lower. Historical records serve as a reasonable guide in estimating these costs.

Operating conditions. Construction equipment which is driven by internal combustion engines requires fuel and lubricating oil, which should be considered as an operating cost. While the amounts consumed and the unit cost of each will vary with the type of equipment, the conditions under which it is used, and the location, it is possible to estimate the cost reasonably accurately for a given project.

The person who is responsible for selecting the equipment should estimate the conditions under which the equipment will operate. There are at least two conditions which will apply to most projects, the extent to which the engine will operate at full power all the time and the actual time that the unit will operate in an hour or a day.

While the power unit in a piece of equipment may be capable of developing a given horsepower when operating at maximum output, it is well known that maximum output usually will not be required at all times. For example, the full power of an engine may be required while a power shovel is loading the dipper, but during the balance of the cycle the demands on the engine are reduced considerably. The full power of a tractor will be required while it is loading a scraper with earth, and possibly while it is climbing an embankment, but for the rest of the round-trip cycle usually less than the maximum power will be required. Consider the gasoline-engine-driven air compressor. For a short time the engine will operate at full power, then it will idle for a while, with these conditions alternating as the air is used.

Horsepower ratings. Because the horsepower ratings specified in the literature of various manufacturers are not determined under the same operating conditions, it is not possible to compare the work capability of different engines with a high degree of accuracy. The power may be specified for standard conditions, namely at a barometric pressure of 29.9 in. of mercury (in. Hg) and at a temperature of 60°F, or it may be specified for normal operating conditions, with altitudes up to 2,000 ft above sea level and at temperatures up to 85°F. The specified power may be the maximum that the bare engine can develop or it may be the flywheel power with all accessories attached to the engine. The accessories will vary with engines but usually include a fan, generator, fuel pump, water pump, air cleaner, and lubricating oil pump. Each of these accessories requires power, for a combined demand that may equal 25% or more of the rated flywheel power of the engine. Thus, an engine rated at 200 flywheel horsepower (fwhp) may develop 250 horsepower (hp) when rated as a bare engine.

Fuel consumed. When operating under standard conditions, a gasoline engine will consume approximately 0.06 gal of fuel per flywheel horsepower hour (fwhp-hr), while a diesel engine will consume approximately 0.04 gal per fwhp-hr. A *horsepower hour* is a measure of the work performed by an engine.

In order to determine the work performed by an engine, we need to know the average power generated by the engine and the duration of this performance. Engines used in the construction industry seldom operate at a constant output or at the rated output, except for short periods of time. A tractor engine may operate at maximum power when it is loading a scraper or negotiating an adverse slope. During the balance of its cycle the demand on the engine will be reduced substantially, resulting in a decreased consumption of fuel. Also, construction equipment is seldom operated the entire 60 min in an hour.

Consider a power shovel with a diesel engine rated at 160 fwhp. When used to load trucks, the engine may operate at maximum power while filling the dipper, requiring 5 sec out of a cycle time of 20 sec. During the other 15 sec the engine may operate at not more than one-half its rated power. Also, the shovel may be idle for 10–15 min, or more, during an hour, with the engine providing only that power required for internal operation.

Assume that this shovel operates 50 min per hour to give an operating factor $= \frac{50}{60} \times 100 = 83.3\%$. The approximate amount of fuel consumed in an hour can be determined as follows:

Rated output at flywheel = 160 hp
Engine Factor:

Filling the dipper, $\frac{5}{20} \times 1$	= 0.250	
Rest of cycles, $\frac{15}{20} \times 0.5 \times 1$	= 0.375	
Total factor	= 0.625	

Time factor $= \frac{50}{60} = 0.833$
Operating factor $= 0.625 \times 0.833 = 0.520$
Fuel consumed per hour $= 0.520 \times 160 \times 0.04 = 3.33$ gal

For other operating factors the quantity of fuel consumed can be estimated in a similar manner.

Lubricants. The quantity of lubricants used by an engine will vary with the size of the engine, the capacity of the crankcase, the condition of the piston rings, and the number of hours between lubricant changes. For extremely dusty operations it may be desirable to change lubricants every 50 hours, but this is an unusual condition. It is common practice to change lubricant every 100–200 hours. The quantity of the lubricant consumed by an engine per change will include the amount added during the change plus the make-up lubricant between changes.

A formula which may be used to estimate the quantity of the lubricant required is

$$q = \frac{\text{hp} \times f \times 0.006 \text{ lb/hp-hr}}{7.4 \text{ lb/gal}} + \frac{c}{t} \tag{3-10}$$

where q = quantity consumed, gph (gal per hours)
   hp = rated horsepower of engine

c = capacity of crankcase, gal

f = operating factor

t = number of hours between changes

It assumes that the quantity of the lubricant consumed per rated horsepower hour, between changes, will be 0.006 lb. Using the formula, for a 100-hp engine with a crankcase capacity of 4 gal, requiring a change every 100 hours, the quantity consumed per hour will be

$$q = \frac{100 \times 0.6 \times 0.006}{7.4} + \frac{4}{100} = 0.049 + 0.04 = 0.089 \text{ gph}$$

EXAMPLES ILLUSTRATING THE COST OF OWNING AND OPERATING CONSTRUCTION EQUIPMENT

Example 3-5. Determine the probable cost per hour for owning and operating a $\frac{3}{4}$-cu-yd diesel-engine-powered crawler-type power shovel. The following information will apply:

Engine, 160 hp
Crankcase capacity, 6 gal
Hours between oil changes, 100
Operating factor, 0.60
Fuel consumed per hr, $160 \times 0.6 \times 0.04 = 3.9$ gal
Lubricating oil consumed per hour

$$\frac{160 \times 0.6 \times 0.006}{7.4} + \frac{6}{100} = 0.138 \text{ gal}$$

Grease consumed per hour, 0.5 lb
Useful life, 5 years, with no salvage value
Hours operated per year, 1,400
Shipping weight, 56,000 lb

Cost to owner:

List price fob factory, including dipper	$= \$119,350$
Freight cost, 56,000 lb @ \$2.40 per cwt[†]	$=\quad 1,344$
Sales tax, \$119,350 @ 5%	$=\quad 5,967$
Unloading and assembling at destination	$=\qquad 359$
Total cost to owner	$= \$127,010$

Ownership cost:

Interest:	$=\quad 9\%$
Risk addition	$=\quad 6\%$
Taxes, insurance, storage	$=\quad 5\%$
Overall i	$= 20\%$

Hourly ownership cost:
$= 127,010(A/P\ 20,5)/1,400 \qquad = \$30.335$

Operating cost:

Maintenance and repairs, assume 100% of annual straight-line depreciation. From Eq. (3-2):
$D = 127,010/5 = \$25,402$

Hourly cost = $25,402/1,400$		=	18.144
Fuel, 3.9 gal @ $1.25		=	4.875
Lubricant, 0.138 gal @ $2.00		=	0.276
Grease, 0.5 lb @ $0.50		=	0.25
Total cost per hour of use (excluding labor)		=	$53.88

†Hundredweight.

Example 3-6. Determine the probable cost per hour for owning and operating a 25-cu-yd heaped capacity bottom-dump truck with six rubber tires. Because the tires will have a different life from the wagon, they should be treated separately. The following information will apply:

Engine, 250-hp diesel
Crankcase capacity, 14 gal
Time between oil changes, 80 hours
Operating factor, 0.60
Fuel consumed per hr, $250 \times 0.6 \times 0.04 = 6.0$ gal
Lubricating oil consumed per hour

$$\frac{250 \times 0.6 \times 0.006}{7.4} + \frac{14}{80} = 0.30 \text{ gal}$$

Other lubricants used per hour, 0.50 lb
Useful life, 5 years, with no salvage value
Hours operated per year, 1,400
Life of tires, 5,000 hours
Repairs to tires, 15% of cost of depreciation of tires

Cost to owner:

Cost delivered, including freight and taxes	=	$92,623
Less cost of tires	=	12,113
Net cost less tires	=	$80,510

Ownership cost:

Interest	=	9%
Risk addition	=	6%
Taxes, insurance, storage	=	5%
Overall i	=	20%

Hourly ownership cost of truck:
= $80,150(A/P, 20, 5)/1,400$ = $19.229
Ownership cost of tires:
Life, $N = 5,000/1,400 = 3.57$ years
Hourly ownership cost of tires:
= $12,133(A/P, 20, 3.57)/1,400$
= $12,133(0.41804)/1,400$ = 3.623
Operating cost:
Maintenance and repairs, assume 50% of annual
straight-line depreciation. From Eq. (3-2):
$D = 80,510/5 = \$16,102$
Hourly cost = $0.5 \times 16,102/1,400$ = 5.751

Tire repair:
  From Eq. (3-2): $D = 12,113/5,000 = \$2.423$

Tire repair $= 0.15 \times 2.423$	=	0.363
Fuel, 6 gal @ \$1.25	=	7.50
Lubricant, 0.30 gal @ \$2.00	=	0.60
Grease, 0.5 lb @ \$0.50	=	0.25
Total cost per hour of use (excluding labor) = 37.316		= \$37.32

Note that the costs determined in the previous examples do not include any allowances for the salvage value of the equipment, if any, at the end of its useful life. If it is anticipated that there will be a realizable salvage value at the end of the indicated useful life, the costs should be adjusted accordingly.

The hourly cost of owning and operating construction equipment, as illustrated in the previous examples, will vary with the conditions under which the equipment is operated, and the job planner should analyze each job to determine the probable conditions.

If a shovel is used to excavate a soft material, the life of the dipper teeth and other parts which are affected by the wear and strain will be relatively long. Repair costs will be relatively low. However, if the shovel is used to excavate rock or other hard materials, the dipper teeth and certain gear parts will be subjected to greater strains and the life of each will be reduced. Repair costs will be correspondingly increased. Likewise, the consumption of fuel will be affected by digging conditions.

If trucks are operated over straight, reasonably level, smooth roads, the cost of repairs will be lower than when the same trucks are operated over poorly maintained roads, with steep hills, ruts, or deep sand. A study of statistical information showing the cost per mile for operating automotive equipment over roads having different types of surfaces will reveal surprisingly large variations in the costs. These variations will apply to trucks used for hauling materials.

ECONOMIC LIFE OF CONSTRUCTION EQUIPMENT

Thus far we have presented a term called *useful life* of a piece of equipment and used it to calculate ownership costs. There are several different "lives" of equipment, including (1) the time it is actually owned (*actual life*), (2) the depreciable life used in depreciation accounting, (3) the life used for tax purposes (*taxable life*), and (4) the optimum time that the equipment should be held from an overall income/cost viewpoint (*economic life*). Obviously, constructors are vitally interested in obtaining the lowest possible overall cost per unit of income production, and equipment costs are an important component. The term encompassing both cost and income (if present) is *worth*. Economic life is defined as the life in which the annual worth is maximized. If no income is generated, the economic life is the life for which the annual costs are minimized. Ideally, when a piece of equipment is purchased, the estimated useful life will equal the actual economic life. Realistically, useful lives are estimated from historical records and manufacturers' data. Seldom are such data accurate because the future is never exactly as planned. Anticipated use levels, operating conditions, technological advancements, and the like are almost impossible to predict with any degree of reliability further than 2 years into the future.

Profitable equipment owners keep accurate records of actual equipment use, equipment charges, ownership costs, and operating costs. Periodically, these actual values are compared with estimated values. If actual values are different, the equipment charges are adjusted. The estimated useful life is also checked with the actual economic life. In order to determine the actual economic life, net annual worth (or cost) calculations are made for several trial time periods using the market value of the equipment, if sold, at the end of these periods. The assumed values, through depreciation accounting, should *not* be used. The following example illustrates the method.

Example 3-7. In Example 3-5 a $\frac{3}{4}$-cu-yd diesel-engine-powered crawler-type shovel was purchased for a total price of $127,010. A 5-year useful life with no salvage value was used to estimate the probable cost per hour of owning and operating the shovel. Two years have elapsed, and the actual operating costs of the shovel (excluding labor) averaged $24.06 per hour the first year and $32.12 per hour the second year. Operating costs are expected to increase about the same amount each year for the next several years. The market value for the shovel, if sold now, is $45,000. The market values of similar shovels 3, 4, and 5 years old are $20,000, $7,000, and $2,000, respectively. Operating cost increase $= 32.12 - 24.06 = \$8.06$ per year.

1. If sold 1 year from now, the hourly cost is:

Ownership $= [45,000(A/P, 20, 1) - 20,000(A/F, 20, 1)]/1,400$

$\qquad\qquad\qquad\qquad\qquad\qquad\qquad\qquad = \$24.29$

Operating $\;= 29.12 + 8.06 \qquad\qquad\qquad\qquad = \underline{\;\;37.18\;\;}$

Total $\qquad\qquad\qquad\qquad\qquad\qquad\qquad\qquad\;\; = \$61.47$

2. If sold 2 years from now, the hourly cost is:

Ownership $= [45,000(A/P, 20, 2) - 7,000(A/F, 20, 2)]/1,400$

$\qquad\qquad\qquad\qquad\qquad\qquad\qquad\qquad = \$18.77$

Operating $\;= (37.18 + 45.24)/2 \qquad\qquad\quad\; = \underline{\;\;41.21\;\;}$

Total $\qquad\qquad\qquad\qquad\qquad\qquad\qquad\qquad\;\; = \$59.98$

3. If sold 3 years from now, the hourly cost is:

Ownership $= [45,000(A/P, 20, 3) - 2,000(A/F, 20, 3)]/1,400$

$\qquad\qquad\qquad\qquad\qquad\qquad\qquad\qquad = \$14.87$

Operating $\;= (37.18 + 45.24 + 53.30)/3 \quad\;\; = \underline{\;\;45.24\;\;}$

Total $\qquad\qquad\qquad\qquad\qquad\qquad\qquad\qquad\;\; = \$60.11$

Based on current estimates the economic life of this equipment is *2 more years*. The hourly charge for the equipment should be changed from $53.88 (Example 3-5) to $59.98 in order to recover actual costs. Furthermore, the profitable equipment owner will continue to reevaluate the costs at least once each year.

Note that the original purchase price was not used in determining the remaining economic life in this example. The difference in the purchase price and current market value is termed a *sunk cost*, in that it cannot be recovered.

EQUIPMENT REPLACEMENT CALCULATIONS

It is important to realize that as equipment ages through time and use, its operating costs always increase. To maintain profitability, equipment owners should periodically compare each piece of equipment's worth with the estimated worth of such alternatives as:

Replacement with a new or used piece of equipment.

Sale without replacement, then either leasing or renting as needed.

When making this comparison, remember the economic life of the existing equipment is *always 1 more year*. The rationale is whether to select one of the alternatives or to keep the existing equipment for *1 more year*. Using the preceding example, the total expected hourly costs of the existing shovel will be $61.48 when comparing it to an alternative. The purchase price of the proposed alternative should be reduced by the expected sale value of the existing equipment. If the alternative resulted in higher costs, the decision will be to keep the existing equipment for 1 more year and then reevaluate. If the alternative resulted in lower costs, the existing equipment will be replaced.

The importance of realistic assumptions cannot be overemphasized. For instance, what if the shovel in Example 3-5 were only used 1,100 hours a year. The result will be (assuming all other estimates are correct):

Actual ownership costs = $30.335 × 1,400   = $42,469.00
Ownership costs recovered = $30.335 × 1,100 = $33,368.50
Loss to equipment owner   = $9,100.50

Remember, ownership costs generally accrue whether or not the equipment is used!

PROBLEMS

3-1. Using the straight-line method of depreciating equipment, determine the annual cost of depreciation for a tractor whose total initial cost is $62,455 if the assumed life is 7 years, with an estimated salvage value of $6,000.

3-2. Using the double-declining-balance method, determine the cost of depreciation each year for 7 years for the tractor of Prob. 3-1.

3-3. Using the sum-of-the-year-digits method, determine the cost of depreciation each year for 7 years for the tractor of Prob. 3-1. What is the book value of the tractor at the end of 3 years?

3-4. A power shovel whose total initial cost was $94,230 was assumed to have a useful life of 6 years, with a salvage value of $8,000. It has been depreciated by the double-declining-balance method for 4 years. What is its book value?

3-5. A loader/hoe whose total initial cost is $70,540 has an estimated useful life of 6 years, with an estimated salvage value of $7,000. Prepare a table listing the annual costs of depreciation and the book value at the end of each of the 6 years based on the straight-line, double-declining-balance, and sum-of-the-years-digits methods of computing the annual cost of depreciation.

3-6. Prepare a graph with curves showing the book values of the loader/hoe of Prob. 3-5 during the 6 years of its life.

Note: Assume an overall cost of money of 20% for the following problems:

3-7. Determine the probable cost per hour for owning and operating a power shovel for the following conditions using straight-line depreciation:

Engine, 180-hp diesel
Crankcase capacity, 5 gal
Time between oil changes, 80 hours
Operating factor, 0.45
Useful life, 6 years
Hours used per year, 1,400
Total initial cost, $92,480
Estimated salvage value after 6 years, $8,000
Annual cost of maintenance and repairs equals 75% of annual depreciation
Cost of fuel, $1.25 per gallon
Cost of lubricating oil, $3.00 per gallon
Cost of other oils and grease, $0.50 per hour

3-8. Determine the probable cost per hour for owning and operating a wheel-type tractor-pulled scraper for the following conditions using straight-line depreciation.

Engine, 240-hp diesel
Crankcase capacity, 6 gal
Time between oil changes, 100 hours
Operating factor, 0.50
Useful life, 5 years
Hours used per year, 1,200
Annual cost of maintenance and repairs equals 75% of annual depreciation
Life of tires, 4,000 hours
Repairs to tires, 15% of the depreciation of tires
Total initial cost, $86,620
Cost of tires, $19,200
Estimated salvage value, $8,000
Cost of fuel, $1.25 per gallon
Cost of lubricating oil, $3.00 per gallon
Cost of other oils and grease, $0.50 per hour

3-9. Determine the probable cost per hour for owning and operating the tractor-pulled scraper of Prob. 3-8 if it will be used only 1,000 hours per year, with all other conditions remaining the same.

CHAPTER
4

ENGINEERING FUNDAMENTALS OF MOVING EARTH

GENERAL INFORMATION

The actual construction process of any project is really a material-handling problem. Some materials will be used only temporarily in support of the construction activities: reusable forms, scaffolding, shoring, and some access roads. Materials such as water for haul roads and fuel will be consumed. Other materials will be permanently incorporated into the structure: steel, timber, concrete, asphalt, rock, and soils. Persons in the construction industry, including constructors and engineers, should understand the effects which the selection of equipment and method have on the cost of handling these materials.

On heavy construction projects the major portion of the work consists of handling and processing bulk materials. The constructor must select the proper equipment to relocate and/or process these materials economically. The decision process for matching the best possible *machine* to the project task requires that the estimator take into account both the properties of the material to be handled and the mechanical capabilities of the machine.

When the estimator considers a construction material-handling problem, there are two primary *material* considerations: the total *quantity* of material and the *size* of the individual pieces. The quantity of material to be handled and the time constraints resulting from the contract or weather influence the selection of equipment as to the type, size, and number of machines. Larger units generally have lower unit-production cost, but there is a trade-off in higher mobilization and fixed costs. The size of the individual material pieces will affect the choice of the machine size. A loader used in a quarry to move shot rock must be able to handle the largest rock sizes produced.

MATERIAL PROPERTIES

In contract documents excavation is typically categorized as common, rock, muck, or unclassified. *Common* refers to ordinary earth excavation, whereas the term *unclassified* reflects the lack of clear distinction between soil and rock. The removal of common excavation will not require the use of explosives, although tractors equipped with rippers may be used to loosen consolidated formations. The specific engineering properties of the soil—plasticity, grain size distribution, and so on—will influence the selection of the appropriate equipment and methods.

In construction *rock* is a material which cannot be removed by ordinary earth-handling equipment.[†] Rock must be removed by drilling and blasting or by some comparable method. This normally results in a considerably greater expense than earth excavation. Rock excavation involves the study of the rock type, faulting, dip and strike, and explosive characteristics as the basis for selecting material removal and aggregate production equipment.

Muck includes materials which will decay or produce subsidence in embankments. It is usually a soft organic material having a high water content. Typically, it would include such things as decaying stumps, roots, logs, and humus. These materials are hard to handle and can present special construction problems both at their point of excavation, and in transportation and disposal.

You should never price an earth- or rock-handling project without first making a thorough study of the materials. In many cases the contract documents include geotechnical information. This owner-furnished information provides a starting point for your *independent* investigation. Other good sources of preliminary information are topographic maps, agriculture maps, geologic maps, well logs, and aerial photographs. The investigation is not complete, however, until you make an on-site visit and conduct either drilling or test pit exploration.

Even though many owners provide good geotechnical data which has been put together by qualified engineers, the design engineer's primary concern has been with how well the material will perform structurally. The constructor is interested in how the material will handle during the construction process and what volume or quantity of material is to be processed in order to yield the desired final structure.

Soil weight-volume relationships. The primary relationships (see Fig. 4-1) are expressed and defined below:

$$\text{Unit weight } (\gamma) = \frac{\text{total weight of soil}}{\text{total soil volume}} = \frac{W}{V} \tag{4-1}$$

$$\text{Dry unit weight } (\gamma_d) = \frac{\text{weight of soil solids}}{\text{total soil volume}} = \frac{W_s}{V} \tag{4-2}$$

$$\text{Water content } (\omega) = \frac{\text{weight of water in soil}}{\text{weight of soil solids}} = \frac{W_w}{W_s} \tag{4-3}$$

[†] It should be noted that this definition of rock will be affected by equipment development. Larger and heavier machines are continually changing the limits of this definition for rock.

$$\text{Void ratio } (e) = \frac{\text{volume of voids}}{\text{volume of soil solids}} = \frac{V_v}{V_s} \qquad (4\text{-}4)$$

$$\text{Porosity } (n) = \frac{\text{volume of voids}}{\text{total soil volume}} = \frac{V_v}{V} \qquad (4\text{-}5)$$

$$\text{Specific gravity } (G_s) = \frac{\text{weight of soil solids/volume of solids}}{\text{unit weight of water}}$$

$$= \frac{W_s/V_s}{\gamma_w} \qquad (4\text{-}6)$$

Many more formulas can be derived from these basic relationships. Two such formulas which are very useful in analyzing compaction specification are

$$\text{Total soil volume } (V) = \text{volume voids } (V_v) + \text{volume solids } (V_s) \qquad (4\text{-}7)$$

$$\text{Weight of solids } (W_s) = \frac{\text{weight of soil } (W)}{(1 + \text{water content } (\omega))} \qquad (4\text{-}8)$$

If unit weights are known, which is the usual case, then Eq. (4-8) becomes

$$\gamma_d = \frac{\gamma}{1 + \omega} \qquad (4\text{-}9)$$

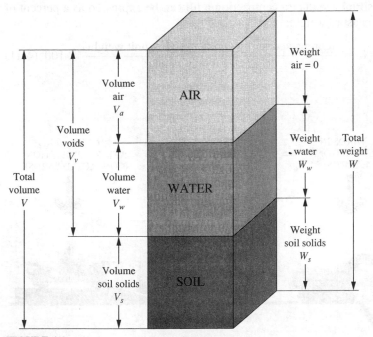

FIGURE 4-1
Soil mass weight and volume relationships.

The usefulness and application of these relationships will be shown by an example problem in the next section.

Volumetric measure. For bulk materials volumetric measure varies with the material's position in the construction process (see Fig. 4-2). The same weight of a material will occupy different volumes as the material is handled on the project. Soil volume is measured in one of three states:

Bank cubic yard	1 cu yd of material as it lies in the *natural* state, bcy
Loose cubic yard	1 cu yd of material after it has been disturbed by a loading process, lcy
Compacted cubic yard	1 cu yd of material in the compacted state, also referred to as a net in-place cubic yard, ccy

In planning or estimating a job, the engineer must use a consistent volumetric state in any set of calculations. The necessary consistency of units is achieved by the use of shrinkage and swell factors.

The *shrinkage factor* is the ratio of the compacted dry weight per unit volume to the bank dry weight per unit volume:

$$\text{Shrinkage factor} = \frac{\text{compacted dry unit weight}}{\text{bank dry unit weight}} \qquad (4\text{-}10)$$

The weight shrinkage due to compacting a fill can be expressed as a percent of the original bank measure weight:

$$\text{Shrinkage \%} = \frac{(\text{compacted unit weight}) - (\text{bank unit weight})}{\text{compacted unit weight}} \times 100 \quad (4\text{-}11)$$

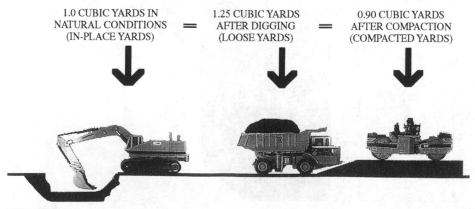

1.0 CUBIC YARDS IN
NATURAL CONDITIONS   =   1.25 CUBIC YARDS
(IN-PLACE YARDS)   AFTER DIGGING   =   0.90 CUBIC YARDS
                                   (LOOSE YARDS)   AFTER COMPACTION
                                                                (COMPACTED YARDS)

FIGURE 4-2
Material volume changes caused by processing.

The *swell factor* is the ratio of the loose dry weight per unit volume to the bank dry weight per unit volume:

$$\text{Swell factor} = \frac{\text{loose dry unit weight}}{\text{bank dry unit weight}} \qquad (4\text{-}12)$$

The percent swell, expressed on a gravimetric basis, is

$$\text{Swell \%} = \left(\frac{\text{bank unit weight}}{\text{loose unit weight}} - 1\right) \times 100 \qquad (4\text{-}13)$$

Table 4-1 gives representative swell values for different classes of earth. These values will vary with the extent of loosening and compaction. If more accurate values are desired for a specific project, tests should be made on several samples of the earth taken from different depths and different locations within the proposed cut. The test can be made by weighing a given volume of undisturbed, loose, and compacted earth.

Example 4-1. An earth fill, when completed, will occupy a net volume of 187,000 cu yd. The borrow material which will be used to construct this fill is a stiff clay. In its "bank" condition, the borrow material has a wet unit weight of 129 lb per cu ft (γ), a moisture content ($\omega\%$) of 16.5%, and an in-place void ratio (e) of 0.620. The fill will be constructed in layers of 8-in. depth, loose measure, and compacted to a dry unit weight (γ_d) of 114 lb per cu ft at a moisture content of 18.3%. Compute the required volume of the borrow pit excavation.

$$\text{Borrow } \gamma_d = \frac{129}{(1 + 0.165)} = 111 \text{ lb/cu ft}$$

$$\text{Fill } \quad \gamma_d \qquad\qquad = 114 \text{ lb/cu ft}$$

$$\overbrace{187{,}000 \text{ cu yd} \times \frac{27 \text{ cu ft}}{\text{cu yd}} \times \frac{114 \text{ lb}}{\text{cu ft}}}^{\text{Fill}} = x \times \overbrace{\frac{27 \text{ cu ft}}{\text{cu yd}} \times \frac{111 \text{ lb}}{\text{cu ft}}}^{\text{Borrow}}$$

$$187{,}000 \times \frac{114}{111} = 192{,}054 \text{ cu yd, borrow required}$$

Note that the element $\frac{114}{111}$ is the shrinkage factor 1.03.

The key to solving this type of problem is the unit weight of the solid particles (dry weight) which make up the soil mass. In the construction process the specifications may demand that the water be either expelled or added to the soil mass. In this example the contractor would be required to add water to the borrow in order to increase the moisture content from 16.5 to 18.3%. Adjusting for the extra borrow cubic yards required to make one cubic yard fill, note the water difference:

	Fill		Borrow
γ 114 × 1.183 =	135 lb/cu ft		129 lb/cu ft
γ_d	114		111
			18
			× 1.03 (shrinkage factor)
Water	21 lb/cu ft		19 lb/cu ft

Now examine what would have happened if the engineer had used wet weights and blindly applied an incorrect shrinkage factor in order to solve for the required volume of borrow:

$$\text{Incorrect shrinkage factor: } \frac{135}{129} = 1.046$$

$$\text{Borrow volume} = 187,000 \text{ cu yd} \times 1.046$$
$$= 195,602 \text{ cu yd}$$

This represents the excavation and hauling of the natural borrow material to the fill, but it assumes that the material reaches the fill at the specified water content. This assumption is not true. To achieve the desired fill density and water content, the contractor will have to add water. This water must be hauled in by water wagon (see Fig. 4-3) and is not part of the in-place borrow unit weight. The quantity of water which must be added is

Fill

Water content = 0.183
$$187,000 \text{ cu yd} \times \frac{114 \text{ lb}}{\text{cu ft}} \times 27 \frac{\text{cu ft}}{\text{cu yd}} \times 0.183 = 105,332,238 \text{ lb, water}$$

Borrow

Water content = 0.165
$$192,054 \text{ cu yd} \times \frac{111 \text{ lb}}{\text{cu ft}} \times 27 \frac{\text{cu ft}}{\text{cu yd}} \times 0.165 = \underline{94,971,663 \text{ lb}}$$
$$10,360,575 \text{ lb, water}$$

This is 1,241,941 gal, or 6.47 gal per cu yd of borrow.

Constructors commonly apply what is referred to as a *swell factor* when estimating jobs. This rule-of-thumb factor should not be confused with the previously defined factors. The term *swell factor* is used in this case because of how the number is applied. The embankment yardage of the job is multiplied by the factor; that is, it is swelled in order to put it in the same reference units as the borrow. The job is then figured in *borrow yards*. This swell factor is strictly a guess based on past experience with similar

TABLE 4-1
Representative properties of earth and rock

Material	Bank weight		Loose weight		Percent swell	Swell factor[†]
	lb/cu yd	kg/m³	lb/cu yd	kg/m³		
Clay, dry	2,700	1,600	2,000	1,185	35	0.74
Clay, wet	3,000	1,780	2,200	1,305	35	0.74
Earth, dry	2,800	1,660	2,240	1,325	25	0.80
Earth, wet	3,200	1,895	2,580	1,528	25	0.80
Earth and gravel	3,200	1,895	2,600	1,575	20	0.83
Gravel, dry	2,800	1,660	2,490	1,475	12	0.89
Gravel, wet	3,400	2,020	2,980	1,765	14	0.88
Limestone	4,400	2,610	2,750	1,630	60	0.63
Rock, well blasted	4,200	2,490	2,640	1,565	60	0.63
Sand, dry	2,600	1,542	2,260	1,340	15	0.87
Sand, wet	2,700	1,600	2,360	1,400	15	0.87
Shale	3,500	2,075	2,480	1,470	40	0.71

[†] The swell factor is equal to the loose weight divided by the bank weight per unit volume.

FIGURE 4-3
Water wagon delivering water to the fill.

materials. It may also reflect consideration of the project design. A case in point would be when the embankment is less than 3 ft in total height, in which case more embankment material will be required to compensate for the compaction of the natural ground below the fill. A higher swell factor would, therefore, be applied by the constructor when calculating the required borrow material for fills of minimum height.

PAYLOAD

The payload of hauling equipment may be expressed either gravimetrically or volumetrically. Volumetric capacity can be stated as struck measure or in terms of loose cubic yard (lcy), bank cubic yard (bcy), or compacted cubic yard (ccy). The payload capacity of a hauling unit is often stated by the manufacturer in terms of the volume of loose material that the unit can hold, assuming that the material is heaped in some specified angle of repose. A gravimetric capacity would represent the safe operational weight which the axles and structural frame of the machine were designed to handle.

HAUL ROUTE

Travel distance. Equipment selection is affected by travel distance because of the time factor it introduces into the production cycle. All other factors being equal, increased travel distances will favor the use of high-speed large capacity units. The difference between the self-loading scraper and a push-loaded scraper can be used as an illustration. The elevating scraper will load, haul, and spread without any assisting equipment, but the extra weight of the loading mechanism reduces the unit's maximum travel speed and load capacity. A scraper, which requires a push tractor to help it load, does not have to expend power to haul a loading mechanism with it on every cycle. It will be more efficient in long-haul situations as it does not have to expend fuel in transporting extra machine weight.

Bearing capacity. A haul route must have sufficient bearing capacity to carry imposed loads. On low-bearing-capacity material, this may dictate the selection of track-type instead of wheel-type running gear. The use of special low-ground-pressure machines using wide tracks or balloon tires may be necessary.

ROLLING RESISTANCE

Rolling resistance is the resistance of a level surface to constant-velocity motion across it. This is sometimes referred to as *wheel resistance* or *track resistance,* which results from friction or the flexing of the driving mechanism plus the force required to shear through or ride over the supporting surface.

This resistance varies considerably with the type and condition of the surface over which a vehicle moves. Soft earth offers a higher resistance than hard-surfaced roads such as concrete pavement. For vehicles which move on rubber tires the rolling resistance varies with the size of, pressure on, and tread design of the tires. For equipment which moves on crawler tracks, such as tractors, the resistance varies primarily with the type and condition of the road surface.

A narrow-tread, high-pressure tire gives lower rolling resistance than a broad-tread, low-pressure tire on a hard-surfaced road. This is the result of the small area of contact between the tire and the road surface. However, if the road surface is soft and the tire tends to sink into the earth, a broad-tread, low-pressure tire will offer a lower rolling resistance than a narrow-tread, high-pressure tire. The reason for this condition is that the narrow tire sinks into the earth more deeply than the broad tire and thus always has to climb out of a deeper hole, which is equivalent to climbing a steeper grade.

The rolling resistance of an earth-haul road probably will not remain constant under varying climatic conditions or for varying types of soil which exist along the road. If the earth is stable, highly compacted, and well maintained by a grader, and if the moisture content is kept near optimum, it is possible to provide a surface with a rolling resistance about as low as that for concrete or asphalt. Moisture can be added, but following an extended period of rain it may be difficult to remove the excess moisture and the haul road will become muddy, thus increasing the rolling resistance. Providing good surface drainage will speed the removal of the water and should permit the road to be reconditioned quickly. For a major earthwork project it is good economy to provide a motor grader, water trucks, and maybe rollers to keep the haul road in good condition. As illustrated under the subject of trucks, the maintenance of low-rolling-resistance haul roads is one of the best financial investments that an earth-moving contractor can make.

TABLE 4-2
Representative rolling resistances for various types of surfaces[†]

	Steel tires, plain bearings		Crawler type track and wheel		Rubber tires, antifriction bearings			
					High pressure		Low pressure	
Type of surface	lb/ton	kg/m ton	lb/ton	kg/m ton	lb/ton	kg/m ton	lb/ton	kg/m ton
Smooth concrete	40	20	55	27	35	18	45	23
Good asphalt	50–70	25–35	60–70	30–35	40–65	20–33	50–60	25–30
Earth, compacted and maintained	60–100	30–50	60–80	30–40	40–70	20–35	50–70	25–35
Earth, poorly maintained	100–150	50–75	80–110	40–55	100–140	50–70	70–100	35–50
Earth, rutted, muddy, no maintenance	200–250	100–125	140–180	70–90	180–220	90–110	150–200	75–100
Loose sand and gravel	280–320	140–160	160–200	80–100	260–290	130–145	220–260	110–130
Earth, very muddy, rutted, soft	350–400	175–200	200–240	100–120	300–400	150–200	280–340	140–170

[†] In pounds per ton or kilograms per metric ton of gross vehicle weight.

A tire sinks into the soil until the product of the bearing area and the bearing capacity is sufficient to sustain the load. Then the tire is always attempting to climb out of the rut. The rolling resistance will increase about 30 lb per ton for each inch of penetration. The total rolling resistance is assumed to be a function of only the riding gear characteristics (independent of speed) and the total weight of the vehicle. It is usually expressed as pounds of resistance per ton of vehicle weight, or as an equivalent grade resistance. For example, if a loaded truck that has a gross weight equal to 20 tons is moving over a level road whose rolling resistance is 100 lb per ton, the tractive effort required to keep the truck moving at a uniform speed will be

$$20 \text{ tons} \times 100 \text{ lb/ton} = 2,000 \text{ lb}$$

Although it is impossible to give complete accurate values for the rolling resistances for all types of haul roads and wheels, the values given in Table 4-2 are reasonably accurate and may be used for estimating purposes.

If desired, one can determine the rolling resistance of a haul road by towing a truck or other vehicle whose gross weight is known along a level section of the haul road at a uniform speed. The tow cable should be equipped with a dynamometer or some other device which will permit determination of the average tension in the cable. This tension is the total rolling resistance of the gross weight of the truck. The rolling resistance in pounds per gross ton will be

$$R = \frac{P}{W} \tag{4-14}$$

where R = rolling resistance, lb per ton
P = total tension in tow cable, lb
W = gross weight of truck, tons

If it is necessary to tow the loaded truck up or down a sloping haul road, an appropriate correction for the effect of the slope may be applied to the tension in the tow cable, as explained in the following section. In order to apply a correction, one needs to know the grade of the haul road over which the test is being conducted.

THE EFFECT OF GRADE ON REQUIRED TRACTIVE EFFORT

The force-opposing movement of a vehicle up a frictionless slope is known as *grade resistance*. When a vehicle moves up a sloping road, the total tractive effort required to keep it moving increases approximately in proportion to the slope of the road. If a vehicle moves down a sloping road, the total tractive effort required to keep it moving reduces approximately in proportion to the slope of the road. The most common method of expressing a slope is by gradient in percent. A 1% slope is one where the surface rises or drops 1 ft vertically in a horizontal distance of 100 ft. If the slope is 5%, the surface rises or drops 5 ft per 100 ft of horizontal distance. If the surface rises, the slope is defined as plus, whereas if it drops, the slope is defined as minus. This is a physical property which is not affected by the type of equipment or the condition or type of road.

For slopes of less than 10%, the effect of grade is to increase, for a plus slope, or decrease, for a minus slope, the required tractive effort by 20 lb per gross ton of weight for each 1% of grade. This can be derived by calculating from elementary mechanics the required driving force.

From Fig. 4-4 the following relationships can be developed:

$$F = W \sin \alpha \tag{4-15}$$

$$N = W \cos \alpha \tag{4-16}$$

For angles less than 10°, $\sin \alpha \approx \tan \alpha$; with that substitution

$$F = W \tan \alpha \tag{4-17}$$

But

$$\tan \alpha = \frac{V}{H} = \frac{G\%}{100}$$

where $G\%$ is the gradient.
Hence,

$$F = W \times \frac{G\%}{100} \tag{4-18}$$

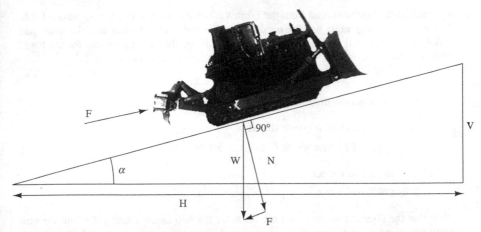

FIGURE 4-4
Frictionless slope–force relationships.

If we substitute $W = 2,000$ lb per ton, the formula reduces to

$$F = 20 \text{ lb/ton} \times G\% \tag{4-19}$$

This formula is valid for a G up to about 10%, that is, the small angle assumption.

With the relationship, a rolling resistance may be equated to an equivalent gradient.

$$\frac{\text{Rolling resistance expressed in lb/ton}}{20 \text{ lb/ton}} = G\% \tag{4-20}$$

Table 4-3 gives values for the effect of slope, expressed in pounds per gross ton or kilograms per metric ton (m ton) of weight of the vehicle.

By combining the rolling resistance, expressed as an equivalent grade, and the grade resistance, one can express the *total resistance* as an effective grade.

TABLE 4-3
The effect of grade on the tractive effort of vehicles

Slope (%)	lb/ton[†]	kg/m ton[†]	Slope (%)	lb/ton	kg/m ton
1	20.0	10.0	12	238.4	119.2
2	40.0	20.0	13	257.8	128.9
3	60.0	30.0	14	277.4	138.7
4	80.0	40.0	15	296.6	148.3
5	100.0	50.0	20	392.3	196.1
6	119.8	59.9	25	485.2	242.6
7	139.8	69.9	30	574.7	287.3
8	159.2	79.6	35	660.6	330.3
9	179.2	89.6	40	742.8	371.4
10	199.0	99.5	45	820.8	410.4
11	218.0	109.0	50	894.4	447.2

[†] Ton or metric ton of gross vehicle weight.

Example 4-2. The haul road from the borrow pit to the fill has an adverse grade of 4%. Wheel-type hauling units will be used on the job and it is expected that the haul road rolling resistance will be 100 lb per ton. What will be the effective grade for the haul? Will the units experience the same effective grade for the return trip?

Using Eq. (4-20), we obtain

$$\text{Equivalent grade} = \frac{100 \text{ lb/ton rolling resistance}}{20 \text{ lb/ton}} = 5\%$$

$$\text{Effective grade (haul)} = 5\% \text{ rr} + 4\% \text{ gr} = 9\%$$

$$\text{Effective grade (return)} = 5\% \text{ rr} - 4\% \text{ gr} = 1\%$$

where rr = rolling resistance
gr = grade resistance

Note that the effective grade is not the same for the two cases. During the haul the unit must overcome the uphill grade; on the return the unit is aided by the downhill grade.

THE EFFECT OF GRADE ON LOCATING HAUL ROUTES

During the life of a project the haul-route grades (and, therefore, grade resistance) may remain constant. One example is trucking aggregate from a rail-yard off-load point to the concrete batch plant. In most cases, however, the haul-route grades change as the project progresses. On a linear highway project, for example, the top of the hills are cut and hauled to the valleys. Early in the project, the grades are steep and reflect the existing natural ground. Over the life of the project the grades begin to assume the final highway profile. Therefore, the estimator must first study the project's mass diagram to determine the *direction* that the material has to be moved. Then the natural ground and the final profiles depicted on the plans must be checked to determine the grades that the equipment will encounter during haul and return cycles.

Site work projects are not usually linear in extent; therefore, a mass diagram is not very useful. The estimator in that case must look at the cut-and-fill areas, lay out probable haul routes, and then check the natural and finish grade contours to determine the haul-route grades.

This process of laying out haul routes is critical to machine productivity. If a route can be found which results in less grade resistance, machine travel speed can be increased and production will likewise increase. In planning a project, a constructor should always check several haul-route options before deciding on a final construction plan.

COEFFICIENT OF TRACTION

The total energy of an engine in any unit of equipment designed primarily for pulling a load can be converted into tractive effort only if sufficient traction can be developed between the driving wheels or tracks and the haul surface. If there is insufficient trac-

FOR TRACK-TYPE TRACTOR	FOR 4-WHEEL TRACTOR	FOR 2-WHEEL TRACTOR
Use total tractor weight.	Use weight on drivers shown on spec sheet or approximately 40% of vehicle gross weight.	Use weight on drivers shown on spec sheet or approximately 50% of vehicle gross weight.

FIGURE 4-5
Weight distribution on powered running gear.

tion, the full power of the engine cannot be used, for the wheels or tracks will slip on the surface.

The *coefficient of traction* may be defined as the factor by which the total load on a driving tire or track is multiplied in order to determine the maximum possible tractive force between the tire or track and the surface just before slippage occurs.

Usable force = coefficient of traction × weight on powered running gear   (4-21)

The power which can be developed at the interface between the running gear and the haul-road surface is often limited by *traction*. The factors controlling usable tractive power are the weight on the powered running gear (drive wheels for wheel-type, total weight for track-type—see Fig. 4-5), the characteristics of the running gear, and the characteristics of the travel surface.

The coefficient of traction between rubber tires and road surfaces will vary with both the type of tread on the tires and the road surface. For crawler tracks it will vary with the design of the grosser and the road surface. These variations are such that exact values cannot be given. Table 4-4 gives approximate values, which are sufficiently accurate for most estimating purposes, for the coefficient of traction between rubber tires or crawler tracks and surfaces.

TABLE 4-4
Coefficients of traction for various surfaces

Surface	Rubber tires	Crawler tracks
Dry, rough concrete	0.80–1.00	0.45
Dry, clay loam	0.50–0.70	0.90
Wet, clay loam	0.40–0.50	0.70
Wet sand and gravel	0.30–0.40	0.35
Loose, dry sand	0.20–0.30	0.30
Dry snow	0.20	0.15–0.35
Ice	0.10	0.10–0.25

Example 4-3. Assume that the rubber-tired tractor has a total weight of 18,000 lb on the two driving tires. The maximum rimpull in low gear is 9,000 lb. If the tractor is operating in wet sand, with a coefficient of traction of 0.30, the maximum possible rimpull prior to slippage of the tires will be

$$0.30 \times 18,000 \text{ lb} = 5,400 \text{ lb}$$

Regardless of the power of the engine, not more than 5,400 lb of tractive effort can be used because of the slippage of the wheels. If the same tractor is operating on dry clay, with a coefficient of traction of 0.60, the maximum possible rimpull prior to slippage of the tires will be

$$0.60 \times 18,000 \text{ lb} = 10,800 \text{ lb}$$

For this surface the engine will not be able to cause the tires to slip. Thus, the full power of the engine can be used.

Example 4-4. A wheel-tractor scraper is used on a road project. When the project initially begins, the scraper will experience high rolling and grade resistance at one work area. The rimpull required to maneuver in this work area is 42,000 lb. In the fully loaded condition 52% of the total vehicle weight is on the drive wheels. The fully loaded vehicle weight is 230,880 lb. What minimum value of the coefficient of traction between the scraper wheels and the traveling surface is needed to maintain maximum possible travel speed?

$$\text{Weight on the drive wheels} = 0.52 \times 230,880 \text{ lb} = 120,058 \text{ lb}$$

$$\text{Minimum required coefficient of traction} = \frac{42,000 \text{ lb}}{120,058 \text{ lb}} = 0.35$$

POWER TRANSMISSION

Most construction equipment is powered by internal combustion engines. Because diesel engines perform better under heavy duty applications than gasoline engines, diesel-powered machines are the workhorses of the construction industry. The characteristics which control the performance differences of these two engines are:

Carburetor	Used on gasoline engines, is an efficient method of regulating fuel.
Injector	Used on diesel engines, is a better method of regulating fuel.
Ignition system	Gasoline engines use spark-ignition; diesel engine meters fuel and air for compression-ignition.

Additionally, diesel engines have longer service lives and lower fuel consumption, and diesel fuel presents less of a fire hazard.

No matter which type of engine serves as the power source, the mechanics of energy transmission are the same. The engine develops a piston force, F_p, which acts on a crankshaft having a radius r, producing a crankshaft torque, T_g, at a governed speed, N_g:

$$T_g = F_p \times r \tag{4-22}$$

The output of the engine at the flywheel at rated revolutions per minute (rpm) and under environmental conditions of testing (temperature and altitude, to be discussed later) can be expressed as a flywheel horsepower (fwhp). This output can be measured by either friction belt or brake, hence the names *belt horsepower* or *brake horsepower* (bhp).

$$\text{fwhp} = \frac{2\pi N_g F_p r}{33,000} = \frac{2\pi N_g T_g}{33,000} \tag{4-23}$$

where N_g is in rpm, F_p is in lb, r is in ft, and T_g is in lb-ft.

Flywheel horsepower is a standard rating used by equipment manufacturers to describe a machine's power. A manufacturer's flywheel horsepower rating is developed based on the engine turning at its rated *rpm* (revolutions per minute) and driving all accessories normal to the machine's standard operational configuration. The power output from the engine, fwhp, becomes the power input to the transmission system. This system consists of the drive shaft, a transmission, planetary gears, drive axles, and drive wheels (see Fig. 4-6).

When analyzing a piece of equipment, we are interested in the usable force developed at the point of contact between the tire and the ground (*rimpull*) for a wheel machine. In the case of a track machine the force in question is that which is available at the drawbar (*drawbar pull*). The difference in the name is a matter of convention; both rimpull and drawbar pull are measured in the same units, pounds pull. Both rimpull and drawbar pull, as discussed earlier, are subject to adequate traction being developed.

In the mechanical process of developing rimpull or drawbar pull there are power losses. For any specified gear or speed-torque position on a torque converter

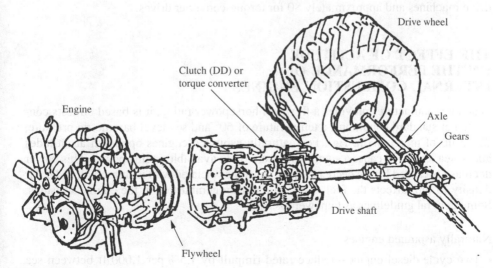

FIGURE 4-6
Power transmission system.

$$\text{Usable horsepower} = \text{fwhp} \times \frac{E\%}{100} \qquad (4\text{-}24)$$

where $E\%$ is the efficiency of the power transmission.

There are two methods for arriving at a machine's developed output force, F_w (force at the wheel):

1. If the whole-body velocity of the machine when operating at governed engine speed N_g is known for a specific gear, the relationship is

$$F_w = \frac{33,000 \times \text{fwhp} \times (E\%/100)}{v} \qquad (4\text{-}25)$$

where v is the velocity in feet per minute, fpm.

2. If the transmission gear ratio and the rolling radius of the wheel are known, v can be computed and then F_w is determined by Eq. (4-25). This assumes that there is no slippage in the gear train:

$$N \text{ drive axle} = N_g \times \text{gear ratio} \qquad (4\text{-}26)$$

where N for the drive axle is in rpm:

$$v = 2\pi \times R \text{ drive wheel} \times N \text{ drive axle} \qquad (4\text{-}27)$$

where R drive wheel is the radius of the drive wheel.

Normally, the F_w and v are measured and then usable horsepower and, ultimately, $E\%$ are backfigured. This mechanical efficiency, $E\%$, is approximately 90 for direct-drive machines and approximately 80 for torque-converter drives.

THE EFFECT OF ALTITUDE ON THE PERFORMANCE OF INTERNAL COMBUSTION ENGINES

When a manufacturer provides a flywheel horsepower rating, it is based on tests conducted at standard conditions, a temperature of 60° and sea-level barometric pressure, 29.92 in. of mercury (in. Hg). For naturally aspirated engines operation at altitudes above sea level will cause a significant decrease in available engine power. This power decrease is caused by the decrease in air density associated with increased altitude. Air density in turn affects the fuel-to-air ratio during combustion in the engine's pistons. Some general guidelines as to power loss are:

Naturally aspirated engines:

- Two-cycle diesel engine—reduce rated rimpull by 1.5% per 1,000 ft between sea level and 6,000 ft. Above 6,000 ft reduce rimpull by 3% per 1,000 ft.
- Four-cycle gasoline and diesel engines—reduce rated rimpull by 3% for every 1,000 ft above 1,000 ft.

Turbocharged engines:

- Two- and four-cycle diesel engines—usually very little or no loss in rated power up to 10,000 ft.

A *turbocharger* is a mechanical component mounted on the engine which forces air to the pistons. Engines without turbochargers rely on the suction of the piston to supply the air for combustion. Thus, for a four-cycle engine with 100 fwhp (flywheel horsepower) at sea level, the power at 10,000 ft above sea level will be determined as follows:

Sea-level power $= 100 \text{ hp}$

Loss due to altitude $\dfrac{0.03 \times 100 \times (10,000 - 1,000)}{1,000} = \underline{\ 27 \text{ hp}}$

Effective power $= 73 \text{ hp}$

The two-cycle engine, which is becoming increasingly popular in the diesel field, has its air supplied, under a slight pressure by a blower whereas the four-cycle engine depends on the suction of the pistons for the supply of air. If the engine described in the previous paragraph is two-cycle, the power at 10,000 ft above sea level will be determined as follows:

Sea-level power $= 100 \text{ hp}$

Loss due to altitude

$\dfrac{0.015 \times 100 \times 6,000}{1,000} + \dfrac{0.03 \times 100 \times (10,000 - 6,000)}{1,000} = \underline{\ 21 \text{ hp}}$

Effective power $= 79 \text{ hp}$

The two previous problems indicate that, other factors being equal, at high altitudes a two-cycle engine will give better performance than a four-cycle engine.

The effect of the loss in power due to altitude may be eliminated by the installation of a supercharger. This is a mechanical unit which will increase the pressure of the air supplied to the engine, thus permitting sea-level performance at any altitude. If equipment is to be used at high altitudes for long periods of time, the increased performance probably will more than pay for the installed cost of a supercharger.

These formulas provide an acceptable starting point in evaluating engine performance at altitudes greater than sea level. However, for specific machine applications the manufacturer's performance data should be consulted. Table 4-5 presents data for selected Caterpillar Inc. machines.

THE COMBINED EFFECT OF PRESSURE AND TEMPERATURE ON THE PERFORMANCE OF INTERNAL COMBUSTION ENGINES

Temperature also affects engine performance. A general formula for estimating purposes which expresses the effect of both temperature and altitude on four-cycle engines follows:

$$\text{Horsepower available} = \text{rated hp} \times \frac{P_{actual}}{P_{std}} \sqrt{\frac{T_{std}}{T_{actual}}} \qquad (4\text{-}28)$$

where P_{actual} = altitude at which the machine will be operated, in in. Hg (inches of mercury), barometric pressure (see Table 4-6)

P_{std} = standard condition altitude, usually sea level, 29.92 in. Hg

T_{actual} = Rankine temperature at which the machine will be operated

T_{std} = standard condition temperature, in Rankine units, usually 60°F, which equals 520°R

TABLE 4-5
Percent flywheel horsepower available for select Caterpillar machines at specified altitudes

Model	0–2,500 ft (0–760 m)	2,500–5,000 ft (760–1,500 m)	5,000–7,500 ft (1,500–2,300 m)	7,500–10,000 ft (2,300–3,000 m)	10,000–12,500 ft (3,000–3,800 m)
Tractors					
D6D, D6E	100	100	100	100	94
D7G	100	100	100	94	86
D8L	100	100	100	100	93
D8N	100	100	100	100	98
D9N	100	100	100	96	89
D10N	100	100	100	94	87
Graders					
120G	100	100	100	100	96
12G	100	100	96	90	84
140G	100	100	100	100	94
14G	100	100	100	94	87
16G	100	100 ·	100	100	100
Excavators					
214B	100	100	100	100	92
235D	100	100	100	98	91
245D	100	100	100	94	87
Scrapers					
615C	100	100	95	88	81
621E	100	100	94	87	80
623E	100	100	94	87	80
631E	100	100	96	88	82
Trucks					
769C	100	100	100	97	89
773B	100	100	100	100	96
Loaders					
966E	100	100	100	93	86
988B	100	100	100	100	93

Source: Caterpillar Inc.

Equation (4-28) may be used to determine the probable effective horsepower of a four-cycle engine at any temperature and altitude. From Table 4-6, determine the probable barometric pressure for the given altitude. Estimate the probable temperature. Apply this information to Eq. (4-28), and solve for the effective horsepower.

Example 4-5. A tractor is powered by a four-cycle diesel engine. When tested under standard conditions, the engine developed 130 fwhp. What is the probable horsepower at an altitude of 3,660 ft, where the average daily temperature is 72°F?

$$\text{fwhp std condition} = 130$$

$$P_{std} = 29.92 \text{ in.}$$

$$P_{actual} = 26.15 \text{ in. (from Table 4-6)}$$

$$T_{std} = 520°R$$

$$T_{actual} = 460 + 72 = 532°R$$

Find the fwhp available. Substituting the given information in Eq. (4-28), we get

$$\text{fwhp} = 130 \times \frac{26.15}{29.92} \sqrt{\frac{520}{532}} = 112.7 \text{ hp}$$

Thus, the probable horsepower of the engine will be reduced to 112.3 as a result of the increased altitude and temperature.

Table 4-7 gives factors by which the horsepower of a four-cycle engine, as determined under standard conditions, may be multiplied to obtain the probable horsepower for various altitudes and temperatures. Owing to variations in the barometric pressure at any altitude as the result of changes in climatic conditions, the factors may vary slightly with climatic conditions.

The two-cycle-diesel engine operates under different conditions from those which apply to a four-cycle engine. Therefore, the correction factors given in Table 4-7 will not apply to two-cycle engines. If similar information is desired, it should be requested from the manufacturer.

In all cases it must be remembered that the *required* power will remain the same at any temperature or altitude. It is the *available* power that changes.

TABLE 4-6
Average barometric pressures for various altitudes

Altitude above sea level (ft)	0	1,000	2,000	3,000	4,000	5,000	6,000
Barometric pressure (in. Hg)	29.92	28.86	27.82	26.80	25.82	24.87	23.95

TABLE 4-7
Correction factors for determining the effective horsepower of four-cycle engines at various altitudes and temperatures

Altitude above sea level (ft)	Temperature (°F)								
	110	90	70	60	50	40	20	0	−20
0	0.954	0.971	0.991	1.000	1.008	1.018	1.039	1.062	1.085
1,000	0.920	0.937	0.955	0.964	0.974	0.984	1.003	1.025	1.048
2,000	0.887	0.904	0.921	0.930	0.938	0.948	0.968	0.988	1.010
3,000	0.855	0.872	0.888	0.896	0.905	0.914	0.933	0.952	0.974
4,000	0.825	0.840	0.856	0.865	0.873	0.882	0.899	0.918	0.938
5,000	0.795	0.809	0.825	0.833	0.842	0.849	0.867	0.885	0.904
6,000	0.767	0.781	0.795	0.803	0.811	0.820	0.836	0.853	0.872
7,000	0.738	0.752	0.767	0.775	0.782	0.790	0.806	0.823	0.840
8,000	0.712	0.725	0.739	0.746	0.754	0.762	0.776	0.793	0.811
9,000	0.686	0.699	0.713	0.720	0.727	0.734	0.748	0.764	0.782
10,000	0.682	0.675	0.687	0.693	0.700	0.707	0.722	0.737	0.753

DRAWBAR PULL

The available pull which a crawler tractor can exert on a load that is being towed is referred to as the *drawbar pull* of the tractor. The pull is expressed in pounds. From the total pulling effort of an engine one must deduct the pull required to move the tractor over a level haul road before the drawbar pull can be determined. If a crawler tractor tows a load up a slope, its drawbar pull will be reduced by 20 lb for each ton of weight of the tractor for each 1% slope.

The performance of crawler tractors, as reported in the specifications supplied by the manufacturer, is usually based on the Nebraska tests. In testing a tractor to determine the maximum drawbar pull at each of the available speeds, the haul road is calculated to have a rolling resistance of 110 lb per ton. If a tractor is used on a haul road whose rolling resistance is higher or lower than 110 lb per ton, the drawbar pull will be reduced or increased, respectively, by an amount equal to the weight of the tractor in tons multiplied by the variation of the haul road from 110 lb per ton.

> **Example 4-6.** A tractor whose weight is 15 tons has a drawbar pull of 5,684 lb in the sixth gear when operated on a level road having a rolling resistance of 110 lb per ton. If the tractor is operated on a level road having a rolling resistance of 180 lb per ton, the drawbar pull will be reduced by 15 tons × (180 − 110) = 1,050 lb. Thus, the effective drawbar pull will be 5,684 − 1,050 = 4,634 lb.

The drawbar pull of a crawler tractor will vary indirectly with the speed of each gear. It is highest in the first gear and lowest in the top gear. The specifications supplied by the manufacturer should give the maximum speed and drawbar pull for each of the gears.

RIMPULL

Rimpull is a term which is used to designate the tractive force between the rubber tires of driving wheels and the surface on which they travel. If the coefficient of traction is high enough to eliminate tire slippage, the maximum rimpull is a function of the power of the engine and the gear ratios between the engine and the driving wheels. If the driving wheels slip on the haul surface, the maximum effective rimpull will be equal to the total pressure between the tires and the surface multiplied by the coefficient of traction. Rimpull is expressed in pounds.

If the rimpull of a vehicle is not known, it may be determined from the equation

$$\text{Rimpull} = \frac{375 \times \text{hp} \times \text{efficiency}}{\text{speed, mph}} \text{ lb} \tag{4-29}$$

The efficiency of most tractors and trucks will range from 0.8 to 0.85. For a rubber-tired tractor with a 140-hp engine and a maximum speed of 3.25 mph in the first gear, the rimpull will be

$$\text{Rimpull} = \frac{375 \times 140 \times 0.85}{3.25} = 13{,}730 \text{ lb}$$

The maximum rimpull in all gear ranges for this tractor will be as follows:

Gear	Speed (mph)	Rimpull (lb)
First	3.25	13,730
Second	7.10	6,285
Third	12.48	3,576
Fourth	21.54	2,072
Fifth	33.86	1,319

In computing the pull which a tractor can exert on a towed load, it is necessary to deduct from the rimpull of the tractor the tractive force required to overcome the rolling resistance plus any grade resistance for the tractor. It should be noted that the rubber-tired tractor differs from the crawler tractor in this respect. For example, if a tractor whose maximum rimpull in the first gear is 13,730 lb, weighs 12.4 tons, and is operated up a haul road with a slope of 2% and a rolling resistance of 100 lb per ton, the pull available for towing a load will be determined as follows:

Max rimpull $\qquad\qquad\qquad\qquad\qquad = \quad$ 13,730 lb

Pull required to overcome grade,
$\qquad\qquad$ 12.4 tn $\times$ 20 lb/tn $\times$ 2% $= \quad$ 496 lb
Pull required to overcome rolling resistance,
$\qquad\qquad$ 12.4 tn $\times$ 100 lb/tn $\quad = \quad$ 1,240 lb
$\qquad$ Total pull to be deducted, 496 lb + 1,240 lb $= \quad -1{,}736$ lb
$\qquad$ Pull available for towing a load $\qquad = \quad$ 11,994 lb

POWER OUTPUT AND TORQUE

Figure 4-7 shows the typical curves for brake horsepower (bhp) and torque as an engine increases its crankshaft speed to the governed rpm value. The important feature of this plot is the shape of the torque curve. Maximum torque is not obtained at maximum rpm. This provides the engine with a power reserve. When a machine is subjected to a momentary overload and this power is brought to bear, we "lug" the engine. The rpm drops but the torque goes up, keeping the engine from stalling under the overload.

Machines can be purchased with either a direct drive (standard) or a torque-converter drive. With a direct-drive machine, the operator must manually shift gears to match the engine output to the resisting load. The difference in power available when considering maximum torque and torque at governed speed is the machine's operating range for a given gear. In those applications where load is constantly changing the operation of a direct-drive machine requires a good operator. Operator skill is a significant factor controlling the amount of wear and tear that a direct-drive machine will experience. Operators of direct-drive machines will be subjected to more operator fatigue than those on power-shift models. This fatigue factor will in turn affect machine productivity.

A *torque converter* is a device which adjusts power output to match the load. This adjustment is accomplished hydraulically by a fluid coupling. As a machine begins to accelerate, the engine rpm will quickly reach the governed crankshaft speed and the torque converter will automatically multiply the engine torque to provide the required acceleration force. In this process there are losses due to hydraulic inefficiencies. If the machine is operating under constant load and at a steady whole-body speed, no torque multiplying is necessary. At this point the transmission of engine torque can be made nearly as efficient as a direct-drive transmission by locking ("lockup") the torque-converter pump and transmission together.

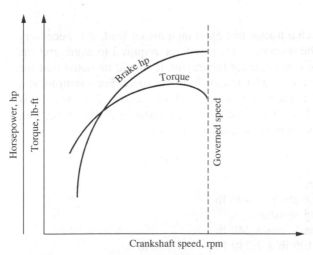

FIGURE 4-7
Engine speed–power relationships.

PERFORMANCE CHARTS

Performance charts for individual machine models are published by equipment manufacturers. These charts allow the equipment estimator/planner to analyze a machine's ability to perform under a given set of job and load conditions.

The performance chart is a graphical representation of the power and corresponding speed that the engine and transmission can deliver. The load condition is stated as either rimpull or drawbar pull. It should be noted that the rimpull-speed relationship is inverse since vehicle speed increases as rimpull decreases. If the gear ratios or rolling radius of a machine is changed, the entire performance curve will shift along both the rimpull and speed axles. Figures 4-8 and 4-10 are rimpull and retarder performance charts for a Caterpillar scraper, whose specifications are:

Engine: flywheel power 450			
Transmission: semiautomatic power shift, eight speeds			
Capacity of scraper:	Struck		– 21 cu yd
	Heaped		– 31 cu yd
Weight distribution:	Empty	Drive axle	– 67%
		Rear axle	– 33%
	Loaded	Drive axle	– 53%
		Rear axle	– 47%
Operating weight:	Empty		– 96,880 lb[†]
Rated load:			– 75,000 lb
Top Speed:	Loaded		– 33 mph

[†]Includes coolant, lubricants, full fuel tank, ROPS canopy, and operator.

A retarder is a dynamic speed-control device. By the use of an oil-filled chamber between the torque converter and the transmission, machine speed is retarded. The retarder will not stop the machine; rather, it provides speed control for long downhill hauls, reducing wear on the service brake.

Each manufacturer has a slightly different graphical layout for presenting performance chart information. However, the procedures for reading a performance chart are basically the same:

1. Ensure that the proposed machine to be utilized has the same engine, gear ratios, and tire size as those identified for the machine on the chart.
2. Determine the machine weight both when the machine is empty and loaded. The empty weight is the operating weight and should include coolants, lubricants, full fuel tanks, and an operator. The loaded weight depends on the density of the loaded material and the proposed load size. These two weights, empty and loaded, are often referred to as the *net vehicle weight* (NVW) and the *gross vehicle weight* (GVW), respectively.

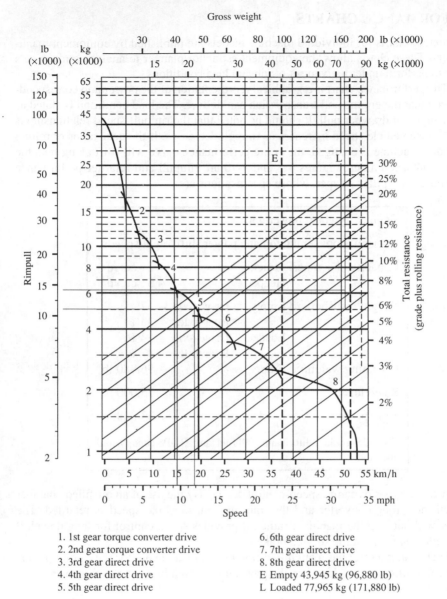

1. 1st gear torque converter drive
2. 2nd gear torque converter drive
3. 3rd gear direct drive
4. 4th gear direct drive
5. 5th gear direct drive

6. 6th gear direct drive
7. 7th gear direct drive
8. 8th gear direct drive
E Empty 43,945 kg (96,880 lb)
L Loaded 77,965 kg (171,880 lb)

FIGURE 4-8
Rimpull performance chart Caterpillar 631E scraper. (*Caterpillar Inc.*)

3. Estimate a total resistance (rolling resistance plus grade resistance) based on the probable job conditions. The intersection of the vehicle weight line and the total resistance line establishes the conditions under which the machine will be operated and correspondingly the power requirement.

4. Extend a line horizontally from the weight-total resistance intersection point. The point of intersection of this horizontal line with the vertical rimpull scale defines

the rimpull force available, between the drive wheels and the ground surface, to propel the vehicle. The rimpull-force value *assumes* that adequate traction can be developed.

5. From the point at which the horizontal line intersects the gear range curve, drop a line vertically to the speed axis. This yields the vehicle speed for the assumed job conditions. Sometimes the horizontal line from the weight-resistance intersection will intersect the gear range curve at two points (see Fig. 4-9). Two interpretations as to the speed can be made when this happens.

A guide in determining the appropriate speed follows:

• If the required rimpull is *less* than that required on the previous stretch of haul, use the higher gear and speed.
• If the required rimpull is *greater* than that required on the previous stretch of haul, use the lower gear and speed.

Performance charts are established assuming machine operation under standard conditions. When the machine is utilized under a differing set of conditions, the

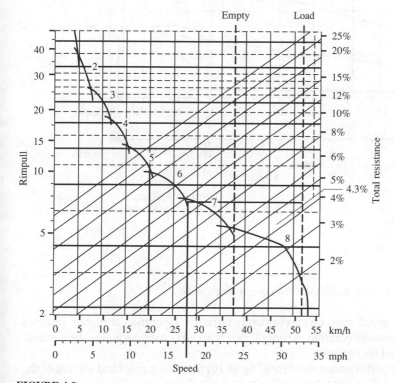

FIGURE 4-9
Rimpull performance chart—gear affect closeup. (*Caterpillar Inc.*)

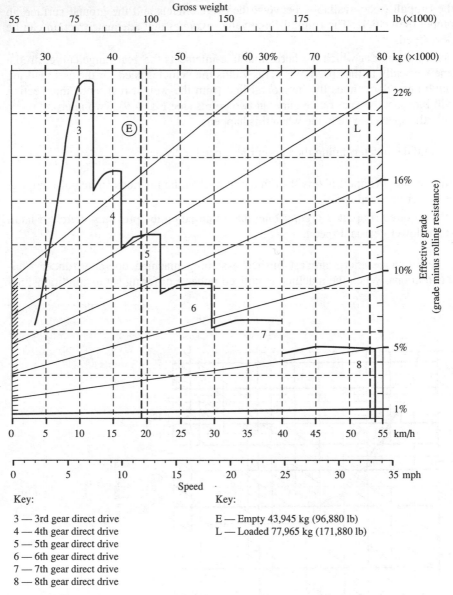

FIGURE 4-10
Retarding performance chart Caterpillar 631E scraper. (*Caterpillar Inc.*)

Key:

3 — 3rd gear direct drive
4 — 4th gear direct drive
5 — 5th gear direct drive
6 — 6th gear direct drive
7 — 7th gear direct drive
8 — 8th gear direct drive

Key:

E — Empty 43,945 kg (96,880 lb)
L — Loaded 77,965 kg (171,880 lb)

rimpull force and speed must be appropriately adjusted. Operation at higher altitudes will require a percentage derating in rimpull that is approximately equal to the percentage loss in flywheel horsepower.

The retarder performance chart (see Fig. 4-10) presents a graphical picture of the speed that can be maintained when a vehicle is descending a grade having a slope such that the magnitude of the grade resistance is greater than the resisting rolling resistance. This retarder-controlled speed is steady state, and use of the service brake will not be necessary to prevent acceleration.

A retarder performance chart is read in a similar manner as described earlier, remembering that the total resistance values are actually negative numbers (Caterpillar uses the term *effective grade*). As with the rimpull chart, the horizontal line can intersect more than one gear. In a particular gear the vertical portion of the retarder curve indicates the maximum retarder effort and the resulting speed. If haul conditions dictate, the operator will shift into a lower gear and a lower speed would be applicable. Many times the decision as to which speed to select is answered by the question: "How much effort will be expended in haul route maintenance?" Route smoothness is often the controlling factor affecting higher operating speeds.

Example 4-7. A constructor proposes to use CAT 631E scrapers on an embankment job and wishes to investigate the performance characteristics of these machines. The CAT 631E has a rated capacity of 21-cu-yd struck. The manufacturer's data states that the machine is powered by an engine which is rated under standard conditions at 450 fwhp. Empty operating weight is 96,880 lb. Loaded weight distribution is 53% on the drive wheels.

The constructor believes that the average load for the material which must be hauled will be 22.8 bank cu yd (bcy). The haul from an excavation area is a uniform adverse gradient of 4.0% with a rolling resistance of 60 lb per ton. The material to be excavated and transported is a common earth with a bank unit weight of 3,000 lb per bcy.

(*a*) Calculate the maximum travel speeds which can be expected.

Machine weight:

Empty operating weight	= 96,880 lb
Payload weight = 22.8 bcy × 3,000 lb per bcy	= 68,400 lb
Total loaded weight	= 165,280 lb

Haul conditions:

	Loaded (haul) (%)	Empty (return) (%)
Grade resistance	4.0	−4.0
Rolling resistance 60/20	3.0	3.0
Total resistance	7.0	−1.0

Loaded (haul): Use Fig. 4-8.
Enter the upper horizontal scale at 165,280 lb, the total loaded weight, and move down to the intersection with the 7.0% total resistance line.

Construct a horizontal line for this vehicle weight–total resistance intersect point. This line yields a rimpull of

$$11.5 \times 1,000 \text{ lb} = 11,500 \text{ lb}$$

The line also intersects the fifth gear. By dropping a vertical line from the fifth gear intersect point to the lower horizontal scale, one can determine the scraper speed: 11.6 mph

Empty (return): Use Fig. 4-10.

Enter the upper horizontal scale at 96,880 lb, the empty operating weight. Because this is a commonly used weight, it is marked on the chart as a heavy dashed line. The intersection with the 1.0% total resistance line defines the point from which to construct the horizontal line. The horizontal line intersects the eighth gear, and the corresponding speed is 33 mph.

(*b*) If the job is at elevation 12,500 ft, what will be the 631E operating speeds when consideration of the nonstandard pressure is included in the analysis?

Operating at an altitude of 12,500 ft, the 631E, which has a turbocharger engine, can deliver 82% of the rated flywheel horsepower (see Table 4-5).

Since we have already worked the problem for standard conditions, the 82% correction can be applied directly to the previously determined rimpull:

$$\frac{11.5}{0.82} = 14.0$$

At an altitude of 12,500 ft the rimpull that is necessary to overcome a total resistance of 7% is

$$14.0 \times 1,000 \text{ lb} = 14,000 \text{ lb}$$

Constructing a horizontal line from 14.0 on Fig. 4-7 yields an intersection with the fourth gear and a speed of 9.5 mph.

If the standard condition problem had not been previously worked, we could have proceeded directly by adjusting the total resistance:

$$\frac{7.0}{0.82} = 8.5 \quad \text{altitude adjusted total resistance}$$

Now proceed as in part (*a*) by locating the intersection of the total loaded weight line and the altitude adjusted total resistance line. Construct the horizontal line; from the intersection with the gear curve read down to determine the speed, 9.5 mph.

In this problem the empty (return) speed will not be affected by the nonstandard altitude because the machine does not require rimpull force for motion. The machine's downhill momentum is controlled by the retarder. Therefore, the empty (return) speed is still 33 mph at a 12,500-ft altitude.

PROBLEMS

4-1. A four-wheel tractor whose operating weight is 46,284 lb is pulled up a road whose slope is +4% at a uniform speed. If the average tension in the towing cable is 4,680 lb, what is the rolling resistance of the road?

4-2. Consider a wheel-type tractor-pulled scraper whose gross weight is 94,170 lb, including the tractor, the scraper, and its load. What is the equivalent gain, in horsepower (hp), resulting from operating this vehicle down a 4% slope instead of up the same slope at a speed of 12 mph?

(*Note:* One horsepower equals 33,000 ft-lb of work per minute.)

4-3. A wheel-type tractor-pulled scraper having a combined weight of 138,000 lb is push-loaded down a 6% slope by a crawler tractor whose weight is 56,240 lb. What is the equivalent gain in loading force for the tractor and scraper resulting from loading the scraper down the slope instead of up the slope?

4-4. A tractor has a 300-hp engine under standard conditions. What is the power of the engine when it is operating at an altitude 8,000 ft above sea level and at a temperature of 85°F?

4-5. A four-cycle gasoline engine was tested under the given conditions and found to develop the indicated horsepower. Determine the horsepower of standard conditions:

Observed horsepower, 112.56
Observed temperature 70°F
Observed atmospheric pressure, 22.14 in. Hg

4-6. A wheel-type tractor with a 210-hp engine has a maximum speed of 4.65 mph in the first gear. Determine the maximum rimpull of the tractor in each of the indicated gears if the efficiency is 90%.

Gear	Speed (mph)
First	4.65
Second	7.60
Third	11.50
Fourth	17.40
Fifth	26.80

4-7. If the tractor of Prob. 4-6 weighs 21.4 tons and is operated over a haul road whose slope is +3% with a rolling resistance of 80 lb per ton, determine the maximum external pull by the tractor in each of the five gears.

4-8. If the tractor of Probs. 4-6 and 4-7 is operated down a 4% slope whose rolling resistance is 80 lb per ton, determine the maximum external pull by the tractor in each of the five gears.

4-9. The soil borrow material to be used to construct a highway embankment has a mass unit weight of 96.0 lb per cu ft (pcf) and a water content of 8%, and the specific gravity of the soil solids is 2.66. The specifications require that the soil be compacted to a dry unit weight of 112 pcf and that the water content be held to 13%.

(a) How many cubic yards of borrow are required to construct an embankment having a 250,000-cu-yd net section volume?

(b) How many gallons of water must be added per cubic yard of borrow material assuming no loss by evaporation?

(c) If the compacted fill becomes saturated at a constant volume, what will be the water content and mass unit weight of the soil?

4-10. The soil borrow material to be used to construct a highway embankment has a mass unit weight of 98.0 pcf and a water content of 9%, and the specific gravity of the soil solids is 2.67. The specifications require that the soil be placed in the fill so that the dry unit weight is 114 pcf and the water content is held to 12%.

(a) How many cubic yards of borrow are required to construct an embankment having a 800,000-cu-yd net section volume?

(b) How many gallons of water must be added per cubic yard of borrow material assuming no loss by evaporation?

(c) If the compacted fill becomes saturated at a constant volume, what will be the water content and mass unit weight of the soil?

4-11. The Society of Automotive Engineers (SAE) supplies the following equation for determining the brake horsepower (bhp) of a four-cycle engine under nonstandard conditions of temperature and pressure:

$$H_t = \frac{1.55 H_s P_t}{\sqrt{T_t}}$$

where H_t = measured, in hp, under actual test conditions

H_s = rated, hp, under standard conditions of 1 atm (atmosphere) of pressure (29.92 in. Hg) and 60°F temperature

P_t = actual atmosphere pressure, in psi (pounds per square inch) absolute

T_t = actual temperature, in degrees absolute

(a) Derive the 1.55 constant in the preceding equation.

(b) A new engine, when tested at an intake-air temperature of 85°F and at an altitude of 6,000 ft (atmospheric pressure of 11.71 psi absolute) is observed to develop 311 hp. Use the SAE equation to calculate its rated horsepower, under standard conditions.

4-12. A wheel-type tractor, operating in its second gear range and at its full rated rpm (revolutions per minute), is observed to maintain a steady speed of 1.50 mph when operating under the conditions described herein. The ambient air temperature is 60°F and the altitude is sea level. The tractor is climbing a uniform 6.5% slope with a rolling resistance of 65 lb per ton, and it is towing a pneumatic-tired trailer loaded with fill material. The two-axle tractor has a total weight of 60,000 lb, 55% of which is distributed to the power axle. The loaded trailer has a weight of 75,000 lb.

(a) The manufacturer for the environmental conditions just described rates the tractive effort of the new tractor at 60 rimpull horsepower. What percentage of this rated rimpull does the tractor actually develop? In performing your calculations, you can assume that the component of weight normal to the traveling surface is equal to the weight itself (i.e., cos 0° is taken as 1.00, where 0° is the angle of total resistance). The "20 lb of rimpull required per ton of weight per percent of slope" approximation will be acceptable. You may also disregard the power required to overcome wind resistance and to provide acceleration. Assume that traction is not a limiting factor.

(b) What is the value of the coefficient of traction if the drive wheels of the tractor are at the point of incipient slippage for the conditions just described?

4-13. A wheel-type tractor unit, operating in its fourth gear range and at its full rated rpm, is observed to maintain a steady speed of 7.50 mph when operating under the conditions described herein. The ambient air temperature is 60°F and the altitude is at sea level. The tractor is climbing a uniform 5.5% slope with a rolling resistance of 55 lb per ton, and it is towing a pneumatic-tired trailer loaded with fill material. The single-axle tractor has an operating weight of 66,000 lb. The loaded trailer has a weight of 48,000 lb. The weight distribution for the combined tractor-trailer unit is 55% to the drive axle and 45% to the rear axle.

(a) The manufacturer for the environmental conditions just described rates the tractive effort of the new tractor at 330 rimpull horsepower. What percentage of this rated rimpull does the tractor actually develop? In performing your calculations, you can assume that the component of weight normal to the traveling surface is equal to the weight itself (i.e., cos 0° is taken as 1.00, where 0° is the angle of total resistance). The "20 lb of rimpull required per ton of weight per percent of slope" approximation will be acceptable. You may also disregard the power required to overcome wind resistance and to provide acceleration. Assume that traction is not a limiting factor.

(b) What is the value of the coefficient of traction if the drive wheels of the tractor are at the point of incipient slippage for the conditions just described?

4-14. A wheel tractor-scraper is operating on a level grade. Assume that no power derating is required for equipment condition, altitude, temperature, and so on. Use equipment data from Fig. 4-8.

(a) Disregarding traction limitations, what is the maximum value of rolling resistance (in lb per ton) over which the fully loaded unit can maintain a speed of 15 mph?

(b) What minimum value of coefficient of traction between the tractor wheels and the traveling surface is needed to satisfy the requirements of part (a)? For the fully loaded condition 67% of the weight is distributed to the drive axle. The operating weight of the empty scraper is 96,880 lb.

4-15. A dragline is excavating a ditch having a cross-sectional area of 120 sq ft. The material swells 28% from the bank to the loose state. The loose material has a 37° angle of repose. What are the height and the width of the spoil pile?

REFERENCES

1. *Caterpillar Performance Handbook,* Caterpillar Inc., Peoria, IL. Published annually.
2. *Production and Cost Estimating of Material Movement with Earthmoving Equipment,* Terex Corporation, Hudson, OH, 1981.
3. Nowatzki, E. A., L. L. Karafiath, and R. L. Wade: "The Use of Mobility Analyses for Selection of Heavy Mining Equipment," in *Proceedings of the Specialty Conference on Construction Equipment and Techniques for the Eighties,* The American Society of Civil Engineers, New York, 1982, pp. 130–145.

CHAPTER
5

TRACTORS AND
RELATED
EQUIPMENT

TRACTOR USES

Tractors are self-contained units that are designed to provide tractive power for drawbar work. Consistent with their purpose as a unit for drawbar work, they are low center of gravity machines. This is a prerequisite of a good machine. The larger the difference between the line-of-force transmission from the machine and the line of resisting force, the less effective the utilization of developed power. Typical project applications are land clearing, bulldozing, ripping, and towing other pieces of construction equipment.

TYPE/PERFORMANCE CHARACTERISTICS
OF TRACTORS

Tractors are classified on the basis of running gear:

1. Crawler (track laying) type (see Fig. 5-1)
2. Wheel type (see Fig. 5-2)
   a. Single-axle—usually part of a unit such as a scraper or bottom dump
   b. Two-axle—single-axle drive; two-axle drive

As discussed in Chap. 4, the usable force available to perform work is often limited by traction. This limitation is dependent on the coefficient of traction of the surface being traversed and on the weight carried by the drive wheels. It is common practice,

FIGURE 5-1
Crawler tractor bulldozer. *(Caterpillar Inc.)*

therefore, to weight the tires of wheel-type tractors in order to overcome tractive-power limitations. A mixture of calcium chloride and water is a recommended tire ballast. Care must be taken to ensure that the new weight distribution is equal between all drive wheels.

FIGURE 5-2
Wheel tractor bulldozer. *(Caterpillar Inc.)*

Traction or flotation requirements can also be met by proper tire selection. Wider tires provide greater contact area and increase flotation. It must be remembered, however, that rimpull charts are based on standard equipment including tires. Larger tires will reduce developed rimpull.

Crawler tractors. The crawler- (track) type unit is designed for those jobs requiring high tractive effort. They are usually rated by size or weight and power. The weight is important on many projects because the maximum tractive effort that a unit can provide is limited to the product of the weight times the coefficient of traction for the particular road surface regardless of the power supplied by the engine. Table 4-4 gives the coefficients of traction for various surfaces.

An advantage of wheel-type tractors as compared with a crawler tractor is the higher speed that is possible with the former tractors—in excess of 30 mph for some models. However, in order to attain a higher speed, a wheel tractor must sacrifice pulling effort. Also, because of the lower coefficient of traction between rubber tires and some soil surfaces, the wheel tractor may slip its wheels before developing its rated pulling effort. Table 5-1 provides a comparison of crawler-tractor and wheel-tractor utilization.

Most tractors used in heavy construction are powered by internal combustion engines, with diesel engines as the most common primary power units. Gasoline engines are used in some smaller machines, and for tunnel work there are electric and air-powered units available.

TABLE 5-1
Tractor-type utilization comparison

Wheel tractor	Crawler tractor
Good on firm soils and concrete and abrasive soils which have no sharp-edged pieces	Can work on a variety of soils. Sharp-edged pieces not as destructive to tractor though fine sand will increase running gear wear
Best on level and downhill work	Can work almost any terrain
Wet weather, causing soft and slick surfaces will stop operation	Can work on soft ground and over mud-slick surfaces; will exert very low ground pressures with special wide tracks and flotation track shoes
The concentrated wheel load will provide compaction and kneading action	
Good for long travel distances	Good for short work distances
Best in loose soils	Can handle tight soils
Has fast return speeds, 8–20 mph	Slow return speeds, 5–7 mph
Can only handle moderate blade loads	Can push large blade loads

Manufacturers make some or all crawler-tractor models with a choice of direct drive or torque-converter and power-shift drives. The smaller (less than 300 hp) diesel-powered machines are commonly available with either direct- or power-shift-type transmissions. Larger machines are always equipped with power-shift transmissions. Both track- and wheel-type tractors are rated by flywheel horsepower (fwhp) and weight. Normally, the weight is an operating weight and includes lubricants, coolants, a full fuel tank, a bulldozer blade, hydraulic fluid, the OSHA rollover protective standards canopy (ROPS), and the operator.

Crawler tractors with direct drive. Table 5-2 gives pertinent information and performance data for three tractors equipped with direct drives. Some manufacturers' specifications list two sets of drawbar pulls—rated and maximum. The rated is the drawbar pull that can be sustained for continuous operation, whereas the maximum is the drawbar pull that the tractor can exert for a short period while lugging the engine, such as when passing over a soft spot in the ground, which requires a temporary higher tractive effort. Thus, the rated pull should be used for continuous operation. Also, the available drawbar pull is subject to the limitations on traction developed between the tracks and the ground.

TABLE 5-2
Representative specifications and performance data for three crawler tractors equipped with direct drive

Approximate			
operating weight (lb)	18,300	32,000	47,000
Flywheel (hp)	93	160	235
Drawbar (hp)	75	128	187
Ratio (lb/hp)	197	200	200

Performance data

	Speed		Drawbar†	Speed		Drawbar†	Speed		Drawbar†
	mph	fpm	pull (lb)	mph	fpm	pull (lb)	mph	fpm	pull (lb)
Gear, forward									
First	1.7	150	17,240	1.5	132	32,500	1.5	132	44,400
Second	2.7	238	10,470	2.2	193	22,700	1.9	167	34,500
Third	3.7	326	7,090	3.1	272	15,000	2.7	238	24,100
Fourth	5.2	458	4,670	4.6	405	9,390	3.5	307	17,750
Fifth	6.8	598	3,190	5.9	518	6,770	4.6	405	13,000
Sixth							6.3	555	8,450
Gear, reverse									
First	2.1	185	13,670	1.8	158	28,470	1.5	132	43,700
Second	3.3	290	8,180	2.5	220	18,935	2.0	176	33,900
Third	4.6	405	5,440	3.7	325	12,390	2.7	238	23,700
Fourth	6.4	563	3,480	5.4	475	7,620	3.6	317	17,400
Fifth							4.6	405	12,700
Sixth							6.4	563	8,250

†Usable pull will depend on weight and traction of the fully equipped tractor.

Crawler tractors with torque converters and power-shift transmissions. Many crawler tractors are available with torque-converter drives and power-shift transmissions, which eliminate shifting gears. These drives provide an efficient flow of power from the engine to the tracks by automatically selecting the speed which is best suited for the load pulled by the tractor.

Figure 5-3 illustrates the performance curves for a tractor equipped with a power-shift transmission.

Wheel tractors. While most wheel tractors are equipped with torque converters and power-shift transmissions, some are direct drive. For this reason performance data will be presented for both types.

Table 5-3 illustrates the specifications for typical wheel tractors equipped with direct drive.

Figure 5-4 illustrates the type of information that may be provided for a wheel tractor by the manufacturer. The unit consists of a two-axle tractor with a dozer blade.

Comparison of performance. Note the caution on Table 5-2 and Fig. 5-4 that "Usable pull/rimpull will depend on the weight and traction of a fully equipped tractor." This is a warning: Even though the engine can develop a certain drawbar pull or rimpull force, all of the pull may not be available to do work. The caution is a restatement of Eq. (4-21). If the project working surface is dry, clay loam, Table 4-4 provides the following coefficient of traction factors:

Rubber tires 0.50–0.70
Track 0.90

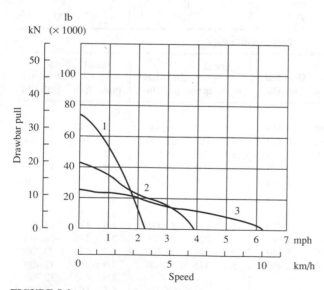

FIGURE 5-3
Performance chart for a 200 HP 45,560 lb track-type tractor with power shift. (*Caterpillar Inc.*)

TABLE 5-3
Representative specifications for single-axle tractors

Approximate weight, lb (kg):	32,200 (14,560)	17,740 (8,050)
Engine hp (kW)	275 (205)	180 (134)
Ratio, lb per hp (kg/kW)	117 (71)	98 (60)
Tire sizes, in. (mm)	24.00 × 29 (610 × 738)	21.00 × 25 (534 × 635)

Performance data

Speed gear	Speed		Rimpull		Speed		Rimpull	
	mph	km/h	lb	kg	mph	km/h	lb	kg
. First	2.16	3.48	25,000†	11,380†	3.41	5.50	15,850	7,175
Second	4.18	6.73	17,100	7,785	7.25	11.70	7,450	3,380
Third	7.15	11.50	10,050	4,560	12.63	20.35	4,280	1,945
Fourth	12.18	19.60	5,880	2,670	22.28	35.90	2,420	1,100
Fifth	20.00	32.20	3,580	1,620	35.03	56.35	1,540	700
Reverse	2.79	4.49	25,000†	11,380†	4.35	7.00	12,440	5,650

†Rimpull limited by the maximum traction resulting from the weights on the tires when pulling loaded scrapers.

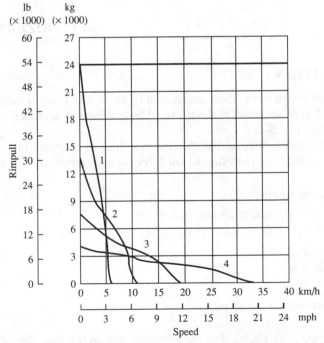

FIGURE 5-4
Performance chart for a 216 HP 45,370 lb two-axle wheel-type tractor
with power shift. Usable rimpull depends upon traction and weight of
tractor. (*Caterpillar Inc.*)

Using the factor for tracks, 0.90, and considering a track-type tractor with a power shift (see Fig. 5-3), we find that the usable drawbar pull is

$$45,560 \text{ lb} \times 0.90 = 41,004 \text{ lb}$$

Now consider a wheel-type tractor (see Fig. 5-4):

$$45,370 \text{ lb} \times 0.60 = 27,222 \text{ lb}$$

The two machines have approximately the same operating weight and flywheel power; yet, because of the effect of traction, the track machine can supply one and a half times the *usable* power.

The coefficient of traction for wheels is less than that of tracks for most soil conditions. Therefore, a wheel-type tractor must be considerably heavier (approximately 50%) than a crawler tractor in order to develop the same amount of usable force.

As the weight of a wheel-type tractor is increased, a larger engine will be required to maintain the weight-to-horsepower ratio. There is a limit to the weight that can be added to the wheel-type tractor and still have a machine with a speed and mobility advantage over track machines.

BULLDOZERS

GENERAL INFORMATION

A *bulldozer* is a tractor unit which has a blade attached to its front. The blade is used to push, shear, cut, and roll material ahead of the tractor. The bulldozer is an effective and versatile earthmover (see Fig. 5-1).

Bulldozers are used as both support and production machines on many construction projects, where they may be used from start to finish for such operations as:

1. Clearing land of timber and stumps
2. Opening up pilot roads through mountains and rock terrain
3. Moving earth for short-haul distances, up to about 300 ft
4. Helping to load tractor-pulled scrapers
5. Spreading earth and rock fills
6. Backfilling trenches
7. Clearing the floors of borrow and quarry pits

Bulldozers are mounted with blades that are perpendicular to the direction of travel, whereas *angle-dozers* are mounted with blades set at an angle with the direction of travel. The former push the earth forward, whereas the latter push it forward and to one side. Some blades may be adjusted to permit their use as bulldozers or as angle-dozers.

Stripping. Bulldozers are good machines for *stripping,* which is the removal of a thin layer of material. On most projects this is a term used to describe the removal of topsoil. As with all earth-moving operations, stripping should be conducted in such a manner that push (haul) distances are minimized. Bulldozers are economical machines for haul distances of less than 300 ft. The exact economical distance will depend on the material being pushed and on the machine size. In situations where the stripped material must be hauled a distance greater than 300 ft, scrapers should be considered. Bulldozers can be very effective support machines for long haul stripping situations when used to create windrows of stripped material which can be more efficiently picked up by the scrapers.

Pioneering and sidehill cuts. It is very difficult to develop the initial working table for excavations made on steep ground. Usually, the excavated material from such a cut is pushed over the side of the hill. The first passes are made perpendicular to the long direction of the project. Starting on the uphill side, short passes are made to push the material across the centerline and over the side. Pushing downhill takes advantage of gravity. Because these perpendicular passes are short, the dozer usually is not able to develop a full blade load. Therefore, once a bench is established, the dozer should push in the long direction of the project, develop a full blade load, and then use turns to push the material over the side (see Fig. 5-5).

In exceptionally steep terrain dozers may not be able to approach the cut area from the front face. The estimator must study the ground conditions and locate approaches with grades that are no greater than those the machines can traverse. Once in position

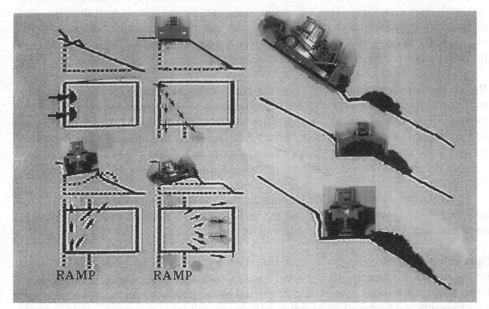

FIGURE 5-5
Techniques for opening a sidehill cut.

above the cut, the bulldozer might be able to make the first downhill push; but because of the steep slope, the tractor is not able to return directly to the top of the hill. In such situations two machines work as a team, with one dozer remaining at the top of the cut and serving as an anchor point for a winch line to the machine which is doing the pushing. After each downhill pass the pusher is winched back up the hill. This is a very slow procedure and should be eliminated as soon as a minimum working table is established. Once the pioneering cut is wide enough and slopes in the long direction are graded, scrapers can be brought in to move the material longitudinally along the project.

Ditching. A bulldozer can be used to accomplish ditching, but this is practical only for very rough ditch sections. Small shallow ditches are usually cut with a motor grader. Large deep ditches are usually cut with excavators, but if the cut can be made in the dry, scrapers may be utilized. A dozer will follow the scrapers and perform the final dressing of the slopes.

If a dozer is used to cut rough ditches, the machine pushes the material out of the cut by working perpendicular to the line of the ditch.

Backfilling. A dozer can efficiently accomplish backfilling a ditch or pushing material against a structure. A dozer equipped with an angle blade can drift backfill material into a ditch or pipe trench while maintaining a forward motion. If a straight blade is used, the dozer will approach at a slight angle and then end the pass with a turn-in toward the ditch. The same movements are used to move material against a structure.

Caution must be exercised in making the initial pass completely across the pipes or culverts. As a minimum, 12 in. of material should cover the pipe or structure before accomplishing a crossing. This minimum is affected by the diameter of the pipe, the distance between the side wall of the excavation and the pipe, and the number of lines of pipe in the excavation. Larger diameter pipe, larger excavation widths, and multiple lines all dictate more cover before crossing the structure.

Rocks and frozen ground. With proper attack techniques, a bulldozer can move rocks and frozen ground. In both cases the blade must be worked under the material to be moved. This can be accomplished by tilting the corner of the blade. To maximize the driving force of the blade, hook only the tilted end under the rock or ground. It may be necessary to use the blade as a pry bar to lift the rock. Once the blade is in contact beneath the rock and the dozer is driving forward, the operator lifts the blade to pry up the rock.

Weak formations of soft rocks, such as shale and sandstone, can be attacked in a similar manner. Work under the outcrop and lift. Once a plane of weakness slides, a track machine can often crush the material by running over it.

Spreading. The spreading of material dumped by trucks or scrapers is a common bulldozer task. Ordinarily, project specifications state a maximum loose lift thickness. Even when lift thickness limits are not stated in the contract specifications, density requirements and proposed compaction equipment will force the contractor to control the height of each lift. Uniform spreading is accomplished with a dozer by keeping the blade straight and at the desired height above the previously placed fill. The dumped material is forced directly under the blade's cutting edge. Fairly uniform spreading can be achieved, even by semiskilled operators if two complete passes are made across the dump area, with the second pass made perpendicular to the first. Today there are also laser-blade controls available for this type of work.

Slot. The dozing method whereby the operator makes use of the sidewalls from previous passes to hold material in front of the dozer blade is known as *slot dozing*. Alternate slots are made between thin-wall sections which are cut last. The technique prevents spillage at each end of the blade and usually increases production by about 20%. The production increase is highly dependent on the slope of the push and the type of material being pushed.

Blade-to-blade dozing. Another technique used to increase bulldozer production is blade-to-blade dozing (see Fig. 5-6). The technique is sometimes referred to as *side-by-side dozing*. As the names imply, two machines maneuver so that their blades are right next to each other during the pushing phase of the production cycle. This reduces the side spillage of each machine by 50%. The extra time necessary to position the machines together increases that phase of the cycle. Therefore, the technique is not

FIGURE 5-6
Blade-to-blade dozing to minimize spillage.

effective on pushes of less than 30 ft because of the excess maneuver time required. When machines operate simultaneously, delay to one machine is in effect a double delay. The combination of less spillage but increased maneuver time tends to make the total increase in production for this technique somewhere between 15 and 25%.

BLADES

The blade attached to the tractor to create a bulldozer must be matched to the expected work task. Basic earth-moving blades are curved in the vertical plane in the shape of a "C." Along the bottom length of the blade hard steel plates are bolted. These plates make up the *cutting edge* of the blade. The term *edge* or *knife* is used to designate these plates. They receive the most abrasion and wear out rapidly, which is the reason they are bolted on so that replacement is easy.

The blade is raised or lowered by hydraulic rams. In past years blades were cable-operated, which meant downward motion was by gravity alone. Today, with hydraulics, the operator can exert a positive downward force.

When the blade is pushed down, the edge cuts into the earth. As the tractor moves forward, the cut material is pushed up the face of the blade. The upper part of the "C" shape rolls this material forward. The total effect is to "boil" the pushed material over and over in front of the blade. The C shape provides the necessary cutting angle for the edge, and at the beginning of the pass the weight of the cut material on the lower half of the C helps to achieve edge penetration. As the push progresses, the load in front of the blade passes the halfway point of the C and exerts an upward force on the blade. This "floats" the blade, reducing the edge's penetration.

The configuration of the connection between the blade and the tractor can be varied to permit one or sometimes two of three possible operational adjustments. The three possible blade adjustments are tilt, pitch, and angle.

Tilt. The vertical movement of a blade end is known as *tilt*. This movement is within the vertical plane of the blade. Tilting permits concentration of tractor driving power on a limited length of blade.

Pitch. The control which allows the operator to vary the angle of attack of the blade's cutting edge with the ground is *pitch*. It is the movement of the top of the blade toward or away from the tractor. This is a pivotal movement about the point of connection between the tractor and the blade. When the top of the blade is pitched forward, the bottom edge moves back; this increases the angle of the cutting edge attack.

Angling. Turning the blade so that it is not perpendicular to the direction of the tractor's travel is *angling*. This causes the pushed material to roll off the trailing end of the blade. The procedure of rolling material off one end of the blade is called *side casting*. Figure 5-7 illustrates tilt, pitch, and angling.

Blade-tractor performance. A bulldozer's pushing potential is measured by two standard ratios:

- Horsepower per foot of cutting edge
- Horsepower per loose cubic yard of material retained in front of the blade.

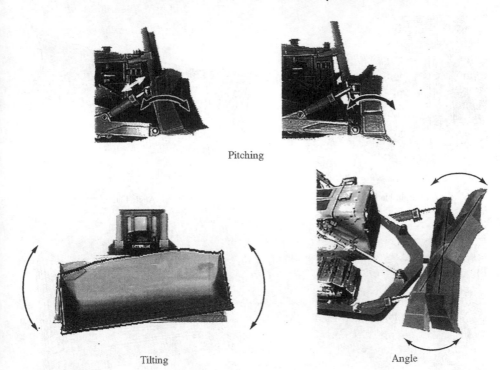

Pitching

Tilting   Angle

FIGURE 5-7
Bulldozer blade adjustments—tilt, pitch, angle.

Horsepower per foot (hp/ft) provides an indication of the ability of the blade to penetrate and obtain a load. The higher this ratio, the more aggressive the blade. Horsepower per loose cubic yard (hp/lcy) measures the blade's ability to push a load. A higher ratio means that the bulldozer can push a load at a greater speed.

Many different special application blades may be attached to a tractor, but basically, only four blades are common to earthwork: the *straight* "S" blade, the *angle* "A" blade, the *universal* "U" blade, and the *cushion* "C" blade (see Fig. 5-8).

Straight blades "S". These are blades used primarily for excavation work. They have no curvature in their length. The blade is normally heavy duty and can be tilted, thus facilitating penetration into hard materials. It may be equipped to pitch. The ability to pitch means that the operator can set the cutting edge to dig hard materials or to move the edge's plane of attack to ease the drifting of light materials.

Angle blades "A". An angle blade is wider by 1–2 ft than an S blade. The angle blade can be operated straight, or angled up to a maximum of 25° left or right of the normal position (perpendicular to the tractor). The blade can be tilted. Because the angle blade is attached to the tractor by a C frame mount, it cannot be pitched. It is designed for side-casting material.

Universal blades "U". This blade is wider than a straight blade and the outside edges are canted forward about 25°. This canting of the edges reduces the spillage of loose material; making the U blade efficient for moving big loads over long distances. The hp/ft ratio is lower for the U than for the S blade mounted on a similar tractor.

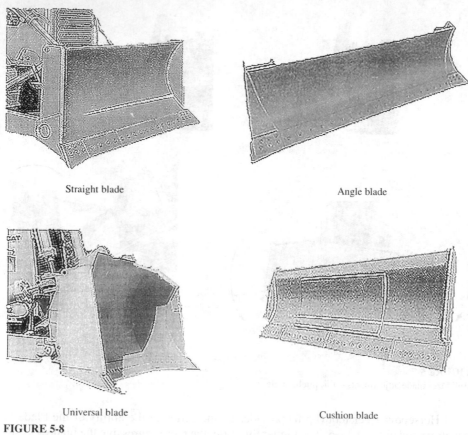

Straight blade

Angle blade

Universal blade

Cushion blade

FIGURE 5-8
Common earthmoving dozer blades.

Penetration is not a prime objective of the U as this ratio relationship indicates. The U blade's hp/lcy ratio is lower than that of an S blade. This denotes that the blade is best suited for lighter materials. Typical usages are working stockpiles and drifting loose or noncohesive materials.

Cushion blades "C". Cushion blades are mounted on large tractors which are used primarily for push-loading scrapers. The C blade is shorter that the S blade. This is to avoid pushing the blade into and cutting the rear tires of the scraper while push-loading. The shorter length facilitates maneuvering into position behind the scrapers. Rubber cushions and springs in the mounting allow the dozer to absorb the impact of contacting the scraper push block. By using a cushion blade instead of a "pusher block" to push scrapers, the dozer can clean up the cut area and increase the total fleet production. The cushion blade has limited utility in pushing material and should not be used for production bulldozing. It cannot be tilted, pitched, or angled.

BULLDOZER PRODUCTION ESTIMATING

A bulldozer has no set volumetric capacity. There is no hopper or bowl to load; instead, the amount of material that the dozer moves depends on the quantity which will remain in front of the blade during the push. The factors that control dozer production rates are:

1. Blade type
2. Type and condition of material
3. Cycle time

Blade type. The description of blade types was presented in the previous section. As stated, an important production estimation characteristic of blades was that straight blades roll material in front of the blade, whereas universal blades control side spillage, thus holding the material within the blade. Because the universal blade forces the material to move to the center, there is a greater degree of swelling. The U blade's quantity of loose material will be greater than that of the S blade. But the ratio of this difference is not the same when considering bank yards. This is because the factor to convert loose cubic yards to bank cubic yards for the universal blade is not the same as that for a straight blade. The difference is caused by the U blade's boiling effect.

The same type of blade comes in different sizes to fit different size tractors. Blade capacity then is a function of blade type and physical size. Manufacturer's specification sheets will provide the necessary information concerning blade dimensions.

Type and condition of material. The shape of the pushed mass in front of the blade is affected by the type and condition of the material being handled. Cohesive materials (clays) will "boil" and heap. Materials which exhibit a slippery quality or those which have a high mica content will ride over the ground and swell out. Cohesionless materials (sands) are known as "dead" materials because they do not exhibit heap or swell properties. Figure 5-9 illustrates these properties.

Blade load. The load that a blade will carry can be estimated by several methods:

1. Manufacturer's blade rating
2. Previous experience (similar material, equipment, and work conditions)
3. Field measurements

Manufacturer's blade ratings. Manufacturers may provide a blade rating based on SAE practice J1265.

$$V_s = 0.8WH^2 \tag{5-1}$$

$$V_u = V_s + ZH(W - Z)\tan x^\circ \tag{5-2}$$

where V_s = capacity of straight or angle blade, in lcy
V_u = capacity of universal blade, in lcy
W = blade width, in yd, exclusive of end bits
H = effective blade height, in yd
Z = wing length measured parallel to the blade width, in yd
x = wing angle

Clay

Top soil

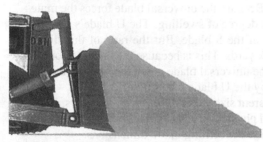

Sand

Coal

FIGURE 5-9
Materials bulking when being pushed.

Previous experience. An excellent estimating method is properly documented past experience. Good documentation requires that the cut be cross-sectioned to determine the total volume of material moved and that the number of push cycles be recorded. Also, studies can be made based on the weight of the material moved. The mechanics of weighing the material is normally harder to accomplish than surveying the volume.

Field measurement. A procedure for measuring blade loads follows:
- Obtain a normal load:
  1. The dozer pushes a normal blade load onto a level area.
  2. Stop the dozer's forward motion. While raising the blade, move forward slightly to create a symmetrical pile.
  3. Reverse and move away from the pile.
- Measurement (see Fig. 5-10):
  4. Measure the height (H) of the pile at the inside edge of each track.
  5. Measure the width (W) of the pile at the inside edge of each track.
  6. Measure the greatest length (L) of the pile. This will not necessarily be at the middle.
- Computation:
  Average both the two-height and the two-width measurements. If the measurements are in feet, the blade load in loose cubic yards (lcy) is calculated by the formula

$$\text{Blade load (lcy)} = 0.0139HWL \qquad (5\text{-}3)$$

Example 5-1. The measurements from a blade-load test were $H_1 = 4.9$ ft, $H_2 = 5.2$ ft, $W_1 = 6.9$ ft, $W_2 = 7.0$ ft, and $L = 12.6$ ft. What is the blade capacity in loose cubic yards for the tested material?

$$H = \frac{4.9 + 5.2}{2} = 5.05 \qquad W = \frac{6.9 + 7.0}{2} = 6.95$$

$$\text{Blade load} = 0.0139 \times 5.05 \times 6.95 \times 12.6 = 6.15 \text{ lcy}$$

Cycle time. The sum of the time required to push, backtrack, and maneuver into position to push represents the complete dozer cycle. The time required to push and backtrack can be calculated for each dozing situation from the travel distance and the machine's performance chart.

However, dozing is generally performed at slow speed, 1.5 to 2 mph. The lower figure is appropriate for very heavy cohesive materials.

Front view

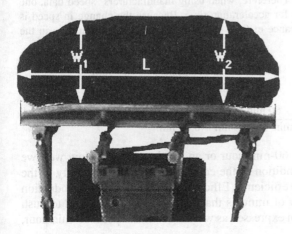

Top view

FIGURE 5-10
Measurement of blade loads.

Return speed is usually the maximum that can be attained in the distance available. When using performance charts to determine possible speeds, remember the chart identifies instantaneous speeds. In calculating durations, the estimator must use an average speed which takes into account the time required to accelerate to the attainable speed as indicated by the chart. Usually for distances less than 100 ft, the operator cannot get the machine past the second gear. If the distance is greater than 100 ft and the ground conditions are relatively smooth and level, maximum machine speed may be obtained. Maneuver time for power-shift tractors is about 0.05 min.

Production. The formula to calculate dozer production in loose cubic yards per a 60-min hour is presented below:

$$\text{Production (lcy per hour)} = \frac{60 \text{ min} \times \text{blade load}}{\text{push time} + \text{return time} + \text{maneuver time}} \quad (5\text{-}4)$$

Example 5-2. Assume that the blade load calculated in the previous example was for a track-type tractor equipped with a power shift (see Fig. 5-3). The tractor will be used to push a silty sand material. The average push distance is 90 ft. What production can be expected in loose cubic yards?

$$\text{Blade load} = 6.15 \text{ lcy} \quad \text{(from previous example)}$$

Push time: 2 mph average speed (sandy material):

$$\text{Push time} = \frac{90 \text{ ft}}{5,280 \text{ ft/mi}} \times \frac{1}{2 \text{ mph}} \times 60 \text{ min/hr} = 0.51 \text{ min}$$

Return time: Figure 5-3, second gear because less than 100 ft
Maximum speed 4 mph:

$$\frac{90 \text{ ft}}{5,280 \text{ ft/mi}} \times \frac{1}{4 \text{ mph}} \times 60 \text{ min/hr} = 0.26 \text{ min}$$

The charts provide information based on a steady-state velocity. The tractor must accelerate to attain that velocity. Therefore, when using manufacturers' speed data, one must always make an allowance for acceleration time. Because the change in speed is very small in this case, an allowance of 0.05 min is made for acceleration time in the example:

$$\text{Return time } (0.26 + 0.05) = 0.31 \text{ min}$$
$$\text{Maneuver time} \qquad\qquad = 0.05 \text{ min}$$

$$\text{Production} = \frac{60 \text{ min} \times 6.15 \text{ lcy}}{0.51 \text{ min} + 0.31 \text{ min} + 0.05 \text{ min}} = 424 \text{ lcy/hr}$$

This production is based on a 60-min hour or an ideal condition. How well we manage our jobs in the field, the condition of the equipment, and the difficulty of the work are factors which will affect job efficiency. Efficiency is included in the production equation by considering the number of minutes that will actually be utilized to push material. The efficiency factor is then expressed as working minutes per a 60-min hour, for example, a 50-min hour.

We may want to express the production in terms of bank cubic yards (bcy). In that case the swell factor, Eq. (4-12), or the percent swell, Eq. (4-13), can be used to make the conversion.

Example 5-3. Assume a percent swell of 0.25 for the silty sand of the previous example and that job efficiency will equal a 50-min hour. What is the actual production that can be expected in bank cubic yards?

$$\text{Production} = \frac{424 \text{ lcy}}{1.25} \times \frac{50 \text{ min}}{60 \text{ min}} = 283 \text{ bcy/hr} \Rightarrow 280 \text{ bcy/hr}$$

The final step is to compute the unit cost for pushing the material. A large machine should be able to push more material per hour than a small one. However, the cost to operate a large machine will be greater than the cost to operate a small one. The ratio of *cost to operate* to *the amount of material moved* determines the most economical machine for the job. This ratio is the cost figure which is used in bidding unit-price work.

Example 5-4. The machine in the previous example has an owning and operating cost of $32.50 per hour. Operators in the area where the proposed work will be performed are making $9.50 per hour. What is the unit cost for pushing the silty sand?

$$\text{Unit cost} = \frac{\$32.50 \text{ per hour} + \$9.50 \text{ per hour}}{280 \text{ bcy/hr}} = \$0.150 \text{ per bcy}$$

Production formulas. Equipment manufacturers have developed production formulas for use in estimating the amount of material that bulldozers can push. Equation (5-5) is a *rule-of-thumb* formula proposed by International Harvester (IH). This formula equates the horsepower for a power-shift crawler tractor to lcy production.

$$\text{Production (lcy per 60-min hr)} = \frac{\text{net hp} \times 330}{(D + 50)} \tag{5-5}$$

where net hp = net horsepower at the flywheel for a power-shift crawler tractor
D = one-way push distance, in ft

Example 5-5. The power-shift tractor whose characteristics are shown in Fig. 5-3 will be used to push material 90 ft. Use the IH formula to calculate the lcy production which can be expected for this operation.
From Fig. 5-3 net hp = 200.

$$\frac{200 \times 330}{(90 + 50)} = 471 \text{ lcy per 60-min hr}$$

Again, the actual production will be less as a 60-min hour is unrealistic.

Production curves. There are production curves for estimating the amount of material that Caterpillar bulldozers can push. These are published in the *Caterpillar Performance Handbook*. A production estimate obtained from those curves is based on a set of ideal conditions:

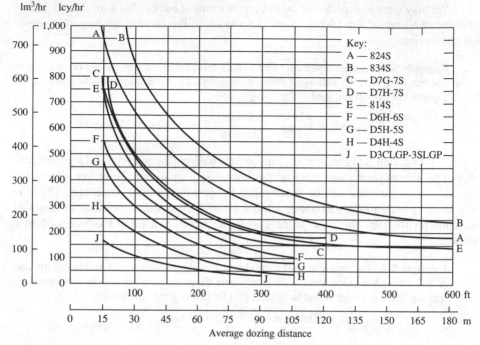

FIGURE 5-11
Dozing production estimating curves for straight blade Caterpillar D3, D4, D5, D6, D7, B14, B24, and B34 tractors. *(Caterpillar Inc.)*

1. A 60-min hour (100% efficiency)
2. Power-shift machines with a 0.05-min fixed time
3. Machine cuts for 50 ft, then drifts blade load to dump over a high wall
4. Soil density of 2,300 lb per lcy
5. Coefficient of traction:
   a. Track machines—0.5 or better
   b. Wheel machines—0.4 or better[†]
6. Hydraulic-controlled blades

To calculate field production rates, one must adjust the curve values by the expected job conditions. Figures 5-11 and 5-12 present the Caterpillar curves, and Table 5-4 lists the correction factors. The formula for the calculation of production from the Caterpillar curves is

Production (lcy per hour)

= maximum production from curve × product of the correction factors (5-6)

[†] Poor traction affects both track and wheel machines, causing smaller blade loads. Wheel units, however, are affected more severely. There are no fixed rules to predict the resulting production loss caused by poor traction. A rough rule of thumb for wheel-dozer production loss is a 4% decrease for each 0.01 decrease in the coefficient of traction below 0.40.

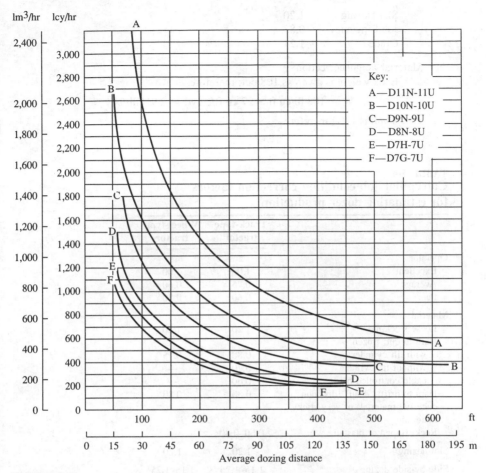

FIGURE 5-12
Dozing production estimating curves for universal blade Caterpillar D7 through D11 tractors. *(Caterpillar Inc.)*

Example 5-6. A D7G crawler tractor with a straight blade is to be used in a slot-dozing operation. The material is a dry, noncohesive silty sand and is to be moved a distance of 300 ft from the beginning of the cut. Dozing is downhill on a 10% grade. The operator will have average skill, the tractor will have a power-shift transmission, and both visibility and traction are assumed to be satisfactory. The material weighs 108 pcf (lb per cu ft) in the bank state and is estimated to swell 12% in the loose state. Job efficiency is assumed to be equivalent to a 50-min hour. Calculate the direct cost of the proposed earth-moving operation in dollars per bcy. Assume that the owning and operating (O&O) cost for the tractor is $32.50 per hour and the operator's wage is $10.85 per hour.

D7G with straight blade:
From Fig. 5-11 ideal production for 300-ft push is 170 lcy per hour
Correction factors from Table 5-4 are:

Operator	0.75
Material (type)	0.80

Slot Dozing 1.20
Job Efficiency 0.83
Grade 1.24

Material weight correction:
Bank weight is given as 108 pcf; therefore,

108 lb/cu ft × 27 cu ft/cu yd = 2,916 lb/bcy

Swell is 12%; therefore,

TABLE 5-4
Caterpillar job condition correction factors for estimating dozer production

	Track-type tractor	Wheel-type tractor
Operator		
Excellent	1.00	1.00
Average	0.75	0.60
Poor	0.60	0.50
Material		
Loose stockpile	1.20	1.20
Hard to cut; frozen		
with tilt cylinder	0.80	0.75
without tilt cylinder	0.70	—
cable controlled blade	0.60	—
Hard to drift; "dead" (dry, non-cohesive material) or very sticky material	0.80	0.80
Rock, ripped or blasted	0.60–0.80	—
Slot dozing	1.20	1.20
Side-by-side dozing	1.15–1.25	1.15–1.25
Visibility		
Dust, rain, snow, fog, or darkness	0.80	0.70
Job efficiency		
50 min/hr	0.83	0.83
40 min/hr	0.67	0.67
Direct drive transmission		
(0.1-min fixed time)	0.80	—
Bulldozer[†]		
Adjust based on SAE capacity relative to the base blade used in the estimated dozing production graphs		
GRADES—see following graph		

[†]*Note:* Angling blades and cushion blades are not considered production-dozing tools. Depending on job conditions, the A blade and C blade will average 50–75% of straight-blade production.
Source: Caterpillar Inc.

TABLE 5-4 (*continued*)
Grade correction factor

% Grade vs. Dozing Factor
(−) Downhill
(+) Uphill

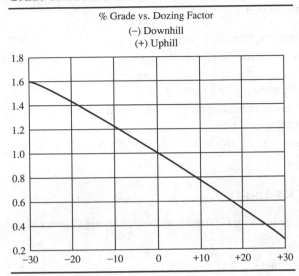

$$\frac{2916}{1.12} = 2,604 \text{ lb/lcy}$$

Standard condition is 2,300 lb/lcy:

$$\text{Material weight correction} = \frac{2,300}{2,604} = 0.88$$

Product correction factors $= 0.75 \times 0.80 \times 1.20 \times 0.83 \times 1.24 \times 0.88 = 0.652$

Production $= 170 \text{ lcy/hr} \times 0.652 = 111 \text{ lcy/hr}$

$$\text{or} \quad \frac{111}{1.12} = 99 \text{ bcy/hr}$$

Cost:

O&O	$32.50 per hour	
Operator	$10.85	
Total	$43.35 per hour	

$$\text{Direct production cost} = \frac{\$43.35 \text{ per hour}}{99 \text{ bcy/hr}} = \$0.438 \text{ per bcy}$$

CLEARING LAND

LAND-CLEARING OPERATIONS

Crawler tractors equipped with either bulldozer blades or special clearing blades are excellent machines for land clearing. Clearing operations are always preferable and usually necessary before undertaking earth-moving operations. Trees, brush, and even grass and weeds make earth handling very difficult. If these organic materials are allowed to become mixed into an embankment, their decay over time will cause settlement of the fill.

Clearing land may be divided into several operations depending on the type of vegetation, the condition of the soil and topography, the amount of clearing required, and the purpose for which the clearing is done:

1. Removing all trees and stumps, including roots
2. Removing all vegetation above the surface of the ground only, leaving stumps and roots in the ground
3. Disposing of vegetation by stacking and burning
4. Knocking all vegetation down, then chopping or crushing it to or into the surface of the ground, or burning it later
5. Killing or retarding the growth of brush by cutting the roots below the surface of the ground

TYPES OF EQUIPMENT USED

Several types of equipment are used for clearing land, with varying degrees of success:

1. Tractor-mounted bulldozers
2. Tractor-mounted clearing blades
3. Tractor-mounted rakes

Bulldozers. In the past bulldozers were used extensively to clear land. They are now being replaced by special blades mounted on tractors. There are at least two valid objections to the use of bulldozers. Prior to felling large trees a bulldozer has to excavate earth from around the tree and cut the main roots; this leaves objectionable holes in the ground and requires considerable time. Also, when stacking the felled trees and other vegetation, bulldozers transport considerable earth to the piles which makes burning more difficult.

Clearing blades. There are blades that have specially designed shapes and edges for use in felling trees. The two basic types of clearing blades are the single-angle blade with the projecting stinger, as shown in Fig. 5-13, and the V blade, as shown in Fig. 5-14. The single-angle blade with the stinger is often referred to as a *"K/G" blade.* This name comes from the highly successful *Rome K/G clearing blade,* manufactured by the Rome Plow Company.

The major components of the Rome or any other stinger-type clearing blade are the stinger, web, cutting edge, and guide bar. The stinger is a protruding vertical knife. It is designed to be used as a knife to cut and split trees, stumps, and roots. The stinger is sharp vertically, whereas the web is sharp horizontally; together they cut the tree in both planes simultaneously (see Fig. 5-15).

The blade can be tilted and is mounted at an angle with the stinger forward. The guide bar serves to protect the tractor and operator and to guide the cut material forward and to the side of the tractor.

The V clearing blade is shaped as the name implies. The point of the V is to the front, allowing debris to be cast off to each side. There is a stinger which protrudes from the lead point. The cutting edges down each side of the V are serrated. As with the single-angle blade, the design is such that vegetation is sheared off at ground level.

FIGURE 5-13
The Rome K/G clearing blade.

FIGURE 5-14
Tractor-mounted V blade for clearing land. *(Fleco Corporation.)*

Large hardwood trees are rammed in their middle and split by the stinger. Simultaneously, the two halves are then sheared off at ground level by the cutting edges on each side of the stinger.

Both types of clearing blades are most efficient when the tractor is operating on level ground and the cutting edges can maintain good contact with the ground surface. It is easier to work with soil types which hold the vegetation's root structure while the trunks are sheared. Large rocks will slow production by damaging the cutting edges.

Rakes. A *rake* is a dozer-mounted tool that is used to grub and pile trees after the clearing blades have worked an area (see Fig. 5-16). The rake has vertical teeth or tines instead of a solid face as with a blade. Like earth-moving blades the teeth of a rake are curved in the vertical plane in the shape of a "C." Rakes have an upward extension brush guard which may be either solid plate or open-spaced ribs.

The size, weight, and spacing of the rake's teeth depend on the intended application. Rakes used to grub out stumps and heavy roots must have teeth of sufficient strength so that a single tooth can take the push of the tractor at full power. Lighter rakes having smaller and closer spaced teeth are used for finish raking and to clear light root systems and small branches on the ground.

Rakes are also used to push, shake, and turn piles of trees and vegetation before and during burning operations. These tasks shake the dirt out of the piles and improve burning.

Tractor-mounted clamp rakes. Figure 5-17 shows a clamp rake which can be used to pick up felled trees and brush and to transport them to sites for burning or disposal. For some projects this method of handling the material is better than using a tractor-mounted rake to push the vegetation over the surface of the ground. Using this type of rake reduces or eliminates soil being transported into the stack. Because of its high reach, the clamp rake can be more effective in reshaping a pile of material in order to increase the rate of burning.

Cutting trees with a shear. Trees can be cut with a shear as illustrated in Fig. 5-18. A tractor-mounted shear may be used to cut trees above the surface of the ground. This machine is especially useful for felling only selected trees without disturbing others.

Disposal of brush. When the brush is to be disposed of by burning, it should be piled, with a minimum amount of soil, into stacks and windrows. Shaking a rake while it is moving the brush will reduce the amount of soil in the pile.

If the brush and trees are burned while the moisture content is high, it may be necessary to provide an external source of fuel, such as diesel, to start combustion. The burner illustrated in Fig. 5-19, which consists of a gasoline-engine-driven pump and a propeller, is capable of maintaining a fire even under adverse conditions. The liquid fuel is blown into the pile of material as a stream while the propeller furnishes a supply of air to assure vigorous burning. Once combustion is started, the fuel is turned off.

Today in many urban areas burning is restricted. Therefore, it is becoming common to chip the brush and trees. Mixed chips, bark, and clean wood can be sold as mulch or as boiler fuel. Clean wood chips without bark are used to manufacture pressed boards.

FIGURE 5-15
Tractor-mounted K/G blade splitting a large tree. *(Fleco Corporation.)*

FIGURE 5-16
Tractor-mounted land-clearing rakes.

FIGURE 5-17
Tractor-mounted clamp rake. *(Fleco Corporation.)*

FIGURE 5-18
Tractor-mounted grapple shear cutting a tree. *(Rome Industries.)*

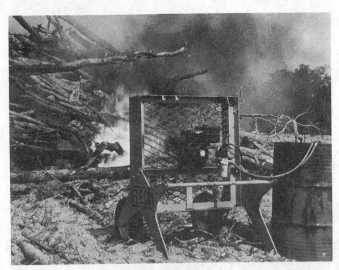

FIGURE 5-19
Burning brush with forced draft. *(Fleco Corporation.)*

CLEARING TECHNIQUES

The job specifications and the nature of the field conditions will dictate the proper clearing techniques to be used on a project. Job specifications may allow shearing of the vegetation and trees at the natural ground level or the contract can require grubbing to include removal of stumps and roots below ground level.

Shearing at ground level and piling operations. Techniques for conducting shearing and piling operations are outlined as follows:

1. Large trees are first cut 2 to 4 ft above ground level by holding the clearing blade in a raised position and by driving the stinger into the tree. This allows the tree to be split both up and down. After the tree is felled, the exposed stump is cut by repeating the splitting with the stinger at ground level.

2. Small-to-medium-diameter vegetation through which the tractor can move almost continuously may be attacked from either the outside or the center of the area. In both types of operations production is best if long areas having widths of between 200 and 400 ft can be worked. The angle-type clearing blade is very efficient for these conditions.

   When working in toward the center of an area, the operator rolls the cut material to the outside and away from the uncut area. After cutting, windrowing is accomplished by working from midwidth and pushing the downed material to the borders of the long dimension (see Fig. 5-20).

   If the shearing is accomplished from the inside toward the outside, the cut material is rolled to the center, which becomes the site for the windrow (see Fig. 5-21).

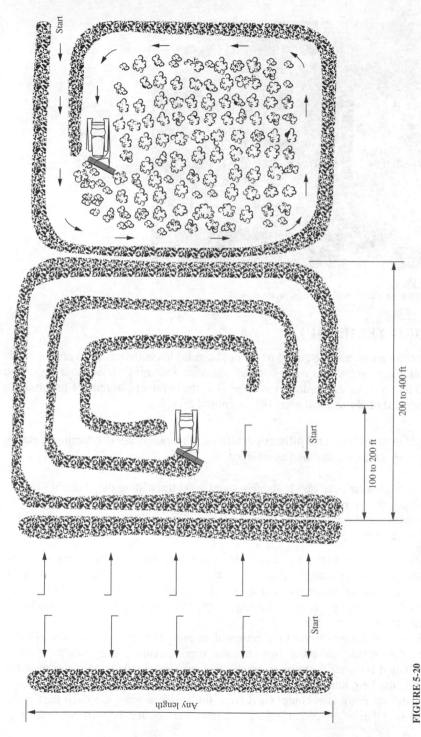

FIGURE 5-20
Shearing small-to-medium-diameter vegetation from the outside of the area to the center. *(Caterpillar Inc.)*

3. In the case of steep slopes or significant numbers of large trees, cutting and windrowing is normally accomplished in one operation. Once a blade load of cut material is obtained, the tractor is turned 90° and the material is deposited in the windrow. All cutting is performed in the direction of the ground's contour, and the windrow is established on the downhill side so that the tractor does not have to work against the natural grade (see Fig. 5-22).

Removal of trees and stumps to below ground level. Stumps can be removed during the clearing operation by the following techniques:

1. To remove stumps, use the stinger of the clearing blade to cut the roots below ground level, then push the stump out of the ground with the edge of the blade. The stinger is designed to be used as a knife or spear, not as a lever. The edge of the blade should be used for pushing.

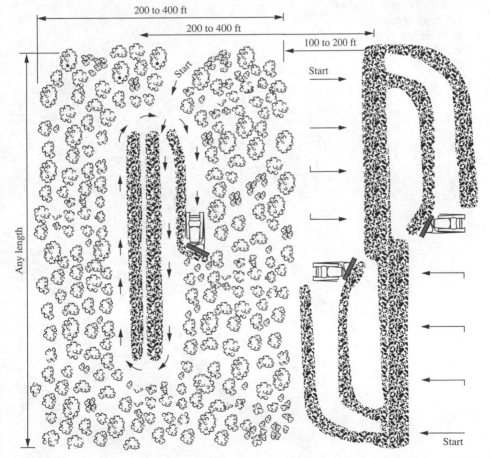

FIGURE 5-21
Shearing small-to-medium-diameter vegetation from the center of the area to the outside. *(Caterpillar Inc.)*

2. Extremely large or hard trees do not split readily. To remove these, first cut the lateral roots around the tree and then push the tree with the blade raised high to provide leverage.

LAND-CLEARING PRODUCTION ESTIMATING

Typically, land clearing of timber is performed with crawler tractors that have between 140 and 350 hp. The speed at which the tractor can move through the vegetation will depend on the nature of the growth and the size of the machine. The best way to estimate land clearing is by using historical data from similar projects. When data from past projects are not available, the estimator can utilize the formula presented in this section as a rough guide for probable production rates. However, production rates calculated strictly from the formula should be used with caution.

Critical factors which must be considered when estimating land clearing are:

1. Nature of the vegetation
   a. Type of trees
   b. Number of trees
   c. Size of the trees

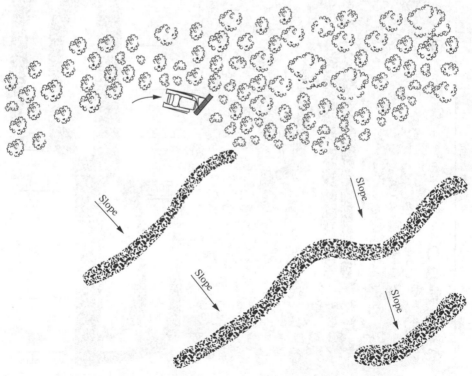

FIGURE 5-22
Cutting on steep slopes or significant amounts of large trees. *(Caterpillar Inc.)*

   d. Density of the trees

   e. Root systems

   f. Undergrowth and vines

2. Soil condition and bearing capacity

   a. Type of soil (cohesive, noncohesive)

   b. Moisture content

   c. Depth to the water table

   d. Presence of rock

3. Topography—level ground, hills, swamps, and so on

4. Climate and rainfall

   a. Temperature, humidity, and wind

   b. Amount of rainfall

   c. Amount of rainfall per rain

   d. Days between rainfalls

   e. Days of sunshine

5. Job specifications

   a. Clear (shear only)

   b. Clear and grub

   c. Size of project

   d. Time available to perform the clearing

Prior to preparing a clearing estimate, the estimator should visit the project site in order to obtain information needed to evaluate the variable factors.

Constant speed clearing. When there is only light vegetation, it is possible to clear at a constant speed; production can be estimated by the tractor speed and the width of the pass:

$$\frac{\text{Production}}{\text{(acre/hr)}} = \frac{\text{width of cut (ft)} \times \text{speed (mph)} \times 5{,}280 \text{ ft/mi} \times \text{efficiency}}{43{,}560 \text{ sq ft/acre}} \quad (5\text{-}7)$$

    The American Society of Agricultural Engineers' formula for estimating land-clearing production at constant speed is based on a 49.5-min hour, which is an 0.825 efficiency. Formula (5-7) then reduces to

$$\text{Production (acre/hr)} = \frac{\text{width of cut (ft)} \times \text{speed (mph)}}{10} \quad (5\text{-}8)$$

    The width of the cut is the resulting cleared width measured perpendicular to the direction of tractor travel. With an angle blade, it is obvious that this is not equal to the width of the blade. Even when working with a straight blade, it may not be the same as the blade width. The width of the cut should be determined by field measurement, but it may have to be estimated.

    Example 5-7. A 200-hp crawler tractor will be used to clear small trees and brush from a 10-acre site. By operating in first gear, the tractor should be able to maintain a continuous forward speed of 0.9 mph. An angle-clearing blade will be used, and from past experience the average resulting clear width will be 8 ft. Assuming normal efficiency, how long will it take to knock down the vegetation?

Using Eq. (5-8), we have

$$\frac{8 \text{ ft} \times 0.9 \text{ mph}}{10} = 0.72 \text{ acre/hr}$$

$$\frac{10 \text{ acres}}{0.72 \text{ acre/hr}} = 13.9 \text{ hr} \Rightarrow 14 \text{ hr}$$

Cutting and piling-up production. Rome Industries has developed a formula for estimating cutting and piling-up production. (Refer to *Caterpillar Performance Handbook*.) The Rome formula and tables of constants provide guidance for variable speed operations, but use of the results should be tempered with field experience.

To develop the necessary input data for the Rome formula, the estimator must make a field survey of the area to be cleared and collect information on the following items:

1. Density of vegetation *less than 12 in.* in diameter:
   Dense—600 trees per acre
   Medium—400 to 600 trees per acre
   Light—less than 400 trees per acre
2. Presence of hardwoods expressed in percent
3. Presence of heavy vines
4. Average number of trees per acre in each of the following ground-level, diameter-size ranges:
   Less than 1 ft
   1–2 ft
   2–3 ft
   3–4 ft
   4–6 ft
5. Sum of diameter of all trees per acre above 6 ft in diameter at ground level

Once the field information is collected, the estimator can enter the table of production factors for cutting (see Table 5-5) to determine the time factors which should be used in the Rome cutting formula, Eq. (5-9):

Time (min) per acre for cutting
$$= H[A(B) + M_1N_1 + M_2N_2 + M_3N_3 + M_4N_4 + DF] \qquad (5\text{-}9)$$

where H = hardwood factor affecting total time
   Hardwoods affect overall time as follows:
   75–100% hardwoods; add 30% to total time ($H = 1.3$)
   25–75% hardwoods; no change ($H = 1.0$)
   0–25% hardwoods; reduce total time 30% ($H = 0.7$)
 A = tree density and presence of vines' effect on base time
   Base time is affected by the density of material less than 1 ft in diameter and the presence of vines

Dense: greater than 600 trees per acre; add 100% to base time ($A = 2.0$)
Medium: 400–600 trees per acre; no change ($A = 1.0$)
Light: less than 400 trees per acre; reduce base time 30% ($A = 0.7$)
Presence of heavy vines; add 100% to base time ($A = 2.0$)

B = base time for each tractor size per acre
M = minutes per tree in each diameter range
N = number of trees per acre in each diameter range, from field survey
D = sum of diameter in foot increments of all trees per acre above 6 ft in diameter at ground level, from field survey
F = minutes per foot of diameter for trees above 6 ft in diameter

When the job specifications require the removal of trees and the grubbing of the roots and stumps greater than 1 ft in diameter in one operation, increase the total time per acre by 25%. When the specifications require the removal of stumps in a separate operation, increase the time per acre by 50%.

Example 5-8. Estimate the rate at which a 215-hp tractor equipped with a K/G blade can fell the vegetation on a highway project. Highway specifications require the grubbing of stumps resulting from trees greater than 12 in. in diameter. Felling and grubbing will be performed in one operation.

The site is reasonably level terrain with firm ground and less than 25% hardwood. The field survey gathered the following tree counts:

Average number of trees per acre, 700
   1–2 ft in diameter,   100 trees
   2–3 ft in diameter,   10 trees
   3–4 ft in diameter,   2 trees
   4–6 ft in diameter,   — trees
Sum of diameter increments above 6 ft, none

TABLE 5-5
Production factors for felling with Rome K/G blades

Tractor (hp)	Base minutes per acre $B^\dagger$	Diameter range				
		1–2 ft M_1	2–3 ft M_2	3–4 ft M_3	4–6 ft M_4	Above 6 ft F
165	34.41	0.7	3.4	6.8	—	—
215	23.48	0.5	1.7	3.6	10.2	3.3
335	18.22	0.2	1.3	2.2	6.0	1.8
460	15.79	0.1	0.4	1.3	3.0	1.0

† Based on power-shift tractors working on reasonably level terrain (10% maximum grade) with good footing and no stones and an average mix of soft and hardwoods.
Source: Caterpillar Inc.

The necessary input values for formula (5-9) are

$$H = 0.7 \quad \text{less than 25\% hardwoods}$$
$$A = 2.0 \quad \text{dense, } > 600 \text{ trees per acre}$$

From Table 5-5 for a 215-hp tractor, $B = 23.48$,

$$M_1 = 0.5, \quad M_2 = 1.7, \quad M_3 = 3.6, \quad M_4 = 10.2, \quad \text{and} \quad F = 3.3$$

Time per acre $= 0.7[2.0(23.48) + 0.5(100) + 1.7(10) + 3.6(2) + 10.2(0) + 0(3.3)]$

Time per acre $= 84.8$ min/acre

Because the operation will include grubbing, the time must be increased by 25%.

$$\text{Time per acre} = 84.8 \times 1.25 = 106.0 \text{ min/acre}$$

Clearing rates are often expressed in acres per hour, so for this example the rate would be $60/106 = 0.57$ acres per 60-min hour.

Table 5-5 and Eq. (5-9) are used to calculate the time for a cutting operation. Usually, the cut material must be piled for burning or so that it can be easily picked up and hauled away. Rome Industries has developed a separate formula and set of constants for estimating piling-up production rates.

$$\text{Time (min) per acre for piling-up} = B + M_1N_1 + M_2N_2 + M_3N_3 + M_4N_4 + DF \tag{5-10}$$

The factors have the same definitions as when used previously in Eq. (5-9), but their values must be determined from Table 5-6 for input into the piling-up Eq. (5-10). Piling-up grubbed vegetation increases the total piling-up time by 25%.

Example 5-9. Consider that the vegetation cut in the previous example must be piled. What is the estimated rate at which piling-up can be accomplished?

$$\text{Time per acre} = 50.61 + 0.4(100) + 0.7(10) + 2.5(2) + 5.0(0) + 0(\text{—})$$
$$= 103 \text{ min/acre}$$

Because the operation will include grubbing, the time must be increased by 25%.

$$103 \text{ min/acre} \times 1.25 = 129 \text{ min/acre} \quad \text{or} \quad 0.47 \text{ acre piled-up per 60-min hr}$$

LAND-CLEARING PRODUCTION STUDY

Land-clearing production varies considerably with the factors previously listed. Very little information on the subject has been released. However, in 1958 the Agricultural Experiment Station of Auburn University, Auburn, AL, conducted tests to determine the cost of clearing land using three sizes of crawler tractors equipped with both bulldozer blades and shearing blades [5].

For test purposes an area of 24 acres was divided into 12 plots of 2 acres each, with the dimensions of 198 ft wide by 440 ft long. Each size tractor cleared two plots using a bulldozer blade and two plots using a shearing blade. The net time required to fell, stack, and burn the material from each plot was determined. The trees consisted of

TABLE 5-6
Production factors for piling-up in windrows[†]

Tractor (hp)	Base minutes per acre $B^†$	Diameter range				
		1–2 ft M_1	2–3 ft M_2	3–4 ft M_3	4–6 ft M_4	Above 6 ft F
165	63.56	0.5	1.0	4.2	—	—
215	50.61	0.4	0.7	2.5	5.0	—
335	44.94	0.1	0.5	1.8	3.6	0.9
460	39.27	0.08	0.1	1.2	2.1	0.3

[†] May be used with most types of raking tools and angled shearing blades. Windrows to be spaced approximately 200 ft apart.
Source: Caterpillar Inc.

pine, oak, hickory, and gum, distributed by species, size, and density as listed in Table 5-7. The diameters of the trees were measured at breast height.

The trees were felled, and then pushed along the surface of the ground and stacked in windrows that were not more than 200 ft apart, after which they were burned. During the burning operation the timber was pushed into tighter stacks to increase the burning effectiveness by using a tractor-mounted blade.

Table 5-8 shows the average time required by each size crawler tractor and type of blade to fell, stack, and dispose of an acre of timber. The smaller amounts of time required to dispose of trees felled with shearing blades were the result of the smaller amounts of soil in the roots of trees felled with this type of blade.

TABLE 5-7
Types of equipment used, species, sizes, and densities of trees

Plot no.	Blade used[†]	Percent by species		Percent by size trees (in.)		No. trees per acre
		Hardwood	Pine	To 6	Above 6	
1	B	79	21	87	13	375
2	B	98	2	74	26	285
3	B	97	3	76	24	385
4	B	56	44	87	13	585
5	B	53	47	93	7	680
6	B	78	22	87	13	755
7	S	80	20	86	14	690
8	S	29	71	98	2	1,545
9	S	72	28	82	18	445
10	S	60	40	98	2	710
11	S	89	11	72	28	410
12	S	75	25	76	24	400

[†] B denotes a bulldozer blade and S denotes a shearing blade.

TABLE 5-8
Average machine time required, in hours, to clear an acre of land based on size tractor and blade used

	Time per acre (hr)					
	93 fwhp		130 fwhp		190 fwhp	
Operation	B†	S†	B	S	B	S
Felling	2.19	1.58	1.71	1.14	0.92	0.71
Stacking	0.52	0.55	0.56	0.60	0.48	0.46
Disposal	1.75	0.84	1.80	0.78	1.93	0.70
Total	4.46	2.97	4.07	2.52	3.33	1.87

† B denotes a bulldozer blade and S denotes a shearing blade.

RIPPING ROCK

GENERAL INFORMATION

Rippers (see Fig. 5-23) are used to tear and split hard ground, weak rock, or old pavements and bases. Heavy ripping is accomplished with crawler tractors because of the power and tractive force available from such machines. Motor graders can also be equipped with rippers for light duty applications.

Although rock has been ripped with varying degrees of success for many years, recent developments in methods, equipment, and knowledge have greatly increased the extent of ripping today. Rock that was considered to be unrippable a few years ago is now ripped with relative ease, and at cost reductions—including ripping and hauling with scrapers—amounting to as much as 50% when compared with the cost of drilling, blasting, loading with loaders, and hauling with trucks.

The major developments responsible for the increase in ripping rock include:

1. Heavier and more powerful tractors
2. Improvements in the sizes and performance of rippers, to include development of impact rippers
3. Better instruments for determining the rippability of rocks
4. Improved techniques in using instruments and equipment

DETERMINING THE RIPPABILITY OF ROCK

Prior to selecting the method of excavating and hauling rock, it is desirable to determine if the rock can be ripped or if it will be necessary to drill and blast. Evaluating rippability of rock involves the study of the rock type and a determination of the rock's

FIGURE 5-23
Tractor-mounted hydraulically operated triple-shank ripper. *(Fiat-Allis Construction Machinery, Inc.)*

density. Because igneous rocks lack stratification and cleavage and are very hard, they are normally impossible to rip. Sedimentary rocks have a layered structure caused by the manner in which they were formed. This characteristic makes them easier to rip. Metamorphic rocks, being a changed form from either igneous or sedimentary rock, vary in rippability.

Because the rippability of most types of rocks is related to the speed at which sound waves travel through rock, it is possible to use seismographic methods to determine with reasonable accuracy if a rock can be ripped. Rocks which propagate sound waves at low velocities are rippable, whereas rocks which propagate waves at high velocities are not rippable. Rocks having intermediate velocities are classified as marginal.

For two different size tractors, Fig. 5-24 indicates rippability based on velocity ranges for various types of soil and rocks encountered on construction projects. The indication that a rock may be rippable, marginal, or nonrippable is based on using multi- or single-shank rippers mounted on a crawler tractor. The information appearing in the figure should be used only as a guide. The decision to rip or not to rip rock should be based on the relative costs of excavating by using the methods under consideration and the equipment that is available. If smaller tractors are to be utilized, the upper limits on the velocities of rock to be ripped will be less than those appearing in Fig. 5-24. Field tests may be necessary to determine if a given rock can be ripped economically.

DETERMINING THE SPEED OF SOUND WAVES IN ROCK

A refraction seismograph can be used to determine the thickness and the degree of consolidation of rock layers at or near the ground surface. The paths followed by sound

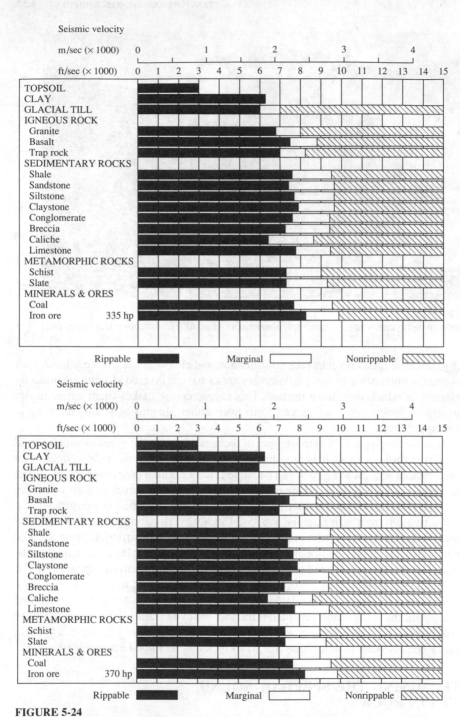

FIGURE 5-24
Ripper performance for Caterpillar 335 & 370 HP crawler tractors with multi- or single-shank rippers.
Estimated by seismic wave velocities. *(Caterpillar Inc.)*

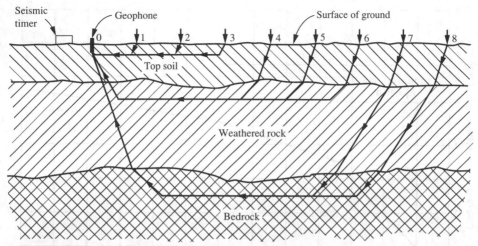

FIGURE 5-25
Path of seismic waves through layers of increasing density with depth.

waves, from a wave-generating source, through a formation to detecting instruments is illustrated in Fig. 5-25.

A geophone, which is a sound sensor, is driven into the ground at station 0. Equally spaced points 1, 2, 3, and so on are located along a line, as indicated. A wire is connected from the geophone to the seismic timer, and another wire is connected from the timer to a sledge hammer, or other impact-producing tool. When the hammer strikes, a switch closes instantly to send an electric signal, which starts the timer. At the same instant the blow from the hammer sends sound waves into the formation, which travel to the geophone. Upon the receipt of the first wave, the geophone signals the timer to stop recording elapsed time. With the distance and the time known, the velocity of a wave can be determined.

As the distance from the geophone to the wave source, namely, the striking hammer, is increased, waves will enter the lower and denser formation, through which they will travel at a higher speed than through the topsoil, and thus the waves will reach the geophone before the waves through the topsoil arrive. When the velocity through the denser formation is determined, note that it has a higher value, which velocity will remain approximately constant as long as the waves travel through a formation of uniform density.

A plot, such as that in Fig. 5-26, yields wave velocity simply by measuring the distance and the time associated with each layer and by dividing the distance by the corresponding time:

$$\text{Velocity, } V_i = \frac{\text{horizontal distance, } L_i}{\text{time to travel distance } L_i} \tag{5-11}$$

The velocity remains constant as the wave passes through the material of uniform density. Breakpoints in the plot indicate changes in material density, and therefore in velocity.

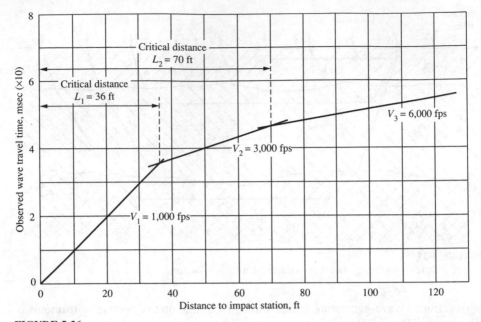

FIGURE 5-26
Plot of seismic wave travel time versus distance between source and the geophone.

The depth to the surface separating the first two strata depends on the critical distance and the velocities in the two materials. It can be computed from the equation

$$D_1 = \frac{L_1}{2} \sqrt{\frac{V_2 - V_1}{V_2 + V_1}} \qquad (5\text{-}12)$$

where D = depth, ft
L_1 = critical distance, ft
V_1 = velocity of wave in top stratum, fps
V_2 = velocity of wave in lower stratum, fps

Solving for D_1 from Fig. 5-26 gives

$$D_1 = \frac{36}{2} \sqrt{\frac{3,000 - 1,000}{3,000 + 1,000}} = 13 \text{ ft}$$

Thus, the top layer has an apparent depth of 13 ft.

Equation (5-13) may be used to determine the apparent thickness of the second stratum.

$$D_2 = \frac{L_2}{2} \sqrt{\frac{V_3 - V_2}{V_3 + V_2}} + D_1 \left[1 - \frac{V_2 \sqrt{V_3^2 - V_1^2} - V_3 \sqrt{V_2^2 - V_1^2}}{V_1 \sqrt{V_3^2 - V_2^2}} \right] \qquad (5\text{-}13)$$

where L_2 is 70 ft, D_1 is 13 ft, V_1 is 1,000 fps, V_2 is 3,000 fps, and V_3 is 6,000 fps. Solving, we obtain

$$D_2 = 31 \text{ ft}$$

Ripping is normally an operation involving the top strata of a formation. Determination of the depth of the upper two layers and the velocity of the upper three layers will provide the necessary data to estimate most jobs. The procedure can become very complicated, however, when dipping strata are encountered. The investigation of complicated formations may require, in addition to seismic studies, the core drilling of samples and the excavation of test pits.

RIPPER ATTACHMENTS

Ripper attachments for tractors are generally rear mounted. The mounting may be either a radial, hinged type or a parallelogram arrangement (see Fig. 5-27). The vertical piece which is forced down into the material to be ripped is known as a *shank*. At the lower cutting end of the shank a tooth (a point, tip, or tap) is mounted. The tooth is detachable for easy replacement as it is the high wear surface of the ripper. A tooth can have a service life from 1,000 hours to only 30 min, depending on the abrasive characteristics of the material being ripped.

There are both straight and curved shanks available. Straight shanks are used for massive or blocky formations. Curved shanks are for bedded or laminated rocks or for pavements where a lifting action will help to shatter the material.

With the radial-type mounting, the beam of the ripper pivots on link-arms about its point of attachment to the tractor; therefore, the angle of tip attack varies with the depth that the shank is depressed. This may make it difficult to achieve penetration in tough materials. The shank may also tend to "dig itself in."

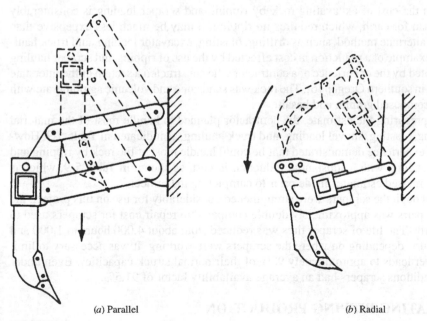

(a) Parallel (b) Radial

FIGURE 5-27
Two types of linkage used to mount rippers on tractors.

The parallelogram-type ripper maintains the shank in a vertical position and keeps the tip at a constant angle. There are adjustable parallelogram-type rippers which allow the tip angle to be controlled by the operator.

Heavy duty rippers have one to three shanks. The shanks are pinned into position on the ripper frame. This allows the ease of removal so that shank arrangement can be matched to material and project requirements. Very heavy work is performed with a single-center-mounted shank. The use of all three shanks will produce more uniform breakage if full penetration can be obtained. A single shank often rolls individual oversized pieces to the side.

The effectiveness of a ripper depends on:

1. Down pressure at the ripper tip
2. The tractor's usable power to advance the tip: function of power available, tractor weight, and coefficient of traction
3. Properties of the material being ripped: laminated, faulted, weathered, and so on

The number of shanks used depends on the size of the tractor, the depth of penetration desired, the resistance of the material being ripped, and the degree of material breakage desired. If the material is to be excavated by scrapers, it should be broken into particles that can be loaded into scrapers, usually not more than 24–30 in. maximum sizes. Only a field test conducted at the project will demonstrate which method, depth, and degree of breakage are most satisfactory and economical.

ECONOMY OF RIPPING ROCK

Although the cost of excavating rock by ripping and scraper loading is considerably higher than for earth, which requires no ripping, it may be much less expensive than using an alternate method, such as drilling, blasting, excavator loading, and truck hauling. An example of a reduction in cost effected by the use of ripping and scraper hauling is illustrated by the experience of a contractor who constructed a section of the interstate highway in southern Oregon [6]. The rock was sandstone and volcanic agglomerate with some decomposed granite and basalt.

In preparing the estimate, the contractor planned to handle most of the material by drilling, blasting, shovel loading, and truck hauling, as indicated in Table 5-9. However, job experience demonstrated that he could handle most of the rock by ripping and scraper loading, with a substantial reduction in cost, as shown in Table 5-9, which is based on revised estimates made prior to completing the project.

Although the scrapers were strengthened considerably for use on this project, the cost of repairs was approximately double compared to repair cost for scrapers used to move earth. The life of scraper tires was reduced from about 4,000 hours to 1,000 and 1,500 hours, depending on where the scrapers were working. It was necessary to limit the scraper loads to approximately 90% of their normal struck capacities. Even under these conditions scrapers had an average availability factor of 91.5%.

ESTIMATING RIPPING PRODUCTION

Estimating ripping production is best accomplished by working a test section and carefully recording the work time and the weight of ripper material. However, the opportunity to conduct such field tests is often nonexistent; therefore, most initial estimates are based on equipment manufacturers' production charts.

By conducting field tests on a variety of materials, the manufacturers have developed relationships between seismic wave velocities and rippability (see Fig. 5-24).

Ripper performance charts, such as those in Fig. 5-24, allow the estimator to make an initial determination of equipment which may be able to perform based on general rock-type classifications. After the initial determination of applicable machines is made, production rates for those particular machines are calculated from production charts.

Ripping production charts (see Fig. 5-28) are based on the physical material properties. The production rates obtained from the charts must be adjusted to reflect the actual field conditions of the project. To consider adequately the possible variations in project conditions and differences in properties even within a basic rock group, we must recognize that ripping production charts are only one indicator of a machine's possible ripping performance. The use of such charts must be tempered with experience.

Owning and operating (O&O) costs of a tractor will increase for machines that are consistently used in ripping operations. Caterpillar warns that normal O&O costs must be increased by 30–40% if the machine is used in heavy ripping applications.

Example 5-9. A contractor encounters a shale formation at shallow depth in a cut section of his project. He performs seismographic tests, which indicate a seismic velocity of 7,000 fps (feet per second) for the shale. On this basis, he proposes to rip the material.

(*a*) Select a tractor-ripper combination for which the material as described is classified as "rippable."

(*b*) Estimate the production in bank cubic yards (bcy) for full-time ripping, with efficiency based on a 45-min hour (a typical factor for ripping operations). Assume that the ripper is equipped with a single shank and that ripping conditions are ideal.

(*c*) The "normal" O&O cost excluding the operator for the tractor-ripper combination which was selected in part (*a*) is $86 per hour. Operator wages are $9.50 per hour. What is the estimated ripping cost in dollars per bcy?

(*a*) From Fig. 5-24, ripper performance:

335 hp—Rippable in shale having a seismic velocity up to 7,500 ft per sec
370 hp—Rippable in shale having a seismic velocity up to 7,500 ft per sec

TABLE 5-9
Ripping rock cost versus alternate methods[†]

	Estimated methods, quantities, and costs			Actual methods and costs	
Method	Cost per cu yd	Volume (cu yd)	Total cost	Volume (cu yd)	Total cost
Blast, shovel, truck	$0.86	3,100,000	$2,666,000	100,000	$ 86,000
Blast, scraper	0.68	none	none	900,000	612,000
Ripper, scraper	0.46	700,000	322,000	2,800,000	1,288,000
Total		3,800,000	$2,988,000	3,800,000	$1,986,000

[†]The costs shown were correct at the time the project was constructed.

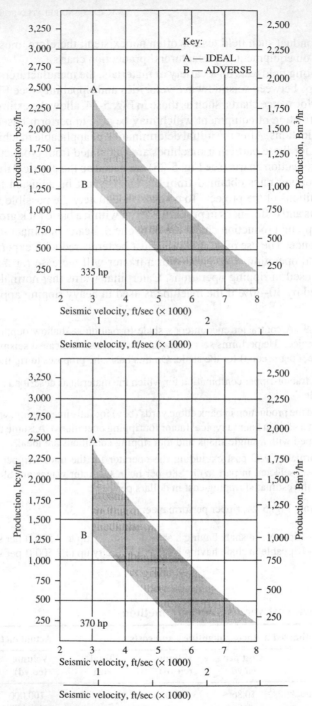

FIGURE 5-28
Ripper production Caterpillar 335 and 370 HP crawler tractors with a single shank. *(Caterpillar Inc.)*

Both tractors are applicable for this situation according to the charts, but both are at the limit of their capability. Therefore, the contractor should consider the larger machine.

(b) Using the 370-hp-tractor-ripper-production chart (see Fig. 5-28) for a seismic velocity of 7,000 ft per sec and ideal conditions, we have

$$\text{Ideal production 370-hp tractor} = 560 \text{ bcy/hr}$$

$$\text{Adjusted production} = 560 \times \frac{45}{60} = 420 \text{ bcy/hr}$$

(c) Increase normal O&O cost because of the ripping application:

$$\$86.50 \text{ per hour} \times 1.35 = \$116.10 \text{ per hour}$$

$$\text{Total cost with operator: } \$116.10 + \$9.50 = \$125.60 \text{ per hour}$$

$$\text{Production cost} = \frac{\$125.60 \text{ per hour}}{420 \text{ bcy/hr}} = \$0.299 \text{ per bcy}$$

PROBLEMS

5-1. A crawler tractor with a universal blade is to be used in a slot-dozing operation. The material is a dry, noncohesive silty sand and is to be moved a distance of 350 ft from the beginning of the cut. The dozing is downhill on a 10% grade. The operator will have average skill, the tractor has a power-shift transmission, and both visibility and traction are assumed to be satisfactory. The material weighs 108 lb per cu ft (pcf) in the bank state and will swell 10% when excavated by dozing. Job efficiency is assumed to be equivalent to a 50-min hour.

(a) Assuming a Caterpillar D8 is used, calculate the direct cost of the proposed earth-moving operation in dollars per bcy (bank cubic yards). Assume that the owning and operating (O&O) cost for the tractor is $64.80 per hour and that the operator's wage is $10.85 per hour plus 36% for fringes, workman's compensation, and so on.

(b) Assume that a CAT 834 wheel-type tractor with a straight blade is substituted for the D8. (The 834 has 58% more flywheel horsepower than the D8.) All other conditions of the job are unchanged, except that the O&O cost for the 834 is $69.95 per hour.

(c) Assume that the 834 tractor, when operating on this particular soil, will have a coefficient of traction of 0.34. Estimate the unit-production cost in dollars per bcy, with all other job conditions remaining unchanged.

5-2. Two CAT D10 (power-shift) tractors are to be used in a side-by-side pushing operation. The tractors are equipped with universal blades. The material, dry and noncohesive, weighs 102 pcf in the bank state. It is estimated that the material will swell 8% in the bank to loose state. The center of mass to the center of the mass-pushing distance is 380 ft downhill on a 5% grade. The operators have average skill and the job will be performed in dusty conditions. Job efficiency can be assumed to be equivalent to a 50-min hour.

Calculate the direct cost of the proposed earth-moving operation in dollars per bcy. The company's normal O&O cost for these machines is $93.82 per hour and the operator's wage is $12.18 per hour plus 42% for fringes, insurance, workman's compensation, and so on.

5-3. A CAT 824C with a straight blade is to be used to push a material which weighs 125 pcf in the bank state. It is estimated that the material will swell 20% in the bank to loose state. This cohesive soil is to be moved an average distance of 100 ft up a 12% grade. The operator is a new hire who has poor skills. Job efficiency is estimated to be equivalent to a 45-min hour.

Assume that the tractor will have a 0.36 coefficient of traction. Calculate the direct cost of the proposed earth-moving operation in dollars per bcy. The (O&O) cost for the tractor is $47.30 per hour and the operator's wage is $8.76 per hour plus 34% for fringes, insurance, workman's compensation, and so on.

5-4. Given the geophone data below, calculate the seismic wave velocity in each layer. Find the bottom depth of each layer, except for the last one.

Distance (ft)	15	30	45	60	75	90	105	125	145
Time (msec.)	7.5	15.0	22.5	26.3	30.0	33.8	37.5	40.4	43.2

5-5. An earth-moving contractor encounters a trap-rock formation at a shallow depth in a rock cut. He performs seismographic tests, which indicate a seismic velocity of 6,500 fps (feet per second) for the material. On this basis, he proposes to rip the material with Caterpillar equipment.

(a) His first step is to select a tractor-ripper combination for which the material as described is classified as rippable. Which tractors should he consider for possible use on the project?

(b) Estimate the production, in bcy, for full-time ripping, with efficiency based on a 50-min hour. Assume that the tractor is equipped with a single shank and that ripping conditions are *average* (i.e., intermediate between extreme conditions).

(c) The *normal* O&O cost per hour, including the operator, for a 335-hp tractor-ripper combination is $63.63 and $95.82 for the 460 hp. This work would be classified as a *heavy ripping* application. Using your estimate of hourly production from part (b), estimate the ripping unit-production cost in dollars per bcy. Which tractor do you recommend for this project and why do you recommend it?

5-6. A limestone formation, with an average depth of 2.4 ft, is exposed over the full 80-ft width and 23,700-ft length of a highway cut. Preliminary seismic investigations indicate that the rock layer has a seismic velocity of 5,500 fps.

The contractor proposes to loosen this rock by using a single-shank ripper on a power-shift track-type tractor. He estimates that job conditions relative to lamination, and so on, are *average* or midway between *adverse* and *ideal*. He believes that he will be able to maintain a 40-min hour working efficiency while the ripper is actually in production, and estimates that the ripper will be out of service for repairs for 5% of the total hours that the ripper could be used on the job (i.e., an availability of 0.95). He further estimates that the ripper will be out of service due to adverse weather for 20% of the same total hours.

The contractor wishes to explore the use of two 370-hp versus three 335-hp tractors for the ripping operations. O&O costs are estimated at $47.63 per working hour for the 335 hp and $79.82 per working hour for each 370 hp, including rippers. Each machine is to be charged against the job at 60% of its normal O&O rate during working hours when the equipment is not used because of adverse weather or scheduling problems, but it will not be charged against the job when the equipment is down for repair.

The operator's wage, paid during hours worked and hours when the equipment is being repaired, is $14.30 per hour. Associated charges against the ripping operation for grade foreman, mechanic, and so on are estimated to be $25 per nominal (i.e., regularly scheduled, including downtime for repairs or adverse weather) working hours. Move-in and move-out costs combined are estimated to be $200 per unit of either type. Calculate the total time in weeks, based on a normal 40-hour workweek, to loosen the rock cut with each of the two alternatives. Calculate the total loosening cost, in dollars per bcy, for each alternative.

5-7. A contract is being bid to clear and grub 147 acres. You are considering the cost associated with using either of two different power-shift tractors. One tractor is a 215-hp model and the other is rated at 335 hp. The 215 hp has an O&O cost, without the operator of $43 per hour and the 335 hp's O&O is $63.96 per hour. The wage determination for heavy duty operators is $10.85 per hour. Project overhead will run $357 per workday. Assume a 10-hour day.

    A field engineer has made a site visit and provided you with the following information. The site is reasonably level and the machines will have no problem with bearing or traction. About 10% of the trees are pines and the rest are oak. The trees per acre are

1–2 ft in diameter	210 trees per acre
2–3 ft in diameter	9 trees per acre
3–4 ft in diameter	1 tree per acre

    You plan to clear and grub in one operation, and then to follow with piling-up in windrows and burning. Burning will require that the tractor be employed twice the time expected for piling-up alone.

    (*a*) What is the estimated clearing and grubbing production rate for each tractor?

    (*b*) What is the cost associated with the total operation, including overhead, when only one 215-hp tractor is used?

    (*c*) What is the cost associated with the total operation, including overhead, when only one 335-hp tractor is used?

    (*d*) Is it cheaper to employ three 215-hp tractors or two 335-hp tractors?

REFERENCES

1. "Alloy Points Rip Hard Sandstone Fast," *Roads and Streets,* vol. 116, p. 114, September 1973.
2. *Caterpillar Performance Handbook,* Caterpillar Inc., Peoria, IL.
3. Church, Horace K., "433 Seismic Excavation Studies: What They Tell about Rippability," *Roads and Streets,* vol. 115, pp. 86–92, January 1972.
4. "Contractor's Own Seismic Study Helps to Set Job Strategy," *Roads and Streets,* vol. 115, pp. 26–28, January 1972.
5. "Cost of Clearing Land," *Circular 133,* Agricultural Experiment Station of Auburn University, Auburn, AL, June 1959.
6. "Factory-Reinforced Scrapers Load and Haul Ripped Rock," *Construction Methods and Equipment,* vol. 47, pp. 95–97, January 1965.
7. *Handbook of Ripping: A Guide to Greater Profits,* 5th ed., Caterpillar Tractor Co., Peoria, IL, 1975.
8. *Land Clearing,* Caterpillar Tractor Co., Peoria, IL.
9. "Rip Basalt with Big Tractor," *Roads and Streets,* vol. 116, pp. 114–115, October 1973.
10. "Rome Training Presentations Nos. 11-A, 11-C, 11-E, 11-F," Rome Industries, Cedartown, GA.
11. *The Rome K/G Clearing Blade, Operator's Handbook,* Rome Plow Company, Cedartown, GA.

CHAPTER

6

SCRAPERS

GENERAL INFORMATION

Tractor-pulled scrapers are designed to load, haul, and dump loose material. The greatest advantage of tractor-scraper combinations is their versatility. They can be used in a wide range of material types (including shot rock) and are economical over a wide range of haul lengths and haul conditions. To the extent that they can self-load, they are not dependent on other equipment. If one machine in the spread experiences a temporary breakdown, it will not shut down the job as would be the case for a machine which is used exclusively for loading. If the loader breaks down, the entire job must stop until repairs can be made. Scrapers are available with loose heaped capacities up to about 44 cu yd, although in the past a few machines as large as 100 cu yd have been offered.

Since scrapers are a compromise between machines designed exclusively for either loading or hauling, they are not superior to function-specific equipment in either hauling or loading. Excavators, such as hydraulic hoes and front shovels, or loaders will usually surpass scrapers in loading. Trucks may surpass them in hauling, especially over long distances. However, for off-highway situations having hauls of less than a mile, their ability both to load and haul gives them an advantage. Additionally, the ability of these machines to deposit their loads in layers of uniform thickness facilitates compaction operations.

SCRAPER TYPES

There are several types of scrapers, primarily classified according to the number of powered axles or by the method of loading. These are all wheel-tractor-pulled machines. In the past crawler-tractor "towed" two-axle scraper bowls were manufactured. They proved effective in short-haul situations, less than 600 ft one-way. Another machine

FIGURE 6-1
Single-powered axle wheel-tractor scraper.

of the past is the two-axle pulling tractor which can now be found only in much older spreads. Machines currently available include:

1. Push-loaded
   a. single-powered axle (see Fig. 6-1)
   b. tandem-powered axles
2. Push-pull, tandem-powered axles (see Fig. 6-2)
3. Elevating (see Fig. 6-3)

Push-loaded scrapers. The wheel-type tractor scraper has the potential for high travel speeds on favorable haul roads. Many models can achieve speeds up to 30 mph when fully loaded. This extends the economic haul distance of the units. However, these units are at a disadvantage when it comes to individually providing the high tractive effort required for economical loading. For the single-powered axle scraper (see Fig. 6-1) only a portion, on the order of 50–55% of the total loaded weight, bears on the drive wheels.

Additionally, in most materials the coefficient of traction for rubber tires is less than that for tracks. Therefore, it is necessary to supplement the loading power of these scrapers. The external source of loading power is usually a crawler-tractor pusher.

FIGURE 6-2
Tandem-powered axles, push-pull wheel-tractor scraper.

Loading costs are still relatively low because both the scraper and the pusher share in providing the total power required to obtain a full load. Even tandem-powered units normally require help in loading (see Fig. 6-2). The tandem-powered units have an initial cost that is up to 25% more than single-powered axle scrapers. For that reason they are commonly considered a specialized unit good for opening up a job, working extremely adverse grades, or working in soft ground conditions.

FIGURE 6-3
Elevating wheel-tractor scraper.

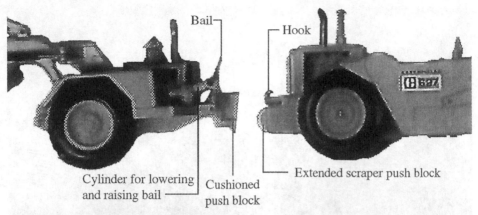

Bail

Hook

Cylinder for lowering and raising bail

Cushioned push block

Extended scraper push block

FIGURE 6-4
Cushioned push block and bail on push-pull wheel-tractor scraper.

Push-pull scrapers. These are basically tandem-axle-powered units having a cushioned push block and bail mounted on the front (see Figs. 6-2 and 6-4), and a hook on the rear above the usual push block. These features allow two scrapers to assist one another during loading by hooking together. The trailing scraper pushes the lead scraper as it loads. Then the lead scraper pulls the trailing scraper to assist it in loading. This feature allows two scrapers to work without assistance from a push tractor.

Elevating scrapers. This is a completely self-contained loading and hauling scraper (see Fig. 6-3). A chain elevator serves as the loading mechanism. The disadvantage of this machine is that the weight of the elevator-loading assembly is deadweight during the haul cycle. Such scrapers are economical in short-haul situations where the ratio of haul time to load time remains low. Elevating scrapers are also used for utility work dressing-up behind high production spreads or shifting material during fine-grading operations. They are very good in small quantity situations. No pusher is required, so there is never a mismatch between the pusher and the number of scrapers. Because of the elevator mechanism, they cannot handle rock or material containing rocks.

Volume of a scraper. The volumetric load of a scraper may be specified as either the struck or heaped capacity of the bowl expressed in cubic yards. The struck capacity is the volume that a scraper would hold if the top of the material were struck off even at the top of the bowl. In specifying the heaped capacity of a scraper, manufacturers usually specify the slope of the material above the sides of the bowl with the designation *SAE.* The Society of Automotive Engineers (SAE) specifies a repose slope of 1 : 1 for scrapers. The SAE standard for other haul units and loader buckets is 2 : 1, as will be discussed in the following chapters. Remember, the actual slope will vary with the type of material handled.

The capacity of a scraper, expressed in cubic yards bank measure (bcy), can be approximated by multiplying the loose volume in the scraper by an appropriate swell factor (see Table 4-1). Because of the compacting effect on the material in a push-loaded scraper, resulting from the pressure required to force additional material into the bowl,

FIGURE 6-5
Weighing a loaded scraper in the field.

the swell is usually less than that for material dropped into a truck by a hoe or loader. Tests indicate that the swell factors in Table 4-1 should be increased by approximately 10% for material push-loaded into a scraper. When computing the bank measure volume for an elevating scraper, no correction is required for the factors in Table 4-1.

If a push-loaded scraper hauls a heaped load measuring 22.5 cu yd and the appropriate swell factor from Table 4-1 is 0.8, the calculated bank measure volume will be

$$22.5 \text{ cu yd} \times 0.8 \times 1.1 = 19.8 \text{ bcy}$$

The use of rated volumetric capacity and swell values from tables provides an estimate of the scraper load. This is satisfactory for small jobs or if the estimator has developed a set of swell values for the materials commonly encountered in the work area. However, over time, actual field weights of loaded scrapers should be obtained for a variety of materials (see Fig. 6-5). From such weights the average carrying capacity of those scrapers actually in the fleet can be calculated directly by the methods outlined in Chap. 4. This can be important on large jobs where the significance of small differences between table values and actual measured values can have large cost effects.

SCRAPER OPERATION

A scraper is loaded by lowering the front end of the bowl until the cutting edge (see Fig. 6-6), which is attached to and extends across the width of the bowl, enters the ground.

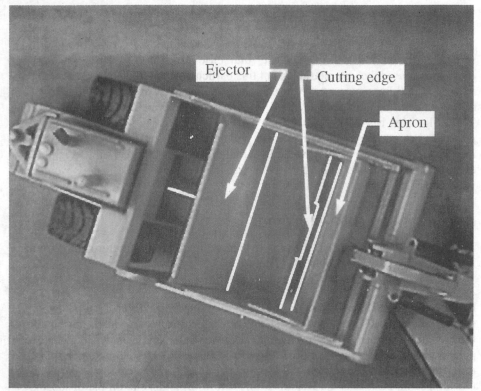

FIGURE 6-6
Scraper bowl, apron, and ejector.

At the same time, the front apron is raised to provide an open slot through which the earth can flow into the bowl. As the scraper moves forward, a horizontal strip of material is forced into the bowl. This is continued until the bowl is filled, at which point the cutting edge is raised and the apron is lowered to prevent spillage during the haul.

The dumping operation consists of lowering the cutting edge to the desired height above the fill, raising the apron, and then forcing the material out by means of a movable ejector mounted at the rear of the bowl.

The elevating scraper is equipped with horizontal flights which are operated by two endless elevator chains to which the ends of the flights are connected. As the scraper moves forward with its cutting edge digging into the earth, the flights rake the material upward into the bowl. The pulverizing action of the flights permits a complete filling of the bowl and enhances uniform spreading of the fill.

SCRAPER PERFORMANCE CHARTS

Manufacturers of scrapers provide performance charts for each of their units. These charts contain information that may be used to analyze the performance of a scraper under various operating conditions. Figures 4-8 and 4-10 in Chap. 4 presented the charts for a single-powered axle scraper. A comprehensive example using the charts was presented in Chap. 4.

It should be noted that owners sometimes add sideboards to the bowls of their scrapers. This practice will increase the volumetric load that the machine can carry. If the boards caused the volumetric load of this particular scraper, which had a rated payload of 75,000 lb, to be increased to 25.8 bcy (bank cubic yards), and the unit weight of the material being hauled is 3,000 lb per cu yd, the weight of the load would be 77,400 lb. This is greater than the rated load. The effect will be a few more yards per load, but in time maintenance costs will increase because of machine overloading. This effect would be aggravated by a material having a higher unit weight. However, if the machine were going to operate in lightweight material, boards would be a valid consideration.

CYCLE TIME FOR A SCRAPER

The *cycle time* for a scraper is the time to load, haul, dump, turn, return, and turn back into position to pick up another load [Eq. (6-1)]:

$$T_s = \text{load}_t + \text{haul}_t + \text{dump}_t + \text{turn}_t + \text{return}_t + \text{turn}_t \tag{6-1}$$

Loading time is fairly consistent regardless of the scraper size. Even though large scrapers carry larger loads, they load just as fast as smaller machines. This is attributable to the fact that the larger scraper has more horsepower and it will be matched with a larger push tractor. The average load time for push-loader scrapers in common earth is 0.85 min. Equipment manufacturers will supply load times for their machines based on the use of specific push tractors. Both haul and return times depend on the distance traveled and the scraper speed. Hauling and returning are usually at different speed ranges. Therefore, it is necessary to determine the time for each separately, as in the Chap. 4 example. If the haul road has multiple grade or rolling resistance conditions, a speed should be calculated for each leg of the route. It is a good practice to use a short distance at a slower speed when coming out of the pit, approaching the dump area, leaving the dump area, and again entering the pit, to account for acceleration/deceleration time. A distance on the order of 200–300 ft in each case is usually appropriate. Extremely steep downhill (favorable) grades can result in longer travel times than those calculated. This is caused by the fact that operators tend to downshift in order to keep speeds from becoming excessive. When using the charts, always consider the human element; do not blindly accept maximum calculable speeds.

Dump times vary with scraper size but project conditions will affect the duration. Average values for dump time are presented in Table 6-1. Physical constraints of the dump area may dictate scraper-dumping techniques. The most common method is for the scraper to dump before turning. This utilizes the haul-speed momentum to carry the scraper through the dump. It reduces the possibility of the scraper becoming stuck in the newly dumped material and yields a fairly even spreading of material, thereby reducing spreading and compaction equipment effort. Sometimes it is necessary to negotiate the turn before dumping. This generally increases dump time and the chances of the scraper becoming stuck while dumping. The last method is to dump during the turning maneuver. This definitely increases dumping time, resulting in uneven spreading and many scrapers becoming bogged down. When access is limited at bridge abutments, or when

TABLE 6-1
Scraper dump cycle times[†]

Scraper size (cu yd) heaped	Scraper type	
	Single engine (min)	Tandem-powered (min)
<25	0.30	—
25–34	0.37	0.26
35–44	0.44	0.28

[†]U.S. Department of Transportation, FHWA.

backfilling culverts, a turning/dumping maneuver may be necessary. Wet material is difficult to eject and will increase the dump time.

Turning time does not seem to be significantly affected by either the type or the size of the scraper. The average turn time in the cut is 0.30 min and on the fill the average time is 0.21 min [2]. The slightly slower turn in the cut is primarily caused by congestion in the area and the necessity to spot the scraper for the pusher.

Example 6-1. Calculate the total time required for a single-engine 31-cu-yd scraper to complete a 2,000-ft haul cycle.

Load$_t$					0.85 min
Haul$_t$	2,000 ft:	accelerate	@ 6 mph[†]	300 ft[†]	0.57
		steady	@ 12 mph[†]	1,500 ft[†]	1.42
		decelerate	@ 8 mph[†]	200 ft[†]	0.28
Dump$_t$		31 cu yd heaped (Table 6-1)			0.37
Turn$_t$		@ fill			0.21
Return$_t$	2,000 ft:	accelerate	@ 8 mph[†]	200 ft[†]	0.28
		steady	@ 18 mph[†]	1,600 ft[†]	1.01
		decelerate	@ 10 mph[†]	200 ft[†]	0.23
Turn$_t$		@ cut			0.30
				Total cycle time	5.52 min

[†]Assumed speeds and distances.

OPERATING EFFICIENCY AND PRODUCTION

If the scraper cycle time of 5.52 min developed in the previous example could be maintained for a period of 60 min, the unit would make 60/5.52 = 10.9 trips per hour. The volume of material hauled would equal the product of the number of trips and the average volume per load. Reality is different from this perfect production. Delays occur on the job; machines break down; men stop for water, or machines cluster causing a queue in the cut for the pusher. Studies of scraper operations suggest that the average productive time is 69% of a perfect 60-min hour (excluding weather delays to the job). The actual number of trips in the real world would be $10.9 \times 0.69 = 7.5$ trips per work hour.

Some people use the term *operating efficiency* and think about actual production in terms of an average number of minutes per hour that the machine will operate. A 50-min hour average would yield a $50/60 = 0.83$ efficiency factor. The 50-min hour is a good starting point if no company/equipment specific efficiency data are available. The estimator should always try to visualize the work site before applying a factor. If the pit will not be congested, and if the dump area is wide open, a 55-min hour may be appropriate. But if the cut involves a tight area, such as a ditch, or if the embankment area is a narrow bridge header, the estimator should consider a 45-min hour.

The minutes-per-hour efficiency factor is a correction for site and management conditions. It does not consider machine availability in terms of major repairs. A machine availability factor is necessary when using efficiency factors. The 50-min hour applied to the 5.52 cycle time in the example will yield $50/5.52 = 9.1$ trips per work hour. But by using the average productive time for scrapers only, we can expect 7.5 trips. What value should be used? The 9.1 value is good assuming that all scrapers in the spread are available mechanically to operate. This is an important consideration. If four scrapers make up the spread, we know that for some period of time each one will be down for major repair. On the average, over the life of a scraper it will be down 10% of the time for such repairs. If we plan to place four machines on a job, then we can assume that, in fact, over the life of the project only 3.6 scrapers will be operationally available. Therefore, a four-scraper spread and a 50-min hour efficiency yields

$$9.1 \text{ trips} \times 3.6 \text{ scrapers} = 32.8 \text{ trips per hour}$$

Considering the 69% average production for scrapers, 7.5×4 scrapers $= 30$ trips per hour. The final resulting values are close, and if a 46-min hour had been used, they would be equal. For estimating cost the efficiency factor and mechanical downtime is perhaps the best approach. The production factor can be used to provide a check. The efficiency approach is better because of how expenses accumulate.

The rent in both cases would be on four scrapers for the life of the job. But the use charge employing the efficiency factor/mechanical availability concept would be on 3.6 scrapers (see Chap. 3). With the production factor approach, use charges for four scrapers might be included mistakenly in the estimate.

PUSH TRACTORS REQUIRED

If push-loaded tractor scrapers are to attain their volumetric capacities, they need the assistance of a push tractor during the loading operation. Such assistance will reduce the loading-time duration, and thereby will reduce the total cycle time. When using push tractors, we should match the number of pushers with the number of scrapers available at a given time. If either the pusher or the scraper must wait for the other, operating efficiency is lowered and production costs are increased.

The pusher cycle time includes the time required to push-load the scraper (the contact time) and the time required to move into position to load the next scraper. The cycle time for a push tractor will vary with the conditions in the loading area, the relative sizes of the tractor and the scraper, and the loading method. Figure 6-7 shows three loading methods. *Backtrack loading* is the most common method employed. It offers the advantage of always being able to load in the direction of the haul. *Chain loading* can be used when the excavation is conducted in a long cut. *Shuttle loading* is utilized infrequently. However, if one pusher can serve scrapers hauling in opposite directions from the cut, it is a viable method. In several past publications Caterpillar recommended calculating backtrack push-tractor cycle time, T_p, by the formula

$$T_p = 1.4L_t + 0.25 \qquad (6\text{-}2)$$

where L_t is the scraper load time (pusher contact time). It is based on the concept that pusher cycle time is a function of four components:

1. Load time of the scraper
2. Boost time, time assisting the scraper out of the cut, 0.15 min
3. Maneuver time, 40% of load time
4. Positioning for contact time, 0.10 min

Pusher cycle time will be less when using the chain or shuttle methods.

The number of scrapers that a push tractor can serve is simply the ratio of the scraper cycle time to the pusher cycle time:

$$N = \frac{T_s}{T_p} \qquad (6\text{-}3)$$

where N is the number of scrapers per one pusher. Rarely, if ever, will the value of N be an integer. This means that either the pusher or a scraper will be idle some of the time.

Favorable loading conditions will reduce loading time and increase the number of scrapers that a pusher can serve. A large pit or cut, ripping hard soil prior to loading, loading downgrade, and using a push tractor whose power is matched with the size of the scraper are all factors which can improve loading times. Likewise, tight soils with no prior ripping, very large scrapers, and loading rock are factors which may create a situation where multiple pushers are required to load a scraper effectively (see Fig. 6-8).

INCREASING SCRAPER PRODUCTION

To obtain a higher profit from earthwork, a constructor must organize and operate the spread in a manner that will ensure maximum production at the lowest cost. There are several methods whereby this objective can be attained.

Ripping. Most types of tight soils will load faster if they are ripped ahead of the scraper. Additionally, delays pertaining to equipment repairs will be reduced substantially as the scraper will not be operated under as much strain. If the value of the increased production resulting from ripping exceeds the ripping cost, the material should be ripped.

When rock is ripped for scraper loading, the depth ripped should always exceed

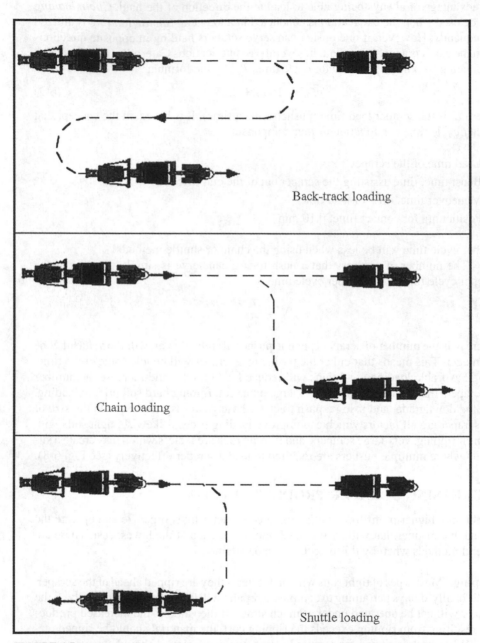

Back-track loading

Chain loading

Shuttle loading

FIGURE 6-7
Methods for push-loading scrapers.

FIGURE 6-8
Three push tractors used loading a very large scraper.

the depth to be excavated. This is in order to leave a loose layer of material under the tires to provide better traction and to reduce the wear on the tracks and tires.

Prewetting the soil. Some soils will load more easily if they are reasonably moist. Prewetting can be performed in conjunction with ripping or ahead of loading, to permit a uniform penetration of the moisture into the soil.

Prewetting the soil in the cut can reduce or eliminate the use of water trucks on the fill, thereby reducing the congestion of equipment on the fill. The elimination of excess moisture on the surface of the fill may facilitate the movement of the scrapers on the fill.

Loading downgrade. When it is practicable to do so, scrapers should be loaded downgrade and in the direction of haul. Downgrade loading results in faster loading times, whereas loading in the direction of haul both shortens the length of haul and eliminates the need to turn in the cut with a loaded scraper. Each 1% of favorable grade is the equivalent of increasing the loading force by 20 lb per ton of gross weight of the push tractor and the scraper unit.

Supervision. Full-time supervisory control should be provided in the cut. A more efficient operation will result through the elimination of confusion and traffic congestion.

A spotter should always control the fill operations, being responsible for coordinating the scrapers with the spreading and compacting equipment. The spotter's job is to keep the scrapers dumping in a specific location and pattern. Typically, the spotter will direct each scraper operator to dump the load at the end of the preceding spread until the end of the fill is reached. Then the next spread is started parallel to the first. This allows compaction equipment to work the freshly dumped material without interfering with the scrapers.

SCRAPER LOAD-GROWTH CURVE

Without a critical evaluation of available information, it might appear that the lowest cost of moving earth with scrapers is to load every scraper to its maximum capacity before it leaves the cut. However, numerous studies of loading practices have revealed that loading scrapers to their maximum capacities usually will reduce rather than increase production. See Table 6-2.

When a scraper starts loading, the earth flows into it rapidly and easily, but as the quantity of earth in the bowl increases, the incoming earth encounters greater resistance and the rate of loading decreases quite rapidly, as illustrated in Fig. 6-9. This figure is a load-growth curve for a specific scraper and pusher combination and material; it shows the relation between the load in a scraper and the loading time. An examination of the curve reveals that during the first 0.5 min the scraper loads about 85% of its maximum possible payload. During the next 0.5 min it loads an additional 12%, and if loading is continued to 1.4 min, the gain in volume during the last 0.4 min is only 3%.

Economical loading time is a function of haul distance. As haul distance increases, economical load time will increase. Figure 6-10 illustrates the relationship between loading time, production, and haul distance; it is presented only to demonstrate those

TABLE 6-2
Variations in the rates of production of scrapers with loading times[†,‡]

Loading time (min)	Other time (min)	Cycle time[†] (min)	Number trips per hr	Payload[‡] (cu yd)	(cu m)	Production per hr[†] cu yd	(cu m)
0.5	5.7	6.2	8.07	17.4	(13.3)	140	(107)
0.6	5.7	6.3	7.93	18.3	(14.0)	145	(111)
0.7	5.7	6.4	7.81	18.9	(14.5)	147	(112)
0.8	5.7	6.5	7.70	19.2	(14.7)	148[§]	(113)
0.9	5.7	6.6	7.57	19.5	(14.9)	147	(112)
1.0	5.7	6.7	7.46	19.6	(15.0)	146	(112)
1.1	5.7	6.8	7.35	19.7	(15.1)	145	(111)
1.2	5.7	6.9	7.25	19.8	(15.2)	143	(109)
1.3	5.7	7.0	7.15	19.9	(15.2)	142	(109)
1.4	5.7	7.1	7.05	20.0	(15.3)	141	(108)

A 2,500-ft one-way haul distance.
[†] For a 50-min hr.
[‡] Determined from measured performance.
[§] The economical loading time is 0.8 min.

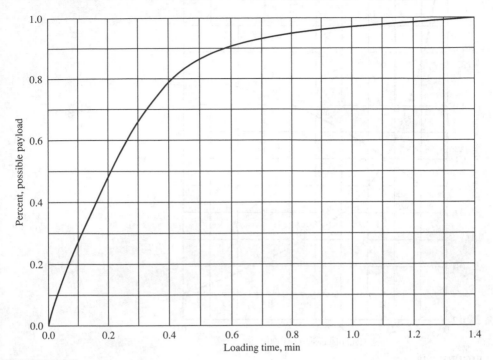

FIGURE 6-9
Load-growth curve for scraper loading.

interrelations. The economical haul distance for scrapers is usually much less than a mile. This can be recognized from the rapid rate at which production falls with increasing haul distance.

ROLLING RESISTANCE AND SCRAPER PRODUCTION

A job condition that is sometimes neglected is the effect of haul-road conditions on rolling resistance, and thereby on the production of scrapers and the cost of hauling earth. A well-maintained haul road permits faster travel speeds and reduces the costs of maintenance and repairs for the scrapers. Figure 6-11 is from a field study of scraper haul times. The shaded area represents the range of average travel times on numerous projects. The lower boundary indicates times on projects having good haul roads. The upper boundary indicates poor haul roads. Considering a haul distance of 4,000 ft, the total time for the haul and return combined on a well-maintained haul road was 5.20 min. Under poor conditions this could be as high as 7.55 min. A difference of 2.35 min in cycle time is a 4.7% production loss in a 50-min hour.

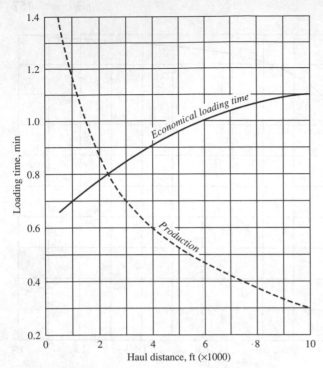

FIGURE 6-10
The effect of haul distance on the economical loading time of a scraper.

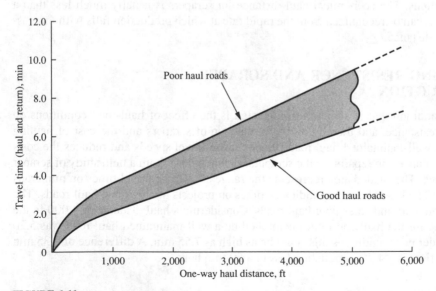

FIGURE 6-11
Average travel times single-powered axle scrapers, capacity < 25 cy, negligible grade.
(*U. S. Department of Transportation, FHWA*)

158

SCRAPER PERFORMANCE CALCULATION

The following example analyzes the performance of a push-loaded single-powered axle scraper for a specific set of job conditions.

Example 6-2. Based on the scraper specified in the section on "Scraper Performance Charts" in this chapter for which the performance charts in Figs. 4-8 and 4-10 are valid, and for haul conditions as stated below, analyze probable scraper production.

The total length of haul when moving from the cut to the fill is 4,000 ft as follows:

1,200 ft	+4% grade
1,400 ft	+2% grade
1,400 ft	−2% grade

Soil:	Clay	3,100 lb per bcy
Rolling resistance:		80 lb per ton or 4%

Assume an average load time of 0.85 min. If it is also assumed that the shape of the load-growth curve, Fig. 6-9, is valid for this machine, the expected load will be 96% of capacity:

Actual load:	$0.96 \times 31 = 29.8$ lcy	
From Table 4-1:	swell factor clay = 0.74	
Load volume in bank measure:	29.8 cu yd $\times 0.74 \times 1.1 = 24.0$ bcy	
Weight of load:	24.3 bcy $\times$ 3,100 lb per bcy =	75,330 lb
Project weight:	Empty	96,880 lb
	Load	75,330 lb
	Gross weight	172,210 lb

Haul and return speeds

Distance (ft)		Grade (%)	Total resistance (%)	Speed (mph)	Travel time (min)
(Haul 172,210 lbs)					
300	acceleration[†]	4	8	5[‡]	0.68
900		4	8	10	1.02
1,400		2	6	15	1.06
1,200		−2	2	30	0.45
200	deceleration[†]	−2	2	12[‡]	0.19
					3.40
Return					
200	acceleration[†]	2	6	10[‡]	0.23
1,200		2	6	21	0.65
1,400		−2	2	32	0.50
1,000		−4	0	32	0.36
200	deceleration[†]	−4	0	12[‡]	0.19
					1.93

[†] Assumed acceleration and deceleration distances.
[‡] Approximately one-half the steady-state speed.

Operation	Cycle time (min)
Load	0.85
Haul	3.40
Dump	0.37
Turn	0.21
Return	1.93
Turn	0.30
Total cycle	7.06 min

Number of trips per 50-min hour:

$$\frac{50}{7.06} = 7.08$$

Volume per scraper per 50-min hour:

$$24.3 \text{ bcy} \times 7.08 \text{ loads per hour} = 172 \text{ bcy per hour}$$

$$\text{Pusher time} = (1.4 \times 0.85) + 0.25 = 1.44 \text{ min}$$

Number of scrapers required:

$$\frac{7.06\text{-min scraper cycle}}{1.44\text{-min pusher cycle}} = 4.9$$

Therefore, use five scrapers, but since there are more scrapers assigned than the pusher can handle, the pusher cycle will control production. Or stated another way, the scrapers will sometimes have to wait on the pusher:

Pusher contacts per a 50-min hour:

$$\frac{50}{1.44} = 34.7$$

Each contact is a 24.3 bcy load. The production will be

$$34.7 \text{ contacts} \times 24.3 \text{ bcy} = 843 \text{ bcy/hr}$$

$$\text{or } 172 \text{ bcy/hr per scraper} \times 4.9 \text{ scrapers} = 843 \text{ bcy/hr}$$

If, mistakenly, the scraper had been thought to control, the calculated production would have been

$$5.0 \times 172 = 860 \text{ bcy/hr}$$

To achieve that production, we will be required to utilize two push tractors. Then the pushers would be waiting for the scrapers. This example did not include the effect of mechanical availability.

PROBLEMS

6-1. Based on the scraper specified in the section on "Performance Charts" in Chapter 4 for which the performance charts in Figs. 4-8 and 4-10 are valid, and for haul conditions as stated below, analyze probable scraper production. The material to be hauled is a sandy clay (dry earth), 2,800 lb per bcy (bank cubic yards). The expected rolling resistance for the well-maintained haul road is 40 lb per ton. Assume an average load of 91% capacity and that 200 ft is required for both acceleration and deceleration at an average speed of 4 mph (miles per hour). The total length of haul when moving from the cut to the fill is 3,200 ft and has the following individual segments:

600 ft	+3% grade
2,200 ft	0% grade
400 ft	+4% grade

6-2. Based on the scraper specified in the section on "Performance Charts" in Chapter 4 for which the performance charts in Figs. 4-8 and 4-10 are valid, and for haul conditions as stated below, analyze probable scraper production. The material to be hauled is cohesive. It has a swell factor of 0.76 and a unit weight of 2,900 lb per bcy. The expected rolling resistance for the well-maintained haul road is +3%. Assume an average load time of 0.80 min and that 200 ft is required for both acceleration and deceleration at an average speed of 5 mph. The total length of haul is 2,600 ft when moving from the cut to the fill and has the following individual segments:

600 ft	+5% grade
1,800 ft	−2% grade
200 ft	−4% grade

6-3. Determine the cycle time for a single-engine scraper rated at 20 cu yd heaped, which is used to haul material from a pit to a fill 1,700 ft away under severe conditions. The average haul speed will be 10 mph and the average return speed will be 16 mph. Use the Eq. (6-1) method of analysis, assuming 200 ft is required both to accelerate and decelerate at an average speed of 5 mph. The operating efficiency will be equal to a 50-min hour.

6-4. A wheel-tractor scraper is operating on a level grade. Assume no power derating is required for equipment condition, altitude, temperature, and so on. Use equipment data from Fig. 4-8.

(*a*) Disregarding traction limitations, what is the maximum value of rolling resistance (in lb per ton) over which the fully loaded unit can maintain a speed of 15 mph?

(*b*) What minimum value of the coefficient of traction between the tractor wheels and the traveling surface is needed to satisfy the requirements of part (*a*)?

REFERENCES

1. *Fundamentals of Earthmoving,* Caterpillar Tractor Co., Peoria, IL, May 1979.
2. *Production Efficiency Study on Rubber-Tired Scrapers,* FHWA DP-PC-920, Federal Highway Administration, Arlington, VA, April 1977.

CHAPTER
7

CRANES

Cranes are a broad class of construction equipment used to hoist and place loads. Each type of machine is designed and manufactured to work economically in a specific site situation. The most common types are:

1. Crawler
2. Hydraulic truck
3. Lattice-boom truck
4. Rough-terrain
5. All-terrain
6. Heavy lift
7. Modified cranes for heavy lift
8. Tower

Many of these machines in their basic configuration can have different front-end operating attachments which allow the unit to be used as an excavator, as a pile driver, or in other specialized tasks. Such diverse usages are discussed in other chapters of this text.

The Power Crane and Shovel Association (PCSA) has conducted and supervised both studies and tests which provide considerable information related to the performance, operating conditions, production rates, economic life, and cost of owning and operating these units. The association has participated in establishing and adopting standards that are applicable to this equipment. These have been published in technical bulletins and booklets.

Some information from the PCSA is reproduced in this book, with permission of the association. Items of particular interest are cited in the bibliography at the end of the chapter.

CRAWLER CRANES

The *full revolving superstructure* of this type of unit is mounted on a pair of continuous, parallel crawler tracks. Many manufacturers have different option packages available which permit the configuration of the crane to a particular application, standard lift, tower unit, or duty cycle. Units in the low-to-middle range of lift capacity have good lifting characteristics and are capable of duty-cycle work such as handling a concrete bucket. Machines of 100-ton capacity and above are built for lift capability and do not have the heavier components required for duty-cycle work. The universal machines incorporate heavier frames, have heavy duty or multiple clutches and brakes, and have more powerful swing systems. These designs allow for quick changing of drum laggings which vary the torque/speed ratio of cables to the application. Figure 7-1 illustrates a crawler crane handling precast panels on a highway project.

The crawlers provide the crane with travel capability around the job site. The tracks provide such a large ground contact area that soil failure under these machines is only a problem when operating on very poor soils. Before hoisting a load the machine must be leveled and ground settlement must be considered. If soil failure or ground settlement is possible, the machine can be positioned and leveled on mats. The distance between crawler tracks affects stability and lift capacity. Some machines have the feature whereby the crawlers can be extended. For many machines this extension of the crawlers can be accomplished without external assistance.

To be transported between projects, the crawler crane must be transported by truck, rail, or barge. As the size of the crane increases, the time and cost to dismantle, load, investigate haul routes, and reassemble the crane increases. The durations and costs can become significant for large machines. Transporting the largest machines can require 15 or more truck trailer units. These machines usually have lower initial cost per rated lift capability, but movement between jobs is more expensive. Therefore, crawler-type machines should be considered for projects requiring long-duration usage at a single site.

Most new models utilize modular components to make dismantling, transporting, and assembling easier. Quick-disconnect locking devices and pin connectors have replaced multiple-bolt connections.

HYDRAULIC TRUCK CRANES

The hydraulic truck crane has a self-contained boom. Most units can travel on the public highways between projects under their own power with a minimum of dismantling. Once the crane is leveled at the new work site, it is ready to work without setup delays.

FIGURE 7-1
Crawler crane handling precast panels.

If a job requires crane utilization for a few hours to a couple of days, a hydraulic truck crane should be given first consideration because of its ease of movement and setup.

The hydraulic multisection telescoping boom is a permanent part of the full revolving superstructure. In this case the superstructure is mounted on a multiaxle truck/carrier. There are three common power and control arrangements for hydraulic truck cranes:

1. A single engine as both the truck and crane power source, with a single, dual-position cab used both for driving the truck and operating the crane.
2. A single engine in the carrier but with both truck and crane operating cabs.
3. Separate power units for the truck and the superstructure. This arrangement is standard for the larger capacity units.

Hydraulic truck crane units have extendable outriggers for stability. In fact, many units cannot be operated safely with a full reach of boom unless the outriggers are fully extended and the machine raised so that the tires are clear of the ground. It should always be remembered that all mobile cranes are stability-sensitive machines. Rated loads are based on ideal conditions, a level machine, calm air, and no dynamic effects.

LATTICE-BOOM TRUCK CRANES

As with the hydraulic truck crane, a full revolving superstructure is mounted on a multiaxle truck/carrier. The advantage of this machine is the *lattice-boom*. A lattice-boom is cable-suspended, and therefore acts as a compression member, *not* a bending member like the telescoping hydraulic boom. The lattice-boom structure is also lightweight. The reduction in boom weight means additional lift capacity as the machine predominately handles hoist load and less weight of boom. The lattice-boom does take longer to assemble. The lightweight boom will give a less expensive lattice-boom machine the same hoisting capacity as a larger hydraulic unit.

The disadvantage of these units is the time and effort required to disassemble them for transport. In the case of the larger units it may be necessary to remove the entire superstructure. Additionally, a second crane is often required for this task. Some newer models are designed so that the machine can separate itself without the aid of another crane.

Figure 7-2 shows a large lattice-boom truck crane working off a city street for a high-rise construction project. Note the extended outriggers and the use of mats to distribute the load and to protect the street.

ROUGH-TERRAIN TRUCK CRANES

These cranes are mounted on two-axle carriers. The operator's cab may be mounted in the upper works allowing the operator to swing with the load (see Fig. 7-3). However, on many models the cab is located on the carrier. This is a simpler design because controls do not have to be routed across the turntable. In turn these units have a lower cost.

The units are equipped with unusually large wheels in order to improve maneuverability at the job site. Most units can travel on the highway but have maximum

FIGURE 7-2
A large lattice-boom truck crane.

speeds of only about 30 mph. In the case of long moves between projects they should be transported on low-bed trailers.

They are sometimes referred to as "cherry pickers." This comes from their use during World War II in handling bombs, as the slang name for a bomb was "cherry."

Many units now have joy stick controls. A *joy stick* allows the operator to manipulate four functions simultaneously. The most common models are in the 18–50-ton capacity range and typically are employed as utility machines. They are primarily lift machines but are capable of light, intermittent duty-cycle work.

ALL-TERRAIN TRUCK CRANES

The *all-terrain crane* is designed with an undercarriage that is capable of long-distance highway travel. Yet, the carrier has four wheel-drive and four wheel-steer, large tires, and high ground clearance. They have dual cabs, a lower cab for fast highway travel, and a superstructure cab which has both drive and crane controls. The machine can, therefore, be used for limited pick-and-carry work. By combining job-site mobility and transit capability, these machines are very good when multiple lifts are required at scattered project sites or at multiple work locations on a single project. Because this machine

FIGURE 7-3
Rough-terrain crane.

is a combination of two features, it has a higher cost than an equivalent capacity hydraulic truck crane or a rough-terrain crane. But all-terrain machines can be positioned on the project without the necessity of having other construction equipment prepare a smooth travel way as truck cranes require. An all-terrain crane does not need a lowboy to haul it between distant project sites as would a rough-terrain machine.

HEAVY LIFT CRANES

These are machines which provide lift capacities in the 600 through 2,000 short-ton range. These cranes consist of a boom and counterweight, each mounted on independent crawlers that are coupled by a stinger (see Fig. 7-4). This configuration utilizes a vertical strut and inclined mast to decrease compressive forces in the boom. The components of a heavy lift crane of this type are illustrated in Fig. 7-5.

FIGURE 7-4
Lampson LTL-1200, with 370 feet of boom and 120 feet of jib setting a 215-ton bridge at 180 feet radius.
(Neil F. Lampson, Inc.)

MODIFIED CRANES FOR HEAVY LIFT

These are basically systems which significantly increase the lift capacity of a crawler crane. A crane's capacity is limited by one of two factors: structural strength or tipping load. If you add counterweight to prevent tipping when hoisting a heavy load, there is a point when the machine is so overbalanced that without a load it would tip backward.

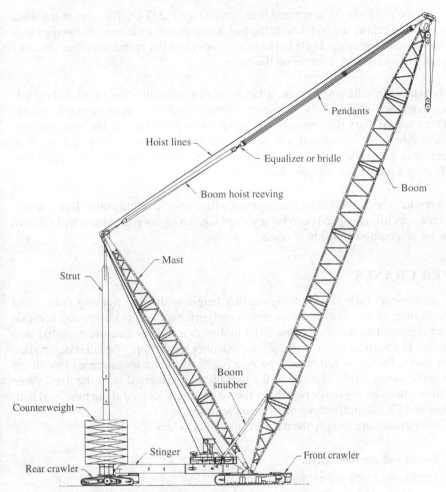

FIGURE 7-5
Components of a heavy lift crane. *(Neil F. Lampson, Inc.)*

At some point, even with sufficient counterweight, the boom is put into such high compression that it will give way at the butt. Manufacturers, understanding both the need of users to make occasional heavy lifts and the users' reluctance to buy a larger machine for a onetime use, have developed systems which provide the capability while maintaining machine integrity. The three principal systems available are:

1. Trailing counterweight
2. Ring system
3. Guy derrick

Trailing counterweight. The trailing counterweight is not carried by the base crane. Instead, the additional counterweight is mounted on a wheeled platform behind the crane, with the platform pin connected to the crane (see Fig. 7-6). The system utilizes a mast positioned behind the *boom,* with the boom suspension lines mounted at the top of the mast. This increases the angle between the boom and the suspension lines, thereby decreasing the compressive forces on the boom.

Ring system. With the ring system, a large circular turntable ring is created outside the base machine (see Fig. 7-7). The heavy counterweight system is supported on this ring. There are auxiliary pin-connected frames at the front and rear of the base machine. These allow both the boom/mast foot and the counterweight to be moved away from the machine. Using rollers or wheels, the auxiliary frames ride the ring. The base crane is really only a power and control source.

Guy derrick. The guy-derrick configuration will immobilize the crane. But a seven-fold increase in lifting capacity can be achieved when a high vertical mast tied off with guy cables is mounted on the base crane.

TOWER CRANES

These are cranes which provide a high-lifting height with good working radius, and take up limited space. The three common configurations are: (1) a special vertical-boom arrangement on a mobile crane, (2) a mobile crane superstructure mounted atop a tower, or (3) a vertical tower with a jib and operator's cab atop. The latter description is often referred to as the European type (see Fig. 7-8). Some tower cranes have fixed towers and a swing circle mounted at the top; these are referred to as the *fixed tower type*. Others, the *slewing tower type,* have the swing circle located at the base, and both the tower and jib assembly rotate relative to the base.

Tower cranes are usually the machine of choice when:

1. Site conditions are restrictive.
2. Lift height and reach are extreme.
3. There is no need for mobility.

Mobile cranes rigged with vertical towers. Vertical tower cranes can be mounted on a mobile crane substructure, a fixed base, or a traveling base, or can be configured to climb within the constructed structure. The crawler or truck-mounted tower cranes use pinned jibs extending from special booms that are set vertically. A crawler-mounted tower crane can travel over firm level ground after the tower is erected, but it has only limited ability to handle loads while moving. A truck-mounted tower crane must have its outriggers extended and down before the tower is raised. Therefore, it cannot travel with a load and the tower must be dismantled before the crane can be relocated.

Fixed base tower cranes. The fixed base-type crane has its tower mounted on an engineered foundation block. By the use of another crane the tower can be erected to its full height at the beginning of the project or the crane can have the mechanical capability, usually hydraulically, to raise itself, allowing for the addition of structural sections to

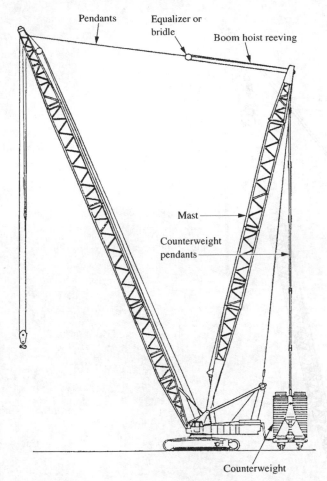

FIGURE 7-6
Trailing counterweight crane modification for heavy lifting. *(Construction Safety Association of Ontario)*

the tower. There is a vertical limit known as the *maximum free-standing* height to which these cranes can safely rise above a base. If it is necessary to raise the tower above this limiting height, lateral bracing must be provided. Even when bracing is provided, there is a *maximum braced height* tower limit. These two limits are dictated by the structural capacity of the tower frame and are machine specific.

A tower which is assembled by the use of other equipment at the beginning of a project cannot have a height greater than the maximum free-standing height as there is no structure into which to tie lateral bracing. If after the building of the structure progresses it is necessary to raise the crane tower, the procedure will require removal of the crane's superstructure from the tower frame before a tower section can be added. This will involve other equipment such as a mobile crane and will be a very costly proposition.

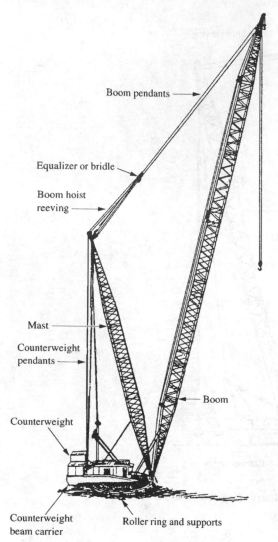

Boom pendants

Equalizer or bridle

Boom hoist reeving

Mast

Counterweight pendants

Boom

Counterweight

Counterweight beam carrier

Roller ring and supports

FIGURE 7-7
Ring system crane modification for heavy lifting. *(Construction Safety Association of Ontario)*

The raising of self-erecting towers to greater vertical heights is fairly easy and economical. A self-erecting crane has a short section of hydraulically operated erecting tower that is situated below the slewing ring for this purpose. The erecting operation is a four-step procedure:

1. The crane hoists a new section of tower and moves it next to its tower.
2. The new tower section is attached to the erecting tower section of the crane.
3. The erecting tower section hydraulically jacks up the slewing ring and jibs, and the new section of tower is positioned on the previously erected tower.
4. The hydraulic jacks are released and the slewing ring and jibs are repositioned on the extended tower.

FIGURE 7-8
Tower crane; static base, fixed tower, European type.

Mobile tower cranes. The ballasted base of this type of tower crane is usually set on a pair of fixed rails. This allows the crane to move along the rails with a load. The advantage is the increased coverage of the work area that can be achieved.

Climbing frame tower crane. The climbing frame-type crane is supported by the floors of the building that it is being used to construct. The reactions of both the weight of the crane and the loads that are lifted are transmitted to the host structure. The crane will have only a short tower section because it moves vertically as construction progresses.

The vertical movement of material in the construction progress creates an *available headroom* clear-distance requirement. This distance is defined as the vertical distance between the maximum achievable crane-hook position and the uppermost work area of the structure. The requirement is set by the dimensions of those loads which must be raised over the uppermost work area during the building process. When selecting a tower crane for a very tall structure, a climbing-type crane may be the only choice that is capable of meeting the available headroom height requirement.

Vertical movement of the climbing base-type crane is achieved by a system of hydraulically activated rams and latchings. Normally, the crane is initially mounted on a fixed base, and as the work progresses, it transfers to the climbing frame mounted on the structure. Usually, a typical floor section cannot safely support the load imposed by the operating crane; therefore, it is imperative for the structural designer to consider the loads imposed by the crane in the area of this opening. Even when consideration for the crane loads is taken into account in the building design, it will usually be necessary to use shoring for several floors below the tower crane frame.

At the end of construction there will be a tower crane at the top of the structure with no means of lowering itself. Removal must be by external methods, such as a mobile crane or by the use of a derrick, and because of the heights involved and the possible physical interference of the completed structure, the dismantling operation must be carefully planned. If two or more tower cranes were used on the project, it may be possible to use the crane with the higher hook height to help dismantle the lower crane, provided there is overlapping hook coverage. Under those circumstances when none of these techniques can be employed, an expensive solution is to use a helicopter.

Jib configurations. The horizontal jib arrangement is commonly known as a "hammerhead," although the proper terminology is *saddle jib*. This type of jib is fixed in a horizontal position by pendants. Actually, there are two jibs: the forward jib with a load block hung from a trolley which moves along the jib in order to change operating radius and an opposite rear counterweight jib. The operator's cab is usually directly below the jib.

If the jib is pinned at its base and supported by cables which are used to control its angle of inclination, it is known as a *luffing jib*. The crane's hook radius is varied by controlling the jib inclination. There are also fixed luffing-jib arrangements. These have the jib supported by jib pendants at a fixed angle of inclination and the hook radius is varied by the use of a trolley traveling along the jib. A saddle-jib machine can handle loads closer to the tower than a luffing-jib machine, a factor which can be important in crane selection. The nomenclature for a tower crane is shown on Fig. 7-9.

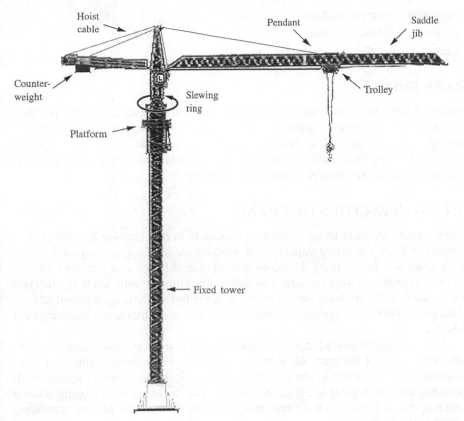

FIGURE 7-9
Nomenclature for a tower crane.

Tower crane selection. The utilization of a tower crane requires considerable planning because the crane is a fixed installation on the site for the duration of the heavy construction activities. It must be able from its fixed position to cover all points from which loads are to be lifted and to reach the locations where the loads must be placed. Therefore, when selecting a crane for a particular project, the engineer must ensure that the weight of the loads can be handled at their corresponding required radius. Individual tower cranes are selected for use based on:

1. Weight, dimension, and lift radii of the heaviest loads
2. Maximum free-standing height of the machine
3. Maximum braced height of the machine
4. Machine-climbing arrangement
5. Weight of machine supported by the structure
6. Available headroom which can be developed

7. Area which must be reached
8. Hoist speeds of the machine
9. Length of cable that the hoist drum can carry

CRANE BOOMS

Most cranes come equipped with standardized booms that are designed to optimize their performance over a range of applications. However, cranes may also utilize optional boom configurations that allow them to adapt to specific lifting conditions. Optional booms and differing boom tops allow a machine to accommodate load clearance, longer reach, or increased lift-capacity requirements (see Fig. 7-10).

LIFTING CAPACITIES OF CRANES

Because cranes are used to hoist and move loads from one location to another, it is necessary to know the lifting capacity and working range of a crane selected to perform a given service. Figure 7-11 shows typical crane-lifting capacities for four specific crawler cranes of varying size. The lifting capacities of units made by different manufacturers will vary from the information in the figure. Individual manufacturers and suppliers will furnish machine-specific information in the literature describing their products.

When a crane lifts a load attached to the hoist line that passes over a sheave located at the boom point of the machine, there is a tendency to tip the machine over. This introduces what is defined as the *tipping condition*. With the crane on a firm level-supporting surface in calm air, it is considered to be at the point of tipping when a balance is reached between the overturning moment of the load and the stabilizing moment of the machine.

During tests to determine the tipping load for wheel-mounted cranes the outriggers should be lowered to relieve the wheels of all weight on the supporting surface or ground. The radius of the load is the horizontal distance from the axis of rotation of the crane to the center of the vertical hoist line or the tackle with the load applied. The *tipping load* is the load that produces a tipping condition at a specified radius. The load includes the weight of the item being lifted plus the weights of the hooks, hook blocks, slings, and any other items used in hoisting the load, including the weight of the hoist rope located between the boom-point sheave and the item being lifted.

RATED LOADS

The rated load for a crane as published by the manufacturer is based on ideal conditions. However, a partial safety factor in respect to tipping is introduced by the PCSA rating standards, which state that the rated load of a lifting crane shall not exceed the following percentages of tipping loads at specified radii [8].

1. Crawler-mounted machines, 75%
2. Rubber-tire-mounted machines, 85%
3. Machines on outriggers, 85%

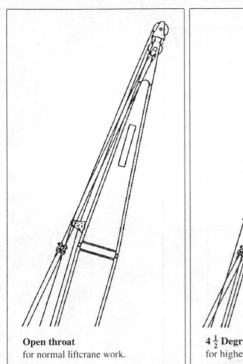

Open throat
for normal liftcrane work.

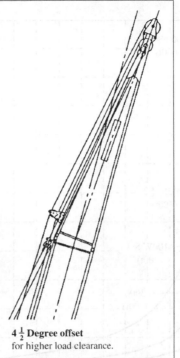

4 ½ Degree offset
for higher load clearance.

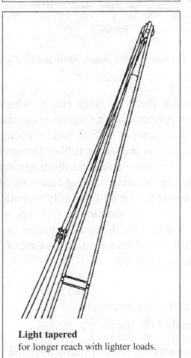

Hammerhead
for heavy lifts and superior
load clearance.

Light tapered
for longer reach with lighter loads.

FIGURE 7-10
Optional crane booms and boom tops. *(Manitowoc Engineering Co.)*

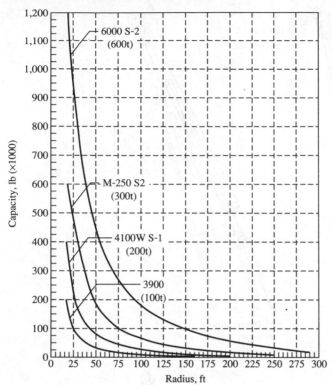

FIGURE 7-11
Safe lifting capacities for four crawler cranes. *(Manitowoc Engineering Co.)*

It should be noted that there are other groups which recommend rating criteria. The Construction Safety Association of Ontario recommends that for rubber-tire-mounted machines, on rubber a factor of 0.75 should be utilized.

One manufacturer is producing rubber-tire-mounted cranes having intermediate outrigger positions. For intermediate positions greater than one-half the fully extended length the manufacturer is using a rating based on 80% of the tipping load. For intermediate positions less than one-half the fully extended length a rating based on 75% is used. At this time there is no standard for this type of machine.

Load capacity will vary depending on the quadrant position of the boom with respect to the machine's undercarriage. In the case of crawler cranes the three quadrants which should be considered are:

1. Over the side
2. Over the drive end of the tracks
3. Over the idler end of the tracks

Crawler-crane quadrants are usually defined by the longitudinal centerline of the machine's crawlers. The area between the centerlines of the two crawlers is considered over the end and the area outside the crawler centerlines is considered over the side.

In the case of wheel-mounted cranes the quadrants of consideration will vary with the configuration of the outrigger locations. If a machine has only four outriggers, two on each side, one located forward and one to the rear, the quadrants are usually defined by imaginary lines running from the superstructure center of rotation through the position of the outrigger support. In such a case the three quadrants to consider are:

1. Over the side
2. Over the rear (of the carrier)
3. Over the front (of the carrier)

Some wheel-mounted cranes have an outrigger directly in the front, or there can be other machine-specific outrigger configurations. Therefore, the best practice is to consult the manufacturer's specifications.

The important point is that the rated load should be based on the direction of minimum stability for the mounting, unless otherwise specified. The minimum stability condition restricts the rated load because the crane must both raise and swing loads. The swinging motion will cause the boom to move through various quadrants, changing the load's effect on the machine. Further, it should be remembered that the rating is based on the fact that the outriggers are fully extended.

Rated loads are based on the assumption that the crane is in a level position (for the full 360° of swing). When a crane is not level, the effect on the lifting capacity can be significant for even small variations. In the case of a short-boom machine operating at minimum radius 3° out of level can result in a 30% loss in capacity. For long-boom machines the loss in capacity can be as great as 50% [6].

Another important consideration with modern cranes is that tipping is not always the critical capacity factor. At short radii, capacity may be dependent on boom or outrigger strength and structural capacity, and at long radii pendant tension can be the controlling element. Manufacturers' load charts will limit the rated capacity to values below the minimum critical condition taking into account all possible factors.

Table 7-1 illustrates the kind of information issued by the manufacturers of cranes. The crane in this example is described as a 200-ton, crawler-mounted cable-controlled crane with 180 ft of boom.

The capacities located in the upper portion of a load chart, Table 7-2, usually defined by either a bold line or by shading, represent structural failure conditions. Operators can feel the loss of stability prior to a tipping condition. But in the case of a structural failure there is no sense of feel to warn the operator; therefore, load charts must be understood and all lifts must be in strict conformance with the ratings.

While the manufacturer will consider crane structural factors when developing a capacity chart for a particular machine, operational factors affect absolute capacity in the field. The manufacturer's ratings can be thought of as valid for a *static* set of conditions. A crane on a project operates in a *dynamic* environment, lifting, swinging, and being subjected to air currents and temperature variations. The load chart provided by the manufacturer does not take into account these dynamic conditions. Factors which will greatly affect actual crane capacity on the job are:

1. Wind forces on the boom or load
2. Swinging the load

TABLE 7-1
Lifting capacities,[†] in pounds, for a 200-ton crawler crane with 180 ft of boom

Radius (ft)	Capacity (lb)	Radius (ft)	Capacity (lb)	Radius (ft)	Capacity (lb)
32	146,300	80	39,200	130	17,900
36	122,900	85	35,800	135	16,700
40	105,500	90	32,800	140	15,500
45	89,200	95	30,200	145	14,500
50	76,900	100	27,900	150	13,600
55	67,200	105	25,800	155	12,700
60	59,400	110	23,900	160	11,800
65	53,000	115	22,200	165	11,100
70	47,600	120	20,600	170	10,300
75	43,100	125	19,200	175	9,600

[†] Specified capacities based on 75% of tipping loads.
Source: Manitowoc Engineering Co.

TABLE 7-2
Lifting capacities,[†] in pounds, for a 25-ton truck-mounted hydraulic crane

Load radius (ft)	Lifting capacity (lb)[‡] Boom length (ft)						
	31.5	40	48	56	64	72	80
12	50,000	45,000	38,700				
15	41,500	39,000	34,400	30,000			
20	29,500	29,500	27,000	24,800	22,700	21,100	
25	19,600	19,900	20,100	20,100	19,100	17,700	17,100
30		14,500	14,700	14,700	14,800	14,800	14,200
35			11,200	11,300	11,400	11,400	11,400
40			8,800	8,900	9,000	9,000	9,000
45				7,200	7,300	7,300	7,300
50				5,800	5,900	6,000	6,000
55					4,800	4,900	4,900
60					4,000	4,000	4,000
65						3,100	3,300
70							2,700
75							2,200

[†] Specified crane capacities based on 85% of tipping loads.
[‡] The loads appearing below the solid line are limited by the machine stability. The values appearing above the solid line are limited by factors other than machine stability.

3. Hoisting speed

4. Hoist-line braking

These dynamic factors should be carefully considered when planning a lift.

RATED LOADS FOR HYDRAULIC CRANES

The rated tipping loads for hydraulic cranes are determined and indicated as for cable-controlled cranes. Table 7-2 lists the rated loads, or maximum safe loads, for a 25-ton truck-mounted crane. The specified loads are limited to 85% of the tipping loads over the sides or rear, with the machine supported and leveled on fully extended outriggers, and standing on a firm, uniform-supporting surface.

In the case of hydraulic cranes the critical load rating is sometimes dictated by hydraulic pressure limits instead of tipping. Therefore, load charts for hydraulic cranes represent the controlling condition lifting capacity of the machine and the governing factor may not necessarily be tipping. The importance of this is that the machine feel cannot be used as a gauge for safe lifting capability.

RATED LOADS FOR TOWER CRANES

Table 7-3 is a capacity chart for a climbing tower crane having a maximum reach of 218 ft. This particular crane can have a stationary free-standing height such that there is 212 ft of clear hook height. Although hook or lift height does not affect capacities directly, there is a relation when hoist speed is considered. Information concerning this relationship between the hoist-line speed and load capacity is shown in Table 7-4.

Tower cranes are usually powered by ac electric motors. A crane having a higher motor horsepower can achieve higher operating speeds. When considering the production capability of a crane for duty-cycle work, hoist-line speed and the effect motor size has on speed, as shown by Table 7-4, can be very important.

Hoist-cable configuration is another factor affecting lifting speed. Cranes can usually be rigged with one of two hoist-line configurations: a two-part line or a four-part line. The four-part-line configuration provides a greater lifting capacity than a two-part line within the structural capacity constraints of the tower and jib configuration. However, the increased lifting capacity is acquired with a resulting loss in vertical hoist speed.

Examination of the Table 7-3 load chart illustrates these points. The upper portion of the table is for a crane rigged with a two-part line. Considering a L7 jib model, a crane so rigged could lift 27,600 lb at a radius of 10 ft 3 in., 25,800 lb at a radius of 94 ft 6 in., and 10,200 lb at a radius of 210 ft 0 in. This same crane rigged with a four-part-line arrangement and a L7 jib can lift 55,200 lb at a radius of 13 ft 6 in., 26,100 lb at a radius of 90 ft 0 in., and 8,300 lb at a radius of 210 ft 0 in.

When the operating radius is less than about 90 ft, the crane has a greater lifting capacity with a four-part line than with the two-part-line arrangement. However, when the operating radius exceeds 90 ft, the crane has a slightly greater lifting capacity with the two-part line. This is because of the increased weight of the four-part rigging system and the fact that structural capacity is the critical factor affecting load-lifting capability.

TABLE 7-3
Lifting capacities, in pounds, for a tower crane

Jib model	L1	L2	L3	L4	L5	L6	L7	Hook
Maximum hook reach	104'-0"	123'-0"	142'-0"	161'-0"	180'-0"	199'-0"	218'-0"	reach
	27,600	27,600	27,600	27,600	27,600	27,600	27,600	10'-3"
	27,600	27,600	27,600	27,600	27,600	27,600	27,600	88'-2"
	27,600	27,600	27,600	27,600	27,600	27,600	25,800	94'-6"
	27,600	27,600	27,600	27,600	27,600	25,800	24,200	101'-0"
	27,600	27,600	27,600	27,600	26,800	24,900	23,400	104'-0"
		27,600	27,600	27,600	25,200	23,600	22,200	109'-8"
		27,600	27,600	25,600	23,300	21,800	20,500	117'-8"
		27,000	27,000	25,100	22,800	21,300	20,100	120'-0"
		26,300	26,300	24,300	22,200	20,700	19,500	123'-0"
Lifting capacities in			24,800	22,800	20,800	19,300	18,300	130'-0"
pounds, two-part line			22,400	20,700	18,700	17,400	16,400	142'-0"
				19,500	17,600	16,300	15,400	150'-0"
				18,800	16,800	15,700	14,800	155'-0"
				17,900	16,200	15,100	14,200	161'-0"
					15,200	14,200	13,300	170'-0"
					14,200	13,200	12,400	180'-0"
						12,300	11,600	190'-0"
						11,700	10,800	199'-0"
							10,200	210'-0"
							9,700	218'-0"

(continued)

However, when operating at a radius of less than 90 ft, the hoisting system controls the load-lifting capability.

As shown in the preceding discussion, tower crane load charts are usually structured assuming that the weight of the hook block is part of the crane's deadweight. But the rigging system is taken as part of the lifted load. When calculating loads, the Construction Safety Association of Ontario recommends that a 5% working margin be applied to computed weight.

Example 7-1. Can the tower crane, whose load chart is shown in Table 7-3, lift a 15,000-lb load at a radius of 142 ft? The crane has a L7 jib and a two-part line hoist. The slings that will be used for the pick weigh 400 lb.

Weight of load	15,000 lb	
Weight of rigging	400 lb	(slings)
	15,400 lb	
	×1.05	working margin
Required capacity	16,170 lb	

TABLE 7-3
(continued)

Jib model	L1	L2	L3	L4	L5	L6	L7	Hook reach
Maximum hook reach	100'-9"	119'-9"	138'-9"	157'-9"	176'-9"	195'-9"	214'-9"	reach
	55,200	55,200	55,200	55,200	55,200	55,200	55,200	13'-6"
	55,200	55,200	55,200	55,200	55,200	55,200	55,200	48'-9"
	55,200	55,200	55,200	55,200	55,200	55,200	51,400	51'-0"
	55,200	55,200	55,200	55,200	55,200	51,500	48,500	53'-6"
	55,200	55,200	55,200	55,200	51,300	48,300	45,600	56'-6"
	55,200	55,200	55,200	50,700	47,100	44,600	42,100	60'-6"
	46,200	46,200	46,200	42,800	39,700	37,400	35,200	70'-0"
	39,400	39,400	39,400	36,500	34,100	31,900	29,900	80'-0"
	34,600	34,600	34,600	31,900	29,700	27,700	26,100	90'-0"
	30,700	30,700	30,700	28,200	26,100	24,100	22,600	100'-9"
		27,800	27,800	25,600	23,600	21,700	20,300	110'-0"
Lifting capacities in		25,400	25,400	23,200	21,300	19,600	18,300	119'-9"
pounds, four-part line			23,100	21,100	19,300	17,700	16,400	130'-0"
			21,300	19,400	17,800	16,300	15,100	138'-9"
				17,600	16,200	14,700	13,600	150'-0"
				16,400	15,100	13,800	12,700	157'-9"
					13,600	12,400	11,400	170'-0"
					12,900	11,800	10,800	176'-9"
						11,500	10,600	180'-0"
						10,700	9,800	190'-0"
						10,200	9,300	195'-9"
							9,100	200'-0"
							8,300	210'-0"
							8,100	214'-9"

Counterweights:

Jib	L1	L2	L3	L4	L5	L6	L7
105-HP hoist unit AC	37,200 lbs	47,600 lbs	50,800 lbs	37,200 lbs	40,800 lbs	44,000 lbs	54,400 lbs
165-HP hoist unit AC	34,000 lbs	44,000 lbs	47,600 lbs	34,000 lbs	40,800 lbs	40,800 lbs	50,800 lbs

Source: Morrow Equipment Company, L. L. C.

TABLE 7-4
Effect of hoist line speed on lifting capacities of a tower crane

105 HP-AC, Eddy Current Brake, with 4 speed remote controlled gear box
Recommended Service = 224 amp

(1) Trolley, 2-Part Line			(2) Trolleys, 4-Part Line		
Gear	Maximum Load	Maximum Speed	Gear	Maximum Load	Maximum Speed
1	27,600 lbs	100 fpm	1	55,200 lbs	50 fpm
2	15,700 lbs	200 fpm	2	31,400 lbs	100 fpm
3	9,300 lbs	300 fpm	3	18,600 lbs	150 fpm
4	5,500 lbs	500 fpm	4	11,000 lbs	250 fpm

165 HP-AC, Eddy Current Brake, with 4 speed remote controlled gear box
Recommended Service = 250 amp

(1) Trolley, 2-Part Line			(2) Trolleys, 4-Part Line		
Gear	Maximum Load	Maximum Speed	Gear	Maximum Load	Maximum Speed
1	27,600 lbs	160 fpm	1	55,200 lbs	80 fpm
2	17,600 lbs	250 fpm	2	35,200 lbs	125 fpm
3	10,600 lbs	400 fpm	3	21,200 lbs	200 fpm
4	6,200 lbs	630 fpm	4	12,400 lbs	315 fpm

Source: Morrow Equipment Company, L.L.C.

From Table 7-3 the maximum lifting capacity at a 142-ft hook reach is 16,400 lb.

$$16,400 \text{ lb} > 16,170 \text{ lb}$$

Therefore, the crane can safely make the lift.

WORKING RANGES OF CRANES

Figure 7-12 shows graphically the height of the boom point above the surface supporting the crane and the distance from the crane center of rotation for various boom angles for the crane whose lifting capacities are given in Table 7-1.

The maximum length of the boom may be increased to 260 ft. The length of the boom is increased by adding sections at or near midlength of the boom, usually in 10-, 20- or 40-ft increments.

Example 7-2. As an example in using the information in Fig. 7-12, determine the minimum boom length that will permit the crane to lift a load which is 34 ft high to a position 114 ft above the surface on which the crane is operating. The length of the block, hook, and slings that are required to attach the hoist rope to the load is 26 ft. The location of the project will require the crane to pick up the load from a truck at a distance of 70 ft from the center of rotation of the crane. Thus, the operating radius will be 70 ft.

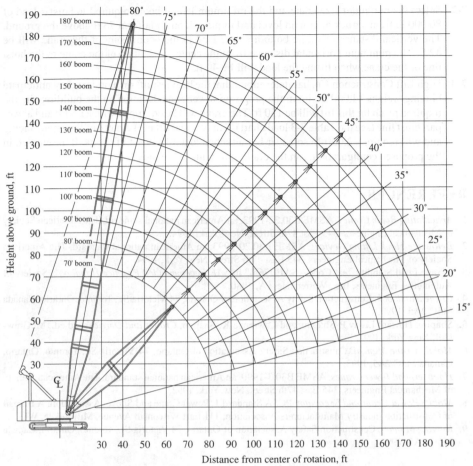

FIGURE 7-12
Working ranges for a 200-ton crawler crane, nominal rating. *(Manitowoc Engineering Co.)*

In order to lift the load to the specified location, the minimum height of the boom point of the crane must be at least 114 + 34 + 26 = 174 ft above the ground supporting the crane. An examination of the diagram in Fig. 7-12 reveals that for a radius of 70 ft the height of the boom point for a 180-ft-long boom is high enough.

If the block, hook, and slings weigh 5,000 lb, determine the maximum net weight of the load that can be hoisted. Using Table 7-1, we find that for a boom length of 180 ft and a radius of 70 ft the maximum total load is 47,600 lb. If the weight of the block, hook, and slings is deducted from the total load, the net weight of the lifted object will be 42,600 lb, which is the maximum safe weight of the object.

PROBLEMS

7-1. Select the minimum size crane required to unload a pipe weighing 166,000 lb per joint and to lower it into a trench when the distance from the centerline of the crane to the trench is 50 ft.

7-2. Select the minimum size crane and the minimum length boom required to hoist a load of 80,000 lb from a truck at ground level and to place it on a platform 76 ft above the ground. The vertical distance from the bottom of the load to the boom point of the crane will be 42 ft. The minimum horizontal distance from the center of rotation of the crane to the hoist line of the crane when lifting the load will be 40 ft.

7-3. High Lift Construction Co. has determined that the heaviest lift on a project they anticipate bidding weighs 14,000 lb. From the proposed tower crane location on the building site the required reach for this lift will be 150 ft. The crane will be equipped with a L5 jib and a two-part hoist line (see the Table 7-3 load chart). This critical lift is of a piece of limestone facing and will require a 2,000-lb spreader bar attached to a 300-lb set of slings. If assembled in the proposed configuration, can the crane safely make the pick?

REFERENCES

1. *Articulating Boom Cranes,* ASME B30.22-1993, an American national standard, The American Society of Mechanical Engineers, 345 East 47th Street, New York, 1994.
2. *Below-the-Hook Lifting Devices,* ASME B30.20-1993, an American national standard, The American Society of Mechanical Engineers, 345 East 47th Street, New York, 1994.
3. "Crane Load Stability Test Code—SAE J765," in *SAE Recommended Practice Handbook,* Society of Automotive Engineers, Inc., Warrendale, PA, 1980.
4. *Crane Handbook,* Construction Safety Association of Ontario, 74 Victoria St., Toronto, Ontario, Canada M5C 2A5, 1990.
5. Shapiro, Howard I., Jay P. Shapiro, and Lawrence K. Shapiro, *Cranes and Derricks,* 2d ed., McGraw-Hill, New York, 1991.
6. *Mobile Crane Manual,* Construction Safety Association of Ontario, 74 Victoria St., Toronto, Ontario, Canada M5C 2A5, 1993.
7. *Hammerhead Tower Cranes,* ASME B30.3-1990, an American national standard, The American Society of Mechanical Engineers, 345 East 47th Street, New York, 1992.
8. *Mobile Power Crane and Excavator,* PCSA Standard 1, Power Crane and Shovel Association, A Bureau of Construction Industry Manufacturers Association, 111 East Wisconsin Avenue, Milwaukee, WI.
9. *Rigging Manual,* Construction Safety Association of Ontario, 74 Victoria St., Toronto, Ontario, Canada M5C 2A5, 1992.

CHAPTER
8

EXCAVATING EQUIPMENT

INTRODUCTION

This chapter deals with types of equipment which are used to excavate earth and rock in construction operations. The equipment includes the following machines:

1. Draglines
2. Clamshells
3. Hydraulic excavators
   a. Front shovels
   b. Hoes
4. Loaders
   a. Wheel
   b. Track
5. Trenching machines

The first two types of machines belong to a group which is frequently identified as the Power Crane and Shovel Association (PCSA) family [1]. This association has conducted and supervised studies and tests which have provided considerable information relating to the performance, operating conditions, production rates, economic life, and cost of owning and operating these machines. The association has participated in establishing and adopting certain standards that are applicable to the equipment. The results of the studies, conclusions and actions, and the standards have been published in technical bulletins and booklets. Some of that information published by the PCSA is reproduced in this book, with the permission of the association.

187

GENERAL INFORMATION

Draglines are used to excavate material and to load it into hauling units, such as trucks or tractor-pulled wagons, or to deposit it in levees, dams, and spoil banks near the pits from which it is excavated. The dragline is designed to excavate below the level of the machine. A dragline usually does not have to go into a pit or hole in order to excavate. It operates adjacent to the pit while excavating material from the pit by casting its bucket. This is very advantageous when earth is removed from a ditch, canal, or pit containing water. If the material is hauled with trucks, they do not have to go into the pit and maneuver through mud. Frequently, it is possible to use a dragline with a long boom to dispose of the earth in one operation if the material can be deposited along the canal or near the pit. This eliminates the need for hauling units, thus reducing the cost of handling the material. Draglines are excellent units for excavating trenches when the sides are permitted to establish their angles of repose, without shoring.

TYPES OF DRAGLINES

Draglines may be divided into three types:

1. Crawler-mounted (see Fig. 8-1).
2. Wheel-mounted, self-propelled (see Fig. 8-2).
3. Truck-mounted (see Fig. 8-3).

Crawler-mounted draglines can operate over soft ground conditions which would not support wheel- or truck-mounted equipment. The travel speed of a crawler machine is very slow, frequently less than 1 mph, and it is necessary to use auxiliary hauling equipment to transport the unit from one job to another. Wheel- and truck-mounted units may have travel speeds in excess of 30 mph.

THE SIZE OF A DRAGLINE

The size of a dragline is indicated by the size of the bucket, expressed in cubic yards (cu yd). However, most draglines may handle more than one size bucket, depending on the length of the boom utilized and the class and weight of the material excavated. The relationship between bucket size and boom length and angle is presented in Fig. 8-4. While a greater boom angle would allow the machine to work with a longer boom, this limits machine reach, thereby negating utility. Because the maximum lifting capacity of a dragline is limited by the force which will tilt the machine over, it is necessary to reduce the size of the bucket when a long boom is used or when the excavated material has a high unit weight. In practice, the combined weight of the bucket and its load should produce a tilting force that is not greater than 75% of the force required to tilt the machine. A longer boom, with a smaller bucket, will be used to increase the digging reach or the dumping radius when it is not desirable to bring in a larger machine.

If the material is difficult to excavate, the use of a smaller bucket, which will reduce the digging resistance, may permit an increase in production.

FIGURE 8-1
Crawler-mounted dragline excavating a ditch.

FIGURE 8-2
Wheel-mounted, self-propelled dragline.

FIGURE 8-3
Truck-mounted dragline.

Typical working ranges for a dragline that will handle buckets varying in size from $1\frac{1}{4}$ to $2\frac{1}{2}$ cu yd are given in Table 8-1 (see Fig. 8-5 for the dimensions given in the table).

BASIC PARTS AND OPERATION OF A DRAGLINE

The basic parts of a dragline are illustrated in Fig. 8-6.

The excavating cycle is started by swinging the empty bucket to the digging position, while at the same time slacking off the drag- and the hoist lines. There are separate drums on the basic unit for each of these cables so that they may be coordinated into a smooth operation. Digging is accomplished by pulling the bucket toward the machine while regulating the digging depth by means of the tension maintained in the hoist line. When the bucket is filled, the operator takes in the hoist line while playing out the drag line. The bucket is so constructed that it will not dump its contents until the drag line tension is released. Hoisting, swinging, and dumping the loaded bucket follow in that order; then the cycle is repeated. An experienced operator can cast the excavated material beyond the end of the boom.

When compared to a hydraulic excavator, it is more difficult to control dumping accurately with a dragline. Therefore, when loading haul units with a dragline, larger haul units should be used in order to reduce the spillage. A size ratio equal to at least 5 to 6 times the capacity of the dragline bucket is recommended.

Figure 8-7 shows the dragline digging zones. The work should be planned to permit most of the digging to be done in the zones which permit the best digging, with the poor digging zone used as little as possible.

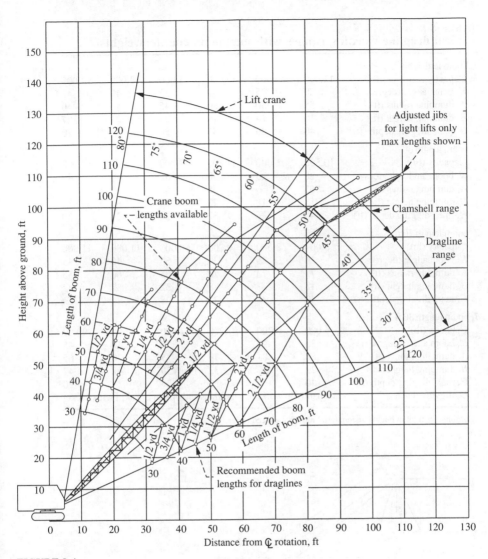

FIGURE 8-4
Working ranges of dragline and clamshell machines.

OUTPUT OF DRAGLINES

The output of a dragline will vary with the following factors:

1. Class of material
2. Depth of cut
3. Angle of swing
4. Size and type of bucket
5. Length of boom

TABLE 8-1
Typical dragline working ranges with maximum counterweights

J, boom length 50 ft						
Capacity (lb)[†]	12,000	12,000	12,000	12,000	12,000	12,000
K, boom angle (degrees)	20	25	30	35	40	45
A, dumping radius (ft)	55	50	50	45	45	40
B, dumping height (ft)	10	14	18	22	24	27
C, max. digging depth (ft)	40	36	32	28	24	20
J, boom length 60 ft						
Capacity (lb)[†]	10,500	11,000	11,800	12,000	12,000	12,000
K, boom angle (degrees)	20	25	30	35	40	45
A, dumping radius (ft)	65	60	55	55	52	50
B, dumping height (ft)	13	18	22	26	31	35
C, max. digging depth (ft)	40	36	32	28	24	20
J, boom length 70 ft						
Capacity (lb)[†]	8,000	8,500	9,200	10,000	11,000	11,800
K, boom angle (degrees)	20	25	30	35	40	45
A, dumping radius (ft)	75	73	70	65	60	55
B, dumping height (ft)	18	23	28	32	37	42
C, max. digging depth (ft)	40	36	32	28	24	20
J, boom length 80 ft						
Capacity (lb)[†]	6,000	6,700	7,200	7,900	8,600	9,800
K, boom angle (degrees)	20	25	30	35	40	45
A, dumping radius (ft)	86	81	79	75	70	65
B, dumping height (ft)	22	27	33	39	42	47
C, max. digging depth (ft)	40	36	32	28	24	20
D, digging reach	Depends on working conditions and operator's skill with bucket					

[†] Combined weight of bucket and material must not exceed capacity.

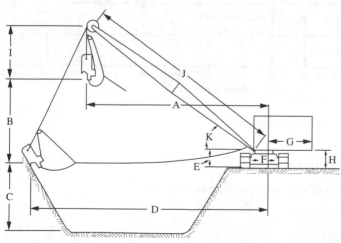

FIGURE 8-5
Dragline range dimensions.

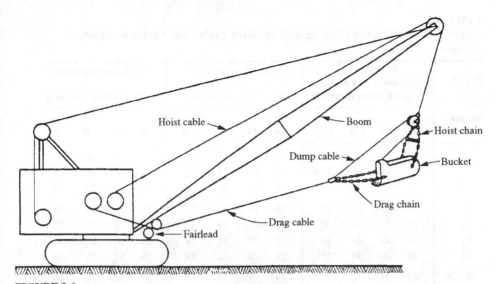

FIGURE 8-6
Basic parts of a dragline.

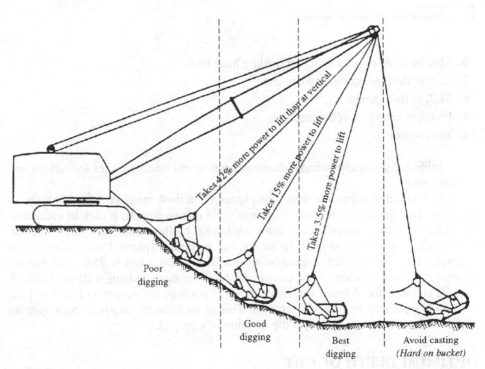

FIGURE 8-7
Dragline digging zones.

193

TABLE 8-2
Approximate dragline digging and loading cycles for various angles of swing[†]

Size of dragline bucket (cu yd)	Easy digging light moist clay or loam angle of swing (degrees)				Sand or gravel angle of swing (degrees)				Good common earth angle of swing (degrees)			
	45	**90**	**135**	**180**	**45**	**90**	**135**	**180**	**45**	**90**	**135**	**180**
$\frac{3}{8}$	16	19	22	25	17	20	24	27	20	24	28	31
$\frac{1}{2}$	16	19	22	25	17	20	24	27	20	24	28	31
$\frac{3}{4}$	17	20	24	27	18	22	26	29	21	26	30	33
1	19	22	26	29	20	24	28	31	23	28	33	36
$1\frac{1}{4}$	19	23	27	30	20	25	29	32	23	28	33	36
$1\frac{1}{2}$	21	25	29	32	22	27	31	34	25	30	35	38
$1\frac{3}{4}$	22	26	30	33	23	28	32	35	26	31	36	39
2	23	27	31	35	24	29	33	37	27	32	37	41
$2\frac{1}{2}$	25	29	34	38	26	31	36	40	29	34	40	44

[†] Time is in seconds with no delays when digging at optimum depths of cut and loading trucks on the same grade as the excavator.
Source: Power Crane and Shovel Association.

6. Method of disposal, casting, or loading haul units
7. Size of the hauling units, when used
8. Skill of the operator
9. Physical condition of the machine
10. Job conditions

Table 8-2 gives approximate dragline digging and loading cycles for various angles of swing.

The output of a dragline should be expressed in bank measure cubic yards (bcy) per hour. This quantity is best obtained from field measurements. It may be estimated by multiplying the average loose volume per bucket by the number of cycles per hour and dividing by 1 plus the swell factor for the material, expressed as a fraction. For example, if a 2-cu-yd bucket, excavating material whose swell is 25%, will handle an average loose volume of 2.4 cu yd, the bank-measure volume will be 2.4/1.25 = 1.92 cu yd. If the dragline can make 2 cycles per min, the output will be 2 × 1.92 = 3.84 bcy per min or 230 bcy per hour. This is an ideal 60-min-hour peak output, which will not be sustainable over the duration of a project.

OPTIMUM DEPTH OF CUT

A dragline will produce its greatest output if the job is planned to permit excavation at the optimum depth of cut where possible. Table 8-3 gives the optimum depth of cut for

TABLE 8-3
Optimum depth of cut and ideal outputs of short-boom draglines[†]

Class of material	Size of bucket [cu yd (cu m)][‡]								
	3.8 (0.29)[‡]	$\frac{1}{2}$ (0.38)[‡]	$\frac{3}{4}$ (0.57)[‡]	1 (0.76)[‡]	$1\frac{1}{4}$ (0.95)[‡]	$1\frac{1}{2}$ (1.14)[‡]	$1\frac{3}{4}$ (1.33)[‡]	2 (1.53)[‡]	$2\frac{1}{2}$ (1.91)[‡]
Moist loam or light sandy clay	5.0 (1.5)[§] 70 (53)[¶]	5.5 (1.7)[§] 95 (72)[¶]	6.0 (1.8)[§] 130 (99)[¶]	6.6 (2.0)[§] 160 (122)[¶]	7.0 (2.1)[§] 195 (149)[¶]	7.4 (2.2)[§] 220 (168)[¶]	7.7 (2.4)[§] 245 (187)[¶]	8.0 (2.5)[§] 265 (202)[¶]	8.5 (2.6)[§] 305 (233)[¶]
Sand and gravel	5.0 (1.5) 65 (49)	5.5 (1.7) 90 (69)	6.0 (1.8) 125 (95)	6.6 (2.0) 155 (118)	7.0 (2.1) 185 (141)	7.4 (2.2) 210 (160)	7.7 (2.4) 235 (180)	8.0 (2.5) 255 (195)	8.5 (2.6) 295 (225)
Good common earth	6.0 (1.8) 55 (42)	6.7 (2.0) 75 (57)	7.4 (2.4) 105 (81)	8.0 (2.5) 135 (104)	8.5 (2.6) 165 (127)	9.0 (2.7) 190 (147)	9.5 (2.8) 210 (162)	9.9 (3.0) 230 (177)	10.5 (3.2) 265 (204)
Hard, tough clay	7.3 (2.2) 35 (27)	8.0 (2.5) 55 (42)	8.7 (2.7) 90 (69)	9.3 (2.8) 110 (85)	10.0 (3.1) 135 (104)	10.7 (3.3) 160 (123)	11.3 (3.5) 180 (139)	11.8 (3.6) 195 (150)	12.3 (3.8) 230 (177)
Wet, sticky clay	7.3 (2.2) 20 (15)	8.0 (2.5) 30 (23)	8.7 (2.7) 55 (42)	9.3 (2.8) 75 (58)	10.0 (3.1) 95 (73)	10.7 (3.3) 110 (85)	11.3 (3.5) 130 (100)	11.8 (3.6) 145 (112)	12.3 (3.8) 175 (135)

[†] In cubic yards (cubic meters) bank measure (bcy) per 60-min hour.
[‡] These values are the sizes of the buckets in cubic meters (cu m).
[§] These values are the optimum depths of cut in meters (m).
[¶] These values are the optimum ideal outputs in cubic meters (cu m).

various sizes of buckets and classes of materials based on using short-boom draglines. Ideal outputs of short-boom draglines, expressed in bcy, for various classes of materials when digging at the optimum depth, with a 90° swing, and no delays are presented in the table. The upper figure is the optimum depth in feet and the lower number is the ideal output in cubic yards.

EFFECT OF THE DEPTH OF CUT AND SWING ANGLE ON DRAGLINE OUTPUT

The outputs of draglines given in Table 8-3 are based on digging at optimum depths with a swing angle of 90°. For any other depth or swing angle the ideal output of the machine must be adjusted by an appropriate depth-swing factor. The effect of the depth of cut and swing angle on dragline production is given in Table 8-4. In the table the

TABLE 8-4
Factors for depth of cut and angle of swing effect on dragline production

Percent of optimum depth	Angle of swing (degrees)							
	30	45	60	75	90	120	150	180
20	1.06	0.99	0.94	0.90	0.87	0.81	0.75	0.70
40	1.17	1.08	1.02	0.97	0.93	0.85	0.78	0.72
60	1.24	1.13	1.06	1.01	0.97	0.88	0.80	0.74
80	1.29	1.17	1.09	1.04	0.99	0.90	0.82	0.76
100	1.32	1.19	1.11	1.05	1.00	0.91	0.83	0.77
120	1.29	1.17	1.09	1.03	0.98	0.90	0.82	0.76
140	1.25	1.14	1.06	1.00	0.96	0.88	0.81	0.75
160	1.20	1.10	1.02	0.97	0.93	0.85	0.79	0.73
180	1.15	1.05	0.98	0.94	0.90	0.82	0.76	0.71
200	1.10	1.00	0.94	0.90	0.87	0.79	0.73	0.69

percent of optimum depth of cut is obtained by dividing the actual depth of cut by the optimum depth for the given material and bucket, then multiplying the result by 100.

Example 8-1. A 2-cu-yd short-boom dragline is to be used to excavate hard, tough clay. The depth of cut will be 15.4 ft, and the swing angle will be 120°. Determine the probable production of the dragline.

Optimum depth of cut (Table 8-3) is 11.8 ft.

The percent of optimum depth: $(15.4/11.8) \times 100 = 130\%$

From Table 8-4 the correction factor is 0.89. The probable production will be $195 \times 0.89 = 173$ bcy per 60-min hour. The production corrected for normal delays, i.e., a 50-min hour would be

$$\text{Production}_{corrected} = 173 \text{ bcy/hr} \times \frac{50}{60} = 144 \text{ bcy/hr}$$

EFFECT OF BUCKET SIZE AND BOOM LENGTH ON DRAGLINE PRODUCTION

In selecting the size and type of bucket to use on a project, one should match the dragline and bucket properly in order to obtain the best action and the greatest operating efficiency, which will produce the greatest output of material. Buckets are generally available in three types: light duty, medium duty, and heavy duty. Light duty buckets are used for excavating materials which are easily dug, such as sandy loam, sandy clay, or sand. Medium duty buckets are used for general excavating service in excavating clay, soft shale, or loose gravel. Heavy duty buckets are used for mine stripping, handling blasted rock, and excavating hardpan and highly abrasive materials. Buckets are sometimes perforated to permit excess water to drain from the loads. Figure 8-8 shows a medium duty dragline bucket.

FIGURE 8-8
Medium duty dragline bucket.

Table 8-5 gives representative capacities, weight, and dimensions for dragline buckets.

The normal size of a dragline bucket is based on its struck capacity, which is expressed more accurately in cubic feet. In selecting the most suitable size bucket for use with a given dragline, one needs to know the loose weight of the material to be handled, expressed in pounds per cubic foot (lb per cu ft). While it is desirable to use the largest bucket possible in the interest of increasing production, a careful analysis should be performed to make sure the combined weight of the load and the bucket does not exceed the recommended safe load for the dragline. The importance of this analysis is illustrated by referring to the information given in Table 8-1.

Example 8-2. Assume that the material to be handled has a loose weight of 90 lb per cu ft. The use of a 2-cu-yd medium duty bucket will be considered. If the dragline is to be operated with an 80-ft boom at a 40° angle, the maximum safe load will be 8,600 lb. The approximate weight of the bucket and its load will be:

Bucket, from Table 8-5	=	4,825 lb
Earth, 60 cu ft @ 90 lb per cu ft	=	5,400 lb
Combined weight	=	10,225 lb
Maximum safe load	=	8,600 lb

As this weight will exceed the safe load of the dragline, it will be necessary to use a smaller bucket. Try a $1\frac{1}{2}$-cu-yd bucket, whose combined weight will be:

Bucket, from Table 8-5	=	3,750 lb
Earth, 47 cu ft @ 90 lb per cu ft	=	4,230 lb
Combined weight	=	7,980 lb
Maximum safe load	=	8,600 lb

TABLE 8-5
Representative capacities, weights, and dimensions of dragline buckets

Size (cu yd)	Struck capacity (cu ft)	Weight of bucket (lb)			Dimension (in.)		
		Light duty	Medium duty	Heavy duty	Length	Width	Height
$\frac{3}{8}$	11	760	880		35	28	20
$\frac{1}{2}$	17	1,275	1,460	2,100	40	36	23
$\frac{3}{4}$	24	1,640	1,850	2,875	45	41	25
1	32	2,220	2,945	3,700	48	45	27
$1\frac{1}{4}$	39	2,410	3,300	4,260	49	45	31
$1\frac{1}{2}$	47	3,010	3,750	4,525	53	48	32
$1\frac{3}{4}$	53	3,375	4,030	4,800	54	48	36
2	60	3,925	4,825	5,400	54	51	38
$2\frac{1}{4}$	67	4,100	5,350	6,250	56	53	39
$2\frac{1}{2}$	74	4,310	5,675	6,540	61	53	40
$2\frac{3}{4}$	82	4,950	6,225	7,390	63	55	41
3	90	5,560	6,660	7,920	65	55	43

If a $1\frac{1}{2}$-cu-yd bucket is used, it may be filled to heaped capacity, without exceeding the safe load of the dragline.

If a 70-ft boom, whose maximum safe load is 11,000 lb, will provide sufficient working range for excavating and disposing of the earth, a 2-cu-yd bucket may be used and filled to heaped capacity. The ratio of the output resulting from the use of a 70-ft boom and a 2-cu-yd bucket, compared with a $1\frac{1}{2}$-cu-yd bucket, should be approximately as follows:

Output ratio, (60 cu ft/47 cu ft) $\times$ 100 = 127%

Increase in production = 27%

This does not consider the cycle time effect of the different boom lengths.

The previous example illustrates the importance of analyzing a job prior to selecting the size excavator to be used. Haphazard selection of equipment can result in a substantial increase in the cost of handling the material.

EFFECT OF MATERIAL CLASS ON THE COST OF EXCAVATING

Figure 8-9 illustrates the effect which the class of material has on the cost per cubic yard bank measure (bcy) when excavating with draglines. The hourly cost of a machine

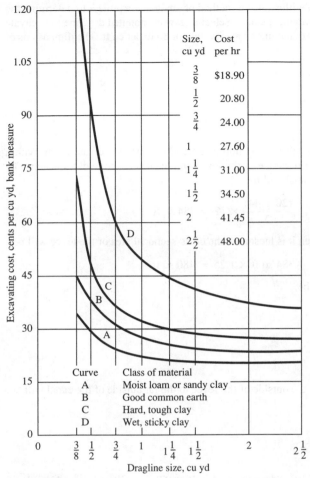

FIGURE 8-9
The effect of material class and size of bucket on the cost of excavating with a dragline.

includes fixed-machine, variable-machine, and labor costs. Each machine is assumed to operate 2,000 hours per year at 75% efficiency. Thus, the probable hourly output of any given size machine is obtained by multiplying the ideal output, as given in Table 8-3, by 75%. For example, the cost of excavating good common earth using a 1-cu-yd machine is determined as follows:

Operating cost per hour	=	$27.60
Ideal output per hour	=	135 cu yd
Probable output, 0.75 × 135 cu yd	=	101 cu yd
Cost per cu yd, $27.60 per 101 cu yd	=	$0.273 per cu yd

Example 8-3. This example illustrates a method of analyzing a project to determine the size dragline required for digging a canal. Select a crawler-mounted dragline to excavate 234,000 bcy of common earth having a loose weight of 80 lb per cu ft. The dimensions of the canal will be:

Bottom width, 20 ft
Top width,   44 ft
Depth,   12 ft
Side slopes,   1:1

The excavated earth will be cast into a levee along one side of the canal, with a berm of at least 20 ft between the toe of the levee and the nearest edge of the canal. The cross-sectional area of the canal will be

$$\frac{(20 + 44)}{2} \times 12 = 384 \text{ sq ft}$$

If the earth swells 25% when it is loosened, the cross-sectional area of the levee will be

$$384 \text{ sq ft} \times 1.25 = 480 \text{ sq ft}$$

The levee dimensions will be:

Height,   12 ft
Base width,   64 ft
Crest width, 16 ft
Side slope,   2:1

The total width from the outside of the levee to the far outside of the canal will be:

Width of levee =   64 ft
Width of berm   =   20 ft
Width of canal =   44 ft
Total   = 128 ft

With a boom angle of 30°, a dragline having 70 ft of boom will be required in order to provide both the necessary digging and dumping reaches, and to permit adequate dumping height and digging depth.

The project must be completed in 1 year. Assume that weather conditions, holidays, and other major losses in time will reduce the operating time to 44 weeks of 40 hours each, or a total of 1,760 working hours. The required production per working hour will be 133 bcy. It should be possible to operate with a 150° maximum swing angle. The efficiency factor should be a 50-min hour.

The required production divided by the efficiency factor is

$$\frac{133}{50/60} = 160 \text{ bcy/hr}$$

Assume the depth-swing factor will be 0.81. The required ideal production is

$$\frac{160}{0.81} = 198 \text{ bcy/hr}$$

Table 8-3 indicates a $1\frac{3}{4}$-cu-yd medium duty bucket will meet the need. The combined weight of the bucket and load will be:

Weight of load, 53 cu ft @ 80 lb per cu ft = 4,240 lb
Weight of bucket = 4,030 lb

Total weight = 8,270 lb

Maximum safe load, from Table 8-1 = 9,200 lb

The equipment selected should be checked to verify whether it will produce the required production:

Ideal output, 210 cu yd per hour
Percent of optimum depth, $(12.0/9.5) \times 100$ = 126
Depth-swing factor, 0.82
Efficiency factor, 50-min hour, or 0.83
Probable output, 210 cu yd per hour $\times$ 0.82 $\times$ 0.83 = 143 cu yd per hour

Thus, the equipment should produce the required output of 133 cu yd, with a slight surplus capacity.

CLAMSHELLS

GENERAL INFORMATION

Clamshells are used primarily for handling loose materials such as sand, gravel, crushed stone, coal, and shells, and for removing materials from cofferdams, pier foundations, sewer manholes, sheet-lined trenches, etc. They are especially suited for lifting materials vertically from one location to another, as in charging hoppers and overhead bins. The vertical movement capability may be relatively large when clamshells are used with long crane booms.

CLAMSHELL BUCKETS

Clamshell buckets are available in various sizes, and in heavy duty types for digging, medium-weight types for general-purpose work, and lightweight types for rehandling light materials. Manufacturers supply buckets either with removable teeth or without teeth. Teeth are used in digging the harder types of materials but are not required when a bucket is used for rehandling purposes. Figure 8-10 illustrates a rehandling and a heavy duty digging bucket.

The capacity of a clamshell bucket is usually given in cubic yards. A more accurate capacity is given as water-level, plate-line, or heaped-measure, generally expressed in cubic feet. The water-level capacity is the capacity of the bucket if it were

FIGURE 8-10
(*a*) Wide rehandling clamshell bucket. (*b*) Heavy duty clamshell bucket.

hung level and filled with water. The plate-line capacity indicates the capacity of the bucket following a line along the tops of the clams. The heaped capacity is the capacity of the bucket when it is filled to the maximum angle of repose for the given material. In specifying the heaped capacity, the angle of repose is usually 45°. The term "deck area" indicates the number of square feet covered by the bucket when it is fully open. Table 8-6 gives representative specifications for medium-weight general-purpose-type buckets furnished by one manufacturer.

PRODUCTION RATES FOR CLAMSHELLS

Because of the variable factors which affect the operations of a clamshell, it is difficult to give dependable production rates. These factors include the difficulty of loading the bucket, the size load obtainable, the height of lift, the angle of swing, the method of disposing of the load, and the experience of the operator. For example, if the material must be discharged into a hopper, the time required to spot the bucket over the hopper and to discharge the load will be greater than when the material is discharged onto a large spoil bank. The following example illustrates one method of estimating the probable output of a clamshell.

Example 8-4. A $1\frac{1}{2}$-cu-yd rehandling-type bucket, whose empty weight is 4,300 lb, will be used to transfer sand from a stockpile into a hopper, 25 ft above the ground. The angle of swing will average 90°. The average loose capacity of the bucket is 48 cu ft.

The specifications for the crane unit give the following information:

Speed of hoist line, 153 fpm (feet per minute)
Swing speed, 4 rpm (revolutions per minute)

TABLE 8-6
Representative specifications for medium-weight general-purpose-type clamshell buckets

	Size (cu yd)								
	$\frac{3}{8}$	$\frac{1}{2}$	$\frac{3}{4}$	1	$1\frac{1}{4}$	$1\frac{1}{2}$	$1\frac{3}{4}$	2	$2\frac{1}{2}$
Capacity (cu ft)									
Water-level	8.0	11.8	15.6	23.2	27.6	33.0	38.0	47.0	52.0
Plate-line	11.0	15.6	21.9	32.2	37.6	43.7	51.5	60.0	75.4
Heaped	13.0	18.8	27.7	37.4	45.8	55.0	64.8	74.0	90.2
Weights (lb)									
Bucket only	1,662	2,120	2,920	3,870	4,400	5,310	5,440	6,000	7,775
Counterweights	230	300	400	400	400	500	500	600	600
Teeth	180	180	180	180	180	190	266	300	390
Complete	2,072	2,600	3,500	4,450	4,980	6,000	6,206	6,900	8,765
Dimensions									
Deck area (sq ft)	13.7	16.0	21.8	24.0	29.0	33.4	36.6	40.0	44.6
Width	2' 6"	2' 6"	3' 0"	3' 0"	3' 5"	3' 9"	4' 0"	4' 3"	4' 6"
Length, open	5' 5"	6' 5"	7' 3"	7' 10"	8' 5"	9' 0"	9' 2"	9' 4"	9' 11"
Length, closed	4' 9"	5' 7"	6' 3"	6' 9"	7' 1"	7' 6"	7' 11"	8' 0"	9' 3"
Height, open	7' 1"	7' 10"	9' 1"	9' 9"	10' 3"	10' 9"	10' 3"	11' 6"	13' 0"
Height, closed	5' 9"	6' 4"	7' 4"	7' 10"	8' 3"	8' 9"	8' 9"	9' 3"	10' 4"

Time per cycle (approx.):

Loading bucket	=	6 sec
Lifting and swing load, $\dfrac{25 \text{ ft} \times 60 \text{ sec per min}}{153 \text{ ft per min}}$	=	10 sec[†]
Dump load	=	6 sec
Swing back to stockpile	=	4 sec
Lost time, accelerating, etc.	=	4 sec
Total cycle time	=	30 sec
		or 0.5 min

[†] A skilled operator should lift and swing simultaneously. If this is not possible, as when coming out of a cofferdam, additional time should be allowed for swinging the load.

Maximum number of cycles per hour, $\dfrac{60 \text{ min}}{0.5 \text{ min cycle}}$ = 120

Maximum volume per hour (120 cycle × 48 cu ft)/27 = 213 lcy

If the unit operates at a 45-min hour efficiency, the probable production will be

$$213 \text{ lcy} \times \frac{45}{60} = 159 \text{ lcy/hr}$$

If the same equipment is used with a general-purpose bucket to dredge muck and sand from a sheet-piling cofferdam partly filled with water, requiring a total vertical lift of 40 ft, and if the muck must be discharged into a barge, the production rate that was previously determined will not apply. It will be necessary to lift the bucket above the top of the dam prior to starting the swing, which will increase the time cycle. Because of the nature of the material, the load will probably be limited to the water-filled capacity of the bucket, which is 33 cu ft. The time per cycle would be approximately:

Loading bucket	=	8 sec
Lifting load, $\dfrac{40 \text{ ft} \times 60 \text{ sec per min}}{153 \text{ ft per min}}$	=	16 sec
Swinging, 90° @ 4 rpm $\dfrac{.25 \text{ rev.} \times 60 \text{ sec per min}}{4 \text{ rev. per min}}$	=	4 sec
Dump load	=	4 sec
Swing back	=	4 sec
Lowering bucket, $\dfrac{40 \text{ ft} \times 60 \text{ sec per min}}{350 \text{ ft per min}}$	=	7 sec
Lost time, accelerating, etc.	=	10 sec
Total cycle time	=	53 sec
		or 0.883 min

Maximum number of cycles per hour, 60 min ÷ 0.883-min cycle   = 68
Maximum volume per hour (68 cycle × 33 cu ft)/27   = 83 lcy

If the unit operates at a 45-min-hour efficiency, the probable production will be

$$83 \text{ lcy} \times \frac{45}{60} = 62 \text{ lcy/hr}$$

HYDRAULIC EXCAVATORS

GENERAL INFORMATION

Machines which make use of hydraulic pressure to develop bucket penetration into materials are classified by the digging motion of the bucket. The hydraulically controlled boom and stick, to which the bucket is attached, may be mounted on either a crawler or a wheel tractor base. A downward arc unit is classified as a "hoe." It develops excavation breakout force by pulling the bucket toward the machine and curling the bucket inward. An upward motion unit is known as a "front shovel." A shovel develops breakout force by crowding material away from the machine. The downward swing of a hoe dictates usage for excavating below the running gear. The boom of a shovel swings upward to load; therefore, the machine requires a material face above the running gear to work against.

FIGURE 8-11
A hydraulic-operated front shovel loading material into a truck. (*Caterpillar Inc.*)

FRONT SHOVELS

Front shovels are used predominately for hard digging above track level, and loading haul units. The loading of shot rock would be a typical application. A shovel is capable of developing a high breakout force. The material being excavated should be such that it will stand with a fairly vertical face. Crawler-mounted shovels have very slow travel speeds, less than 3 mph. Figure 8-11 illustrates a crawler-mounted shovel.

SIZE OF A FRONT SHOVEL

The size of a shovel is indicated by the size of the bucket, expressed in cubic yards. There are three different bucket rating standards, PCSA Standard No. 3, Society of Automotive Engineers (SAE) Standard J-296, and the Committee on European Construction Equipment (CECE) method. All the methods are based only on the physical dimensions of the bucket and do not address the "bucket loading motion" of a specific machine. For buckets greater than a 3-cu-yd capacity, ratings are on $\frac{1}{4}$-cu-yd intervals and they are on $\frac{1}{8}$-cu-yd intervals for buckets less than 3 cu yd in size.

Struck capacity. The volume actually enclosed by the bucket with no allowance for bucket teeth is the struck capacity.

Heaped capacity. Both PCSA and SAE use a 1:1 angle of repose for evaluating heaped capacity. CECE specifies a 2:1 angle of repose.

Fill factors. Rated heaped capacities represent a net section bucket volume; therefore, they must be corrected to average bucket payload based on the characteristics of the material being handled. Manufacturers usually suggest factors, commonly named "fill

TABLE 8-7
Fill factors for front shovel buckets†

Material	Fill factor‡ (%)
Bank clay; earth	100–110
Rock-earth mixture	105–115
Rock—poorly blasted	85–100
Rock—well blasted	100–110
Shale; sandstone—standing bank	85–100

† Caterpillar Inc.
‡ Percent of heaped bucket capacity.

factors," for making such corrections. Fill factors are percentages which, when multiplied by a rated heaped capacity, adjust the volume by accounting for how the specific material will load into the bucket (see Table 8-7).

It is always best to conduct field tests based on the weight of material per bucket load to validate fill factors.

BASIC PARTS AND OPERATION OF A FRONT SHOVEL

The basic parts of a front shovel include the mounting, cab, boom, stick, and bucket (see Fig. 8-12).

With a shovel in the correct position, near the face of the material to be excavated, the bucket is lowered to the floor of the pit, with the teeth pointing into the face. A

FIGURE 8-12
Basic parts of a hydraulic front shovel.

crowding force is applied by hydraulic pressure to the stick cylinder at the same time the bucket cylinder rotates the bucket through the face. If the height of the face is just right, considering the type of material and the size of the bucket, the bucket will be filled when it reaches the top of the face. If the height of the face, referred to as the "height of cut," is too shallow, it will not be possible to fill the bucket completely without making a second pass at the face. If the height of the face is greater than required to fill the bucket, it will be necessary to reduce the depth of penetration of the bucket into the face if the full face is to be excavated in one pass or to start the excavation above the floor of the pit. Material left near the floor of the pit will be excavated after the upper portion of the face is removed.

SELECTING A FRONT SHOVEL

In selecting a shovel, the user should consider the probable concentration of work to be performed. Two fundamental factors which should be taken into account are the cost per cubic yard of material excavated and the job conditions under which the shovel will operate.

In estimating the cost per cubic yard, one should consider the following factors:

1. The size of the job, as a larger job may justify the higher cost of a large shovel.
2. The cost of transporting the machine (a large shovel will involve more cost than a small one).
3. The combined cost of drilling, blasting, and excavating. For a large shovel these costs may be less than for a small shovel, as a large machine will handle more massive rocks than a small one. Large shovels may permit savings in drilling and blasting costs.
4. The direct unit cost per cubic yard for the excavation (less for a large shovel than for a small one).

The following job conditions should be considered in selecting the size of a shovel:

1. If the material to be excavated is hard and tough, the bucket of the large shovel, which exerts higher digging pressures, will handle the material more easily.
2. If blasted rock is to be excavated, the large-size bucket will handle bigger individual pieces.
3. If the time allotted for the completion of a project requires a high hourly production, either multiple small shovels or a large shovel must be used.
4. The size of available hauling units should be considered in selecting the size of a shovel. If small hauling units must be used, the size of the shovel should be small, whereas if large hauling units are available, a large shovel should be used.

Manufacturers' specifications should always be consulted for the exact values of machine clearances. The maximum bucket dumping height is especially important when the shovel is loading haul units.

SHOVEL PRODUCTION

There are four elements in the production cycle of a shovel:

1. Load bucket
2. Swing with load
3. Dump load
4. Return swing

It should be noted that a shovel does not travel during the digging and loading cycle. Travel is limited to moving into or along the face as the excavation progresses.

Typical cycle element times under average conditions, for 3- to 5-cu-yd-size shovels, will be:

1. Load bucket   7–9 sec
2. Swing with load   4–6 sec
3. Dump load   2–4 sec
4. Return swing   4–5 sec

The actual production of a shovel is affected by numerous factors, including the:

1. Class of material
2. Height of cut
3. Angle of swing
4. Size of hauling units
5. Operator skill
6. Physical condition of the shovel

The production of a shovel should be expressed in cubic yards per hour based on bank-measure volume (bcy per hour). The capacity of a bucket is based on its heaped volume. In order to obtain the bank-measure volume of a bucket of material, the average loose volume should be divided by 1 plus the swell, expressed as a fraction. For example, if a 2-cu-yd bucket, excavating material whose swell is 25%, will handle an average loose volume of 2.25 cu yd, the bank-measure volume will be 2.25/1.25 = 1.8 cu yd. If this shovel can make 2.5 cycles per min, which includes no allowance for lost time, the output will be 2.5 × 1.8 = 4.5 bcy per min, or 270 bcy per hour. This is an ideal production, which will seldom, if ever, be experienced on a project. Ideal production is based on digging at optimum height with a 90° swing and no delays.

The actual production of a shovel will be significantly lower than the ideal because operators do not operate continuously at peak efficiency, nor do they operate a full 60 minutes every hour. Machines require minor repairs, haul units tend to bunch together, and other minor delays *always* affect production.

Ideal production assumes no interruption of the loading cycle. Transportation Research Board (TRB) studies have shown that actual production times for shovels used in highway construction excavation operations are 50–75% of the available working time. Therefore, production efficiency is only 30–45 min per hour. The factors causing this loss of production are:

1. Short moves to position for digging
2. Handling oversize material
3. Cleanup of the loading area
4. Haul-unit exchange
5. Lack of haul unit to load
6. Operator breaks

In the field the machine will require time to move into the digging position as the face is advanced. One study found this type of motion to be required after about 20 bucket loads, and on the average it required 36 sec. When handling shot rock, carefully evaluate the amount of oversize material to be moved. A machine with a bucket whose bite width and pocket are satisfactory for the average size pieces may spend too much time handling individual oversize pieces. A larger bucket, or a larger machine, or changing the blasting pattern should be considered when there is a large percentage of oversize material.

The use of auxiliary equipment in the loading area, such as a dozer, can reduce cleanup delays. Control of haul units and operator breaks are within the control of field management.

THE EFFECT OF THE HEIGHT OF CUT ON SHOVEL PRODUCTION

If the height of the face from which a shovel is excavating material is too shallow, it will be difficult or impossible to fill the bucket in one pass up the face. The operator will have a choice of making more than one pass to fill the bucket, which will increase the time per cycle, or with each cycle he may carry a partly filled bucket to the hauling unit. In either case the effect will be to reduce the production of the shovel.

If the height of the face is greater than the minimum required to fill the bucket, with favorable crowding and hoisting forces, the operator may do one of three things. He may reduce the depth of the bucket penetration into the face in order to fill the bucket in one full stroke. This will increase the time for a cycle. He may start digging above the base of the face, and then remove the lower portion of the face later. Or he may run the bucket up the full height of the face and let the excess earth spill down to the bottom of the face, to be picked up later. The choice of any one of the procedures will result in lost time, based on the time required to fill the bucket when it is digging at optimum height.

The PCSA has published findings on the optimum height of cut based on data from studies of cable-operated shovels (see Table 8-8). In the table the percent of optimum height of cut is obtained by dividing the actual height of cut by the optimum height for the given material and bucket, then multiplying the result by 100. Thus, if the actual height of cut is 6 ft and the optimum height is 10 ft, the percent of optimum height of cut is $(6/10) \times 100 = 60\%$.

TABLE 8-8
Factors for height of cut and angle of swing effect on shovel production

Percent of optimum depth	Angle of swing (degrees)						
	45	60	75	90	120	150	180
40	0.93	0.89	0.85	0.80	0.72	0.65	0.59
60	1.10	1.03	0.96	0.91	0.81	0.73	0.66
80	1.22	1.12	1.04	0.98	0.86	0.77	0.69
100	1.26	1.16	1.07	1.00	0.88	0.79	0.71
120	1.20	1.11	1.03	0.97	0.86	0.77	0.70
140	1.12	1.04	0.97	0.91	0.81	0.73	0.66
160	1.03	0.96	0.90	0.85	0.75	0.67	0.62

Much of the PCSA work concerned smaller size machines, less than 3 cu yd. In most cases those small shovels have been replaced by other types of excavators, track or rubber tire loaders. But some general guidelines can still be gleaned from the studies.

The optimum height of cut ranges from 30 to 50% of the maximum digging height, with the lower percentage being representative of easy to load materials, such as loam, sand, or gravel. Hard to load materials, sticky clay or blasted rock, necessitate a greater optimum height, in the range of 50% of the maximum digging height value. Common earth would require slightly less than 40% of the maximum digging height.

THE EFFECT OF THE ANGLE OF SWING ON SHOVEL PRODUCTION

The angle of swing of a shovel is the horizontal angle, expressed in degrees, between the position of the bucket when it is excavating and the position when it is discharging the load. The total time in a cycle includes digging, swinging to the dumping position, dumping, and returning to the digging position. If the angle of swing is increased, the time for a cycle will be increased, whereas if the angle of swing is decreased, the time for a cycle will be decreased. The ideal production of a shovel is based on operating at a 90° swing and the optimum height of cut. The effect of the angle of swing on the production of a shovel is illustrated in Table 8-8. The ideal production should be multiplied by the proper conversion factor in order to correct the production for any given height and swing angle. For example, if a shovel which is digging at optimum depth has the angle of swing reduced from 90° to 60°, the production will be increased by 16%.

Example 8-5. A 5-cu-yd shovel having a maximum digging height of 34 ft is being used to load poorly blasted rock. The face being worked is 12 ft high and the haul units can be positioned so that the swing angle is only 60°. What is the adjusted ideal production if the ideal cycle time is 21 sec.

Optimum height for this machine and material (poorly blasted rock):

$$0.50 \times 34 \text{ ft (max. height)} = 17 \text{ ft}$$

Fill factor Table 8-7: 85–100%, use 90%

Ideal production per 60-min hour:

$$(60 \text{ min-hr} \div (21 \text{sec}/60 \text{ sec-min})) \times 5 \text{ cu yd} \times 0.9 = 771 \text{ lcy/hr}$$

Percent optimum height, $\frac{12 \text{ ft}}{17 \text{ ft}} = 0.71$

Correcting for height and swing, from Table 8-8, by interpolation, 1.08

The adjusted ideal production of the shovel is

$$771 \times 1.08 = 833 \text{ lcy per 60-min hr}$$

Although the information given in the text and in Tables 8-7 and 8-8 is based on extensive field studies, the reader is cautioned against using it too literally without adjusting for conditions which will probably exist on a particular project.

PRODUCTION EFFICIENCY FACTOR

As every constructor knows, no two projects are alike. There are certain conditions at every job over which the constructor has no control. These conditions must be considered in estimating the probable production of any piece of equipment including shovels.

A shovel may operate in a large, open quarry situation with a firm well-drained floor, where trucks can be spotted on either side of the machine to eliminate lost time waiting for haul units. The terrain of the natural ground may be uniformly level so that the height of cut will always be close to optimum. The haul road is not affected by climatic conditions, such as rains. These would be excellent working conditions.

Another shovel may be used to excavate material for a highway cut through a hill. The height of cut may vary from zero to considerably more than the optimum height. The sides of the cut must be carefully sloped. The cut may be so narrow that a loaded truck must be moved out before an empty truck can be backed into the loading position. As the truck must be spotted behind the shovel, the angle of swing will approximate 180°. The floor of the cut may be muddy, which will delay the movement of the trucks. On a project of this type the shovel will have a severely reduced productivity.

Besides project-specific factors, there are constructor or management factors which will suppress or enhance production efficiency. The advance planning and foresight of the constructor in controlling the work and organizing the job will affect production. Factors that should always be considered and addressed are:

1. Maintenance of equipment
2. Availability of repair parts
3. Project housekeeping
4. Haul-road condition
5. Loading area layout
6. Haul-unit sizing and number
7. Competency of field management

The estimator must consider all these factors and decide upon an efficiency factor with which to adjust peak production. To select the precisely correct efficiency factor every time is very difficult. Experience and good judgment are essential to selecting the appropriate efficiency factor. Sometimes it will be found that actual job production is below the estimated production; in such cases the selected factor should be reconsidered to guide future estimating, but the job conditions should also be carefully examined.

Example 8-6. A 3-cu-yd shovel, having a maximum digging height of 30 ft, will be used on a highway project to excavate well-blasted rock. The average face height is expected to be 22 ft. Most of the cut will require a 140° swing of the shovel in order to load the haul units. Determine the estimated production in cubic yards bank measure.

Fill factor: From Table 8-7, well-blasted rock 100–110%, use 100%:

Load	9 sec	(because of material)
Swing loaded	4 sec	
Dump	4 sec	(into haul units)
Swing empty	4 sec	
	21 sec or 0.35 min	

Ideal production:

$$(60 \text{ min-hour}/0.35 \text{ min}) \times 3 \text{ cu yd} \times 1.0 = 514 \text{ lcy/hr}$$

Optimum height, 50% of max.: $0.5 \times 30 \text{ ft} = 15 \text{ ft}$

Percent optimum height: $\dfrac{22 \text{ ft}}{15 \text{ ft}} = 147\%$

Height and swing factor: From Table 8-8, for 147% and 140°, by interpolation, 0.73

Adjusted production:

$$514 \text{ lcy} \times 0.73 = 375 \text{ lcy/hr}$$

Percent swell, Table 4-1:

$$\text{Well-blasted rock} = 60\%$$

$$375 \text{ lcy/hr} \div 1.6 = 234 \text{ bcy/hr}$$

If the TRB information is used, the efficiency would be 30–45 working minutes per hour.

$$234 \text{ bcy/hr} \times \frac{45}{60} = 175 \text{ bcy/hr}$$

The best estimating method is to develop specific historical data by type of machine and project factors. But information such as the TRB study, which presents data from thousands of shovel cycles, provides a good bench mark for selecting an efficiency factor.

HOES

Hoes are used primarily to excavate below the natural surface of the ground on which the machine rests. A hoe is sometimes referred to by other names, such as backhoe or

FIGURE 8-13
Crawler-mounted hydraulic hoe loading a truck.

back shovel. Hoes are adapted to excavating trenches and pits for basements, and the smaller machines can handle general grading work. Because of their positive control, they are superior to draglines in operating on close-range work and loading into haul units (see Fig. 8-13). In storm drain and utility work the hoe can perform the trench excavation and handle the pipe, eliminating a second machine (see Fig. 8-14).

THE BASIC PARTS AND OPERATION OF A HOE

The basic parts and operating ranges of a hoe are illustrated in Fig. 8-15.

Table 8-9 gives representative dimensions and clearances for hydraulic crawler-mounted hoes. Buckets are available in varying widths to suit the job requirements.

Wheel-mounted hydraulic hoes are available with buckets up to $1\frac{1}{2}$ cu yd. The maximum digging depth for the larger machines is about 25 ft. With all four outriggers down, the large machines can handle 10,000 lb loads at a 20-ft radius. These are not production excavation machines. They are designed for mobility and general-purpose work.

FIGURE 8-14
Crawler-mounted hydraulic hoe handling 72-in. reinforced concrete pipe.

The penetration force into the material being excavated is achieved by the stick cylinder and the bucket cylinder. The maximum crowd force is developed when the stick cylinder operates perpendicular to the stick (see Fig. 8-16). As in the case of the dragline (see Fig. 8-7), the best digging is therefore at the bottom of the arc because the geometry of the boom, stick, bucket, and the hydraulic cylinders at that point exerts the maximum force drawing the stick in and curling the bucket.

BUCKET RATING FOR HYDRAULIC HOES

Hoe buckets are rated like shovel buckets by PCSA and SAE standards using a 1 : 1 angle of repose for evaluating heaped capacity (see Fig. 8-17). Buckets should be selected based on the material being excavated. The hoe can develop high penetration forces. By matching bucket width and bucket tip radius to the resistance of the material, one can take full advantage of the hoe's potential. For easily excavated materials wide buckets should be utilized. When excavating rocky material or blasted rock, a narrow bucket with a short tip radius is best. In utility work the width of the required trench may be the critical consideration. Fill factors for hydraulic hoe buckets are presented in Table 8-10.

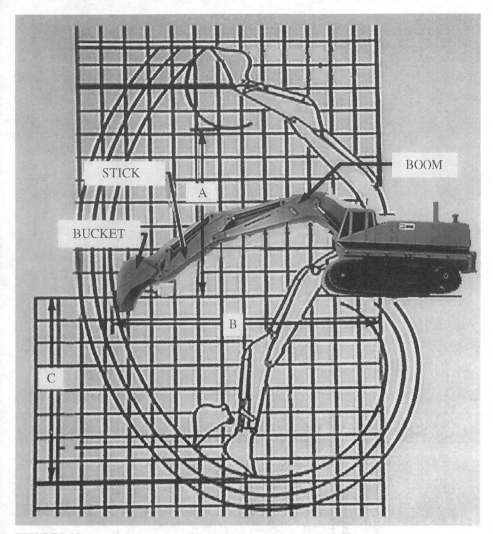

FIGURE 8-15
Basic parts and operating ranges of a hydraulic hoe. A, dumping height; B, digging reach; C, max. digging depth.

HOE OPERATING EFFICIENCY AND PRODUCTION

The same elements which affect shovel production are applicable to hoe excavation operations. The optimum depth of cut will depend on the type of material being excavated and bucket selection. As a rule, the optimum depth of cut for a hoe is usually in the range of 30–60% of the machine's maximum digging depth. Table 8-11 presents cycle times for hydraulic track hoes based on bucket size and average conditions.

Example 8-7. A $3\frac{1}{2}$-cu-yd crawler hoe is being considered for use on a project to excavate very hard clay from a borrow pit. The clay will be loaded into trucks having a loading

TABLE 8-9
Representative dimensions, loading clearance, and lifting capacity for hydraulic crawler hoes

Size bucket (cu yd)	Stick length (ft)	Maximum reach @ ground level (ft)	Maximum digging depth (ft)	Maximum loading height (ft)	Lifting capacity @ 15 ft			
					Short stick		Long stick	
					Front (lb)	Side (lb)	Front (lb)	Side (lb)
$\frac{3}{8}$	5– 7	19–22	12–15	14–16	2,900	2,600	2,900	2,600
$\frac{3}{4}$	6– 9	24–27	16–18	17–19	7,100	5,300	7,200	5,300
1	5–13	26–33	16–23	17–25	12,800	9,000	9,300	9,200
$1\frac{1}{2}$	6–13	27–35	17–21	18–23	17,100	10,100	17,700	11,100
2	7–14	29–38	18–27	19–24	21,400	14,500	21,600	14,200
$2\frac{1}{2}$	7–16	32–40	20–29	20–26	32,600	21,400	31,500	24,400
3	10–11	38–42	25–30	24–26	32,900†	24,600†	30,700†	26,200†
$3\frac{1}{2}$	8–12	36–39	23–27	21–22	33,200†	21,900†	32,400†	22,000†
4	11	44	29	27	47,900†	33,500†		
5	8–15	40–46	26–32	25–26	34,100‡	27,500‡	31,600‡	27,600‡

† Lifting capacity @ 20 ft.
‡ Lifting capacity @ 25 ft.

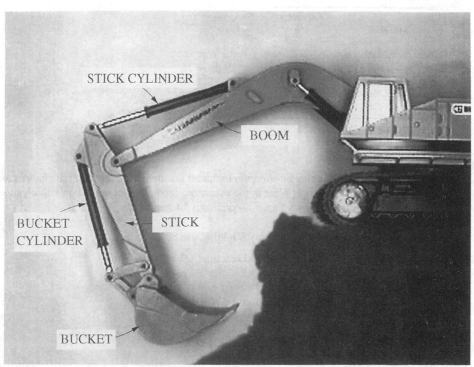

FIGURE 8-16
Arrangement of a hoe's hydraulic cylinders to develop digging forces.

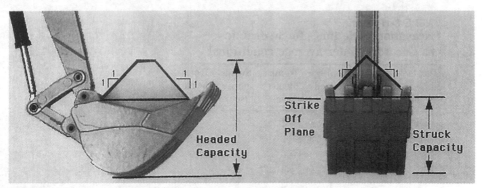

FIGURE 8-17
Hydraulic hoe bucket capacity rating dimensions.

TABLE 8-10
Fill factors for hydraulic hoe buckets[†]

Material	Fill factor[‡] (%)
Moist loam/sandy clay	100–110
Sand and gravel	95–110
Rock—poorly blasted	40– 50
Rock—well blasted	60– 75
Hard, tough clay	80– 90

[†] Caterpillar Inc.
[‡] Percent of heaped bucket capacity.

height of 9 ft 9 in. Soil-boring information indicates that below 8 ft the material changes to an unacceptable silt material. What is the estimated production of the hoe in cubic yards bank measure, if the efficiency factor is equal to a 50-min hour?

Fill factor: From Table 8-10, hard clay 80–90%, use 80%

Cycle time: From Table 8-11, $3\frac{1}{2}$-cu-yd machine, 22 sec or 0.37 min

Ideal production:

$$(60 \text{ min-hr}/0.37 \text{ min cycle}) \times 3\frac{1}{2} \text{ cu yd} \times 0.8 = 454 \text{ lcy/hr}$$

From Table 4-1,

$$\text{Percent swell dry clay} = 0.35$$

Adjusted production:

$$\frac{454 \text{ cy/hr}}{1.35} \times \frac{50 \text{ min hr}}{60 \text{ min hr}} = 280 \text{ bcy/hr}$$

TABLE 8-11
Excavation cycle times for hydraulic crawler hoes under average conditions[†]

Bucket size (cu yd)	Load bucket (sec)	Swing loaded (sec)	Dump bucket (sec)	Swing empty (sec)	Total cycle (sec)
< 1	5	4	2	3	14
$1–1\frac{1}{2}$	6	4	2	3	15
$2–2\frac{1}{2}$	6	4	3	4	17
3	7	5	4	4	20
$3\frac{1}{2}$	7	6	4	5	22
4	7	6	4	5	22
5	7	7	4	6	24

[†] Depth of cut 40–60% of maximum digging depth; swing angle 30–60°; loading haul units on the same level as the excavator.

Checks: Optimum depth, 30–60% maximum digging depth
from Table 8-9, 23–27 ft

$$8/23 = 34\% \geq 30\% \text{ okay}$$
$$8/27 = 30\% \geq 30\% \text{ okay}$$

Maximum loading height, from Table 8-9, 21–22 ft
9 ft 9 in. < 21   okay

Hoe cycle times are usually of greater duration than those for shovels, because, after making the cut, the hoe bucket must be raised above the ground level in order to load a haul unit or to get above a spoil pile. If in Example 8-7 the trucks can be spotted on the floor of the pit, the bucket will be above the truck when the cut is completed. Then it would not be necessary to raise the bucket any higher before swinging and dumping. The spotting of haul units below the level of the hoe will increase production.

A study by the author found a 12.6% total cycle time savings between loading at the same level and working the hoe from a bench above the haul units [4]. Factors to be carefully considered in selecting a hoe and planning its utilization are:

1. Maximum digging depth required
2. Minimum digging depth available
3. Working radius for digging and dumping
4. Dumping height required
5. Digging width required (trench operations)
6. Clearance for carrier, superstructure, and boom
7. Hoisting capability

In trenching operations the primary concern is to match the hoe's ability to excavate linear feet of trench per unit of time with the pipe-laying production. Usually, the volume of material moved is not the question.

GRADALLS

The *gradall* is a utility machine which combines the operating features of the hoe, dragline, and motor grader (see Fig. 8-18). The full revolving superstructure of the unit can be mounted on either crawler tracks or wheels. The unit is designed as a versatile machine for both excavation and finishing work. Being designed as a multi-use machine affects production efficiency in respect to individual applications, when compared to a unit designed specifically for a particular application. The gradall will have lower production capability than those single purpose units.

The bucket of a gradall can be rotated (that is, the gradall's arm can rotate) 90° or more, allowing it to be effective in reaching restricted working areas and where special shaping of slopes is required. Note its use in Fig. 8-18. The three-part telescoping boom can be hydraulically extended or retracted to vary digging or shaping reach. It can exert breakout force both above and below ground level.

FIGURE 8-18
Gradall shaping the side slopes of a ditch.

When used in a hoe application to excavate below the running gear, its production rate will be less than a hoe equipped with an equal size bucket. Similarly, it can perform dragline-type tasks, but it does have limited reach compared to a dragline. Because the machine provides the operator with positive hydraulic control of the bucket it can be used as a finishing tool for fine-grading slopes and confined areas, tasks which would normally be motor grader work if there were no space constraints.

LOADERS

GENERAL INFORMATION

Loaders are used extensively in construction work to handle and transport bulk material, such as earth and rock, to load trucks, to excavate earth, and to charge aggregate bins at asphalt and concrete plants.

TYPES AND SIZES

There are basically two types of loaders, the crawler-tractor-mounted type and the wheel-tractor-mounted type, as illustrated in Figs. 8-19 and 8-20, respectively. They

FIGURE 8-19
Track-type loader.

may be further classified by the capacity of the bucket or the weight that the bucket can lift. Wheel loaders may be steered by the rear wheels, or they may be articulated to permit steering as indicated in Fig. 8-21. The figure gives important dimensional specifications.

BUCKET RATINGS FOR LOADERS

The heaped capacity of a loader bucket is based on SAE standards. That standard specifies a 2:1 angle of repose for the material above the struck load. This repose angle (2:1) is different from that specified by both SAE and PCSA for shovel and hoe buckets (1:1). The fill factor correction for a loader bucket (see Table 8-12) adjusts heaped capacity to loose cubic yards (lcy) based on the type of material being handled.

 Once the bucket volumetric load is determined, a check must be made of payload weight. Unlike a shovel or hoe, to position the bucket to dump, a loader must maneuver and travel with the load. A shovel or hoe simply swings about its center pin and does not require track travel when moving the bucket from loading to dump position. SAE has established operating load weight limits for loaders. A wheel loader is limited to an operating load, by weight, which is less than 50% of the rated full-turn static tipping load considering the combined weight of the bucket and the load, measured from the center of gravity of the extended bucket at its maximum reach, with standard counterweights and nonballasted tires. In the case of track loaders the operating load is limited to less than 35% of the static tipping load. The term "operating capacity" is sometimes used interchangeably for operating load. Most buckets are sized based on standard 3,000 lb per loose cu yd material.

FIGURE 8-20
Wheel-tractor loader.

OPERATING SPECIFICATIONS

Representative operating specifications for a wheel loader furnish information such as listed below:

Engine flywheel horsepower 119 @ 2,300 rpm
    Speeds, forward and reverse:
    Low,   0– 3.9 mph
    Intermediate, 0–11.1 mph
    High,   0–29.5 mph

Operating load (SAE),   6,800 lb
Tipping load, straight ahead, 17,400 lb
Tipping load, full-turn,   16,800 lb
Lifting capacity,   18,600 lb
Breakout force, maximum, 30,000 lb

Tables 8-13 and 8-14 present the operating specifications across the range of commonly available wheel and track loaders.

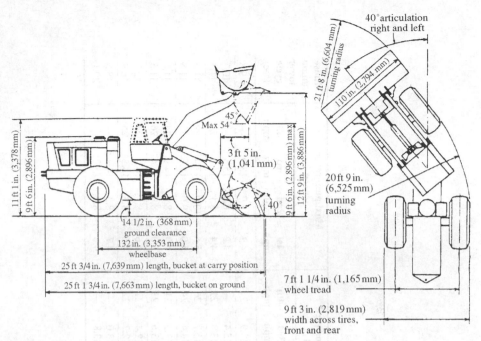

FIGURE 8-21
Articulated wheel loader. (International Harvester Company.)

TABLE 8-12
Bucket fill factors for wheel and track loaders[†]

Material	Wheel loader fill factor[‡] (%)	Track loader fill factor[‡] (%)
Loose material		
Mixed moist aggregates	95–100	95–100
Uniform aggregates: up to $\frac{1}{8}$ in.	95–100	95–110
$\frac{1}{8}-\frac{3}{8}$ in.	90–95	90–110
$\frac{1}{2}-\frac{3}{4}$ in.	85–90	90–110
1 in. and over	85–90	90–110
Blasted rock		
Well blasted	80–95	80–95
Average	75–90	75–90
Poor	60–75	60–75
Other		
Rock dirt mixtures	100–120	100–120
Moist loam	100–110	100–120
Soil	80–100	80–100
Cemented materials	85–95	85–100

[†] Caterpillar Inc.
[‡] Percent of heaped bucket capacity, adjusted to loose cubic yards (lcy).

223

TABLE 8-13
Representative specifications for wheel loaders

Size, heaped bucket capacity (cu yd)	Bucket dump clearance (ft)	Static tipping load, @ full turn (lb)	Maximum forward speed				Maximum reverse speed				Raise/dump/lower cycle (sec)
			1st mph	2nd mph	3rd mph	4th mph	1st mph	2nd mph	3rd mph	4th mph	
1.25	8.4	9,600	4.1	7.7	13.9	21	4.1	7.7	13.9	—	9.8
2.00	8.7	12,700	4.2	8.1	15.4	—	4.2	8.3	15.5	—	10.7
2.25	9.0	13,000	4.1	7.5	13.3	21	4.4	8.1	14.3	23	11.3
3.00	9.3	17,000	5.0	9.0	15.7	26	5.6	10.0	17.4	29	11.6
3.75	9.3	21,000	4.6	8.3	14.4	24	5.0	9.0	15.8	26	11.8
4.00	9.6	25,000	4.3	7.7	13.3	21	4.9	8.6	14.9	24	11.6
4.75	9.7	27,000	4.4	7.8	13.6	23	5.0	8.9	15.4	26	11.5
5.50	10.7	37,000	4.0	7.1	12.4	21	4.6	8.1	14.2	24	12.7
7.00	10.4	50,000	4.0	7.1	12.7	22	4.6	8.2	14.5	25	16.9
14.00	13.6	98,000	4.3	7.6	13.0	—	4.7	8.3	14.2	—	18.5
23.00	19.1	222,000	4.3	7.9	13.8	—	4.8	8.7	15.2	—	20.1

TABLE 8-14
Representative specifications for track loaders

Size, heaped bucket capacity (cu yd)	Bucket dump clear- ance (ft)	Static tipping load (lb)	Maximum forward speed (mph)	Maximum reverse speed (mph)	Raise/ dump/ lower cycle (sec)
1.00	8.5	10,500	6.5	6.9	11.8
1.30	8.5	12,700	6.5	6.9	11.8
1.50	8.6	17,000	5.9†	5.9†	11.0
2.00	9.5	19,000	6.4†	6.4†	11.9
2.60	10.2	26,000	6.0†	6.0†	9.8
3.75	10.9	36,000	6.4†	6.4†	11.4

†Hydrostatic drive.

PRODUCTION RATES FOR WHEEL LOADERS

The production rate for a wheel loader will depend on: (1) the fixed time required to load the bucket, shift gears, turn, and dump the load, (2) the time required to travel from the loading to the dumping position, (3) the time required to return to the loading position, and (4) the actual volume of material hauled each trip. Table 8-15 gives fixed cycle times for both the wheel and track loaders. Figure 8-22 illustrates a typical loading situation. Because wheel loaders are more maneuverable and can travel faster on smooth haul surfaces, their production rates should be higher than for track units under favorable conditions requiring longer maneuver distances.

Consider a wheel loader with a $2\frac{1}{2}$-cu-yd-heaped capacity bucket, handling well-blasted rock weighing 2,700 lb per lcy, for which the swell is 25%. This unit, equipped with a torque converter and a power-shift transmission, has the following speed ranges, forward and reverse:

Low,	0– 3.9 mph
Intermediate,	0–11.1 mph
High,	0–29.5 mph

TABLE 8-15
Fixed cycle times for loaders

Machine size, heaped bucket capacity (cu yd)	Wheel loader cycle time† (min)	Track loader cycle time† (min)
1.00– 3.75	0.45–0.50	0.25–0.35
4.00– 5.50	0.50–0.55	
6.00– 7.00	0.55–0.60	
14.00–23.00	0.60–0.70	

†Includes load, maneuver with four reversals of direction (minimum travel), and dump.

When hauling a loaded bucket, the unit should travel at an average speed of about 80% of its maximum speed in the low range. When returning empty, the unit should travel at an average speed of about 60% of its maximum speed in the intermediate range for distances less than 100 ft, and at about 80% of its maximum speed in the same range for distances of 100 ft and over. The average speeds [in feet per minute (fpm)] should be about as follows:

Hauling, all distances, 0.8×3.9 mph $\times 88$ fpm per mph $= 274$ fpm
Returning, 0–99 ft, 0.6×11.1 mph $\times 88$ fpm per mph $= 586$ fpm
Returning, 100 ft and over, 0.8×11.1 mph $\times 88$ fpm per mph $= 781$ fpm

If the haul surface is not well maintained, or is rough, these speeds should be reduced accordingly to realistic values. The effect of increased haul distance on production is shown by the following calculations:

Cycle time

Haul distance (ft)	25	50	100	150	200
Fixed time	0.45	0.45	0.45	0.45	0.45
Haul time	0.09	0.18	0.36	0.55	0.73
Return time	0.04	0.09	0.13	0.19	0.26
Cycle time (min)	0.58	0.72	0.94	1.19	1.44
Trips per 50-min hour	86.2	69.4	53.2	42.0	34.7
Production (tons)[†]	262	210	161	127	105

[†] The 0.9 bucket fill factor.

FIGURE 8-22
Loading travel cycle for a track loader.

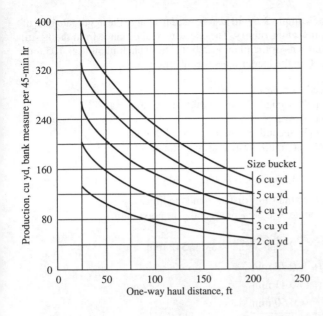

FIGURE 8-23
Effect of bucket size and haul distance on wheel loader production.

Figure 8-23 illustrates the variations in production by sizes of buckets and one-way haul distances.

The following example demonstrates the process for estimating loader production.

Example 8-8. A 4-cu-yd wheel loader will be used to load trucks from a quarry stockpile of processed aggregate having a maximum size of $1\frac{1}{4}$ in. The haul distance will be negligible. The aggregate has a loose unit weight of 3,100 lb per cu yd. Estimate the loader production in tons based on a 50-min-hour efficiency factor.

From Table 8-12: Fill factor for uniform aggregate > 1 in.,
85–90%; use 85%

$$4 \text{ cu yd} \times 0.85 = 3.4 \text{ lcy}$$

From Table 8-13: 4-cu-yd machine static tipping load @ full turn,
25,000 lb

Therefore, operating load is

$$0.5 \times 25,000 \text{ lb} = 12,500 \text{ lb}$$

Check tipping:

$$3.4 \times 3,100 \text{ lb/cu yd} = 10,540 \text{ lb} < 12,500 \text{ lb} \quad \text{okay}$$

From Table 8-15: Fixed cycle time for a 4-cu-yd wheel loader,

0.50–0.55 min; use 0.50 min

Production:

$$\frac{50 \text{ min-hr}}{0.50 \text{ min/cycle}} \times 3.4 \text{ cu yd/cycle} \times \frac{3,100 \text{ lb/cu yd}}{2,000 \text{ lb/ton}} = 527 \text{ ton/hr}$$

Example 8-9. The loader in Example 8-6 will also be used to charge the aggregate bins of an asphalt plant which is located at the quarry. The one-way haul distance from the $1\frac{1}{4}$-in. aggregate stockpile to the cold bins of the plant is 220 ft. The asphalt plant uses 105 tons per hour of $1\frac{1}{4}$-in. aggregate. Can the loader meet this requirement?

From Table 8-13: Travel speeds forward
> First, 4.3 mph; second, 7.7 mph; third, 13.3 mph
> Travel speeds reverse
> First, 4.9 mph; second, 8.6 mph; third, 14.9 mph

Travel loaded: 220 ft, @ 80% maximum first, to account for acceleration and breaking.

$$4.3 \text{ mph} \times 0.8 \times 88 = 303 \text{ fpm}$$

Return empty: 220 ft; because of the short distance and the time required to accelerate and brake, use 80% of second gear maximum speed.

$$7.7 \text{ mph} \times 0.8 \times 88 = 542 \text{ fpm}$$

Travel time loaded (220 ft) $= 0.73$ min

empty (220 ft) $= 0.41$ min

Fixed time $= \underline{0.50 \text{ min}}$

Total cycle time $= 1.64$ min

Production:

$$\frac{50 \text{ min-hour}}{1.64 \text{ min/cycle}} \times 3.4 \text{ lcy/cycle} \times \frac{3,100 \text{ lb/lcy}}{2,000 \text{ lb/ton}} = 160 \text{ ton/hr}$$

160 tons per hour $>$ 105 tons per hour required

The loader will meet the requirement.

PRODUCTION RATES FOR TRACK LOADERS

The production rates for track loaders are determined in the same manner as for wheel loaders.

Example 8-10. A track loader having the following specifications is used to load trucks from a bank of moist loam:

Bucket capacity, heaped, $2\frac{1}{4}$-cu-yd travel speed by gear

Gear	mph	fpm
Forward		
First	1.9	167
Second	2.9	255
Third	4.0	352
Reverse		
First	2.3	202
Second	3.6	317
Third	5.0	440

Assume that the loader will travel at an average of 80% of the specified speeds in the second gear, forward and reverse. The fixed time should be based on time studies for the particular equipment and job; Table 8-15 provides average times by loader size.

The cycle time per load will be:

Fixed time to load, turn, and dump	0.35 min
Haul time, 30 ft ÷ 204 fpm	0.15 min
Return time, 30 ft ÷ 254 fpm	0.12 min
Total cycle time	0.62 min

Although the rated heaped capacity of the bucket is $2\frac{1}{4}$ cu yd, it is probable that the average volume will be about 100–120% (Table 8-12) of this capacity for sustained loading. Assume an average capacity of 110%:

$$1.1 \times 2.25 \text{ cu yd} = 2.48 \text{ lcy}$$

The production rate in a 60-min hour will be:

Number of cycles, 60 min ÷ 0.62 min per cycle = 97 cycles per hr
Volume, 97 cycles × 2.48 lcy per cycle = 240 lcy per hr

If the material has a swell of 17%, and the loader has an operating efficiency equal to a 45-min hour, the volume per hour in bank measure will be

$$\frac{240 \text{ lcy/hr}}{1.17} \times \frac{45}{60} = 154 \text{ bcy/hr}$$

The chart in Fig. 8-24 gives the production rates for track loaders based on handling earth having a swell of 25% and an operating factor of 45 min per hour. The loose weight of the material is 2,700 lb per cu yd. It is assumed that the actual average volume of material in a bucket is 90% of its heaped capacity.

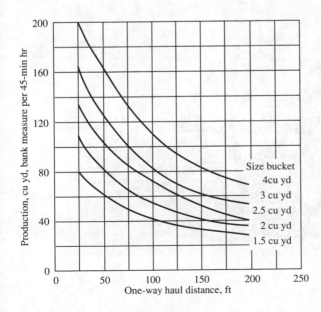

FIGURE 8-24
Effect of bucket size and haul distance on track loader production.

GENERAL INFORMATION

The term "trenching machine," as used in this book, applies to the wheel- and ladder-type machines shown in Figs. 8-25 and 8-26, respectively. These machines are satisfactory for digging utility trenches for water, gas, and oil pipelines; shoulder drains on highways; drainage ditches; and sewers where the job and soil conditions are such that they may be used. They provide relatively fast digging, with positive controls of depths and widths of trenches, reducing expensive finishing. These machines are capable of digging any type of soil but are generally not suitable for rock. They are available in various sizes for digging trenches of varying depths and widths. They are usually crawler-mounted to increase their stability and to distribute the weight over a greater area.

WHEEL-TYPE TRENCHING MACHINES

Figure 8-25 illustrates a wheel-type trenching machine. These machines are available with maximum cutting depths exceeding 8 ft, with trench widths from 12 in. to approximately 60 in. Many are available with 25 or more digging speeds to permit the selection of the most suitable speed for almost any job condition.

The excavating part of the machine consists of a power-driven wheel, on which are mounted a number of removable buckets, equipped with cutter teeth. Buckets are available in varying widths to which side cutters may be attached when it is necessary to increase the width of a trench. The machine is operated by lowering the rotating

FIGURE 8-25
Wheel-type trenching machine.

FIGURE 8-26
Ladder-type trenching machine.

wheel to the desired depth, while the unit moves forward slowly. The earth is picked up by the buckets and deposited onto an endless belt conveyor, which can be adjusted to discharge the earth on either side of the trench.

Table 8-16 gives representative specifications for wheel-type trenching machines. As these specifications do not necessarily include all machines that are available, a prospective purchaser should consult the manufacturer's specifications for the particular machine under consideration. The various trench widths for a given machine are obtained by using different bucket widths and installing side cutters.

Wheel-type machines are especially suited to excavating trenches for water, gas, and oil pipelines, and pipe drains which are placed in relatively shallow trenches. They may be used to excavate trenches for sewer pipes up to the maximum digging depths.

LADDER-TYPE TRENCHING MACHINES

Figure 8-26 illustrates a ladder-type trenching machine. By installing extensions to the ladders or booms, and by adding more buckets and chain links, it is possible to dig trenches in excess of 30 ft deep with large machines. Trench widths in excess of 12 ft may be dug. Most of these machines have booms whose lengths may be varied, thereby permitting a single machine to be used on trenches varying considerably in depth. This eliminates the need of owning a different machine for each depth range. A machine may have 30 or more digging speeds to suit the needs of a given job.

The excavating part of the machine consists of two endless chains, which travel along the boom, to which there are attached cutter buckets equipped with teeth. In addition, shaft-mounted side cutters may be installed on each side of the boom to increase the width of a trench. As the buckets travel up the underside of the boom, they bring

TABLE 8-16
Representative specifications for wheel-type trenching machines

Max. trench depth [ft (m)]	Trench width [in. (mm)]	Engine power [hp (kW)]	Wheel speed [fpm (m/sec)]	Travel speed [mph (km/hr)]	Digging speed [fpm (m/min)]
5.5 (1.67)	15–18–21 (380–450–532) 20–23–26 (507–583–660)	55 (41)	36–266 (0.18–1.35)	0.5–2.7 (0.8–4.3)	0.2–10 (0.06–0.30)
6.0 (1.82)	16–18–20 (405–457–517) 20–22–24 (507–559–610) 24–26–28 (610–660–710) 28–30 (710–760)	67 (50)	153–410 (0.78–2.08)	0.16–4.6 (0.26–7.4)	2.8–57.5 (0.08–17.4)
8.5 (2.58)	38–40 (965–1,015) 40–51 (1,015–1,290)	110 (82)	243 (1.23)	1.9 (3.1)	1.3–35.0 (0.42–10.8)

out earth and deposit it on a belt conveyor, which discharges it along either side of the trench. As a machine moves over uneven ground, it is possible to vary the depth of cut by adjusting the position, but not the length of the boom.

Table 8-17 gives representative specifications for ladder-type trenching machines. The prospective purchaser of a machine should check the manufacturer's specifications for the particular machine under consideration. The various trench widths for a given machine are obtained by using different bucket widths and installing side cutters.

As can be seen from Table 8-17, ladder-type trenching machines have considerable flexibility with regard to trench depths and widths. However, the machines are

TABLE 8-17
Representative specifications for ladder-type trenching machines

Max. trench depth [ft (m)]	Trench width [in. (mm)]	Engine power [hp (kW)]	Bucket speed [fpm (m/sec)]	Travel speed [mph (km/hr)]	Digging speed [fpm (m/min)]
4.5 (1.37)	6–8 (152–203)	47 (35)	245–538 (1.24–2.72)	0.7–3.4 (1.1–5.5)	2.2–21.8 (0.67–6.6)
8.5 (2.58)	16–36 (407–920)	55 (41)	96–225 (0.48–1.14)	1.4–3.2 (2.2–5.1)	0.5–13.8 (0.15–4.2)
12.5 (3.81)	16–42 (407–1,070)	74 (55)	135–542 (0.68–2.74)	1.4–3.2 (2.2–5.1)	0.3–9.7 (0.09–2.95)
15.0 (4.57)	18–54 (457–1,370)	90 (67)	103–168 (0.52–0.85)	1.7 (2.7)	0.7–15.5 (0.21–4.75)

not suitable for excavating trenches in rock or where large quantities of groundwater, combined with unstable soil, prevent the walls of a trench from remaining in place. If the soil, such as loose sand or mud, tends to flow into the trench, it may be desirable to adopt some other method of excavating the trench.

SELECTING THE MOST SUITABLE EQUIPMENT FOR EXCAVATING TRENCHES

The choice of equipment to be used in excavating a trench will depend on the job conditions, the depth and width of the trench, the class of soil, the extent to which groundwater is present, the width of the right-of-way for disposal of excavated earth, and the type of equipment already owned by a contractor.

If a relatively shallow and narrow trench is to be excavated in firm soil, the wheel-type machine is probably the most suitable. However, if the ground is rock, which requires blasting, the most suitable excavator will be a hoe. If the soil is an unstable, water-saturated material, it may be necessary to use a hoe or a clamshell and let the walls establish a stable slope. If it is necessary to install solid sheeting to hold the walls in place, either a hoe or a clamshell, which can excavate between the trench braces that hold the sheeting in place, will probably be the best equipment for the job.

Example 8-11. Consider the selection of a machine to excavate a trench 24 ft deep and 10 ft wide in soil which is sufficiently firm to require only shoring to hold the walls in place. A trench of this size can be excavated with a ladder-type machine, provided that the length and height of the conveyor belt are adequate to dispose of the earth along one side of the trench. The cross-sectional area of the trench will be 240 sq ft. If the loose earth has a 30% swell, the cross-sectional area of the spoil pile will be

$$240 \times 1.3 = 312 \text{ sq ft}$$

If the excavated earth reposes with 1:1 side slopes, the pile will have a height of 17.6 ft and a base width of 35.2 ft. If a minimum of 4 ft of clear berm is required along the side of the trench, the end of the conveyor must have a height clearance of 17.6 ft and a length of approximately 27 ft, measured from the center of the trench. The casting effect on the earth, as it leaves the end of the conveyor belt, may permit the use of a shorter conveyor. Unless the machine under consideration satisfies these clearances, it is probable that difficulties will be experienced in disposing of the earth.

PRODUCTION RATES OF TRENCHING MACHINES

Many factors influence the production rates of trenching machines. These include the class of soil; the depth and width of the trench; the extent of shoring required; the topography; climatic conditions; the extent of vegetation such as trees, stumps, and roots; physical obstructions such as buried pipes, sidewalks, paved streets, buildings; and the speed with which the pipe can be placed in the trench. Any factor that may affect the progress of the work should be considered in estimating the probable digging speed of a trenching machine.

In laying oil and gas pipelines through open, level country, with no physical obstructions to interfere with the progress, it is possible to install in excess of 6,000 ft of pipe in an 8-hour day. This is equivalent to approximately 800 ft per hour, which is not excessive for a wheel-type machine. However, if a trench must be excavated into rock over rough terrain covered with heavy timber, it may not be possible to excavate more than a few hundred feet per day.

If a trench is dug for the installation of sewer pipe under favorable conditions, it is possible that the machine can dig 300 ft of trench per hour. However, an experienced pipe-laying crew may not be able to lay more than 25 joints of small-diameter pipe, 3 ft long, in an hour. Thus, the speed of the machine will be limited to about 75 ft per hour regardless of its ability to dig more trench. In estimating the probable rate of digging a trench, one must apply an appropriate operating factor to the speed at which the machine can dig if there were no interferences.

Example 8-12. Estimate the probable average production rate, in feet per hour, in excavating a trench 36 in. wide, with a maximum depth of 12 ft, in hard, tough clay. The trench will be dug for the installation of a 21-in.-diameter sewer pipe, which can be laid at a rate of approximately 30 ft per hour. An examination of the site along the trench reveals obstructions which will reduce the digging speed to approximately 60% of the theoretically possible speeds. This will require the application of an operating factor of 0.6 to the speed of the machine.

Table 8-17 presents information on a ladder-type machine with a maximum digging depth of 12.5 ft. Considering the class of soil and the depth and width of the trench, one finds that the maximum digging speed should be about 1 fpm, or 60 ft per hour. The application of the operating factor will reduce the average speed to 36 ft per hour. However, since only 30 ft per hour of pipe can be laid, this will be the controlling speed.

The probable cost per linear foot of trench, for excavating only, should be as follows:

Trenching machine	=	$29.60
Operator	=	14.20
Helpers, three men @ $8.00 per hour	=	24.00
Foreman, one-half time charged to excavating	=	9.00
Total cost excavation	=	$76.80
Cost per linear feet, $76.80 per 30 ft per hour	=	$ 2.56

EARTH-AND-ROCK SAWS

As illustrated in Fig. 8-27, a rock saw consists of a vertical wheel attached to a horizontal shaft which is supported on an adjustable boom mounted on the rear of a track-type or wheel-type power unit such as a tractor. The machine is used to cut narrow trenches, up to about 6 in. in width and 30 in. or more in depth, in frozen earth, caliche, coral or other rocks, and concrete.

The sawing is performed by round carbide-tipped or diamond-tipped cutters attached to the wheel, with the type selected depending on the properties of the material to be sawed. The teeth, which are replaceable, rotate freely in their mounting pockets to maintain even tooth wear.

FIGURE 8-27
Crawler-mounted cutting wheel.

PROBLEMS

8-1. Determine the probable production in cubic yard bank measure (bcy) for a 2-cu-yd dragline when excavating and casting good common earth. The average depth of dig will be 12 ft, and the average angle of swing will be 120°. The efficiency factor will be a 55-min hour.

8-2. Determine the largest capacity medium duty dragline bucket that can be used with a dragline equipped with an 80-ft boom when the boom is operating at an angle of 45°. The earth will weigh 98 lb per cu ft loose measure.

8-3. A contractor has both a 3-cu-yd and a 5-cu-yd shovel in his equipment fleet. Select the minimum size shovel that will excavate 600,000 cu yd bank measure (bcy) of common earth in 130 working days of 8 hours each. The average height of excavation will be 15 ft, and the average angle of swing will be 120°. The 3-cu-yd shovel has a maximum digging height of 30 ft and the 5-cu-yd machine's maximum digging height is 34 ft. The efficiency factor will be a 45-min hour.

8-4. For each of the stated conditions, determine the probable production of a 3-cu-yd shovel expressed in bcy per hour. The shovel has a maximum digging height of 32 ft.

	Class of material			
Condition	Common earth	Common earth	Rock–earth	Shale
Height of excavation (ft)	12	8	12	19
Angle of swing (degrees)	90	120	60	130
Efficiency factor (min-hr)	50	50	50	45

8-5. A 5-cu-yd shovel, whose cost per hour including the wages to an operator is $96, is assumed to excavate well-blasted rock under each of the stated conditions. The maximum digging height of the machine is 35 ft. Determine the cost per cubic yard for each condition.

Condition	(1)	(2)	(3)	(4)
Height of excavation (ft)	10	18	24	28
Angle of swing (degrees)	60	90	120	150
Efficiency factor (min-hr)	45	40	50	45

REFERENCES

1. Power Crane and Shovel Association, A Bureau of Construction Industry Manufacturers Association, 111 East Wisconsin Avenue, Milwaukee, WI 53202.
2. "Crane Load Stability Test Code—SAE J765," in *SAE Recommended Practice Handbook,* Society of Automotive Engineers, Inc., 1967.
3. Stewart, Rita F., and Cliff J. Schexnayder: "Production Estimating for Draglines," *Journal of Construction Engineering and Management,* American Society of Civil Engineers, vol. 111, no. 1, March 1985, pp. 101–104.
4. Lewis, Chris R., and Cliff J. Schexnayder: "Production Analysis of the CAT 245 Hydraulic Hoe," in *Proceedings of Earthmoving and Heavy Equipment Specialty Conference,* American Society of Civil Engineers, February 1986, pp. 88–94.

CHAPTER 9

TRUCKS AND WAGONS

TRUCKS

In handling earth, aggregate, rock, ore, coal, and other materials, trucks serve one purpose. They are hauling units which, because of their high travel speeds when operating on suitable roads, provide relatively low hauling costs. They provide a high degree of flexibility, as the number in service can usually be increased or decreased easily to permit modifications in the total hauling capacity of a fleet and adjustments for changing haul distances. Most trucks may be operated over any haul road for which the surface is sufficiently firm and smooth and on which the grades are not excessively steep. Some units now in use are designated as off-highway trucks because their size and total load are larger than that permitted on public highways (see Fig. 9-1). These trucks are used for hauling materials on large project sites, where their size and costs are justified.

Trucks may be classified according to a great many factors, including:

1. The size and type of engine—gasoline, diesel, butane, propane
2. The number of gears
3. The kind of drive—two-wheel, four-wheel, six-wheel, etc.
4. The number of wheels and axles and arrangement of driving wheels
5. The method of dumping the load—rear-dump, side-dump
6. The class of material hauled—earth, rock, coal, ore, etc.
7. The capacity, in tons or cubic yards

If trucks are to be purchased for general material hauling, the purchaser should select units that are adaptable to the multipurposes for which they will be used. However, if trucks are to be used on a given project for a single purpose, the purchaser should select trucks that specifically fit the requirements of the project.

FIGURE 9-1
Off-highway quarry truck.

GLOSSARY OF TERMS

The following glossary defines the important terms that are used in describing trucks and wagons.

Curb weight. Sometimes called "chassis weight," a curb weight usually refers to the weight of a base chassis of a truck or tractor.

Fifth wheel. A circular metal plate used to connect the semitrailer to the tractor. The lower fifth wheel, which is secured to the tractor frame, consists of a base, a rocking plate, and a locking mechanism. The upper fifth wheel, mounted to the underside of the semitrailer near the nose, consists of a circular plate and a kingpin.

Gross axle weight rating. The manufacturer's rating for the maximum amount of weight that can be supported by an "axle system." The axle system includes the axle, suspension system, tires, and wheels. The lowest-capacity component in the "system" will determine the gross axle weight rating.

Gross combination weight. The actual loaded weight of a tractor and trailer or semi-trailer combination.

Gross combination weight rating. The manufacturer's rating for the maximum allowable weight of a tractor and a loaded trailer or semitrailer.

Gross vehicle weight. The actual loaded weight of a straight truck, including the tare weight, the cargo weight, and the weight of the occupants.

Gross vehicle weight rating. The manufacturer's estimate of the maximum amount that a loaded straight truck should weigh. It includes the tare weight and the weight added by the cargo and occupants.

Kingpin. A hardened steel pin, attached to the upper fifth wheel, that engages and locks into the lower fifth wheel.

Landing gear. Retractable supports under the front of a semitrailer that keep the trailers level when the tractor is removed.

Semitrailer. A trailing load carrier that has axles only at the rear. The front of the semi-trailer is supported by the tractor's fifth wheel.

Straight truck. A straight truck carries the cargo-handling device completely on its own frame, such as a rear-dump body, a mixer barrel, or a flat bed.

Tare weight. The work-ready weight of a truck or tractor, including fuel.

Tractor. The truck portion of a vehicle that pulls a trailer or a semitrailer.

Trailer. A trailing load carrier that is completely supported on its own axles (two or more) and attached to the tractor with a drawbar/pintle hook arrangement.

REAR-DUMP TRUCKS

Rear-dump trucks are suitable for use in hauling many types of materials. The shape of the body, such as the extent of sharp angles, corners, and the contour of the rear, through which the materials must flow during dumping, will affect the ease or diffi-culty of dumping. The bodies of trucks that will be used to haul wet clay and similar materials should be free of sharp angles and corners. Dry sand and gravel will flow eas-ily from almost any shape of body (see Fig. 9-2). If quarry rock is to be hauled, bodies should be shallow with sloping sideboards. Figure 9-3 shows a hydraulic hoe loading an articulated rear-dump truck.

Rear-dumps should be considered when:

1. The material to be hauled is free-flowing or has bulky components.
2. The hauling unit must dump into restricted locations or over the edge of a bank or fill.
3. Maximum maneuverability in the loading or dumping area is required.

When hauling rock, the impact loading on the truck body is extremely severe. Con-tinuous use under such conditions will require a heavy duty rock body. Even with the special body, the loader operator must use care in placing a load in the truck.

BOTTOM-DUMP WAGONS

If units are to be used to haul materials which flow easily, such as sand, gravel, reason-ably dry earth, coal, etc., the use of bottom-dump wagons will reduce the time required

FIGURE 9-2
Highway rear-dump, dumping a load.

to unload the material. There are both large off-highway units (see Fig. 9-4), and highway sized units (see Fig. 9-5). They are particularly suitable for use when the materials are to be distributed in layers on a fill or when material is to be discharged through grizzlies into hoppers. When discharging the loads onto fills, the wagons can dump their loads in windrows while moving. When discharging through grizzlies, they will need to stop for only a few seconds. The rapid rate of discharging the load gives the wagons a time advantage over rear-dump trucks.

The doors through which these units discharge their loads have a limited opening width. Difficulties may be experienced in discharging such materials as wet, sticky clay, especially if the material is in large lumps.

These wagons are satisfactory hauling units on projects such as earthen dams, levees, highways, and airports, where large quantities of materials are to be transported and haul roads can be kept in reasonably good condition. They may be loaded by shovels, draglines (see Fig. 9-6), or belt loaders (see Fig. 9-5).

Bottom-dumps should be considered when:

1. The material to be hauled is free-flowing.
2. There are unrestricted loading and dump sites.

FIGURE 9-3
An articulated rear-dump truck being loaded by a hydraulic hoe.

FIGURE 9-4
Loaded bottom-dump wagon approaching the dump.

FIGURE 9-5
Highway bottom-dump being loaded by a fine-grade machine.

3. The haul route grades are less than about 5%. Because of its unfavorable power-weight ratio, the unit has limited ability to pull steep grades and there is less weight on the drive wheels of the tractor unit, thereby limiting traction.

CAPACITIES OF TRUCKS AND WAGONS

There are at least three methods of expressing the capacities of trucks and wagons: (1) by the load which it will carry, expressed *gravimetrically* in tons; (2) by its struck volume; and (3) by its heaped volume. The latter two are expressed in cubic yards or cubic meters.

The struck capacity of a truck is the volume of material which it will haul when it is filled level to the top of the sides of the body. The heaped capacity is the volume of material which it will haul when the load is heaped above the sides. While the struck capacity remains fixed for any given unit, the heaped capacity will vary with the height and angle at which the material may extend above the sides. Wet earth or sandy clay may be hauled with a slope of about 1:1, whereas dry sand or gravel may not permit a slope greater than about 3:1. In order to determine the probable heaped capacity of a unit, one needs to know the struck capacity, the length and width of the body, and the slope at which the material will remain stable while the unit is moving. Smooth haul roads will permit a larger heaped capacity than rough haul roads. Because of variations

FIGURE 9-6
Bottom-dump wagon being loaded by a dragline.

in the heaping capacities of units, it may be better to compare them on the basis of their struck capacities. In any event the capacities should be determined or compared in a realistic manner.

The weight capacity may limit the volume of the load when a unit is used to haul heavy material, such as iron or even wet sand. However, when the specific gravity of the materials is such that the safe load is not exceeded, a unit may be filled to its heaped capacity.

In some instances it is possible to add sideboards to increase the depth of the body of a truck or wagon, thereby permitting it to haul a larger load. When this is done, the weight of the new volumes must be checked against the vehicle's load capacity. This practice probably will increase the hourly cost of operating a unit because of higher fuel consumption; reduced tire life; more frequent failures of parts, such as axles, gears, brakes, and clutches; and higher maintenance costs. However, if the value of the extra material hauled is greater than the total increase in the cost of operating the vehicle, overloading is justified. In considering the option of sideboarding and hauling larger volumes of materials, one must check the maximum safe loads on the tires to prevent excessive loading, which might result in lost time due to tire failures.

PERFORMANCE CAPABILITIES OF TRUCKS AND WAGONS

The productive capacity of a truck or wagon depends on the size of its load and the number of trips it can make in an hour. The size of the load can be determined from the specifications furnished by the manufacturer. The number of trips per hour will depend on the weight of the vehicle, the horsepower of the engine, the haul distance, and the condition of the haul road.

The productivity may be determined as illustrated in Example 9-4 by using vehicle rimpull, the weight of the vehicle, and the condition of the haul road.

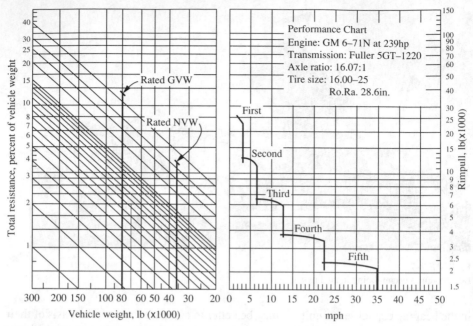

FIGURE 9-7
Performance chart for a 22-ton rear-dump truck.

Another method of determining the production is to use the vehicle's performance chart furnished by the manufacturer. Such a chart, for a 22-ton rear-dump truck, is illustrated in Fig. 9-7.

Example 9-1. The specifications for the truck are as follows:

Engine, 239 fwhp (flywheel horsepower)

Capacity
Struck, 14.7 cu yd
Heaped, 2:1, 18.3 cu yd

Net weight empty   = 36,860 lb
Payload   = 44,000 lb
Gross vehicle weight   = 80,860 lb

Determine the maximum speed for the truck when it is hauling a load of 22 tons up a 6% grade on a haul road having a rolling resistance of 60 lb per ton, equivalent to a 3% adverse grade. Because the chart is based on zero rolling resistance, it is necessary to combine the grade and the rolling resistance, which gives an equivalent total resistance equal to $6 + 3 = 9$% of the vehicle weight.

The procedure for using Fig. 9-7 is:

1. Find the vehicle weight on the lower left horizontal scale.
2. Read up the weight line to the intersection with the slanted total resistance line.

3. From this intersection, read horizontally to the right to the intersection with the performance curve.
4. From this intersection, read down to find the vehicle's speed.

Following these four steps, one finds that the truck will operate in the second speed range, and that its maximum speed will be 6.5 mph.

The chart should be used to determine the maximum speed for each section of a haul road having a significant difference in the grade or the rolling resistance.

Although a performance chart indicates the maximum speed at which a vehicle can travel, the vehicle will not necessarily travel at this speed. If conditions other than total resistance limit the speed to less than the value given in the chart, the anticipated effective speed should be used.

BALANCING THE CAPACITIES OF HAULING UNITS WITH EXCAVATOR SIZE

When loading with hoes, shovels, draglines, or belt loaders, it is desirable to use haul units whose capacities balance the output of the excavator. If this is not done, operating difficulties will develop and the combined cost of excavating and hauling material will be higher than when balanced units are used. For example, when an excavator is used to load earth into trucks, the size of the trucks may introduce several factors which will affect the production rate and the cost of handling earth:

1. Advantages of using small trucks compared with large trucks:
   a. They are more flexible in maneuvering, which may be an advantage on short hauls.
   b. They may have higher speeds.
   c. There is less loss in production when one truck in a fleet breaks down.
   d. It is easier to balance the number of trucks with the output of the excavator, which will reduce the time lost by the trucks or the excavator.
2. Disadvantages of using small trucks compared with large trucks:
   a. A small truck is more difficult for the excavator to load owing to the small target for depositing the bucket load.
   b. More total spotting time is lost in positioning the trucks because of the larger number required.
   c. More drivers are required to haul a given output of material.
   d. The greater number of trucks increases the danger of units bunching at the pit, along the haul road, or at the dump.
   e. The greater number of trucks required may increase the total investment in hauling equipment, with more expensive maintenance and repairs, and more parts to stock.
3. Advantages of using large trucks compared with small trucks:
   a. Fewer trucks are required, which may reduce the total investment in hauling units and the cost of maintenance and repairs.
   b. Fewer drivers are required.

   c. The smaller number of trucks facilitates synchronizing the equipment and reduces the danger of bunching by the trucks. This is especially true for long hauls.

   d. There is a larger target for the excavator during loading.

   e. The frequency of spotting trucks under the excavator is reduced.

   f. There are fewer trucks to maintain and repair, and fewer parts to stock.

   g. The engines ordinarily use cheaper fuels, i.e., gasoline versus diesel, but this must be based on fuel prices at the specific project location.

4. Disadvantages of using large trucks compared with small trucks:

   a. The cost of truck time at loading is greater, especially with small excavators.

   b. The heavier loads may cause more damage to the haul roads, thus increasing the cost of mechanical maintenance to the trucks and requiring more support equipment for maintenance of the haul road.

   c. It is more difficult to balance the number of trucks with the output of the excavator.

   d. Repair parts may be more difficult to obtain.

   e. The largest sizes may not be permitted to haul on highways.

A rule-of-thumb practice that is frequently used in selecting the size of trucks is to use trucks with a minimum capacity of 4 to 5 times the capacity of the excavator bucket, when loading with an excavator. The dependability of this practice is discussed in the following analysis.

Example 9-2. Consider a $\frac{3}{4}$-cu-yd shovel excavating good common earth with a 90° swing, with no delays waiting for hauling units, and with a 21-sec-cycle time. If the bucket and the trucks are operated at their heaped capacities, the swelling effect of the earth should permit each truck to carry its rated or struck capacity, expressed in cubic yards bank measure (bcy). Assume that the number of buckets required to fill a truck will equal the capacity of the truck divided by the size of the bucket, both expressed in cubic yards. The sizes of the trucks considered are based on the struck capacities. Assume that the time for a travel cycle, *excluding the time for loading,* will be the same for the several sizes of trucks considered. The time for a travel cycle, which includes traveling to the dump, dumping, and returning to the shovel, will be 6 min.

   If 6-cu-yd trucks are used, it will require eight buckets ($6 \div \frac{3}{4}$) to fill a truck. The time required to load a truck will be 168 sec, or 2.8 min. The minimum round-trip cycle for a truck will be 8.8 min. The minimum number of trucks required to keep the shovel busy will be $8.8 \div 2.8 = 3.15$. For this condition it will probably be cheaper to provide three trucks and to let the shovel remain idle a short period of time between the trucks' arrivals. The time required to load three trucks will be $3 \times 2.8 = 8.4$ min. Thus, the shovel will lose $8.8 - 8.4 = 0.4$ min when only three trucks are used. The percentage of time lost will be $(0.4 \div 8.8) \times 100 = 4.5\%$, which is not serious. If four trucks are used, the total loading time required will be $4 \times 2.8 = 11.2$ min. As this will increase the total round-trip cycle of each truck from 8.8 to 11.2 min, the lost time per truck cycle will be 2.4 min per truck. This will result in a loss of

$$\frac{2.4}{11.2} \times 100 = 21.4\%, \text{ for each truck}$$

which is equivalent to an operating factor of 78.6% for the trucks.

   If 15-cu-yd trucks are used, it will require 20 buckets to fill a truck. The time required to load a truck will be 420 sec, or 7 min. The minimum round-trip cycle for a truck will be 13 min. The minimum number of trucks required to keep the shovel busy will be $13 \div 7 = 1.86$. Using two trucks, the time required to load will be $2 \times 7 = 14$ min; the lost time per truck cycle will be $14 - 13 = 1$ min per truck. This will produce an operating factor of $(13/14) \times 100 = 93\%$ for the trucks.

In the previous example note that the production of the shovel is based on a 60-min hour. This policy should be followed when balancing a servicing (loading) unit with the units being served (hauling) because at times both types of units will operate at maximum capacity if the number of units is properly balanced. However, the average production of a unit, shovel or truck, for a sustained period of time, should be based on applying an appropriate efficiency factor to the maximum productive capacity.

Attention must be called to the fact that in this example truck sizes have been chosen which exactly match the loader; i.e., to load a 6-cu-yd truck with a $\frac{3}{4}$-cu-yd shovel results in an integer number of bucket swings. In practice, this is not always the case, but physically only an integer number of swings can be used in loading the truck. Therefore, if the division of truck volume by bucket volume is rounded to the next higher integer and that higher number of bucket swings is used to load the truck, some material falls off the truck. In such a case the loading duration equals the bucket cycle time multiplied by the number of bucket swings. But the truck load equals the truck capacity, not the number of bucket swings multiplied by the bucket volume. If one less bucket load is placed on the truck, the loading time will be reduced; but the truck load is also reduced. The truck load in that case will equal the bucket volume multiplied by the number of bucket swings.

THE EFFECT OF TRUCK SIZE ON THE COST OF HAULING

A comparison of the cost of hauling with each of several different sized trucks, based on the previous analysis, is illustrated in Table 9-1. The information appearing in the table is obtained as illustrated in the following example.

Example 9-3. Assume that the shovel operates at 80% efficiency while it is excavating, but there is no lost time waiting for trucks.

No. of cycles per min: $\dfrac{60 \text{ sec per min}}{21 \text{ sec per cycle}} = 2.86$

No. cycles per hour: 60-min hour $\times$ 2.86 cycles per min = 171.6

Ideal output per hour: 171.6 cycles per hour $\times \frac{3}{4}$ cu yd per cycle = 128 cu yd

Output at 80% efficiency: $0.8 \times 128 = 102$ cu yd per hour

Travel cycle for each truck, 6 min

If 6-cu-yd trucks are used,

No. of cycles per hour: 60 min per hour $\div$ (6 min, haul + 2.8 min, load) = 6.82

Ideal output per hour, 3 trucks, 6 cu yd: $3 \times 6 \times 6.82 = 122.7$

Output at 80% efficiency: $0.8 \times 122.72 = 98$ cu yd per hour

Cost per hour for a truck and driver $= \$22$

Total cost per hour for trucks, $3 \times \$22 = \$66$

Truck cost while loading, $\dfrac{2.8 \times \$22}{60} = \$1.03$

TABLE 9-1
Comparison of the cost of hauling with various size trucks, using a $\frac{3}{4}$-cu-yd shovel for loading

Size of truck (cu yd)	No. of trucks	Output (cu yd/hr)	Loading time (min)	Truck cost ($) Per hr Per truck ($)	Truck cost ($) Per hr Total ($)	Truck cost ($) At loading Per truck ($)	Truck cost ($) At loading Per cu yd ($)	Hauling cost per cu yd ($)
6	3	98	2.8	22.00	66.00	1.03	0.171	0.673
6	4	102	2.8	22.00	88.00	1.03	0.171	0.863
9	2	85	4.2	31.80	63.60	2.23	0.247	0.748
9	3	102	4.2	31.80	95.40	2.23	0.247	0.935
15	2	102	7.0	48.50	97.00	5.67	0.378	0.951

Truck cost per cubic yard of earth loaded, $\dfrac{\$1.03}{6 \text{ cu yd}} = \$0.171$ per cu yd

The hauling cost per cubic yard equals the total cost per hour divided by the output per hour:

$$\frac{\$66}{98 \text{ cu yd}} = \$0.673 \text{ per cu yd}$$

The information given in Table 9-1 indicates that, for the given size excavator and project situation, the lowest hauling cost will be obtained if three 6-cu-yd trucks are used. For other sizes of excavators and truck travel cycles the comparative costs given in the table will not hold true. If the travel cycle for the larger trucks is greater than for the 6-cu-yd trucks, namely, 6 min, the actual time should be used in preparing information similar to that given in the table.

If the size of the excavator is increased, the time lost by the larger trucks at loading will be reduced, which will reduce their hauling cost per cubic yard. One disadvantage in using large trucks, for which costs are paid by the hour, is that the cost of the trucks while they are being loaded will be higher than for smaller trucks. This results from two factors, the longer time required to load and the higher hourly cost of the larger trucks. Since it is desirable to have a truck under the excavator at all times, the total hourly truck cost while loading 15-cu-yd trucks will be $48.50, compared with $22 for 6-cu-yd trucks, regardless of the size of the excavator. In the case of a *fixed size* excavator this higher cost for the larger trucks must be recovered by more economical performance during the travel cycle; otherwise the use of the larger trucks will not be justified.

THE EFFECT OF EXCAVATOR SIZE ON THE COST OF EXCAVATING AND HAULING

If the size of the excavator is increased, while the size of trucks remains constant, the resulting increase in the output of the shovel will reduce the time required to load a

TABLE 9-2
The effect of excavator size on the cost of hauling with 15-cu-yd trucks

| Shovel size (cu yd) | Output per hr (cu yd) | Truck time | | No. of trucks | Truck cost per hr ($) | Truck cost at loading ($) | | Cost per cu yd ($) |
		Load (min)	Round trip (min)			Per truck	Per cu yd	
1	125†	6.4	14.4	2	97.20	5.18	0.346	0.777
1	140	6.4	14.4	3	145.80	5.18	0.346	1.041
1½	191	4.7	12.7	3	145.80	3.81	0.254	0.763
2	231†	3.8	11.8	3	145.80	3.08	0.205	0.631
2	240	3.8	11.8	4	194.40	3.08	0.205	0.810
2½	280	3.2	11.2	4	194.40	2.59	0.173	0.694
3	312	2.9	10.9	4	194.40	2.35	0.157	0.623

†These values are reduced because the hauling capacities of the trucks limit the outputs.

truck. This will reduce the truck cost per cubic yard during loading. The effect which the size of a loading unit has on the truck cost at loading and the hauling cost is illustrated in Table 9-2. In this example the material is good common earth, the height of cut is optimum, and the angle of swing is 90°. The operating factor for the shovel is 80%, with no lost time waiting for trucks. Trucks with a heaped capacity of 15 bcy will be used to haul the earth. The travel cycle for the trucks is 8 min. The cost per hour for a truck and driver will be $48.60.

Sample calculations using a 1-cu-yd shovel are:

Ideal output of the shovel, 175 cu yd per hour
Output at 80% efficiency, $0.80 \times 175 = 140$ cu yd per hour

Time required to load a truck:

$$\frac{15 \text{ cu yd} \times 60 \text{ min-hr}}{140 \text{ cu yd/hr}} = 6.4 \text{ min}$$

Round-trip time per truck, with no delays waiting for the shovel:

$$6.4 \text{ min, load} + 8.0 \text{ min, travel and dump} = 14.4 \text{ min}$$

Number of trucks needed, $\dfrac{14.4 \text{ min per cycle}}{6.4 \text{ min per load}} = 2.25$

Output using two trucks, truck controls system production:

$$\frac{2 \text{ trucks} \times 60 \text{ min-hr} \times 15 \text{ cu yd per truck}}{14.4 \text{ min/cycle}} = 125 \text{ cu yd/hr}$$

Output using three trucks, shovel controls system production, 140 cu yd per hour

Cost per hour for two trucks, $2 \times \$48.60$ $= \$\ 97.20$
Cost per hour for three trucks, $3 \times \$48.60$ $= \$145.80$

TABLE 9-3
The effect of excavator size on the cost of loading and hauling, with
15-cu-yd trucks

Shovel size (cu yd)	Output per hr (cu yd)	Shovel cost per hr ($)	No. of trucks	Truck cost per hr ($)	Excavating cost per cu yd ($)	Hauling cost per cu yd ($)	Total cost per cu yd ($)
1	125†	43.20	2	97.20	0.346	0.777	1.123
1	140	43.20	3	145.80	0.309	1.041	1.350
$1\frac{1}{2}$	191	64.20	3	145.80	0.336	0.763	1.100
2	231†	89.70	3	145.80	0.388	0.631	1.020
2	240	89.70	4	194.40	0.374	0.810	1.184
$2\frac{1}{2}$	280	101.10	4	194.40	0.361	0.694	1.055
3	312	121.50	4	194.40	0.389	0.623	1.013

†These values are reduced because the hauling capacities of the trucks limit the outputs.

Cost per truck during loading, $\dfrac{6.4 \text{ min}}{60 \text{ min-hr}} \times \$48.60$ per hour $= \$5.19$

Truck cost on a cubic yard basis during loading:

$$\$5.19 \div 15 \text{ cu yd} = \$0.346 \text{ per cu yd}$$

Hauling cost per cubic yard, using two trucks:

$$\$97.20 \div 125 \text{ cu yd} = \$0.777 \text{ per cu yd}$$

Hauling cost per cubic yard, using three trucks:

$$\$145.80 \div 140 \text{ cu yd} = \$1.041 \text{ per cu yd}$$

While the information given in Table 9-2 indicates that the cost of hauling earth is reduced as the size of the shovel is increased, the job planner is concerned with the combined cost of excavating and hauling earth. This cost may be obtained by adding the cost of operating the shovel, including labor, to the cost of the trucks. Table 9-3 gives this information. The costs given in the table do not include the cost of moving the equipment to the project and setting it up. The cost of a shovel is based on the cost of owning and operating, with an allowance for the operator and an oiler.

THE EFFECT OF GRADE ON THE COST OF HAULING WITH TRUCKS

In constructing a fill, one frequently can obtain the necessary material from a borrow pit located either above or below the fill. If the borrow pit is above the fill, the effect of the favorable grade on the loaded truck is to reduce the required rimpull by 20 lb per gross ton for each 1% of grade. If the borrow pit is below the fill, the effect of the adverse grade on the loaded truck is to increase the required rimpull by 20 lb per gross ton for each 1% grade. Obviously, the grade of the haul road will affect the hauling capacity of a truck, its performance, and the cost of hauling material. It may be more economical to obtain material from a borrow pit above, instead of below, the fill, even though the haul distance from the higher pit is greater than that from the lower pit. This is an item which should be given consideration in locating borrow pits.

If material is hauled downhill, it may be possible to add sideboards to the vehicle to increase the hauling capacity, up to the maximum load which the truck frame, dumping system, and the tires can carry. In some instances it will be desirable to use larger tires to permit the trucks to haul even greater loads. If the material is hauled uphill, it may be necessary to reduce the size of the load or the travel speed of the truck, either of which will increase the cost of hauling.

Example 9-4. This example illustrates the effect of grade on the cost of hauling.

The project requires 1,000,000 bcy of earth. The material will be good common earth, weighing 2,700 lb per bcy, with a swell of 25%. Two borrow pits are available.

Borrow pit 1 will require an average haul of 0.66 mi up an average grade of 2.2%. Borrow pit 2 will require an average haul of 0.78 mi down an average slope of 1.4%.

Both borrow pits are easily accessible to the trucks, which will permit spotting on either side of the shovel, whose angle of swing will not exceed 90°. Excavating can be done at optimum height. The production efficiency factor should not be less than 0.80.

The earth will be excavated with a 3-cu-yd shovel, with a probable output of $0.80 \times 390 = 312$ bcy per hour. The average rolling resistance of the haul road is estimated to be 60 lb per ton.

The coefficient of traction between the truck tires and the haul road will average 0.60.

The earth will be hauled with bottom-dump wagons, whose estimated heaped capacity will be 15 bcy.

The average elevation is 600 ft above sea level.

The specifications for the trucks are:

Payload capacity, 40,000 lb
Engine, diesel, 200 hp
Empty weight, 36,800 lb
Gross weight, loaded, 76,800 lb

Gross weight distribution
    Front axle, 12,000 lb
    Drive axle, 32,400 lb
    Trailer axle, 32,400 lb

Size of tires on drive and trailer axles, 24 × 25

Gear	Speed (mph)	Rimpull (lb)
First	3.2	19,900
Second	6.3	10,100
Third	11.9	5,350
Fourth	20.8	3,060
Fifth	32.7	1,945

The maximum usable rimpull of a loaded truck, as limited by the coefficient of traction, will be $32,400 \times 0.6 = 19,440$ lb. This is sufficiently high to eliminate the danger of tire slippage, except possibly in first gear.

Borrow pit 1

The combined effect of the rolling resistance and grade on a *loaded* truck will be:

Rolling resistance = 60 lb per ton
Grade resistance, 2.2 × 20 = 44 lb per ton

Total resistance = 104 lb per ton

Gross weight of truck, 76,800 ÷ 2,000 = 38.4 tons
Required rimpull, 38.4 × 104 = 3,994 lb
Maximum speed of loaded truck, 11.9 mph

The combined effect of the rolling resistance and grade on an *empty* truck will be:

Rolling resistance = 60 lb per ton
Grade resistance, 2.2 × 20 = −44 lb per ton

Total resistance = 16 lb per ton

Weight of empty truck, 36,800 ÷ 2,000 = 18.4 tons
Required rimpull, 18.4 × 16 = 294 lb
Maximum speed of an empty truck, 32.7 mph

The time required for each operation in a round-trip cycle should be about:

Loading, 15 cu yd ÷ 312 cu yd per hour = 0.0481 hour
Lost time in pit and accelerating, 1.5 min = 0.0250 hour
Travel to the fill, 0.66 mi ÷ 11.9 mph = 0.0555 hour
Dumping, turning, and accelerating, 1 min = 0.0167 hour
Travel to pit, 0.66 mi ÷ 32.7 mph = 0.0202 hour

Total round-trip time = 0.1655 hour

Assume that the trucks will operate an average of 50 min per hour:

No. of trips per hour, $\dfrac{1 \text{ hour}}{0.1655 \text{ hour}} \times \dfrac{50}{60} = 5.04$

Volume of material hauled per truck, 15 × 5.04 = 75.6 cu yd per hour

No. of trucks required, 312 cu yd per hour ÷ 75.6 cu yd per hour = 4.13

Use four trucks, which will reduce the output of the shovel slightly. If a truck and driver cost $32.40 per hour, the hauling cost will be

$$\frac{\$32.40}{75.6 \text{ cu yd}} = \$0.429 \text{ per cu yd}$$

Borrow pit 2

The combined effect of the rolling resistance and grade on a *loaded* truck will be:

Rolling resistance = 60 lb per ton
Grade resistance, 1.4 × 20 = −28 lb per ton

Total resistance = 32 lb per ton

Gross weight of truck, 38.4 tons

Required rimpull, 38.4 × 32 = 1,229 lb

The available rimpull in the fifth gear is 1,945 lb, which is more than will be required by the truck. Sideboards can be installed to increase the hauling capacity of the truck. The gross load should be limited to a weight that can be pulled by not over 80% of the rimpull, with the remaining rimpull reserved to accelerate the truck and to be used on sections of the haul road having a higher rolling resistance or grades less than the 1.4% negative.

Net available rimpull,	$0.8 \times 1,945$ =	1,556 lb
Required rimpull for 15 cu yd	=	1,229 lb
Surplus rimpull	=	327 lb

Possible additional load, 327 lb ÷ 32 lb per ton = 10.2 tons

Possible additional volume:

$$\frac{10.2 \text{ tons} \times 2,000 \text{ lb/ton}}{2,700 \text{ lb/cu yd}} = 7.55 \text{ cu yd}$$

In order to compensate for the additional weight of the sideboards, the volume of the earth should be increased by no more than 7 cu yd. This will give a total volume of 22 cu yd per load.

The combined effect of the rolling resistance and grade on the *empty* truck will be:

Rolling resistance	=	60 lb per ton
Grade resistance, 1.4×20	=	28 lb per ton
Total resistance	=	88 lb per ton

Weight of empty truck, including sideboards, 19 tons

Required rimpull, 19 tons $\times$ 88 lb per ton = 1,672 lb

Maximum speed of an empty truck, 32.7 mph

The time required for each operation in a round-trip cycle should be about:

Loading, 22 cu yd ÷ 312 cu yd per hour	= 0.0705 hour
Lost time in pit and accelerating, 2 min[†]	= 0.0333 hour
Travel to fill, 0.78 mi ÷ 32.7 mph	= 0.0239 hour
Dumping, turning, and accelerating, 1.5 min[†]	= 0.0250 hour
Travel to pit, 0.78 mi ÷ 32.7 mph	= 0.0239 hour
Total round-trip time	= 0.1766 hour

[†]Note 0.5 min has been added to both "lost time" and "dump, turning" to compensate for the increased load.

Assume that the trucks will operate an average of 50 min per hour:

No. of trips per hour, $\dfrac{1 \text{ hour}}{0.1766 \text{ hour}} \times \dfrac{50}{60} = 4.72$

Volume of material hauled per truck, $22 \times 4.72 = 103.8$ cu yd per hour

No. of trucks required, 312 cu yd per hour ÷ 103.8 cu yd per hour = 3.01

Use three trucks.

If a truck and driver cost $32.40 per hour, the cost of hauling the earth will be $32.40 ÷ 103.8 = $0.312 per cubic yard.

A comparison of the hauling cost for the two pits reveals the extent of savings that may be affected by using pit 2.

Hauling cost from pit 1   = $0.429 per cu yd
Hauling cost from pit 2   = $\underline{0.312 \text{ per cu yd}}$

     Difference in hauling cost   = $0.117 per cu yd

Another item that is favorable to pit 2 is the reduction in the number of trucks from four to three units.

THE EFFECT OF ROLLING RESISTANCE ON THE COST OF HAULING

An important factor which affects the production capacity of a truck or a tractor-pulled wagon is the rolling resistance of the haul road. The rolling resistance is determined primarily by two factors, the physical condition of the road and the tires used on the hauling unit. The rolling resistance can be greatly reduced by both properly maintaining the road and by properly selecting tire sizes and keeping them inflated to the correct pressure. Money spent for these purposes will return dividends, through reduced hauling costs, far in excess of the expenditures. This is one field where the application of engineering knowledge will yield excellent returns.

A haul road which is given little or no maintenance will soon become rough, loose, and soft, and may develop a rolling resistance of 150 lb per ton or more, depending on the type of material and weather conditions. If a road is properly maintained with a grader, sprinkled with water, and compacted as required, it may be possible to reduce the rolling resistance to 50 lb per ton or less. Sprinkling the road will reduce the damage to hauling equipment from dust. It will reduce the danger of vehicular collision by improving visibility and it will prolong the life of tires because of the cooling effect which the moisture has on the tires.

The selection of proper tire sizes and the practice of maintaining correct air pressure in the tires will reduce that portion of the rolling resistance due to the tires. A tire supports its load by deforming where it contacts the road surface until the area in contact with the road will produce a total force on the road equal to the load on the tire. Neglecting any supporting resistance furnished by the side walls of the tire, if the load on a tire is 5,000 lb and the air pressure is 50 psi, the area of contact will be 100 sq in. If, for the same tire, the air pressure is permitted to drop to 40 psi, the area contact will be increased to 125 sq in. The additional area of contact will be produced by additional deformation of the tire. This will increase the rolling resistance because the tire will be continually climbing a steeper grade as it rotates. The tire size selected and the inflated pressure should be based on the resistance which the surface of the road offers to penetration by the tire. For rigid road surfaces, such as concrete, small-diameter high-pressure tires will give a lower rolling resistance, whereas for soft road surfaces, large-diameter low-pressure tires will give a lower rolling resistance because the larger areas of contact will reduce the tire penetration depth.

Example 9-5. This example illustrates the effect which the rolling resistance has on the cost of hauling.

A project requires a constructor to excavate and haul 1,900,000 cu yd of common earth. The contract must be completed within 1 year. By operating three shifts, with 7 hours actual working time per shift, 6 days per week, it is estimated that there will be 5,600 working hours, allowing for lost time due to bad weather. This will require an output of approximately 350 bcy per hour, which should be obtainable with a 4-cu-yd shovel.

The job conditions are:

Length of haul, one way, 3.5 mi
Slope of haul road, minus 0.5% from borrow pit to the fill
Weight of earth in place, 2,600 lb per cu yd
Swell, 30%
Weight of loose earth, $2,600 \div 1.3 = 2,000$ lb per lcy
Elevation, 800 ft above sea level

For hauling the earth the constructor considers using rubber-tire-equipped tractor-pulled bottom-dump wagons, which may be purchased with standard or optional gears. The optional gears will permit the unit to operate at a higher speed. Specifications and performance data are:

	Standard tractor	Optional tractor
Tractor engine	150 bhp	150 bhp
Maximum speed	19.8 mph	27.4 mph
Mechanical efficiency	82%	82%
Rimpull at maximum speed	2,330 lb	1,685 lb

Heaped capacity of *standard wagon,* 32,000 lb or 16 lcy, based on 3:1 slope
Heaped capacity of *wagon with sideboard extensions, 2 ft 0 in. high,* 46,800 lb, or 23.4 lcy, based on 3:1 slope

	Standard equipment	Optional equipment
Gross weight		
Tractor and wagon	29,400 lb	29,400 lb
Sideboards	—	1,600 lb
Payload	32,000 lb	46,800 lb
Total weight	61,400 lb	77,800 lb
Gross weight, tons	30.7	38.9
Delivered cost	$36,200	$36,900
Cost per hour, including driver	$27.40	$28.80[†]

[†] The higher cost per hour for the optional equipment is due to the more severe conditions to which it will be subjected.

Standard Equipment. An analysis of the performance of the standard equipment, operating on a haul road with an estimated rolling resistance of 80 lb per ton, will give the probable hauling cost per cubic yard. This rolling resistance is representative of haul roads which are not carefully maintained.

The combined effect of the rolling resistance and grade on a loaded unit will be:

Rolling resistance	=	80 lb per ton
Grade,	-0.5×20 =	-10 lb per ton
	Total =	70 lb per ton

Gross weight of vehicle,   30.7 tons

Required rimpull, $30.7 \times 70 = 2,149$ lb

Available rimpull at 19.8 mph $= 2,330$ lb

The tractor can pull the loaded wagon, with a surplus rimpull for acceleration. The rimpull required for the return trip to the shovel will be

$$14.7 \text{ tons} \times (80 + 10) \text{ lb/ton} = 1,323 \text{ lb}$$

which will permit travel at maximum speed.

The time required for each operation in a round-trip cycle should be about:

Volume of earth per load, 16 lcy $\div$ 1.30 $= 12.3$ bcy

Loading, 12.3 bcy ÷ 350 bcy per hour	= 0.0351 hour
Lost time in pit and accelerating, 1.5 min	= 0.0250 hour
Travel to the fill, 3.5 mi ÷ 19.8 mph	= 0.1768 hour
Dumping, turning, and accelerating, 1.0 min	= 0.0167 hour
Travel to pit, 3.5 mi ÷ 19.8 mph	= 0.1768 hour
Total round-trip time	= 0.4304 hour

Assume that the wagons will operate an average of 45 min per hour:

No. of trips per hour, $\dfrac{1 \text{ hr}}{0.4304 \text{ hr}} \times \dfrac{45}{60} = 1.74$

Volume of earth hauled per wagon, 12.3 bcy $\times$ 1.74 $=$ 21.4 bcy per hour

No. of wagons required:

$$\frac{350 \text{ bcy/hr}}{21.4 \text{ bcy/hr}} = 16.4$$

It will be necessary to provide 17 wagons if the specified output is to be maintained. The actual volume of earth hauled per wagon will be

$$\frac{350 \text{ cu yd/hr}}{17 \text{ wagons}} = 20.6 \text{ cu yd/hr per wagon}$$

Hauling cost per cubic yard:

$$\frac{\$27.40}{20.6 \text{ cu yd}} = \$1.330 \text{ per cu yd}$$

Optional Equipment. Let us analyze the performance of the optional equipment to determine whether it will operate at the maximum possible speed while hauling 23.4 lcy. It will be necessary to reduce the rolling resistance of the haul road by providing continuous maintenance. This haul road maintenance will cost an additional $0.10 per cu yd hauled. While it is possible to reduce the rolling resistance to 40 lb per ton during most of the time that the project is in operation, a value of 50 lb per ton will be used in order to provide a margin of safety.

The combined effect of the rolling resistance and grade on a loaded unit will be:

Rolling resistance		=	50 lb per ton
Grade,	-0.5×20 =		-10 lb per ton
	Total	=	40 lb per ton

Gross weight of vehicle,	38.9 tons
Required rimpull,	38.9×40 = 1,556 lb
Available rimpull at 27.4 mph	= 1,685 lb

The tractor can pull the load at the maximum speed, with a surplus for acceleration. The rimpull required for the return trip to the shovel will be

$$15.5 \text{ tons} \times (50 + 10) \text{ lb/ton} = 930 \text{ lb}$$

which will permit travel at maximum speed.

The time required for each operation in a round-trip cycle should be about:

Volume of earth per load, 23.4 lcy ÷ 1.30 = 18.0 bcy

Loading, 18 bcy ÷ 350 bcy per hour	= 0.0515 hour
Lost time in pit and accelerating, 2 min[†]	= 0.0333 hour
Travel to the fill, 3.5 mi ÷ 27.4 mph	= 0.1277 hour
Dumping, turning, and accelerating, 1.5 min[†]	= 0.0250 hour
Travel to pit, 3.5 mi ÷ 27.4 mph	= 0.1277 hour
Total round-trip time	= 0.3652 hour

[†] Note 0.5 min has been added to compensate for the increased load.

Assume that the wagons will operate an average of 45 min per hour.

No. of trips per hour, $\dfrac{1 \text{ hr}}{0.3652 \text{ hr}} \times \dfrac{45}{60} = 2.05$

Volume of earth hauled per wagon, 18 bcy × 2.05 = 36.9 bcy per hour

No. of wagons required:

$$\frac{350 \text{ bcy/hr}}{36.9 \text{ bcy/hr}} = 9.52$$

It will be necessary to provide 10 wagons if the specified output is to be maintained. The actual volume of earth hauled per hour per wagon will be 350 ÷ 10 = 35 cu yd:

Hauling cost per cubic yard, $28.80 ÷ 35 cu yd	= $0.825 per cu yd
Plus haul road maintenance	= 0.100 per cu yd
Total	= $0.925 per cu yd

The reduction in the cost of hauling the earth with the optional equipment will be:

Cost using standard equipment   = $1.330 per cu yd
Cost using optional equipment   = 0.925 per cu yd

Reduction in cost   = $0.405 per cu yd

Total reduction for project, 1,900,000 × $0.405 = $769,500

The reduction in the hauling cost and in the amount of money invested in hauling equipment resulting from the improvement in the rolling resistance of the haul road illustrates the value of analyzing a project. Although the reduction may appear to be unreasonably large, it is possible to produce similar results for many projects involving material hauling. Even the cost of paving the haul road can be justified in some situations.

Most manufacturers of trucks and tractor-pulled wagons can furnish units with standard or optional gears. For equipment already in service the standard gears may be replaced with optional gears at reasonable costs. Sideboards may be purchased from the equipment manufacturer, or they may be made locally in a machine shop.

Example 9-6. The effect of the rolling resistance on the performance of equipment and the cost of hauling earth is further illustrated in Table 9-4. The information given in the table is based on using the optional tractor-pulled wagons of the previous analysis, an output of 350 bcy of earth per hour, a one-way haul distance of 3.5 mi, and a level haul road. If the haul road is not level, similar information may be obtained by combining the effect of the rolling resistance and grade.

The speeds and rimpulls of the hauling units are:

Gear	Speed (mph)	Rimpull (lb)
First	4.1	11,250
Second	6.5	7,120
Third	10.6	4,360
Fourth	17.0	2,720
Fifth	27.4	1,685

TABLE 9-4
The effect of rolling resistance on hauling cost

Item	Rolling resistance (lb/ton)			
	40	60	100	150
Maximum speed loaded (mph)	27.4	17.0	10.6	6.5
Maximum speed empty (mph)	27.4	27.4	27.4	17.0
Number of trucks required	10	12	15	22
Cost of trucks required	$288.00	$345.60	$518.40	$633.60
Volume of material hauled per hr (cu yd)	350	350	350	350
Hauling cost per cu yd	$0.822	$0.987	$1.481	$1.810

The following sample calculations will show how the information given in Table 9-4 is obtained. Consider a haul road with a rolling resistance of 100 lb per ton.

Gross weight of loaded unit, 38.9 tons

Weight of empty unit, 15.5 tons

Required rimpull for loaded unit, $38.9 \times 100 = 3,890$ lb

Maximum speed, 10.6 mph

Required rimpull for empty unit, $15.5 \times 100 = 1,550$ lb

Maximum speed, 27.4 mph

The round-trip time will include fixed time, which should be reasonably constant regardless of the condition of the haul road, plus the travel time to and from the fill.

The fixed time will be:

Loading, 18 cu yd ÷ 350 cu yd per hour	= 0.0514 hour
Lost time in pit and accelerating, 2 min	= 0.0333 hour
Dumping, turning, and accelerating, 1.5 min	= 0.0250 hour
Total fixed time	= 0.1097 hour
Travel to the fill, 3.5 mi ÷ 10.6 mph	= 0.3302 hour
Travel to shovel, 3.5 mi ÷ 27.4	= 0.1277 hour
Total round-trip time	= 0.5676 hour

Trips per 45-min hour, $\dfrac{1 \text{ hr}}{0.5676 \text{ hr}} \times \dfrac{45}{60} = 1.32$

Volume per wagon, $\qquad 18 \times 1.32 = 23.78$ cu yd per hour

No. of wagons required, $\qquad 350 \div 23.78 = 14.7$, use 15

Actual volume per wagon, $\qquad 350 \div 15 = 23.3$ cu yd per hour

Hauling cost per cubic yard, $28.80 \div 23.3 = \$1.236$ per cu yd

THE EFFECT OF ALTITUDE ON THE PERFORMANCE OF HAULING EQUIPMENT

Constructors who have established satisfactory production rates for hauling equipment at one altitude frequently find it desirable to bid on a project located at a different altitude. Unless an adjustment is made for the performance of the equipment at the higher altitude, it is possible that a substantial error may be made in estimating the cost of hauling. As previously discussed, the effect of altitude is to reduce the sea-level power of 4-cycle internal-combustion engines by approximately 3% for each additional 1,000 ft of altitude above 1,000 ft unless a supercharger is installed on the engine. Power losses of this magnitude are too large to ignore in analyzing a project for bid purposes.

Example 9-7. This example illustrates the effect of altitude on the performance of hauling equipment and the cost of hauling.

The job conditions are as follows:

Weight of earth, 2,700 lb per bcy
Swell, 25%
Weight of loose earth

$$\frac{2,700 \text{ lb/bcy}}{1.25} = 2,160 \text{ lb/lcy}$$

Haul distance, 1.5 mi, over level road
Rolling resistance, 50 lb per ton

The earth will be excavated with a shovel, whose output will be 280 bcy per hour.

The specifications for the hauling units are as follows:

Type, tractor-pulled bottom-dump wagons
Tractor engine, 200 bhp
Wagon capacity, 16 cu yd heaped volume

Wagon capacity:

$$\frac{16 \text{ lcy heaped}}{1.25} = 12.8 \text{ bcy}$$

Weight of tractor and wagon   = 36,800 lb
Weight of load, 16 lcy @ 2,160 lb = 34,560 lb

Gross loaded weight   = 71,360 lb, or 35.68 tons

Cost per hour, including operator, $31.60

Tractor performance data at sea level

Gear	Speed (mph)	Rimpull (lb)
First	3.0	20,250
Second	5.8	10,450
Third	11.1	5,520
Fourth	19.4	3,130
Fifth	30.5	1,990

Compare the performance of a hauling unit at sea level with its performance at 5,000 ft above sea level, all other conditions remaining constant.

Performance at sea level:

Required rimpull for loaded unit, $35.68 \times 50 = 1,784$ lb
Maximum speed loaded, 30.5 mph
Maximum speed empty, 30.5 mph

The probable round-trip time should be:

Loading, 12.8 bcy ÷ 280 bcy per hour = 0.0458 hour
Lost time in pit and accelerating, 1.5 min = 0.0250 hour
Travel to the fill, 1.5 mi ÷ 30.5 mph = 0.0493 hour
Dumping, turning, and accelerating, 1.5 min = 0.0250 hour
Travel to pit, 1.5 mi ÷ 30.5 mph = 0.0493 hour

Total round-trip time = 0.1944 hour

Assume that units will operate an average of 45 min per hour:

No. of trips per hour, $\dfrac{1 \text{ hour}}{0.1944 \text{ hour}} \times \dfrac{45}{60} = 3.86$

Volume per hour, $12.8 \times 3.86 = 49.5$ bcy

No. units required:

$$\frac{280 \text{ bcy/hr}}{49.5 \text{ bcy/hr}} = 5.7$$

It will be necessary to use six units.

Volume hauled per unit:

$$\frac{280 \text{ bcy/hr}}{6 \text{ units}} = 46.7 \text{ bcy/hr per unit}$$

Hauling cost per bcy:

$$\frac{\$31.60}{46.7 \text{ bcy/hr}} = \$0.677$$

Performance at 5,000-ft elevation:

Loss in available rimpull, $\dfrac{0.03(5,000 - 1,000)}{1,000} \times 100 = 12\%$

Correction factor for rimpull at 5,000 ft, 0.88

Available rimpull

Gear	Speed (mph)	Rimpull at sea level (lb)	Rimpull at 5,000 ft (lb)
First	3.0	20,250	17,820
Second	5.8	10,450	9,196
Third	11.1	5,520	4,620
Fourth	19.4	3,130	2,772
Fifth	30.5	1,990	1,751

Required rimpull for loaded unit, 1,784 lb
Maximum speed loaded, 19.4 mph
Required rimpull empty, $15.5 \times 50 = 775$ lb
Maximum speed empty, 30.5 mph

The probable round-trip time should be:

Loading, 12.8 bcy ÷ 280 bcy per hour	= 0.0458 hour
Lost time in pit and accelerating, 1.5 min	= 0.0250 hour
Travel to the fill, 1.5 mi ÷ 19.4 mph	= 0.0773 hour
Dumping, turning, and accelerating, 1.5 min	= 0.0250 hour
Travel to pit, 1.5 mi ÷ 30.5 mph	= 0.0493 hour
Total round-trip time	= 0.2224 hour

No. of trips per hour, $\dfrac{1}{0.2224} \times \dfrac{45}{60} = 3.37$

Volume per hour, $12.8 \times 3.37 = 43.1$ bcy
No. of units required, $280 \div 43.1 = 6.5$

It will be necessary to use seven units.

Volume hauled per unit, $280 \div 7 = 40$ bcy per hour

Hauling cost per bcy, $31.60 ÷ 40 = \$0.790$

PROBLEMS

9-1. A truck for which the information in Fig. 9-6 applies operates over a haul road with a +4% slope and a rolling resistance of 90 lb per ton. If the gross vehicle weight is 70,000 lb, determine the maximum speed of the truck.

9-2. If the truck of Prob. 9-1 operates on a haul road having a −4% slope, determine the maximum speed.

9-3. Prepare a table similar to Table 9-1, using a $1\frac{1}{2}$-cu-yd shovel whose adjusted production will be 160 cu yd per hour, and 6-, 10-, 15-cu-yd size trucks. Assume a 21-sec bucket cycle time and that the number of buckets required to fill a truck will equal the capacity of the truck divided by the size of the bucket, both expressed in cubic yards (no consideration of swell). Assume that the time for a travel cycle, *excluding the time for loading,* will be the same for the several sizes of trucks considered. The time for a travel cycle, which includes traveling to the dump, dumping, and returning to the shovel, will be 6 min.

9-4. A 2-cu-yd shovel will be used to load common earth into trucks whose capacities are 15.0 bcy. Determine the number of trucks required to haul the earth for the following conditions:

For the shovel:
Ideal output, 300 cu yd per hour
Height of dig, 12 ft
Optimum digging height, 10.2 ft
Angle of swing, 90°
Operating efficiency is equal to a 45-min hour

For the trucks:
Weight of earth, 2,900 lb per bcy
Empty weight of truck, 34,820 lb
Performance chart of Fig. 9-6 applies.
Assume that the time at the dump will be 1.75 min.
Rolling resistance of the haul road, 80 lb per ton
Distance to dump, 1 mi of minus 2% slope and $\frac{3}{4}$
mi of plus 4% slope.

Assume the operating conditions limit the average speed of the trucks to 75% of the maximum possible speed.

CHAPTER
10

COMPACTION AND SOIL STABILIZATION

INTRODUCTION

Soils are the principal component of many construction projects. They are used to support structures, static load; to support pavements for highways and airport runways, dynamic loads; and in dams and levees, as impoundments, to resist the passage of water. Some soils may be suitable for use in their natural state, whereas others must be excavated, processed, and compacted in order to serve their purposes.

A knowledge of the properties, characteristics, and behavior of different soil types is important to those persons who are associated with the design or construction of projects involving the use of soils. A great deal of useful knowledge related to the properties and characteristics of soils has been developed since 1933 when R. R. Proctor initiated a scientific study to determine the density-moisture relationship of soils. His original methods or modifications thereof are still used in construction to specify the placement and compaction criteria of soils.

GLOSSARY OF TERMS

The following glossary defines the important terms that are used in discussing compaction and stabilization.

AASHTO. American Association of State Highway and Transportation Officials.

Aggregate, coarse. Crushed rock or gravel, generally greater than $\frac{1}{4}$ in. in size.

Aggregate, fine. The sand or fine crushed stone used for filling voids in coarse aggregate. Generally, less than $\frac{1}{4}$ in. and greater than the No. 200 sieve in size.

ASTM. American Society for Testing and Materials.

Backfill. The material used in refilling a cut or other excavation.

Bank. A mass of soil rising above an average level, or any soil which is excavated from its original position.

Bank measure. A measure of the volume of earth in its natural position before it is excavated.

Base. The layer of material in a roadway or runway section on which the pavement is placed.

Binder. Fine aggregate or other materials which fill voids and hold coarse aggregate together.

Borrow pit. An excavation from which fill material is excavated.

Cohesion. The quality of some soil particles to be attracted to like particles, manifested in a tendency to stick together, as in clay.

Cohesive materials. A soil having properties of cohesion.

Compacted volume. A measurement of the volume of a soil after it has been subjected to compaction.

Core. The impervious portion of an embankment, such as a dam.

Density. The ratio of the weight of a material to its volume.

Embankment. A fill whose top is higher than the adjoining natural ground.

Fines. Soil whose particles are smaller in size than the No. 200 sieve.

Grain-size curve. A graph of the analysis of a soil showing the percentage of sizes by weight.

Granular material. A soil, such as sand, whose particle sizes and shapes are such that they do not stick together.

Impervious. A material that resists the flow of water through it.

In situ. Soil in its original or undisturbed position.

Lift. A layer of soil placed on top of soil previously placed in an embankment.

Liquid limit (LL). The water content, expressed as a percent of the weight of water to the dry weight of the soil, at which the soil passes from a plastic to a liquid state.

Optimum moisture content. The water content at which the greatest density of a soil can be obtained at a given compactive effort.

Pavement. A layer of rigid surfacing material, usually asphalt or concrete, above the base which provides high bending resistance and distributes loads to the base over a comparatively large area.

Pass. A working trip or passage of an excavating, grading, or compaction machine.

Plastic limit (PL). The lowest water content, expressed as a percent of the weight of water to the dry weight of the soil, at which the soil remains in a plastic state.

Plasticity. The capability of being molded; does not assume original shape after force causing the deformation is removed.

Plasticity index (PI). The numerical difference between a soil's liquid limit water content and its plastic-state water content.

Proctor, or Proctor test. A method developed by R. R. Proctor for determining the moisture-density relationship of soils subjected to compaction.

Proctor, modified. A moisture-density test involving a higher compactive effort than the standard Proctor test.

Rock. The hard, mineral matter of the earth's crust, occurring in masses and often requiring blasting to be broken up before excavation in the field.

Soil. The loose surface material of the earth's crust, created naturally from the disintegration of rocks or the decay of vegetation, that can be excavated easily using power equipment in the field.

Stabilize. To make a soil stronger, to increase its strength and stiffness, and to decrease its sensitivity to volume changes with changes in moisture content.

Subbase. The layer of selected material placed to furnish strength to the base of a road. In areas where the construction goes through marshy, swampy, unstable land it is often necessary to excavate the natural materials in the areas of the roadway and to replace them with more stable materials. The material used to replace the unsuitable natural soils is generally called subbase material, and when compacted it is known as the subbase.

Subgrade. The surface produced by grading native earth, or imported materials which serve as the foundation layer for a paving structural section.

Surface layer. The top layer of a road, street, parking lot, runway, etc., that covers and protects the sublayers from the action of traffic and weather. If the layer has structural strength properties, it is often referred to as a pavement layer.

PROPERTIES OF SOILS

Before discussing earth-handling techniques or analyzing problems involving earthwork, it is necessary to become familiar with some of the physical properties of soils. These properties have a direct effect on the ease or difficulty of handling the material, on the selection of equipment, and on production rates.

Types of soils. Soils may be classified according to the sizes of the particles of which they are composed, by their physical properties, or by their behavior when the moisture content varies.

A constructor is concerned primarily with five types of soils: gravel, sand, silt, clay, organic matter, and combinations of these types. Different agencies and specification groups denote the sizes of these types of soil differently, causing some confusion. The following size limits represent those set forth by ASTM:

Gravel is rounded or semiround particles of rock that will pass a 3-in. and be retained on a 2.0-mm No. 10 sieve. Sizes larger than 10 in. are usually called boulders.

Sand is disintegrated rock whose particles vary in size from the lower limit of gravel 2.0 mm down to 0.074 mm (No. 200 sieve). It may be classified as coarse or fine sand, depending on the sizes of the grains. Sand is a granular noncohesive material.

Silt is a material finer than sand, and thus its particles are smaller than 0.074 mm but larger than 0.005 mm. It is a noncohesive material that has little or no strength. It compacts very poorly.

Clay is a cohesive material whose particles are less than 0.005 mm. The cohesion between the particles gives a clay high strength when air-dried. Clay can be subject to considerable changes in volume with variations in moisture content. They will exhibit plasticity within a range of "water contents."

Organic matter is a partly decomposed vegetable matter. It has a spongy, unstable structure that will continue to decompose and is chemically reactive. If present in soil that is used for construction purposes, organic matter should be removed and replaced with a more suitable soil.

Soils existing under natural conditions may not contain the relative amounts of desired types to produce the properties required for construction purposes. For this reason it may be necessary to obtain soils from several sources and then to blend them for use in a fill.

If the material in a borrow pit consists of layers of different types of soils, the specifications for the project may require the use of excavating equipment that will dig vertically through the layers in order to mix the soil.

Soil tests. Before the specifications for a project are prepared, representative soil samples are usually collected and tested in the laboratory to determine material properties. Normal testing would include grain-size analysis because the size of the grains and the distribution of those sizes are important properties which affect a soil's suitability. Another critical test is the construction of a compaction curve. From such curves the maximum dry unit weight (density) and the percent water required to achieve maximum density can be determined. This percent of water, which corresponds to the maximum dry density (for a given compactive effort), is known as the *optimum water content*.

Figure 10-1 shows compaction curves which illustrate the effect of varying amounts of moisture on the density of a soil subjected to given compactive efforts. The two energy levels depicted are known as standard and modified Proctor tests. It should be noted that the modified Proctor, which is a higher energy level, gives a higher density at a lower moisture content than the standard Proctor. In this example, the optimum moisture for the standard Proctor is 16%, versus 12% for the modified Proctor.

Compaction tests. The laboratory compaction test that is accepted by many highway departments and other agencies is the Proctor test. For this test a sample of soil consisting of $\frac{1}{4}$ in. and finer material is used. The sample is placed in a steel mold in three equal layers. The cylindrical steel mold has an inside diameter of 4.0 in. and a height of 4.59 in. In the standard test each layer is compacted by dropping a 5.5-lb rammer, with a 2-in. circular base, 25 times from a height of 12 in. above the specimen. The specimen is removed from the mold and the entire specimen is immediately weighed. Then a sample of the specimen is taken and weighed. That sample is dried to a constant weight to remove all moisture and weighed again to determine the water content. With this water content information, the dry weight can be determined. The test is repeated, using

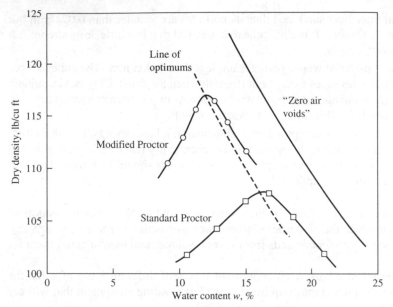

FIGURE 10-1
Standard and modified compaction curves.

varying water content specimens, until the water content that produces the maximum density is determined. This test is designated as ASTM D-698 or AASHTO T 99.

The modified Proctor test, designated as ASTM D-1557 or AASHTO T 180, is performed in a similar manner, except that the applied energy is greater because a 10-lb rammer is dropped 18 in. on each of five equal layers.

Compaction control. The specifications for a project may require a contractor to compact the soil to a 100% relative density, based on the standard Proctor test or a laboratory test at some other energy level. If the maximum laboratory density of the soil is determined to be 120 lb per cu ft, the contractor must compact the soil to a density of 120 lb per cu ft.

Field verification tests of achieved compaction can be conducted by any of several accepted methods: sandcone, balloon, or nuclear. The first two methods are destructive tests. They involve excavating a hole in the compacted fill and weighing the excavated material, determining the water content of the excavated material, measuring the volume of the resulting hole by the use of the sandcone or a water-filled balloon, and finally computing the density based on the obtained total weight of the excavated material and the volume of the hole. The dry density conversion can be made because the water content is known. Problems associated with such methods are: (1) too time-consuming to conduct sufficient tests for statistical analysis, (2) problems with oversized particles, and (3) the determination of the water content takes time. Because the tests are usually conducted on each placement lift, delays in testing and acceptance can delay construction operations.

FIGURE 10-2
Nuclear gauge for density and water content. (*Troxler Electronic Laboratories, Inc.*)

Nuclear compaction test. Nuclear methods are used extensively to determine the water content and density of soils. The instrument required for this test can be easily transported to the fill, placed at the desired test location, and within a few minutes the results can be read directly from the digital display (see Fig. 10-2).

The device utilizes the Compton effect of gamma-ray scattering for density determinations and hydrogenous thermalization of fast neutrons for moisture determinations. The emitted rays enter the ground, where they are partially absorbed and partially reflected. Reflected rays pass through Geiger-Müller tubes in the surface gauge. Counts per minute are read directly on a reflected-ray countergauge and related to moisture and density calibration curves.

Advantages of the nuclear method when compared with other methods include the following:

1. Decreases the time required for a test from as much as a day to a few minutes, thereby eliminating potentially excessive construction delays.
2. Is nondestructive in that it does not require the removal of soil samples from the site of the tests.
3. Provides a means of performing density tests on soils containing large-sized aggregates and on frozen materials.
4. Reduces or eliminates the effect of the personal element, and possible errors. Erratic results can be easily and quickly rechecked.

Because nuclear tests are conducted with instruments that present a potential source of radiation, an operator should exercise care to ensure that no harm can result from the use of the instruments. However, by following the instructions furnished with the instruments and by exercising proper care, exposure can be kept well below the limits set by the Nuclear Regulatory Commission (NRC). In the United States and in most individual states a license is required to own, possess, or use nuclear-type instruments.

Laboratory versus field. Maximum dry density is only a maximum for a specific compaction effort (input energy level) and the method by which that effort is applied. If more energy is applied in the field, a density greater than 100% of the laboratory value can be achieved. Dissimilar materials have individual curves and maximum values for the same input energy (see Fig. 10-3). Well-graded sands have a higher dry density

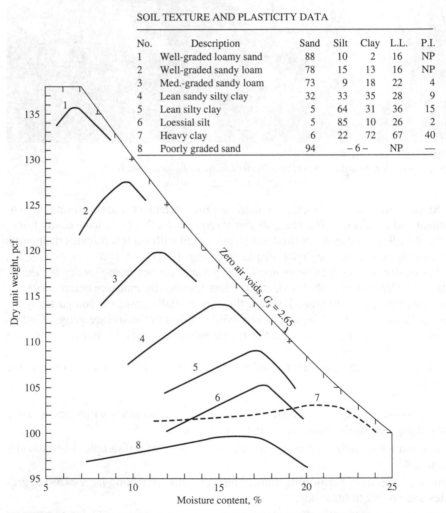

SOIL TEXTURE AND PLASTICITY DATA

No.	Description	Sand	Silt	Clay	L.L.	P.I.
1	Well-graded loamy sand	88	10	2	16	NP
2	Well-graded sandy loam	78	15	13	16	NP
3	Med.-graded sandy loam	73	9	18	22	4
4	Lean sandy silty clay	32	33	35	28	9
5	Lean silty clay	5	64	31	36	15
6	Loessial silt	5	85	10	26	2
7	Heavy clay	6	22	72	67	40
8	Poorly graded sand	94	– 6 –		NP	—

FIGURE 10-3
Compaction curves for eight soils compacted according to AASHTO T99. (Highway Research Board) [6]

than uniform soils. As plasticity increases, the dry density of clay soil decreases. It should be noted that at some point higher moisture contents result in decreased density. This is because initially the water serves to "lubricate" the soil grains and helps the mechanical compaction operation to move them into a compact physical arrangement. But the density of water is less than that of the soil solids and at water contents above optimum, water is replacing soil grains in the matrix. If compaction is attempted at a water content that is much above optimum, no amount of effort will overcome these physical facts. Under such conditions extra compactive effort will be wasted work. In fact soils can be "overcompacted." Shear planes are established and there is a large reduction in strength.

COMPACTION

SOIL COMPACTION

Engineering properties of soils can be improved by compaction. Compaction can:

Reduce or prevent settlements
Increase strength
Improve bearing capacity
Control volume changes
Lower permeability

Because there is a correlation between these properties and dry density, construction documents usually call for achieving a specified density. There may be other methods whereby the desired properties can be attained, but by far the most widely used method of soil strengthening for use as a subgrade under a pavement structure or other foundation is compaction of the soil at optimum moisture. The benefits of proper compaction are enormous, far outweighing their costs. Typically, a uniform layer, or lift, of soil from 4 to 12 in. thick is compacted by means of several passes of heavy mechanized compaction equipment. In terms of strength an often overlooked fact is that the denser the soil is compacted, the better it will perform in service. Of course, compaction costs money, and an owner is interested in achieving the most economical construction that will perform as intended. The constructor is concerned with meeting the specifications. What is altogether too often overlooked is the intended purpose and the increased benefits to be derived by obtaining greater densification.

Specifications governing compaction may be one of the following types:

1. Method only (often termed "recipe")
2. End result only (often termed "performance")
3. Method and end result

Method only specifications. If the specifications for a project direct the constructor to place the soil in lifts of a specified depth, with the soil having a specified moisture content, with the provision that a specified type of roller having a specified weight is to be used to compact the soil by making a specified number of passes over each lift, the constructor will have no choice except to comply with the requirements of the specifications. If the owner prescribes this type of specifications, he assumes responsibility for the results.

End result only specifications. If the specifications dictate that the soil shall be compacted to 95% relative density, based on the modified Proctor test, such a specification would be "end result." Several states and agencies are moving toward a policy of using this type of specification. The argument for the use of this policy is that the owner is interested primarily or solely in the end result. Unless there are justified reasons for prescribing the methods to be used, the constructor should be permitted to select his own methods, which may be substantially less expensive than other prescribed methods.

Methods and end results specifications. For most projects this is not a satisfactory specification. Unless extensive predesign tests have been performed on soil samples, which eliminate the possibility of the soil behaving differently than expected, it is probable that a specified method of compacting the soil will result in excessive costs because compacting operations will continue after adequate compaction is attained. Another result may be that compaction operations are discontinued before adequate density is attained. For these specifications the contractor should not be held responsible for the end results.

A further objection to the use of this type of specification is that it may not permit a constructor to make use of methods which he has found to be economical and effective. Thus, the use of this type of specification may result in an unnecessarily high cost for the project.

TYPES OF COMPACTING EQUIPMENT

Compaction is attained by applying energy to a soil by one or more of the following methods:

1. Kneading
2. Static weight
3. Vibration
4. Impact
5. Explosives

Many types of compacting equipment are available, including:

1. Tamping rollers
2. Modified tamping rollers
3. Smooth-wheel rollers
4. Pneumatic-tired rollers
5. Vibrating compactors, including tamping, smooth-wheel, and pneumatic

TABLE 10-1
Types of equipment suited for compacting soils

Type of compactor	Soil best suited for	Maximum effect in loose lift (in.)	Density gained in lift	Maximum weight (tons)
Sheep's foot	Clay, silty clay, gravel with clay binder	7–12	Nearly uniform	20
Steel tandem two-axle	Sandy silts, most granular material with some clay binder	4–8	Average[†]	16
Steel tandem three-axle	Same as above	4–8	Average[†]	20
Steel three-wheel	Granular or granular-plastic material	4–8	Average[†] to uniform	20
Pneumatic, small-tire	Sandy silts, sandy clays, gravelly sand and clays with few fines	4–8	Average[†] to uniform	12
Pneumatic large-tire	All types	?–24	Uniform	50
Vibratory	Sand, silty sands, silty gravels	3–6	Uniform	30

[†] The density may decrease with depth.

6. Manually propelled vibrating plates

7. Manually propelled compactors

Table 10-1 summarizes the types of equipment suited for compacting soils. On some projects it may be desirable to use more than one type of equipment to attain the desired results and to achieve the greatest economy.

Tamping rollers. Tamping rollers (see Fig. 10-4) are of the sheep's-foot type or modifications thereof. This roller, which may be towed by a tractor or self-propelled, consists of a hollow steel drum on whose outer surface a number of projecting steel feet are welded. The feet on individual rollers may be of varying lengths and cross sections. A unit may consist of one or several drums mounted on one or more horizontal axles. The weight of a drum may be varied by adding water or sand to produce unit pressures under the feet up to 750 psi or more.

As a tamping roller moves over the surface, the feet penetrate the soil to produce a kneading action and a pressure to mix and compact the soil from the bottom to the top of the layer. With repeated passages of the roller over the surface, the penetration of the feet decreases until the roller is said to "walk out" of the fill. If it does not walk out, the roller is too heavy or the soil is too wet and the roller is shearing the soil.

The specifications may prescribe one of the following as a means of attaining the desired compaction:

1. The *number of passes* of a roller, producing a specified unit pressure under the feet, over each layer of soil

FIGURE 10-4
Self-propelled tamping roller with blade.

2. Repeated passes of a roller, producing a specified unit pressure under the feet, over each layer of soil *until the penetration of the feet does not exceed a stated depth*
3. Repeated passes of a roller over each layer until the soil is compacted to *a specified density*

These rollers are quite effective in compacting clays and mixtures of sand and clay. However, they cannot compact granular soils such as sand and gravel. The depth of a layer of soil to be compacted is limited to approximately the foot length of the tamping feet.

Modified tamping rollers. A modification of the tamping roller, designated as a grid roller, is illustrated in Fig. 10-5. When this roller is ballasted with concrete blocks, it is capable of producing very high soil pressures, and when it is used to compact soil containing rocks, the high concentration of pressure on rocks projecting above the surface of the soil is effective in shattering the rocks and forcing the broken pieces into the soil to produce a relatively smooth surface.

Smooth-wheel rollers. These rollers may be classified by type or by weight. A diesel-powered dual-drum self-propelled roller is shown in Fig. 10-6. Note that the front wheel is used for steering, whereas the rear wheel is powered for driving.

FIGURE 10-5
Tractor-pulled ballasted grid roller. (*Hyster Company.*)

Smooth-wheel rollers may be classified by weight, which is usually stated in tons. The rolls are steel drums, which may be ballasted with water or sand to increase the unit's weight. If a machine is designated as 8–14 tons, it means that the minimum weight of the machine is 8 tons and that it can be ballasted to give a maximum weight of 14 tons.

Specifications governing these rollers may be of two types: one type simply designating the weight and the other type designating the weight per linear inch of drum, such as 300 lb per in. of roller width. Specifying only weight does not necessarily indicate the compressive pressure under the wheels. Specifying the minimum weight per linear inch of width is a more definitive method.

When compacting cohesive soils, these rollers tend to form a crust over the surface, which may prevent adequate compaction in the lower portions of a lift. However, these rollers are effective in compacting granular soils, such as sand, gravel, and crushed stone. They are effective in smoothing surfaces of soils that have been compacted by tamping rollers.

Pneumatic-tired rollers. These are surface rollers which apply the principle of kneading action to effect compaction below the surface. They may be self-propelled or towed. They may be small- (see Fig. 10-7) or large-tired units.

The small-tired units usually have two tandem axles with four to nine tires on each axle. The rear tires are spaced to travel over the surfaces between the front tires, which produces a complete coverage of the surface. The wheels may be mounted in a manner that will give them a wobbly wheel effect to increase the kneading action of the soil. Usually, by adding ballast the weight of a unit may be varied to suit the material being compacted.

Large-tired rollers are available in sizes varying from 15 to 200 tons gross weight (see Fig. 10-8). They utilize two or more big earth-moving tires on a single axle. The

FIGURE 10-6
Smooth-wheel roller, diesel powered. (*Ferguson Manufacturing and Equipment Co., Inc.*)

FIGURE 10-7
Self-propelled pneumatic roller. (*Ferguson Manufacturing and Equipment Co., Inc.*)

FIGURE 10-8
Fifty-ton pneumatic roller being used to proof roll a roadway subgrade.

air pressure in the tires may vary from 80 to 150 psi (pounds per square inch). Because of the heavy loads and high tire pressures, they are capable of compacting all types of soils to greater depths. These units are frequently used to proof roll roadway subgrades and airfield bases, and on earth-fill dams.

Because the area of contact between a tire and the ground surface over which it passes varies with the air pressure in the tire, specifying the total weight or the weight per wheel is not necessarily a satisfactory method of indicating the compacting ability of a pneumatic roller. Four parameters must be known to determine the compacting ability of pneumatic rollers:

1. Wheel load
2. Tire size
3. Tire ply
4. Inflation pressure

Table 10-2 illustrates the effect of gross vehicle weight and tire inflation pressure on the ground contact pressure and the load per inch of tire width.

Figure 10-9 illustrates a graphical method of determining the ground contact pressure for a 7.50 × 15 14-ply smooth compactor tire subjected to varying loads and in-

TABLE 10-2
Effect of variations in gross weight and tire inflation pressure on ground contact pressure

Gross weight (lb)		7,650		15,300		22,500		25,000	
Tire size	Inflation pressure (psi)	Ground contact pressure							
		psi[†]	pli[‡]	psi	pli	psi	pli	psi	pli
7.50 × 15	35	33	125	39	237	44	333	46	369
4 or 6 ply	45	38	127	45	241	50	338	51	374
	55	44	129	50	243	55	341	57	377
	60	46	131	53	245	58	344	61	380
7.50 × 15	50	43	145	50	250	56	342	58	378
10 ply	60	47	152	54	254	60	347	62	382
	70	50	162	58	258	64	350	66	385
	80	54	175	62	264	68	354	70	389
	90	58	183	65	272	71	359	74	392
7.50 × 15	50	43	153	50	250	57	343	59	378
12 ply	60	47	164	55	256	61	347	64	383
	70	51	170	59	264	66	351	68	386
	80	55	184	62	270	70	357	72	392
	90	58	202	66	276	73	364	76	397
	100	62	218	69	289	76	369	79	402
	110	65	224	72	293	79	375	82	406
7.50 × 15	50	47	158	57	253	63	348	65	385
14 ply	60	50	170	59	260	67	353	68	389
	70	52	181	62	268	69	358	72	394
	80	55	192	65	276	73	365	75	399
	90	57	210	68	281	76	370	78	405
	100	61	225	71	290	79	377	82	408
	110	65	230	75	293	83	385	85	417
	120	68	239	79	301	87	391	89	423
	130	71	243	82	318	90	400	93	431

[†] Ground contact pressure in psi.
[‡] Ground contact pressure in lbs per in. of tire width.
Source: Firestone Tire and Rubber Company.

flated to varying air pressures. Similar information is available from tire manufacturers for other tire sizes and loads.

As indicated by the dashed lines in Fig. 10-9, a wheel load of 4,000 lb and an inflation pressure of 90 psi gives a ground contact pressure of 86 psi. The contact area for the tire will be 4,000 lb ÷ 86 psi = 46.5 sq in. not accounting for sidewall stiffness.

Pressure bulb theory of load distribution. This theory is related to the distribution of a load, and thus to the unit soil pressure when the load is applied to the soil through a circular object. Because the contact area between a tire and the ground approximates a circle, the theory can be applied to pressures in the soil under tires with slight modifi-

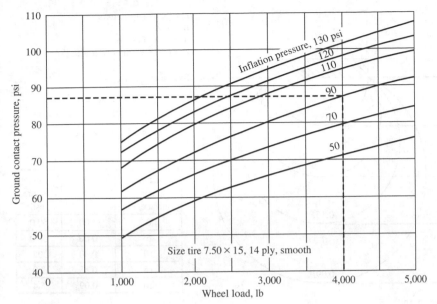

FIGURE 10-9
Ground pressure at varying wheel loads and air pressures.

cations. Figure 10-10 illustrates the ratios of unit pressures to ground contact pressure at varying depths below the surface of the ground.

Pneumatic-tire rollers with variable inflation pressures. When a pneumatic-tired roller is used to compact soil through all stages, the first passes over a lift should be made with relatively low tire pressures to increase flotation and ground coverage. However, as the soil is compacted, the air pressure in the tires should be increased up to the maximum specified value for the final pass. Prior to the development of rollers having the capability of varying their tire pressure while in operation, it was necessary either to stop the rolling and (1) adjust the pressure in the tires, (2) vary the weight of the ballast on the roller, or (3) keep rollers of different weights and tire pressures on a project in order to provide units to fit the particular needs of a given compaction condition.

Several manufacturers produce rollers that are equipped to permit the operator to vary the tire pressure without stopping the machine. The first passes are made with relatively low tire pressures. As the soil is compacted, the tire pressure is increased to suit the particular conditions of the soil. The use of this type of roller usually permits adequate compaction in less time than required by constant pressure rollers.

Vibrating compactors. Certain types of soils such as sand, gravel, and relatively large shot rock respond quite well to compaction produced by a combination of pressure and vibration. When these materials are vibrated, the particles shift their positions and nestle more closely with adjacent particles to increase the density of the mass.

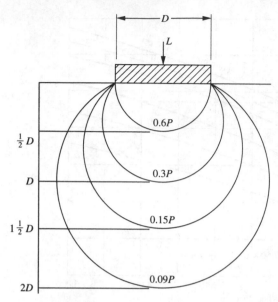

D = diameter of circle
L = load
A = area of circle
P = unit pressure under area

Example: $D = 10$ in.
$A = 78.5$ sq in.
$L = 4,710$ lb
$P = \dfrac{4,710}{78.5} = 60$ psi

Distance under surface, in.	Factor	Soil pressure, psi
0	1.00	60.0
5	0.60	36.0
10	0.30	30.0
15	0.15	9.0
20	0.09	5.4

FIGURE 10-10
Variations in pressure with depth under a load.

Several types of compactors have demonstrated their abilities to produce excellent densification of these soils. They include:

1. Vibrating padded drum rollers (see Fig. 10-11)
2. Vibrating steel-drum rollers (see Fig. 10-12)
3. Vibrating pneumatic-tired rollers

In order to rate vibratory compactors, four parameters must be known:

1. Unsprung drum weight
2. Rated dynamic force
3. Frequency at which the rated dynamic force is developed
4. Drum width

Vibrating padded drum, steel-drum, pad-type, and pneumatic-tired rollers are actuated by an eccentric shaft which produces the vibratory action. The eccentric shaft needs to be only a body which rotates about an axis other than the one through the center of mass. The vibrating mass (drum) is always isolated from the main frame of the roller. Vibrations normally vary from 1,000 to 5,000 per minute. The impacts imparted by the vibrations produce pressure waves that set the soil particles in motion, thus producing compaction. Compactor speed is important because it controls the number of impacts for each pass. Most vibratory compactors operate in the 2–3 mph speed range. Large steel-drum vibratory rollers can be effective on rock lifts as thick as 3 ft.

FIGURE 10-11
Vibrating padded drum roller.

Manually operated vibratory plate compactors. Figure 10-13 illustrates a self-propelled vibratory-plate compactor that is used for consolidating soils and asphalt concrete (hot or cold mix) in locations where large units are not practical. These gasoline- or diesel-powered units are rated by centrifugal force, exciter revolutions per minute (rpm), depth of vibration penetration (lift), feet per minute (fpm) travel, and area of coverage per hour.

Manually operated rammer compactors. Figure 10-14 illustrates a gasoline-engine-driven rammer that is used for compacting cohesive or mixed soils in confined areas. These units range in impact from about 300 to 900 or more ft-lb per sec at an impact rate up to 850 per min, depending on the specific model. Performance criteria include pounds per blow, area covered per hour, and depth of compaction (lift) in inches. Rammers are self-propelled in that each blow moves them ahead slightly to contact new area.

ROLLER PRODUCTION ESTIMATING

The compaction equipment used on a project must have a production capability matched to that of the excavation, hauling, and spreading equipment. Usually, excavation or

FIGURE 10-12
Vibrating steel-drum roller.

hauling capability will set the expected maximum production for the job. The production formula for a compactor is

$$\text{Compacted cubic yards per hour} = \frac{W \times S \times L \times 16.3}{P} \qquad (10\text{-}1)$$

where W = compacted width per roller pass, ft

S = average roller speed, mph

L = compacted lift thickness, in.

P = number of roller passes required to achieve the required density

The computed production is in compacted cubic yards so that it will be necessary to apply a shrinkage factor to convert the production to bank cubic yards (bcy), which is how the excavation and hauling production is usually expressed.

Example 10-1. A self-propelled tamping foot compactor will be used to compact a fill being constructed of clay material. Field tests have shown that the required density can be achieved with four passes of the roller operating at an average speed of $1\frac{1}{2}$ mph. The compacted lift will have a thickness of 5 in. The compacting width of this machine is 7 ft. One bcy equals 0.83 compacted cubic yards. The scraper production estimated for the project is 510 bcy per hour. How many rollers will be required to maintain this production?

FIGURE 10-13
Self-propelled Vibro-plate. (*Wacker Corporation.*)

$$\text{Compacted cubic yards per hour} = \frac{7 \times 1\frac{1}{2} \times 5 \times 16.3}{4} = 214 \text{ cu yd/hr}$$

$$\frac{214 \text{ compacted cu yd per hour}}{0.83} = 258 \text{ bcy/hr}$$

$$\frac{510 \text{ cu yd/hr required}}{258 \text{ cu yd/hr}} = 1.98 \quad \text{or two rollers required}$$

DENSIFICATION OF SOILS BY EXPLOSIVE VIBRATIONS

In clean saturated, uncemented, granular soils a sudden shock or vibration causes localized spontaneous liquefaction and displacement of the soil grains. The weight of the soil is temporarily transferred to the liquid, and the soil particles fall into a much denser pattern, aided by the weight of the overlying soil mass. The method is not commonly used because of the uncertainty in the attainable results, caused by nonuniformity of soil strata, and the possibility of damage to adjacent structures in built-up areas. Field test programs are always recommended to verify process design.

There will be an immediate settlement of the ground surface, in the order of 2–10% of the layer thickness subjected to this process. The densification, verified by penetration resistance testing techniques, will develop slowly over time. A significant

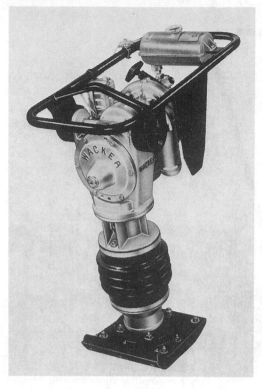

FIGURE 10-14
Manually operated rammer. (*Wacker Corporation.*)

improvement from the conditions noted before the process will result, but the change may not manifest itself for several weeks. Some dense zones may lose strength but the total layer will be improved. Surface layer soils will be loosened. As a result, compaction of the surface by conventional methods will have to be undertaken after the blasting.

Spacings, depths, and sizes of explosive charges. The densification of soils by means of explosives is different from regular blasting in that no craters can be blown in the soil and there must be no debris from the explosion of the charges. The energy from an explosion must be contained entirely within the ground.

The approximate sizes and depths of charges can be determined from existing formulas, tempered with experience and checked by trial tests conducted at the site of the operation. The amount of each charge will vary according to the type of soil, depth of strata, desired amount of densification, spacing of holes, groundwater level, nearness of structures, overlapping effect of charges, and type of explosive used. Experience has indicated that the depth of an explosive charge should be below the center of the mass of the soil to be densified. A placement depth between one-half and three-fourths the thickness of the mass is common. Horizontal spacings of holes may vary from 5.0 to 15 m and are governed by the depth of the strata, the size of the charge, and the overlapping effect of adjacent charges. Spacings closer than 3.0 m in saturated soils should be avoided, unless carefully investigated for safety, because of possible propagation of sensitive explosives of adjacent charges. The final spacing pattern should be based on field blasting tests.

The firing pattern should allow a number of charges to act on one particular area. However, the pattern should leave an area on one or two sides to permit excess pore water to escape. The reduction of the voids in a volume of soil results in the release or displacement of a large volume of water, the quantity of which will depend on the depth, the original void ratio, and the amount of densification of the soil.

It is normal to use two or three separate explosive blasts to treat an area. The firing of individual coverages or blasting patterns in an area should be separated by hours or days. This does not mean that the entire area to be treated is covered in a single blast. As in the case of a large area, a single blast will cause problems in allowing escape paths for the pore water. It is usually necessary to divide the total area into manageable units, each of which is subjected to two or three blasts. Each successive blast will produce a smaller effect. The ratio for any series of charges, empirically obtained, shows that the first quarter of the total explosive used causes approximately 60% of the densification; the second quarter, 25% more; the third quarter, 10% more; and the last quarter, 5% more. The total amount of explosive used is generally 10–30 g/m^3 (grams per cubic meter) in two to three blasts.

VIBROCOMPACTION METHODS [4,13]

There are two distinct vibrocompaction techniques: the vibrating pile method, which utilizes a top-mounted vibrator to create vibration in a vertical mode, and vibroflotation equipment, which develops horizontal motion in the penetrator. Both are applicable for densification of saturated cohesionless soils having no more than 20% fines.

Vibrating pile method. Vibrator compaction is accomplished by the use of a vibratory pile-driving apparatus, together with an open-end tubular pile, Fig. 10-15. Using a square spacing pattern the pile is driven into and extracted from the soil to be compacted. The spacing is usually determined based on project specific test panel construction. When the driving and extracting phases are accomplished, densification of the soil occurs both inside and outside the pile, with the concentration of vibratory energy creating extreme densification inside the pile and with densification outside the pile diminishing with distance.

To date, the vibratory pile-driving apparatuses used have been in the frequency ranges of 720–1,100 cycles per minute (cpm) (11–19 Hz), the normal operating frequency being 900 cpm (15 Hz). The vibrator has been able to create amplitudes of $\frac{3}{8}$ to 1 in. (9.5–25 mm). The vibrator creates vertical energy by counterrotating eccentric weights, which cancel out the horizontal effects and give vertical vibrations only.

The best pile configuration used has been an open-end 30-in. (760-mm) pipe of $\frac{3}{8}$-in. (9.5-mm) wall thickness with 4- to 6-in. (100- to 150-mm) wide and $\frac{1}{2}$-in. (13-mm) thick steel bands spaced 5–10 ft (1.5–3 m) apart on the outside of the pipe, together with wider driving and clamping bands at the bottom and top of the pile. Tests using other diameters have revealed that smaller diameters give less densification inside the pipe, whereas larger diameters require more vibratory energy and thicker and heavier pile. The pile is usually 10–15 ft (3–4.6 m) longer than the maximum penetration depth, to

FIGURE 10-15
Vibratory pile in position to densify the soil. (*L. B. Foster Company.*)

allow for any flexing of the pile, particularly when piles more than 50–55 ft long (15–17 m) are used. This allows for any cutoff requirements during application.

The pile is attached to the vibrator by means of a hydraulic clamp; this permits the vertical vibratory energy produced to travel to the pile material undiminished, as the pile, hydraulic clamping head, and vibrating transmission case act as a unit.

A mobile crane of sufficient size and capacity is required to handle the vibrating unit and the pile length during driving and extracting operations. An overburden of sand is required before beginning the operation to compensate for the settling that will result from the compaction. About a 12% shrinkage allowance has been satisfactory for most applications, but a hydraulic fill with a relatively low density may require a 15% allowance.

Spacing of the piles. The dimensions of the spacing pattern of the piles are dependent on the required relative density of the soil. Test patterns of several different spacings should be run initially to determine the required spacing which yields the desired density. Square patterns with spacings varying from 3 to 8 ft (0.9 to 2.4 m) have been successfully used to give the desired density. Square spacings seem to offer better results and faster operations than other patterns. Also, if additional probes are needed, they can be placed in the centers of the square patterns. Small lathing stakes are generally used to indicate the location of each probe setting.

Production rates obtained with vibrating pile. Working in saturated sands or hydraulically placed cohesionless materials, compaction by this method is very expeditious. For 50- to 55-ft piles an average rate of about 15 pile penetrations per hour can be achieved. For projects requiring shallow piles in loose soils the rate can be higher, whereas for projects requiring deeper piles in denser soils the rate can be lower.

During early applications of this method tests were conducted whereby the vibrating pile was held at full penetration depth and vibration was continued for several minutes. It was thought that such a procedure would produce additional densification. The tests revealed that little, if any, additional densification resulted from the full-depth vibration. The significant compaction is achieved during the penetration and extraction process.

On some projects, in which the upper layers of soil consist of mud, muck, and silt, it will be necessary to remove all the undesirable material because it will not be densified by the vibratory method. The replacement material should be granular, cohesionless soil that will respond to vibratory densification. In some instances it may require screening the replacement material in order to remove any silt or clay balls.

Vibroflotation. This method utilizes a vibrator penetrator which has water jets at both the top and bottom. As the penetrator is lowered, extension tubes are added. The vibrator penetrator requires a crane of sufficient size and capacity to handle both the penetrator and the extensions. The penetrator actually settles into the soil by its own weight as the lower water jet creates a "quick" condition. Typical penetration is 3–6 ft per min. To begin compaction, the lower jets are turned off and the water is directed to the upper jets at a reduced pressure. The penetrator is then withdrawn in 1 ft per min lifts, and sand is continuously fed as backfill. The lifts method of raising the penetrator ensures compaction for the entire depth. The soil will be compacted in a radial zone extending 5–13 ft from the vibratory penetrator. This method is effective with greater spacing patterns than the vibrating pile method and is much more efficient in finer granular formations.

Cost considerations. In all applications of the numerous techniques and methods available the consideration of costs becomes important. The vibrating methods, because they are applicable to some very difficult situations, have some interesting cost considerations. An overall cost consideration should include the following items:

1. Cost of soil removal, if required
2. Cost of replacement soil, if required
3. Cost of necessary soil overburden, if required
4. Cost of a testing program
5. Cost of the vibratory compaction method

The first four costs will be uniquely related to each project site, as each may or may not be applicable.

The cost of the vibratory compaction method can vary depending on the size of the area, the initial soil density, the required density, and the depth to be compacted. Because the mobilization and demobilization costs will be the same for a small or a large project, the unit cost for a small project will be higher. With other conditions remaining the same, the cost per unit volume should be less for projects requiring deep probes. A higher specified density, requiring closer spacing of probes, will result in a higher cost per unit of volume than the wider spacing permitted with lower density requirements.

The depth of compaction is a factor for consideration, but it is less significant than other factors because of the speed provided by the vibratory device used. Overall probing time for a hole 25 ft (7.6 m) deep will not be doubled if the depth is increased to 50 ft (15 m) under the same soil conditions because the time required to move between the probes will be the same for both depths and the time required to penetrate the additional depth will be a matter of a few seconds for most projects.

The employment of this method provides the following advantages:

1. An effective means for compacting a range of saturated sands
2. An expedient method of deep compaction because of the speed of driving and extracting made available by the vibratory pile-driving device
3. Adjustable modular spacings to adapt to final density requirements and job-site conditions
4. An effective method of compacting soil to substantial depths
5. A compaction method where a lower initial density can make the method more expedient than a higher initial density
6. A means of densification of some soils to reduce the soil liquefaction hazards of earthquakes

DYNAMIC COMPACTION

The densification technique of repeatedly dropping a heavy weight onto the ground surface is commonly referred to as "dynamic compaction" although the process has also been described as heavy tamping, impact densification, dynamic consolidation, pounding, and dynamic precompression. For either a natural soil deposit or a placed fill the method can produce densification to depths of greater than 35 ft. Most projects have used drop weights weighing from 6 to 30 tons and typical drop heights ranging from 30 to 75 ft.

Conventional cranes are used for drop weights of up to 20 tons and for drop heights below 100 ft. The weight is attached to a single hoist line. During the drop the hoist drum to which the line is attached is allowed to free spool, releasing the line. When heavier

FIGURE 10-16
Dynamic compaction using a special Lampson Thumper.

weights are used, specially designed dropping machines are required (see Fig. 10-16). With this densification technique, the material is compacted from the ground surface at its prevailing water content throughout the entire thickness. A possible disadvantage is that ground vibrations can be produced which travel significant distances from the impact point.

The most successful projects have been those where coarse-grained pervious soils were present. The position of the water table will have a major influence on the construction operations and project success. It is better to be at least 6.5 ft above the water table. Operations on saturated impervious deposits have resulted in only minor improvement at high cost and should be considered noneffective.

The depth of improvement which can be achieved is a function of the weight of the tamper and the drop height:

$$D = n(W \times H)^{1/2} \qquad (10\text{-}2)$$

where D = depth of improvement, meters (m)

n = an empirical coefficient which is less than 1.0

W = weight of tamper, metric tons

H = drop height, m

An n value of 0.5 has been suggested for many soil deposits. That value is a reasonable starting point; however, the coefficient is affected by:

The type and characteristics of the material being compacted

The applied energy

The contact pressure of the tamper

The influence of cable drag

The presence of energy-absorbing layers

SOIL STABILIZATION

GENERAL INFORMATION

Many soils are subject to differential expansion and shrinkage when undergoing changes in moisture content. Many soils also shift and rut when subjected to moving wheel loads. If pavements are to be constructed on such soils, it is usually necessary to stabilize them to reduce the volume changes and to strengthen them to the point where they can carry the imposed load, even under adverse weather and climatic conditions. In the broadest sense *stabilization* refers to any treatment of the soil which increases its natural strength. There are two kinds of stabilization—mechanical and chemical. In engineering construction, however, stabilization most often refers to when compaction is preceded by the addition and mixing of an inexpensive admixture, termed a "stabilization agent," which alters the chemical makeup of the soil, resulting in a more stable material.

FIGURE 10-17
Disk harrow used to blend soil. (*Rome Industries.*)

Stabilization may be applied in place to a soil in its natural position or mixing can take place on the fill. Also, stabilization may be applied in a plant and then the blended material is transported to the job site for placement and compaction.

Methods of stabilizing soils include, but are not limited to, the following operations:

1. Blending and mixing heterogeneous soils to produce more homogeneous soils
2. Incorporating lime or lime–fly ash into soils that have a high clay content
3. Blending asphalt with the soil
4. Incorporating portland cement (with or without fly ash) with soils that are largely granular in nature
5. Incorporating various salts into the soil
6. Incorporating certain chemicals into the soil
7. Compacting the soils after they are processed

BLENDING AND MIXING SOILS

If the soils that are to be used in a fill are heterogeneous in their original states, such as in a borrow pit, they may be mixed during excavation by using equipment such as a hoe or shovel to excavate through several horizontal layers in one operation. When such material is placed on a fill, it may be subjected to further blending by several passes with a disk harrow (see Fig. 10-17).

STABILIZING SOILS WITH LIME

In combination with compaction, soil stabilization with lime involves a chemical process whereby the soil is improved by the addition of lime. In this content the most troublesome soils are the clays and silty clays with a plasticity index (PI) greater than about 10. Unless stabilized, these soils usually become very soft when water is introduced. Lime, in its hydrated form [Ca(OH)$_2$], will rapidly cause cation exchange and flocculation/agglomeration, provided it is intimately mixed with the soil (see Fig. 10-18). A high PI clay soil will then behave much like a material having a lower PI. This reaction begins to occur within an hour after mixing, and significant changes are realized within a very few days, depending on the PI of the soil, the temperature, and the amount of lime used. The observed effect in the field is one of a drying action.

According to Krebs and Walker [7]:

> Clay otherwise in a plastic condition may become semisolid or friable in consistency. Moreover, normal clay-water interactions are inhibited. Plasticity index decreases. . . . The reactions that cause amelioration effects in lime-clay mixtures are not clearly known, but it is thought that sufficient lime dissolves in the soil water to create a highly alkaline environment and to crowd calcium ions onto the clay exchange complex, causing severe flocculation.

Following this rapid soil improvement, a longer, slower soil improvement takes place, termed "pozzolanic reaction." In this reaction the lime chemically combines with siliceous and aluminous constituents in the soil to cement the soil together. Here some confusion exists. Some people refer to this as a "cementitious reaction," which is a term normally associated with the hydraulic action occurring between portland cement and water, in which the two constituents chemically combine to form a hard, strong product. The confusion is increased by the fact that almost two-thirds of portland cement is lime (CaO). But the lime in portland cement starts out already chemically combined during

FIGURE 10-18
Self-propelled soil-pulverized stabilizer. (*RayGo, Inc.*)

the manufacture with silicates and aluminates, and thus is not in an available or "free" state to combine with the clay.

The cementing reaction of the lime, as $Ca(OH)_2$, with the clay is a very slow process, quite different from the reaction of portland cement and water, and the final form of the products is thought to be somewhat different. The slow strength with time experienced with lime stabilization of clay provides flexibility in the manipulation of the soil. Lime can be added and the soil mixed and compacted, initially drying the soil and causing flocculation. Several days later the soil can be remixed and compacted to form a dense stabilized layer that will continue to gain strength for many years. The resulting stabilized soils have been shown to be extremely durable.

LIME–FLY ASH STABILIZATION

This type of stabilization, although not new, has only recently become widely used. The primary reason is that fly ash, which is the residue that would "fly" out the stack in a coal-fired power plant if it were not captured, is becoming extremely plentiful throughout the United States and, in fact, throughout many parts of the world. Fly ash is a by-product in the production of electricity from burning coal. As such, it can be a highly variable product, and its engineering usefulness can range from superior to extremely poor. Today, in the United States alone, there is in excess of 90 million tons of fly ash being collected each year [2]. The newer, more modern power plants literally pulverize the coal until almost all of it passes the No. 200-mesh sieve before it is used as fuel. The resulting fly ash is extremely fine in size (often finer than portland cement) and contains the silicates and aluminates that are necessary to combine with the lime in soil stabilization. Laboratory and field results indicate that fly ash, of suitable quality, can replace a *portion* of the lime needed to stabilize a clay-type soil. Because lime is relatively expensive and fly ash is often quite inexpensive, lime–fly ash stabilization of soils is being increasingly utilized. The major drawback to the use of fly ash is that two stabilizing agents are being used instead of only one, which means more manipulation of the soil and more chance of error. There are a number of excellent references on the use of lime–fly ash stabilization [10,11].

ASPHALT–SOIL STABILIZATION

When asphalts, such as an emulsion or a cutback, are mixed with granular soils, usually in amounts of 5–7% of the volume of the soil, this treatment will produce a much more durable and stable soil. Some soils have been stabilized by adding 10–15% of minus No. 200-mesh fines to fill the interstices in the soils and then by mixing this blend with asphalt.

The moisture content of the soil must be low at the time that the asphalt is added. Also, it is necessary to allow the volatile oils to evaporate from the bitumen before finishing and rolling the material.

Soils treated in this manner may be used as finished surfaces for low-traffic-density secondary roads, or they may serve as base courses for high-type pavements.

CEMENT–SOIL STABILIZATION

Stabilizing soils with portland cement is an effective method of strengthening certain soils. As long as the soils are predominately granular with only minor amounts of clay particles, the use of portland cement has been found to be effective. A good rule of thumb is that soils with a PI less than about 10 are likely candidates for this type of stabilization. Soils with higher amounts of clay-sized particles are very difficult to manipulate and thoroughly mix with the cement before the cement sets. The terms "soil cement" and "cement-treated base" are often used interchangeably, and generally describe this type of stabilization. However, in some areas the term "soil cement" refers strictly to the mixing and treatment of in-place soils on the grade. The term "cement-treated base" is then used to describe an aggregate/cement blend produced in a pugmill plant and hauled onto the grade. The amount of cement mixed with the soil is usually 3–7% by the dry weight of the soil.

As discussed in connection with lime stabilization, fly ash is becoming plentiful in many areas of the world, and it can be effectively utilized to replace a portion of the portland cement in a soil cement. Replacement percentages on an equal weight basis or on a 1.25:1.0 fly ash/portland cement replacement ratio have been used. There are a number of excellent references on this subject [9–11].

The construction methods involve spreading the portland cement uniformly over the surface of the soil (see Fig. 10-19), then mixing it into the soil, preferably with a pulverizer-type machine to the specified depth, followed by compaction and fine

FIGURE 10-19
Flynn spreader being used to uniformally apply cement during a 'soil cement' stabilization project.

FIGURE 10-20
Water truck connected to a soil stabilizer for adding water during a 'soil-cement' pulverizing and mixing operation.

grading. If the moisture content of the soil is low, it will be necessary to add water during the mixing operation (see Fig. 10-20). The material should be compacted within 30 min after it is mixed, using tamping or pneumatic-tired rollers, followed by final rolling with smooth-wheel rollers. A seal of asphalt or other acceptable material may have to be applied to the surface to retain the moisture in the mix.

PROBLEMS

10-1. If the earth is placed in fill at the rate of 190 cu yd per hour, compacted measure at 10% moisture content, and the dry weight of the compacted earth is 2,890 lb per cu yd, how many gallons of water must be supplied each hour to increase the moisture content of the earth from 4 to 10% by weight?

10-2. The earth whose in situ weight is 112 lb per cu ft, loose weight is 95 lb per cu ft, and compacted weight is 120 lb per cu ft is placed in a fill at the rate of 240 cu yd per hour, measured as compacted earth, in layers whose compacted thickness is 6 in. Towed sheep's-foot roller drums, each 5 ft wide, are pulled by a tractor at a speed of 2 mph, with a 45-min-hour operating efficiency. Determine the number of drums required to provide the necessary compaction if eight drum passes are specified for each layer of earth.

10-3. If a multiwheel pneumatic roller whose 7.50 × 15-14-ply tires are inflated to 90 psi, and whose wheel loads are 2,800 lb each, is used to compact a soil, what is the maximum compacted depth of a layer of earth that can be compacted to a unit pressure of not less than 50 psi at the bottom of the layer? Assume that the ground contact area for a tire is a circle whose area in square inches equals the wheel load divided by the ground contact pressure.

REFERENCES

1. American Society for Testing and Materials: *Compaction of Soils*, STP 377, ASTM, Philadelphia, PA, 1964, 135 pp.
2. Covey, James N.: "An Overview of Ash Utilization in the United States," in *Proceedings of the Fly Ash Applications in 1980 Conference*, Texas A&M University, May 1980.
3. *Guide to Earthwork Construction*, State of the Art Report 8, TRB, National Research Council, Washington, DC, 1990.
4. Holtz, R. D.: *NCHRP, Synthesis of Highway Practice 147: Treatment of Problem Foundations for Highway Embankments*, TRB, National Research Council, Washington, DC, 1989, 72 pp.
5. Johnson, A. W., and J. R. Sallberg: "Factors that Influence Field Compaction of Soils," *Bulletin 272*, HRB, National Research Council, Washington, DC, 1960, 206 pp.
6. Johnson, A. W., and J. R. Sallberg: "Factors Influencing Compaction Test Results," *Bulletin 319*, HRB, National Research Council, Washington, DC, 1962, 148 pp.
7. Krebs, Robert D., and Richard D. Walker: *Highway Materials*, McGraw-Hill, New York, 1971, 428 pp.
8. Lukas, Robert G.: "Dynamic Compaction for Highway Construction Vol. I: Design and Construction Guidelines," U.S. Department of Transportation, Federal Highway Administration, July 1986.
9. McKerall, W. C., and W. B. Ledbetter: "Variability and Control of Class C Fly Ash," *Cement, Concrete, and Aggregates*, CCAGDP, vol. 4, no. 2, winter 1982, ASTM, Philadelphia, PA.
10. Meyers, J. F., R. Pichumami, and B. S. Kapples: "Fly Ash as a Highway Construction Material," U.S. Department of Transportation, Federal Highway Administration, June 1976.
11. Terrel, R. L.: "A Guide Users Manual for Soil Stabilization," U.S. Department of Transportation, Federal Highway Administration, April 1979.
12. Wahls, H. E.: *NCHRP Synthesis of Highway Practice 8: Construction of Embankments*, TRB, National Research Council, Washington, DC, 1971, 38 pp.
13. Welsh, Joseph P.: *Soil Improvement—A Ten Year Update*, Geotechnical Special Publication No. 12, American Society of Civil Engineers, New York, 1987.

CHAPTER
11

BELT-CONVEYOR SYSTEMS

GENERAL INFORMATION

Belt-conveyor systems are used extensively in the field of construction. They frequently provide the most satisfactory and economical method of handling and transporting materials, such as earth, sand, gravel, crushed stone, mine ores, cement, concrete, etc. Because of the *continuous* flow of materials at relatively high speeds, belt conveyors have high capacities. During the construction of the Channel Tunnel (between England and France) conveyors were used to move up to 2,400 tonnes of spoil per hour from the tunnel headings.

The essential parts of a belt-conveyor system include a continuous belt, idlers, a driving unit, driving and tail pulleys, take-up equipment, and a supporting structure. Additional accessories, as described later, may be included when desirable or necessary.

A conveyor for transporting materials a short distance may be a portable unit or a fixed installation. Figure 11-1 illustrates a portable conveyor used to stockpile aggregate which is delivered by trucks. This machine is available in lengths of 33–60 ft, with belt widths of 18, 24, and 30 in. It is self-powered with a gasoline-engine drive through a shaft and gearbox to the driving pulley. The operating features include swivel wheels, a V-type truck, a hydraulic hoist, a low mast height, and antifriction bearings throughout.

When a belt-conveyor system is used to transport materials a considerable distance, up to several miles in some instances, the system should consist of a number of different flights, as there is a limit to the maximum length of a belt. Each flight is a complete conveyor unit which discharges its load onto the tail end of the succeeding unit. Such a system will operate over any terrain, provided the slopes do not exceed those for which the given material may be transported.

The limestone rock for the Bull Shoals Dam in Texas, whose maximum size was 6 in., was transported 7 mi from the primary crushing plant at the quarry to the dam site. The conveyor system consisted of 21 flights, varying in length from 600 to 2,800 ft, each powered with a 100-hp electric motor. The belts, which were 30 in. wide, were

FIGURE 11-1
Portable belt conveyor.

operated at a speed of 525 fpm to deliver 350 cu yd of material per hour. The entire system required 14,000 idlers, which were supported primarily by wood structures.

Figure 11-2 illustrates two conveyor systems at an aggregate plant. One belt is open whereas the second belt is covered for most of its length to the stockpiles.

THE ECONOMY OF TRANSPORTING MATERIALS WITH A BELT CONVEYOR

One of the first questions that arises in considering the use of a belt conveyor is whether this method of transportation is the most dependable and economical when compared with other methods. The proper way to answer this question is to estimate the cost of transporting the material by each method under consideration. Assume that a belt conveyor is to be compared with trucks for hauling aggregate on a large concrete project.

The net total cost of the conveyor system will include the installed cost of the system, an access road for installing and servicing the system, maintenance, replacements and repairs, fuel, or electrical energy, and labor, less the net salvage value of the system upon completion of the project. Interest on the investment, plus taxes and insurance, if they apply, should be included. Likewise, any cost of obtaining a right-of-way for the system should be included. The unit cost of moving the material, per ton or cubic yard, may be obtained by dividing the net total cost of the system by the quantity of material to be transported.

The cost of transporting the materials by truck will include the cost of constructing and maintaining a haul road, plus the cost of owning and operating the trucks. The unit cost of moving the materials may be obtained by dividing the net total cost by the quantity of material to be transported.

FIGURE 11-2
Two operating conveyor systems at an aggregate plant.

If either method requires additional handling costs at the source or at the destination, these costs should be included prior to determining the unit cost of moving the materials.

In the construction of the Bull Shoals Dam more than 4,500,000 tons of aggregate was transported on belt conveyors at a reported cost of $0.045 per ton-mile. It was estimated that the contractors saved $560,000 on the purchase and installation of the conveyor system compared with a fleet of trucks, plus a haul road and incidentals required for the trucks. In addition, it was estimated that there was a saving of $375,000 on labor operating the system compared with trucks.

CONVEYOR BELTS

The "belt" is the moving and supporting surface on which the material is transported. Many types, sizes, and grades are available from which the most suitable belt for a given service may be selected. Figure 11-3 illustrates four belt-conveyor systems based on the location of the drive pulley, the number of drive pulleys, and the take-up method of maintaining the necessary tension in the belt.

Belts are manufactured by joining several layers or plies of woven cotton duck into a carcass which provides the necessary strength to resist the tension in the belt. The layers are covered with an adhesive which combines them into a unified structure. Special types of reinforcing, such as rayon, nylon, and steel cables, are sometimes employed to increase the strength of a belt. High tenacity fibers such as Du Pont's Kevlar® are beginning to be used for heavy duty conveyor belts. They have the advantage of a relatively low resistance to longitudinal splitting compared to steel cord belts and there is reduced danger of corrosion.

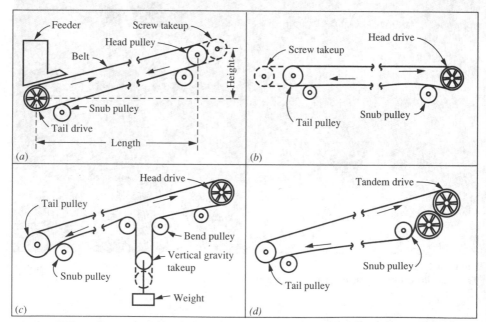

FIGURE 11-3
Representative belt-conveyor systems.

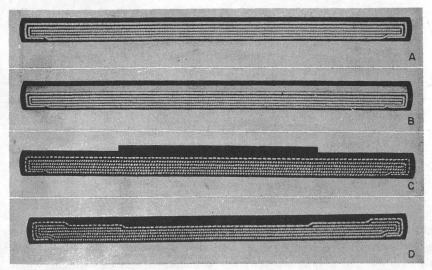

FIGURE 11-4
Types of conveyor belt construction. (*a*) Standard. (*b*) Shock pad. (*c*) Stepped pad. (*d*) Stepped ply.

A measure of the strength of a belt is indicated by the number and weight of the several layers of fabric. The number of layers is expressed as 4, 6, 7, 8, etc. ply. The weight of each layer of fabric is expressed as 28, 32, 36, 42, etc. oz; the number indicates the weight of a piece of duck 42 in. wide and 36 in. long. The width of a belt is expressed in inches. Thus, a belt might be specified as a 36-in.-wide 6-ply 42-oz belt.

The top and bottom surfaces of a belt are covered with rubber to protect the carcass from abrasion and injury from the impact at loading. Various thicknesses of covers may be specified. Figure 11-4 illustrates cross sections of belts having different types of construction.

It is necessary to select a belt with sufficient strength to resist the maximum tension to which it will be subjected, as determined by methods which will be developed later.

Also, a belt should be selected that is wide enough to transport the material at the required rate. Most belts used on construction projects travel over troughing rollers to increase the carrying capacities. The number of tons that can be transported in an hour is determined by using Eq. (11-1).

$$T = \frac{60ASW}{2,000}$$ (11-1)

where T = weight of material, tons per hour
$\quad A$ = cross-sectional area of material, sq ft
$\quad S$ = speed of the belt, ft per min
$\quad W$ = weight of material, lb per cu ft

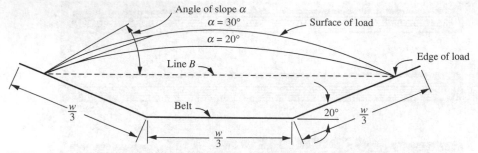

FIGURE 11-5
Cross-section area of a load on a conveyor belt.

The area of the cross section will depend on the width of the belt, the depth of troughing, the angle of repose for the material, and the extent to which the belt is loaded to capacity. Figure 11-5 illustrates how the cross-sectional area may vary with the width of a belt and the angle of repose for the material. In the figure the troughing idlers are set at an angle of 20° above the horizontal. In order to eliminate side spillage, it is assumed that materials will not be placed closer than $0.05W + 1$ in. from the sides of the belt, where W is the width of the belt in inches. It is assumed that the top surface of the material will be an arc of a circle. Table 11-1 gives the cross-sectional areas for various belt widths and loading conditions. These areas are subject to variation and should not be considered as exact unless the loading conditions are as stated. The area of surcharge is the area above the B line of Fig. 11-5. The angle of slope is about 15° less than the angle of repose of the material.

The carrying capacity of a 42-in. belt, moving 100 fpm, loaded with sand weighing 100 lb per cu ft, with a 20° angle of repose, will be 100 fpm × 100 lb per cu ft ×

TABLE 11-1
Loaded belt material cross-sectional area for troughing idlers at an angle of 20°

Width of belt (in.)	$0.05W + 1$, (in.)	Area of level load (sq ft)	Area of surcharge (sq ft) for angle of repose (degrees)			Total area (sq ft) for angle of repose (degrees)		
			10	20	30	10	20	30
16	1.8	0.072	0.029	0.059	0.090	0.101	0.131	0.162
18	1.9	0.096	0.038	0.078	0.118	0.134	0.174	0.214
20	2.0	0.122	0.048	0.098	0.150	0.170	0.220	0.272
24	2.2	0.185	0.072	0.146	0.225	0.257	0.331	0.410
30	2.5	0.303	0.118	0.238	0.365	0.421	0.541	0.668
36	2.8	0.450	0.174	0.351	0.540	0.624	0.801	0.990
42	3.1	0.627	0.241	0.488	0.749	0.868	1.115	1.376
48	3.4	0.833	0.321	0.649	0.992	1.154	1.482	1.825
54	3.7	1.068	0.408	0.826	1.264	1.476	1.894	2.332
60	4.0	1.333	0.510	1.027	1.575	1.843	2.360	2.908

TABLE 11-2
Carrying capacities of troughed conveyor belts, in tons per hour, for a speed of 100 fpm

Width of belt (in.)	Max lumps Sized (in.)	Max lumps Un-sized (in.)	Weight of material (lb/cu ft) 30	50	90	100	125	150	160	180	200
14	2	$2\frac{1}{2}$	9	15	28	31	39	46	49	56	62
16	$2\frac{1}{2}$	3	13	21	38	42	52	63	67	75	83
18	3	4	16	27	48	54	67	81	86	97	107
20	$3\frac{1}{2}$	5	20	33	60	67	83	100	107	120	133
24	$4\frac{1}{2}$	8	30	50	90	100	125	150	160	180	200
30	7	14	47	79	142	158	197	236	252	284	315
36	9	18	70	117	210	234	292	351	374	421	467
42	11	20	100	167	300	333	417	500	534	600	667
48	14	24	138	230	414	460	575	690	736	828	920
54	15	28	178	297	534	593	741	890	948	1,070	1,190
60	16	30	222	369	664	738	922	1,110	1,180	1,330	1,480

Courtesy Hewitt-Robins.

1.115 sq ft $\times$ 60 min $\div$ 2,000 lb per ton = 334.5 tons per hour. The carrying capacity of this belt for other speeds may be obtained by multiplying 334.5 by the ratio of the two speeds.

Table 11-2 gives the approximate carrying capacities of troughed conveyor belts, in tons per hour, for various widths and materials for a speed of 100 fpm. Table 11-3 gives the suggested maximum speeds which are considered good practice for conveyor belts of different widths when handling various kinds of materials. Table 11-4 gives representative allowable working tensions in duck belts for various thicknesses and

TABLE 11-3
Maximum speeds, fpm, of conveyor belts

Kind and condition of material handled	Width of belt (in.) 14	16	18	20	24	30	36	42	48	54	60
Unsized coal, gravel, stone, ashes, ore, or similar material	300	300	350	350	400	450	500	550	600	600	600
Sized coal, coke, or other breakable material	250	250	250	300	300	350	350	400	400	400	400
Wet or dry sand	400	400	500	600	600	700	800	800	800	800	800
Crushed coke, crushed slag, or other fine abrasive material	250	250	300	400	400	500	500	500	500	500	500
Large lump ore, rock, slag, or other large abrasive material	—	—	—	—	350	350	400	400	400	400	400

Courtesy Hewitt-Robins.

TABLE 11-4
Allowable working tension and pulley diameter for conveyor belts

No. of plies	Weight per ply (oz)	Width of belt (in.) Allowable working tension (lb)								Diameter of pulley (in.)		
		16	18	20	24	30	36	42	48	Head, drive, tripper	Tail, take-up, snub	Bend
3	32	1,440	1,620	—	—	—	—	—	—	16	12	12
3	36	—	—	1,800	2,160	—	—	—	—	20	16	12
3	42	—	—	2,200	2,640	3,300	—	—	—	20	16	12
3	48	—	—	—	3,840	—	—	—	—	24	20	16
4	28	1,600	1,800	2,000	2,400	3,000	—	—	—	20	16	12
4	32	1,920	2,160	2,400	2,880	3,600	4,320	—	—	20	16	12
4	36	—	—	2,600	3,120	3,900	4,680	—	—	24	20	16
4	42	—	—	—	—	4,800	5,760	6,720	—	24	20	20
4	48	—	—	—	—	6,450	7,750	9,020	—	30	24	20
5	28	2,000	2,250	2,500	3,000	3,750	4,500	—	—	24	20	16
5	32	—	2,700	3,000	3,480	4,500	5,400	—	—	24	20	16
5	36	—	—	3,400	4,080	5,100	6,120	7,140	—	30	24	20
5	42	—	—	—	—	6,600	7,920	9,240	10,560	30	24	20
5	48	—	—	—	—	8,700	10,400	12,180	13,920	36	30	24
6	28	—	—	3,000	3,600	4,500	5,400	—	—	30	24	20
6	32	—	—	—	4,320	5,400	6,480	7,560	—	30	24	20

TABLE 11-4 *(continued)*
Allowable working tension and pulley diameter for conveyor belts

No. of plies	Weight per ply (oz)	Width of belt (in.)								Diameter of pulley (in.)		
		16	18	20	24	30	36	42	48	Head, drive, tripper	Tail, take-up, snub	Bend
		Allowable working tension (lb)										
6	36	—	—	—	—	6,300	7,560	8,820	10,080	36	30	24
6	42	—	—	—	—	—	9,720	11,340	12,900	36	30	24
6	48	—	—	—	—	—	13,000	15,120	17,300	42	36	30
7	28	—	—	—	—	5,250	6,300	—	—	36	30	24
7	32	—	—	—	—	6,300	7,560	8,820	10,080	36	30	24
7	36	—	—	—	—	—	8,820	10,300	11,780	42	36	30
7	42	—	—	—	—	—	—	13,200	15,140	42	36	30
7	48	—	—	—	—	—	—	17,640	20,180	48	42	36
8	32	—	—	—	—	—	8,640	10,080	11,520	42	30	24
8	36	—	—	—	—	—	—	11,760	13,450	48	42	30
8	42	—	—	—	—	—	—	—	17,300	48	42	30
8	48	—	—	—	—	—	—	—	23,050	54	48	42
9	32	—	—	—	—	—	—	11,340	12,900	48	36	30
9	36	—	—	—	—	—	—	13,200	15,140	54	48	36

Courtesy Hewitt-Robins.

widths. The pulley diameter is the minimum size that should be used for the indicated service.

IDLERS

Idlers provide the supports for a belt conveyor. For the load-carrying portion of a belt the idlers are designed to provide the necessary troughing, whereas for the return portion of a belt idlers provide flat supports. The essential parts of a troughing idler include the rolls, brackets, and base. Antifriction bearings are generally used in idlers, with high-pressure grease fittings to permit periodic lubrication of the bearings. The rolls may be made of steel tubing or cast iron, either plain or covered with a composition, such as rubber, where it is necessary to protect a belt against damage due to impact. The diameters of the rolls most commonly used are 4, 5, 6, and 7 in. Large-diameter rolls give lower friction and better belt protection, especially when the load includes large lumps of material. Figure 11-6 illustrates troughing and return idlers.

Spacing of idlers. Troughing idlers should be spaced close enough to prevent excessive deflection of the loaded belt between the idlers. As indicated in Table 11-5, the maximum spacing will vary with the width of the belt and the weight of the load carried. The idler spacing should be reduced at the point where the load is fed onto the belt.

   As the sole function of the return idlers is to support the empty belt, the spacing can be increased to approximately 10 ft.

FIGURE 11-6
Belt idlers. (*a*) Heavy-duty troughing. (*b*) Return.

TABLE 11-5
Recommended maximum spacing of troughing idlers

Width of belt (in.)	Weight of material (lb/cu ft)		
	30–70	70–120	120–150
14	5 ft 6 in.	5 ft 0 in.	4 ft 9 in.
16	5 ft 6 in.	5 ft 0 in.	4 ft 9 in.
18	5 ft 6 in.	5 ft 0 in.	4 ft 9 in.
20	5 ft 6 in.	5 ft 0 in.	4 ft 9 in.
24	5 ft 6 in.	5 ft 0 in.	4 ft 9 in.
30	5 ft 0 in.	4 ft 6 in.	4 ft 3 in.
36	5 ft 0 in.	4 ft 6 in.	4 ft 3 in.
42	4 ft 6 in.	4 ft 0 in.	3 ft 9 in.
48	4 ft 0 in.	3 ft 3 in.	3 ft 0 in.
24	4 ft 0 in.	2 ft 9 in.	2 ft 6 in.
60	4 ft 0 in.	2 ft 3 in.	2 ft 0 in.

Courtesy Hewitt-Robins.

Training idlers. Sometimes a conveyor belt is operated under conditions which make it difficult to keep the belt centered on the troughing idlers. If the conditions cannot be corrected sufficiently to keep the belt centered, it may be necessary to install training idlers, spaced 50–60 ft apart. Figure 11-7 illustrates a set of training idlers.

Idler friction. In analyzing a belt conveyor to determine the horsepower required, it is necessary to include the power needed by the idlers. This power will depend on the type and size of idler, the kind of bearings, the weight of the revolving parts, the weight of the belt, and the weight of the load. Table 11-6 gives representative friction factors for idlers equipped with antifriction bearings. Manufacturers of idlers will furnish information giving the weights of the revolving parts of their idlers.

The information in Table 11-6 is used in the following example.

Example 11-1. Consider a conveyor 100 ft long, with a 5-ply, 32-oz, 30-in.-wide belt weighing 6.8 lb per ft. The load will weigh 100 lb per cu ft, or 54 lb per foot of conveyor. The revolving parts will weigh 50 lb for a troughing idler and 31 lb for a return idler. Both idlers are 6 in. in diameter.

From Table 11-6 the idler friction factor is 0.030.

No. of troughing idlers required,

$$100 \text{ ft} \div 4.5 \text{ (from Table 11-5)} = 22$$

Add extra idlers at loading point $\quad = \underline{\quad 3}$

Total no. of troughing idlers $\quad = 25$

No. of return idlers, $100 \text{ ft} \div 10 = 10$

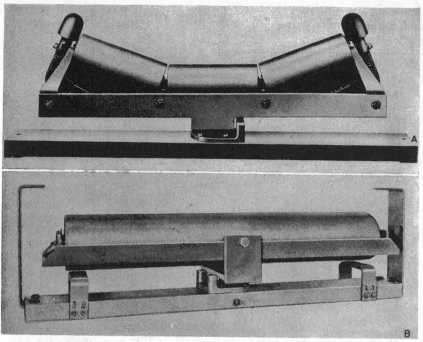

FIGURE 11-7
Training idlers. (*a*) Reversible troughing. (*b*) Return.

Total weight of the revolving parts of idlers will be:

Troughing, 25 idlers × 50 lb per idler = 1,250 lb
Return, 10 idlers × 31 lb per idler   = 310 lb
Weight of belt, 200 ft × 6.8 lb per ft = 1,360 lb
Weight of load, 100 ft × 54 lb per ft   = 5,400 lb

Total weight   = 8,320 lb

The force required to overcome idler friction:

$$8,320 \times 0.03 = 249.6 \text{ lb}$$

TABLE 11-6
Friction factors for conveyor-belt idlers equipped with antifriction bearings

Diameter of idler pulley	4 in.	5 in.	6 in.	7 in.
Friction factor	0.0375	0.036	0.030	0.025

Courtesy Hewitt-Robins.

For a belt speed of 100 fpm the energy required per minute will be

$$100 \times 249.6 = 24{,}960 \text{ ft-lb}$$

The horsepower required to overcome idler friction will be

$$P = \frac{24{,}960 \text{ ft-lb/min}}{33{,}000 \text{ ft-lb/min per hp}} = 0.76 \text{ hp}$$

For other belt speeds the required horsepower will be

$$P = \frac{0.76 \times \text{speed, fpm}}{100}$$

POWER REQUIRED TO DRIVE A BELT CONVEYOR

POWER REQUIREMENT COMPONENTS

The total external power required to drive a loaded belt conveyor is the algebraic sum of the power required by each of the following:

1. To move the empty belt over the idlers
2. To move the load horizontally
3. To lift or lower the load vertically
4. To turn all pulleys
5. To compensate for drive losses
6. To operate a tripper, if one is used

The power required for each of these operations can be determined with reasonable accuracy for any given conveyor system, as explained in the following sections.

POWER REQUIRED TO MOVE AN EMPTY BELT

The power required to move an empty conveyor belt over the idlers will vary with the type of idler bearings; the diameter and spacing of the idlers; and the length, weight, and speed of the belt. The energy required to move an empty belt is given by the equation

$$E = LSCQ \tag{11-2}$$

where E = energy, ft-lb per min
L = length of conveyor, ft
S = belt speed, fpm
C = idler-friction factor, from Table 11-6
Q = weight of moving parts per foot of conveyor

This is valid for systems which operate at temperatures above freezing (32°F). A correction factor must be added to Eq. 11-2 for cold weather applications. The factor is about 1.2 at 0°F and goes to 1.5 at −15°F.

Equation (11-2) may be expressed as horsepower by dividing by 33,000, to give

$$P = \frac{LSCQ}{33,000} \tag{11-3}$$

Representative values of Q are given in Table 11-7. If more accurate values are desired for a given conveyor, they may be determined from the design of the particular conveyor and the weight of the belt used.

Example 11-2. The use of Eq. (11-3) is illustrated by determining the horsepower required to move a 30-in.-wide belt on a conveyor whose length is 1,800 ft, equipped with 5-in.-diameter idler pulleys, with antifriction bearings. Assume a belt speed of 100 fpm.

From Table 11-6 the value of C will be 0.036.
From Table 11-7 the value of Q will be 26 lb per ft of conveyor length.

The power required to move the empty belt will be

$$P = \frac{1,800 \times 100 \times 0.036 \times 26}{33,000} = 5.10 \text{ hp}$$

Table 11-8 gives representative values for the horsepower required to move empty conveyor belts. The values are based on using 5-in.-diameter idlers with antifriction bearings.

POWER REQUIRED TO MOVE A LOAD HORIZONTALLY

The power required to move a load horizontally may be expressed by Eq. (11-4) if Q is replaced by W, the weight of the load in pounds per foot of belt.

$$P = \frac{LSCW}{33,000} \tag{11-4}$$

This equation may be expressed in terms of the load moved in tons per hour. Let

T = tons of material moved per hour
SW = pounds of material moved per minute
$60SW$ = pounds of material moved per hour

$$T = \frac{60SW}{2,000} = \frac{3SW}{100}$$

Solving, we get

$$SW = \frac{100T}{3} \tag{11-5}$$

TABLE 11-7
Representative values of Q

| Width of belt (in.) | Idlers, 5-in.-diameter, steel pulleys | | | | Weight of belt (lb/ft) | Weight of conveyor (lb/ft) | | | Q (lb/ft) |
| | Troughing | | Return | | | Idlers | | Belt | |
	Weight of revolving parts (lb)	Spacing	Weight of revolving parts (lb)	Spacing		Troughing	Return		
14	18	5 ft 0 in.	9	10 ft 0 in.	2.8	3.6	0.9	5.6	10.1
16	20	5 ft 0 in.	11	10 ft 0 in.	3.3	4.0	1.1	6.6	11.7
18	22	5 ft 0 in.	12	10 ft 0 in.	4.1	4.4	1.2	8.2	13.8
20	24	5 ft 0 in.	14	10 ft 0 in.	4.6	4.8	1.4	9.2	15.4
24	26	5 ft 0 in.	17	10 ft 0 in.	7.0	5.2	1.7	14.0	20.9
30	31	4 ft 6 in.	21	10 ft 0 in.	8.5	6.9	2.1	17.0	26.0
36	36	4 ft 6 in.	25	10 ft 0 in.	11.3	8.0	2.5	22.6	33.1
42	40	4 ft 0 in.	29	10 ft 0 in.	17.0	10.0	2.9	34.0	46.0
48	45	3 ft 3 in.	34	10 ft 0 in.	23.8	13.8	3.4	47.6	64.8
54	74	2 ft 9 in.	54	10 ft 0 in.	29.2	26.9	5.4	73.2	105.5
60	80	2 ft 3 in.	60	10 ft 0 in.	32.5	35.6	6.0	74.0	115.6

Courtesy Hewitt-Robins.

TABLE 11-8
Horsepower required to move empty conveyor belts for a speed of 100 fpm

Length of conveyor (ft)	Width of belt (in.)										
	14	16	18	20	24	30	36	42	48	54	60
50	0.05	0.06	0.07	0.08	0.11	0.14	0.18	0.25	0.35	0.54	0.63
100	0.11	0.13	0.15	0.17	0.23	0.28	0.36	0.51	0.70	1.14	1.25
150	0.16	0.19	0.22	0.25	0.34	0.42	0.53	0.76	1.05	1.71	1.88
200	0.22	0.25	0.30	0.33	0.45	0.56	0.71	1.01	1.40	2.28	2.50
250	0.27	0.32	0.37	0.42	0.56	0.70	0.89	1.27	1.75	2.85	3.13
300	0.33	0.38	0.45	0.50	0.68	0.84	1.07	1.52	2.10	3.42	3.76
400	—	—	0.60	0.66	0.90	1.12	1.43	2.03	2.80	4.56	5.01
500	—	—	—	0.83	1.13	1.40	1.79	2.53	3.50	5.70	6.26
600	—	—	—	1.00	1.35	1.68	2.14	3.04	4.20	6.84	7.51
800	—	—	—	—	1.80	2.25	2.86	4.05	5.60	9.12	10.00
1,000	—	—	—	—	2.26	2.81	3.57	5.07	7.00	11.40	12.50
1,200	—	—	—	—	—	3.37	4.29	6.08	8.40	13.70	15.00
1,400	—	—	—	—	—	3.93	5.00	7.09	9.80	16.00	17.50
1,600	—	—	—	—	—	4.49	5.72	8.10	11.20	18.30	20.10
1,800	—	—	—	—	—	5.05	6.43	9.12	12.60	20.50	22.60
2,000	—	—	—	—	—	5.62	7.15	10.10	14.00	22.80	24.90
2,200	—	—	—	—	—	—	7.86	11.10	15.40	25.10	27.60
2,400	—	—	—	—	—	—	8.58	12.20	16.80	27.40	30.10
2,600	—	—	—	—	—	—	9.29	13.20	18.20	29.60	32.60
2,800	—	—	—	—	—	—	10.00	14.20	19.60	31.90	35.00
3,000	—	—	—	—	—	—	10.70	15.20	21.00	34.20	37.60

Courtesy Hewitt-Robins.

Substituting this value of SW into Eq. (11-4), we determine that the horsepower required to move a load horizontally is

$$P = \frac{100LCT}{3 \times 33,000} = \frac{LCT}{990} \tag{11-6}$$

Table 11-9 gives values for the horsepower required to move loads horizontally on conveyor belts. The values are based on using 5-in.-diameter idlers with antifriction bearings.

POWER REQUIRED TO MOVE A LOAD UP AN INCLINED BELT CONVEYOR

When a load is moved up an inclined belt conveyor, the power required may be divided into two components: the power required to move the load horizontally and the power required to lift the load through the net change in elevation. The power required to move the load horizontally may be determined from Eq. (11-6). The power required to lift the

TABLE 11-9
Horsepower required to move loads horizontally on conveyor belts

Length of conveyor (ft)	Load (tons/hr)													
	50	100	150	200	250	300	350	400	500	600	700	800	900	1,000
50	0.09	0.18	0.27	0.36	0.46	0.55	0.64	0.73	0.91	1.1	1.3	1.5	1.6	1.8
100	0.18	0.36	0.55	0.74	0.91	1.1	1.3	1.5	1.8	2.2	2.6	2.9	3.3	3.6
150	0.27	0.55	0.82	1.1	1.4	1.6	1.9	2.2	2.7	3.3	3.8	4.4	4.9	5.5
200	0.36	0.73	1.1	1.5	1.8	2.2	2.6	2.9	3.6	4.4	5.1	5.8	6.6	7.3
250	0.46	0.91	1.4	1.8	2.3	2.7	3.2	3.6	4.6	5.5	6.4	7.3	8.2	9.1
300	0.55	1.1	1.6	2.2	2.7	3.3	3.8	4.4	5.5	6.6	7.7	8.8	9.9	10.9
400	0.73	1.5	2.2	2.9	3.6	4.4	5.1	5.8	7.3	8.7	10.2	11.6	13.1	14.6
500	0.91	1.8	2.7	3.6	4.6	5.5	6.4	7.3	9.1	10.9	12.7	14.5	16.4	18.2
600	1.10	2.1	3.2	4.2	5.3	6.4	7.4	8.5	10.6	12.7	14.8	17.0	19.1	21.0
800	1.40	2.7	4.1	5.5	6.8	8.2	9.5	10.8	13.7	16.4	19.1	22.0	25.0	27.0
1,000	1.70	3.3	5.0	6.7	8.3	10.0	11.7	13.3	16.7	20.0	23.0	27.0	30.0	33.0
1,200	2.0	3.9	5.9	7.9	9.8	11.8	13.8	15.7	19.8	24.0	28.0	32.0	36.0	39.0
1,400	2.3	4.5	6.8	9.1	11.4	13.7	15.9	18.1	23.0	27.0	32.0	36.0	41.0	45.0
1,600	2.6	5.2	7.7	10.3	12.9	15.5	18	21	26	31	36	41	46	52
1,800	2.9	5.8	8.7	11.5	14.4	17.3	20	23	28	35	40	46	52	58
2,000	3.2	6.4	9.6	12.7	15.9	19.1	22	25	32	38	45	51	57	64
2,200	3.5	7.0	10.5	13.9	17.4	21.0	24	28	35	42	49	56	63	70
2,400	3.9	7.6	11.4	15.2	18.9	23.0	27	30	38	46	53	61	68	76
2,600	4.1	8.2	12.3	16.4	20.0	25.0	29	33	41	49	57	65	74	82
2,800	4.4	8.8	13.2	17.6	22.0	26.0	31	35	44	53	62	70	79	88
3,000	4.7	9.4	14.1	18.8	23.0	28.0	33	37	47	56	66	75	85	94

Courtesy Hewitt-Robins.

TABLE 11-10
Horsepower required to lift a load

Net lift (ft)	Load (tons/hr)											
	50	100	150	200	250	300	350	400	500	600	800	1,000
5	0.3	0.5	0.8	1.0	1.3	1.5	1.8	2.0	2.5	3.0	4.0	5.1
10	0.5	1.0	1.5	2.0	2.5	3.0	3.5	4.0	5.1	6.1	8.1	10.0
15	0.8	1.5	2.3	3.0	3.8	4.5	5.3	6.1	7.6	9.1	12.0	15.0
20	1.0	2.0	3.0	4.0	5.1	6.1	7.1	8.1	10.0	12.0	16.0	20.0
25	1.3	2.5	3.8	5.1	6.3	7.6	8.8	10.0	13.0	15.0	20.0	25.0
30	1.5	3.0	4.5	6.1	7.6	9.1	11.0	12.0	15.0	18.0	24.0	30.0
40	2.0	4.0	6.1	8.1	10.0	12.0	14.0	16.0	20.0	24.0	32.0	40.0
50	2.5	5.1	7.6	10.0	13.0	15.0	18.0	20.0	25.0	30.0	40.0	51.0
75	3.8	7.6	11.0	15.0	19.0	23.0	27.0	30.0	38.0	45.0	61.0	76.0
100	5.1	10.0	15.0	20.0	25.0	30.0	35.0	40.0	51.0	61.0	81.0	101
125	6.3	13.0	19.0	25.0	32.0	38.0	44.0	51.0	63.0	76.0	˙101	126
150	7.6	15.0	23.0	30.0	38.0	45.0	53.0	61.0	76.0	91.0	121	152
200	10.0	20.0	30.0	40.0	51.0	61.0	71.0	81.0	101	121	162	202
300	15.0	30.0	45.0	61.0	76.0	91.0	106	121	152	185	242	303
400	20.0	40.0	61.0	81.0	101	121	141	162	202	242	323	404
500	25.0	51.0	76.0	101	126	151	177	202	252	303	404	505

Courtesy Hewitt-Robins.

load through the net change in elevation may be determined by using Eq. (11-5) and letting H = net change in elevation, in ft.

$$\frac{100TH}{3} = \text{energy, ft-lb/min}$$

Dividing by 33,000 gives the horsepower,

$$P = \frac{100TH}{3 \times 33,000} = \frac{TH}{990} \tag{11-7}$$

If the load is moved up an inclined conveyor, the power given in Eq. (11-7) must be supplied from an outside source. If the load is moved down an inclined conveyor, the power will be supplied to the belt by the load. Table 11-10 gives representative horsepower requirements for lifting a load on a belt conveyor.

DRIVING EQUIPMENT

A belt conveyor may be driven through the head or tail pulley or through an intermediate pulley. In the event that high driving forces are required, it may be necessary to use more than one pulley, with the pulleys arranged in tandem to increase the area of contact with the belt. Smooth-faced or lagged pulleys may be used, depending on the desired coefficient of friction between the belt and the pulley surface. The pulley may be driven by an electric motor, or a gasoline or diesel engine. It is usually necessary to install a suitable speed reducer, such as gears, chain drives, or belt drives, between the power unit and the driving pulley. The power loss in the speed reducer should be included in determining the total power required to drive a belt conveyor. This power loss may be 5–10% or more, depending on the type of speed reducer.

The coefficient of friction between a steel shaft and babbitted bearings will be approximately 0.10.

When power is transmitted from a driving pulley to a belt, the effective driving force, which is transmitted to the belt, is equal to the tension in the tight side less the tension in the slack side of the belt, expressed in pounds.

$$T_e = T_1 - T_2 \tag{11-8}$$

where T_e = effective tension or driving force between the pulley and the belt
  T_1 = tension in the tight side of the belt
  T_2 = tension in the slack side of the belt

The coefficient of friction between a rubber belt and a bare steel or cast-iron pulley is approximately 0.25. If the surface of a pulley is lagged with a rubberized fabric, the coefficient of friction will be increased to approximately 0.35.

When power is transmitted from a pulley to a belt, the tension in the slack side of the belt should not exceed the amount required to prevent slippage between the pulley and the belt. For a driving pulley with a given diameter and speed, the effective tension T_e required to transmit a given horsepower to the belt may be determined from the following equation:

$$P = \frac{\pi D T_e N}{33,000} \tag{11-9}$$

where P = horsepower transmitted to belt
  D = diameter of pulley, ft
  T_e = effective force between pulley and belt, lb
  N = rpm (revolutions per minute)

The equation may be rewritten as

$$T_e = \frac{33,000P}{\pi D N} \tag{11-10}$$

The ratio T_1/T_e is defined as the pulley tension factor F. This factor varies with the type of pulley surface, bare or lagged, and the arc of contact between the belt and the pulley. Values for the factor are given in Table 11-11.

The factor may be expressed as

$$F = \frac{T_1}{T_e} \tag{11-11}$$

TABLE 11-11
Tension factors for driving pulleys

Arc of contact (degrees)	Bare pulley	Lagged pulley	Arc of contact (degrees)	Bare pulley	Lagged pulley
Single-pulley drive			Tandem drive		
200	1.72	1.42	360	1.26	1.13
210	1.70	1.40	380	1.23	1.11
215	1.65	1.38	400	1.21	1.10
220	1.62	1.35	450	1.18	1.09
240	1.54	1.30	500	1.14	1.06

Courtesy Hewitt-Robins.

If the required effective force T_e between a pulley and a belt, whose arc of contact is 210°, is 3,000 lb, the minimum tension in the tight side of the belt may be determined from Eq. (11-11) and the factor in Table 11-11. From Table 11-11, $F = 1.70$ for a bare pulley, and

$$T_1 = FT_e$$
$$= 1.70 \times 3,000 = 5,100 \text{ lb}$$

If the same pulley is lagged, the value of F will be 1.40 and

$$T_1 = 1.40 \times 3,000 = 4,200 \text{ lb}$$

For these conditions the minimum of T_1, T_2, and T_e will be:

	Bare pulley (lb)	Lagged pulley (lb)
T_1	5,100	4,200
T_e	3,000	3,000
T_2	2,100	1,200

Thus, it is evident that by lagging a drive pulley, the tension in a belt may be reduced, possibly enough to permit the use of a lighter and less expensive belt.

POWER REQUIRED TO TURN PULLEYS

A belt conveyor includes several pulleys, around which the belt is bent. For the shaft of each pulley there is a bearing friction that requires the consumption of power. The power required will vary with the tension in the belt, the weight of the pulley and shaft, and the type of bearing, babbitted or antifriction. For a given conveyor the friction factors for each pulley may be determined reasonably accurately, and from this information the additional power required to compensate for the loss due to pulley friction may be obtained. Table 11-12 gives the percent of the power delivered to a conveyor required

TABLE 11-12
**Percent of shaft horsepower required to overcome pulley friction
for conveyors with head drive and babbitted bearings**

Length of conveyor (ft)	Slope of conveyor[†] (%)				
	0	2–10	10–19	19–29	29–36
20	112	93	53	35	28
30	76	63	36	25	19
50	45	38	22	15	13
75	30	25	15	12	9
100	22	19	11	8	7
150	15	14	9	7	6
200	14	11	8	6	5
250	12	10	7	5	5
300	11	8	6	5	4
400	9	6	5	4	4
500	7	6	5	4	3
600	6	5	4	3	3
700	5	4	4	3	3
800	4	4	3	3	3
1,000	4	4	3	3	3
2,000	4	4	3		
3,000	4	3	3		

[†]For antifriction bearings, use one-half the above percentages.
Courtesy Hewitt-Robins.

to overcome pulley friction for conveyors with head drive and babbitted bearings for
all pulley shafts.

CONVEYOR BELT TAKE-UPS

Because of the tendency of a conveyor belt to elongate after it is put into operation, a
method of adjusting for the increase in length must be provided.

A screw take-up may be used to increase the length of the conveyor by moving
the head or tail pulley. This adjustment may be sufficient for a short belt but not for a
long belt.

Another take-up, which is more satisfactory, depends on forcing the returning
belt to travel under a weighted pulley, which provides a uniform tension in the belt
regardless of the variation in length.

HOLDBACKS

If a belt conveyor is operated on an incline, it is advisable to install a holdback on the
driving pulley to prevent the load from causing the belt to run backward in the event
of a power failure. A *holdback* is a mechanical device which permits a driving pulley to

rotate in the normal direction but prevents it from rotating in the opposite direction. The operation of a holdback should be automatic. At least three types are available. They are the roller, ratchet, and differential band brake, all of which operate automatically.

A holdback must be strong enough to resist the force produced by the load less the sum of the forces required to move the empty belt, to move the load horizontally, to turn the pulleys, to drive the tripper, and to overcome drive losses.

If a belt conveyor is operated on a decline, the effect of the load is to move the belt forward. If this effect exceeds the total forces of friction, it will be necessary to install a suitable braking unit to regulate the speed of the belt. To overcome this difficulty, an electric motor or generator may be used as the driving unit. In starting an empty belt, the unit will act as a motor, but when the effect of the load is sufficient to overcome all resistances, the unit will act as a generator to regulate the belt speed.

FEEDERS

The purpose of a feeder is to deliver material to a belt at a uniform rate. A feeder may discharge directly onto a belt, or it may discharge the material through a chute in order to reduce the impact of the falling material on the belt. Several types of feeders are available, each of which has advantages and disadvantages when compared with another type. Among the more popular types are the following:

1. Apron
2. Reciprocating
3. Rotary vane
4. Rotary plow

An *apron* feeder usually receives the material from a gated hopper, which regulates the flow onto the feeder. The feeder consists of a moving, flat, rubber-covered belt or a number of flat steel plates connected to two moving chains. This feeder moves the material from under the hopper and discharges it through a receiving unit onto the conveyor belt. A belt feeder is suitable for handling material consisting of relatively small pieces. If the material contains large pieces of highly abrasive rock or stone, a steel-plate-type feeder will usually prove more satisfactory than a belt type.

A *reciprocating* feeder consists of a steel plate placed under a hopper. The plate is operated through an eccentric drive to produce the reciprocating effect, which moves the material onto the conveyor belt.

A *rotary-vane* feeder consists of a number of vanes mounted on a horizontal shaft. As the material flows down an inclined plane, the rotating vanes deliver measured amounts to the conveyor. The rate of feeding may be regulated by varying the speed of the rotating vanes.

A *rotary-plow* feeder consists of a number of plows, or vanes, mounted on a vertical shaft. The plows rotate over a horizontal table onto which the material is allowed to flow. The rate of feeding may be regulated by varying the speed of the plows.

FIGURE 11-8
Belt-propelled automatically controlled tripper.

TRIPPERS

When it is necessary to remove material from a belt conveyor before the material reaches the end of the belt, a tripper should be installed on the conveyor. A tripper consists of a pair of pulleys which are so located that the loaded belt must pass over one pulley and under the other. As the belt passes over the top pulley, the load will be discharged from the belt into an auxiliary hopper or chute.

A tripper may be stationary or a traveling type. The latter type may be propelled by a hand-operated crank, a separate motor, or the conveyor belt. If a tripper is installed on a conveyor, additional power should be provided to operate it. Figure 11-8 illustrates a belt-propelled automatically controlled tripper.

Example 11-3. Belt-conveyor design. Design a belt conveyor to transport unsized crushed limestone. The essential information is as follows:

Capacity, 300 tons per hour
Horizontal distance, 360 ft
Vertical lift, 40 ft
Maximum size stone, 6 in.
Weight of stone, 100 lb per cu ft
Required belt width, from Table 11-2, 24 in.

Maximum speed, from Table 11-3, 400 fpm

Capacity at 400 fpm, Table 11-2, $4 \times 100 = 400$ tons per hour

Required belt speed, $\dfrac{400 \times 300}{400} = 300$ fpm

This speed, 300 fpm, will be satisfactory, provided the feeder supplies material at a uniform rate. If the rate of feeding is irregular, it may be necessary to increase the speed to assure the specified rate of delivery. The design will be based on a speed of 350 fpm to provide a margin of safety.

The power required to operate the loaded conveyor will be:

To drive the empty belt, Table 11-8,
$0.81 \times 350/100$	$=$	2.84 hp[†]
To move the load horizontally, from Table 11-9	$=$	3.92 hp[†]
To lift the load, from Table 11-10	$=$	12.00 hp
Subtotal	$=$	18.76 hp
For pulley friction, from Table 11-2, 4% of 18.76	$=$	0.75 hp
Subtotal required by belt	$=$	19.51 hp
For drive losses, 10% of 19.51	$=$	1.95 hp
Total power required	$=$	21.46 hp

[†]These values are obtained by interpolating in the tables.

Determine the type, size, and number of driving pulleys required to operate the belt. The belt will be driven through a head pulley. When a belt is driven by a pulley, the effective driving force transmitted to the belt is equal to the difference in the belt tensions on the tight side and the slack side, expressed in pounds. This difference is referred to as the effective driving force or tension. Let

T_1 = tight-side tension
T_2 = slack-side tension
T_e = effective tension
$T_e = T_1 - T_2$

The value of T_e can be determined from the horsepower transmitted to the belt and the belt speed in fpm.

$$T_e = \frac{\text{hp} \times 33{,}000}{\text{belt speed, fpm}} = \frac{19.5 \times 33{,}000}{350} = 1{,}838 \text{ lb}$$

$$T_1 - T_2 = 1{,}838 \text{ lb}$$

It is desirable to operate the belt at the lowest practical tight-side and slack-side tensions. The necessary tensions are maintained by the take-ups. The maximum slack-side tension will occur as the belt leaves the driving pulley. This tension will equal the tension at the tail pulley plus the weight of the vertical component of the belt. Field observations indicate that the tension in the belt at the loading point should be no less than 20 lb per in. of belt width. This tension will be transmitted to the slack side of the belt at the tail pulley. The minimum possible slack-side tension will be:

Tension at tail pulley, 20 × 24   = 480 lb
Weight of belt, 40 ft × 6 lb per ft   = 240 lb

    Total tension   = 720 lb

The values of T_1 and T_2 for each of three driving arrangements will be:

Arc of contact (degrees)	T_1 (lb)	T_2 (lb)
Single bare drive		
215	1,838 × 1.65 = 3,035	3,035 − 1,838 = 1,197
220	1,838 × 1.62 = 2,980	2,980 − 1,838 = 1,142
Single lagged drive		
215	1,838 × 1.38 = 2,538	2,538 − 1,838 = 700
220	1,838 × 1.35 = 2,480	2,480 − 1,838 = 642
Tandem bare drive		
400	1,838 × 1.21 = 2,225	2,225 − 1,838 = 387
450	1,838 × 1.18 = 2,170	2,170 − 1,838 = 332

Regardless of the type of drive selected, the minimum slack-side tension in the belt just as it leaves the head pulley will be 720 lb. Adding the effective tension T_e gives a minimum tight-side tension of $720 + 1,838 = 2,558$ lb. If, for a single lagged drive, with an arc of contact of 215°, T_2 is increased to 720 lb, T_1 will be 2,558 lb, which satisfies the tension requirements. Thus, a single lagged pulley will be used to drive the belt.

Reference to Table 11-4 indicates that a 3-ply 42-oz belt has a safe working stress of 2,640 lb, which is satisfactory. The thickness of this belt will permit it to trough satisfactorily. Reference to Table 11-4 indicates that the minimum pulley diameters should be head, 20 in.; tail, take-up, and snub, 16 in.; bend, 12 in.

The troughing idlers should be 5 in. in diameter, spaced 5 ft 0 in. apart, with a maximum spacing of 1 ft 6 in. at the loading point. The return idlers should be 5 in. in diameter, spaced 10 ft 0 in. apart.

Illustrative example 11-4. The use of belt-conveyor systems. When the Los Angeles County Flood Control District prepared an estimate covering the cost of removing 7,300,000 tons of silt, sand, and gravel from the lake bed above the San Gabriel Dam in California, the estimate was based on the use of conventional equipment for excavating and hauling the material to a dump site some 800 ft above the lake. It was estimated that the project would cost $7,977,000, and that it would require 857 days to complete the job. The project was awarded to a contractor at a cost of $4,593,000. He completed the project in some 200 days less than the allotted time.

The contractor installed a belt-conveyor system consisting of 165 flights of belts, each 105 ft long and 48 in. wide, to transport the material from the lake to the disposal area. The electric motor selected to power each flight varied from 40 to 100 hp, depending on the slope of the flight. In order to ensure the same rate of flow of the material on each flight, all belts operated at the same speed.

A feature of the system was the continuous weighing of the material as it moved along on the belt, giving a metered readout of the total tonnage measured from the start of a shift, with another meter showing the cumulative total from the beginning of the week. Still another meter indicated continuously the percent of maximum capacity that the belt was carrying at any given time.

The conveyor was loaded at two separate portable stations by tractor-mounted front-end loaders. The method permitted one station to be moved to another location as necessary, while loading was continued at the other station. Grizzlies were installed at the loader stations to remove any boulders that were too large for the conveyor to handle [2].

PROBLEMS

11-1. Determine the minimum belt width and the minimum belt speed, in fpm, required to transport 300 tons per hour (tph) of unsized crushed stone weighing 100 lb per cu ft. The maximum size of the stone is 4 in.

11-2. What is the capacity of a 36-in.-wide belt, in tph, when the belt is transporting gravel weighing 100 lb per cu ft and is moving at the maximum recommended speed?

11-3. A conveyor 500 ft long with a 30 in.-wide 5-ply 36-oz belt is used to transport material weighing 125 lb per cu ft. The angle of repose for the material is 20°. The revolving parts will weigh 36 lb for each troughing idler and 25 lb for each return idler. Both sides are 5 in. in diameter and are equipped with antifriction bearings. Determine the horsepower required to move this belt at a speed of 300 fpm.

11-4. Using the information given in Table 11-7, determine the horsepower required to move an empty conveyor belt 30 in. wide on a 900-ft-long conveyor equipped with 5-in.-diameter idlers with antifriction bearings when the belt is moving at a speed of 300 fpm.

11-5. If the belt of Prob. 11-4 transports 300 tph up a 5% slope, determine the horsepower required when the belt is moving at the minimum speed necessary to transport the material. The material will weigh 125 lb per cu ft.

11-6. A 4-ply, 36-in.-wide belt on a conveyor 500 ft long will be used to transport its maximum capacity of unsized gravel weighing 125 lb per cu ft up a 4% slope, using 5-in. antifriction idlers. Determine the power required to operate the belt when it is traveling at its maximum recommended speed.

11-7. Design a conveyor-belt system to transport 300 tph of crushed stone under the following conditions:

> Weight of stone, 125 lb per cu ft
> Horizontal distance, 600 ft
> Vertical lift, 60 ft

Use 5-in.-diameter idlers with antifriction bearings.
The design should furnish the following information:

> The required width of the belt
> The number of plies required for the belt
> The required belt speed
> The number of 5-in. diameter troughing and return idlers required
> The spacing of the idlers
> The minimum diameters of the head, tail, take-up, snub, and bend pulleys

REFERENCES

1. "Belt Conveyors for Bulk Materials," *CEMA Handbook,* Conveyor Equipment Manufacturers Association, Stamford, CT, 1980.
2. "Belt-Conveyor System Wins Cleanout Job," *Construction Methods Equipment,* vol. 51, pp. 154–157, March 1969.
3. Golosinski, T. S., J. Wedzicha, and W. Cholewa: "Power Requirements and Resistance to Motion of Oil Sand Conveyors during Winter Operations," *CIM Bulletin,* vol. 84, no. 959, pp. 45–51, April 1992.
4. Lock, Jim: "Belting Up for Muck Removal," *Tunnels & Tunnelling,* vol. 20, no. 10, pp. 47–51, October 1988.
5. Low, W. Irvine: "Portage Mountain Dam Conveyor System," *Journal of the Construction Division, American Society of Civil Engineers,* vol. 95, pp. 126–127, July 1969.
6. Rukavina, Mitchell: "Special Report: Conveyor Trends," *Rock Products,* vol. 93, no. 3, pp. 46–56, March 1990.

CHAPTER
12

COMPRESSED AIR

GENERAL INFORMATION

Compressed air is used extensively on construction projects for drilling rock; loosening earth; operating air motors, hand tools, pile drivers, pumps, and mucking equipment; and cleaning. In many instances the energy supplied by compressed air is the most convenient method of operating equipment and tools.

When air is compressed, it receives energy from the compressor. This energy is transmitted through a pipe or hose to the operating equipment, where a portion of the energy is converted into mechanical work. The operations of compressing, transmitting, and using air will always result in a loss of energy, which will give an overall efficiency less than 100%, sometimes considerably less.

As air is a gas, it obeys the fundamental laws which apply to gases. The laws with which we are concerned are those related to the pressure, volume, temperature, and transmission of air.

GLOSSARY OF GAS-LAW TERMS

The following glossary defines the important terms that are used in developing and applying the laws which relate to compressed air.

Absolute pressure. This is the total pressure measured from absolute zero. It is equal to the sum of the gauge and the atmospheric pressure, corresponding to the barometric reading. The absolute pressure is used in dealing with the gas laws.

Absolute temperature. This is the temperature of a gas measured above absolute zero. It equals degrees Fahrenheit plus 459.6 or, as more commonly used, 460.

Atmospheric pressure. The pressure exerted by the earth's atmosphere at any given position. Also referred to as barometric pressure.

Celsius temperature. This is the temperature indicated by a thermometer calibrated according to the Celsius scale. For this thermometer pure water freezes at 0°C and boils at 100°C, at a pressure of 14.7 psi.

Fahrenheit temperature. This is the temperature indicated by a thermometer calibrated according to the Fahrenheit scale. For this thermometer pure water freezes at 32°F and boils at 212°F, at a pressure of 14.7 psi. Thus, the number of degrees between the freezing and boiling point of water is 180.

Gauge pressure. This is the pressure exerted by the air in excess of atmospheric pressure. It is usually expressed in psi or inches of mercury and is measured by a pressure gauge or a mercury manometer.

Psf. The abbreviation for pounds per square foot of pressure.

Psi. The abbreviation for pounds per square inch of pressure.

Relation between Fahrenheit and Celsius temperatures. A difference of 180° on the Fahrenheit scale equals 100° on the Celsius scale; 1°C equals 1.8°F. A Fahrenheit thermometer will read 32° when a Celsius thermometer reads 0°.

Let T_F = Fahrenheit temperature and T_C = Celsius temperature. For any given temperature the thermometer readings are expressed by the following equation:

$$T_F = 32 + 1.8T_C \tag{12-1}$$

Standard conditions. Because of the variations in the volume of air with pressure and temperature, it is necessary to express the volume at standard conditions if it is to have a definite meaning. Standard conditions are an absolute pressure of 14.696 psi (14.7 psi is commonly used in practice) and a temperature of 60°F.

Temperature. Temperature is a measure of the amount of heat contained by a unit quantity of gas (or other material). It is measured with a thermometer or some other suitable temperature-indicating device.

Vacuum. This is a measure of the extent to which pressure is less than atmospheric pressure. For example, a vacuum of 5 psi is equivalent to an absolute pressure of $14.7 - 5 = 9.7$ psi.

TYPES OF COMPRESSION

Isothermal compression. When a gas undergoes a change in volume without any change in temperature, this is referred to as *isothermal expansion* or *compression*.

Adiabatic compression. When a gas undergoes a change in volume without gaining or losing heat, this is referred to as *adiabatic expansion* or *compression*.

Boyle's law states that when a gas is subjected to a change in volume due to a change in pressure, at a constant temperature, the product of the pressure times the volume will remain constant. This relation is expressed by the equation

$$P_1V_1 = P_2V_2 = K \tag{12-2}$$

where P_1 = initial absolute pressure

$\quad\quad V_1$ = initial volume

$\quad\quad P_2$ = final absolute pressure

$\quad\quad V_2$ = final volume

$\quad\quad K$ = a constant

Example 12-1. Determine the final volume of 1,000 cu ft of air when the gauge pressure is increased from 20 to 120 psi, with no change in temperature. The barometer indicates an atmospheric pressure of 14.7 psi.

$$P_1 = 20 + 14.7 \;\; = 34.7 \text{ psi}$$
$$P_2 = 120 + 14.7 = 134.7 \text{ psi}$$
$$V_1 = 1,000 \text{ cu ft}$$

From Eq. (12-2)

$$V_2 = \frac{P_1 V_1}{P_2} = \frac{34.7 \times 1,000}{134.7} = 257.6 \text{ cu ft}$$

BOYLE'S AND CHARLES' LAWS

When a gas undergoes a change in volume or pressure with a change in temperature, Boyle's law will not apply. Charles' law determines the effect of absolute temperature on the volume of a gas when the pressure is maintained constant. It states that the volume of a given weight of gas at constant pressure varies in direct proportion to its absolute temperature. It may be expressed mathematically by the equation

$$\frac{V_1}{T_1} = \frac{V_2}{T_2} = C \tag{12-3}$$

where V_1 = initial volume

$\quad\quad T_1$ = initial absolute temperature

$\quad\quad V_2$ = final volume

$\quad\quad T_2$ = final absolute temperature

$\quad\quad C$ = a constant

The laws of Boyle and Charles may be combined to give the equation

$$\frac{P_1 V_1}{T_1} = \frac{P_2 V_2}{T_2} = \text{a constant} \tag{12-4}$$

Equation (12-4) may be used to express the relations between pressure, volume, and temperature for any given gas, such as air. It is illustrated by the following example.

Example 12-2. One thousand cubic feet of air, at an initial gauge pressure of 40 psi and temperature of 50°F, is compressed to a volume of 200 cu ft at a final temperature of 110°F. Determine the final gauge pressure. The atmospheric pressure is 14.46 psi.

$$P_1 = 40 + 14.46 = 54.46 \text{ psi}$$
$$V_1 = 1{,}000 \text{ cu ft}$$
$$T_1 = 460 + 50 = 510°F$$
$$V_2 = 200 \text{ cu ft}$$
$$T_2 = 460 + 110 = 570°F$$

Rewriting Eq. (12-4) and substituting these values, we get

$$P_2 = \frac{P_1 V_1}{T_1} \times \frac{T_2}{V_2} = \frac{54.46 \times 1{,}000}{510} \times \frac{570}{200} = 304.34 \text{ psi}$$

Final gauge = 304.34 − 14.46 = 289.88 psi or 290 psi

ENERGY REQUIRED TO COMPRESS AIR

Equation (12-2) may be expressed as $PV = K$, where K is a constant so long as the temperature remains constant. However, in actual practice the temperature usually will not remain constant, and the equation must be modified to provide for the effect of changes in temperature. The effect of temperature may be provided for by introducing an exponent n to V. Thus, Eq. (12-2) may be rewritten as

$$P_1 V_1^n = P_2 V_2^n = K \tag{12-5}$$

For air the values of n will vary from 1.0 for isothermal compression to 1.4 for adiabatic compression. The actual value for any compression condition may be determined experimentally from an indicator card obtained for a given compressor.

When the pressure of a given volume of air is increased by an air compressor, it is necessary to furnish energy to the air. Consider a single compression cycle for an air compressor, as indicated in Fig. 12-1. Air is drawn into the cylinder at pressure P_1

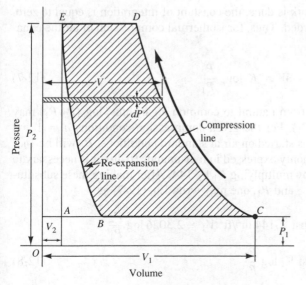

FIGURE 12-1
Cycle for isothermal compression of air.

and is discharged at pressure P_2. P_1 does not need to be atmospheric pressure. The initial volume is V_1. As the piston compresses the air, the pressure-volume will follow the curve CD. At D, when the pressure is P_2, the discharge valve will open and the pressure will remain constant while the volume decreases to V_2, as indicated by line DE. Point E represents the end of the piston stroke. At point E the discharge valve will close, and as the piston begins its return stroke, the pressure will decrease along line EB to a value of P_1, when the intake valve will open and allow additional air to enter the cylinder. This will establish line BC.

The work done along the line CD may be obtained by integrating the equation $dW = V\,dP$.

From Eq. (12-5), $V^n = K/P$. If both sides of the equation are raised to the $1/n$ power, the equation will be

$$V = \left(\frac{K}{P}\right)^{1/n}$$

Substituting this value of V gives

$$dW = \left(\frac{K}{P}\right)^{1/n} dP$$

Integrating yields

$$W = K^{1/n} \int_1^2 \frac{dP}{P^{1/n}} \tag{12-6}$$

For isothermal compression $n = 1$. Substituting this value in Eq. (12-6) gives

$$W = K \int_1^2 \frac{dP}{P} = -K \log_e \frac{P_2}{P_1} + C$$

When $P_2 = P_1$ and no work is done, the constant of integration is equal to zero. The minus sign may be disregarded. Thus, for isothermal compression of air the equation may be written as

$$W = K \log_e \frac{P_2}{P_1} \tag{12-7}$$

If it is desired to convert from natural to common logarithms, $\log_e(P_2/P_1)$ may be replaced by $2.3026 \log(P_2/P_1)$. For the given compression conditions $n = 1$ and $K = P_1 V_1$. If the compression is started on air at standard conditions, P_1 will be 14.7 psi at 60°F. Since work is commonly expressed in foot-pounds (ft-lb), it is necessary to express P_1 in psf. This is done by multiplying P_1 by 144. After making these substitutions and using exact values for e and P_1, one may write Eq. (12-7) as

$$W = 14.696 \text{ psi} \times 144 \text{ in}^2/\text{ft}^2 \; V_1 \times 2.3026 \log \frac{P_2}{P_1}$$

$$= 4{,}873 \text{ psf } V_1 \log \frac{P_2}{P_1} \tag{12-8}$$

The value of W will be in foot-pounds per cycle when V_1 is expressed as cubic feet. One horsepower is equivalent to 33,000 ft-lb per min. If V_1 in Eq. (12-8) is replaced by V, the volume of free air per minute at standard conditions, the horsepower required to compress V cu ft of air from an absolute pressure of P_1 to P_2 psi will be

$$hp = \frac{4,873V \log(P_2/P_1)}{33,000}$$

$$= 0.1477V \log \frac{P_2}{P_1} \qquad (12\text{-}9)$$

Example 12-3. Determine the theoretical horsepower required to compress 100 cu ft of free air per minute, measured at standard conditions, from atmospheric pressure to 100 psi gauge pressure. Substituting in Eq. (12-9), we get

$$hp = 0.1477 \times 100 \times \log \frac{114.7}{14.7}$$

$$= 14.77 \times \log 7.8$$

$$= 14.77 \times 0.892$$

$$= 13.2$$

If air is compressed under other than isothermal conditions, the equation for the required horsepower may be derived in a similar manner. However, since n will not equal 1, it must appear as an exponent in the equation. Equation (12-10) gives the horsepower for nonisothermal conditions.

$$hp = \frac{n}{n-1}0.0642V\left[\left(\frac{P_2}{P_1}\right)^{(n-1)/n} - 1\right] \qquad (12\text{-}10)$$

where the terms are the same as those used in Eq. (12-9).

Example 12-4. Determine the theoretical horsepower required to compress 100 cu ft of free air per minute, measured at standard conditions, from atmospheric pressure 100 psi gauge pressure, under adiabatic conditions. The value n will be 1.4 for air for adiabatic compression. Substituting in Eq. (12-10), we get

$$hp = \frac{1.4}{1.4-1} \times 0.0642 \times 100(7.8^{0.4/1.4} - 1)$$

$$= 22.5(7.8^{0.286} - 1)$$

$$= 22.5 \times 0.798$$

$$= 17.9$$

For air compressors used on construction projects the compression will be performed under conditions between isothermal and adiabatic. Thus, the theoretical horsepower will be between 13.2 and 17.9, the actual value depending on the extent to which the compressor is cooled during operation. The difference in the horsepowers required (almost 35% in this example) illustrates the importance of operating an air compressor at the lowest practical temperature.

TABLE 12-1
Theoretical horsepower required to compress 100 cu ft of free air per minute at different altitudes

Altitude (ft)	Isothermal compression—Single- and two-stage gauge pressure (psi)				Adiabatic compression						
					Single-stage gauge pressure (psi)			Two-stage gauge pressure (psi)			
	60	80	100	125	60	80	100	60	80	100	125
0	10.4	11.9	13.2	14.4	13.4	15.9	18.1	11.8	13.7	15.4	17.1
1,000	10.2	11.7	12.9	14.1	13.2	15.6	17.8	11.6	13.5	15.1	16.8
2,000	10.0	11.4	12.6	13.8	13.0	15.4	17.5	11.4	13.2	14.8	16.4
3,000	9.8	11.2	12.3	13.5	12.8	15.2	17.2	11.2	13.0	14.5	16.1
4,000	9.6	11.0	12.1	13.2	12.6	14.9	16.9	11.0	12.7	14.2	15.7
5,000	9.4	10.7	11.8	12.8	12.4	14.7	16.5	10.8	12.5	13.9	15.4
6,000	9.2	10.5	11.5	12.5	12.2	14.4	16.2	10.6	12.2	13.6	15.1
7,000	9.0	10.3	11.2	12.2	12.0	14.2	16.0	10.4	12.0	13.4	14.8
8,000	8.9	10.0	11.0	11.9	11.8	14.0	15.7	10.2	11.8	13.1	14.5
9,000	8.7	9.8	10.7	11.6	11.6	13.7	15.4	10.0	11.6	12.8	14.1
10,000	8.5	9.6	10.4	11.4	11.5	13.5	15.1	9.8	11.3	12.6	13.8

Source: Compressed Air and Gas Institute.

EFFECT OF ALTITUDE ON THE POWER REQUIRED TO COMPRESS AIR

When a given volume of air, measured as free air prior to its entering a compressor, is compressed, the original pressure will average 14.7 psi absolute pressure at sea level. If the same volume of free air is compressed to the same gauge pressure at a higher altitude, the volume of the air after being compressed will be less than the volume compressed at sea level. The reason for this difference is that the density of a cubic foot of free air at 5,000 ft is less than at sea level. Thus, while a compressor may compress air to the same discharge pressure at a higher altitude, the volume supplied in a given time interval will be less at the higher altitude. This is demonstrated by the use of Eq. (12-2) and information on pressure variation with altitude.

Because a compressor of a specified capacity actually supplies a smaller volume of air at a given discharge pressure at a higher altitude, it requires less power to operate a compressor at a higher altitude, as illustrated in Table 12-1.

GLOSSARY OF AIR-COMPRESSOR TERMS

The following glossary defines the important terms that relate to air compressors and compressed air.

Aftercooler. This is a heat exchanger which cools the air after it is discharged from a compressor.

Air compressor. This is a machine which is used to increase the pressure of air by reducing its volume.

Brake horsepower. Brake horsepower is the actual horsepower input required by a compressor.

Capacity. Capacity is the volume of air delivered by a compressor, expressed in cfm of free air.

Centrifugal compressor. This compressor is a machine in which the compression is effected by a rotating vane or impeller that imparts velocity to the flowing air to give it the desired pressure.

Cfm. The abbreviation for cubic feet per minute.

Compressor efficiency. This is the ratio of the theoretical horsepower to the brake horsepower requirement.

Compression ratio. This is the ratio of the absolute discharge pressure to the absolute inlet pressure.

Density of air. This is the weight of a unity volume of air, usually expressed as pounds per cubic foot (pcf). Density varies with the pressure and temperature of the air. The weight of air at 60°F and 14.7 psi absolute pressure, is 0.07658 lb per cu ft. The volume per pound is 13.059 cu ft.

Discharge pressure. Discharge pressure is the absolute pressure of the air at the outlet from a compressor.

Diversity factor. This is the ratio of the actual quantity of air required for all uses to the sum of the individual quantities required for each use.

Double-acting compressor. The double-acting compressor is a machine which compresses air in both ends of a cylinder.

Free air. Free air is air as it exists under atmospheric conditions at any given location.

Inlet pressure. This is the absolute pressure of the air at the inlet to a compressor.

Intercooler. The intercooler is a heat exchanger which is placed between two compression stages to remove the heat of compression from the air.

Load factor. The load factor is the ratio of the average load during a given period of time to the maximum rated load of a compressor.

Multistage compressor. This is a compressor which produces the desired final pressure through two or more stages.

Reciprocating compressor. This is a machine which compresses air by means of a piston reciprocating in a cylinder.

Rotary compressor. The rotary compressor is a machine in which the compression is effected by the action of rotating elements.

Single-acting compressor. This compressor is a machine which compresses air in only one end of a cylinder.

Single-stage compressor. This is a machine which compresses air from atmospheric pressure to the desired discharge pressure in a single operation.

Theoretical horsepower. This is the horsepower required to compress adiabatically the air delivered by a compressor through the specified pressure range, without any provision for lost energy.

Two-stage compressor. This is a machine which compresses air in two separate operations. The first operation compresses the air to an intermediate pressure, whereas the second operation further compresses it to the desired final pressure.

Volumetric efficiency. This is the ratio of the capacity of a compressor to the piston displacement of the compressor.

STATIONARY COMPRESSORS

Stationary compressors are generally used for installations where there will be a requirement for compressed air over a long duration of time at fixed locations. The compressors may be reciprocating or rotary types, single-stage or multistage. The total quantity of air may be supplied by one or more compressors. The installed cost of a single compressor will usually be less than that for several compressors having the same capacity. However, several compressors provide better flexibility for varying load demands, and in the event of a shutdown for repairs the entire plant does not need to be stopped.

Stationary compressors may be driven by steam, electric motors, or internal-combustion engines.

PORTABLE COMPRESSORS

Portable compressors are more commonly used on construction sites where it is necessary to meet frequently changing job demands. The compressors may be mounted on rubber tires (see Fig. 12-2), steel wheels, or skids. They are usually powered by gasoline or diesel engines and are available in single- or two-stage, reciprocating or rotary types.

Reciprocating compressors. A reciprocating compressor depends on a piston, which moves back and forth in a cylinder, for the compressing action. The piston may compress air while moving in one or both directions. For the former it is defined as single-acting, whereas for the latter it is defined as double-acting. A compressor may have one or more cylinders.

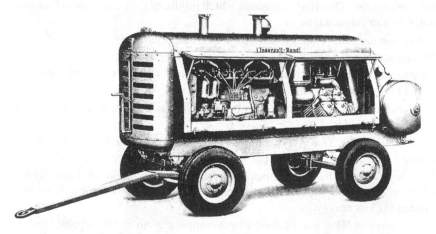

FIGURE 12-2
Two-stage diesel-engine-operated portable air compressor. (*Ingersoll-Rand Company.*)

FIGURE 12-3
Two-stage rotary air compressor. (*Ingersoll-Rand Company.*)

Rotary compressors. These machines offer several advantages compared with reciprocating compressors, such as compactness, light weight, uniform flow, variable output, maintenance-free operation, and long life.

Figure 12-3 illustrates a 600-cfm two-stage rotary compressor which has given excellent performance in the construction industry. Its operating weight is 9,500 lb, which is comparable to the weight of a 315-cfm portable reciprocating unit. The cost is approximately the same as that for a 600-cfm reciprocating compressor.

Rotary screw compressors. The working parts of a screw compressor are two helical rotors as illustrated in Fig. 12-4. The male rotor has four lobes and rotates 50% faster than the female rotor, which has six flutes, with which the male motor meshes. As the air enters and flows through the compressor, it is compressed in the space between the lobes and the flutes. The inlet and outlet ports are automatically covered and uncovered by the shaped ends of the rotors as they turn.

These compressors are available in a relatively wide range of capacities, with single-stage or multistage compression and with rotors which operate under oil-lubricated conditions or with no oil, the latter to produce oil-free air.

They offer several advantages when compared with other types of compressors, including but not limited to:

1. Quiet operation, with little or no loss in output, to satisfy a wide range of legal requirements limiting permissible noise
2. Few moving parts, with minimum mechanical wear and few maintenance requirements
3. Automatic controls actuated by the output pressure, which regulate the speed of the driving unit and the compressor to limit the output to only the demand required
4. Little or no pulsation in the flow of air, and hence reduced vibrations

FIGURE 12-4
The operation of the helical rotors of a screw compressor. (*Atlas Copco, Inc.*)

TABLE 12-2
Representative specifications for rotary screw air compressors

Capacity of free air		Normal operating pressure		Number of compression stages
cfm	cu m/min	psi	kp/cm²	
125	3.5	102	7	1
170	4.8	102	7	1
250	7.1	102	7	1
335	9.5	102	7	1
365	10.3	100	7	2
425	12.0	100	7	2
600	17.0	100	7	2
700	19.8	100	7	2
900	25.5	102	7	2
1,200	34.0	102	7	2
1,500	42.5	102	7	2

Source: Atlas Copco, Inc.

Table 12-2 lists information that is applicable for representative screw compressors operated under absolute inlet air pressure equal to 1 bar (1.02 kp/sq cm or 14.5 psi) and inlet air temperature and inlet coolant temperature equal to 15°C (60°F).

COMPRESSOR CAPACITY

Air compressors are rated by the piston displacement, in cfm. However, the capacity of a compressor will be less than the piston displacement because of valve and piston leakage and the air left in the end-clearance spaces of the cylinders.

The capacity of a compressor is the actual volume of free air drawn into a compressor in a minute. It is expressed in cubic feet. For a reciprocating compressor in good mechanical condition the actual capacity should be 80–90% of the piston displacement. This is illustrated by an analysis of a 315-cfm two-stage portable compressor. The manufacturer's specifications give the following information:

No. of low-pressure cylinders, 4
No. of high-pressure cylinders, 2
Diameter of low-pressure cylinders, 7 in.
Diameter of high-pressure cylinders, $5\frac{3}{4}$ in.
Length of stroke, 5 in.
rpm, 870

Consider only the piston displacement of the low-pressure cylinders as they determine the capacity of the unit.

Area of cylinder, $\dfrac{\pi \times 7^2}{4 \times 144}$ = 0.267 sq ft

Displacement per cylinder per stroke, $0.267 \times \dfrac{5}{12}$ = 0.111 cu ft

Displacement per minute, $4 \times 0.111 \times 870$ = 388 cu ft
Specified capacity, 315 cu ft
Volumetric efficiency, $\dfrac{315}{388} \times 100$ = 81.3%

EFFECT OF ALTITUDE ON CAPACITY OF COMPRESSORS

The capacity of an air compressor is rated on the basis of its performance at sea level, where the normal absolute barometric pressure is about 14.7 psi. If a compressor is operated at a higher altitude, such as 5,000 ft above sea level, the absolute barometric pressure will be about 12.2 psi. Thus, at the higher altitude, density is less and the weight of air in a cubic foot of free volume is less than at sea level. If the air is discharged by the compressor at a given pressure, the compression ratio will be increased, and the capacity of the compressor will be reduced. This may be demonstrated by applying Eq. (12-2).

Assume the 100 cu ft of free air at sea level is compressed to 100-psi gauge with no change in temperature. Applying Eq. (12-2), we obtain

$$V_2 = \frac{P_1 V_1}{P_2}$$

where V_1 = 100 cu ft
P_1 = 14.7 psi absolute
P_2 = 114.7 psi absolute
$V_2 = \dfrac{14.7 \times 100}{114.7} = 12.82$ cu ft

At 5,000 ft above sea level

V_1 = 100 cu ft
P_1 = 12.2 psi absolute
P_2 = 112.2 psi absolute
$V_2 = \dfrac{12.2 \times 100}{112.2} = 10.87$ cu ft

TABLE 12-3
The effect of altitude on the capacity of single-stage air compressors

| Altitude above sea level | | Operating pressure: psi gauge [psi absolute], (Pa) | | | | | | | |
| | | 80 [94.7] (6.53 × 10⁵) | | 90 [104.7] (7.23 × 10⁵) | | 100 [114.7] (7.91 × 10⁵) | | 125 [139.7] (9.65 × 10⁵) | |
ft	m	Compressor ratio[†]	Factor[‡]	Compressor ratio	Factor	Compressor ratio	Factor	Compressor ratio	Factor
0	0	6.44	1.000	7.12	1.000	7.81	1.000	9.51	1.000
1,000	305	6.64	0.992	7.34	0.988	8.05	0.987	9.81	0.982
2,000	610	6.88*	0.977	7.62	0.972	8.35	0.972	10.20	0.962
3,000	915	7.12	0.967	7.87	0.959	8.63	0.957	10.55	0.942
4,000	1,220	7.36	0.953	8.15	0.944	8.94	0.942	10.92	0.923
5,000	1,525	7.62	0.940	8.44	0.931	9.27	0.925	11.32	0.903
6,000	1,830	7.84	0.928	8.69	0.917	9.55	0.908	11.69	0.883
7,000	2,135	8.14	0.915	9.03	0.902	9.93	0.890	12.17	0.863
8,000	2,440	8.42	0.900	9.33	0.886	10.26	0.873	12.58	0.844
9,000	2,745	8.70	0.887	9.65	0.868	10.62	0.857	13.02	0.824
10,000	3,050	9.00	0.872	10.00	0.853	11.00	0.840	13.50	0.804
11,000	3,355	9.34	0.858	10.38	0.837	11.42	0.823	14.03	
12,000	3,660	9.70	0.839	10.79	0.818	11.88	0.807	14.60	
14,000	4,270	10.42	0.805	11.60		12.78		15.71	
15,000	4,575	10.88	0.784	12.12		13.36		16.43	

[†] The compressor ratio is the ratio of the volume of free air divided by the volume of the same air at the indicated pressure.
[‡] When this factor is multiplied by the specified capacity of the compressor, at sea level, it will give the capacity at the indicated altitude and operating pressure.
Source: Compressed Air and Gas Institute.

Table 12-3 lists the factors that should be applied to single-stage compressors to correct for the loss in capacity at various altitudes. For example, a compressor having a sea-level capacity of 600 cfm operating at a pressure of 100 psi gauge will have a capacity at 5,000 ft equal to $600 \times 0.925 = 555.0$ cfm if the operating pressure is 100 psi gauge. At an altitude of 10,000 ft the capacity will be reduced to $600 \times 0.840 = 504$ cfm.

INTERCOOLERS

Frequently intercoolers are installed between the stages of a compressor to reduce the temperature of the air and to remove moisture from the air. The reduction in temperature prior to additional compression can reduce the total power required by as much as 10 to 15%. Unless an intercooler is installed, the power required by a two-stage compressor will be the same as that for a single-stage compressor.

An intercooler requires a continuous supply of circulating cool water to remove the heat from the air. It will require 1.0 to 1.5 gal of water per minute for each 100 cfm of air compressed, the actual amount depending on the temperature of the water.

AFTERCOOLERS

Aftercoolers are sometimes installed at the discharge side of a compressor to cool the air to the desired temperature and to remove moisture from the air. It is highly desirable to remove excess moisture from the air, as it tends to freeze during expansion in air tools, and it washes the lubricating oil out of tools, thereby reducing the lubricating efficiency.

RECEIVERS

An air receiver should be installed on the discharge side of a compressor to equalize the compressor pulsations and to serve as a condensing chamber for the removal of water and oil vapors. A receiver should have a drain cock at its bottom to permit the removal of the condensate. Its volume should be one-tenth to one-sixth the capacity of the compressor. A blowoff valve, to limit the maximum pressure, is desirable.

LOSS OF AIR PRESSURE IN PIPE DUE TO FRICTION

The loss in pressure due to friction as air flows through a pipe or a hose is a factor which must be considered in selecting the size of a pipe or hose. Failure to use a sufficiently large line may cause the air pressure to drop so low that it will not satisfactorily operate the tool to which it is providing power.

The selection of the size of line is a problem in economy. The efficiency of most equipment operated by compressed air drops off rapidly as the pressure of the air is reduced. When the cost of lost efficiency exceeds the cost of providing a larger line, it is cost-effective to install a larger line. The manufacturers of pneumatic equipment generally specify the minimum air pressure at which the equipment will operate satisfactorily. However, these values should be considered as minimum and not desirable operating pressures. The actual pressure should be higher than the specified minimum.

> **Example 12-5.** The cost of lost efficiency on a project resulting from the operation of pneumatic equipment at reduced pressure is estimated to be $1,000. The lost efficiency can be eliminated by installing a larger line at an additional cost of $600. In this instance the contractor will save $400 by installing the larger pipe. Thus, it is cost-effective to spend $600 to eliminate an operating loss of $1,000.

Several formulas are used to determine the loss of pressure in a pipe due to friction. The following equation has been used extensively:

$$f = \frac{CL}{r} \times \frac{Q^2}{d^5} \qquad (12\text{-}11)$$

where f = pressure drop, psi
$\quad L$ = length of pipe, ft
$\quad Q$ = cu ft of free air per sec
$\quad r$ = ratio of compression
$\quad d$ = actual ID of pipe, in.
$\quad C$ = experimental coefficient

For ordinary steel pipe the value of C has been found to equal $0.1025/d^{0.31}$. If this value is substituted in Eq. (12-11), we get

$$f = \frac{0.1025L}{r} \times \frac{Q^2}{d^{5.31}} \qquad (12\text{-}12)$$

A chart for determining the loss in pressure in a pipe is given in Fig. 12-5.

> **Example 12-6.** This example illustrates the use of the chart in Fig. 12-5. Determine the pressure loss per 100 ft of pipe resulting from transmitting 1,000 cfm of free air, at 100 psi gauge pressure, through a 4-in. standard-weight steel pipe. Enter the chart at the top at 100 psi; then proceed vertically downward to a point opposite 1,000 cfm; then proceed parallel to the sloping guide lines to a point opposite the 4-in. pipe; and then proceed vertically downward to the bottom of the chart, where the pressure drop is indicated to be 0.225 psi.

Table 12-4 gives the loss of air pressure in 1,000 ft of standard-weight pipe due to friction. For longer or shorter lengths of pipe the friction loss will be in proportion to the length. The losses given in the table are for an initial gauge pressure of 100 psi. If the initial pressure is other than 100 psi, the corresponding losses may be obtained by multiplying the values in Table 12-4 by a suitable factor. Reference to Eq. (12-12) reveals that for a given rate of flow through a given size pipe the only variable is r, which is the ratio of compression, based on absolute pressures. For a gauge pressure of 100 psi, $r = 114.7/14.7 = 7.8$, whereas for a gauge pressure of 80 psi, $r = 94.7/14.7 = 6.44$. The ratio of these values of $r = 7.8/6.44 = 1.211$. Thus, the loss for an initial pressure

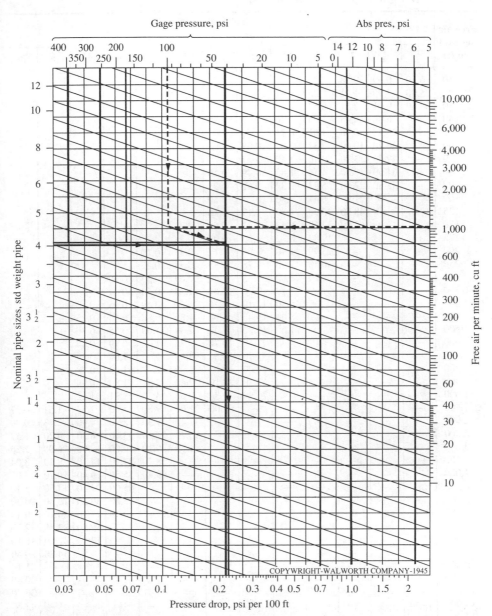

FIGURE 12-5
Compressed-air flow chart.

TABLE 12-4
Loss of pressure, in psi, in 1,000 feet of standard-weight pipe due to friction for an initial gauge pressure of 100 psi

Free air per min (cu ft)	$\frac{1}{2}$	$\frac{3}{4}$	1	$1\frac{1}{4}$	$1\frac{1}{2}$	2	$2\frac{1}{2}$	3	$3\frac{1}{2}$	4	$4\frac{1}{2}$	5	6
						Nominal diameter (in.)							
10	6.50	0.99	0.28										
20	25.90	3.90	1.11	0.25	0.11								
30	68.50	9.01	2.51	0.57	0.26								
40	—	16.00	4.45	1.03	0.46								
50	—	25.10	6.96	1.61	0.71	0.19							
60	—	36.20	10.00	2.32	1.02	0.28							
70	—	49.30	13.70	3.16	1.40	0.37							
80	—	64.50	17.80	4.14	1.83	0.49	0.19						
90	—	82.80	22.60	5.23	2.32	0.62	0.24						
100	—	—	27.90	6.47	2.86	0.77	0.30						
125	—	—	48.60	10.20	4.49	1.19	0.46						
150	—	—	62.80	14.60	6.43	1.72	0.66	0.21					
175	—	—	—	19.80	8.72	2.36	0.91	0.28					
200	—	—	—	25.90	11.40	3.06	1.19	0.37	0.17				
250	—	—	—	40.40	17.90	4.78	1.85	0.58	0.27				
300	—	—	—	58.20	25.80	6.85	2.67	0.84	0.39	0.20			
350	—	—	—	—	35.10	9.36	3.64	1.14	0.53	0.27			
400	—	—	—	—	45.80	12.10	4.75	1.50	0.69	0.35	0.19		
450	—	—	—	—	58.00	15.40	5.98	1.89	0.88	0.46	0.25		
500	—	—	—	—	71.60	19.20	7.42	2.34	1.09	0.55	0.30		
600	—	—	—	—	—	27.60	10.70	3.36	1.56	0.79	0.44		
700	—	—	—	—	—	37.70	14.50	4.55	2.13	1.09	0.59		
800	—	—	—	—	—	49.00	19.00	5.89	2.77	1.42	0.78		
900	—	—	—	—	—	62.30	24.10	7.60	3.51	1.80	0.99		
1,000	—	—	—	—	—	76.90	29.80	9.30	4.35	2.21	1.22		
1,500	—	—	—	—	—	—	67.00	21.00	9.80	4.90	2.73	1.51	0.57
2,000	—	—	—	—	—	—	—	37.40	17.30	8.80	4.90	2.73	0.99
2,500	—	—	—	—	—	—	—	58.40	27.20	13.80	8.30	4.20	1.57
3,000	—	—	—	—	—	—	—	84.10	39.10	20.00	10.90	6.00	2.26
3,500	—	—	—	—	—	—	—	—	58.20	27.20	14.70	8.20	3.04
4,000	—	—	—	—	—	—	—	—	69.40	35.50	19.40	10.70	4.01
4.500	—	—	—	—	—	—	—	—	—	45.00	24.50	13.50	5.10
5,000	—	—	—	—	—	—	—	—	—	55.60	30.20	16.80	6.30
6,000	—	—	—	—	—	—	—	—	—	80.00	43.70	24.10	9.10
7,000	—	—	—	—	—	—	—	—	—	—	59.50	32.80	12.20
8,000	—	—	—	—	—	—	—	—	—	—	77.50	42.90	16.10
9,000	—	—	—	—	—	—	—	—	—	—	—	54.30	20.40
10,000	—	—	—	—	—	—	—	—	—	—	—	—	25.10
11,000	—	—	—	—	—	—	—	—	—	—	—	—	30.40
12,000	—	—	—	—	—	—	—	—	—	—	—	—	36.20
13,000	—	—	—	—	—	—	—	—	—	—	—	—	42.60
14,000	—	—	—	—	—	—	—	—	—	—	—	—	49.20
15,000	—	—	—	—	—	—	—	—	—	—	—	—	56.60

of 80 psi will be 1.211 times the loss for an initial pressure of 100 psi. For other initial pressures the factors are given below:

Gauge pressure (psi)	Factor
80	1.211
90	1.095
100	1.000
110	0.912
120	0.853
125	0.822

LOSS OF AIR PRESSURE THROUGH FITTINGS AND HOSE

In order to provide for the loss of pressure resulting from the flow of air through screw-pipe fittings, it is common practice to convert a fitting to its equivalent length of pipe having the same nominal diameter. This equivalent length should be added to the actual length of the pipe in determining pressure loss. Table 12-5 gives the equivalent length of standard-weight pipe for computing pressure losses. The loss of pressure resulting from the flow of air through a hose is given in Table 12-6.

TABLE 12-5
Equivalent length, in feet, of standard-weight pipe having the same pressure losses as screwed fittings

Nominal pipe size (in.)	Gate valve	Globe valve	Angle valve	Long-radius ell or on run of standard tee	Standard ell or on run of tee	Tee through side outlet
$\frac{1}{2}$	0.4	17.3	8.6	0.6	1.6	3.1
$\frac{3}{4}$	0.5	22.9	11.4	0.8	2.1	4.1
1	0.6	29.1	14.6	1.1	2.6	5.2
$1\frac{1}{4}$	0.8	38.3	19.1	1.4	3.5	6.9
$1\frac{1}{2}$	0.9	44.7	22.4	1.6	4.0	8.0
2	1.2	57.4	28.7	2.1	5.2	10.3
$2\frac{1}{2}$	1.4	68.5	34.3	2.5	6.2	12.3
3	1.8	85.2	42.6	3.1	6.2	15.3
4	2.4	112.0	56.0	4.0	7.7	20.2
5	2.9	140.0	70.0	5.0	10.1	25.2
6	3.5	168.0	84.1	6.1	15.2	30.4
8	4.7	222.0	111.0	8.0	20.0	40.0
10	5.9	278.0	139.0	10.0	25.0	50.0
12	7.0	332.0	166.0	11.0	29.8	59.6

TABLE 12-6
Loss of pressure, in psi, in 50 feet of hose and end couplings

Size of hose (in.)	Gauge pressure at line (psi)	Volume of free air through hose (cfm)													
		20	30	40	50	60	70	80	90	100	110	120	130	140	150
$\frac{1}{2}$	50	1.8	5.0	10.1	18.1										
	60	1.3	4.0	8.4	14.8	23.5									
	70	1.0	3.4	7.0	12.4	20.0	28.4								
	80	0.9	2.8	6.0	10.8	17.4	25.2	34.6							
	90	0.8	2.4	5.4	9.5	14.8	22.0	30.5	41.0						
	100	0.7	2.3	4.8	8.4	13.3	19.3	27.2	36.6						
	110	0.6	2.0	4.3	7.6	12.0	17.6	24.6	33.3	44.5					
$\frac{3}{4}$	50	0.4	0.8	1.5	2.4	3.5	4.4	6.5	8.5	11.4	14.2				
	60	0.3	0.6	1.2	1.9	2.8	3.8	5.2	6.8	8.6	11.2				
	70	0.2	0.5	0.9	1.5	2.3	3.2	4.2	5.5	7.0	8.8	11.0			
	80	0.2	0.5	0.8	1.3	1.9	2.8	3.6	4.7	5.8	7.2	8.8	10.6		
	90	0.2	0.4	0.7	1.1	1.6	2.3	3.1	4.0	5.0	6.2	7.5	9.0		
	100	0.2	0.4	0.6	1.0	1.4	2.0	2.7	3.5	4.4	5.4	6.6	7.9	9.4	11.1
	110	0.1	0.3	0.5	0.9	1.3	1.8	2.4	3.1	3.9	4.9	5.9	7.1	8.4	9.9
1	50	0.1	0.2	0.3	0.5	0.8	1.1	1.5	2.0	2.6	3.5	4.8	7.0		
	60	0.1	0.2	0.3	0.4	0.6	0.8	1.2	1.5	2.0	2.6	3.3	4.2	5.5	7.2
	70	—	0.1	0.2	0.4	0.5	0.7	1.0	1.3	1.6	2.0	2.5	3.1	3.8	4.7
	80	—	0.1	0.2	0.3	0.5	0.7	0.8	1.1	1.4	1.7	2.0	2.4	2.7	3.5
	90	—	0.1	0.2	0.3	0.4	0.6	0.7	0.9	1.2	1.4	1.7	2.0	2.4	2.8
	100	—	0.1	0.2	0.2	0.4	0.5	0.6	0.8	1.0	1.2	1.5	1.8	2.1	2.4
	110	—	0.1	0.2	0.2	0.3	0.4	0.6	0.7	0.9	1.1	1.3	1.5	1.8	2.1
$1\frac{1}{4}$	50	—	—	0.2	0.2	0.2	0.3	0.4	0.5	0.7	1.1				
	60	—	—	—	0.1	0.2	0.3	0.3	0.5	0.6	0.8	1.0	1.2	1.5	
	70	—	—	—	0.1	0.2	0.2	0.3	0.4	0.4	0.5	0.7	0.8	1.0	1.3
	80	—	—	—	—	0.1	0.2	0.2	0.3	0.4	0.5	0.6	0.7	0.8	1.0
	90	—	—	—	—	0.1	0.2	0.2	0.3	0.3	0.4	0.5	0.6	0.7	0.8
	100	—	—	—	—	—	0.1	0.2	0.2	0.3	0.4	0.4	0.5	0.6	0.7
	110	—	—	—	—	—	0.1	0.2	0.2	0.3	0.3	0.4	0.5	0.5	0.6
$1\frac{1}{2}$	50	—	—	—	—	—	0.1	0.2	0.2	0.2	0.3	0.3	0.4	0.5	0.6
	60	—	—	—	—	—	—	0.1	0.2	0.2	0.2	0.3	0.3	0.4	0.5
	70	—	—	—	—	—	—	—	0.1	0.2	0.2	0.2	0.3	0.3	0.4
	80	—	—	—	—	—	—	—	—	0.1	0.2	0.2	0.2	0.3	0.4
	90	—	—	—	—	—	—	—	—	—	0.1	0.2	0.2	0.2	0.2
	100	—	—	—	—	—	—	—	—	—	—	0.1	0.2	0.2	0.2
	110	—	—	—	—	—	—	—	—	—	—	0.1	0.2	0.2	0.2

RECOMMENDED SIZES OF PIPE FOR TRANSMITTING COMPRESSED AIR

In transmitting air from a compressor to pneumatic equipment, it is necessary to limit the pressure drop along the line. If this precaution is not taken, the pressure may drop below that for which the equipment was designed and production will suffer.

At least two factors should be considered in determining the minimum size pipe: (1) the necessity of supplying air at the required pressure and (2) the desirability of supplying energy (compressed air) at the lowest total cost, taking into account the cost of the pipe and the cost of production obtained from the equipment. Considering the first factor, a smaller pipe may be used for a short run rather than for a long run. While this is possible, it may not be economical. For the latter factor, economy may dictate the use of a pipe larger than the minimum possible size. The cost of installing a large pipe will be more fully justified for an installation that will be used for a long period of time than for one that will be used for a short period of time.

No book, table, or fixed data can give the correct pipe size for all installations. The correct method of determining the size pipe for a given installation is to make a complete engineering analysis of the particular operations required.

Table 12-7 gives recommended sizes of pipe for transmitting compressed air for various lengths of run. This information is useful as a guide in selecting pipe sizes.

RECOMMENDED SIZES OF HOSE FOR TRANSMITTING COMPRESSED AIR

Most pneumatic equipment and tools require a length of flexible hose between the source of air and the equipment. As the loss of pressure in the hose is relatively high, the length should be no greater than is required for satisfactory operation.

TABLE 12-7
Recommended pipe sizes for transmitting compressed air at 80 to 125 psi gauge

Volume of air (cfm)	Length of pipe (ft)				
	50–200	200–500	500–1,000	1,000–2,500	2,500–5,000
	Nominal size pipe (in.)				
30–60	1	1	$1\frac{1}{4}$	$1\frac{1}{2}$	$1\frac{1}{2}$
60–100	1	$1\frac{1}{4}$	$1\frac{1}{4}$	2	2
100–200	$1\frac{1}{4}$	$1\frac{1}{2}$	2	$2\frac{1}{2}$	$2\frac{1}{2}$
200–500	2	$2\frac{1}{2}$	3	$3\frac{1}{2}$	$3\frac{1}{2}$
500–1,000	$2\frac{1}{2}$	3	$3\frac{1}{2}$	4	$4\frac{1}{2}$
1,000–2,000	$2\frac{1}{2}$	4	$4\frac{1}{2}$	5	6
2,000–4,000	$3\frac{1}{2}$	5	6	8	8
4,000–8,000	6	8	8	10	10

TABLE 12-8
Recommended sizes of hose, in inches, for transmitting compressed air at 80 to 125 psi gauge

Volume of air (cfm)	Types of air tools	Length of hose (ft)		
		0–25	25–50	50–200
0–15	Spray guns $\frac{1}{4}$-in. drills Light chipping and scaling hammers $\frac{3}{8}$-in. impact wrenches	$\frac{5}{16}$	$\frac{3}{8}$	$\frac{1}{2}$
15–30	$\frac{5}{16}$–$\frac{1}{2}$-in. drills $\frac{5}{8}$-in. impact wrenches Chipping hammers 15-lb rock drills	$\frac{3}{8}$	$\frac{1}{2}$	$\frac{1}{2}$
30–60	$\frac{5}{8}$–1-in. drills $\frac{3}{4}$-in. impact wrenches Light grinders Rivet hammers Clay diggers Backfill tampers Small concrete vibrators Light and medium demolition tools 25-lb rock drills	$\frac{1}{2}$	$\frac{3}{4}$	$\frac{3}{4}$
60-100	1–2-in. drills $1\frac{1}{4}$–$1\frac{3}{4}$-in. impact wrenches Heavy grinders Large concrete vibrators Sump pumps 35–55-lb rock drills Heavy demolition tools	$\frac{3}{4}$	$\frac{3}{4}$	1
100–200	Winches and hoists Drifters Wagon drills 75-lb rock drills	1	1	$1\frac{1}{4}$

Table 12-8 gives the recommended sizes of hose based on transmitting the specified quantities of compressed air to various types of pneumatic equipment and tools frequently used on construction projects.

DIVERSITY OR CAPACITY FACTOR

While it is necessary to provide as much compressed air as will be required to supply the needs of all operating equipment, providing more air capacity than is actually needed is extravagant. It is probable that all equipment nominally used on a project will not be in operation at any given time. An analysis of the job should be made to determine the probable maximum *actual* need prior to designing the compressed-air system.

TABLE 12-9a
Quantities of compressed air required by pneumatic equipment and tools[†]

Equipment or tools	Capacity or size		Air consumption (cfm)
	Weight (lb)	Depth of hole (ft)	
Jackhammers	10	0–2	15–25
	15	0–2	20–35
	25	2–8	30–50
	35	8–12	55–75
	45	12–16	80–100
	55	16–24	90–110
	75	8–24	150–175
Paving breakers	35	—	30–35
	60	—	40–45
	80	—	50–50

[†] Air pressure at 90 psi guage.

If 10 jackhammers are nominally drilling, normally no more than 5 or 6 will be consuming air at a given time. The others will be out of use temporarily for changes in bits or drill steel or moving to new locations. Thus, the *actual* amount of air demand should be based on 5 or 6 drills instead of 10. The same condition applies to other pneumatic tools.

The *capacity factor* is the ratio of the actual load to the maximum mathematical load that will exist if all tools are operating at the same time. This ratio is also referred to as a *diversity factor*. For example, if a jackhammer required 90 cfm of air, 10 hammers would require a total of 900 cfm if they were all operated at the same time. However, with only 5 hammers operating at one time, the demand for air would be 450 cfm. Thus, the diversity factor would be $450 \div 900 = 0.5$.

AIR REQUIRED BY PNEUMATIC EQUIPMENT AND TOOLS

The approximate quantities of compressed air required by pneumatic equipment and tools are given in Table 12-9. The quantities are based on continuous operation at a pressure of 90 psi gauge.

EFFECTS OF ALTITUDE ON THE CONSUMPTION OF AIR BY ROCK DRILLS

As previously explained in this chapter, the capacity of an air compressor is the volume of free air that enters the compressor during a stated time, usually expressed in cfm. Because of the lower atmospheric pressure at higher altitudes, the quantity of air supplied by a compressor at a given gauge pressure will be less than at sea level. It is necessary to provide more compressor capacity at higher altitudes to assure an adequate supply of air at the specified pressure to rock drills.

TABLE 12-9b
Quantities of compressed air required by pneumatic equipment and tools[†]

Equipment or tools	Capacity or size	Air consumption (cfm)
Chipping hammers	Light	15–25
	Heavy	25–30
Clay diggers	Light, 20 lb	20–25
	Medium, 25 lb	25–30
	Heavy, 35 lb	30–35
Concrete vibrators	$2\frac{1}{2}$-in.-tube diameter	20–30
	3-in.-tube diameter	40–50
	4-in.-tube diameter	45–55
	5-in.-tube diameter	75–85
Drills or borers	1-in. diameter	35–40
	2-in. diameter	50–75
	4-in. diameter	50–75
Hoist	Single-drum, 2,000-lb pull	200–220
	Double-drum, 2,400-lb pull	250–260
Impact wrenches	$\frac{5}{8}$-in. bolt	15–20
	$\frac{3}{4}$-in. bolt	30–40
	$1\frac{1}{4}$-in. bolt	60–70
	$1\frac{1}{2}$-in. bolt	70–80
	$1\frac{3}{4}$-in. bolt	80–90
Saws:		
Circular	12-in. blade	40–60
Chain	18–30-in. blade	85–95
	36-in. blade	135–150
	48-in. blade	150–160
Reciprocating	20-in.	45–50
Spray guns	Light duty	2–3
	Medium duty	8–15
	Heavy duty	14–30
Sump pump	Single-stage, 10–40-ft head	80–90
	Single-stage, 100–150-ft head	150–170
	Two-stage, 100–150-ft head	160–180
Trampers, earth	35 lb	30–35
	60 lb	40–45
	80 lb	50–60
Wagon drills—drifters	3-in. piston	150–175
	$3\frac{1}{2}$-in. piston	180–210
	4-in. piston	225–275

[†] Air pressure at 90 psi gauge.

TABLE 12-10
Factors to be used in determining the capacities of compressed air required by rock drills at different altitudes

Alti- tude (ft)	Number of drills									
	1	2	3	4	5	6	7	8	9	10
	Factor									
0	1.0	1.8	2.7	3.4	4.1	4.8	5.4	6.0	6.5	7.1
1,000	1.0	1.9	2.8	3.5	4.2	4.9	5.6	6.2	6.7	7.3
2,000	1.1	1.9	2.9	3.6	4.4	5.1	5.8	6.4	7.0	7.6
3,000	1.1	2.0	3.0	3.7	4.5	5.3	5.9	6.6	7.2	7.8
4,000	1.1	2.1	3.1	3.9	4.7	5.5	6.1	6.8	7.4	8.1
5,000	1.2	2.1	3.2	4.0	4.8	5.6	6.3	7.0	7.6	8.3
6,000	1.2	2.2	3.2	4.1	4.9	5.8	6.5	7.2	7.8	8.5
7,000	1.2	2.2	3.3	4.2	5.0	5.9	6.6	7.4	8.0	8.7
8,000	1.3	2.3	3.4	4.3	5.2	6.1	6.8	7.6	8.2	9.0
9,000	1.3	2.3	3.5	4.4	5.3	6.2	7.0	7.7	8.4	9.2
10,000	1.3	2.4	3.6	4.5	5.4	6.3	7.1	7.9	8.6	9.4
12,000	1.4	2.5	3.7	4.6	5.6	6.6	7.4	8.2	8.9	9.7
15,000	1.4	2.6	3.9	4.7	5.9	6.9	7.7	8.6	9.3	10.2

Source: Compressed Air and Gas Institute.

Table 12-10 gives representative factors to be applied to specified compressor capacities to determine the required capacities at different altitudes. For example, if a single drill requires a capacity of 600 cfm of air at sea level, it will require a capacity of $600 \times 1.2 = 720$ cfm at an altitude of 5,000 ft, and $600 \times 1.3 = 780$ cfm at an altitude of 10,000 ft.

The values of the factors are adjusted to reflect representative diversity factors for the use of multidrills. Because these factors will not necessarily apply to all drills and projects, they should be used only as a guide.

THE COST OF COMPRESSED AIR

The cost of compressed air may be determined at the compressor or at the point of use. The former will include the cost of compressing plus transmitting, including line losses.

The cost of compressing should include the total cost of the compressor, both ownership and operation. The cost is usually based on 1,000 cu ft of free air.

Example 12-7. Determine the cost of compressing 1,000 cu ft of free air to a gauge pressure of 100 psi by using a 600-cfm, two-stage portable compressor driven by a 180-hp diesel engine.
The following information will apply:

Annual ownership cost = $19,686
Based on a 5-year life at 1,400 hours per year
Fuel consumed per hour, $0.04 \times 180 = 7.2$ gal
Lubricating oil consumed per hour, 0.125 gal

Hourly costs:

$$
\begin{array}{ll}
\text{Fixed cost, } \$19,686 \div 1,400 \text{ hour} & = \$14.06 \\
\text{Fuel, 7.2 gal @ } \$1.00 & = \quad 7.20 \\
\text{Lubricating oil, 0.125 gal @ } \$3.20 & = \quad 0.40 \\
\text{Operator, } \tfrac{1}{2} \text{ time @ } \$16.00 \text{ per hour} & = \quad 8.00^\dagger \\
\hline
\text{Total cost per hour} & = \$29.66
\end{array}
$$

† This cost will vary with location and company benefit packages.

Volume of air compressed per 50-min hour, $50 \times 600 = 30,000$ cu ft.

Cost per 1,000 cu ft, $\$29.66 \div 30 = \$0.989$ or $\$0.99$

The cost per 1,000 cu ft of air for a compressor operating under various load factors might be as follows:

	Load factor (%)		
	100	**75**	**50**
Hours costs:			
Fixed cost†	$14.06	$14.06	$14.06
Fuel	7.20	5.38	4.28
Lubricating oil	0.40	0.30	0.24
Operator, $\tfrac{1}{2}$ time‡	8.00	8.00	8.00
Total cost per hour	$29.66	$27.74	$26.58
Volume of air per hour (cu ft)	30,000	22,500	15,000
Cost per 1,000 cu ft	$0.99	$1.23	$1.77

† This cost may vary slightly with the load factor.
‡ This cost may vary with the locations.

THE COST OF AIR LEAKS

The loss of air through leakage in a transmission line can be surprisingly large and costly. Leakage results from poor pipe connections, loose valve stems, deteriorated hose,

TABLE 12-11
Cost per month for air leakage

Size of opening (in.)	Cubic feet of air lost per month at 100 psi	For indicated cost per 1,000 cu ft			
		$ 0.45	**$ 0.60**	**$ 0.75**	**$ 1.20**
$\frac{1}{32}$	45,500	$ 19.14	$ 27.30	$ 34.14	$ 45.50
$\frac{1}{16}$	182,300	82.20	109.50	136.95	182.30
$\frac{1}{8}$	740,200	333.00	444.00	555.00	740.20
$\frac{1}{4}$	2,920,000	1,314.00	1,782.00	2,190.00	2,920.00

and loose hose connections. If the cost of such leaks were more fully known, most of them would be eliminated. The rate of leakage through an opening of known size can be determined by applying a formula for the flow of air through an orifice.

Table 12-11 illustrates the cost of air leakage for various sizes of openings and costs per 1,000 cu ft of air.

THE COST OF USING LOW AIR PRESSURE

The effect on the cost of production of operating pneumatic equipment at less than the recommended air pressure can be demonstrated by analyzing the performance of a group of jackhammers under different pressures. Similar results would be obtained when using other kinds of pneumatic equipment. The hammers receive the air from a common header-type pipeline.

Example 12-8. Determine the economy of using a 3-in. pipe instead of a $2\frac{1}{2}$-in. pipe to transmit compressed air to jackhammers. The air will be supplied to the entrance of each pipe at a pressure of 100-psi gauge. The stated conditions will apply:

Length of pipe, 1,000 ft
Installed cost of 3-in. pipe, $7,550
Installed cost of $2\frac{1}{2}$-in. pipe, $5,665

Extra cost of 3-in pipe, $1,885

Extra cost chargeable to this project, considering the salvage value of the pipe, $1,200
Estimated length of project, 4 months
Hours worked per month, 180
No. of jackhammers on the job, 16
No. of jackhammers operating at one time, 8
Size of jackhammers, 55 lb

Air required per hammer at 90 psi, 100 cfm
    Total air required, $8 \times 100 = 800$ cfm

Loss of pressure in 3-in. pipe, from Table 12-4, is $1.0 \times 5.89 = 5.9$ psi

Loss of pressure in 50 ft of the $\frac{3}{4}$-in. hose, from Table 12-6, is 4.7 psi, interpolated for 100 cfm at a pressure of 94 psi

Total loss in pressure through the pipe and hose, 10.6 psi
Air pressure at the hammer, $100.00 - 10.6 = 89.4$ psi

Loss in pressure through the $2\frac{1}{2}$-in. pipe, from Table 12-4, 19.0 psi
Pressure entering the $\frac{3}{4}$-in. hose, 81 psi
Loss of pressure in 50 ft of $\frac{3}{4}$-in. hose, 5.8 psi

Total loss in pressure through the $2\frac{1}{2}$-in. pipe and hose, 24.8 psi
Pressure at the hammer, $100.00 - 24.8 = 75.2$ psi

If the pressure of air at the hammer is reduced to 75.2 psi, the quantity of air required to operate each hammer will be 90 cfm instead of 100 cfm.

The total quantity of air required will be $8 \times 90 = 720$ cfm.

The hammer efficiency at 75.2 psi will be about 80% of that at 90 psi.

Assume that the cost of air will be $0.87 per 1,000 cu ft. Consider the effect of using each size pipe for 1 hour, as it applies to the rate of drilling rock, and the indicated costs. The results will be:

Item	Size of pipe (in.)	
	$2\frac{1}{2}$	3
Volume of air consumed, cu ft per hour		
by $2\frac{1}{2}$-in.-pipe, 60×72	43,200	
by 3-in. pipe		48,000
Cost of air @ $0.87 per 1,000 cfm	$37.58	$41.76
Cost of labor, 20 men @ $12.00		
per hour	240.00	240.00
Cost of jackhammers, steel, and bits[†]	36.00	42.00
Total cost per hour	$313.58	$323.76

[†] The cost per hour for jackhammers, steel, and bits is increased to compensate for the greater wear and reduced life of the units operated at the higher pressure provided by the 3-in. pipe.

Tests conducted on drilling equipment indicate that the drills operating at lower pressure, namely, 75.2 psi, will have an efficiency equal to about 80% of those operating at 89.4 psi. Thus, the increase in the depth of holes drilled at the higher pressure will be $100 - 80 = 20\%$.

Value of increased production as related to total	
cost per hour, $0.20 \times \$313.58$	= $62.70
Increased cost per hour with 3-in. pipe,	
$\$323.76 - \$313.55$	= -10.18
Net value of increased production per hour	= $52.52

The total value of the increased rate of production during the project will be:

Length of project, 4 months × 180 hours = 720 hours
Value of increased production, 720 hours @ $52.52 = $37,814.40
or $37,800

Thus, it is evident that spending an extra $1,200 to provide the larger pipe is an excellent investment. If the length of the project is greater than 4 months, the value of using the larger pipe will be proportionally greater.

PROBLEMS

12-1. An air compressor draws in 1,000 cu ft of air at a gauge pressure of 0 psi and a temperature of 70°F. The air is compressed to a gauge pressure of 100 psi at a temperature of 140°F. The atmospheric pressure is 14.0 psi. Determine the volume of air after it is compressed.

12-2. An air compressor draws in 1,000 cu ft of free air at a gauge pressure of 0 psi and a temperature of 60°F. The air is compressed to a gauge pressure of 100 psi at a temperature of 130°F. The atmospheric pressure is 12.30 psi. Determine the volume of air after it is compressed.

12-3. Determine the theoretical horsepower required to compress 600 cfm of free air, measured at standard conditions, from atmospheric pressure to 100 psi gauge pressure when the compression is performed under isothermal conditions.

12-4. Solve Prob. 12-3 if the air is compressed under adiabatic conditions.

12-5. Determine the difference in horsepower required to compress 600 cfm of free air under adiabatic conditions for altitudes of 3,000 and 8,000 ft. The air will be compressed in a single stage to 100 psi gauge pressure at each altitude.

12-6. A compressor has a capacity of 500 cfm of free air at 100 psi gauge pressure at zero altitude. If the compressor is operating at an altitude of 8,000 ft, determine the capacity when the air is compressed to 100 psi gauge pressure, with no change in temperature.

12-7. Compressors operating at zero altitude will supply enough air to operate eight drills. If the compressors and drills are operated at an altitude of 6,000 ft, how many drills can the compressor serve?

12-8. A 3-in. pipe with screwed fittings is used to transmit 1,000 cfm of free air at an initial pressure of 100 psi gauge pressure. The pipeline includes the following items:

900 ft of pipe
three gate valves
eight on-run tees
six standard ells

Determine the total loss of pressure in the pipeline.

12-9. If the air from the end of the pipeline of Prob. 12-8 is delivered through 50 ft of 1-in. hose to a rock drill that requires 160 cfm of air, determine the pressure at the drill.

REFERENCES

1. Atlas Copco, Inc., 70 Demarest Drive, Wayne, NJ 07470.
2. Chicago Pneumatic Tool Company, 6 East 44th Street, New York, NY 10017.
3. Ingersoll-Rand Company, Phillipsburg, NJ 08865.
4. "Selecting a Compressor," *Equipment Guide News,* May 1986, pp. 26–27.

CHAPTER
13

DRILLING ROCK AND EARTH

INTRODUCTION

This chapter deals with the equipment and methods used by the construction and mining industries to drill holes in both rock and earth. Although the same or similar equipment may in some instances be used for drilling both materials, they are treated separately in this chapter.

Because the purposes for which drilling is performed vary a great deal from general to highly specialized applications, it is desirable to select the equipment and methods that are best suited to the specific service. A contractor engaged in highway construction must usually drill rock under varying conditions; therefore, equipment that is suitable for various services would be selected. However, if equipment is needed to drill rock in a quarry where the material and conditions will not vary, specialized equipment should be considered. In some instances custom-made equipment designed for use on a single project may be justified.

GLOSSARY OF TERMS

The following glossary defines the important terms that are used in describing drilling equipment and procedures.

Bit. This is the portion of a drill which contacts the rock and disintegrates it. Many types are used.

    Carbide-insert bit. The carbide-insert bit is a detachable bit whose cutting edges consist of tungsten carbide embedded in a softer steel base.

    Detachable bit. This is a bit which may be attached to or removed from the drill steel or drill stem.

    Diamond bit. The diamond bit is a detachable bit whose cutting elements consist of diamonds embedded in a metal matrix.

352

Forged bit. This is a bit which is forged on the drill steel.

Burden. This is the horizontal distance from a rock face to the first row of drill holes or the distance between rows of drill holes.

Coupling. A short, hollow steel pipe having interior threads. The coupling is used to hold pieces of drill steel together or to the shank. The percussion energy is transferred through the steel, not the coupling; therefore, the coupling *must* allow the drill steel to butt together.

Cuttings. These are the disintegrated rock particles that are removed from a hole.

Depth per bit. This is the depth of hole that can be drilled by a bit before it is replaced.

Drifter. A drifter is an air-operated percussion-type drill, similar to a jackhammer; it is so large, however, that it requires mechanical mounting.

Drills:

Abrasion. This drill grinds rock into small particles through the abrasive effect of a bit that rotates in the hole.

Blast-hole. This is a rotary drill consisting of a steel-pipe drill stem on the bottom of which is a roller bit that disintegrates the rock as it rotates over the rock. The cuttings are removed by a stream of compressed air.

Churn. The churn drill is a percussion-type drill consisting of a long steel bit that is mechanically lifted and dropped to disintegrate the rock. It is used to drill deep holes, usually 6 in. in diameter or larger.

Core. This drilling equipment is designed for obtaining samples of rock from a hole, usually for exploratory purposes. Diamond and shot drills are used for core drilling.

Diamond. The diamond drill is a rotary abrasive-type drill whose bit consists of a metal matrix in which a large number of diamonds are embedded. As the drill rotates, the diamonds disintegrate the rock. This drill is used extensively to obtain core samples from hard rock.

Dry. This is a drill which uses compressed air to remove the cuttings from a hole.

Percussion. This is a drill which breaks rock into small particles by impact from repeated blows. It can be powered by compressed air or hydraulic fluids.

Shot. This is a rotary abrasive-type drill whose bit consists of a section of steel pipe with a roughened surface at the bottom. As the bit is rotated under pressure, chilled-steel shot are supplied under the bit to accomplish the disintegration of the rock. The cuttings are removed by water.

Wagon. This is a drifter mounted on a mast supported by two or more wheels.

Wet. A wet drill is one that uses water to remove the cuttings from a hole.

Drilling pattern. This is the spacing of the drill holes.

Drilling rate. This is the number of feet of hole drilled per hour per drill.

Drill steel, or *rods.* These are rods which transmit the blow energy and drill rotation from the shank to the bit. Drill steel is threaded on both ends and usually comes in standard 10-, 12-, and 20-ft lengths.

Face. This is the approximately vertical surface extending upward from the floor of a pit to the level at which drilling is accomplished.

FIGURE 13-1
Dimensional terminology for drilling rock.

Jackhammer, or *sinker.* This device is an air-operated percussion-type drill that is small enough to be handled by one worker.

Stoper. A stoper is an air-operated percussion-type drill, similar to a drifter, that is used for overhead drilling, as in a tunnel.

Striker bar, or *shank.* A short piece of steel which attaches to the percussion drill piston for receiving the blow and transferring the energy to the drill steel.

The dimension terminology that is frequently used for drilling is illustrated in Fig. 13-1.

BITS

The *bit* is the essential part of a drill, as it is the part which must engage and disintegrate the rock. The success of a drilling operation depends on the ability of the bit to remain sharp under the impact of the drill. Many types and sizes are available. Most bits are units which screw mount to the drill steel. They are easily replaced and some can be resharpened. Bits are available in various sizes, shapes, and hardnesses.

Steel bits for jackhammers and drifters are available in sizes from 1 to $4\frac{1}{2}$ in., the gauge size varying in steps of $\frac{1}{8}$ in. These bits may be resharpened 2 to 6 times.

The depth of the hole that can be drilled with a steel bit will vary from a few inches to 40 ft or more, depending on the type of rock.

Carbide-insert bits. Some types of rock are so abrasive that steel bits must be replaced after they have drilled only a few inches of the hole. The cost of the bits and lost time to production in changing bits is so great that it will usually be economical to use carbide-insert bits. This bit is illustrated in Figs. 13-2 and 13-3. As noted in the figures, the actual drilling points consist of a very hard metal, tungsten carbide, which is embedded in steel. Although these bits are considerably more expensive than steel bits, the increased drilling rate and depth of hole obtained per bit give an overall economy in drilling hard rock.

A contractor on a highway project in Pennsylvania found that when drilling diabase rock, the depth per steel bit was $\frac{1}{2}$ to 2 in. When he changed to carbide bits, he obtained an average depth per bit of 1,992 ft.

Tapered socket bits. Figure 13-2 illustrates removable tapered socket bits, which are available in gauge sizes varying in $\frac{1}{8}$-in. (3.2-mm) steps from about 1 in. (25 mm) to 4 in. (102 mm).

Bottom-drive bits. Figure 13-3 illustrates removable bottom-drive bits, which are available in gauge sizes varying from about $1\frac{1}{2}$ in. (38 mm) to 6 in. (152 mm).

Button bits. Figure 13-4 illustrates removable button bits, which are available in numerous sizes. These bits, which are available in different cutting face designs with a choice of insert grades, require no regrinding or sharpening. Their demonstrated performance has been superior to that of other types of bits when used to drill rocks that are more suitable for them, as indicated in Table 13-7.

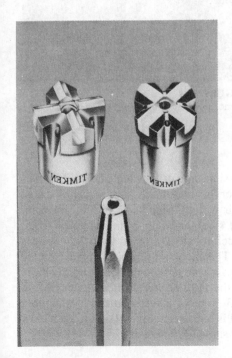

FIGURE 13-2
Removable tapered-socket-type rock bits. *(The Timken Company.)*

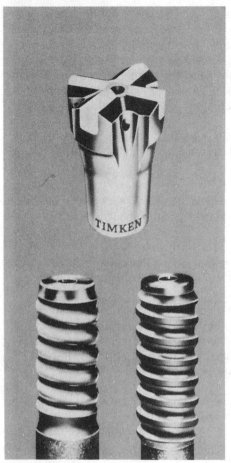

FIGURE 13-3
Removable bottom-drive-type carbide insert rock bit. *(The Timken Company.)*

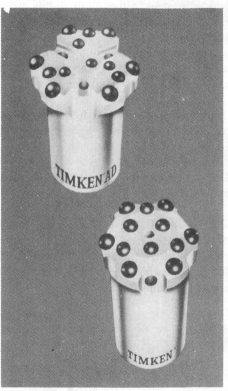

FIGURE 13-4
Removable button bits. *(The Timken Company.)*

JACKHAMMERS

Jackhammers are hand-held air-operated percussion-type drills which are used primarily for drilling holes in a downward direction. For this reason they are frequently called "sinkers." They are classified according to their weight, such as 45 or 55 lb. A complete drilling unity consists of a hammer, drill steel, and bit. As the compressed air flows through a hammer, it causes a piston to reciprocate at a speed up to 2,200 blows per minute, which produces the hammer effect. The energy of this piston is transmitted to a bit through the drill steel. Air flows through a hole in the drill steel and the bit to remove the cuttings from the hole and to cool the bit. For wet drilling, water is used instead of air to remove the cuttings. Figure 13-5 shows a sectionalized jackhammer with the essential parts indicated. The drill steel is rotated slightly following each blow so that the points of the bit will not strike at the same spot each time.

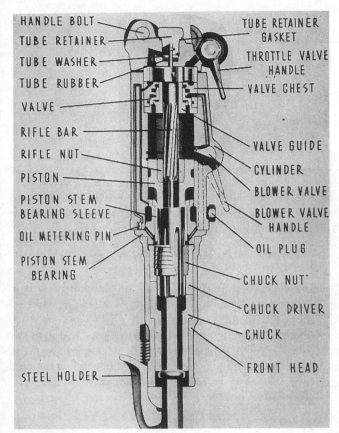

HANDLE BOLT
TUBE RETAINER
TUBE WASHER
TUBE RUBBER
VALVE
RIFLE BAR
RIFLE NUT
PISTON
PISTON STEM
BEARING SLEEVE
OIL METERING PIN
PISTON STEM
BEARING
STEEL HOLDER

TUBE RETAINER
GASKET
THROTTLE VALVE
HANDLE
VALVE CHEST
VALVE GUIDE
CYLINDER
BLOWER VALVE
BLOWER VALVE
HANDLE
OIL PLUG
CHUCK NUT
CHUCK DRIVER
CHUCK
FRONT HEAD

FIGURE 13-5
Section through a jackhammer.

Although jackhammers may be used to drill holes in excess of 20 ft deep, they seldom are used for holes exceeding 10 ft in depth. The heavier hammers will drill holes up to $2\frac{1}{2}$ in. in diameter. Drill steel usually is supplied in 2-ft-length variations, but longer lengths are available. Representative specifications for jackhammers are listed in Table 13-1.

DRIFTERS

Drifter drills are similar to jackhammers in operation, but they are larger and used as mounted tools for drilling down, horizontal, or up holes. They vary in weight from 75 to 260 lb and are capable of drilling holes up to $4\frac{1}{2}$ in. in diameter. These tools are used extensively in rock excavation, mining, and tunneling. Either air or water may be used to remove the cuttings.

The drifter's weight is usually sufficient to supply the necessary feed pressure for down drilling. But when used for horizontal or up drilling, the feed pressure is

TABLE 13-1
Representative specifications for jackhammers

Model	S33	S55	S73
Length overall (in.)	$20\frac{1}{8}$	$23\frac{3}{8}$	25
Cylinder bore (in.)	$2\frac{3}{8}$	$2\frac{5}{8}$	$2\frac{3}{4}$
Weight (lb)	31	$56\frac{1}{2}$	67
Size steel recommended (in.)	$\frac{7}{8}$	$\frac{7}{8}-1$	$\frac{7}{8}-1\frac{1}{4}$
Size air hose recommended (in.)	$\frac{3}{4}$	$\frac{3}{4}-1$	$\frac{3}{4}-1$
Size water hose recommended (in.)	$\frac{1}{2}$	$\frac{1}{2}$	$\frac{1}{2}$

supplied by a hand-operated screw or a pneumatic or hydraulic piston. Steel changes may be obtained in lengths of 24, 30, 36, 45, and 60 in. Representative specifications for automatic-feed drifters are listed in Table 13-2.

WAGON DRILLS

Wagon drills consist of drifters mounted on masts which are mounted on wheels to provide portability. They are used extensively to drill holes up to $4\frac{1}{2}$ in. in diameter and up to 30 ft or more in depth. They give better performance than jackhammers when used on terrain where it is possible for them to operate. They may be used to drill at any angle from down to slightly above horizontal. The length of drill steel is usually 6, 10, or 15 ft, but longer lengths are available. The length selected will depend on the feed reach of the particular wagon drill.

TRACK-MOUNTED DRILLS

The track-mounted drills illustrated in Figs. 13-6 and 13-7 have substantially replaced the wagon drill on construction projects. Their production rate may be 3 or more times that of a wagon drill because of their ability to move quickly to a new location and the use of the hydraulically operated boom for positioning the drill. Holes can be drilled at any angle from under 15° back from vertical to above the horizontal, ahead, or on either side of the unit. All operation, including tramming, can be powered by compressed

TABLE 13-2
Representative specifications for automatic-feed drifters

Model	79	89	93	99
Cylinder bore (in.)	3	$3\frac{1}{2}$	$3\frac{1}{2}$	4
Size chuck available (in.)	$\frac{7}{8}-1\frac{1}{4}$	$\frac{7}{8}-1\frac{1}{4}$	$\frac{7}{8}-1\frac{1}{4}$	$\frac{1}{4}-1\frac{1}{2}$
Size air hose recommended (in.)	1	1	1	1
Size water hose recommended (in.)	$\frac{1}{2}$	$\frac{1}{2}$	$\frac{1}{2}$	$\frac{1}{2}$
Weight of drill, less mounting (lb)	111	134	140	181
Overall length (in.)	$31\frac{3}{4}$	34	35	$35\frac{1}{8}$

FIGURE 13-6
Track-mounted drill equipped with dust collector.

air. There are also hydraulic-powered drills, but compressed air is still used for hole cleaning.

WHEEL-MOUNTED DRILLS

Figure 13-8 illustrates a wheel-mounted drill. Wheel-mounted drills are similar in sizes and capacities to the track-mounted drills. However, these drills require a more nearly level ground surface to operate.

ROTARY-PERCUSSION DRILLS

These drills combine the hard-hitting reciprocal action of the percussion drill with the turning-under-pressure action of the rotary drill. Whereas the percussion drill only has a rotary action to reposition the bit's cutting edges, the rotation of this combination drill, with the bit under constant pressure, has demonstrated its ability to drill much faster than the regular percussion drill (see Fig. 13-9). On one project rotary-percussion drills are reported to have drilled blastholes 3 times as fast as regular percussion drills. These drills require special carbide bits, with the carbide inserts set at a different angle from those used with standard carbide bits.

FIGURE 13-7
Air-track drill and air compressor.

In the Smith Power tunnel [1] four of these drills operating on a two-deck rail-mounted jumbo are reported to have drilled $1\frac{3}{4}$-in.-diameter holes at rates that varied from 5 to 10 fpm, depending on the hardness of the rock.

PISTON DRILLS

These are percussion-type drills with the hollow drill tube attached to the piston. The stroke and rotation of the piston are adjustable in order to give the best performance for the particular type of rock being drilled. They are available with carbide-insert bits which are up to 6 in. in diameter. The drill has a practical depth limit of approximately 70 ft.

ROTARY DRILLS

The rotary or blasthole drill is a self-propelled drill which is mounted on a truck or on crawler tracks (see Fig. 13-10). Drilling is accomplished with a tricone roller-type bit (see Fig. 13-11) attached to the lower end of a drill pipe. As the bit is rotated in the

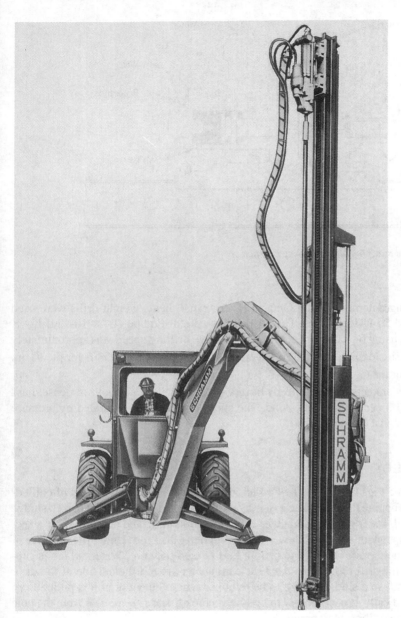

FIGURE 13-8
Wheel-mounted drill. *(Schramm, Inc.)*

hole, a continuous blast of compressed air is forced down through the pipe and the bit to remove the rock cuttings and to cool the bit. Rigs are available to drill holes to different diameters and to depths up to approximately 300 ft. This drill is suitable for drilling soft to medium rock, such as hard dolomite and limestone, but usually is not suitable for drilling the harder igneous rocks.

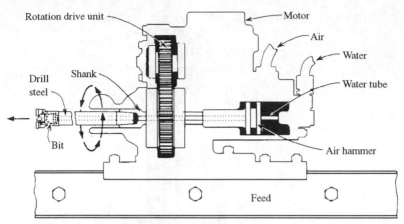

FIGURE 13-9
Rotary-percussion drill. *(Joy Manufacturing Company.)*

In drilling dolomite for the Ontario Hydro-canal, heavyweight drills were used to drill 25- and 50-ft-deep holes. The 25-ft holes were drilled on 10- × 10- and 12- × 12-ft patterns, using $6\frac{1}{4}$- and $6\frac{3}{4}$-in. bits. The average drilling speed was approximately 30 ft per hour, including moving. The average life of the bits was 958 ft for the $6\frac{1}{4}$ in. and 1,374 ft for the $6\frac{3}{4}$ in. bits.

On other projects drilling speeds have varied from $1\frac{1}{2}$ ft per hour in dense, hard dolomite to 50 ft per hour in limestone. The speed of drilling is regulated by pressure delivered through a hydraulic feed.

SHOT DRILLS

A shot drill (see Fig. 13-12) is a tool which depends on the abrasive effect of chilled-steel shot to penetrate the rock. The essential parts include a shot bit, core barrel, sludge barrel, drill rod, water pump, and power-driven rotation unit. The bit consists of a section of steel pipe, with a serrated lower end through the drill rod. Under the pressure of the bit these shots erode the rock to form a kerf around the core. Water, which is supplied through the drill rod, forces the rock cuttings up around the outside of the drill, where they settle in a sludge barrel, to be removed when the entire unit is pulled from the hole. Periodically, it is necessary to break the core off and to remove it from the hole in order that the drilling may proceed.

Standard shot drills are capable of drilling holes up to 600 ft or more in depth, with diameters varying from $2\frac{1}{2}$ to 20 in. Special equipment has been used to drill up to 6 ft in diameter and depths in excess of 1,000 ft.

A primary purpose of small, hole shot drilling is to provide continuous cores for examination to determine structural information, as rock of any hardness may be drilled.

The rate of drilling with a shot drill is relatively slow, sometimes less than 1 ft per hour, depending on the size of the drill and the hardness of the rock.

FIGURE 13-10
Two rotary (blasthole) drills working on a highway project.

On a project for an electric utility company near Oak Park, Ohio, the contractor used a shot drill to drill 100 large-diameter footings for columns in hard limestone rock. The holes varied from 30 in. (76 cm) to 60 in. (152 cm) in diameter and averaged about 12 ft (3.7 m) in depth. Holes 42 in. (107 cm) in diameter were drilled at an average rate of 1 to $1\frac{1}{2}$ ft (0.3–0.5 m) per hour, whereas holes 60 in. (152 cm) in diameter were drilled at an average rate of about 1 ft (0.3 m) per hour [2].

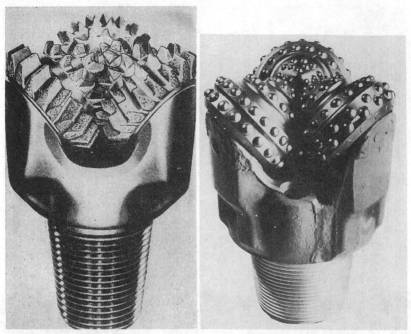

FIGURE 13-11
Representative rotary bits. (*a*) Tricone bit. (*Joy Manufacturing Company.*) (*b*) Button-type bit. (*Reed Tool Company.*)

DIAMOND DRILLS

Diamond drills are used primarily for exploration drilling, where cores are desired for the purpose of studying the rock structure. The Diamond Core Drill Manufacturers' Association lists four sizes as standard—$1\frac{1}{2}$, $1\frac{7}{8}$, $2\frac{3}{8}$, and 3 in. Larger sizes are available, but the investment in diamonds increases so rapidly with an increase in size that shot drills may be more economical for larger diameter holes.

A drilling rig consists of a diamond bit, a core barrel, a jointed driving tube, and a rotary head to supply the driving torque (see Fig. 13-13). Water is pumped through the driving tube to remove the cuttings. The pressure on the bit is regulated through a screw or hydraulic-feed swivel head. Core barrels are available in lengths varying from 5 to 15 ft. When the bit advances to a depth equal to the length of the core barrel, the core is broken off and the drill is removed from the hole. Diamond drills can drill in any desired direction from vertically downward to upward.

The selection of the size of diamonds depends on the nature of the formation to be drilled. Large stones are preferred for the softer formations and small stones for fine-grained solid formations. A selection of diamond point bits is shown in Fig. 13-14.

Diamond drills are capable of drilling to depths in excess of 1,000 ft. Bit speeds may vary from approximately 200 to 1,200 rpm. The drilling rate will vary from less than a foot to several feet per hour, depending on the type of rock.

Table 13-3 gives information on the dimensions and diamond content of bits.

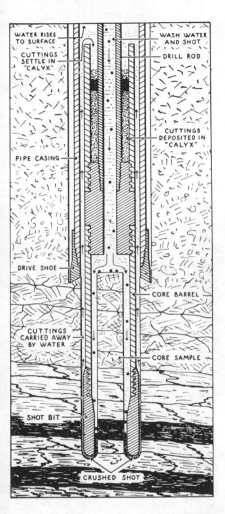

FIGURE 13-12
Shot or calyx core drill. *(Ingersoll-Rand Company.)*

MANUFACTURERS' REPORT ON DRILLING EQUIPMENT AND TECHNIQUES [3]

A magazine devoted primarily to construction methods and equipment published an article presenting the views of representatives of drilling equipment manufacturers, with suggestions listed for selecting and using drilling equipment to achieve increased production at reduced costs. Some of those ideas are presented here.

The manufacturers' representatives who assessed drilling productivity included as important factors: maintainability, mobility, operator expertise, the operability of equipment, the use of auxiliary attachments, the method of drilling employed, and the interrelationship between the drill bit and the drilling rig. Each user or prospective user of drilling equipment should examine these ideas and adopt the ones that apply to the particular operations being considered.

FIGURE 13-13
Drilling unit for diamond core drill.
(Acker Drill Company.)

FIGURE 13-14
Diamond-point bits. *(Sprague & Henwood, Inc.)*

TABLE 13-3
Representative information for standard diamond coring bits

Size of bit (in.)	Nominal		Net dimension		Minimum carat content
	Hole diameter (in.)	Core diameter (in.)	OD (in.)	ID (in.)	
EX	$1\frac{1}{2}$	$\frac{7}{8}$	1.460	0.845	6.75
AX	$1\frac{7}{8}$	$1\frac{1}{8}$	1.865	1.185	10.00
BX	$2\frac{3}{8}$	$1\frac{5}{8}$	2.330	1.655	14.00
NX	3	$2\frac{1}{8}$	2.945	2.155	18.00
$2\frac{3}{4} \times 3\frac{7}{8}$	$3\frac{7}{8}$	$2\frac{3}{4}$	3.840	2.690	36.00
$4 \times 5\frac{1}{2}$	$5\frac{1}{2}$	4	5.435	3.970	60.00
$6 \times 7\frac{3}{4}$	$7\frac{3}{4}$	6	7.655	5.970	90.00

The user of drills to be operated in a quarry should select equipment that will maximize productivity within the limits of the loading, hauling, and crushing equipment. The equipment selected must work under the most severe and grueling conditions of the given project. Before any equipment is selected, it should be tested for performance.

It was suggested that when drilling holes deeper than about 50 ft, down-the-hole drilling, i.e., the process of moving the cylinder and its percussive impact into the hole, should be considered. This move can increase the effective energy by as much as 10% by eliminating the loss of energy in extended lengths of drill rods.

Another suggestion was that more tests could be conducted to determine the best sizes of blastholes, ratios of burden to spacing, density of explosives, and delay patterns to increase the yield of blasted rock per foot of hole to determine the effect which such actions would have on the cost of production.

Greater care perhaps could be exercised by the drill operators as they add sections of steel rods to produce deeper holes. The *abutting ends* of drill rods must *bear tightly* against each other to transmit the drilling forces to the bits. If these forces are transmitted by the couplings, they may cause excessive splitting of the couplings, with possible loss of bits and drill rods down the hole.

The use of button bits as a means of more evenly distributing the forces of the drills on the rock may be desirable on some projects. The superior geometric pattern of the buttons can help to increase the penetration by as much as 20%, to smooth the drilling operation, and to reduce the stress on the drilling equipment when compared with conventional blade bits. However, button bits are not recommended for drilling long, close, parallel holes, as in presplitting. Holes drilled with button bits may drift or even cross each other. Moreover, their small contact surface may cause greater wear in drilling hard abrasive rock.

In some drilling operations productivity has been increased by increasing the pressure and volume of air supplied to the drill. This maintains a cleaner blasthole. At the same time, increasing the down pressure on the bit has improved the cutting action of the bit.

Maintenance and repair services for equipment can be improved, with less downtime for repairs and replacement of parts if the equipment is standardized to the extent permitted by the operations for which it is used. With fewer models of equipment to be serviced, an inventory of spare parts that fail most frequently can be maintained on the job.

The availability of extendable booms on track drills increases the service ranges and performance of drills. The availability of drills with dust control systems permits the use of drills in locations where environmental restrictions would otherwise preclude their operation.

Because of the high cost, complexity, and sophistication of drilling equipment, some manufacturers have developed training programs to assist the users and operators of their equipment in increasing its efficiency.

SELECTING THE DRILLING METHOD AND EQUIPMENT

Holes are drilled for various purposes, such as to receive charges of explosives, for exploration, or for ground modification by the injection of grout. Within practical limits, the equipment which will produce the greatest overall economy for the particular project is the most satisfactory. Many factors affect the selection of equipment. Among these are:

1. The nature of the terrain. Rough surfaces may dictate jackhammers regardless of other factors.
2. The required depth of holes.
3. The hardness of the rock.
4. The extent to which the formation is broken or fractured.
5. The size of the project.
6. The extent to which the rock is to be broken for handling or crushing.
7. The availability of water for drilling purposes. Lack of water favors dry drilling.
8. The purpose of the holes, such as blasting, exploration, or grout injection.
9. The size of cores required for exploration. Small cores permit the use of diamond drills, whereas large cores suggest shot drills.

For small-diameter shallow blastholes, especially on rough surfaces where larger drills cannot operate, it is usually necessary to use jackhammers or track-mounted drills even though the production rates will be low and the costs will be higher.

For blastholes up to about 6 in. in diameter and up to about 50 ft deep, where machines can operate, the choice may be between track-mounted, rotary-percussion, or piston drills.

For drilling holes from 6 to 12 in. in diameter, from 50 to 300 ft deep, the rotary or blasthole drill is usually the best choice, but this is affected by the type of rock.

If cores up to 3 in. are desired, the diamond coring drill is the most satisfactory.

If intermediate-size cores, 3- to 8-in. outside diameter, are desired, the choice will be between a diamond drill and a shot drill. A diamond drill will usually drill faster than a shot drill. Also, a diamond drill can drill holes in any direction, whereas a shot drill is limited to holes that are vertically down, or nearly so.

SELECTING THE DRILLING PATTERN

The pattern selected for drilling holes to be loaded with explosives will vary with the type and size drill used, the depth of the holes, the kind of rock, the maximum rock breakage size permissible, and other factors.

Drilling operations for rock excavation where the material will be used in an embankment fill must consider the fill specifications concerning the maximum physical size. The drilling pattern should be planned to produce rock sizes that are small enough to permit most of them to be handled by the excavator, such as a loader or shovel, or to pass into the crusher opening without secondary blasting. While meeting either condition is possible, the cost of excess drilling and greater amounts of explosives to produce it may be so high that the production of some oversize rocks may be cost-effective. The oversize rock will still have to be handled on an individual basis, possibly with a headache ball.

If small-diameter holes are spaced close together, the better distribution of the explosives will result in a more uniform rock breakage. However, if the added cost of drilling exceeds the value of the benefits resulting from better breakage, the close spacing is not justified.

Large-diameter holes permit greater explosive loading per hole, making it possible to increase the spacing between holes and thereby reduce the cost of drilling.

In analyzing a job for drilling and blasting operations, there are four factors which should be considered:

1. The cubic yards of rock per linear foot of hole.
2. The number of pounds of explosive per cubic yard of rock.
3. The number of pounds of explosive per linear foot of hole.
4. Will the resulting breakage meet the job requirements?

The value of each of the first three factors may be estimated in advance of drilling and blasting operations, but after experimental drilling operations are conducted, it probably will be desirable to modify the values to give better results. The fourth factor is more subjective, but the relationship between hole size and spacing gives some indication of expected results.

The relationships between the first three factors are illustrated in Table 13-4. The volumes of rock per linear foot of hole are based on the net depth of holes and do not include subdrilling, which usually will be necessary. The pounds of explosive per linear foot of hole are based on filling the holes completely with 60% dynamite. The pounds of explosive per cubic yard of rock are based on filling each hole to 100, 75, and 50% of its total capacity with dynamite. When a hole is not filled completely with dynamite, the surplus volume is filled with stemming. See Chap. 14 on "Blasting Rock."

RATES OF DRILLING ROCK

The rates of drilling rock will vary with a number of factors such as the type of drill and bit size, hardness of the rock, depth of holes, drilling pattern, terrain, and time lost waiting for other operations. If pneumatic drills are used, the rate of drilling will vary with the pressure of the air, as demonstrated in Chap. 12 on "Compressed Air."

Another item that influences the rate of drilling is the availability factor. Because of the nature of the work that they do, drills are subjected to severe vibration and wear, which may result in frequent failures of critical parts, or a deterioration of the whole unit, entailing mechanical delays. The portion of time that a drill is operative is defined

TABLE 13-4
Drilling and blasting data

Size hole (in.)	Hole pattern (ft)	Area per hole (sq ft)	Volume of rock per lin. ft of hole‡ (cu yd)	Pounds of explosive per lin. ft of hole†	Pounds of explosive per cu yd of rock† % of hole filled		
					100	75	50
$1\frac{1}{2}$	4×4	16	0.59	0.9	1.52	1.14	0.76
	5×5	25	0.93	0.9	0.97	0.73	0.48
	6×6	36	1.33	0.9	0.68	0.51	0.34
	7×7	49	1.81	0.9	0.50	0.38	0.25
2	5×5	25	0.93	1.7	1.83	1.37	0.92
	6×6	36	1.33	1.7	1.28	0.96	0.64
	7×7	49	1.81	1.7	0.94	0.71	0.47
	8×8	64	2.37	1.7	0.72	0.54	0.36
3	7×7	49	1.81	3.9	2.15	1.61	1.08
	8×8	64	2.37	3.9	1.65	1.24	0.83
	9×9	81	3.00	3.9	1.30	0.97	0.65
	10×10	100	3.70	3.9	1.05	0.79	0.53
	11×11	121	4.48	3.9	0.87	0.65	0.44
4	8×8	64	2.37	7.5	3.16	2.37	1.58
	10×10	100	3.70	7.5	2.03	1.52	1.02
	12×12	144	5.30	7.5	1.42	1.06	0.71
	14×14	196	7.25	7.5	1.03	0.77	0.52
	16×16	256	9.50	7.5	0.79	0.59	0.40
5	12×12	144	5.30	10.9	2.05	1.54	1.02
	14×14	196	7.25	10.9	1.50	1.13	0.75
	16×16	256	9.50	10.9	1.15	0.86	0.58
	18×18	324	12.00	10.9	0.91	0.68	0.46
	20×20	400	14.85	10.9	0.73	0.55	0.37
6	12×12	144	5.30	15.6	2.94	2.20	1.47
	14×14	196	7.25	15.6	2.05	1.54	1.02
	16×16	256	9.50	15.6	1.64	1.23	0.82
	18×18	324	12.00	15.6	1.30	0.97	0.65
	20×20	400	14.85	15.6	1.05	0.79	0.53
	24×24	576	21.35	15.6	0.73	0.55	0.37
9	20×20	400	14.85	35.0	2.36	1.77	1.18
	24×24	576	21.35	35.0	1.64	1.23	0.82
	28×28	784	29.00	35.0	1.21	0.91	0.61
	30×30	900	33.30	35.0	1.05	0.79	0.53
	32×32	1,024	37.90	35.0	0.92	0.69	0.46

† Based on using dynamite weighing 80 lb per cu ft.
‡ Does not account for subdrilling.

as the *availability factor,* which is usually expressed as a percent of the total time that the drill is expected to be working.

Historical drill penetration rates based on very general rock-type classification is shown in Table 13-5. These rates should be used only as an order-of-magnitude guide. Actual project estimates need to be based on drilling tests of the specific rock which will be encountered.

Drill bits, rods, and couplings are high wear items, and the time required to replace or change each affects the drilling production. Table 13-6 gives the average life of these high wear items based on the drill footage and the type of rock.

The effect of air pressure on the rate of drilling rock. The cost of energy furnished by compressed air is high when compared with the cost of energy supplied by electricity or diesel fuel. The ratio of costs may be as high as 6 : 1. For this reason it is essential that every reasonable effort be made to increase the efficiency of the compressed air system and the equipment which uses compressed air as a source of energy. One method of increasing the efficiency of pneumatic drills is to be certain that the specified air pressure at the drill is available.

It has been shown that the energy of a rock drill can be represented by the following equation [5, 6]

$$E \propto \frac{P^{1.5} A^{1.5} S^{0.5}}{W^{0.5}} \tag{13-1}$$

where E = energy per blow
  P = air pressure
  A = area of piston stroke
  S = length of piston stroke
  W = weight of piston

With all the factors constant in a given drill except the pressure of the air, this equation indicates that the energy delivered per blow varies with the 1.5 power of the pressure.

In the past, factors discouraging the use of higher pressures to increase the rate of drilling have been the limitations imposed by the design of the drills and reduced life spans of the drill steel and bits. These limitations to a large extent have been overcome today.

The potential increase in production of a drill when operating at a higher pressure should not be the sole factor in a decision to use higher pressure. The value of the increased production should be compared with the probable increase in the cost of air and maintenance and repairs for the drill, including drill steel and bits. Any increase in maintenance and repairs may reduce the availability factor for the drill. The optimum pressure is the pressure that will result in the minimum cost of drilling a unit of hole depth, taking into account all factors related to the drilling, including, but not limited to:

1. The value of the increased production.
2. The increased cost of providing air at a higher pressure.

TABLE 13-5
Order-of-magnitude drilling production rates

Bit size	Drill type Compressed air	Direct penetration rate		Estimated[†] production rate good conditions	
		Granite (ft/hr)	Dolomite (ft/hr)	Granite (ft/hr)	Dolomite (ft/hr)
	Rotary-percussion				
$3\frac{1}{2}$	750 cfm @ 100 psi	65	125	35	55
$3\frac{1}{2}$	900 cfm @ 100 psi	85	175	40	65
	Downhole drill				
$4\frac{1}{2}$	600 cfm @ 250 psi	70	110	45	75
$6\frac{1}{2}$	900 cfm @ 350 psi	100	185	65	90
	Rotary				
$6\frac{1}{4}$	30,000 pulldown	NR	100	NR	65
$6\frac{3}{4}$	40,000 pulldown	75	120	30	75
$7\frac{7}{8}$	50,000 pulldown	95	150	45	85

NR-Not recommended.
[†]Estimated productions are for ideal conditions, but they do account for all delays including blasting.

3. The cost of increased line leakage.

4. The increased cost of maintenance and repairs for the drill.

5. The adverse effect, if any, of increased noise in some instances such as tunneling.

6. The effect which a higher pressure may have on the availability factor for the drill or air compressor.

On most construction projects it is not practical to conduct studies to evaluate each of these factors. However, a limited number of studies have been made under conditions that did permit the evaluation of the effects of varying the pressure of the air.

Determining the optimum air pressure for drilling rock. This is a report on the results of tests that were conducted in a mine in Ontario, Canada [3]. The walls of the test station were marked off in panels, so that by drilling in each of the panels at every stage of testing, variations in the drillability of the rock were minimized. Stopwatches, an air flowmeter, pressure-reducing valves, pressure gauges, micrometer gauges, and tools were used to ensure good control and information.

Prior to starting the tests, seven new jackleg drills were obtained from five manufacturers and divided into two groups. Table 13-7 lists bore and stroke data for the seven drills. Holes were drilled at pressures varying from 90 to 140 psi. For each pressure increment a new carbide-insert bit was used on both 6-ft and 12-ft steel. All bits were $1\frac{1}{4}$ in. in diameter. Table 13-8 lists the volume of air consumed, in cubic feet of free air per minute, for each drill and pressure.

Figure 13-15 shows the relationship between the average rate of penetration and the operating pressure for each group of drills. Figure 13-16 is a nomogram based on the information appearing in Fig. 13-15 which indicates the percent increase in penetration

TABLE 13-6a
Igneous rock: Average life, in feet, for drill bits and steel

Drill bits (in.)	Type	High silica LA < 20 (Rhyolite) (ft)	High silica 20 < LA < 50 (Granite) (ft)	Medium silica LA < 50 (Granite) (ft)	Low silica LA < 20 (Basalt) (ft)	Low silica LA > 20 (Diabase) (ft)
3	B	250	500	750	750	1,000
3	STD	NR	NR	NR	NR	750
$3\frac{1}{2}$	STD	NR	NR	NR	750	1,500
$3\frac{1}{2}$	HD	200	575	1,000	1,400	2,000
$3\frac{1}{2}$	B	550	1,200	2,500	2,700	3,200
4	B	750	1,500	2,800	3,000	3,500
Rotary bits						
5	ST	NR	NR	NR	NR	NR
$5\frac{7}{8}$	ST	NR	NR	NR	NR	NR
$6\frac{1}{4}$	ST	NR	NR	NR	NR	NR
$6\frac{3}{4}$	ST	NR	NR	NR	NR	800
$6\frac{3}{4}$	CB	NR	NR	1,500	2,000	4,000
$7\frac{7}{8}$	CB	NR	1,700	2,400	3,500	6,000
Down hole bits						
$6\frac{1}{2}$	B	500	1,000	1,800	2,200	3,000
Drill steel						
Shanks		2,500	4,500	5,800	5,850	6,000
Couplings		700	700	800	950	1,100
Steel 10 ft		1,450	1,500	1,600	1,650	2,200
Steel 12 ft		2,200	2,600	3,000	3,500	5,000
5 in. 20 ft		25,000	52,000	60,000	75,000	100,000

B = button, CB = carbide button, HD = heavy duty, ST = steel tooth,
STD = standard, NR = not recommended.

resulting from an increase in air pressure. For example, if the pressure is increased from 90 to 100 psi, the increase in penetration will be 38%.

DETERMINING THE INCREASE IN PRODUCTION RESULTING FROM AN INCREASE IN AIR PRESSURE

If a drill is presently operating at a given air pressure, such as 90 psi, Fig. 13-16 indicates that if the pressure is increased to 110 psi, the rate of penetration of the drill will be increased 38%. This will not result in an increase of 38% in the production on the project. The increased rate of penetration is effective only during the time that the drill

TABLE 13-6b
Metamorphic rock: Average life, in feet, for drill bits and steel

Drill bits (in.)	Type	Metamorphic rock				
		High silica LA < 35 (Quartzite) (ft)	Medium silica low mica (Schist) (Gneiss) (ft)	Medium silica high mica (Schist) (Gneiss) (ft)	Medium silica LA < 25 (Metala-) (tite) (ft)	Low silica LA > 45 (Marble) (ft)
3	B	200	1,200	1,500	800	1,300
3	STD	NR	800	900	400	850
3½	STD	NR	1,300	1,700	850	1,600
3½	HD	NR	1,800	2,200	1,200	2,100
3½	B	450	3,000	3,500	2,000	3,300
4	B	600	3,300	3,800	2,300	3,700
Rotary bits						
5	ST	NR	NR	NR	NR	NR
5⅞	ST	NR	NR	NR	NR	1,200
6¼	ST	NR	NR	NR	NR	2,000
6¾	ST	NR	NR	750	NR	4,500
6¾	CB	NR	3,700	4,200	1,200	9,000
7⅞	CB	NR	5,500	6,500	2,200	13,000
Down hole bits						
6½	B	500	2,700	3,200	1,500	4,500
Drill steel						
Shanks		5,000	5,700	6,200	5,550	5,800
Couplings		900	1,000	1,200	750	800
Steel	10 ft	1,700	2,100	2,300	1,500	1,600
Steel	12 ft	3,000	3,300	3,800	2,800	3,000
5 in.	20 ft	50,000	90,000	100,000	85,000	175,000

B = button, CB = carbide button, HD = heavy duty, ST = steel tooth, STD = standard, NR = not recommended.

is *actually* producing the hole or drilling. Thus, the increase does not apply to the time that the drill is not, in fact, drilling. This nonproductive time will generally remain the same regardless of the rate of penetration.

Let us develop an equation which can be used to determine the increase in production resulting from an increase in the rate of penetration. The following symbols will be used:

T = elapsed time that the drill is on the job, hour

T_1 = time actually devoted to drilling, hour

D = drilling factor, the portion of the elapsed time devoted to drilling = $\dfrac{T_1}{T}$

TABLE 13-6c
Sedimentary rock: Average life, in feet, for drill bits and steel

		Sedimentary				
Drill bits (in.)	Type	High silica fine grain (Sandstone) (ft)	Medium silica coarse grain (Sandstone) (ft)	Low silica fine grain (Dolomite) (ft)	Low silica fine-med. grain (Shale) (ft)	Low silica coarse grain (Conglomerate) (ft)
3	B	800	1,200	1,300	2,000	1,800
3	STD	NR	850	900	1,500	1,200
$3\frac{1}{2}$	STD	NR	1,500	1,800	3,000	2,500
$3\frac{1}{2}$	HD	850	2,000	2,200	3,500	3,000
$3\frac{1}{2}$	B	2,000	3,100	3,500	4,500	4,000
4	B	2,500	3,500	2,000	5,000	4,800
Rotary bits						
5	ST	NR	1,000	NR	8,000	6,000
$5\frac{7}{8}$	ST	NR	2,500	NR	15,000	13,000
$6\frac{1}{4}$	ST	NR	4,000	4,000	18,000	14,000
$6\frac{3}{4}$	ST	500	6,000	8,000	20,000	15,000
$6\frac{3}{4}$	CB	2,000	8,000	10,000	25,000	20,000
$7\frac{7}{8}$	CB	3,000	10,000	15,000	25,000	20,000
Down hole bits						
$6\frac{1}{2}$	B	2,500	3,500	5,500	7,500	6,000
Drill steel						
Shanks		5,000	5,500	6,000	7,000	6,500
Couplings		1,000	1,200	1,500	2,000	1,750
Steel	10 ft	2,000	2,300	2,500	4,000	3,500
Steel	12 ft	4,500	5,000	6,000	7,500	7,000
5 in.	20 ft	65,000	250,000	200,000	300,000	250,000

B = button, CB = carbide button, HD = heavy duty, ST = steel tooth,
STD = standard, NR = not recommended.

Q_1 = total depth of hole drilled during T hours, ft

R_1 = average rate of drilling during T hours = $\dfrac{Q_1}{T}$, ft per hour

P = increase in rate of penetration resulting from increase in pressure, expressed as a fraction

R_2 = average rate of drilling resulting from increase in pressure = $R_1(1 + P)$

T_2 = time required to drill Q_1 ft of hole at increased rate R_2, hours = $\dfrac{T_1}{1 + P}$

T_s = time saved by increased rate of drilling

TABLE 13-7
Bore and stroke data for drills used in Ontario, Canada, optimum air pressure for drilling test

Drill group	Bore [(in.) (mm)]	Stroke [(in.) (mm)]	Drill group	Bore [(in.) (mm)]	Stroke [(in.) (mm)]
A_1	$2\frac{21}{32}$ (67.4)	$2\frac{7}{8}$ (73.0)	B_1	$3\frac{1}{8}$ (79.5)	$2\frac{3}{8}$ (60.5)
A_2	$2\frac{11}{16}$ (68.3)	$2\frac{9}{16}$ (65.2)	B_2	3 (76.0)	$2\frac{9}{16}$ (65.2)
A_3	$2\frac{3}{4}$ (69.7)	$2\frac{3}{4}$ (69.7)	B_3	3 (76.0)	$2\frac{5}{8}$ (66.6)
			B_4	3 (76.0)	$1\frac{15}{16}$ (49.2)

TABLE 13-8
Variations in the volume of air consumed with varying air pressures

Drill group	Dynamic air pressure (psi gauge (Pa))[†]					
	90 (7.2)[‡]	100 (7.9)[‡]	110 (8.6)[‡]	120 (9.3)[‡]	130 (10.0)[‡]	140 (10.6)[‡]
	Volume of air consumed [cfm (cu m/sec)]					
A_1	132.2 (0.062)	154.2 (0.073)	160.5 (0.076)	178.5 (0.084)	185.0 (0.087)	210.0 (0.099)
A_2	133.5 (0.063)	150.6 (0.071)	162.5 (0.077)	182.5 (0.086)	193.0 (0.091)	221.0 (0.104)
A_3	159.2 (0.075)	171.0 (0.081)	193.2 (0.091)	214.0 (0.102)	228.5 (0.108)	255.7 (0.121)
Average for group A	141.6 (0.067)	158.6 (0.075)	172.1 (0.081)	191.7 (0.090)	202.2 (0.095)	228.9 (0.108)
Percent increase	—	12.0	21.5	35.4	42.8	61.7
B_1	185.2 (0.087)	207.3 (0.098)	233.6 (0.111)	257.0 (0.121)	284.5 (0.134)	302.4 (0.143)
B_2	165.1 (0.078)	188.2 (0.089)	208.5 (0.098)	241.3 (0.114)	252.5 (0.119)	273.0 (0.129)
B_3	163.0 (0.077)	183.0 (0.086)	206.7 (0.097)	226.5 (0.107)	255.0 (0.121)	267.7 (0.126)
B_4	182.2 (0.086)	195.2 (0.092)	213.8 (0.102)	241.2 (0.114)	269.5 (0.127)	290.5 (0.137)
Average for group B	173.9 (0.082)	193.4 (0.091)	215.6 (0.103)	241.5 (0.114)	265.4 (0.125)	283.4 (0.133)
Percent increase	—	11.21	24.0	38.9	52.6	63.0

[†] Psi pressures are gauge, whereas Pa pressures are absolute. Thus, 14.7 must be added to the psi values before multiplying by the conversion factor to obtain Pa units.

[‡] Each of the listed values is multiplied by 10^5 to obtain the correct Pa units. Thus, (7.2) is 7.2×10^5, (7.9) is 7.9×10^5, etc.

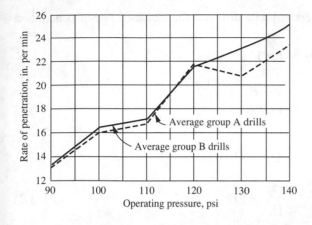

FIGURE 13-15
Variations in the rate of penetration with air pressure.

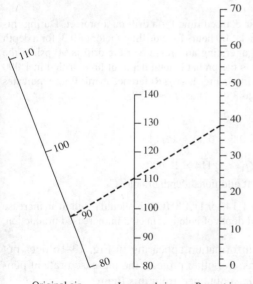

Original air pressure, psi   Increased air pressure, psi   Percent increase in penetration

FIGURE 13-16
Variations in the rates of penetration with air pressure.

$$T_s = T_1 - T_2 = T_1 - \frac{T_1}{1 + P}$$

$$= \frac{T_1(1 + P) - T_1}{1 + P} = \frac{T_1 + T_1P - T_1}{1 + P} = \frac{T_1P}{1 + P}$$

But $T_1 = TD$. Thus,

$$T_s = \frac{TDP}{1 + P}$$

Let Q_2 = the increased depth of hole drilled at the increased rate of penetration during time T. Thus,

$$Q_2 = T_s R_2$$
$$= \frac{TDP}{1 + P} \times R_1(1 + P)$$
$$= TDPR_1$$

But $Q_1 = TR_1$. Thus,

$$Q_2 = Q_1 DP$$

and

$$\frac{Q_2}{Q_1} = DP \tag{13-2}$$

which is the ratio of the increased production divided by the original production, expressed as a fraction.

Example 13-1. Consider a 1,000-hour elapsed time for a drill on a project. During this time the drill actually penetrates the rock 300 hours for a drilling factor of 0.3, for a depth of hole equal to 10,000 ft. The initial operating air pressure at the drill is 90 psi. If the pressure is increased to 110 psi, what is the probable total depth of hole drilled in 1,000 hours, based on the information appearing in Fig. 13-16? Reference to this figure indicates an increased rate of penetration equal to 38%. Thus, $P = 0.38$.

Applying Eq. (13-2), we get

$$\frac{Q_2}{Q_1} = DP = 0.3 \times 0.38 = 0.114$$
$$Q_2 = 0.114Q_1 = 0.114 \times 10,000$$
$$= 1,140 \text{ ft additional depth of hole}$$

The total depth of hole will be $10,000 + 1,140$ or 11,140 ft. This should result in an increase of 11.4% in production if the increased depth of hole is reflected in increased production.

It should be emphasized that the information appearing in Fig. 13-16 does not necessarily apply to all drilling conditions. For other projects the increased rate of penetration may be more or less than the values obtained from this figure.

During the time that tests were conducted by the mining company to evaluate the effect of increasing air pressure on the rate of penetration, the company also determined the effect of increased pressure on the cost of providing compressed air and the cost of drills, bits, and drill steel (see Table 13-9).

CONDUCTING A STUDY TO DETERMINE THE ECONOMY OF INCREASING AIR PRESSURE

The decision to increase the air pressure at the drills should not be determined solely on the basis of the anticipated increase in production and the increase in the cost of compressed air and drilling equipment. Drilling is only one item in a chain of operations, which includes drilling, blasting, loading, and hauling. The cost effect which operating

TABLE 13-9
**Increase in drilling expense resulting
from using increased air pressure**

| | Percent increase in expense | | | |
| | Operating air pressure (psi gauge) | | | |
Item	90	100	110	120
Compressor operation and maintenance	0	13.0	26.0	39.5
Drills	0	27.0	55.0	83.0
Bits	0	21.5	43.0	64.5
Steel	0	21.5	43.5	66.0

at an increased pressure will have on the rate of production and on the cost of the related operations should be considered in reaching a decision. The objective is to provide rock at its disposal point, at a waste area, in a fill, or as crushed stone in stockpiles at the lowest practical cost per unit of material.

Figure 13-17 presents a curve that establishes the lowest total cost of producing the end product of a drilling operation. The curve is plotted to indicate this cost for varying air pressures. As noted, the optimum pressure is 102 psi, based on the tests described earlier.

ESTIMATING DRILLING PRODUCTION

The first step in estimating drilling production is to make an assumption about the type of equipment which will be used. That first assumption will be guided by the type of

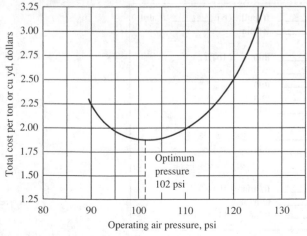

FIGURE 13-17
Variation in the total cost of rock product with air pressure.

rock to be drilled. Both Tables 13-5 and 13-6 give information that is useful in making such a decision. However, it must again be emphasized, the final decision on the type of equipment should only be made after test drilling the specific formation. The drilling test should yield data on the penetration rate based on bit size and type. Once a drill type and bit is selected, the format given in Fig. 13-18 can be used to estimate the hourly production.

Usually, when drilling for loading explosives and blasting, it is necessary to sub-drill below the desired final bottom or floor elevation. This extra depth is dependent on the blasting design. The controlling factors include hole diameter, hole spacing, pounds of explosive per cubic yard, and firing sequence. Normally, 2 or 3 ft of extra depth is required. Therefore, if the depth to the finish grade is 25 ft, (1a) pull depth, it may be necessary to actually drill 28 ft, (1b) drilling depth.

The penetration rate will be an average rate developed from the test drilling program based on a specific bit size and type. With these two pieces of information, drilling time can be calculated.

If the drilling depth is greater than the steel length, it will be necessary to add steel during the drilling and to remove steel when coming out of the hole. For track-mounted rotary-percussion drills, standard steel lengths are 10 or 12 ft. They require about 0.5 min or less to add or remove a length. The single pass capability of rotary drills varies considerably, in the range of 20 to 60 ft. A limited study by the author found that it took an average of 1.1 min to add a 20-ft length of steel and 1.5 min to remove the same on such units.

After the actual drilling is completed, it is good practice to blow out the hole to ensure that all cuttings are removed. Some drillers prefer simply to drill an extra foot and to pull the drill out without blowing the hole clean.

The time required to move between drill hole locations is a function of the distance (blasting pattern) and the terrain. Track-mounted rotary-percussion drills have travel

(1)	Depth of hole:	(a) _____	ft pull,	(b) _____	ft drill
(2)	Penetration rate:	_____	ft/min		
(3)	Drilling time:	_____	min	(1b)/(2)	
(4)	Change steel:	_____	min		
(5)	Blow hole:	_____	min		
(6)	Move to next hole:	_____	min		
(7)	Align steel:	_____	min		
(8)	Change bit:	_____	min		
(9)	Total time:	_____	min		
(10)	Operating Rate:	_____	ft/min	(1b)/(9)	
(11)	Production efficiency:	_____	min/hr		
(12)	Hourly production:	_____	ft/hr	(11)×(10)	

FIGURE 13-18
Format for estimating drilling production.

speeds of from 1 to 3 mph. Track-mounted rotary drills with their high masts can move at a maximum speed of about 2 mph. It should be remembered that hole spacing is often less than 20 ft and the operator is maneuvering to place the drill over an exact spot, so travel speed is slow. Once over the drilling location, the mast or steel must be aligned. In the case of rotary drills the entire machine is leveled by the use of hydraulic jacks. This usually takes about 1 min.

A time allowance must be made for changing bits, shanks, couplings, and steel. Table 13-6 provides information for determining the frequency of such changes.

Finally, as with all production estimating, the effect of job and management factors must be taken into account. With experienced drillers working on a large project, a 50-min production hour should be achievable. If the situation is sporadic drilling with knowledgeable people, a 40-min production hour might be more appropriate. The estimator needs to consider the specific project requirements and the skill of the available labor pool before deciding on the appropriate production efficiency.

Example 13-2. A project utilizing experienced drillers will require the drilling and blasting of high silica, fine-grained sandstone rock. From field drilling tests it was determined that a direct drilling rate of 120 ft per hour could be achieved with a $3\frac{1}{2}$ HD bit on a rotary percussion drill @ 100 psi. The drills to be used take 10-ft steel. The blasting pattern will be a 10- × 10-ft grid with 2 ft of subdrilling required. On the average the specified finish grade is 16 ft below the existing ground surface. Determine the drilling production.

Using the Fig. 13-18 format:

(1)	Depth of hole (a) 16-ft pull	(b) 18-ft drill (16 + 2 ft)	
(2)	Penetration	2.00 ft/min	(120 ft ÷ 60 min)

(3)	Drilling time:	9.00 min	(18 ft ÷ 2 ft/min)
(4)	Change steel:	0.60 min	(1 add and 1 remove @ 0.3 ea.)
(5)	Blow hole:	0.10 min	
(6)	Move 10 ft:	0.45 min	(10 ft @ $\frac{1}{4}$ mph)
(7)	Align steel:	0.50 min	(not a high mast drill)
(8)	Change bit:	0.09 min	
(9)	Total time:	10.74 min	
(10)	Operating rate:	1.68 ft/min	(18 ft ÷ 10.74 min)
(11)	Production efficiency:	50 min/hr	
(12)	Hourly production:	84.0 ft/hr	[(50 min/hr) × (1.68 ft/min)]

From Table 13-6c the expected life of the high wear items of the drill can be found. For an average hole depth of 18 ft the following number of holes can be completed per each replacement.

$3\frac{1}{2}$-HD bit	850-ft life	47 holes
Shanks	5,000-ft life	278 holes
Couplings	1,000-ft life	56 holes
Steel	2,000-ft life	111 holes

If it takes 4 min to change a bit, the time per hole is 4 min divided by 47 holes per bit or the 0.09 min per hole used in this example.

Drilling is only one part of the process of excavating rock, so when considering production, it is good to consider the cost and output in terms of cubic yards of rock. With the 10- × 10-ft pattern, the 18 ft of drilling yields 16 ft of excavation. Therefore, each foot of *drill* hole produces 3.29 cu yd of bank measure (bcy) rock.

$$\frac{10 \text{ ft} \times 10 \text{ ft} \times 16 \text{ ft}}{27 \text{ cu ft/cu yd}} \times \frac{1}{18 \text{ ft}} = 3.29 \text{ cu yd/ft}$$

If the hourly drilling production is 84.0 ft, then the rock production is 84.0 × 3.29, which equals 276 cu yd. This should be matched to the blasting production and to the loading and hauling production. For example, if the loading and hauling capability is 500 cu yd per hour, it will be necessary to employ two drills.

In calculating cost, one will find it good practice to make the analysis in terms of both feet of the hole drilled and cubic yards of the rock produced. Considering only the high wear items of the last example, if bits cost $200 each, shanks $105, couplings $50, and a 10-ft steel $210, what is the cost per cubic yard of the rock produced?

Bits	$200 ÷ 850 ft	=	$0.235 per ft
Shanks	$105 ÷ 5,000 ft	=	$0.021 per ft
Couplings	$ 50 ÷ 1,000 ft	=	$0.050 per ft
Steel	$210 ÷ 2,000 ft	=	$0.105 per ft
			$0.411 per ft

or $\dfrac{\$0.411 \text{ per ft}}{3.29 \text{ cu yd per ft}} = \$0.125 \text{ per cu yd}$

DRILLING EARTH

General information. This section discusses various types of equipment used to drill holes in earth, as distinguished from rock. Some equipment, such as that used for exploratory purposes in securing core samples and similar operations, may be used for drilling rock or earth.

Purposes for drilling holes in earth. In the construction and mining industries holes are drilled into the earth for many purposes, including, but not limited to:

1. Obtaining samples of soil for test purposes.
2. Locating and evaluating deposits of aggregate suitable for mining.
3. Locating and evaluating deposits of minerals.
4. Permitting the installation of cast-in-place piles or shafts to support structures.
5. Enabling the driving of load-bearing piles into hard and tough formations.
6. Providing wells for supplies of water or for deep drainage purposes.
7. Providing shafts for ventilating mines, tunnels, and other underground facilities.
8. Providing horizontal holes through embankments, such as those for the installation of utility conduits.

Sizes and depths of holes drilled into earth. Most holes are drilled by rotating bits or heads attached to the lower end of a shaft called a "kelly bar." This bar, which is

FIGURE 13-19
Tractor-mounted auger-type earth drill. *(Acker Drill Company.)*

supported by a truck, a tractor, or a skid mount, is rotated by an external motor or engine (see Figs. 13-19 and 13-20).

The sizes of holes drilled may vary from a few inches to more than 12 ft (3.7 m). Drills may be equipped with a device attached to the lower end of the drill shaft, known as an *underreamer,* which will permit a gradual increase in the diameter of the hole, as illustrated in Fig. 13-21. This enlargement permits a substantial increase in the bearing area under a shaft-type concrete footing. Underream diameters as great as 144 in. or more have been drilled. Under favorable conditions it is possible to drill holes as deep as 200 ft for underreamed foundations.

The holes are drilled by a truck-mounted rig, whose essential parts include a power unit, cable drum, boom, rotary table, drill stem, and drill. The shaft is drilled first with a large earth auger or a bucket drill, equipped with cutting blades at the bottom, and then the bottom portion of the hole is enlarged with the underreamer.

Figure 13-21 illustrates a method used to drill these holes through unstable soils, such as mud, sand, or gravel, containing water. If it is possible to do so, the shaft is drilled entirely through the unstable soil; then a temporary steel casing is installed in the hole to eliminate groundwater and caving. An alternate method is to add sections to the casing as drilling progresses until the full depth of bad soil is cased off. Then the

FIGURE 13-20
Truck-mounted auger-type earth drill. *(Mobile Drilling Company.)*

hole is completed and filled with concrete, and the casing is pulled before the concrete sets.

This type of foundation has been used extensively in areas whose soils are subject
to changes in moisture content to considerable depth. By placing the footings below the
zone of moisture change, the effects of soil movements due to changes in moisture are
minimized.

Among the advantages of drilled and underreamed foundations, compared with
piles and conventional spread footings, are:

1. They are less expensive for some soils and projects.

2. For varying soil conditions, they make it easy to adjust the depth.

3. They permit inspection of soil prior to establishing the depth or placing concrete.

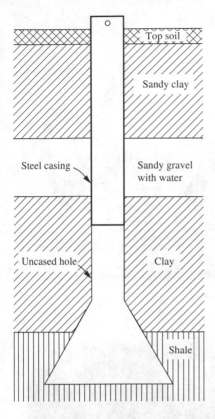

FIGURE 13-21
Steel casing used to permit footing to be drilled through unstable soil.

4. They eliminate damage to adjacent structures due to the vibration of the pile hammer.

5. They eliminate the use of forms for concrete.

Removal of cuttings. Several methods are used to remove the cuttings from the holes. One method of removing the cuttings is to attach an auger to the drill head. The drill head (see Fig. 13-22) is the actual cutting tool at the bottom of the drill stem. The auger extends from the drill head to above the surface of the ground. As the drill shaft and the auger rotate, the earth is forced to the top of the hole, where it is removed and wasted. However, the depth of a hole for which this method may be used is limited by the diameter of the hole, the class of soil, and the moisture content of the soil.

Another method of removing the cuttings is to attach the drill head to only a section of the auger. When the auger section is filled with cuttings, it is raised above the surface of the ground and rotated rapidly to free it of the cuttings.

A third method of removing the cuttings is to use a combination of a drill head with a cylindrical bucket, whose diameter is the same as the diameter of the hole. As the bucket is rotated, steel cutting blades attached to the bottom of the bucket force the cuttings up and into the bucket. When the bucket is filled, it is raised to the surface of the ground and emptied.

A fourth method of removing the cuttings is to force air and water through the hollow kelly bar and drill shaft to the bottom of the hole and then upward around the

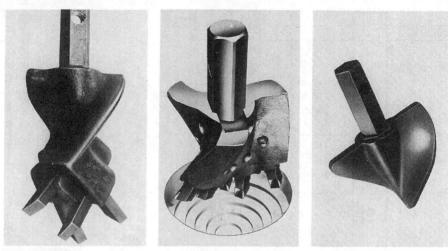

FIGURE 13-22
Drill heads or bits to be attached to the bottom of a drill kelly for drilling earth or soft rock. *(Mobile Drilling Company.)*

FIGURE 13-23
Gasoline-engine-powered auger-type boring machine with the auger enclosed in steel casing. *(McLaughlin Manufacturing Company.)*

drill shaft, so that the cuttings are carried to the surface of the ground, by the air or water.

Earth-boring machines. Figure 13-23 illustrates a self-contained gasoline-engine-powered auger-type boring machine with the auger enclosed in a steel pipe or casing, which is forced through the hole excavated by the auger. The machine illustrated is capable of boring holes for casing sizes varying from 4 to 30 in. (102 to 762 mm) or more and lengths up to 200 ft (61 m), depending on the type and condition of the soil and job. As the boring advances, the machine automatically maintains a forward thrust on the casing and the auger.

These machines are powered hydraulically, by air, or by electric motors.

PROBLEMS

13-1. A project utilizing experienced drillers will require the drilling and blasting of medium silica granite. No field drilling tests were conducted. It is proposed to use a $6\frac{1}{2}$-B downhole drill @ 350 psi. The drills to be used have a single pass capability of 20 ft and take steel in 20-ft lengths. The blasting pattern will be a 10- $\times$ 12-ft grid with 3 ft of subdrilling required. On the average the specified finish grade is 20 ft below the existing ground surface. Determine the drilling production, assuming it takes 30 min to change a $6\frac{1}{2}$-in. downhole hammer.

13-2. A project in medium silica sandstone is being investigated. Field drilling tests proved that air-track drills with $3\frac{1}{2}$-in.-HD bits can achieve a penetration rate of 2.5 ft per min. The drills use 12-ft steel. The blasting pattern will be 6 $\times$ 8 ft with 2 ft of subdrilling. The average depth to finish grade is 8 ft. The drilling production must match that of the loading and hauling, which is 210 bcy per hour. How many drill units will be required?

13-3. A highway cut through shale is being constructed. Drilling tests indicate that air-track drills with $3\frac{1}{2}$-in.-STD bits can penetrate 3.5 ft per min. The drills use 10-ft steel. The blasting pattern will be 8 $\times$ 10 ft with 2 ft of subdrilling. The average depth to finish grade is 15 ft. The project labor scale is $16 per hour for drillers. The air-track drill and compressor cost is $46 per hour; bits are $185 each; shanks, $115; couplings, $54; and 10-ft steel, $200. Because of very difficult job conditions, use a 45-min production hour. What is the drilling cost per cubic yard of rock?

13-4. The president of the "Low Bid" construction company has just visited one of his jobs. At the project he found most of the rock trucks parked. When he questioned the foreman as to why this new equipment with the capability of hauling 600 cu yd per hour was not working, the foreman replied that the drilling could not keep up. The president has told you to solve the problem immediately.

The project is in a dolomite formation. Company drilling experience in this area indicates that compressed-air rotary-percussion drills with $3\frac{1}{2}$-in. button bits can average 1.5 ft of penetration per minute. Drilling efficiency is typically a 50-min hour. These drills use 12-ft drill steel. The best blasting pattern has proven to be 10 $\times$ 10 ft with 2 ft of subdrilling. The average excavation depth is 8 ft. How many drills will you recommend for use on the job, to the president?

13-5. Buffet Inc. has determined that there is an untapped party market at the north pole. Intensive marketing studies indicate that a "Margaritaville Bar & Grille" will be very successful during the long, dark arctic winters. Joe Cool, now living in Key West, has been employed to manage the construction of this project and has employed you to analyze the foundation drilling program.

The plan is to construct the establishment 20 ft below the surface of the ice. This will require an extra 2 ft of drilling to ensure that the final floor can be excavated to the required depth after blasting. From field testing with a 90-psi rotary-percussion drill, it has been determined that a direct drilling rate, through the ice, of 175 ft per hour can be achieved when using a $3\frac{1}{2}$-HD bit. This drill uses 12-ft drill steel. Studies have indicated that ice acts similar to low silica, LA > 20, diabase. The blasting pattern will be on a 12- × 12-ft grid. The cool climate will affect production.

Because of the high freight cost to the site, $3\frac{1}{2}$-in. bits cost $500 each; shanks, $400; coupling, $150; and steel, $600. All prices are FOB (free on board) at the north pole. What drilling production can be expected and what will be the cost on a per cubic yard basis for the drill's high wear items that you should tell Mr. Cool to use in the project's construction cost estimate?

REFERENCES

1. Smith, Gordon R.: "Drilling, New Equipment, New Techniques," *Construction Methods and Equipment,* vol. 44, pp. 110–115, August 1962.
2. "Shot-drill Cuts Hard Rock Sockets for Footings," *Construction Methods and Equipment,* vol. 53, pp. 84–85, May 1971.
3. Higgins, Lindley R.: "Drills Play Dramatic Role in Profit Production," *Construction Methods and Equipment,* vol. 58, pp. 54–61, September 1976.
4. "The Cost of Drilling and Blasting Today's Pits," *Engineering and Mining Journal,* vol. 166, pp. 110–113, September 1965.
5. Pasieka, A. R., and J. C. Wilson: "The Importance of High-Pressure Compressed Air to Mining Operations," *The Canadian Mining and Metallurgical Bulletin,* vol. 59, pp. 1093–1102, September 1966.
6. Knox, John: "Factors Influence the Design and Application of Downhole Drills," *The Canadian Mining and Metallurgical Bulletin,* vol. 58, pp. 547–550, May 1965.
7. Dick, Richard A., Larry R. Fletcher, and Dennis W. D'Andrea: "Explosives and Blasting Procedures," GPO No. 024-004-02115-6, Government Printing Office, Washington, DC.
8. Nelmark, Jack D.: "Large Diameter Blast Hole Drills," *Journal of the Mining Congress,* August 1980.

CHAPTER 14

BLASTING ROCK

BLASTING

The operation referred to as "blasting" is performed to break rock so that it may be quarried for processing in an aggregate production operation, or to excavate a right-of-way. Blasting is accomplished by discharging an explosive that has either been placed in an unconfined manner, such as mud capping boulders, or is confined as in a borehole. There are two forms of energy released when high explosives are detonated, shock and gas. An unconfined charge works by shock energy, whereas a confined charge has a high gas energy output.

There are many types of explosives and methods for using them. A full treatment of each explosive and method is too comprehensive for inclusion in this book. A complete discussion of explosives can be found in handbooks on blasting that are published by manufacturers of explosives.

GLOSSARY OF TERMS

The following glossary defines the important terms that are used in describing blasting operations.

ANFO. A blasting agent that is produced by mixing prilled ammonium nitrate and fuel oil.

Back break. The rock broken beyond the last row of holes.

Bench height. The vertical distance between the floor or base of an excavation and the berm or ledge above, where the blastholes are drilled and shot.

Blasthole (borehole). A hole that is drilled into the rock to permit placement of an explosive.

Blasting (shot). The detonation of an explosive to fracture the rock.

Blasting agent. An explosive classification from the standpoint of storage and transportation. It is a material or mixture intended for blasting, consisting of an oxidizer and a fuel. It is less sensitive to initiation and cannot be detonated with a No. 8 blasting cap when unconfined. Therefore, blasting agents are covered by different federal handling regulations.

Blasting cap. A hollow metal cap which is filled with a high explosive and is detonated within or adjacent to the blasting agent as a means of detonating the agent.

Blasting machine. A machine used to generate the electric current that detonates an electric blasting cap.

Block holing. A hole or holes drilled into a boulder or individual oversize rock to permit placement of a small charge for secondary blasting.

Booster. A chemical agent used to intensify an explosive reaction. A booster does not include an initiating device.

Burden. The distance from the explosive charge to the nearest free or open face is referred to as the burden or a burden distance. There can be an apparent burden and a true burden. True burden is in the direction that the displacement of broken rock will move following the firing of the charge.

Charge. The total explosive loaded in a blasthole, which includes the blasting agent, booster, and primer.

Coyote blasting. The horizontal drilling of blastholes at the foot of a rock face for a shot.

Crimping. An operation of reducing the diameter of a cap near the open end to hold the fuse securely in the cap.

Cutoff. The breaking of a fuse or electric circuit to a cap in a primer resulting in a portion of a column of explosives failing to detonate.

Decking (deck stemming). The operation of placing inert material in a blasthole at spacings to separate explosive charges in the hole.

Delay. The term used to describe noninstantaneous firing of a charge or group of charges usually by blasting caps having predetermined built-in time delays.

Density. A measure of the mass of an explosive per unit volume.

Detonating cord (Primacord). A plastic covered fabric braid cord of a high-velocity explosive (PETN) used to detonate explosives.

Detonation rate. A measure of the speed at which an explosion travels within a column of explosive.

Downline. Primacord lines extending into the blasthole from a trunkline on the surface at the top of the hole. At the bottom end the cord is attached to the primer.

Electric blasting cap (EBC). A small metal tube loaded with a powder charge. It is detonated by the heat produced from an electric current flowing through a wire bridge inside the cap.

Explosive. A chemical mixture that reacts at high speed, liberating gas and heat, thus causing very high pressure. High explosives contain at least one ingredient characterized by a very high rate of reaction and development of high pressure. Low explosives contain no ingredients which by themselves can explode. Both can be initiated by a single No. 8 blasting cap.

Flammability. The characteristic of an explosive which describes its ease of initiation from a spark, fire, or flame.

Floor. The horizontal, or nearly so, bottom plane of an excavation.

Flyrock. The rock that is ejected into the air by an explosion. It is an indication of wasted energy.

Fracture. The breaking of rock without the movement of individual pieces.

Fragmentation. The degree to which rock is broken by blasting.

Fumes. The amount of toxic gases produced by an explosive in the detonation process.

Highwall. The common name for the vertical face of an excavation; the term comes from coal strip mining.

Initiation. The act of detonating a high explosive.

Lead wires. The wires that conduct the electric current from its source to the leg-wires of the electric blasting caps.

Leg-wires. The wires that conduct the electric current from the lead wires to an electric blasting cap.

Mat (blasting mat). A blanket, usually of woven wire rope, used to restrict or contain flyrock.

MS delay cap (millisecond). A cap which has a built-in delay element. It is commonly available in 25/1,000-sec increments.

Misfire. When a charge or part of a charge fails to fire. Such a situation should be considered extremely dangerous.

Mud capping (plaster shot). An operation where an explosive is placed in contact with the surface of a boulder or rock and covered with mud or earth for firing.

Nitroglycerin. A colorless explosive liquid obtained by treating glycerol with a mixture of nitric and sulfuric acids.

Overbreak. A rock which is fractured outside the desired excavation limits. (Many construction contracts stipulate nonpayment for rock beyond a specified overbreak line.)

Overburden. The depth of material lying above the rock which is to be shot.

PETN. The abbreviation for the chemical content (pentaerythritol tetranitrate) of a high explosive having a very high rate of detonation, commonly used in detonating cord.

Powder factor. The quantity of explosive used to fracture a specific volume of rock, e.g., pounds of explosive per cubic yard of rock.

Premature. A charge which detonates before it is intended to explode.

Presplitting. A stress relief line of small-diameter drill holes at close intervals which are lightly loaded and detonated to rupture the remaining web of rock. The main charge is fired after firing the presplit holes.

Prill. In the United States most ammonium nitrate, both agricultural and blasting grade, is produced by the prill tower method. Ammonium nitrate liquor is released as a spray at the top of a prilling tower. Prills of ammonium nitrate congeal in the upcoming steam and air of the tower. The moisture driven out by the dropping process leaves voids within the prills.

Primer. The portion of a charge, consisting of a cap-sensitive explosive loaded with a firing device, which initiates the explosion.

Propagation. The movement of a detonation wave, either in the hole or from hole to hole.

Rounds. A term which includes all the blastholes that are drilled, loaded, and fired in one shot.

Safety fuse. A fuse containing a low explosive enclosed in a suitable covering. When the fuse is ignited, it will burn at a predetermined speed. It is used to initiate explosions under certain conditions.

Secondary blasting. An operation performed to reduce to desirable size the oversize material remaining after the primary explosion.

Sensitiveness. A measure of an explosive's cartridge-to-cartridge propagating ability.

Sensitizer. An ingredient used in explosive compounds to promote greater ease in initiation or propagation of the reactions.

Stemming. The adding of an inert material, such as drill cuttings, on top of the explosive in a blasthole for the purpose of confining the energy of the explosion.

Subdrill. The practice of extending the depth of drilled blastholes beyond the planned grade lines or below floor elevation.

Tamping. The process of compacting the stemming or explosive in a blasthole.

Throw/Heave. The displacement of rock as a result of a detonation and the expansion of gases.

TNT. A high explosive whose chemical content is trinitrotoluene, or trinitrotoluol.

Toe. The burden distance if the blasthole is vertical or the distance from the bottom of a borehole to the vertical free face of a bench.

Trunkline. The main line of a detonating cord on the surface, in the case of a nonelectric system, extending from the ignition point to the blastholes containing explosives to be detonated. Secondary lines (downlines) of detonating cord attached to the trunkline are used to detonate the blasting caps in the primers.

COMMERCIAL EXPLOSIVES

There are four main categories of commercial high explosives: dynamite, slurries, ANFO, and two-component explosives. To be a high explosive, the material must be cap-sensitive, react at a speed faster than the speed of sound, and the reaction must be accompanied by a shock wave. The first three categories, dynamite, slurries, and ANFO, are the principal explosives used for borehole charges. Two-component or binary explosives are normally not classified as an explosive until mixed. Therefore, they offer advantages in shipping and storage which make them attractive alternatives on small jobs. But their unit price is significantly greater than that of other explosives.

Dynamite. This nitroglycerin-based product is the most sensitive of all the generic classes of explosives in use today. It is available in many grades and sizes to meet the requirements of a particular job. Straight dynamite is not appropriate for construction applications because it is very sensitive to shock. With straight dynamite, sympathetic detonation can result from adjacent holes, which were fired on an earlier delay.

The most widely used product is known as "high-density extra dynamite." In this product, which is less sensitive to shock than straight dynamite, some of the nitroglycerin has been replaced with ammonium nitrate.

The approximate strength of a dynamite is specified as a percentage, which is an indication of the ratio of the weight of nitroglycerin to the total weight of a cartridge. Individual cartridges vary in size from approximately 1 to 8 in. in diameter and 8 to 24 in. long.

Dynamite is used extensively for charging boreholes, especially for the smaller sizes. As cartridges are placed in a hole, they are tamped sharply with a wooden pole, expanding the cartridges to fill the hole. For this purpose it may be desirable to split the sides of a cartridge or to use cartridges with perforated shells. The dynamite may be fired by a blasting cap or a Primacord fuse. If a blasting cap is used, one of the cartridges serves as a primer. The cap is placed within a hole made in this cartridge.

Slurries. This is a generic term for both water gels and emulsions. They are water-resistant explosive mixtures of ammonium nitrate and a fuel sensitizer. The primary sensitizing methods are the introduction of air throughout the mixture, the addition of aluminum particles, or the addition of nitrocellulose. In comparison to ANFO (see next section), slurries have a higher cost per pound and have less energy. However, in wet conditions they are very competitive with ANFO because the ANFO is water-sensitive and must be protected in lined holes or a bagged product has to be used. Both of these measures add to the total cost of the ANFO. Emulsions will have a somewhat higher detonation velocity than water gels.

An advantage of slurries over dynamite is that the separate ingredients can be hauled to the project in bulk and mixed immediately before loading the blastholes. The mixture may be poured directly into the hole. Some emulsions tend to be wet and will adhere to the blasthole, causing bulk loading problems. Slurries may be packaged in plastic bags for placement in the holes. Because they are denser than water, they will sink to the bottom of holes containing water.

Slurries are detonated by special primers, such as dynamite, or PETN, using electric blasting caps or Primacord.

ANFO. This explosive is used extensively on construction projects and represents about 80% of all explosives used in the United States. "ANFO" is an ammonium nitrate and fuel oil mixture and is synonymous with dry blasting agents. This explosive is the cheapest source of explosive energy. Because it must be detonated by special primers, it is much safer than dynamite.

The explosive is made by blending $3\frac{1}{2}$ quarts of fuel oil with 100 lb of ammonium nitrate blasting prills. This is the optimum mixture ratio. The detonation efficiency is controlled by this ratio. It is less detrimental to have a fuel deficiency but both fuel extremes affect the blast. With too little fuel, the explosive will not perform properly. With too much fuel, maximum energy output is reduced. The prills should not be confused with ammonium nitrate fertilizer prills. A blasting prill is porous in order to distribute the fuel oil better.

Because the mixture is free-flowing, it can be either blown or augered from bulk trucks directly into the blastholes. It is detonated by primers consisting of charges of dynamite placed at the bottoms of the holes and sometimes at intermediate depths. Electric blasting caps or Primacord may be used to detonate the dynamite.

ANFO is not water-resistant. Detonation will be marginal if ANFO is placed in water and shot, even if the interval between loading and shooting is very short. If it is to be used in wet holes, there is a *densified* ANFO cartridge. This product has a density greater than water, so it will sink to the bottom of a wet hole. Normal bulk ANFO has a density of 0.8. Cartridges or bulk product sealed in plastic bags will not sink. Another method to permit use in wet conditions is to preline the holes with plastic tubing, closed at the bottom, to exclude the water. The tubes, whose diameters should be slightly smaller than the holes, are installed in the holes by placing rocks or other weights in their bottoms.

INITIATING AND DELAY DEVICES

It is common practice to fire several holes or rows of holes at one time. Fragmentation, backbreak, vibration, and violence of a blast are all controlled by the firing sequence of the individual blastholes. The order and timing of the detonation of individual holes is regulated by the initiation system. Electric and nonelectric initiation systems are available. When selecting the proper system, one should consider both blast design and safety. Electrical systems are more sensitive to lightning than nonelectric systems, but both are susceptible.

Electric blasting caps. With an electric cap an explosion is caused by passing an electric current through a wire bridge, similar to an electric light bulb filament. The current, approximately 1.5 amps, heats the bridge to incandescence and ignites a heat-sensitive flash compound. The ignition sets off a primer which in turn fires a base charge in the cap. This charge detonates with sufficient violence to fire a charge of explosive.

Electric caps are supplied with two leg-wires in lengths varying from 2 to 100 ft. These wires are connected with the wires from other holes to form a closed electric circuit for firing purposes. The leg-wires of electric blasting caps are made of either iron or copper. For ease in wiring a blast, each leg-wire on an electric cap is a different color. Regular electric blasting caps are made to fire within a few milliseconds after current is applied. ·

Delay blasting systems. Delay blasting caps are used to obtain a specified firing sequence. Such caps are available for delay intervals varying from a small fraction of a second to about 7 sec. When explosive charges in two or more rows of holes parallel to a face are fired in one shot, it is desirable to fire the charges in the holes nearest the face a short time ahead of those in the second row. This procedure will reduce the apparent burden for the holes in the second row, and thereby will permit the explosive in the second row to break the rock more effectively. In the case of more than two rows this same delayed firing sequence will be followed for each successive row.

In construction and surface blasting applications millisecond delay electric blasting caps are frequently used. They have individual intervals ranging from 25 to about 650 milliseconds (msec). Long period delay electric blasting caps have individual intervals ranging from about $\frac{2}{10}$ sec to over 7 sec. They are primarily used in tunneling and underground mining.

Detonating cord. This is a nonelectric initiation system consisting of a flexible cord having a center core of high explosive, usually PETN. It is used to detonate dynamite and other cap-sensitive explosives. The explosive core is encased within textile fibers and covered with a waterproof sheath for protection. Detonating cord is insensitive to ordinary shock or friction. The explosive has a detonation rate of approximately 21,000 ft per sec. Delays can be achieved by attaching in-line delay devices. When several blastholes are fired in a round, the cord is laid on the surface between the holes as a trunkline. At each hole one end of a detonating cord downline is attached to the trunkline, whereas the other end of the downline extends into the blasthole. If it is necessary to use a blasting cap and/or a primer to initiate the blast in the hole, the bottom end of the downline may be cut square and securely inserted into the cap.

Sequential blasting machine. There are condenser-discharge blasting machines for firing electric blasting caps. These special machines have sequential timers permitting precisely timed firing intervals for blasting circuits. This provides the blaster the option of many delays within a blast. Since many delays are available, the pounds of explosive fired per delay can be reduced to control noise and vibration better.

ROCK BREAKAGE

The major mechanisms of rock breakage result from the sustained gas pressure buildup in the borehole by the explosion. First, this pressure will cause radial cracking. Such cracking is similar to what happens in the case of frozen water pipes—a longitudinal split occurs parallel to the axis of the pipe. A borehole is analogous to the frozen pipe in that it is a cylindrical pressure vessel. But there is a difference in the rate of loading. A blasthole is pressurized instantaneously. Failure, therefore, instead of being at the one weakest seam, is in *many* seams parallel to the borehole. Burden distance and direction to the free face will control the course and extent of the radial crack pattern.

When the radial cracking takes place, the rock mass is transformed into individual rock wedges. If relief is available perpendicular to the axis of the blasthole, the gas pressure pushes against these wedges, putting their opposite sides into tension and compression. The exact distribution of such stresses are affected by the location of the charge in the blasthole. In this second breakage mechanism, flexural rupture is controlled by the burden distance and bench height. The ratio of the bench height divided by the burden distance is known as the "stiffness ratio." This is the same mechanism that a structural engineer is concerned with when analyzing the length of a column in relation to its thickness.

There is a greater degree of difficulty in breaking rock when the burden distance is equal to the bench height. As bench height increases compared to burden distance, the rock is more easily broken. If the blast is not designed properly and the burden distance is too great, relief will not be available and the hole will either crater or the stemming will blow out.

BLAST DESIGN

Every blast must be designed to meet the existing conditions of the rock formation and overburden, and to produce the desired final result. There is no single solution to this

FIGURE 14-1
Blasthole dimensional terminology.

problem. Rock is not a homogeneous material. There are fracture planes, seams, and changes in burden to be considered. Wave propagation is faster in hard rock than in soft rock. Initial blast designs use idealized assumptions. The engineer does this realizing that discontinuities will be encountered in the field. Because of these facts, it must always be understood that the theoretical blast design is only the starting point for blasting operations in the field. A trial blast should always be performed. It will either validate the initial assumptions or provide the information needed for final blast design.

Burden. The most critical dimension in blast design is the burden distance. This is the shortest distance to stress relief at the time a blasthole detonates. It is normally the distance to the free face in an excavation, whether a quarry situation or a highway cut (see Fig. 14-1). Internal faces can be created by blastholes fired on an earlier delay within a shot. When the burden distance is insufficient, rock will be thrown for excessive distances from the face, fragmentation may be excessively fine, and air blast levels will be high.

An empirical formula for approximating a burden distance to be used on a first trial shot is

$$B = \left(\frac{2SG_e}{SG_r} + 1.5\right)D_e \qquad (14\text{-}1)$$

where B = burden, ft

SG_e = specific gravity of the explosive

SG_r = specific gravity of the rock

D_e = diameter of explosive, in.

The actual explosive diameter will depend on the manufacturer's packaging container thickness. If the specific product is known, the exact information should be used; but in the case of developing a design before settling on a specific product an allowance should be made. Rock density is an indicator of strength, which in turn governs the amount of energy required to cause breakage. The approximate specific gravities of rocks are given in Table 14-1.

Example 14-1. A contractor plans to use dynamite, specific gravity 1.3, to open an excavation in granite rock. The drilling equipment available will drill a 3-in. blasthole. Dynamite comes packaged in $2\frac{3}{4}$-in. diameter sticks. What is the recommended burden distance for the first trial shot?

From Table 14-1, specific gravity of granite 2.6 to 2.9, use 2.8:

$$B = \left(\frac{2 \times 1.3}{2.8} + 1.5\right) \times 2.75 = 6.1 \text{ ft}$$

Explosive density is used in Eq. (14-1) because of the proportional relationship between explosive density and strength. There are, however, some explosive emulsions which exhibit differing strengths at equal densities. In such a case Eq. (14-1) will not be valid. An equation based on relative bulk strength instead of density can be used in such situations.

Relative bulk strength is the strength ratio for a constant volume compared to a standard explosive. ANFO, ammonium nitrate and fuel oil, is the standard explosive with an energy-level rating of 100.

TABLE 14-1
Density by nominal rock classifications

Rock classification	Specific gravity	Density broken (ton/cu yd)
Basalt	2.8–3.0	2.57
Diabase	2.6–3.0	2.36
Diorite	2.8–3.0	2.50
Dolomite	2.8–2.9	2.43
Gneiss	2.6–2.9	2.43
Granite	2.6–2.9	2.30
Hematite	4.5–5.3	4.12
Limestone	2.4–2.9	2.23
Marble	2.1–2.9	2.09
Mica schist	2.5–2.9	2.30
Quartzite	2.0–2.8	2.16
Sandstone	2.0–2.8	2.03
Shale	2.4–2.8	2.16
Slate	2.5–2.8	2.23
Trap rock	2.6–3.0	2.36

The relative bulk strength rating should be based on test data under specified conditions, but sometimes the rating is based on calculations. Manufacturers will supply specific values for their individual products. Again, a caution is important: These design equations only provide a starting point for blasting activities in the field. The relative energy equation for burden distance is

$$B = 0.67D_e \sqrt[3]{\frac{St_v}{SG_r}} \qquad (14\text{-}2)$$

where St_v = relative bulk strength compared to ANFO = 100.

When one or two rows of blastholes are used, the burden distance between rows will usually be equal. If more than two rows are to be fired in a single shot, either the burden distance of the rear holes must be adjusted or delay devices must be used to allow the face rock from the front rows to move.

The burden distance may have to be adjusted because of geological variations. Rock is not the homogeneous material assumed by all the formulas; therefore, it is often necessary to employ correction factors for specific geological conditions. Table 14-2 provides burden distance correction factors for rock deposition, Kd, and rock structure, Ks.

$$B_{\text{corrected}} = B \times Kd \times Ks \qquad (14\text{-}3)$$

Example 14-2. A new quarry is being opened in a limestone formation having horizontal bedding with numerous weak joints. From a borehole test drilling program it is believed that the limestone is highly laminated with many weakly cemented layers. Because of possible wet conditions, a cartridged slurry (relative bulk strength of 140) will be used as the explosive. The 6.5-in. blastholes will be loaded with 5-in. diameter cartridges. What is the calculated burden distance to be used initially?

From Table 14-1, specific gravity of limestone 2.4 to 2.9, use 2.6:

$$B = 0.67 \times 5 \times \sqrt[3]{\frac{140}{2.6}} = 12.65 \text{ ft}$$

Correction factors $Kd = 1$, horizontal bedding, and $Ks = 1.3$, numerous weakly cemented layers.

$$B_{\text{corrected}} = 12.65 \times 1 \times 1.3 = 16.4 \text{ ft}$$

TABLE 14-2
Burden distance correction factors

Rock deposition	Kd
Bedding steeply dipping into cut	1.18
Bedding steeply dipping into face	0.95
Other cases of deposition	1.00

Rock structure	Ks
Heavily cracked, frequent weak joints, weakly cemented layers	1.30
Thin, well-cemented layers with tight joints	1.10
Massive intact rock	0.95

Stemming. The purpose of stemming is to confine the explosive energy to the blast-hole. To function properly the material used for stemming must lock into the borehole. It is common practice to use drill cuttings as the stemming material. Very fine cuttings or drill cuttings which are only dust will not accomplish the desired purpose. It may be necessary in such cases to bring in crushed stone. Likewise, very coarse materials do not make good stemming because they tend to bridge and will be ejected from the hole. To function properly, the stemming material should have an average diameter 0.05 times the diameter of the hole and should be angular.

If the stemming distance is too great, there will be poor top breakage from the explosion and backbreak will increase. When the stemming distance is inadequate, the explosion will escape prematurely from the hole. Under normal conditions, properly designed burden and explosive, and good stemming material, a stemming distance, T, of 0.7 times the burden distance, B, will be satisfactory.

$$T = 0.7 \times B \qquad (14\text{-}4)$$

When drilling dust is used for stemming material, the stemming distance will have to be increased by another 30% of the burden distance because the dust will not lock into the hole.

Subdrilling. A shot will normally not break to the very bottom of the blasthole. This can be understood by remembering that the second mechanism of breakage is flexural rupture. To achieve a specified grade, one will need to drill below the desired floor elevation. This portion of the blasthole below the desired final grade is termed "subdrilling." The subdrilling distance, J, required can be approximated by the following formula:

$$J = 0.3 \times B \qquad (14\text{-}5)$$

Subdrilling represents the depth required for explosive placement, not a field drilling depth. During the drilling operation there will be random drilling depth errors, holes will slough, and material will accidentally fall into some holes. Therefore, for practical reasons drilling should be to a depth slightly greater than that calculated. An extra foot of drilling depth for holes greater than 12 ft in required depth should be considered for economical reasons. The blaster can always add cutting to the hole to load explosive from the proper elevation, but he does not have the ability to increase the depth. It is costly to have to stop the loading operation and to bring a drill back to increase the depth of a hole. It is also costly and hazardous to perform secondary blasting.

Blasthole size. The size (diameter) of the blasthole will affect blast considerations concerning fragmentation, air blast, flyrock, and ground vibration. The economics of drilling is the second consideration in determining blasthole size. Larger holes are usually more economical to drill but they introduce possible blast problems. Once again, the second mechanism of rupture and the stiffness ratio need to be considered. The *stiffness ratio* for blasting purposes is the bench height divided by the burden distance. In some situations, as in a quarry, the blaster can adapt the bench height to optimize the blast, but on a road project the existing ground and the specified final roadway grades

TABLE 14-3
Stiffness ratio's effect on blasting factors

Stiffness ratio	1	2	3	4 and higher[†]
Fragmentation	Poor	Fair	Good	Excellent
Air blast	Severe	Fair	Good	Excellent
Flyrock	Severe	Fair	Good	Excellent
Ground vibration	Severe	Fair	Good	Excellent

[†] Stiffness ratios above 4 yield no increase in benefit.

set limits on any bench height modification. Table 14-3 gives the relationship between the stiffness ratio and the critical blasting factors.

One of the parameters in both Eqs. (14-1) and (14-2) was the diameter of the explosive, D_e. The diameter of the explosive is limited by the diameter of the blasthole. If it is desirable to drill larger blastholes for economic reasons, the burden distance will be affected. Consider Example 14-1: If the contractor had wanted to use a 5-in. bit, the charge could possibly have been increased to $4\frac{1}{2}$ in. in diameter in the case of a packaged explosive or the full 5-in. diameter if bulk ANFO were loaded into an unlined hole.

Using the $4\frac{1}{2}$-in. assumption, one would find the burden distance to be

$$B = \left(\frac{2 \times 1.3}{2.8} + 1.5\right) \times 4.5 = 10.9 \text{ ft}$$

If the extent of the excavation perpendicular to the face is 100 ft, the original burden distance will require 17 rows [(100/6.1) + 1]. Using larger holes, the calculated burden distance is increased to 10.9 ft and only 10 rows will be required [(100/10.9) + 1]. By increasing the blasthole diameter, the number of holes which will have to be drilled and loaded has been reduced.

However, the question of bench height has not been considered in either example. If the bench height was limited to 13 ft because that was the specified excavation depth, which size blasthole should be utilized? The stiffness ratio (SR) for the two blasthole diameters under consideration are

3-in. blasthole: 13-ft height/6.1-ft burden = 2.1 SR
5-in. blasthole: 13-ft height/10.9-ft burden = 1.2 SR

Table 14-3 indicates that for the 5-in. blasthole there will be blasting problems. Even the 3-in. blasthole can only be expected to yield fair results, which indicates that the shot should be redesigned.

It will be good to have a SR value of at least 3. Such a value is necessary for the blast to yield good results. Try a 2-in. blasthole and assume an explosive diameter of $1\frac{3}{4}$ in.

$$B = \left(\frac{2 \times 1.3}{2.8} + 1.5\right) \times 1.75 = 4.25 \text{ ft}$$

2-in. blasthole: 13-ft height/4.25-ft burden = 3.1 SR

This means that more rows will be required but better breakage will result. Drilling cost will be increased but secondary blasting and handling cost should be minimized.

Spacing. Proper spacing of blastholes is controlled by the initiation timing and the stiffness ratio. When holes are spaced too close and fired instantaneously, venting of the energy will occur with resulting air blast and flyrock. When the spacing is extended, there is a limit beyond which fragmentation will become harsh. Before beginning a spacing analysis, two questions must be answered concerning the shot: (1) Will the charges be fired instantaneously or will delays be used? (2) Is the stiffness ratio greater than 4? A SR of less than 4 is considered a low bench and a high bench is a SR value of 4 or greater. This means that there are four cases to be considered:

1. *Instantaneous initiation*, with the SR greater than 1 but less than 4.

$$S = \frac{L + 2B}{3} \tag{14-6}$$

where S = spacing
L = bench height

2. *Instantaneous initiation*, with the SR equal to or greater than 4.

$$S = 2B \tag{14-7}$$

3. *Delayed initiation*, with the SR greater than 1 but less than 4.

$$S = \frac{L + 7B}{8} \tag{14-8}$$

4. *Delayed initiation*, with the SR equal to or greater than 4.

$$S = 1.4B \tag{14-9}$$

The actual spacing utilized in the field should be within 15% plus or minus the calculated value.

Example 14-3. It is proposed to load 4-in.-diameter blastholes with bulk ANFO. The contractor would like to use a 8 × 8 drill pattern (8-ft burden and 8-ft spacing). Assuming the burden distance is correct, will the 8-ft spacing be acceptable? The bench height is 35 ft and each hole is to be fired on a separate delay.

Check the stiffness ratio, L/B for high or low bench:

$L/B = 35/8 = 4.4 > 4$; therefore, high bench.

Delay timing; therefore, use Eq. (14-9).

$S = 1.4 \times 8 = 11.2$ ft
Range, $11.2 \pm 15\%$: $9.5 \leq S \leq 12.9$

The proposed spacing of 8 ft does not appear to be sufficient. As a minimum, the pattern should be changed to 8-ft burden × 9.5-ft spacing for the first trial shot in the field.

Example 14-4. A project in granite rock will have an average bench height of 20 ft. An explosive having a specific gravity of 1.2 has been proposed. The contractor's equipment can easily drill 3-in.-diameter holes. Assume the packaged diameter of the explosives will be 2.5 in. Delay blasting techniques will be utilized. Develop a blast design for the project.

The specific gravity of granite is between 2.6 and 2.9 (see Table 14-1). Use the average, 2.75.

Using Eq. (14-1), we obtain

$$B = \left(\frac{2 \times 1.2}{2.75} + 1.5\right) \times 2.5 = 5.93 \text{ ft}$$

Use 6 ft for the burden distance.

The stiffness ratio: $L/B = 20/6 = 3.3$
From Table 14-3, the stiffness ratio is good.

The stemming depth, from Eq. (14-4), is

$T = 0.7 \times 6 = 4.2 \text{ ft}$

Use 4 ft for stemming.

The subdrilling depth, from Eq. (14-5) is

$J = 0.3 \times 6 = 1.8 \text{ ft}$

Use 2 ft for subdrilling.

The spacing for a SR greater than 1 but less than 4 and using delay initiation, from Eq. (14-8), is

$$S = \frac{20 + (7 \times 6)}{8} = 7.75 \text{ ft}$$

$7.75 \pm 15\%$: The range for S is 6.6–8.9 ft
As a first try, use a 6-ft burden × 8-ft spacing pattern.

Note that we have attempted to design a blast which will require only integer measurements in the field.

Powder factor. The amount of explosive required to fracture a cubic yard of rock is a measure of the economy of a blast design. Table 14-4 is a loading density chart which allows the engineer to easily calculate the weight of explosive required for a blasthole. In Example 14-4 the diameter of the explosive was 2.5 in. and the explosive had a density of 1.2. Using Table 14-4, one finds that the loading density is 2.55 lb per ft of charge. The powder column length is the total hole length less the stemming, 18 ft in this case [20 ft + 2 ft (subdrilling) − 4 ft (stemming)]. The total weight of explosive used per blasthole will be 18 ft × 2.55 lb per ft = 45.9 lb.

The amount of rock fractured by one blasthole is the pattern area times the depth to grade. For the 6 × 8 ft pattern having a 20-ft depth, each hole will have an affected volume of 35.6 cu yd[(6 × 8 × 20 ft)/27 cu ft per cu yd]. The powder factor will be 1.29 lb per cu yd[45.9 lb /35.6 cu yd]. With experience, this number provides the engineer a check on the blast design.

TABLE 14-4
Explosive loading density chart in lb per ft of column for a given explosive specific gravity

Column diam. (in.)	Explosive specific gravity							
	0.80	0.90	1.00	1.10	1.20	1.30	1.40	1.50
1	0.27	0.31	0.34	0.37	0.41	0.44	0.48	0.51
$1\frac{1}{4}$	0.43	0.48	0.53	0.59	0.64	0.69	0.74	0.80
$1\frac{1}{2}$	0.61	0.69	0.77	0.84	0.92	1.00	1.07	1.15
$1\frac{3}{4}$	0.83	0.94	1.04	1.15	1.25	1.36	1.46	1.56
2	1.09	1.23	1.36	1.50	1.63	1.77	1.91	2.04
$2\frac{1}{2}$	1.70	1.92	2.13	2.34	2.55	2.77	2.98	3.19
3	2.45	2.76	3.06	3.37	3.68	3.98	4.29	4.60
$3\frac{1}{2}$	3.34	3.75	4.17	4.59	5.01	5.42	5.84	6.26
4	4.36	4.90	5.45	6.00	6.54	7.08	7.63	8.17
$4\frac{1}{2}$	5.52	6.21	6.89	7.58	8.27	8.96	9.65	10.34
5	6.81	7.66	8.51	9.36	10.22	11.07	11.92	12.77
$5\frac{1}{2}$	8.24	9.27	10.30	11.33	12.36	13.39	14.42	15.45
6	9.81	11.03	12.26	13.48	14.71	15.93	17.16	18.39
$6\frac{1}{2}$	11.51	12.95	14.39	15.82	17.26	18.70	20.14	21.58
7	13.35	15.02	16.68	18.35	20.02	21.69	23.36	25.03
8	17.43	19.61	21.79	23.97	26.15	28.33	30.51	32.69
9	22.06	24.82	27.58	30.34	33.10	35.85	38.61	41.37
10	27.24	30.64	34.05	37.46	40.86	44.26	47.67	51.07

In all the examples and discussion up to this point it has been assumed that only one explosive was used in a blasthole. This is not true; if a hole is loaded with ANFO, it will require a primer to initiate the explosion. When it is expected that the bottom of some holes will be wet, an allowance must be made for a water-resistant explosive, such as a slurry in those locations. In the case of a powder column that is 18 ft, and that will be loaded with ANFO, specific gravity 0.8, a primer will have to be placed at the bottom of the hole. A stick of dynamite, specific gravity 1.3, will require a minimum of 8 in. Therefore, there will be 216 in. of ANFO and 8 in. of dynamite. This is about 4% primer.

The determination of wet holes usually has to be made strictly as a percentage guess based on limited geotechnical information. This percentage is added to the percentage calculated for the initiator because the initiator is required whether or not the holes are wet. In this case, assuming all dry holes, the weight of explosives based on a 2.5-in. explosive diameter will be:

ANFO   1.70 lb/ft × (208 in. ÷ 12 in. per ft) = 29.46 lb
Dynamite   2.77 lb/ft × (8 in. ÷ 12 in. per ft)   = 1.85 lb
                                                      31.31 lb

The total per hole is 31.31 lb for 18 ft of powder column.

It is necessary to know the total weight in order to check the powder factor and vibration, as will be discussed later. The breakout as to how much is agent and initiator is important because the price of the two is considerably different. The initiator can cost up to 9 times the unit price of the agent.

Material handling considerations. The economics of handling the fractured rock is a factor which should be considered in blast design. Although it is critical to achieve good breakage, the blast pattern will affect such considerations as the type of equipment and the bucket fill factor. The appropriate piling of the blasted rock by the shot is dependent on the blast design. To utilize the blast to accomplish both objectives, one should apply the following principles:

1. Rock movement will be parallel to the burden dimension.
2. Instantaneous initiation along a row causes more displacement than delayed initiation.
3. Shots delayed row-by-row scatter the rock more than shots fired in a V pattern (see Fig. 14-2).
4. Shots designed in a V-pattern firing sequence (see Fig. 14-2) give maximum piling close to the face.

Trench rock. In the case of excavating trench rock the diameter or width of the structural unit, whether a pipe or conduit, is the principal consideration. When considering the necessary trench width, the space required for working and backfill placement requirements must be taken into account. Many specifications will specifically address backfill. Another important consideration is the size of the excavation equipment.

Geology will have a significant impact on the blast design. Trenches are at the surface; usually, they will extend through soil overburden and weathered unstable rock into solid rock. This nonuniform condition must be recognized. The blaster must check each individual hole to determine the actual depth of rock. Explosives are placed only in rock, not in the overburden.

If only a narrow trench in an interbedded rock mass is required, a single row of blastholes located on the trench centerline is usually adequate. Equation (14-1) will provide a first try for hole spacing. The timing of the shot should sequence down the row. The firing of the first hole provides the free face for the progression, which is why Eq. (14-1) is applicable. In the situation where the trench is shallow or there is little overburden, blasting mats may be necessary. In the case of a wide trench or when solid rock is encountered, a double row of blastholes is common.

PRESPLITTING ROCK

This is a technique of drilling and blasting which breaks rock along a relatively smooth surface, as illustrated in Fig. 14-3. The formulas in the next section provide guidance for selecting presplitting hole spacing and determining the amount of explosive with which each hole should be loaded. Usually, the holes are $2\frac{1}{2}$ to 3 in. in diameter and are drilled along the desired surface at spacings varying from 18 to 36 in., depending on the

FIGURE 14-2
V-pattern (square corner) firing sequence with progressive delays, numbers indicate firing order.

characteristics of the rock. These holes are loaded with one or two sticks of dynamite at the bottoms, with smaller charges, such as $1\frac{1}{4}$-×4-in. sticks spaced at 12-in. intervals, to the top of the portion of the holes to be loaded. The sticks may be attached to Primacord with tape, or hollow sticks may be used, which permits the Primacord to pass through the sticks with cardboard tube spacers between the charges. It is important that the charges be less than half the blasthole diameter and they should not touch the walls of the hole.

When the explosives in these holes are detonated ahead of the production blast, the webs between the holes will fracture, leaving a surface joint which serves as a barrier

FIGURE 14-3
A presplit rock face. (*E. I. du Pont de Nemours & Company.*)

to the shock waves from the production blast. This will eliminate most breakage beyond the fractured surface.

Explosive load and spacing. The approximate load of explosive per foot of presplit blasthole is given by Eq. (14-10).

$$d_{ec} = \frac{D_h^2}{28}$$ (14-10)

where d_{ec} = explosive load, lb per ft
D_h = diameter of blasthole, in.

When this formula is used to arrive at an explosive loading, the spacing between blast-holes can be determined by the equation

$$Sp = 10D_h$$ (14-11)

where Sp = presplit blasthole spacing, in.

Because of the variations in the characteristics of rocks, the final determination of the spacings of the holes and the quantity of explosive per hole should be determined by tests conducted at the project. Many times field trials will allow the constant in Eq. (14-11) to be increased from 10 to as much as 14.

Presplit blastholes are not extended below grade. In the bottom of the hole a con-centrated charge of 2 to 3 times d_{ec} should be placed instead of subdrilling.

Because a presplit blast is only intended to cause fracture, drill cutting can be used as stemming. The purpose is to only momentarily confine the gases and to reduce noise. Two to five feet of stemming is normal. This technique has been used successfully with vertical holes and with slanted holes whose slopes are not less than about 1 to 1. It has been used with limited success in tunnel work.

Example 14-5. By contract specification the walls of a highway excavation through rock must be presplit. The contractor will be using drilling equipment capable of drilling a 3-in. hole. What explosive load and hole spacing should he try for the first presplit shot on the project?

Using Eqs. (14-10) and (14-11), one gets

$$d_{ec} = \frac{3^2}{28} = 0.32 \text{ lb/ft}$$

$$Sp = 10 \times 3 = 30 \text{ in.}$$

The bottom load should be $3 \times 0.32 = 0.96$ lb

SAFETY

An accident involving explosives may easily kill or cause serious injury. The prevention of such accidents depends on careful planning and faithful observation of proper blasting practices. There are federal and state regulations concerning the transportation and handling of explosives. Safety information on specific products is provided by the manufacturer. In addition to regulations and product information, there are recommended practices, such as the evacuation of the blast area during the approach of an electrical storm whether electric or nonelectric initiation systems are used. A good source for material on recommended blasting safety practices is the Institute of Makers of Explosives in New York City.

Misfires. In shooting charges of explosives, one or more charges may fail to explode. This is referred to as a "misfire." It is necessary to dispose of this explosive before excavating the loosened rock. The most satisfactory method is to shoot it if possible.

If electric blasting caps are used, the leading wires should be disconnected from the source of power prior to investigating the cause of the misfire. If the leg-wires to the cap are available, test the cap circuit; and if the circuit is satisfactory, try again to set off the charge.

When it is necessary to remove the stemming to gain access to a charge in a hole, the stemming should be removed with a wooden tool instead of a metal tool. If water or compressed air is available, either one may be used with a rubber hose to wash the stemming out of the hole. A new primer, set on top of or near the original charge, may be used to fire the charge.

SEISMIC EFFECT

Because blasting operations may cause actual or alleged damages to buildings, structures, and other properties located in the vicinity of the blasting operations, it may be desirable to examine, and possibly photograph, any structures for which charges of damages may be made later. Before beginning blasting operations, seismic recording instruments can be placed in the vicinity of the shots to monitor the magnitudes of vibrations caused by the blasting. The monitoring may be conducted by the persons responsible for the blasting, or if insurance covering this activity is carried by the company responsible for the blasting, a representative of the insurance carrier may provide this service [6].

Factors affecting vibration. Rock exhibits the property of elasticity. When explosives are detonated, elastic waves are produced as the rock is deformed and then regains its shape. The two principal factors which will affect how this motion is perceived at any discrete point are the size of the explosive charge detonated and the distance to the charge. It is, therefore, obvious that delays in initiation will reduce the effect because the individual charges are less than the total which would have been fired without the delays.

The U.S. Bureau of Mines has proposed a formula to evaluate vibration and as a way to control blasting operations.

$$D_s = \frac{d}{\sqrt{W}} \tag{14-12}$$

where D_s = scaled distance (nondimensional factor)

d = distance from shot to a structure, ft

W = maximum charge weight per delay, lb

A scaled distance value of 50 or greater indicates that a shot is safe with respect to vibration according to the Bureau of Mines. Some regulatory agencies require a value of 60 or greater.

The statement can be made that two identical blasts cause different effects. Excessive burden distances will cause high levels of ground vibration per pound of explosive and burden is never constant across a project. Some of the critical factors effecting vibration which should be carefully considered are:

1. Burden	10. Rock type
2. Spacing	11. Rock physical properties
3. Subdrilling	12. Geological features
4. Stemming depth	13. Number of holes in a row
5. Type of stemming	14. Number of rows
6. Bench height	15. Row-to-row delays
7. Number of decks	16. Initiator precision
8. Charge geometry	17. Face angle to structure
9. Powder column length	18. Explosive energy

Preblast surveys. Prior to exposing a structure to the vibration caused by blasting operations it is good practice to make a preblast survey and to document its condition.

To be of value, the survey must be thorough and accurate. Structures are subjected to many dynamic forces. However, because many of these act over long time periods, the effects often go unobserved. Temperature, humidity, wind, soil conditions, and operating equipment can all cause the cracking of a structure. In many cases the effect is seasonal and the cracks will open and close with changing conditions. Besides the condition of the structure, possible contributing soil conditions should be noted during the survey; e.g., drainage problems, pooling of water, and seepage.

PROBLEMS

14-1. A project in limestone will have an average bench height of 16 ft. An emulsion relative bulk strength 105, specific gravity 0.8, will be the explosive used on the project. The contractor's equipment can easily drill 3-in.-diameter holes. It is assumed that single rows of no more than 10 holes will be detonated instantaneously. The excavation site has structures within 900 ft. The local regulatory agency specifies a scaled distance factor of no less than 60. Even though an emulsion is being used because of expected wet conditions, the holes will be lined. The thickness of the lining material is $\frac{1}{4}$ in. Develop a blast design for the project.

14-2. The blasting in Prob. 14-1 must be conducted so as to limit overbreakage. Develop a presplitting blast plan.

14-3. An investigation of a highway project revealed a sandstone formation with steeply dipping bedding into the face. Many weak joints were identified. An analysis of the plan and profile sheets and the cross sections showed that the average bench height will be about 12 ft. Bulk ANFO, specific gravity 0.8, and dynamite, specific gravity 1.3, will be the explosives used on the project. The dynamite comes in 8-in.-long $\times 1\frac{3}{4}$-in.-diameter sticks. The contractor's equipment can easily drill 6-in.-diameter holes. It is assumed that delayed initiation will be utilized.

   (*a*) Develop a blast design for the project.
   (*b*) If the burden distance is held constant at 5 ft but the hole spacing is varied in 1-ft increments across the range of *S* developed in part (*a*), what is the cost per cubic yard of rock if the ANFO is $0.166 per lb, and dynamite is $1.272 per lb?
   (*c*) What is the cost per cubic yard of rock if it is expected that 15% of the holes will be wet?

14-4. A materials company is opening a new quarry in a limestone formation. Tests have shown that the specific gravity of this formation is 2.7. The initial mining plan envisions an average bench height of 24 ft based on the loading and hauling equipment capabilities. Bulk ANFO, specific gravity 0.8, and dynamite, specific gravity 1.5, will be the explosives used. The contractor's equipment can drill 6-in.-diameter holes. Delayed initiation will be utilized. Develop a blasting plan for the first shot.

REFERENCES

1. *Blasters' Handbook,* E. I. du Pont de Nemours & Co. (Inc.), Wilmington, DE, 1977.
2. *Explosive and Rock Blasting,* Atlas Powder Company, Dallas, TX, 1987.
3. *Handbook of Electric Blasting,* Atlas Powder Company, Dallas, TX, 1985.
4. Hemphill, G. B.: *Blasting Operations,* McGraw-Hill, New York, 1981.
5. Konya, C. J., and E. J. Walter: "Blasthole Timing Controls Vibration, Airblast and Flyrock," *Coal Mining,* January 1988.

6. "Precision Blasting for Highway Cut Protects Old Rail Tunnel Nearby," *Construction Methods and Equipment*, vol. 59, pp. 53–55, February 1977.
7. *Rock Blasting and Overbreak Control*, National Highway Institute, U.S. Department of Transportation, Federal Highway Administration, Pub. No. FHWA-HI-92-001, 1991.
8. *Rock Fragmentation Prediction (Breaker)*, Computer Software Package, Precision Blasting Services, Montville, OH, 1989.

CHAPTER 15

PILES AND PILE-DRIVING EQUIPMENT

INTRODUCTION

This chapter deals with the selection of piles and the equipment used to drive piles (see Fig. 15-1). Load-bearing piles, as the name implies, are used primarily to transmit structural loads, through soil formations with poor supporting properties, into or onto soil strata that are capable of supporting the loads. If the load is transmitted to the soil through skin friction between the surface of the pile and the soil, the pile is called a *friction pile*. If the load is transmitted to the soil through the lower tip, the pile is called an *end-bearing pile*. Many piles depend on a combination of friction and end bearing for their supporting strengths.

TYPES OF PILES

Piles may be classified on the basis of either their use or the materials from which they are made. On the basis of use, there are two major classifications, *sheet* and *load bearing*.

Sheet piling is used primarily to resist the flow of water and loose soil. Typical uses include cutoff walls under dams, cofferdams, bulkheads, and trench sheeting. On the basis of the materials from which they are made, sheet pilings may be classified as *steel, wood, concrete,* or *composite.*

Considering both the type of the material from which they are made, and the method of constructing and driving them, load-bearing piles may be classified as follows:

411

FIGURE 15-1
Crawler crane driving 12 in. concrete piles utilizing a single acting air hammer and hydraulic leads. (*Tidewater Construction Corporation.*)

1. Timber
   a. Untreated
   b. Treated with a preservative
2. Concrete
   a. Precast-prestressed
   b. Cast-in-place with shells
   c. Augered cast-in-place
3. Steel
   a. H section
   b. Steel pipe
4. Composite
5. Sheet
   a. Steel
   b. Prestressed concrete
   c. Timber

Each type of load-bearing pile has a place in engineering practice, and for some projects more than one type may seem satisfactory. It is the responsibility of the engineer to select the pile type which is best suited for a given project, taking into account all the factors that affect both installation and performance. Factors that will influence the decision are:

1. The type, size, and weight of the structure to be supported.
2. The physical properties of the soil stratum at the site.
3. The depth to a stratum capable of supporting the piles.
4. The variations across the site in the depth to a supporting stratum.
5. The availability of materials for piles.
6. The number of piles required.
7. The driving equipment.
8. The comparative in-place costs.
9. The durability required.
10. The types of structures adjacent to the project.
11. The depth and kind of water, if any, above the ground into which the piles will be driven.

To illustrate the effect which these factors have on pile-type selection, consider factor number 4. If soil borings at a project site indicate that the depth to a stratum capable of supporting piles varies considerably, precast piles normally will not be selected. Regardless of other desirable factors, the difficulty and expense of increasing or decreasing the length of such piles can eliminate them from consideration. If concrete piles are desired, one of the cast-in-place types might be considered.

SITE INVESTIGATION AND
A TEST PILE PROGRAM

For projects of intermediate to large scale a thorough site investigation can be very cost-effective. The geotechnical information gathered from borings can be used to determine the soil characteristics and the depths to strata capable of supporting the design loads. The number of blows per foot, from geotechnical tests such as the standard penetration test, is normally recorded during the soil sampling operations and can be extremely valuable for use in predicting pile lengths. From this information pile types, sizes, and capacities may be chosen. Once a pile type has been selected, or if several types are deemed practical for use on a particular project, a test pile program should be conducted.

Pile lengths to be used for the test pile program are generally somewhat longer than the anticipated lengths as determined from the borings. This permits driving the test piles to greater depths if necessary and allows additional pile length for installing the load test apparatus. Several test piles should be driven and carefully monitored at selected locations within the project area. Dynamic testing equipment and testing techniques, discussed in further detail in this chapter, can be utilized to gather significant information pertaining to the combined characteristics of the pile, the soil, and the pile-driving equipment. This information will greatly enhance the engineer's ability to predict the required pile lengths for the project and the number of blows per foot required to obtain the desired bearing capacity.

Depending on the size of the project, one or more of the test piles will be selected for load testing. To apply a load to the selected piles, static test weights, water tanks, or reaction piles and jacks may be employed. Static weights or water tanks allow the loading weight to be incrementally applied directly to the test pile by adding either weights or water. In the case of the reaction pile method steel H piles can be used as reaction piles. They are driven in relatively close proximity to the pile to be tested. Since the test load will be applied to these reaction piles in tension, the number of reaction piles is determined by the magnitude of the test load to be applied and the friction characteristics of the soil.

A reaction frame or beam is attached to the reaction piles and spans over the top of the test pile so that the test load may be applied by utilizing an hydraulic jack (see Fig. 15-2). The jack is located between the reaction beam and the top of the test pile. As the load is applied by the jack, the reaction beam transfers the load to the test pile, putting it in compression and putting the reaction piles in tension.

Calibrated hydraulic gauges are used to measure the amount of load applied. The test load is applied in increments over a period of time and the pile is continuously monitored for movement. For either type test, direct load or reaction, the magnitude of the applied test load is normally 2 to 3 times the design bearing capacity of the pile. Any sudden or rapid movement of the pile indicates a failure of the pile.

Once a test pile program has been completed, pile lengths and supporting bearing capacities can be predicted with reasonable accuracy. Where precast concrete piles are determined to be an economical alternative at a particular site, a test pile program can verify with suitable accuracy the required pile lengths. Therefore, when good geotechnical and load test data are available, piles can be cast to calculated lengths with little risk of their being either too short or too long.

FIGURE 15-2
Load test of a 54-in. concrete cylinder pile utilizing reaction piles, beams, and a jack. (*Tidewater Construction Corporation.*)

TIMBER PILES

Timber piles are made from the trunks of trees. While such piles are available in most sections of the country and the world, it is becoming more difficult and costly to obtain long, straight timber piles. Pine piles are reasonably available in lengths up to 80 ft, whereas Douglas fir piles are available in lengths in excess of 100 ft from the Pacific northwest. Preservative treatments, such as salt or creosote, are used to reduce the rate of decay and to fight the attacks of marine borers. These preservatives should be carefully selected, as they may have environmentally detrimental effects.

The advantages of timber piles include the following:

1. The more popular lengths and sizes are available on short notice.
2. They are economical in cost.
3. They are handled easily, with little danger of breakage.
4. After driving they can be easily cut off to any desired length.
5. Usually they can be extracted easily in the event that removal is necessary.

The disadvantages of timber piles include the following:

1. It may be difficult to economically obtain piles that are sufficiently long and straight.
2. They may be difficult or impossible to drive into hard formations.
3. They are difficult to splice when increased lengths are necessary.
4. While they are satisfactory when used as friction piles, they are not usually suitable for use as end bearings under heavy loads.
5. The duration over which they maintain their structural capacity may be short unless the piles are treated with a preservative, and preservatives may have undesirable environmental effects. ·

PRECAST-PRESTRESSED CONCRETE PILES

Precast-prestressed concrete piles are normally manufactured at established plants utilizing approved methods in accordance with the PCI MNL-116-85 "Manual for Quality Control" [14]. Specifications for many projects, such as those used by state highway departments, require the piles to be manufactured at PCI certified plants. However, for projects with a large quantity of piles, transportation costs from existing manufacturing plants may be significant. Therefore, it may be cost-effective to set up a casting facility on the job or in the general vicinity of the project. The establishment of such a facility requires a substantial investment in special equipment and casting forms, as well as a sufficient amount of space for the casting beds, curing area, and storage yard.

Square and octagonal piles are cast in horizontal forms on casting beds, whereas cylinder piles are cast in cylindrical forms and then centrifugally spun. After the piles are cast, they are normally steam cured until they have reached sufficient strength to allow them to be removed from the forms. Under controlled curing conditions and utilizing concrete with compressive strengths of 5,000 psi or greater, the piles may be removed from the forms in as little as 24 hours or as soon as the concrete has developed a compressive strength of 3,500 psi. The piles are then stored and allowed to cure for 21 days or more before reaching driving strengths.

Prestressed concrete piles are reinforced with either $\frac{1}{2}$ in. or $\frac{7}{16}$ in. 270-ksi high-strength stress relieved or low relaxation tendons or strands. The number and type of strand is determined by the design properties of the pile. In addition, the piles are reinforced with spiral reinforcing. The amount of spiral reinforcing is increased at the ends of the pile to resist cracking and spalling during driving. Piling for marine applications may require that the spirals be epoxy coated. Pile dowels may be cast in the tops of the piles for uplift reinforcing, or dowel sleeves may be cast in the top of the pile and the dowels can then be grouted into the pile after driving. Figures 15-3 and 15-4 show the details for typical 12- and 20-in. sq. prestressed concrete piles.

The square and octagonal piles are traditionally cast on beds 200–600 ft long in order that multiple piles may be cast and prestressed simultaneously (see Fig. 15-5). The prestressing strand will be as long as the casting bed and bulkheads will be placed in the forms as determined by the desired pile lengths. Utilizing stressing jacks, each strand will be pretensioned to between 20 and 35 kips prior to the concrete placement. Immediately following the concrete placement the piles are covered with curing blankets and steam is introduced. The steam raises the air temperature at a rate of 30–60°F per hour until a maximum temperature of 140–160°F is reached. The curing continues and the prestressing forces are not released until the concrete has attained a minimum compressive strength of 3,500 psi.

Cylinder piles are cast in short sections of up to 16 ft in length with prestressing sleeves or ducts cast into the wall of the pile. The wall thickness can vary from 5 in. up to $6\frac{1}{2}$ in., depending on the design properties of the pile. Once the concrete is placed in the form, the concrete and the form are centrifugally spun, causing the concrete to consolidate. After the sections have been steam cured and the concrete has obtained sufficient strength, the sections are assembled to the proper pile lengths. The prestressing strand is pulled through the sleeves or ducts and then tensioned with jacks. Finally, the tensioned strands are pressure grouted in the sleeves.

The precast-prestressed piles may be transported by truck to land-based projects, or they can be moved by barge in the case of marine projects. For handling concrete piles care must be exercised to prevent breakage or damage due to flexural stresses. Long piles should be picked up at several points to reduce the unsupported lengths (see Fig. 15-6). When piles are stored or transported, they must be supported continuously or at the pickup points.

Precast concrete piles may be cast in any desired size and length. Those used in constructing the Morganza Floodway on the Mississippi River in Louisiana had square and octagonal cross sections, 20 in. wide and varied in length to more than 100 ft. Almost 360,000 linear feet (lin ft) of piles were driven on the project. The piles were cast in prefabricated steel forms, loaded on railroad cars by a gantry crane with a 135-ft span, and hauled to the driving site, where they were driven by special rigs.

To support the trestle bents of the Chesapeake Bay Bridge Tunnel project across the mouth of the Chesapeake Bay in Virginia, 2,500 cylinder piles 54 in. in diameter, totaling approximately 320,000 lin ft, were utilized. These cylinder piles were cast at a nearby casting yard constructed specifically for the project. The piles were loaded onto barges which were towed to the bridge site. Driving was performed primarily with a

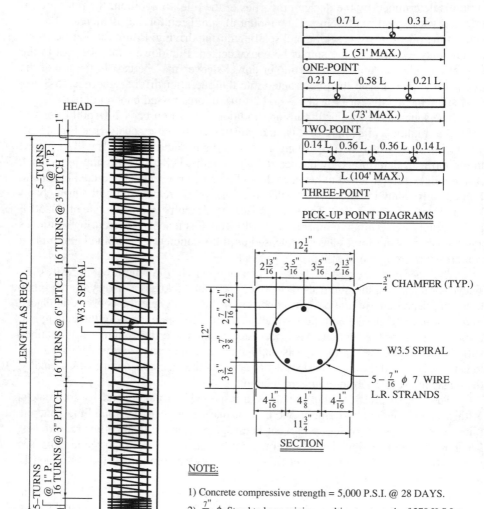

PICK-UP POINT DIAGRAMS

0.7 L | 0.3 L

L (51' MAX.)

ONE-POINT

0.21 L | 0.58 L | 0.21 L

L (73' MAX.)

TWO-POINT

0.14 L | 0.36 L | 0.36 L | 0.14 L

L (104' MAX.)

THREE-POINT

HEAD

5–TURNS @ 1" P.

16 TURNS @ 3" PITCH

16 TURNS @ 6" PITCH

W3.5 SPIRAL

16 TURNS @ 3" PITCH

16 TURNS @ 3" PITCH

LENGTH AS REQ'D.

5–TURNS @ 1" P.

TIP

1"

$12\frac{1}{4}"$

$2\frac{13}{16}"$ | $3\frac{5}{16}"$ | $3\frac{5}{16}"$ | $2\frac{13}{16}"$

$-\frac{3}{4}"$ CHAMFER (TYP.)

12"

$2\frac{1}{2}"$ $2\frac{7}{16}"$

$3\frac{7}{8}"$ $3\frac{3}{16}"$

W3.5 SPIRAL

$5 - \frac{7}{16}"$ ϕ 7 WIRE L.R. STRANDS

$4\frac{1}{16}"$ | $4\frac{1}{8}"$ | $4\frac{1}{16}"$

$11\frac{3}{4}"$

SECTION

NOTE:

1) Concrete compressive strength = 5,000 P.S.I. @ 28 DAYS.

2) $\frac{7}{16}"$ ϕ Stand to have minimum ultimate strength of 270 K.S.I., as per A.S.T.M. A416.

3) Spiral wire to be w3.5 cold-drawn wire as per A.S.T.M. A82.

4) Strands to be cut off flush w/pile ends.

5) Initial tension per stand = 23.3 K.

6) Transfer of present force @ 3,500 P.S.I. concrete strength.

FIGURE 15-3
Typical details of a 12-in. square prestressed concrete pile. (*Bayshore Concrete Products, Chesapeake, Inc.*)

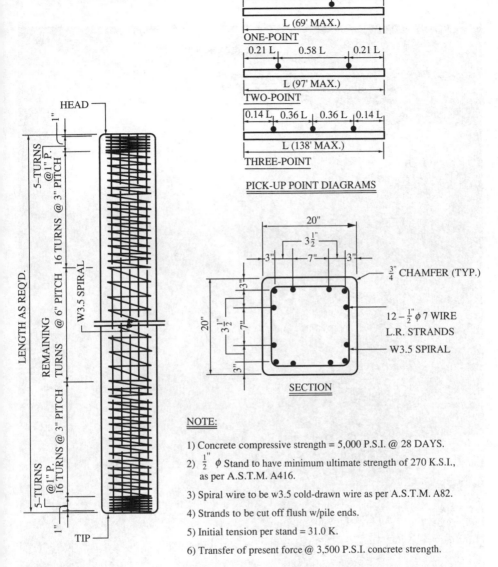

FIGURE 15-4
Typical details of a 20-in. square prestressed concrete pile. (*Bayshore Concrete Products, Chesapeake, Inc.*)

150-ton barge-mounted Whirley crane. The driving barge was outfitted with four jack-up spuds to allow it to hold position and to be jacked-up out of the water when the crane was driving piles. For such big projects as these, the large investment in special equipment is justified, but for a small project such an investment would probably be cost-prohibitive. Thus, the maximum-size concrete piles that can be used on a project may be determined by the economy of construction equipment.

FIGURE 15-5
Casting bed for 12-in. prestressed concrete piles showing bulkheads and strands. (*Tidewater Construction Corporation.*)

FIGURE 15-6
Barge-mounted Whirley crane using a three-point pickup to lift a 36-in. cylinder pile off a barge
and into the leads. (*Tidewater Construction Corporation.*)

One of the disadvantages of using precast-prestressed concrete piles, especially for a project where different lengths of piles are required, is the difficulty of reducing or increasing the lengths of piles. It is for this reason that on major piling projects, it is cost-effective to perform a site investigation program and to conduct a test pile program in order to predict more precisely the correct lengths for the precast concrete piles.

If a pile proves to be too long, it is necessary to cut off the excess length. This is done after a pile is driven to its maximum penetration by chipping the concrete away from the reinforcing steel, by cutting the reinforcing steel with a gas torch, and then by removing the surplus length of concrete core. Hydraulic concrete crushing machines can also be used to cut off the excess length of pile. Such a method requires substantially less time and is less expensive than the chipping method. But either operation represents a waste of material and time, and adds to project cost.

When a precast concrete pile does not develop sufficient driving resistance to support the design load, it may be necessary to increase the length and drive the pile to a greater depth. Unless the reinforcing dowels extend above the top of the pile, it will be necessary to drill holes in the top of the pile to allow the insertion and grouting of reinforcing dowels. Then the added length of pile can be mated to the original.

There are a number of suggested rules for driving prestressed concrete piles:

1. Adequate cushioning material must be used between the pile driver's steel helmet or cap and the head or top of the concrete pile. Usually, a wood cushion is used and may vary in thickness from 4 to 8 in., depending on the length of the pile and the characteristics of the soil. This is a very economical way of reducing driving stresses in the pile.

2. Driving stresses may be reduced by using a hammer with a heavy ram and a low impact velocity or large stroke. Driving stresses are proportional to the ram impact velocity.

3. Care must be taken when driving piles through soils or soil layers with low resistance. If such soils are anticipated or encountered, it is important to reduce the ram velocity or stroke of the hammer to avoid critical tensile stresses in the pile.

4. In the case of cylinder piles, it is important to prevent the soil plug inside the pile from rising to an elevation above the level of the existing soil on the outside of the pile, thus creating unequal stresses in the pile. This should be monitored, and, in the event that the plug does rise inside the pile, it should be excavated down to the level of the existing soil outside of the pile.

5. The pile-driving helmet should fit loosely around the top of the pile so that the pile may rotate slightly without binding within the driving head to prevent torsional stress.

6. The top of the pile must be square or perpendicular to the longitudinal axis of the pile to eliminate eccentricity, which causes stress.

7. The ends of the prestressing strand or reinforcing must either be cut off flush with the top of the pile or the driving helmet must be designed so that the reinforcing threads through the pile cap in order that the hammer's ram does not directly contact the reinforcing during driving. The driving energy must be delivered to the top of the concrete.

The advantages of concrete precast piles include the following:

1. They have high resistance to chemical and biological attacks.
2. They have great strength.
3. A pipe may be installed along the center of the pile to facilitate jetting.

The disadvantages of precast concrete piles include the following:

1. It is difficult to reduce or increase the length.
2. Large sizes require heavy and expensive handling and driving equipment.
3. The inability to obtain piles quickly by purchase may delay the starting of a project.
4. Possible breakage of piles during handling or driving produces a delay hazard.

CAST-IN-PLACE CONCRETE PILES

As the name implies, cast-in-place concrete piles are constructed by depositing the freshly mixed concrete in place in the ground and letting it cure there. The two principal methods of constructing such piles are:

1. Driving a metallic shell and leaving it in the ground, and then filling the shell with concrete.
2. Driving a metallic shell and filling the resulting void with concrete as the shell is pulled from the ground.

There are several modifications for each of the two methods. The more commonly used piles constructed by these two methods are described in the following sections:

Raymond step-taper concrete piles. The step-taper pile is installed by driving a spirally corrugated steel shell, made up of sections 4, 8, 12, and 16 ft long, with successive increases in a diameter for each section. A corrugated sleeve at the bottom of each section is screwed into the top of the section immediately below it. Piles of the necessary length, up to a maximum of 80 ft, are obtained by joining the proper number of sections at the job site. The shells are available in various gauges of metal to fit different job conditions. The bottom of the shell, whose diameter can be varied from $8\frac{5}{8}$ to $13\frac{3}{8}$ in., is closed prior to driving by a flat steel plate or a hemispherical steel boot.

After a shell is assembled to the desired length, a step-tapered rigid-steel core or mandrel is inserted and the shell is driven to the desired penetration. The core is removed, and the shell is filled with concrete. Figure 15-7 gives the dimensions of a step-taper pile shell. Figure 15-8 illustrates steps in driving these piles. Figure 15-9 shows the installation sequence for step-taper piles.

Monotube piles. The monotube pile is obtained by driving a fluted, tapered steel shell, closed at the tip with an 8-in.-diameter driving point, to the desired penetration. The shell is driven without a mandrel, is inspected, and is filled with concrete. Any desired length of shell, up to approximately 125 ft, may be obtained by welding extensions to a standard length shell.

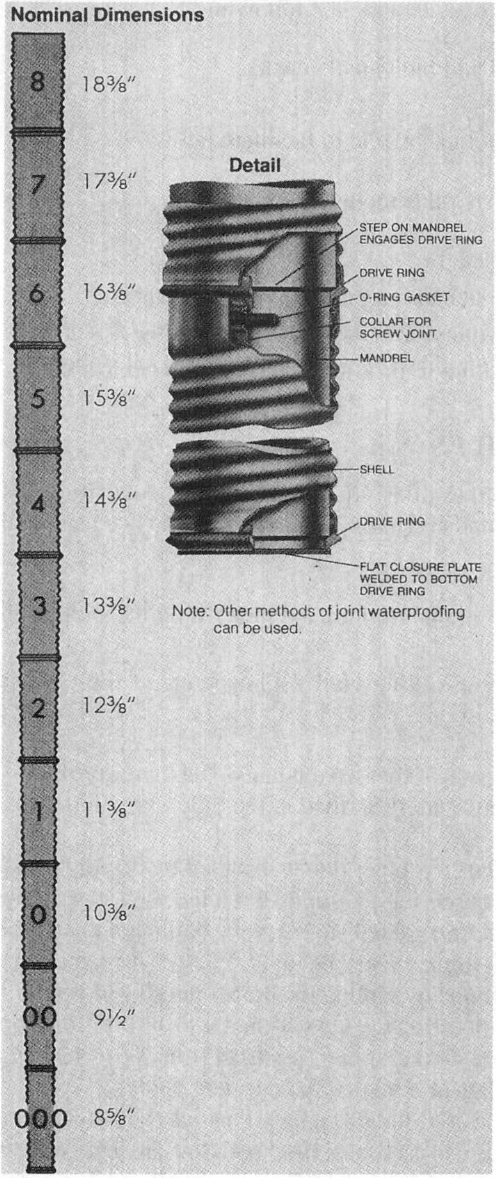
Nominal Dimensions
8 18⅜″
7 17⅜″
6 16⅜″
5 15⅜″
4 14⅜″
3 13⅜″
2 12⅜″
1 11⅜″
0 10⅜″
00 9½″
000 8⅝″
Detail
STEP ON MANDREL ENGAGES DRIVE RING
DRIVE RING
O-RING GASKET
COLLAR FOR SCREW JOINT
MANDREL
SHELL
DRIVE RING
FLAT CLOSURE PLATE WELDED TO BOTTOM DRIVE RING
Note: Other methods of joint waterproofing can be used.

FIGURE 15-7
Dimensions and detail for Raymond step-taper piles.

Table 15-1 gives dimensions and other information on specific monotube pile types. Figure 15-10 illustrates a crawler crane driving one of these piles; Fig. 15-11 shows monotube piles used to support a bridge.

Augered cast-in-place piles. Another form of cast-in-place concrete pile is the augered cast-in-place pile. These piles differ from the previously discussed cast-in-place piles since they do not require a shell or pipe. A continuous flight, hollow shaft auger

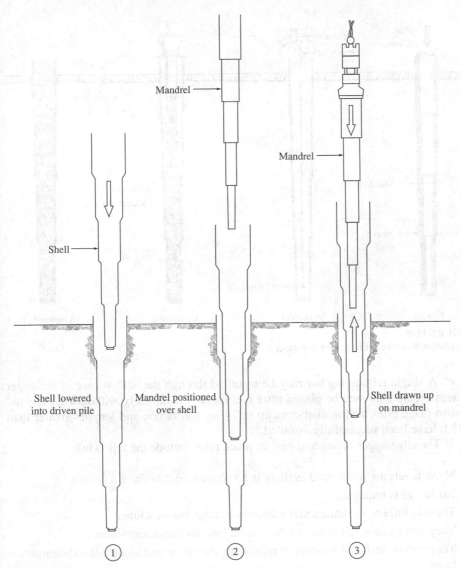

Mandrel

Mandrel

Shell

| Shell lowered into driven pile | Mandrel positioned over shell | Shell drawn up on mandrel |

① ② ③

FIGURE 15-8
Shell-up procedure for Raymond step-taper piles.

with a minimum inside diameter of $2\frac{1}{2}$ in. is rotated into the soil to a predetermined tip elevation or refusal, whichever occurs first. As the auger is slowly rotated and withdrawn from the hole, grout is injected under pressure through the hollow shaft. The rate of injection is carefully coordinated with the auger withdrawal rate to ensure that the hole is completely filled with grout. The displaced soil is removed as the auger is rotated and withdrawn.

The concrete can be placed to the ground elevation and then cut off to the required elevation. Sometimes it is necessary to build up the pile to an elevation above ground

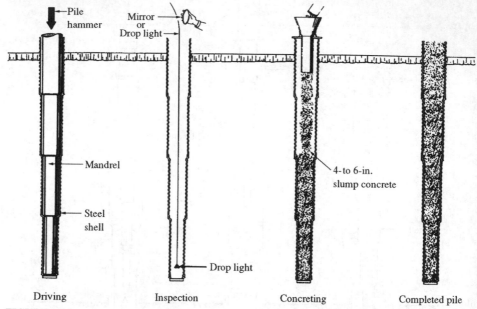

FIGURE 15-9
Installation sequence for Raymond step-taper piles.

level. A single reinforcing bar may be installed through the hollow core of the auger or reinforcing bars may be placed after the auger is completely withdrawn. Augered cast-in-place piles having diameters up to 24 in. and larger, and lengths greater than 125 ft have been successfully installed.

The advantages of augered cast-in-place piles include the following:

1. Noise levels are minimized as there is no requirement to drive a casing.
2. No casing is required.
3. There is little or no detrimental vibration to adjacent structures.
4. They can be installed in areas which have low overhead restrictions.
5. They can be installed in areas of minimum clearance and alongside existing structures.
6. There is little or no detrimental soil upheaval or displacement.
7. Pile splicing is eliminated.

The disadvantages of augered cast-in-place piles include the following:

1. They require very careful placement of the concrete to ensure a structurally sound shaft.
2. Soil and groundwater conditions can greatly affect installation time and cost.
3. Vertical or horizontal ground movement from adjacent pile construction can damage completed piles.

TABLE 15-1
Data on monotube piles

Type	Size, point diameter × butt diameter × length	Weight (lb per ft)				Volume of concrete (cu yd)
		9 ga	7 ga	5 ga	3 ga	
F	$8\frac{1}{2}$ in. × 12 in. × 25 ft	17	20	24	28	0.43
Taper	8 in. × 12 in. × 30 ft	16	20	23	27	0.55
0.14 in.	$8\frac{1}{2}$ in. × 14 in. × 40 ft	19	22	26	31	0.95
per ft	8 in. × 16 in. × 60 ft	20	24	28	33	1.68
	8 in. × 18 in. × 75 ft		26	31	35	2.59
J	8 in. × 12 in. × 17 ft	17	20	23	27	0.32
Taper	8 in. × 14 in. × 25 ft	18	22	26	30	0.58
0.25 in.	8 in. × 16 in. × 33 ft	20	24	28	32	0.95
per ft	8 in. × 18 in. × 40 ft		26	30	35	1.37
Y	8 in. × 12 in. × 10 ft	17	20	24	28	0.18
Taper	8 in. × 14 in. × 15 ft	19	22	26	30	0.34
0.40 in.	8 in. × 16 in. × 20 ft	20	24	28	33	0.56
per ft	8 in. × 18 in. × 25 ft		26	31	35	0.86

Extensions (overall lengths 1 ft greater than indicated)						
Type	Diameter × length	9 ga	7 ga	5 ga	3 ga	cu yd/ft
N 12	12 in. × 12 in. × 20 ft/40 ft	20	24	28	33	0.026
N 14	14 in. × 14 in. × 20 ft/40 ft	24	29	34	41	0.035
N 16	16 in. × 16 in. × 20 ft/40 ft	28	33	39	46	0.045
N 18	18 in. × 18 in. × 20 ft/40 ft		38	44	52	0.058

4. There are insufficient data concerning pile behavior under seismic loading conditions.

5. Because of the construction technique, no penetration resistance correlation can be made about pile capacity.

6. Their use in instances where uplift forces can be encountered requires installation of reinforcing steel and the process of installing the steel is somewhat difficult.

Franki pressure-injected footings. The Franki pressure-injected footing technique is illustrated in Fig. 15-12. As shown in Fig. 15-12(*a*), a steel-drive tube of the desired diameter and length is fitted with an expendable steel boot to close the bottom end. Using a pile-driving hammer of adequate size, usually with 50,000 to 100,000 ft-lb per blow, the tube is driven to the desired depth. As illustrated in Fig. 15-12(*b*), after the tube is driven to the desired depth, the hammer is removed and a charge of dry concrete is dropped into the tube and compacted with a drop hammer to form a compact watertight plug. Following step (*b*), the tube is raised slightly and held in that position while repeated blows of the drop hammer expel the plug of concrete from the lower end of the tube, leaving in the tube sufficient concrete to prevent the intrusion of water or soil. Additional concrete is dropped into the tube and forced by the drop hammer to flow out the bottom of the tube to form an enlarged bulb or pedestal, as illustrated by step (*c*).

FIGURE 15-10
Driving No. 5 gauge 12-in. monotube piles up to 200 ft long with a 37,000 ft-lb
steam hammer. (*The Union Metal Manufacturing Company.*)

The final step in this operation consists of raising the tube in increments. After
each incremental upward movement additional dry concrete is dropped into the tube
and is hammered with sufficient energy to force it to flow out the tube and to fill the
exposed hole [see Fig. 15-12(*d*)]. This operation cycle is repeated until the hole is filled
to the desired elevation. The shaft may be reinforced by inserting a spirally wound steel
cage, embedded in the bulb and extended upward for the full height of the shaft.

FIGURE 15-11
Monotube piles used to support a bridge structure. (*The Union Metal Manufacturing Company.*)

Advantages and disadvantages of cast-in-place concrete piles
The advantages of cast-in-place concrete piles include the following:

1. The lightweight shells may be handled and driven easily.
2. The variations in length do not present a serious problem. The length of a shell may be increased or decreased easily.
3. The shells may be shipped in short lengths and assembled at the job.
4. The excess reinforcing, to resist stresses caused only by handling the pile, is eliminated.
5. The danger of breaking a pile while driving is eliminated.
6. Additional piles may be provided quickly if they are needed.

The disadvantages of cast-in-place concrete piles include the following:

1. A slight movement of the earth around an unreinforced pile may break it.
2. An uplifting force, acting on the shaft of an uncased and unreinforced pile, may cause it to fail in tension.
3. The bottom of a pedestal pile may not be symmetrical.

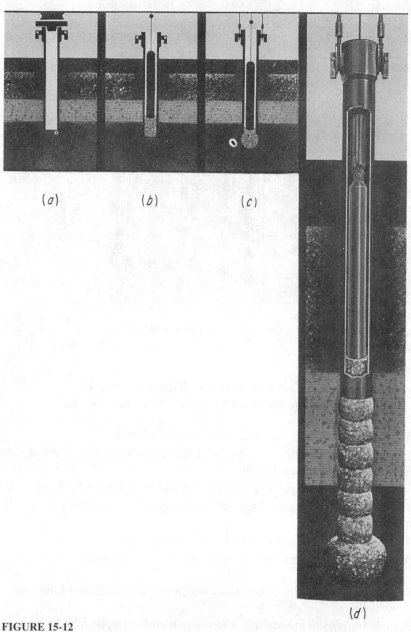

FIGURE 15-12
Steps in providing Franki pressure injected footing: (*a*) The drive tube driven to the desired depth. (*b*) Concrete dropped into the drive tube and compacted. (*c*) Drop hammer expels concrete from the tube. (*d*) Additional steps complete the footing.

STEEL PILES

In constructing foundations that require piles driven to great depths, steel piles probably are more suitable than any other type (see Fig. 15-13).

Steel H section piles. Steel piles may be driven through hard materials to a specified depth to eliminate the danger of failure due to scouring, such as under a pier in a river. Steel piles may be driven to great depths through poor soils to bear on a solid rock stratum. The great strength of steel combined with small displacement of soil permits a large portion of the energy from a pile hammer to be transmitted to the bottom of a pile. As a result, one can drive steel piles into soils which cannot be penetrated by any other type of pile. However, in spite of the great strength of these piles, sometimes it is necessary to drill pilot holes, into compacted sand, ahead of steel H piles in order to obtain the specified penetration. By weld-splicing sections together, lengths in excess of 200 ft can be driven.

Because the steel H piles may be driven in short lengths and additional lengths then welded on top of the previously driven section, they may be utilized more readily in situations where height restrictions limit the length of piles that may be driven in one piece.

Steel-pipe piles. These piles are installed by driving pipes to the desired depth and, if desired, filling them with concrete. A pipe may be driven with the lower end closed

FIGURE 15-13
Diesel hammer driving steel H pile on 1:1 batter. (*Pilco, Inc.*)

with a plate or steel driving point, or the pipe may be driven with the lower end open. Pipes varying in diameter from 6 to 42 in. have been driven in lengths varying from a few feet to several hundred feet.

A closed-end pipe pile is driven in any conventional manner, usually with a pile hammer. If it is necessary to increase the length of a pile, two or more sections may be welded together or sections may be connected by using an inside sleeve for each joint. This type of pile is particularly advantageous for use on jobs when the headroom for driving is limited and short sections must be added to obtain the desired total length.

An open-end pipe pile is installed by driving the pipe to the required depth and then removing the soil from the inside. Removal methods include bursts of compressed air, a mixture of water and compressed air, or the use of an earth auger or a small orange-peel bucket. Finally, the hollow pipe is filled with concrete.

Because open-end pipe piles offer less driving resistance than closed-end piles, a smaller pile hammer may be used. The use of a light hammer is desirable when piles are driven near a structure whose foundation might be damaged by vibrations from the blows of a large hammer. Open-end piles may be driven to depths which can never be reached with closed-end piles.

COMPOSITE PILES

When extremely hard soils or soil layers are encountered, it may be cost-effective to consider the use of a composite pile. The top portion of the pile would be a prestressed concrete pile and the tip would be a steel H pile embedded into the end of the concrete pile. This composite design is suggested for marine applications, where the concrete pile section offers resistance to deterioration and the steel pile tip enables penetration of hard underlying soils.

SHEET PILES

Sheet piles are used primarily to retain or support earth. They are commonly used for bulkheads and cofferdams and when excavation depths or soil conditions require temporary or permanent bracing to support the lateral loads imposed by the soil or by the soil and adjacent structures. Supported loads include any live loads imposed by construction operations. Sheet piles can be made of steel, concrete, or timber. Each of these types can support limited loads without additional bracing or tieback systems. When the depth of support is large or when the loads are great, it is necessary to incorporate a tieback or bracing system with the sheet piles.

Steel sheet piles. In the United States steel sheet piling is manufactured in both flat and Z section sheets which have interlocking longitudinal edges. Most steel sheet piles are supplied in standard ASTM 328 grade steel, but high strength low alloy grades ASTM A572 and ASTM A690 are available for use when large loads must be supported or where corrosion is a concern. In marine applications epoxy coated piles may be used to resist corrosion.

The flat sections are designed for interlocking strength which makes them suitable for the construction of cellular structures. The Z sections are designed for bending, which makes them more suitable for use in the construction of retaining walls, bulk-heads, cofferdams, and for use as excavation support. Figure 15-14 shows various configurations of domestically produced steel sheet piles and their corresponding properties. Several overseas manufacturers produce steel sheet piles with properties that are similar to the domestic sheets. These piles sometimes utilize a different interlocking design from the domestic sheets. Careful attention should be given to this design feature in order to assure that sheets will perform in the intended usage and that the interlocking system allows the sheets to be threaded and driven easily.

Sheet piles are driven individually or in pairs frequently with the use of a vibratory hammer and a guide frame or template. Automatic sheet pile threading devices can be utilized to thread the new sheet into the previously threaded or driven sheet. These devices allow the sheets to be threaded without the assistance of a person working at the top of the previously placed sheet. If the steel sheet piling is used for temporary support, the individual sheets can be extracted ("pulled") by using a vibratory hammer after construction and backfilling has been completed.

Prestressed concrete sheet piles. Concrete sheet piles are best suited for applications where corrosion is a concern such as marine bulkheads. The prestressed concrete sheets are precast in thicknesses ranging from 6 to 24 in. and usually have widths of 3 to 4 ft. Figure 15-15 shows the dimensions and properties of various size concrete sheet piles. Conventional steam, air, or diesel hammers can be used to drive concrete sheet piles. However, jetting is often required to attain the proper tip elevation. Once the piles have been driven, the slots between sections are filled with grout.

Timber sheet piles. When supported loads are minimal, timber sheet piles can be used. Commonly, timbers of 3 to 4 in. thickness are used in an overlapping pattern three timbers thick. Such a pattern is commonly called "Wakefield sheeting." The timbers are driven with a light hammer or are jetted into place. Timber wales and piles may be used to add support to the system. Traditionally, timber sheets have been used for bulkheads and to construct groins. When utilized in permanent marine applications, they should be pressure treated to resist deterioration and borers.

THE RESISTANCE OF PILES TO PENETRATION

In general, the forces which enable a pile to support a load also cause the pile to resist the efforts made to drive it. The total resistance of a pile to penetration will equal the sum of the forces produced by skin friction and end bearing. The relative portions of the resistance contributed by either skin friction or end bearing may vary from almost 0 to 100%, depending more on soil type than on the type of pile. A steel H pile driven to refusal in stiff clay should be classified as a skin friction pile, whereas the same pile driven through a mud deposit to rest on solid rock should be classified as an end-bearing pile.

Numerous tests have been conducted to determine values for skin friction for various types of piles and soils. A representative value for skin friction can be obtained by determining the total force required to cause a small incremental upward movement of the pile by using hydraulic jacks with calibrated pressure gauges.

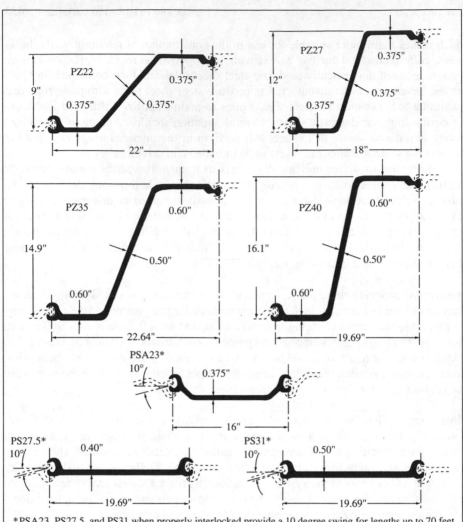

*PSA23, PS27.5, and PS31 when properly interlocked provide a 10 degree swing for lengths up to 70 feet. The dimensions given on this page are nominal.

Properties and Weights

Section designation	Area, sq in.	Nominal width, in.	Weight, lb		Moment of inertia, in.⁴	Section modulus, in.³		Surface area sq ft per lin. ft of bar	
			Per lin. ft of bar	Per sq ft of wall		Single section	Per lin. ft of wall	Total area	Nominal coating area*
PZ22	11.86	22	40.3	22.0	154.7	33.1	18.1	4.94	4.48
PZ27	11.91	18	40.5	27.0	276.3	45.3	30.2	4.94	4.48
PZ35	19.41	22.64	66.0	35.0	681.5	91.4	48.5	5.83	5.37
PZ40	19.30	19.69	65.6	40.0	805.4	99.6	60.7	5.83	5.37
PSA23	8.99	16	30.7	23.0	5.5	3.2	2.4	3.76	3.08
PS27.5	13.27	19.69	45.1	27.5	5.3	3.3	2.0	4.48	3.65
PS31	14.96	19.69	50.9	31.0	5.3	3.3	2.0	4.48	3.65

*Excludes socket interior and ball of interlock.

FIGURE 15-14
Domestically produced steel sheet piles and their corresponding properties and weights. (*Bethlehem Steel Corporation.*)

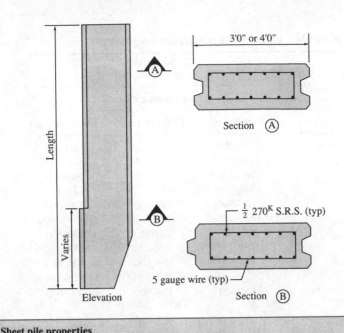

Elevation

3'0" or 4'0"

Section (A)

½ 270ᴷ S.R.S. (typ)

5 gauge wire (typ)

Section (B)

Sheet pile properties
(per L.F. of width)

T Thickness	Area in.^{2}	I, in.^{4}	S, in.^{3}	Max allowable Bending moment (ft kips) $f'c = 5,000$ psi $_{(2)}$	$f'c = 6,000$ PSI	Approx. weight per $_{(1)}$ l.f.
6"	72"	216	72	6.0	7.2	75#
8"	96"	512	128	10.6	12.8	100#
10"	120"	1,000	200	16.6	20.0	125#
12"	144"	1,728	288	24.0	28.8	150#
16"	192"	4,096	512	42.7	51.2	200#
18"	216"	5,832	648	54.0	64.8	225#
20"	240"	8,000	800	66.7	80.0	250#
24"	288"	13,824	1,152	96.0	115.2	300#

I - Moment of inertia.
S - Section modulus.

(1) Weights based on 150 pcf of regular concrete.
(2) Based on 'o' psi allowable stress on tensile face and 0.4f'c allowable stress on compression face.

FIGURE 15-15
Prestressed concrete sheet piles and their corresponding properties and weights. (*Bayshore Concrete Products, Chesapeake, Inc.*)

TABLE 15-2
Approximate allowable value of skin friction on piles†

Material	Skin friction [psf (kg/sq m)] Approximate depth		
	20 ft (6.1 m)	60 ft (18.3 m)	100 ft (30.5 m)
Soft silt and dense muck	50–100 (244–488)	50–120 (244–586)	60–150 (273–738)
Silt (wet but confined)	100–200 (488–976)	125–250 (610–1,220)	150–300 (738–1,476)
Soft clay	200–300 (976–1,464)	250–350 (1,220–1,710)	300–400 (1,476–1,952)
Stiff clay	300–500 (1,464–2,440)	350–550 (1,710–2,685)	400–600 (1,952–2,928)
Clay and sand mixed	300–500 (1,464–2,440)	400–600 (1,952–2,928)	500–700 (2,440–3,416)
Fine sand (wet but confined)	300–400 (1,464–1,952)	350–500 (1,710–2,440)	400–600 (1,952–2,928)
Medium sand and small gravel	500–700 (2,440–3,416)	600–800 (2,928–3,904)	600–800 (2,928–3,904)

†Some allowance is made for the effect of using piles in small groups.

The value of the skin friction is a function of the coefficient of friction between the pile and the soil and the pressure of the soil normal to the surface of the pile. However, for a soil, such as some clays, the value of the skin friction may be limited to the shearing strength of the soil immediately adjacent to the pile. Consider a concrete pile driven into a soil that produces a normal pressure of 100 psi on the vertical surface of the pile. This is not an unusually high pressure for certain soils such as compacted sand. If the coefficient of friction is 0.25, the value of the skin friction will be $0.25 \times 100 \times 144 = 3,600$ psf (pounds per square foot). Table 15-2 gives representative values of skin friction on piles. The author of the table states that the information is intended as a qualitative guide, not as correct information to be used in any and all cases.

The magnitude of end-bearing pressure can be determined by driving a button-bottom-type pile and leaving the driving casing in place. A second steel pipe, slightly smaller than the driving casing, is lowered onto the bottom button. The force, applied through the second pipe, required to drive the button into the soil is a direct measure of the supporting strength of the soil, because there is no skin friction on the inside pipe.

PILE HAMMERS

The function of a pile hammer is to furnish the energy required to drive a pile. Pile-driving hammers are designated by type and size. The hammer types commonly used include the following:

1. Drop
2. Single-acting steam or compressed air
3. Double-acting steam or compressed air
4. Differential-acting steam or compressed air
5. Diesel
6. Hydraulic
7. Vibratory drivers

For each of the first six pile hammer types listed the driving energy is supplied by a falling mass, which strikes the top of the pile. The size of a drop hammer is designated by its weight, whereas the size of each of the other hammers is designated by theoretical energy per blow, expressed in foot-pounds (ft-lb).

Drop hammers. A *drop hammer* is a heavy metal weight that is lifted by a hoist line, then released and allowed to fall onto the top of the pile. Because of the high dynamic forces, a pile cap is positioned between the hammer and the pile head. The pile cap serves to uniformally distribute the blow to the pile head and to serve as a "shock absorber." The cap contains a cushion block which is commonly fabricated from wood.

The hammer may be released by a trip and fall freely, or it may be released by loosening the friction band on the hoisting drum and permitting the weight of the hammer to unwind the rope from the drum. The latter type of release reduces the effective energy of a hammer because of the friction loss in the drum and rope. Leads are used to hold the pile in position and to guide the movement of the hammer so that it will strike the pile axially.

Standard drop hammers are made in sizes which vary from about 500 to 3,000 lb. The height of drop or fall most frequently used varies from about 5 to 20 ft. The maximum recommended drop height varies with the pile type, 15 ft for timber piles and 8 ft for concrete piles. When a large energy per blow is required to drive a pile, it is better to use a heavy hammer with a small drop than a light hammer with a large drop.

Drop hammers are suitable for driving piles on remote projects which require only a few piles and for which the time of completion is not an important factor. A drop hammer normally can deliver four to eight blows per minute.

The advantages of drop hammers include the following:

1. Small investment in equipment.
2. Simplicity of operation.
3. Ability to vary energy per blow by varying the height of fall.

The disadvantages of drop hammers include the following:

1. Slow rate of driving piles.
2. Danger of damaging piles by lifting a hammer too high.
3. Danger of damaging adjacent buildings as a result of the heavy vibration caused by a hammer.
4. Unable to use directly for underwater driving.

Single-acting steam/air hammers. A single-acting steam/air hammer (see Fig. 15-16) has a freely falling weight, called a "ram," which is lifted by steam or compressed air, whose pressure is applied to the underside of a piston that is connected to the ram through a piston rod. When the piston reaches the top of the stroke, the steam or air pressure is released and the ram falls freely to strike the top of a pile. The energy supplied by this type of hammer is delivered by the heavy weight striking with a low velocity, due to the relatively short fall distance, usually 3 ft; but fall can vary from 12 to 60 in. for specific hammers. Whereas a drop hammer may strike four to eight blows per minute, a single-acting steam/air hammer will strike 40 to 60 blows per minute when delivering the same energy per blow.

A pile cap is used with a single-acting steam/air hammer. The cap is mated to the case of the hammer. This cap is commonly called an "anvil" or a "helmet."

Single-acting steam/air hammers may be open or enclosed (see Fig. 15-17). These hammers are usually used in a pile lead, although they can be fitted to operate free hung. The hammers are available in sizes varying from a few thousand to 1,000,000 ft-lb of energy per blow. Table 15-3a gives data on several of the more popular sizes of single-acting steam/air hammers. The length of the stroke and the energy per blow for this type of hammer may be decreased slightly by reducing the steam or air pressure below that recommended by the manufacturer. The reduced pressure has the effect of decreasing the height to which the piston will rise before it begins to fall.

The advantages of single-acting steam/air compared with drop hammers include the following:

1. The greater number of blows per minute permits faster driving.
2. The greater frequency of blows reduces the increase in skin friction between blows.
3. The heavier ram falling at lower velocity transmits a greater portion of the energy to driving piles.
4. The reduction in the velocity of the ram decreases the danger of damage to piles during driving.
5. The enclosed types may be used for underwater driving.

The disadvantages of single-acting steam/air hammers compared with drop hammers include the following:

1. They require more investment in equipment such as a steam boiler or air compressor.
2. They are more complicated, with higher maintenance cost.
3. They require more time to set up and take down.
4. They require a larger operating crew.
5. They require a crane having a greater lifting capacity.

Double-acting steam/air hammers. In the double-acting steam/air hammer, steam or air pressure is applied to the underside of the piston to raise the ram; then during the downward stroke steam is applied to the top side of the piston to increase the energy per blow. Thus, with a given weight of ram, it is possible to attain a desired amount of energy per blow with a shorter stroke than with a longer single-acting hammer. The

FIGURE 15-16
Raymond 60X steam hammer driving 54-inch cylinder pile. (*Tidewater Construction Corporation.*)

FIGURE 15-17
Single-acting steam hammers. (*a*) Open type. (*Vulcan Iron Works.*)
(*b*) Enclosed type. (*MKT Geotechnical Systems.*)

number of blows per minute will be approximately twice as great as for a single-acting hammer with the same energy rating.

Double-acting hammers commonly deliver 95 to 300 blows per minute. These hammers do not require cushion blocks. The ram strikes upon an alloy steel anvil which fits the pile head.

The lighter ram and higher striking velocity of the double-acting hammer may be advantageous when driving light- to medium-weight piles into soils having normal frictional resistance. It is claimed that the high frequency of blows will keep a pile moving downward continuously, thus preventing static skin friction from developing between blows. However, when heavy piles are driven, especially into soils having high frictional resistance, the heavier weight and slower velocity of a *single-acting* hammer will transmit a greater portion of the rated energy into driving the piles. Figure 15-18 shows the essential parts of a double-acting hammer. The hammer is fully enclosed by a steel case.

TABLE 15-3a
Specifications for air or steam pile-driving hammers

Rated energy	Model	Manufacturer	Type	Style	Blows per min	Wt. of striking parts	Total weight (lb)	Hammer length (ft-in.)	Jaw dimensions	Boiler HP required (ASME)	Steam consump. (lb/hr)	Air consump. (cfm)	Inlet pressure (psi)	Inlet size (in.)
1,800,000	6300	VULCAN	SGL.-ACT.	OPEN	42	300,000	575,000	30'0"	22"×144"(M)	2,804	43,873	19,485(A)	235	2@6"
1,582,220	MRBS 12500	MENCK	SGL.-ACT.	OPEN	36	275,580	540,130	35'9"	CAGE	2,400	52,910	26,500	171	2@6"
867,960	MRBS 8000	MENCK	SGL.-ACT.	OPEN	38	176,370	330,690	30'10"	CAGE	1,380	30,860	15,900	171	8"
750,000	5150	VULCAN	SGL.-ACT.	OPEN	46	150,000	275,000	26'3 1/2"	22"×120"(M)	1,317	45,426	9,535(A)	175	2@6"
500,000	5100	VULCAN	SGL.-ACT.	OPEN	48	100,000	197,000	27'4"	22"×120"(M)	1,043	35,977	7,620(A)	150	2@5"
499,070	MRBS 4600	MENCK	SGL.-ACT.	OPEN	42	101,410	176,370	27'5"	CAGE	850	19,840	9,900	142	6"
325,480	MRBS 3000	MENCK	SGL.-ACT.	OPEN	42	66,135	108,025	25'0"	CAGE	520	12,130	6,000	142	5"
325,000	5650	CONMACO	SGL.-ACT.	OPEN	45	65,000	139,300	23'0"	18 3/4"×100"	606	20,907	—	160	3@4"
300,000	3100	VULCAN	SGL.-ACT.	OPEN	60	100,000	195,500	23'3"	18 3/4"×88"(M)	900	30,153	6,644(A)	130	3@4"
300,000	560	VULCAN	SGL.-ACT.	OPEN	47	62,500	134,060	23'0"	18 3/4"×88"(M)	606	20,897	4,427(A)	150	2@5"
200,000	540	VULCAN	SGL.-ACT.	OPEN	48	40,900	102,980	22'7"	14"×80"(M)	409	14,126	3,022(A)	130	2@5"
189,850	MRBS 1800	MENCK	SGL.-ACT.	OPEN	44	38,580	64,590	22'5"	CAGE	295	7,060	3,700	142	4"
180,000	360	VULCAN	SGL.-ACT.	OPEN	62	60,000	124,830	19'0"	18 3/4"×88"(M)	506	17,460	3,736(A)	130	2@4"
180,000	060	VULCAN	SGL.-ACT.	OPEN	62	60,000	128,840	19'0"	18 3/4"×88"(M)	506	17,460	3,736(A)	130	2@4"
150,000	5300	CONMACO	SGL.-ACT.	OPEN	46	30,000	62,000	20'9 1/2"	14"×80"(M)	234	12,296	2,148(A)	160	4"
150,000	530	VULCAN	SGL.-ACT.	OPEN	42	30,000	57,680	20'5"	10 1/2"×54"(M)	234	8,064	1,711	150	3"
120,000	340	VULCAN	SGL.-ACT.	OPEN	60	40,000	98,180	18'7"	14"×80"(M)	354	12,230	2,628(A)	120	2@3"
120,000	040	VULCAN	SGL.-ACT.	OPEN	60	40,000	87,673	17'11"	14"×80"(M)	354	12,230	2,628(A)	120	2@3"
93,340	MRBS 850	MENCK	SGL.-ACT.	OPEN	45	18,960	27,890	19'8"	CAGE	150	3,530	1,950	142	3"
90,000	030	VULCAN	SGL.-ACT.	OPEN	54	30,000	55,410	16'5"	10 1/4"×54"(M)	201	6,944	1,471(A)	150	3"
90,000	300	CONMACO	SGL.-ACT.	OPEN	55	30,000	55,390	16'10"	11 1/4"×56"(F)	201	6,944	1,833(A)	150	3"
81,250	8/0	RAYMOND	SGL.-ACT.	OPEN	40	25,000	34,000	19'4"	10 1/4"×25"	172	5,950	—	135	3"
75,000	30X	RAYMOND	SGL.-ACT.	OPEN	70	30,000	52,000	19'1"	—	246	8,500	—	150	3"
60,000	S-20	MKT	SGL.-ACT.	CLOSED	60	20,000	38,650	15'5"	-×36"	190	—	—	150	3"
60,000	020	VULCAN	SGL.-ACT.	OPEN	59	20,000	43,785	14'8"	10 1/4"×54"(M)	161	5,563	1,195(A)	120	3"
60,000	200	CONMACO	SGL.-ACT.	OPEN	60	20,000	44,560	15'0"	11 1/4"×56"(F)	161	7,500	1,634(A)	120	3"
56,875	5/0	RAYMOND	SGL.-ACT.	OPEN	44	17,500	26,450	16'9"	10 1/4"×25"	100	4,250	—	150	3"
50,200	200-C	VULCAN	DIFFER.	OPEN	98	20,000	39,000	13'11"	11 1/4"×37"	260	8,970	1,746(A)	142	4"
48,750	016	VULCAN	SGL.-ACT.	OPEN	58	16,250	33,340	13'8"	10 1/4"×54"(M)	121	4,182	899(A)	120	3"
48,750	4/0	RAYMOND	SGL.-ACT.	OPEN	46	15,000	23,800	16'1"	—	85	—	—	120	2 1/2"
48,750	150-C	RAYMOND	DIFFER.	OPEN	95-105	15,000	32,500	15'9"	—	—	—	—	120	3"

(continued)

TABLE 15-3a (*continued*)

Rated energy	Model	Manufac-turer	Type	Style	Blows per min	Wt. of striking parts	Total weight (lb)	Hammer length (ft-in.)	Jaw dimensions	Broiler HP required (ASME)	Steam consump. (lb/hr)	Air consump. (cfm)	Inlet pressure (psi)	Inlet size (in.)
48,750	160	CONMACO	SGL.-ACT.	OPEN	60	16,250	33,200	13'8"	11 1/4" × 42"(F)	121	6,950	1,290(A)	120	3"
46,350	MS-500	MKT	SGL.-ACT.	OPEN	40	11,300	15,550	16'8"	-× 26"	64	2,200	1,060	115	3"
45,200	MRBS 500	MENCK	SGL.-ACT.	OPEN	48	11,020	15,210	16'8"	-× 26"	90	2,200	1,100	142	2 1/2"
42,000	014	VULCAN	SGL.-ACT.	OPEN	59	14,000	29,590	13'8"	10 1/4" × 54"(M)	111	3,844	829(A)	110	3"
42,000	140	CONMACO	SGL.-ACT.	OPEN	60	14,000	30,850	13'10 1/4"	11 1/4" × 42"(F)	111	6,920	1,282(A)	110	3"
41,280	160D	CONMACO	DIFFER.	OPEN	103	16,000	35,400	13'7 1/2"	11 1/4" × 42"(F)	237	8,175	1,550(A)	160	3"
40,600	3/0	RAYMOND	SGL.-ACT.	OPEN	50	12,500	21,000	15'7"	10 1/4" × 25"	—	3,000	—	120	2 1/2"
37,500	S-14	MKT	SGL.-ACT.	CLOSED	60	14,000	31,700	13'7"	-× 36"	155	—	—	100	3"
37,375	115	CONMACO	SGL.-ACT.	OPEN	50	11,500	20,830	14'2"	9 1/4" × 32"(C)	*99	*3,425	*910(A)	120	2 1/2"
37,375	115	CONMACO	SGL.-ACT.	OPEN	50	11,500	20,250	15'0"	9 1/4" × 26"(K)	116	3,980	1,060(A)	120	2 1/2"
36,000	140-C	VULCAN	DIFFER.	OPEN	103	14,000	27,984	12'3"	11 1/4" × 32"	211	7,279	1,425(A)	140	3"
36,000	140D	CONMACO	DIFFER.	OPEN	103	14,000	31,200	12'3"	11 1/4" × 42"(F)	211	7,279	1,425(A)	140	2 1/2"
32,885	100C	VULCAN	DIFFER..	OPEN	103	10,000	22,200	14'0"	9 1/4" × 26"	180	6,210	1,245(A)	140	2 1/2"
32,500	100	CONMACO	SGL.-ACT.	OPEN	50	10,000	19,280	14'2"	9 1/4" × 32"(C)	*85	*2,945	*820(A)	100	2 1/2"
32,500	100	CONMACO	SGL.-ACT.	OPEN	50	10,000	18,700	15'0"	9 1/4" × 26"(K)	101	3,425	950(A)	100	2 1/2"
32,500	2/0	RAYMOND	SGL.-ACT.	OPEN	50	10,000	18,550	15'7"	10 1/4" × 25"	—	2,400	—	110	2"
32,500	010	VULCAN	SGL.-ACT.	OPEN	57	10,000	19,500	14'11"	10 1/4" × 40"(M)	101	3,498	753(A)	105	2 1/2"
32,500	S-10	MKT	SGL.-ACT.	CLOSED	55	10,000	22,380	14'1"	-× 30"	130	—	1,000	80	2 1/2
27,121	BB3000	BRONS	SGL.-ACT.	CLOSED	42-65	6,615	12,790	18'6"	9" × 26"	—	—	706	90	2"
26,000	80	CONMACO	SGL.-ACT.	OPEN	50	8,000	17,280	14'2"	9 1/4" × 32"(C)	*75	*2,580	*730(A)	85	2 1/2"
26,000	80	CONMACO	SGL.-ACT.	OPEN	50	8,000	16,700	15'0"	9 1/4" × 26"(K)	127	3,000	850	85	2 1/2"
26,000	85C	VULCAN	DIFFER.	OPEN	111	8,525	19,020	12'7"	9 1/4" × 26"	180	6,210	1,245(A)	128	2 1/2"
26,000	08	VULCAN	SGL.-ACT.	OPEN	50	8,000	16,750	14'10"	9 1/4" × 26"	127	4,380	880(A)	83	2 1/2"
26,000	S-8	MKT	SGL.-ACT.	CLOSED	55	8,000	18,300	14'4"	-× 26"	120	4,140	850	80	2 1/2"
24,450	80-C	VULCAN	DIFFER.	OPEN	111	8,000	17,885	12'1"	9 1/4" × 26"	180	6,210	1,245(A)	120	2 1/2"
24,450	80-CHYD	RAYMOND	DIFFER.	OPEN	110-120	8,000	17,780	11'10"	—	N/A	N/A	—	5,100	—
24,450	80-C	RAYMOND	DIFFER.	OPEN	95-105	8,000	17,885	12'2"	—	80	—	—	120	2 1/2"
24,375	0	RAYMOND	SGL.-ACT.	OPEN	50	7,500	16,000	15'0"	10 1/4" × 25"	—	—	750	110	2"
24,375	0	VULCAN	SGL.-ACT.	OPEN	50	7,500	16,250	15'0"	9 1/4" × 26"	125	9,320	841(A)	80	2 1/2"
24,000	C-826	MKT	COMPOUND	CLOSED	85-95	8,000	17,750	12'2"	-× 26"	120	—	875	125	2 1/2"
19,500	65-C	RAYMOND	DIFFER.	OPEN	110	6,500	14,675	11'8"	9 1/4" × 19"	—	3,100	—	120	2"
19,500	1-S	RAYMOND	SGL.-ACT.	OPEN	58	6,500	12,500	12'9"	7 1/2" × 28 1/4"	—	1,500	—	100	1 1/2"

(*continued*)

TABLE 15-3a (continued)

Rated energy	Model	Manufacturer	Type	Style	Blows per min	Wt. of striking parts	Total weight (lb)	Hammer length (ft-in.)	Jaw dimensions	Broiler HP required (ASME)	Steam consump. (lb/hr)	Air consump. (cfm)	Inlet pressure (psi)	Inlet size (in.)
19,500	06(106)	VULCAN	SGL.-ACT.	OPEN	60	6,500	11,200	13'0"	8 1/4" × 20"	94	3,230	625(A)	100	2"
19,500	65	CONMACO	SGL.-ACT.	OPEN	60	6,500	12,100	13'0"	9 1/4" × 26"(C)	94	3,230	625(A)	100	2"
19,500	65	CONMACO	SGL.-ACT.	OPEN	60	6,500	11,200	13'0"	8 1/4" × 20"(K)	94	2,300	625(A)	100	2"
19,500	65-CHYD	RAYMOND	DIFFER.	OPEN	130	6,500	14,615	12'1"	—	N/A	5,244	—	5,000	2"
19,200	65-C	VULCAN	DIFFER.	OPEN	117	6,500	14,886	12'1"	8 1/4" × 20"	152	5,244	991(A)	150	2 1/2"
19,150	11B3	MKT	DBL.-ACT.	CLOSED	95	5,000	14,000	11'2"	-× 26"	126	—	900	100	2 1/2"
19,150	1100	BSP	DBL.-ACT.	CLOSED	95	5,000	14,000	11'2"	-× 26"	126	—	900	90	2 1/2"
16,250	S-5	MKT	SGL.-ACT.	CLOSED	60	5,000	12,460	13'3"	-× 24"	85	—	600	80	2 1/2"
16,000	C-5(STM)	MKT	DBL.-ACT.	CLOSED	100-110	5,000	11,880		-× 26"	80	—	—	100	2"
15,100	50-C	VULCAN	DIFFER.	OPEN	120	5,000	11,782		8 1/4" × 20"	125	4,312	880(A)	120	2"
15,000	1 (106)	VULCAN	SGL.-ACT.	OPEN	60	5,000	9,700		8 1/4" × 20"	81	2,794	565(A)	80	2"
15,000	1	RAYMOND	SGL.-ACT.	OPEN	60	5,000	11,000	12'9"	7 1/2" × 28 1/4"	—	1,400	500	80	1 1/2"
15,000	50	CONMACO	SGL.-ACT.	OPEN	60	5,000	10,600	13'0"	9 1/4" × 26"(C)	81	2,794	565(A)	80	2"
15,000	50	CONMACO	SGL.-ACT.	OPEN	60	5,000	9,700	13'0"	8 1/4" × 20"(K)	81	1,925	565(A)	80	2 1/2"
14,200	C-5(AIR)	MKT	COMPOUND	CLOSED	100-110	5,000	11,880	8'9"	-× 26"	—	—	585	100	1 1/2"
13,560	BB1500	BRONS	SGL.-ACT.	CLOSED	42-65	3,307	6,285	17'7"	8" × 20"	—	—	353	90	1 1/2"
13,100	10B3	MKT	DBL.-ACT.	CLOSED	105	3,000	10,850	9'2"	-× 24"	104	—	750	100	2 1/2"
13,100	1000	BSP	DBL.-ACT.	CLOSED	105	3,000	10,850	9'2"	-× 24"	104	—	750	90	2 1/2"
8,750	900	BSP	DBL.-ACT.	CLOSED	145	1,600	7,100	8'2"	-× 20"	85	—	600	90	2"
8,750	9B3	MKT	DBL.-ACT.	CLOSED	145	1,600	7,000	8'4"	8 1/2" × 20"	85	—	600	120	1 1/2"
7,260	30-C	VULCAN	DIFFER.	OPEN	133	3,000	7,036	8'11"	7 1/4" × 19"	70	2,412	488	80	1 1/2"
7,260	2	VULCAN	SGL.ACT.	OPEN	70	3,000	6,700	11'7"	7 1/4" × 19"	49	1,690	336(A)	90	2"
4,700	700N	BSP	DBL.-ACT.	CLOSED	225	850	6,500	5'5"	-× 15"	—	—	600	100	1 1/2
4,150	7	MKT	DBL.-ACT.	CLOSED	225	800	5,000	6'1"	-× 21"	65	—	450	78	1 1/2"
4,000	DGH-900	VULCAN	DIFFER.	CLOSED	328	900	5,000	6'9"	VARIES	75	2,620	580(A)	90	1 1/2"
3,000	600N	BSP	DBL.-ACT.	CLOSED	250	500	3,800	5'0"	-× 15"	—	—	365	100	1 1/4"
2,500	6	MKT	DBL.-ACT.	CLOSED	275	400	2,900	5'3"	-× 15"	45	—	400	100	1 1/4"
1,200	500N	BSP	DBL.-ACT.	CLOSED	330	200	2,000	3'11"	-× 12"	—	—	250	90	1 1/4"
1,000	5	MKT	DBL.-ACT	CLOSED	300	200	1,500	4'7"	6'× 11"	35	—	250	100	1 1/4"
386	DGH-100D	VULCAN	DIFFER.	CLOSED	303	100	786	4'2"	4 1/4" × 8 3/4"	5	—	74	60	1"

(A) ADIABATIC COMPRESSION (C) CONMACO CABLE HAMMER (K) CONMACO KEY HAMMER (F) FEMALE JAWS SPECIAL SHORT CYLINDER (M) MALE JAWS

TABLE 15-3b
Specifications for diesel pile-driving hammers

Energy range (ft-lb)	Model	Manufacturer	Single/double acting	Blows per min	Piston weight (lb)	Total weight (lb)	Maximum Stroke (ft-in.)	Total length (ft-in.)	Width between jaws (in.)	Fuel used (gph)
280,000-	K150	KOBE	SINGLE	45-60	33,100	80,500	8'6"	29'8"	CAGE	16-20
161,300-80,600	D62-02	DELMAG	SINGLE	36-53	13,670	28,000	12'8"	17'9"	32	5.3
141,000-63,360	MB70	MITSUBISHI	SINGLE	38-60	15,840	46,000	8'6"	19'6"	—	7-10
135,200	MH72B	MITSUBISHI	SINGLE	38-60	15,900	44,000	8'6"	19'6"	—	7-10
117,175-62,566	D55	DELMAG	SINGLE	36-47	11,860	26,300	9'10"	17'9"	32	5.54
105,600-	K60	KOBE	SINGLE	42-60	13,200	37,500	8'0"	24'3"	42	6.5-8.0
105,000-48,400	D46-02	DELMAG	SINGLE	37-53	10,100	19,900	10'8"	17'3"	32	3.3
92,752	KC45	KOBE	SINGLE	39-60	9,920	24,700	9'4"	17'11"	—	4.5-5.5
91,100-	K45	KOBE	SINGLE	39-60	9,900	25,600	9'2"	18'6"	36	4.5-5.5
87,000-43,500	D44	DELMAG	SINGLE	37-56	9,460	22,440	9'2"	15'10"	32	4.5
84,300	MH45	MITSUBISHI	SINGLE	42-60	9,920	24,500	8'6"	17'11"	37	4.0-5.8
84,000-37,840	M43	MITSUBISHI	SINGLE	40-60	9,460	22,660	8'10"	16'3"	37	4.0-5.8
83,100-38,000	D36-02	DELMAG	SINGLE	37-53	7,900	17,700	10'8"	17'3"	32	3.0
79,500-	J44	IHI	SINGLE	42-70	9,720	21,500	8'2"	14'10"	37	6.86
79,000-	K42	KOBE	SINGLE	40-60	9,260	24,000	8'6"	17'8"	36	4.5-5.5
78,800-	B45	BSP	DOUBLE	80-100	10,000	27,500	—	19'3"	36	5.5
73,780-30,380	D36	DELMAG	SINGLE	37-53	7,940	17,780	9'3"	14'11"	32	3.7
72,182	KC35	KOBE	SINGLE	39-60	7,720	17,400	9'4"	16'10"	—	3.2-4.3
70,800-	K35	KOBE	SINGLE	39-60	7,700	18,700	9'2"	17'8"	30	3.0-4.0
65,600-	MH35	MITSUBISHI	SINGLE	42-60	7,720	18,500	8'6"	17'3"	32	3.4-5.3
64,000-29,040	M33	MITSUBISHI	SINGLE	40-60	7,260	16,940	8'0"	13'2"	32	3.4-5.3
63,900-	B35	BSP	DOUBLE	80-100	7,700	21,200	—	18'5"	36	4.5
63,500-	J35	IHI	SINGLE	72-70	7,730	16,900	8'3"	14'6"	32	4.76
63,000-42,000	DE70/50B	MKT	SINGLE	40-50	7,000	14,600	10'6"	15'10"	26	3.3
62,900-31,800	D30-02	DELMAG	SINGLE	38-52	6,600	13,150	10'7"	17'2"	26	1.7
60,100-	K32	KOBE	SINGLE	40-60	7,050	17,750	8'6"	17'8"	30	2.75-3.5
54,200-23,870	D30	DELMAG	SINGLE	39-60	6,600	12,346	8'3"	14'2"	26	2.9
51,518-	KC25	KOBE	SINGLE	39-60	5,510	12,130	9'4"	16'10"	—	2.4-3.2
50,700-	K25	KOBE	SINGLE	39-60	5,510	13,100	9'3"	17'6"	26	2.5-3.0
48,400-24,600	D22-02	DELMAG	SINGLE	38-52	4,850	11,400	10'7"	17'2"	26	1.6
46,900	MH25	MITSUBISHI	SINGLE	42-60	5,510	13,200	8'6"	16'8"	28	2.4-3.7

(continued)

444

TABLE 15-3b *(continued)*

Energy range (ft-lb)	Model	Manufacturer	Single/double acting	Blows per min	Piston weight (lb)	Total weight (lb)	Maximum Stroke (ft-in.)	Total length (ft-in.)	Width between jaws (in.)	Fuel used (gph)
45,700-	B25	BSP	DOUBLE	80-100	5,510	15,200	—	17'9"	30	3.5
45,000-30,000	DE70/50B	MKT	SINGLE	40-50	5,000	12,600	10'6"	15'10"	26	3.3
45,000-30,000	DE50B	MKT	SINGLE	40-50	5,000	12,000	10'6"	14'9"	26	3.0
45,000-30,000	DA55B	MKT	SINGLE	40-50	5,000	18,300	10'9"	17'4"	26	2.7
45,000-20,240	M23	MITSUBISHI	SINGLE	42-60	5,060	11,220	8'10"	14'1"	26	2.4-3.7
45,000-	660	ICE	DOUBLE	84	7,564	23,423	—	15'1"	30	3.25
41,300-	K22	KOBE	SINGLE	40-60	4,850	12,350	9'2"	17'6"	26	2.0-2.75
39,780-	D22	DELMAG	SINGLE	42-60	4,850	11,150	8'2"	14'2"	26	3.44
39,100	J22	IHI	SINGLE	42-70	4,850	10,800	10'0"	14'0"	26	3.2
38,200-31,200	DA55B	MKT	DOUBLE	78-82	5,000	18,300	—	17'4"	26	3.0
36,000-24,000	DE40	MKT	SINGLE	40-50	4,000	11,275	10'6"	15'0"	26	3.0
31,000-17,700	520	ICE	DOUBLE	80-84	5,070	12,545	—	16'6"	26	1.35
28,100-	MH15	MITSUBISHI	SINGLE	42-60	3,310	8,400	8'6"	16'1"	26	1.3-2.1
27,100-	D15	DELMAG	SINGLE	40-60	3,300	6,615	8'3"	13'11"	20	1.75
26,200-	B15	BSP	DOUBLE	80-100	3,300	9,000	—	17'0"	26	2.5
26,000-11,800	M14S	MITSUBISHI	SINGLE	42-60	2,970	7,260	8'9"	13'7"	20	1.3-2.1
25,200-16,800	DE30/20B	MKT	SINGLE	40-50	2,800	7,250	10'0"	15'4"	20	2.0
25,200-16,800	DA35B	MKT	SINGLE	40-50	2,800	10,000	10'9"	17'0"	20	1.7
25,200-	DE30	MKT	SINGLE	40-50	2,800	8,125	10'9"	15'0"	20	2.0
24,400-	K13	KOBE	SINGLE	40-60	2,860	7,300	8'6"	16'8"	26	.57-2.0
22,500-	D12	DELMAG	SINGLE	40-60	2,750	6,050	8'2"	13'11"	20	2.11
21,000-16,000	DA35B	MKT	DOUBLE	78-82	2,800	10,000	—	17'0"	20	2.0
19,840-7,700	440	ICE	DOUBLE	86-90	4,000	9,840	—	13'9"	20	1.6
18,000-12,000	DE20	MKT	SINGLE	40-50	2,000	6,325	9'5"	13'3"	20	1.6
18,000-	312	ICE	DOUBLE	100-105	3,857	10,375	—	10'9"	26	1.1
16,000-12,000	DE30/20B	MKT	SINGLE	40-50	2,000	6,450	10'0"	15'4"	20	2.0
9,100	D5	DELMAG	SINGLE	40-60	1,100	2,730	8'3"	12'2"	19	1.32
8,800-	DE10	MKT	SINGLE	40-50	1,100	3,100	8'0"	12'2"	10" BP	0.9
8,100-	180	ICE	DOUBLE	90-95	1,725	4,550	—	11'7"	18	0.65
3,630-	D4	DELMAG	SINGLE	50-60	836	1,360	4'4"	7'9"	BEAM	0.21
1,815-	D2	DELMAG	SINGLE	60-70	484	792	4'1"	6'9"	BEAM	0.075

TABLE 15-3c
Specifications for hydraulic vibratory pile-driver/extractors

Dynamic forces (tons)	Model	Manufacturer	Frequency (vpm)	Amplitude (in.)	HP	Max. pull extraction (tons)	Pile clamp force (tons)	Suspended weight (lb)	Shipping weight (lb)	Height (ft-in.)	Depth (ft-in.)	Width	Throat width (in.)
182	V-36	MKT	1600	.75	550	80	80	18,800	36,300	13-1	1-0	12-0	14
145.4	812	ICE	750-1500	1/2-1	330	40	100	14,700	30,200	9-0	2-0	8-0	12
139	50H1	PTC	1500	1.25	370	44							
100.5	V-20	MKT	1650	.66	295	40	75	12,500	23,900	5-3	1-2		14
111.4	4000	FOSTER	1400	.72	299	40	100/200	18,800	32,300	9-10	1-10	9-10	12
78.3	V-16	MKT	1750	.47	161	50	75	11,700	20,600	5-3	1-2		14
71.0	V-14	MKT	1500	.32	140	50	75	10,000	29,500	5-3	1-2		14
65.2	416	ICE	800-1600	1/4-1	175	40	100	12,200	26,200	8-9	1-10	8-0	12
55	20H6	PTC	1500	.88	185	22							
48.5	1700	FOSTER	1400	.39	147	30	80/100	12,900	26,900	7-0	1-10		12
38.8	14H2	PTC	1500	.85	120	16.5							
36.4	216	ICE	800-1600	1/4-3/4	115	20	50	4,500	12,500	6-6	5-0	3-11	12
35.2	1200	FOSTER	1425	.34	85	20	60	6,700	11,670	5-0	1-11		12
34.4	7H4	PTC	2000	.50	115	16.5							
30.0	V-5	MKT	1450	.50	59	20	31	6,800	10,800	5-4	1-2		14

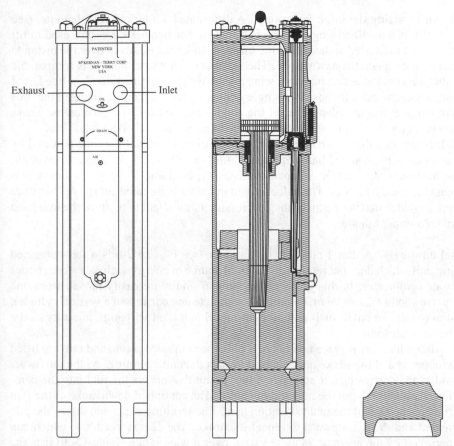

FIGURE 15-18
Section through a double-acting pile hammer. (*MKT Geotechnical Systems.*)

Table 15-3a gives dimensions and other data for several of the more popular sizes of double-acting hammers.

The advantages of double-acting compared with single-acting hammers include the following:

1. The greater number of blows per minute reduces the time required to drive piles.
2. The greater number of blows per minute reduces the development of static skin friction between blows.
3. Piles can be driven more easily without leads.

The disadvantages of double-acting compared with single-acting hammers include the following:

1. The relative light weight and high velocity of the ram make this type of hammer less suitable for use in driving heavy piles into soils having high frictional resistance.
2. The hammer is more complicated.

Differential-acting steam/air hammers. A differential-acting steam/air hammer (see Fig. 15-19), is a modified single-acting hammer in that steam/air pressure used to lift the ram is not exhausted at the end of the upward stroke but is valved over the piston to accelerate the ram on the downstroke. The number of blows per minute is comparable with that for a double-acting hammer, whereas the weight and the equivalent free fall of the ram are comparable to those of a single-acting hammer. Thus, it is claimed that this type of hammer has the advantages of the single- and double-acting hammers. These hammers require the use of a pile cap with cushioning material and a set of leads.

It is reported that this hammer will drive a pile in one-half the time required by the same-size, single-acting hammer and in doing so will use 25–35% less steam or air. These hammers are available in open or closed types. Table 15-3a gives dimensions and data for these hammers. The values given in the table for rated energy per blow are correct, provided that the steam or the air pressure is sufficient to produce the indicated normal blows per minute.

Diesel hammers. A diesel pile-driving hammer (see Fig. 15-20) is a self-contained driving unit which does not require an external source of energy such as a steam boiler or an air compressor. In this respect it is simpler and more easily moved from one location to another than a steam hammer. A complete unit consists of a vertical cylinder, a piston or ram, an anvil, fuel- and lubricating-oil tanks, a fuel pump, injectors, and a mechanical lubricator.

After a hammer is placed on top of a pile, the combined piston and ram are lifted to the upper end of the stroke and released to start the unit operating. As the ram nears the end of the downstroke, it activates a fuel pump that injects the fuel into the combustion chamber between the ram and the anvil. The continued downstroke of the ram compresses the air and the fuel to ignition heat. The resulting explosion drives the pile downward and the ram upward to repeat its stroke. The energy per blow, which can be controlled by the operator, may be varied over a wide range. Table 15-3b lists the specifications for several makes and models of diesel hammers. Figure 15-21 illustrates the operation of a diesel hammer.

Open-end diesel hammers deliver 40 to 55 blows per minute. The closed end models operate at 75 to 85 blows per minute. In the United States diesel hammers are almost always used in a set of leads, yet in other parts of the world they are commonly used free-hanging. These hammers require a pile cap with good "live" cushioning material.

A time plot of the force applied to the pile for a diesel hammer is quite different from those for the previously discussed hammers. In the case of a diesel hammer the force begins to build as soon as the falling ram closes the exhaust ports of the cylinder and compresses the trapped air. With the explosion of the fuel at the bottom of the stroke, there is a force spike which decays as the ram travels upward. The important point is that the loading to the pile spans time and changes magnitude across the time span.

Advantages of the diesel hammer. When compared with the steam/air hammer, the diesel hammer has several potential advantages, including the following:

1. The hammer needs no external source of energy. Thus, it is more mobile and it requires less time to set up and start operation.

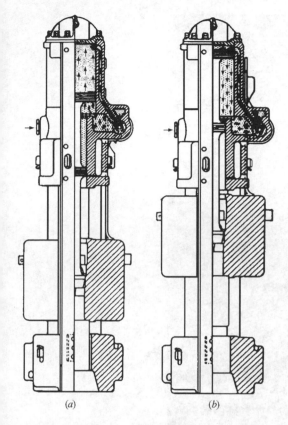

(a)   (b)

FIGURE 15-19
Section through a differential-acting steam hammer. (*a*) Piston in lower position. (*b*) Piston in upper position. (*Vulcan Iron Works.*)

2. The hammer is economical to operate. The rated fuel consumption for a 24,000-ft-lb hammer is 3 gal per hour (gph) when it is operating. Because a hammer does not operate continuously, the actual consumption is less.

3. The hammer is convenient to operate in remote areas. Because the hammer uses diesel oil as a source of energy, it is not necessary to provide a boiler, water for steam, and fuel.

4. The hammer operates well in cold weather. Diesel hammers have been used at temperatures well below 0°F, where it would be difficult or impossible to provide steam.

5. The hammer is light in weight when compared with the weight of a steam hammer of equal rating.

6. The maintenance and service of the hammer are simple and fast.

7. The energy per blow increases as the driving resistance of a pile increases.

8. Because the resistance of a pile to driving is necessary for the continuous operation of a diesel hammer, this hammer will not operate if a pile breaks or falls out from under the hammer.

FIGURE 15-20
Diesel hammer driving sheet piling. (*Pileco, Inc.*)

9. Because of the low velocity in easy driving, and because the piston reacts to the impact needed for each blow by rebounding up its cylinder, a diesel hammer is less likely to batter the piles when driving them.

10. The energy per blow and the number of blows per minute can be varied easily to permit a diesel hammer to operate most effectively for an existing condition [18].

Disadvantages of the diesel hammer. The disadvantages of a diesel hammer include the following:

1. It is difficult to determine the energy per blow for this hammer because the height to which the piston ram will rise following the explosion of the fuel in the combustion chamber is a function of the driving resistance. For this reason there is uncertainty about the accuracy of applying dynamic pile-driving formulas to diesel hammers.

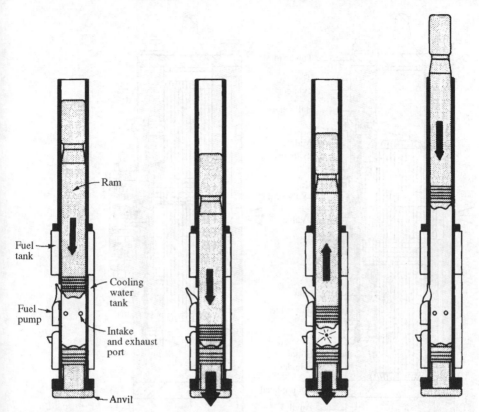

FIGURE 15-21
The operation of a diesel hammer. (*L. B. Foster Company.*)

2. The hammer may not operate well when driving piles into soft ground. Unless a pile offers sufficient driving resistance to activate the ram, the hammer will not operate.

3. The number of strokes per minute is less than for a steam hammer. This is especially true for a diesel hammer with either an open end or top.

4. The length of a diesel hammer is slightly greater than the length of a steam hammer of comparable energy rating.

Hydraulic hammers. These hammers operate on the differential pressure of hydraulic fluid instead of steam or compressed air used by conventional hammers (see Fig. 15-22). Dynamic pile-driving equations in current use are applicable to these hammers.

Another type of hydraulic pile hammer which can be utilized for driving and extracting steel H piles and steel sheet piles incorporates a gripping and pushing or pulling technique. This pile driver grips the pile and then pushes the pile down approximately 3 ft. At the end of the downstroke the pile is released and the gripper slides up the pile 3 ft to begin the process of another push. The equipment can be used in reverse for extracting piles. These drivers develop up to 140 tons of pressing or extracting force,

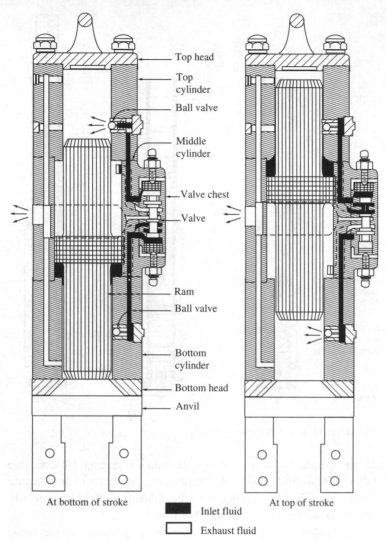

At bottom of stroke   At top of stroke

■ Inlet fluid

□ Exhaust fluid

FIGURE 15-22
Operation of a fluid-valve double-acting hammer. (*MKT Geotechnical Systems.*)

are compact, make minimal noise, and cause very little vibration. They are well suited for driving piles in areas where there is restricted overhead space since piles may be driven in short lengths and spliced.

Vibratory pile drivers. Vibratory pile hammers have demonstrated their effectiveness in speed and economy in driving piles into certain types of soil. These drivers are especially effective when the piles are driven into water-saturated noncohesive soils. The drivers may experience difficulty in driving piles into dry sand, or similar materials, or into cohesive soils that do not respond to the vibrations.

The drivers are equipped with horizontal shafts, to which eccentric weights are attached. As the shafts rotate in pairs, in opposing directions, at speeds that can be varied in excess of 1,000 rpm, the forces produced by the rotating weights produce vibrations that are transmitted to the pile which is rigidly connected to the driver by clamps. Thence the vibrations are transmitted into the soil adjacent to the pile. The agitation of the soil, especially when it is saturated with water, materially reduces the skin friction between the soil and the pile. The combined weight of the pile and the driver resting on the pile will drive the pile quite rapidly.

Figure 15-23 illustrates the basic principle of the rotating weights, using six shafts. As noted in the figure, the two inner shafts, with lighter weights, rotate at twice the speeds of the top and bottom shafts. During each revolution of two top and bottom shafts the forces contributed by all weights will act downward at 0 and 360°, whereas at 180° the forces tend to counteract each other, as indicated in the exciting force curve [12]. Figure 15-24 illustrates a vibratory driver driving sheet piling.

Leads are rarely employed with vibratory drivers. The driver is powered either electrically or hydraulically; therefore, a generator or hydraulic power pack is needed as an energy source. Because leads are not required, a smaller crane can usually be employed to handle vibratory driver work.

Performance factors for vibratory drivers. There are five performance factors that determine the effectiveness of a vibratory driver:

1. *Amplitude.* This is the magnitude of the vertical movement of the pile produced by the vibratory unit. It may be expressed in inches (in.) or millimeters (mm).
2. *Eccentric moment.* The eccentric moment of a vibratory unit is a basic measure or indication of the size of a driver. It is the product of the weight of the eccentricities multiplied by the distance from the center of rotation of the shafts to the center of gravity of the eccentrics. The heavier the eccentric weights and the farther they are from the center of rotation of the shaft, the greater the eccentric moment of the unit.
3. *Frequency.* This is expressed as the number of vertical movements of the vibrator per minute, which is also the number of revolutions of the rotating shafts per minute. Tests conducted on piles driven by vibratory drivers have indicated that the frictional forces between the piles being driven and the soil into which they are driven are at minimum values when frequencies are maintained in the range of 700 to 1,200 vibrations per minute. In general, the frequencies for piles driven into clay soils should be lower than for piles driven into sandy soils.
4. *Vibrating weight.* The vibrating weight includes the vibrating case and the vibrating head of the vibrator unit, plus the pile being driven.
5. *Nonvibrating weight.* This is the weight of that part of the system which does not vibrate, including the suspension mechanism and the motors. Nonvibrating weights push down on and aid in driving the piles.

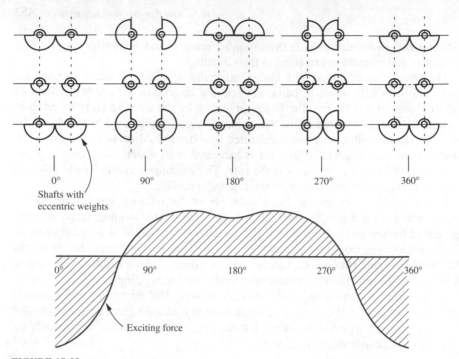

FIGURE 15-23

Operation of the eccentric weights for a vibratory pile driver. Diagram shows how exciting force of a six-shaft vibrator varies with the position of the eccentric weights attached to the shafts.

FIGURE 15-24

A vibratory driver driving sheet piling. (*L. B. Foster Company.*)

METHODS OF SUPPORTING AND POSITIONING PILES DURING DRIVING

When driving piles, it is necessary to have a method which will position the pile in the proper location with the required alignment or batter, and which will support the pile during driving. The following methods are utilized to accomplish such alignment and support.

Fixed leads. Normally, a set of leads consists of a three-sided steel lattice frame similar in construction to a crane boom with one side open. The open side allows positioning of the pile in the leads and under the hammer. The leads have a set of rails or guides for the hammer. Running on the rails, the hammer is lifted above the pile height when a new pile is threaded into the leads. During driving the hammer descends along the lead rails as the pile moves downward into the ground. When driving batter piles, the leads are positioned at an angle.

The term "fixed" is used to indicate that the leads are held in a fixed position by the pile-driving rig or by some other means. The bottom of the leads is commonly attached to the crane or to the driving platform to assure proper positioning of the pile during driving.

Swing leads. Leads which are not attached, at their bottom, to the crane or driving platform are known as "swing leads." Such an arrangement allows the driving rig to position a pile at a location that is farther away than would be possible with fixed leads. This is not generally the preferred method of driving a pile since it is more difficult to position the pile accurately and to maintain vertical alignment during driving. If for any reason the pile tends to twist or run off the intended alignment, it is difficult to control the pile with swing leads.

Hydraulic leads. To control pile position, hydraulic leads utilize a system of hydraulic cylinders connected between the bottom of the leads and the driving rig (see Fig. 15-25). This system allows the operator to position the pile very quickly and accurately. Hydraulic leads are extremely useful in driving batter piles since the system can rapidly and easily adjust the angle of the leads for the required batter. The system is more costly than standard fixed leads but that dollar difference is quickly recovered by any contractor who is regularly involved in pile-driving operations. This is because of the increased driving productivity.

Templates. Many times a template is used to support and hold the pile in position during driving. Templates are usually constructed from steel pipe or beams and may have several levels of framing to support long piles or piles on a batter (see Fig. 15-26). In marine work templates are used regularly where access to the pile groups is restricted. Frequently, a set of leads can be fixed or attached to a template beam and the combined systems are used to support and guide the pile during driving. Templates or guide frames are commonly used when driving sheet piling. When driving sheet pile cells, circular templates are used to maintain proper alignment.

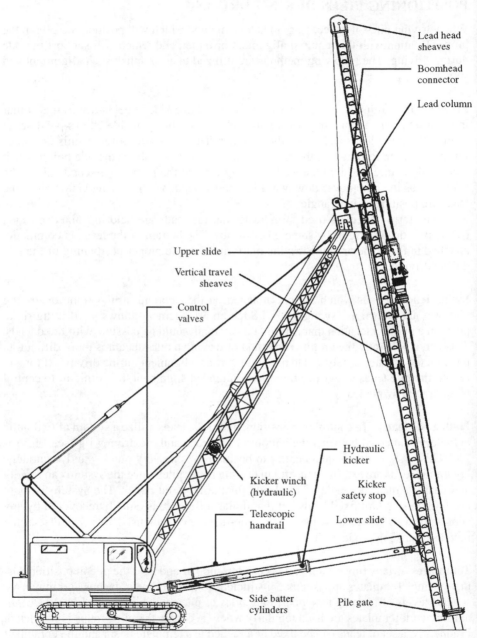

FIGURE 15-25
Vertical travel leads (hydraulic) attached to a crawler crane. (*Berminghammer Corporation Limited.*)

FIGURE 15-26
Barge mounted Whirley crane driving concrete piles on a batter utilizing a template. (*Tidewater Construction Corporation.*)

JETTING PILES

The use of a water jet to assist in driving piles into sand or fine gravel frequently will speed the driving operation. The water, which is discharged through a nozzle at the lower end of a jet pipe, keeps the soil around the pile in agitation, thereby reducing the resistance due to skin friction. Successful jetting requires a plentiful supply of water at a pressure high enough to loosen the soil and to remove it from the hole ahead of the penetration of the pile. Commonly used jet pipes vary in size from 2 to 4 in. in diameter, with nozzle diameters varying from $\frac{1}{2}$ to $1\frac{1}{2}$ in. The water pressure at the nozzle may vary from approximately 100 to more than 300 psi, with the water quantity usually varying from 300 to 500 gallons per minute (gpm), but as high as 1,000 gpm in some instances.

Although some piles have been jetted to final penetration, this is not considered good practice primarily because it is impossible to determine the safe supporting capacity of a pile so driven. Most specifications require that piles shall be driven the last few feet without the benefit of jetting. The Foundation Code of the City of New York requires a contractor to obtain special permission prior to jetting piles and specifies that piles shall be driven the last 3 ft with a pile hammer.

SPUDDING AND PREAUGERING

At proposed pile locations where there is evidence of previous construction or when it is suspected that the preexisting foundations may interfere with driving operations, it may be prudent to preauger or predrive a short H pile section to below the depth of the suspected interference. If there is evidence of very hard overlying soil strata, it may be necessary to preauger or predrill through the strata prior to beginning the pile-driving operation.

Preaugering should also be considered where piles are to be driven through an earth fill and into natural soil. This is often the case at bridge abutments where the embankment fill is placed prior to construction of the bridge. The depth of the preaugering should coincide with the depth of the placed fill in order that the piles develop their full bearing capacity in the natural soil.

DRIVING PILES BELOW WATER

If it is necessary to drive piles below water, either of two methods may be used. When the driving unit is a drop hammer, an open-type steam hammer, or a diesel hammer, the pile is driven until the top is just above the surface of the water. Then a follower is placed on top of the pile, and the driving is continued through the follower. The follower may be made of wood or steel and must be strong enough to transmit the energy from the hammer to the pile.

When the driving unit is an enclosed steam hammer, the driving may be continued below the surface of the water, without a follower. It is necessary to install an exhaust hose to the surface of the water for the steam, as well as to supply about 60 cubic feet per minute (cfm) of compressed air to the lower part of the hammer housing to prevent water from flowing into the casing and around the ram. An air pressure of $\frac{1}{2}$ psi for each foot of depth below the surface of water should be satisfactory.

PILE-DRIVING EQUATIONS

There are many pile-driving equations, each of which is intended to give the supporting strength of a pile. The equations are empirical, with coefficients that have been determined for certain existing or assumed conditions under which they were developed. None of the equations will give dependable values for the supporting strength of the piles for all the varying conditions that exist on foundation jobs.

It is not within the scope of this book to analyze the various pile-driving equations or the theory related to them. For a more comprehensive study of this subject we suggest that the reader consult the books listed at the end of this chapter. Perhaps the most popular equation in the United States is the *Engineering News* equation. Its popularity seems to be due primarily to its simplicity rather than to its accuracy. For the three types of pile-driving hammers in common use the *Engineering News* equation has the following forms:

For a drop hammer

$$R = \frac{2WH}{S + 1.0} \tag{15-1}$$

For a single-acting steam hammer

$$R = \frac{2WH}{S + 0.1} \tag{15-2}$$

For a double- and differential-acting steam hammer

$$R = \frac{2E}{S + 0.1} \tag{15-3}$$

where R = safe load on a pile, lb
  W = weight of a falling mass, lb
  H = height of free fall for mass W, ft
  E = total energy of ram at the bottom of its downward stroke, ft-lb
  S = average penetration per blow for last 5 or 10 blows, in.

MICHIGAN PILE-DRIVING TESTS

In 1961 the Michigan Highway Department and the U.S. Bureau of Public Roads began the most comprehensive tests ever conducted to investigate pile driving [1,12,16]. The eight main objectives of the tests were:

1. To develop a method for determining the pile-driving energy output of various types of pile-driving hammers, including air, single- or double-acting steam, and diesel hammers.
2. To determine by load tests the load-bearing capacities of piles driven under test conditions.
3. To determine what factors, if any, relate the measured pile-driving energy to the load-bearing capacity of a pile.

4. To determine the proper wall thickness of pipe piles under certain driving conditions.
5. To determine the correlations between the tested load-bearing capacity and estimates of load-bearing capacity as obtained by nine of the best-known pile-driving formulas.
6. To determine the best methods or procedures for jetting piles through intermediate soil layers when the driving resistance is larger but the bearing capacity of the pile in these layers is not satisfactory.
7. To determine the effect of the pile cross section or the surface configuration on the energy required for driving piles.
8. To determine the effect of the pile cross section or surface configuration on the load-bearing capacity of the pile.

   A total of 88 piles were driven for the tests and analysis program. They included 12-in.-diameter pipe, open-end and closed-end, and 12-in. WF sections. The results of the tests appear in Table 15-4. Enthru, as used in the table, is the actual energy delivered to a pile by a hammer, which was determined by instruments. As noted in the table, there was considerable variation in the net energy delivered to the piles by any given hammer. The tests revealed that no dynamic formula in use at that time could consistently provide an accurate estimate of the bearing capacity of a pile [22]. While advances have been made in developing more reliable methods of predetermining the bearing capacity of a pile, dynamic formulas are not infallible prediction tools. The formulas must be used with an understanding of the affects of input variable errors and a realization of how such input will affect predicted pile capacities.

   After observing the tests and analyzing the results, the highway department modified the *Engineering News* equation as follows:

$$R = \frac{2.5E}{S + 0.1} \times \frac{W_r + e^2 W_p}{W_r + W_p} \qquad (15\text{-}4)$$

where R = computed design pile load capacity, lb
$\quad E$ = manufacturer's maximum-rated energy per blow, ft-lb
$\quad S$ = final average penetration of pile per blow, in.
W_r = weight of ram, lb
W_p = weight of pile, including driving appurtenances, lb
$\quad e$ = coefficient of restitution, whose values are:
   0.55 for steel hammer on steel pile, with no cushion
   0.50 for well-compacted cushion in driving pipe piles
   0.50 for double-acting steel hammer striking on steel anvil and driving steel piles or precast concrete piles
   0.40 for ram of double-acting steam hammer striking steel anvil and driving wood piles
   0.40 for medium-compacted wood cushion in driving steel or pipe piles
   0.40 for ram of single-acting steam hammer or drop hammer striking directly on head of precast concrete pile

TABLE 15-4
Results of Michigan State Highway Department pile tests

Site	Hammer model	Maximum rated energy (ft-lb)	Type pile	Accepted enthru determinations	Peak force (kips)	Peak acceleration (G's)	Average enthru (ft-lb)	Ratio enthru/enthru		
								Minimum	Maximum	Average
1	Vulcan No. 1	15,000	H	11	230	90	5,283	0.27	0.45	0.35
			Pipe	5	180	75	5,094	0.26	0.41	0.34
	Link-belt 312	18,000	H	27	380	170	7,726	0.28	0.56	0.43
			Pipe	12	440	210	8,226	0.32	0.62	0.46
	McKiernan-Terry DE-30	22,400	H	22	390	270	5,769	0.19	0.36	0.26
			Pipe	9	490	240	8,682	0.31	0.59	0.39
	Delmag D-12	22,500	H	30	800	360	9,123	0.19	0.53	0.41
			Pipe	13	690	350	11,870	0.39	0.64	0.53
2	Vulcan No. 1	15,000	H Pipe}	12	200	110	5,339	0.30	0.43	0.36
	Vulcan 50C	15,100	Pipe	3	490	270	9,822	0.55	0.76	0.65
	Link-belt 312	18,000	H Pipe}	3	200	100	7,554	0.37	0.50	0.42
	McKiernan-Terry DE-30	22,400	H Pipe}	14	370	190	8,417	0.31	0.46	0.38
	Delmag D-12	22,500	H Pipe}	9	600	320	10,033	0.24	0.60	0.45
3	Vulcan No. 1	15,000	Pipe	10	220	80	6,359	0.32	0.48	0.42
	Vulcan 80C	24,500	Pipe	6	650	310	13,872	0.52	0.64	0.57
	Link-belt 520	30,000	Pipe	8	560	150	16,637	0.44	0.66	0.55
	McKiernan-Terry DE-40	32,000	Pipe	4	700	310	18,088	0.52	0.65	0.57
	Delmag D-22	39,700	Pipe	9	1,050	470	24,660	0.53	0.78	0.62

0.25 for ram of single-acting steam hammer or drop hammer striking on well-conditioned wood cap in driving precast concrete piles or directly on wood-pile heads

0.00 for badly broomed wood piles

DYNAMIC FORMULAS

During the past 30 years considerable progress has been made in the conduct of tests and studies analyzing the properties of piles.

In 1964 the Ohio Department of Transportation sponsored a research program at the Case Western Reserve University, Cleveland, Ohio, whose objective was to develop reliable techniques to predict static capacities for load-bearing piles. One of the systems developed by this program was a Pile-Driving Analyzer, a programmed field computer used to analyze a pile during the driving operation.

The Pile-Driving Analyzer processes the strain and acceleration signals from two strain transducers and two accelerometers which are attached to the pile during driving. For each hammer blow the Analyzer converts the analog strain and acceleration signals into digital force and velocity data plotted against time. These traces are displayed on an oscilloscope during driving so that the quality of the data can be instantly evaluated. This allows for immediate correction of the driving operations if necessary. Specific data from each hammer blow can be selected from a menu of 36 possible dynamic quantities for print out on a paper tape. Additionally, the signals can be recorded on a magnetic tape or digitally stored so that further analyses of the data can be performed if necessary.

Wave equation analysis of piles. As a result of the ability to test a pile dynamically during the driving process, a new generation of formulas has been developed to predict pile load-bearing capacities. One analysis method makes use of a differential equation describing the wave propagation process. This equation, commonly known as the "wave equation" can be written in the form

$$\frac{\partial^2 u}{\partial t^2} = \frac{E}{p} \frac{\partial^2 u}{\partial x^2} \tag{15-5}$$

where x defines a position on the rod

u = displacement of the rod at point x

t = time

E = elastic modulus of the rod material

p = mass density of the rod

Solutions of the wave equation have been employed for the analysis of pile driving, but this is a difficult process because of the boundary conditions encountered during driving. Working under contract for the Federal Highway Administration, Rausche and Goble developed a pile wave equation program named WEAP. This program is in the public domain and operates on a wide variety of computers.

This wave equation program models the total pile-driving system. The pile hammer, hammer cushion, helmet, and pile are each represented by a series of masses and springs. The size of each of the masses is determined from the weight of the piece of the system represented. For example, if the pile is divided into discrete lengths of 5 ft, then the equivalent mass element will have the same mass as 5 ft of pile. Similarly, the discrete spring will have the same stiffness as 5 ft of pile. Some of the elements of the system are naturally discrete. An example of a discrete element is the hammer cushion. It has the function of behaving like a spring to soften the effect of the impact on the ram and to protect the ram from damage. It can be easily represented by a spring in the computer model. The helmet is a very compact element that contributes little or no flexibility to the system, so it can be treated as only a mass element.

Wave equation limitations. A wave equation analysis requires input assumptions that can significantly affect the program results. Potential sources of error include assumptions about hammer performance, the hammer and pile cushion properties, the soil resistance distribution, as well as soil quake and damping characteristics. However, insight into these assumptions can be obtained through dynamic measurement and analysis.

Dynamic measurements of force, velocity, and energy at the point on the pile where the transducers and accelerometers are attached can readily be compared to the wave equation values computed for a corresponding model pile segment. Adjustments to the wave equation input parameters can then be made depending on the agreement between the measured and computed values. This approach is the simplest use of the data available from the dynamic measurements and is an easy way to "calibrate" the wave equation, thereby reducing potential errors.

CAPWAP analysis. In pile-driving analysis three unknowns exist: pile forces, pile motions, and pile boundary conditions. If any two of the three are known, the remaining unknown can be determined. CAPWAP is a computer program that was first developed by Rausche at Case Western Reserve University. The CAPWAP program uses the continuous pile model and applies the records of force and velocity obtained with the Pile-Driving Analyzer to an assumed soil model consisting of the soil resistance distribution, quakes, and damping characteristics at each soil segment and at the pile toe. With this input data of pile motion and assumed boundary conditions, the program computes a force wave trace at the pile head. This computed force wave trace is compared to the force wave trace measured in the field by the Pile-Driving Analyzer.

Therefore, with pile force and pile motion quantified, the CAPWAP program and an experienced engineer can determine the boundary conditions through a trial-and-error process of signal matching. The boundary conditions include the pile capacity, the soil resistance distribution, and soil quake and damping characteristics. The CAPWAP model uses this iteration process of computer runs matched to field-measured force wave traces to predict pile conditions and capacity.

SELECTING A PILE-DRIVING HAMMER

Selecting the most suitable pile-driving hammer for a given project involves a study of several factors, such as the size and type of piles, the number of piles, the character of the soil, the location of the project, the topography of the site, the type of rig available, whether driving will be done on land or in water, etc. A pile-driving contractor is usually concerned with selecting a hammer that will drive the piles for a project at the lowest practical cost. As most contractors must limit their ownership to a few representative sizes and types of hammers, a selection should be made from hammers already owned unless conditions are such that it is economical or necessary to secure an additional size or type. Naturally, more consideration should be given to the selection of a hammer for a project that requires several hundred piles than for a project that has only a few piles.

As previously stated, the function of a pile hammer is to furnish the energy required to drive a pile. This energy is supplied by a weight which is raised and permitted to drop onto the top of a pile, under the effect of gravity alone or with steam/air acting during the downward stroke. The theoretical energy per blow will equal the product of the weight times the equivalent free fall. Since some of this energy is lost in friction as the weight travels downward, the net energy per blow will be less than the theoretical energy. The actual amount of net energy depends on the efficiency of the particular hammer. The efficiencies of the pile hammers vary from 50 to 100%.

Table 15-5 gives recommended sizes of hammers for different types and sizes of piles and driving resistances. The sizes are indicated by the theoretical foot-pounds (ft-lb) of the energy delivered per blow. The theoretical energy per blow given in Table

TABLE 15-5
Recommended sizes of hammers for driving various types of piles[†]

Length of piles (ft)	Depth of penetration	Weight of various types of piles (lb/lin ft)						
		Steel Sheet[‡]			Timber		Concrete	
		20	30	40	30	60	150	400
Driving through ordinary earth, moist clay, and loose gravel, normal frictional resistance								
25	$\frac{1}{2}$	2,000	2,000	3,600	3,600	7,000	7,500	15,000
	Full	3,600	3,600	6,000	3,600	7,000	7,500	15,000
50	$\frac{1}{2}$	6,000	6,000	7,000	7,000	7,500	15,000	20,000
	Full	7,000	7,000	7,500	7,500	12,000	15,000	20,000
75	$\frac{1}{2}$	—	7,000	7,500	—	15,000	—	30,000
	Full	—	—	12,000	—	15,000	—	30,000
Driving through stiff clay, compacted sand, and gravel, high frictional resistance								
25	$\frac{1}{2}$	3,600	3,600	3,600	7,500	7,500	7,500	15,000
	Full	3,600	7,000	7,000	7,500	7,500	12,000	15,000
50	$\frac{1}{2}$	7,000	7,500	7,500	12,000	12,000	15,000	25,000
	Full	—	7,500	7,500	—	15,000	—	30,000
75	$\frac{1}{2}$	—	7,500	12,000	—	15,000	—	36,000
	Full	—	—	15,000	—	20,000	—	50,000

[†] Size expressed in foot-pounds of energy per blow.

[‡] The indicated energy is based on driving two steel sheet piles simultaneously. In driving single piles, use approximately two-thirds the indicated energy.

15-3 is correct, provided the hammer is operated at the designated number of strokes per minute.

In general, it is good practice to select the largest hammer that can be used without overstressing or damaging a pile. As previously shown, when a large hammer is used, a greater portion of the energy is effective in driving the pile, which produces a higher operating efficiency. Therefore, the hammer sizes given in Table 15-5 should be considered as the minimum sizes. In some instances hammers as much as 50% larger may be used advantageously.

PROBLEMS

15-1. The falling ram of a drop hammer used to drive a timber pile is 5,000 lb. The free-fall height during driving was 19 in., and the average penetration for the last eight blows was $\frac{1}{2}$ in. per blow. What is the safe rated load using the *Engineering News* equation?

15-2. If the hammer in Prob. 15-1 had been a single-acting steam type what will be the safe rated load using the *Engineering News* equation?

15-3. If the hammer in Prob. 15-1 had been a double-acting steam type having a rated total energy of ram at the bottom of a stroke of 19,150 ft-lb, what will be the safe rated load using the *Engineering News* equation?

15-4. If a BSP 1000 double-acting steam hammer is used to drive a pile and the average penetration per blow for the last 10 blows is $\frac{1}{4}$ in., what will be the safe rated load using the *Engineering News* equation?

REFERENCES

1. "A Performance Investigation of Pile-Driving Hammers and Piles, Final Report," Michigan State Highway Commission, Lansing, MI, March 1965.
2. Bayshore Concrete Products, P.O. Box 230, Cape Charles, VA 23310.
3. Berkel & Company Contractors, Inc., 2649 South 142nd St., Bonner Springs, KS 66012.
4. Berminghammer Corporation Limited, Wellington St. Marine Terminal, Hamilton, Ontario L8L 4Z9, Canada.
5. Bethlehem Steel Corporation, Piling Products, Bethlehem, PA 18016.
6. Bruce, R. N., Jr., and D. C. Hebert: "Splicing of Precast Prestressed Concrete Piles: Part 1—Review and Performance of Splices," *Journal of the Prestressed Concrete Institute*, Prestressed Concrete Institute, vol. 19, no. 5, September–October 1974.
7. Deep Foundation Institute, P.O. Box 281, Sparta, NJ 07871.
8. *Design of Pile Foundations, Technical Engineering and Design Guides as Adapted from the U.S. Army Corps of Engineers, no. 1,* American Society of Civil Engineers, New York, NY 10017, 1993.
9. Gendron, G. J.: "Pile Driving: Hammers and Driving Methods," *Highway Research Record No. 333,* Transportation Research Board, Washington, DC, 1970.
10. Goble, G. G., K. Fricke, and G. E. Likens, Jr.: "Driving Stresses in Concrete Piles," *Journal of Prestressed Concrete Institute,* vol. 21, pp. 70–88, January–February 1976.
11. Goble, G. G., G. E. Likens, and F. Rausche: "Bearing Capacity of Piles from Dynamic Measurements," Final Report, Department of Civil Engineering, Case Western Reserve University, Cleveland, OH 44106, March 1975.
12. Housel, W. S., "Michigan Study of Pile-Driving Hammers," *Journal of the Soil Mechanics and Foundation Division,* in *Proceedings of the ASCE,* vol. 91, pp. 37–64, September 1965.
13. Ken-Jet Industries Ltd., 1275 Cardiff Blvd., Mississauga, Ontario L5S 1R1, Canada.
14. "Manual for Quality Control," PCI MNL-116-85, Prestressed Concrete Institute, 201 N. Wells St., Chicago, IL 60606.

15. McClelland, B., J. A. Focht, Jr., and W. J. Emrich: "Problems in Design and Installation of Offshore Piles," *Journal of the Soil Mechanics and Foundation Division*, in *Proceedings of the ASCE*, vol. 95, pp. 1491–1514, November 1969.
16. "Michigan Pile Test Program Results Are Released," *Engineering News-Record*, vol. 164, pp. 26–34, May 20, 1965.
17. "Practical Guidelines for the Selection, Design and Installation of Piles," American Society of Civil Engineers, New York, NY 10017, 1984.
18. Rausche, Frank, and George G. Goble: "Performance of Pile-Driving Hammers," *Journal of the Construction Division*, in *Proceedings of the ASCE*, vol. 98, pp. 201–218, September 1972.
19. Rausche, F., Fred Moses, and G. G. Goble: "Soil Resistance Predictions from Pile Dynamics," *Journal of the Soil Mechanics and Foundation Division*, in *Proceedings of the ASCE*, vol. 98, pp. 917–937, September 1972.
20. "Recommended Practice for Design, Manufacture, and Installation of Prestressed Concrete Piling," *Journal of the Prestressed Concrete Institute*, Prestressed Concrete Institute, vol. 22, no. 2, March–April, 1977.
21. Rempe, D. M., and M. T. Davisson: "Performance of the Diesel Pile Hammer," In *Proceedings of the Ninth International Conference of Soil Mechanics and Foundation Engineering*, ISSMFE, Tokyo, Japan, 1977.
22. Samson, C. H., T. J. Hirsch, and L. L. Lowery: "Computer Study of Dynamic Behavior of Piling," *Journal of the Structural Division*, in *Proceedings of the ASCE*, vol. 89, pp. 413–440, August 1963.
23. Sandhu, Balbir S.: "Predicting Driving Stresses in Piles," *Journal of the Construction Division*, In *Proceedings of the ASCE*, vol. 108, pp. 485–503, December 1982.
24. Sullivan, Richard A., and Charles J. Ehlers: "Planning for Driving Offshore Piles," *Journal of the Construction Division*, in *Proceedings of the ASCE*, vol. 49, pp. 59–79, July 1973.
25. Thorburn, S., and J. Q. Thorburn: "Review of Problems Associated with the Construction of Cast-in-Place Concrete Piles," *Report PG2*, Construction Industry Research and Information Association, London, January 1977.
26. Tidewater Construction Corporation, P.O. Box 57, Norfolk, VA 23501.

CHAPTER 16

PUMPING EQUIPMENT

INTRODUCTION

Pumps are used extensively on construction projects for such operations as:

1. Removing water from pits, tunnels, and other excavations.
2. Dewatering cofferdams.
3. Furnishing water for jetting and sluicing.
4. Furnishing water for many types of utility services.
5. Lowering the water table for excavations.
6. Foundation grouting.

Most projects require the use of one or more water pumps at various stages during the period of construction. Construction pumps must frequently perform under severe conditions, such as those resulting from variations in the pumping head or from handling water that is muddy, sandy and trashy, or highly corrosive. The required rate of pumping may vary considerably during the duration of a construction project. The most satisfactory solution to the pumping problem may be a single all-purpose pump, or possibly the use of several types and sizes of pumps, to permit operational flexibility. The proper solution is to select the equipment which will take care of the pumping needs adequately at the lowest total cost, taking into account the investment in pumping equipment, the cost of operating the pumps, and any losses that will result from possible failure of the pumps to operate satisfactorily. This last fact can be critical when considering dewatering applications.

For some projects a pump may be the most critical item of construction equipment, even though it is not a direct production machine. In constructing a multimillion-dollar concrete and earth-filled dam, a contractor used a single centrifugal pump to supply water from a nearby stream. The water was used to wash all concrete aggregate, for mixing and curing the concrete, and for compaction moisture in the earth-filled dam. When the pump developed mechanical trouble and the rate of pumping dropped below the job requirements for several days, progress on the project suffered a loss of approximately 25%. With the fixed costs exceeding $4,000 per day, the loss due to the partial failure of the pump exceeded $1,000 per day.

The factors that should be considered in selecting pumps for construction applications include:

1. Dependability.
2. Availability of repair parts.
3. Simplicity to permit easy repairs.
4. Economical installation and operation.
5. Operating power requirements.

CLASSIFICATION OF PUMPS

The pumps commonly used on construction projects may be classified as:

1. Displacement
   a. Reciprocating
   b. Diaphragm
2. Centrifugal
   a. Conventional
   b. Self-priming
   c. Air-operated

Reciprocating pumps. A reciprocating pump operates as the result of the movement of a piston inside a cylinder. When the piston is moved in one direction, the water ahead of the piston is forced out of the cylinder. At the same time additional water is drawn into the cylinder behind the piston. Regardless of the direction of movement of the piston, water is forced out of one end and drawn into the other end of the cylinder. This is classified as a double-acting pump. If water is pumped during a piston movement in one direction only, the pump is classified as single-acting. If a pump contains more than one cylinder, mounted side by side, it is classified as a duplex for two cylinders, triplex for three cylinders, etc. Thus, a pump might be classified as duplex double-acting, duplex single-acting.

The volume of water pumped in one stroke will equal the area of the cylinder times the length of the stroke, less a small deduction for slippage through the valves or past the piston, usually about 3 to 5%. If this volume is expressed in cubic inches, it may be converted to gallons by dividing by 231, the number of cubic inches in a gallon. The volume pumped in gallons per minute (gpm) by a simplex double-acting pump will be

$$Q = c\frac{\pi d^2 ln}{4 \times 231} \qquad (16\text{-}1)$$

where Q = capacity of a pump, gpm

c = one-slip allowance; varies from 0.95 to 0.97

d = diameter of cylinder, in.

l = length of stroke, in.

n = number of strokes per min (*Note:* The movement of the piston in either direction is a stroke.)

The volume pumped per minute by a multiplex double-acting pump will be

$$Q = Nc\frac{\pi d^2 ln}{4 \times 231} \qquad (16\text{-}2)$$

where N = number of cylinders in pump.

The energy required to operate a pump will be

$$W = \frac{wQh}{e}$$

where W = energy, ft-lb per min

w = weight of one gallon of water, lb

h = total pumping head, in ft, including friction loss in pipe

e = efficiency of the pump, expressed decimally

The horsepower required by the pump will be

$$P = \frac{W}{33,000} = \frac{wQh}{33,000e} \qquad (16\text{-}3)$$

where P = power, hp.

33,000 = ft-lb of energy per minute for 1 hp

Example 16-1. How many gallons of freshwater will be pumped per minute by a duplex double-acting pump, size 6 × 12 in., driven by a crankshaft making 90 rpm? If the total head is 160 ft and the efficiency of the pump is 60%, what is the minimum horsepower required to operate the pump? The weight of water is 8.34 lb per gal.

Assume a water slippage of 4%. If we apply Eq. (16-2), the rate of pumping will be

$$Q = Nc\frac{\pi d^2 ln}{924}$$

$$= \frac{2 \times 0.96 \times \pi \times 36 \times 12 \times 180}{924} = 508 \text{ gpm}$$

Applying formula (16-3), the power required by the pump will be

$$P = \frac{wQh}{33,000e}$$

$$= \frac{8.34 \times 508 \times 160}{33,000 \times 0.60} = 34.2 \text{ hp}$$

The capacity of a reciprocating pump depends essentially on the speed at which the pump is operated and is independent of the head. The maximum head at which a reciprocating pump will deliver water depends on the strength of the component parts of the pump and the power available to operate the pump. The capacity of this type of pump may be varied considerably by varying the speed of the pump.

Because the flow of water from each cylinder of a reciprocating pump stops and starts every time the direction of piston travel is reversed, a characteristic of this type of pump is to deliver water with pulsations. The amplitude of the pulsations may be reduced by using more cylinders and by installing an air chamber on the discharge side of a pump.

The advantages of reciprocating pumps are:

1. They are able to pump at a uniform rate against varying heads.
2. Their capacity can be increased by increasing the speed.
3. They have reasonably high efficiency regardless of the head and speed.
4. They are usually self-priming.

The disadvantages of reciprocating pumps are:

1. The heavy weight and large size for the given capacity.
2. The possibility of valve trouble, especially in pumping water containing abrasive solids.
3. The pulsating flow of water.
4. The danger of damaging a pump when operating against a high head.

Diaphragm pumps. The principle under which a diaphragm pump operates is illustrated in Fig. 16-1. The central portion of the flexible diaphragm is alternately raised and lowered by the pump rod, which is connected to a walking beam. This action draws water into and discharges it from the pump. Because this type of pump will handle clear water or water containing large quantities of mud, sand, sludge, and trash, it is popular as a construction pump. It is suitable for use on jobs where the quantity of water varies considerably, as the loss of prime during low flow does not prevent the pump from automatically repriming when the quantity of water increases. The accessible diaphragm may be replaced easily.

The Contractors Pump Bureau specifies that diaphragm pumps shall be manufactured in the size and capacity ratings given in Table 16-1.

Centrifugal pumps. A centrifugal pump contains a rotation element, called an "impeller," which imparts to water passing through the pump a velocity sufficiently great

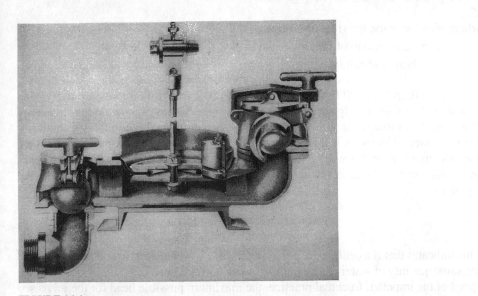

FIGURE 16-1
Section through a diaphragm pump.

to cause it to flow from the pump, even against considerable pressure. A mass of water may possess energy due to either its height above a given datum or its velocity. The former is potential, whereas the latter is kinetic energy. One type of energy can be converted into the other under favorable conditions. The kinetic energy imparted to a particle of water as it passes through the impeller is sufficient to cause the particles to rise to some determinable height.

The principle of the centrifugal pump may be illustrated by considering a drop of water at rest at a height h above a surface. If the drop of water is permitted to fall freely, it will strike the surface with a velocity given by the equation

$$V = \sqrt{2gh} \qquad (16\text{-}4)$$

TABLE 16-1
Minimum capacities for diaphragm pumps at 10-ft suction lifts[†]

Size	Capacity (gph)
Two-in. single	2,000
Three-in. single	3,000
Four-in. single	6,000
Four-in. double	9,000

[†] Diaphragm pumps shall be tested with standard contractor's type suction hose 5 ft longer than the suction lift shown.
Source: Courtesy Contractors Pump Bureau.

where V = velocity, fps (feet per second)

g = acceleration of gravity, equal to 32.2 ft per sec at sea level

h = height of fall, ft

If the drop falls 100 ft, the velocity will be 80.2 fps. If the same drop is given an upward velocity of 80.2 fps, it will rise 100 ft. These values assume no loss in energy due to friction through air. It is the function of the centrifugal pump to give the water the necessary velocity as it leaves the impeller. If the speed of the pump is doubled, the velocity of the water will increase from 80.2 to 160.4 fps, neglecting any increase in friction losses. With this velocity, the water can be pumped to a height given by the equation

$$h = \frac{V^2}{2g} = \frac{(160.4)^2}{64.4} = 400 \text{ ft}$$

This indicates that if a centrifugal pump is pumping water against a total head of 100 ft, the same quantity of water can be pumped against a total head of 400 ft by doubling the speed of the impeller. In actual practice, the maximum possible head for the increased speed will be less than 400 ft because of increases in losses in the pump due to friction. These results illustrate the effect which increasing the speed or the diameter of an impeller has on the performance of a centrifugal pump.

A centrifugal pump may be equipped with an open or an enclosed impeller. Although an enclosed impeller usually has higher efficiency, it will not handle water containing trash as well as an open impeller.

The power required to operate a centrifugal pump is given by Eq. (16-3). The efficiencies of these pumps may be as high as 75%.

Self-priming centrifugal pumps. On construction projects pumps frequently must be set above the surface of the water which is to be pumped. Consequently, self-priming centrifugal pumps are more suitable than the conventional types for use on construction projects. The operation of a self-priming pump is illustrated in Fig. 16-2. A check valve on the suction side of the pump permits the chamber to be filled with water prior to starting the pump. When the pump is started, the water in the chamber produces a seal flow through channel A into the chamber, where the air escapes through the discharge, and the water flows down through channel B to the impeller. This action continues until all the air is exhausted from the suction line and water enters the pump. When a pump is stopped, it will retain its charge of priming water indefinitely. Such a pump is self-priming to heights in excess of 25 ft when in good mechanical condition.

Submersible pumps. Figure 16-3 illustrates an electric-motor-operated submersible pump which can be very useful in dewatering tunnels, foundation pits, trenches, and similar places. Figure 16-4 is a performance curve for this pump when operated against varying heads of water. The figure includes pertinent information related to the pump. Other types and models have different performance characteristics.

Multistage centrifugal pumps. If a centrifugal pump has a single impeller, it is described as a single-stage pump, whereas if there are two or more impellers and the water

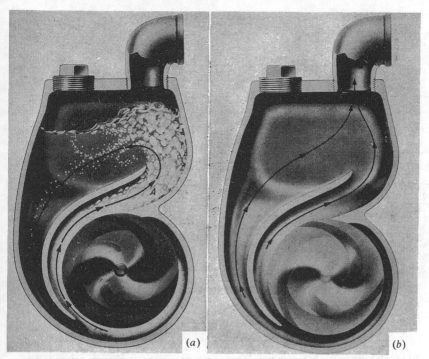

FIGURE 16-2
Section through a self-priming centrifugal pump. (*a*) Priming action. (*b*) Pumping action.

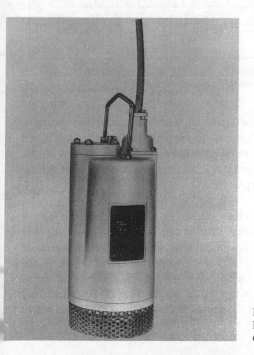

FIGURE 16-3
Electric-motor-operated submersible pump. (*The Gorman-Rupp Co.*)

473

Model S3B1 .... Centrifugal, single stage

Discharge .... 3 in.

Solids handled .... 3/8 in.

Horsepower 6

Hertz 60

RPM 3,450

Voltage .... 230 volt, 1 phase, 7.2 kW
230/460 dual voltage, 3 phase, 6.8 kW
or 575 volt, 3 phase, 6.8 kW

Cable .... #10 gauge, 50-ft length

Weight (pump and cable) .... 125 lb (approx.)

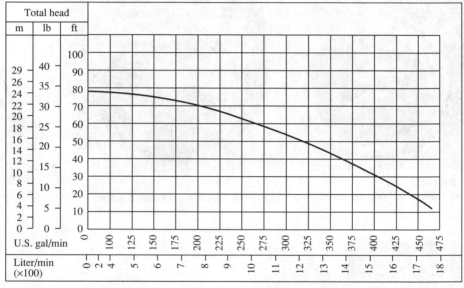

FIGURE 16-4
Performance curve for Gorman-Rupp submersible pump. (*The Gorman-Rupp Co.*)

discharge from one impeller flows into the suction of another, it is described as a multi-stage pump. Multistage pumps are especially suitable for pumping against high heads or pressures, as each stage imparts an additional pressure to the water. Pumps of this type are used frequently to supply water for jetting, where the pressure may run as high as several hundred pounds per square inch (psi).

Performance of centrifugal pumps. Pump manufacturers will furnish sets of curves showing the performance of their pumps under different operating conditions. A set of curves for a given pump will show the variations in capacity, efficiency, and horsepower for different pumping heads. These curves can be very helpful in selecting the pump that is most suitable for a given pumping condition. Figure 16-5 illustrates a set of performance curves for a 10-in. centrifugal pump. For a total head of 60 ft the capacity will be 1,200 gpm, the efficiency 52%, and the required power 35 brake horsepower

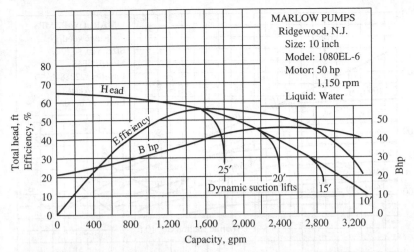

FIGURE 16-5
Performance curves for centrifugal pump.

(bhp). If the total head is reduced to 50 ft and the dynamic suction lift does not exceed 23 ft, the capacity will be 1,930 gpm, the efficiency 55%, and the required power 44 bhp. This pump will not deliver any water against a total head in excess of 66 ft, which is called the "shutoff head."

Since a construction pump frequently is operated under varying heads, it is desirable to select a pump with relatively flat head capacity and horsepower curves, even though efficiency must be sacrificed in order to obtain these conditions. A pump with a flat horsepower demand permits the use of an engine or an electric motor that will provide adequate power over a wide pumping range, without a substantial surplus or deficiency regardless of the head.

The effect of varying the speed of a centrifugal pump is illustrated by the curves in Fig. 16-6.

The Contractors Pump Bureau publishes pump standards for several types of pumps, including self-priming centrifugal pumps, given in Tables 16-2 and 16-3 [1].

LOSS OF HEAD DUE TO FRICTION IN PIPE

Table 16-4 gives the nominal loss of head due to water flowing through clean iron or steel pipe. The actual losses may differ from the values given in the table because of variations in the diameter of a pipe and in the condition of the inside surface.

The relationship between the head of freshwater in feet and pressure in psi is given by the equation

$$h = 2.31p \tag{16-5}$$

or

$$p = 0.433h \tag{16-6}$$

where h = depth of water or head, ft

p = pressure at depth h, psi

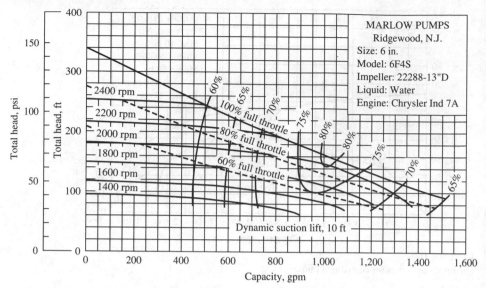

FIGURE 16-6
The effect of varying the speed on the performance of a centrifugal pump.

Table 16-5 gives the equivalent length of straight steel pipe having the same loss in head due to water friction as fittings and valves.

LOSS OF HEAD DUE TO FRICTION IN RUBBER HOSE

The flexibility of rubber hose makes it a desirable substitute for pipe for use with pumps on many jobs. Such a hose may be used on the suction side of a pump if it is constructed with a wire insert to prevent collapse under partial vacuum. Rubber hose is available with end fittings corresponding with those for iron or steel pipe.

Table 16-6 gives the loss in head in feet per 100 ft due to friction caused by water flowing through the hose. The values in the table apply for rubber substitutes.

SELECTING A PUMP

Before a pump for a given job is selected, it is necessary to analyze all information and conditions that will affect the selection. The most satisfactory pumping equipment will be the combination of pump and pipe that will provide the required service for the least total cost. The total cost includes the installed and operating cost of the pump and pipe for the period that it will be used, with an appropriate allowance for salvage value at the

TABLE 16-2a
Minimum capacities for M-rated self-priming centrifugal pumps manufactured in accordance with standards of the Contractors Pump Bureau

Model 6-M ($1\frac{1}{2}$-in.)

Total head including friction [ft (m)]		Height of pump above water [ft (m)]								
		5	(1.5)	10	(3.0)	15	(4.6)	20	(6.1)	25	(7.6)
		Capacity [gpm (l/min)†]									
5	(1.5)	100	(379)								
10	(3.0)	96	(363)								
15	(4.6)	93	(352)	85	(322)						
20	(6.1)	89	(337)	84	(318)	68	(257)				
25	(7.6)	85	(322)	82	(310)	67	(254)				
30	(9.1)	80	(303)	79	(299)	66	(250)	49	(186)	35	(133)
40	(12.2)	71	(269)	71	(269)	60	(227)	46	(174)	33	(125)
50	(15.2)	59	(223)	59	(223)	52	(197)	41	(155)	28	(106)
60	(18.3)	42	(159)	42	(159)	40	(151)	32	(121)	22	(83)
70	(21.3)	22	(83)	22	(83)	22	(83)	20	(75)	12	(45)

Model 8-M (2-in.)

Total head including friction [ft (m)]		Height of pump above water [ft (m)]								
		5	(1.5)	10	(3.0)	15	(4.6)	20	(6.1)	25	(7.6)
		Capacity [gpm (l/min)†]									
5	(1.5)	140	(530)								
10	(3.0)	137	(519)								
20	(6.1)	135	(511)	117	(443)						
25	(7.6)	133	(503)	116	(439)						
30	(9.1)	132	(500)	116	(439)	102	(386)	82	(310)		
40	(12.2)	123	(466)	105	(397)	100	(379)	80	(303)	58	(220)
50	(15.2)	109	(413)	92	(348)	90	(341)	76	(288)	55	(208)
60	(18.3)	90	(341)	70	(265)	70	(265)	70	(265)	55	(208)
70	(21.3)	66	(250)	40	(151)	40	(151)	40	(151)	40	(151)
80	(24.4)	40	(151)	40	(151)	40	(151)	40	(151)	40	(151)

† Liters per minute.
Courtesy Contractors Pump Bureau.

TABLE 16-2b
Minimum capacities for M-rated self-priming centrifugal pumps manufactured in accordance with standards of the Contractors Pump Bureau

Model 12-M (2-in.)									
Total head including friction [ft (m)]		Height of pump above water [ft (m)]							
	5	(1.5)	10	(3.0)	15	(4.6)	20	(6.1)	25	(7.6)
				Capacity [gpm (l/min)[†]]					

Total head including friction [ft (m)]	5	(1.5)	10	(3.0)	15	(4.6)	20	(6.1)	25	(7.6)
5 (1.5)	200	(757)								
10 (3.0)	196	(742)								
20 (6.1)	190	(719)	167	(632)						
25 (7.6)	185	(700)	166	(628)						
30 (9.1)	174	(659)	165	(625)	140	(530)	110	(416)		
40 (12.2)	158	(598)	158	(598)	140	(530)	110	(416)	75	(284)
50 (15.2)	145	(549)	145	(549)	130	(492)	106	(401)	70	(265)
60 (18.3)	126	(477)	126	(477)	117	(443)	97	(367)	68	(257)
70 (21.3)	102	(386)	102	(386)	100	(379)	85	(322)	60	(227)
80 (24.4)	74	(280)	74	(280)	74	(280)	68	(257)	48	(181)
90 (27.4)	40	(151)	40	(151)	40	(151)	40	(151)	32	(121)

Model 18-M (3-in.)									

Total head including friction [ft (m)]	5	(1.5)	10	(3.0)	15	(4.6)	20	(6.1)	25	(7.6)
				Capacity [gpm (l/min)[†]]					
5 (1.5)	300	(1,136)								
10 (3.0)	295	(1,117)								
20 (6.1)	277	(1,048)	259	(980)						
30 (9.1)	260	(984)	250	(946)	210	(795)	200	(757)		
40 (12.2)	241	(912)	241	(912)	207	(784)	177	(670)	160	(606)
50 (15.2)	225	(852)	225	(852)	202	(765)	172	(651)	140	(530)
60 (18.3)	197	(746)	197	(746)	197	(746)	169	(640)	140	(530)
70 (21.3)	160	(606)	160	(606)	160	(606)	160	(606)	138	(522)
80 (24.4)	125	(473)	125	(473)	125	(473)	125	(473)	125	(473)
90 (27.4)	96	(363)	96	(363)	96	(363)	96	(363)	96	(363)

[†] Liters per minute.
Courtesy Contractors Pump Bureau.

TABLE 16-2c
Minimum capacities for M-rated self-priming centrifugal pumps manufactured in accordance with standards of the Contractors Pump Bureau

Model 20-M (3-in.)

Total head including friction [ft (m)]		Height of pump above water [ft (m)]							
		10	(3.0)	15	(4.6)	20	(6.1)	25	(7.6)
		Capacity [gpm (l/min)†]							
30	(9.1)	333	(1,260)	280	(1,060)	235	(890)	165	(625)
40	(12.2)	315	(1,192)	270	(1,022)	230	(871)	162	(613)
50	(15.2)	290	(1,098)	255	(965)	220	(833)	154	(583)
60	(18.3)	255	(965)	235	(890)	205	(776)	143	(541)
70	(21.3)	212	(802)	209	(791)	184	(696)	130	(492)
80	(24.4)	165	(625)	165	(625)	157	(594)	114	(432)
90	(27.4)	116	(439)	116	(439)	116	(439)	94	(356)
100	(30.5)	60	(227)	60	(227)	60	(227)	60	(227)

Model 40-M (4-in.)

Total head including friction [ft (m)]		Height of pump above water [ft (m)]							
		10	(3.0)	15	(4.6)	20	(6.1)	25	(7.6)
		Capacity [gpm (l/min)†]							
25	(7.6)	667	(2,525)						
30	(9.1)	660	(2,498)	575	(2,176)	475	(1,798)	355	(1,344)
40	(12.2)	645	(2,441)	565	(2,139)	465	(1,760)	350	(1,325)
50	(15.2)	620	(2,347)	545	(2,063)	455	(1,722)	345	(1,306)
60	(18.3)	585	(2,214)	510	(1,930)	435	(1,647)	335	(1,268)
70	(21.3)	535	(2,025)	475	(1,798)	410	(1,552)	315	(1,192)
80	(24.4)	465	(1,760)	410	(1,551)	365	(1,382)	280	(976)
90	(27.4)	375	(1,419)	325	(1,230)	300	(1,136)	220	(833)
100	(30.5)	250	(946)	215	(815)	195	(738)	145	(549)
110	(33.5)	65	(246)	60	(227)	50	(189)	40	(151)

†Liters per minute.
Courtesy Contractors Pump Bureau.

TABLE 16-2d
Minimum capacities for M-rated self-priming centrifugal pumps manufactured in accordance with standards of the Contractors Pump Bureau

Model 90-M (6-in.)

Total head including friction [ft (m)]		Height of pump above water [ft (m)]							
		10	(3.0)	15	(4.6)	20	(6.1)	25	(7.6)
		Capacity [gpm (l/min)[†]]							
25	(7.6)	1,500	(5,678)						
30	(9.1)	1,480	(5,602)	1,280	(4,845)	1,050	(3,974)	790	(2,990)
40	(12.2)	1,430	(5,413)	1,230	(4,656)	1,020	(3,861)	780	(2,952)
50	(15.2)	1,350	(5,110)	1,160	(4,391)	970	(3,672)	735	(2,782)
60	(18.3)	1,225	(4,637)	1,050	(3,974)	900	(3,407)	690	(2,612)
70	(21.3)	1,050	(3,974)	900	(3,407)	775	(2,933)	610	(2,309)
80	(24.4)	800	(3,028)	680	(2,574)	600	(2,271)	490	(1,855)
90	(27.4)	450	(1,703)	400	(1,514)	365	(1,382)	300	(1,136)
100	(30.5)	100	(379)	100	(379)	100	(379)	100	(379)

Model 125-M (8-in.)

Total head including friction [ft (m)]		Height of pump above water [ft (m)]							
		10	(3.0)	15	(4.6)	20	(6.1)	25	(7.6)
		Capacity [gpm (l/min)[†]]							
25	(7.6)	2,100	(7,949)	1,850	(7,002)	1,570	(5,943)		
30	(9.1)	2,060	(7,797)	1,820	(6,889)	1,560	(5,905)	1,200	(4,542)
40	(12.2)	1,960	(7,419)	1,740	(6,586)	1,520	(5,753)	1,170	(4,429)
50	(15.2)	1,800	(6,813)	1,620	(6,132)	1,450	(5,488)	1,140	(4,315)
60	(18.3)	1,640	(6,207)	1,500	(5,678)	1,360	(5,148)	1,090	(4,126)
70	(21.3)	1,460	(5,526)	1,340	(5,072)	1,250	(4,731)	1,015	(3,841)
80	(24.4)	1,250	(4,731)	1,170	(4,429)	1,110	(4,201)	950	(3,596)
90	(27.4)	1,020	(3,861)	980	(3,709)	940	(3,558)	840	(3,179)
100	(30.5)	800	(3,028)	760	(2,877)	710	(2,687)	680	(2,574)
110	(33.5)	570	(2,158)	540	(2,044)	500	(1,893)	470	(1,779)
120	(36.6)	275	(1,041)	245	(927)	240	(908)	240	(908)

[†]Liters per minute.
Courtesy Contractors Pump Bureau.

TABLE 16-2e
Minimum capacities for M-rated self-priming centrifugal pumps manufactured in accordance with standards of the Contractors Pump Bureau

Total head including friction [ft (m)]	Model 200-M (10-in.)							
	Height of pump above water [ft (m)]							
	10	**(3.0)**	**15**	**(4.6)**	**20**	**(6.1)**	**25**	**(7.6)**
	Capacity [gpm (l/min)[†]]							
20 (6.1)	3,350	(12,680)	3,000	(11,355)				
30 (9.1)	3,000	(11,355)	2,800	(10,598)	2,500	(9,463)	1,550	(5,867)
40 (12.2)	2,500	(9,463)	2,500	(9,463)	2,250	(8,516)	1,500	(5,678)
50 (15.2)	2,000	(7,570)	2,000	(7,570)	2,000	(7,570)	1,350	(5,110)
60 (18.3)	1,300	(4,921)	1,300	(4,921)	1,300	(4,921)	1,150	(4,353)
70 (21.3)	500	(1,893)	500	(1,893)	500	(1,893)	500	(1,893)

[†]Liters per minute.
Courtesy Contractors Pump Bureau.

completion of the project. In order to analyze the cost of pumping water, it is necessary to have certain information, such as:

1. The rate at which the water is pumped.

2. The height of the lift from the existing water surface to the point of discharge.

3. The pressure head at discharge, if any.

4. The variations in water level at suction or discharge.

5. The altitude of the project.

6. The height of the pump above the surface of water to be pumped.

7. The size of pipe to be used, if already determined.

8. The number, sizes, and types of fittings and valves in the pipeline.

The examples which follow illustrate the methods of selecting pumps and pumping systems.

Example 16-2. Select a self-priming centrifugal pump, with a capacity of 600 gpm, for the project illustrated in Fig. 16-7. All the pipe, fittings, and valves will be 6 in. with threaded connections. Use the information in Table 16-5 to convert the fittings and valves into equivalent lengths of pipe.

(Example continues)

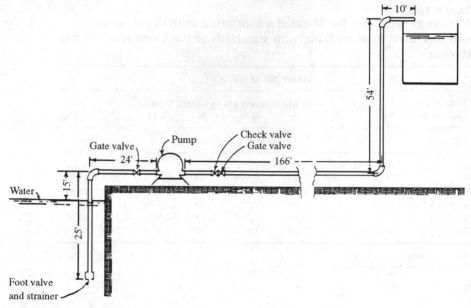

FIGURE 16-7
Pump and pipe installation for Example 16-2.

Item	Equivalent length of pipe (ft)
One foot valve and strainer	76
Three elbows @ 16 ft	48
Two gate valves @ 3.5 ft	7
One check valve	63
Total	194
Add length of pipe (25 + 24 + 166 + 54 + 10)	279
Total equivalent length of 6-in pipe	473

From Table 16-4 the friction loss per 100 ft of 6-in. pipe will be 3.10 ft. The total head, including lift plus head lost in friction, will be:

Lift,	15 + 54	= 69.0 ft
Head lost in friction, 473 ft @ 3.10 ft per 100 ft		= 14.7 ft
Total head		= 83.7 ft

Table 16-2d indicates that a model 90-M pump will deliver the required quantity of water.

TABLE 16-3a
Minimum capacities for MT-rated solids handling, self-priming centrifugal pumps manufactured in accordance with standards of the Contractors Pump Bureau

Model 6-MT ($1\frac{1}{2}$-in.)

Total head including friction [ft (m)]		Height of pump above water [ft (m)]									
		5	(1.5)	10	(3.0)	15	(4.6)	20	(6.1)	25	(7.6)
		Capacity [gpm (l/min)[†]]									
5	(1.5)	100	(379)								
10	(3.0)	96	(363)								
20	(6.1)	89	(337)	84	(318)	68	(257)				
30	(9.1)	80	(303)	79	(299)	66	(250)	49	(186)	35	(133)
40	(12.2)	71	(269)	71	(269)	60	(227)	46	(174)	33	(125)
50	(15.2)	59	(223)	59	(223)	52	(197)	41	(155)	28	(106)
60	(18.3)	42	(159)	42	(159)	40	(151)	32	(121)	22	(83)
70	(21.3)	22	(83)	22	(83)	22	(83)	20	(75)	12	(45)

Model 11-MT (2-in.)

Total head including friction [ft (m)]		Height of pump above water [ft (m)]									
		5	(1.5)	10	(3.0)	15	(4.6)	20	(6.1)	25	(7.6)
		Capacity [gpm (l/min)[†]]									
5	(1.5)	185	(700)								
10	(3.0)	183	(693)								
20	(6.1)	178	(674)	164	(621)	132	(500)				
30	(9.1)	169	(640)	164	(621)	132	(500)	105	(397)	75	(284)
40	(12.2)	164	(621)	164	(621)	132	(500)	105	(397)	75	(284)
50	(15.2)	150	(568)	150	(568)	132	(500)	105	(397)	75	(284)
60	(18.3)	135	(511)	135	(511)	132	(500)	105	(397)	75	(284)
70	(21.3)	88	(333)	88	(333)	88	(333)	88	(333)	68	(257)
80	(24.4)	40	(151)	40	(151)	40	(151)	40	(151)	40	(151)

[†]Liters per minute.
Courtesy Contractors Pump Bureau.

TABLE 16-3b

Minimum capacities for MT-rated solids handling, self-priming centrifugal pumps manufactured in accordance with standards of the Contractors Pump Bureau

Model 18-MT (3-in.)

Total head including friction [ft (m)]	Height of pump above water [ft (m)]							
	10	(3.0)	15	(4.6)	20	(6.1)	25	(7.6)
	Capacity [gpm (l/min)†]							
20 (6.1)	310	(1173)	265	(1003)				
30 (9.1)	305	(1154)	265	(1003)	200	(757)	115	(435)
40 (12.2)	300	(1136)	265	(1003)	200	(757)	110	(416)
50 (15.2)	275	(1041)	260	(984)	200	(757)	105	(397)
60 (18.3)	215	(814)	215	(814)	200	(757)	100	(379)
70 (21.3)	170	(644)	170	(644)	170	(644)	100	(379)
80 (24.4)	87	(329)	87	(329)	87	(329)	87	(329)
90 (27.4)	25	(95)	25	(95)	25	(95)	25	(95)

Model 33-MT (4-in.)

Total head including friction [ft (m)]	Height of pump above water [ft (m)]							
	10	(3.0)	15	(4.6)	20	(6.1)	25	(7.6)
	Capacity [gpm (l/min)†]							
30 (9.1)	550	(2,082)	460	(1,741)	350	(1,325)	240	(908)
40 (12.2)	540	(2,044)	455	(1,722)	350	(1,325)	240	(908)
50 (15.2)	500	(1,893)	430	(1,628)	340	(1,287)	230	(871)
60 (18.3)	450	(1,703)	395	(1,495)	320	(1,211)	220	(833)
70 (21.3)	370	(1,401)	360	(1,363)	300	(1,136)	210	(795)
80 (24.4)	275	(1,041)	275	(1,041)	260	(984)	180	(681)
90 (27.4)	190	(719)	190	(719)	190	(719)	150	(568)
100 (30.5)	100	(379)	100	(379)	100	(379)	100	(379)

† Liters per minute.
Courtesy Contractors Pump Bureau.

TABLE 16-3c

Minimum capacities for MT-rated solids handling, self-priming centrifugal pumps manufactured in accordance with standards of the Contractors Pump Bureau

Model 35-MT (4-in.)

Total head including friction [ft (m)]		Height of pump above water [ft (m)]							
		10	(3.0)	15	(4.6)	20	(6.1)	25	(7.6)
		Capacity [gpm (l/min)†]							
30	(9.1)	585	(2,214)	500	(1,893)	350	(1,325)	240	(908)
40	(12.2)	585	(2,214)	500	(1,893)	350	(1,325)	240	(908)
50	(15.2)	585	(2,214)	500	(1,893)	350	(1,325)	240	(908)
60	(18.3)	545	(2,063)	500	(1,893)	350	(1,325)	240	(908)
70	(21.3)	495	(1,874)	480	(1,817)	350	(1,325)	240	(908)
80	(24.4)	430	(1,628)	420	(1,590)	340	(1,287)	240	(908)
90	(27.4)	320	(1,211)	320	(1,211)	260	(984)	220	(833)
100	(30.5)	100	(379)	100	(379)	100	(379)	100	(379)

Model 70-MT (6-in.)

Total head including friction [ft (m)]		Height of pump above water [ft (m)]							
		10	(3.0)	15	(4.6)	20	(6.1)	25	(7.6)
		Capacity [gpm (l/min)†]							
30	(9.1)	1,180	(4,466)	975	(3,690)	715	(2,706)	350	(1,325)
40	(12.2)	1,175	(4,447)	950	(3,596)	715	(2,706)	350	(1,325)
50	(15.2)	1,160	(4,391)	935	(3,539)	715	(2,706)	350	(1,325)
60	(18.3)	1,150	(4,353)	925	(3,501)	715	(2,706)	350	(1,325)
70	(21.3)	1,120	(4,239)	900	(3,407)	715	(2,706)	350	(1,325)
80	(24.4)	950	(3,596)	875	(3,312)	700	(2,650)	350	(1,325)
90	(27.4)	700	(2,650)	700	(2,650)	600	(2,271)	350	(1,325)
100	(30.5)	450	(1,703)	450	(1,703)	450	(1,703)	300	(1,136)
110	(33.5)	200	(757)	200	(757)	200	(757)	200	(757)

†Liters per minute.
Courtesy Contractors Pump Bureau.

TABLE 16-4
Water friction loss, in feet per 100 ft for clean iron or steel pipe[†]

Flow in U.S. (gpm)	Nominal diameter of pipe (in.)													
	$\frac{1}{2}$	$\frac{3}{4}$	1	$1\frac{1}{4}$	$1\frac{1}{2}$	2	$2\frac{1}{2}$	3	4	5	6	8	10	12
5	26.5	6.8	2.11	0.55										
10	95.8	24.7	7.61	1.98	0.93	0.31	0.11							
15		52.0	16.3	4.22	1.95	0.70	0.23							
20		88.0	27.3	7.21	3.38	1.18	0.40							
25			41.6	10.8	5.07	1.75	0.60	0.25						
30			57.8	15.3	7.15	2.45	0.84	0.35						
40				26.0	12.2	4.29	1.4	0.59						
50				39.0	18.5	6.43	2.2	0.9	0.22					
75					39.0	13.6	4.6	2.0	0.48	0.16				
100					66.3	23.3	7.8	3.2	0.79	0.27	0.09			
125						35.1	11.8	4.9	1.2	0.42	0.18			
150						49.4	16.6	6.8	1.7	0.57	0.21			
175						66.3	22.0	9.1	2.2	0.77	0.31			
200							28.0	11.6	2.9	0.96	0.40			
225							35.3	14.5	3.5	1.2	0.48			
250							43.0	17.7	4.4	1.5	0.60	0.15		
275								21.2	5.2	1.8	0.75	0.18		
300								24.7	6.1	2.0	0.84	0.21		
350								33.8	8.0	2.7	0.91	0.27		
400									10.4	3.5	1.4	0.35		
500									15.6	5.3	2.2	0.53	0.18	0.08
600									22.4	6.2	3.1	0.74	0.25	0.10
700									30.4	9.9	4.1	1.0	0.34	0.14
800											5.2	1.3	0.44	0.18
900											6.6	1.6	0.54	0.22
1,000											7.8	2.0	0.65	0.27
1,100											9.3	2.3	0.78	0.32
1,200											10.8	2.7	0.95	0.37
1,300											12.7	3.1	1.1	0.42
1,400											14.7	3.6	1.2	0.48
1,500											16.8	4.1	1.4	0.55
2,000												7.0	2.4	0.93
3,000													5.1	2.1
4,000														3.5
5,000														5.5

[†] For old or rough pipes, add 50% to friction values.
Courtesy Contractors Pump Bureau.

TABLE 16-5
Length of steel pipe, in feet, equivalent to fittings and valves

Item	1	$1\frac{1}{4}$	$1\frac{1}{2}$	2	$2\frac{1}{2}$	3	4	5	6	8	10	12
						Nominal size (in.)						
90° elbow	2.8	3.7	4.3	5.5	6.4	8.2	11.0	13.5	16.0	21.0	26.0	32.0
45° elbow	1.3	1.7	2.0	2.6	3.0	3.8	5.0	6.2	7.5	10.0	13.0	15.0
Tee, side outlet	5.6	7.5	9.1	12.0	13.5	17.0	22.0	27.5	33.0	43.5	55.0	66.0
Close return bend	6.3	8.4	10.2	13.0	15.0	18.5	24.0	31.0	37.0	49.0	62.0	73.0
Gate valve	0.6	0.8	0.9	1.2	1.4	1.7	2.5	3.0	3.5	4.5	5.7	6.8
Globe valve	27.0	37.0	43.0	55.0	66.0	82.0	115.0	135.0	165.0	215.0	280.0	335.0
Check valve	10.5	13.2	15.8	21.1	26.4	31.7	42.3	52.8	63.0	81.0	105.0	125.0
Foot valve	24.0	33.0	38.0	46.0	55.0	64.0	75.0	76.0	76.0	76.0	76.0	76.0

Courtesy The Gorman-Rupp Company.

Sometimes the problem is to select the pump and pipeline that will permit water to be pumped at the lowest total cost. The following example illustrates a method that may be used to select the most economical pumping system.

Example 16-3. In operating a rock quarry, it is necessary to pump 400 gpm of clear water. The pump and pipeline selected will be installed as illustrated in Fig. 16-8. It is estimated that the pump will be operated a total of 1,200 hours per year. Compare the economy of using 4- and 6-in. steel pipe for the water line. Assume that the pump will have an economic life of 5 years and that the pipeline and fittings will have a life of 10 years. Also, assume that the cost of installing the pipeline will be the same regardless of the size so that this cost may be disregarded.

Consider the use of 4-in. pipe. The total length of pipe will be:

Item	Equivalent length of pipe (ft)
One foot valve and strainer	75
Three elbows @ 11 ft	33
Two gate valves @ 2.5 ft	5
Pipe (20 + 40 + 176 + 44 + 40)	320
Total equivalent length	433

The total head, including lift and head lost in friction, will be:

Lift,   10 + 44   = 54.0 ft
Head lost in friction, 433 ft @ 10.4 ft per 100 ft = 45.0 ft
      Total head   = 99.0 ft

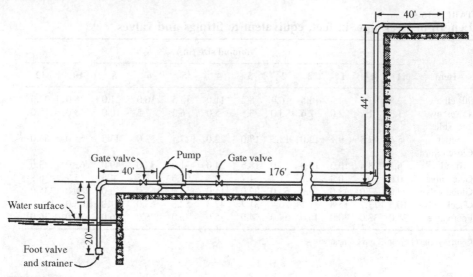

FIGURE 16-8
Pump and pipe installation for Example 16-3.

A model 125-M self-priming pump, with a capacity of approximately 800 gpm, will be required for this installation.

Consider the use of 6-in. pipe. The total equivalent length of pipe will be:

Item	Equivalent length of pipe (ft)
One foot valve and strainer	76
Three elbows @ 16 ft	48
Two gate valves @ 3.5 ft	7
Pipe	320
Total equivalent length	451

The total head, including lift and head lost in friction, will be:

Lift,   10 + 44   = 54.0 ft
Head lost in friction, 451 ft @ 1.4 ft per 100 ft =   6.3 ft
       Total head   = 60.3 ft

A model 40-M self-priming pump, with a capacity of approximately 585 gpm, will be satisfactory for this installation. The excess capacity of this pumping system is an advantage in favor of using 6-in. pipe.

TABLE 16-6
Water friction loss, in feet per 100 ft of smooth bore hose

Flow in U.S. (gpm)	Actual inside diameter of hose (in.)											
	$\frac{5}{8}$	$\frac{3}{4}$	1	$1\frac{1}{4}$	$1\frac{1}{2}$	2	$2\frac{1}{2}$	3	4	5	6	8
5	21.4	8.9	2.2	0.74	0.3							
10	76.8	31.8	7.8	2.64	1.0	0.2						
15		68.5	16.8	5.7	2.3	0.5						
20			28.7	9.6	3.9	0.9	0.32					
25			43.2	14.7	6.0	1.4	0.51					
30			61.2	20.7	8.5	2.0	0.70	0.3				
35			80.5	27.6	11.2	2.7	0.93	0.4				
40				35.0	14.3	3.5	1.2	0.5				
50				52.7	21.8	5.2	1.8	0.7				
60				73.5	30.2	7.3	2.5	1.0				
70					40.4	9.8	3.3	1.3				
80					52.0	12.6	4.3	1.7				
90					64.2	15.7	5.3	2.1	0.5			
100					77.4	18.9	6.5	2.6	0.6			
125						28.6	9.8	4.0	0.9			
150						40.7	13.8	5.6	1.3			
175						53.4	18.1	7.4	1.8			
200						68.5	23.4	9.6	2.3	0.8	0.32	
250							35.0	14.8	3.5	1.2	0.49	
300							49.0	20.3	4.9	1.7	0.69	
350								27.0	6.6	2.3	0.90	
400									8.4	2.9	1.1	0.28
450									10.5	3.6	1.4	0.35
500									12.7	4.3	1.7	0.43
1,000										15.6	6.4	1.6

Courtesy Contractors Pump Bureau.

The cost of each size pipeline, fittings, and valves will be:

Item	Size pipe	
	4 in.	6 in.
A 320-ft pipeline	$776.00	$1,340.00
Three elbows	12.00	24.00
One foot valve	24.00	36.00
Two gate valves	168.00	216.00
Total cost	$980.00	$1,616.00
Depreciation cost per year, based on 10-yr life	98.00	161.60
Depreciation cost per hr, based on 1,200 hr/yr	0.08	0.14

The combined cost per hour for each size pump and pipeline system will be:

Item	Cost per hr	
	4-in. pipe	6-in. pipe
Pump	$2.62	$1.74
Pipe, fittings, and valves	0.08	0.14
Total cost per hr	$2.70	$1.88

This analysis shows that the additional cost of the 6-in. pipe is more than offset by the reduction in the cost of the smaller pump.

WELLPOINT SYSTEMS

In excavating below the surface of the ground, the constructor may encounter ground-water prior to reaching the bottom of a pit. For pits excavated into sand and gravel the flow of water will be large if some method is not adopted to remove the water before it enters the pit. While the water may be permitted to flow into sumps located in the pit and then removed by pumps, the presence of such water usually creates a nuisance and interferes with the construction operations. The installation of a wellpoint system along or around the pit may lower the water table below the bottom of the excavation, thus permitting the work to take place under relatively dry conditions.

A *wellpoint* is a perforated tube enclosed in a screen, which is installed below the surface of the ground in order to collect and remove water from the ground. The essential parts of a wellpoint are illustrated in Fig. 16-9. The top of a wellpoint is attached to a riser pipe. The riser extends to a short distance above the surface of the ground, where

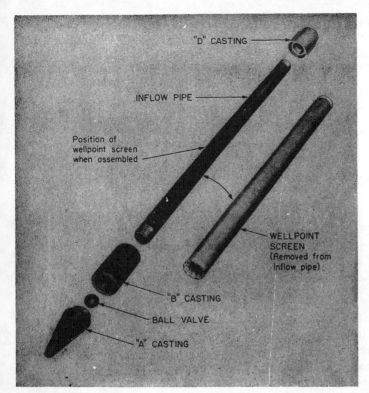

FIGURE 16-9
The essential parts of a wellpoint system.

it is connected to a large pipe called a "header." The header pipe is connected to the suction of a centrifugal pump. A wellpoint system may include a few or several hundred wellpoints, all connected to one or more headers and pumps.

The principle by which a wellpoint system operates is illustrated in Fig. 16-10. Figure 16-10(*a*) shows how a single point will lower the surface of the water table in the soil adjacent to the point. Figure 16-10(*b*) shows how several points, installed reasonably close together, lower the water table over an extended area. A group of wellpoints properly installed along a trench or around a foundation pit can lower the water table below the depth of excavation.

Wellpoints will operate satisfactorily if they are installed in a permeable soil such as sand or gravel. If they are installed in a less permeable soil, such as silt, it may be necessary first to sink a large pipe, say, 6 to 10 in. in diameter, for each point, remove the soil from inside the pipe, install a wellpoint, fill the space inside the pipe with sand or fine gravel, and then withdraw the pipe. This leaves a volume of sand around each wellpoint to act as a water collector and a filter to increase the rate of flow for each point.

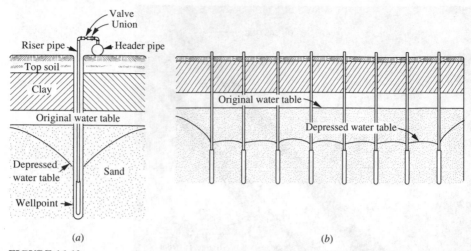

(a)   (b)

FIGURE 16-10
Lowering the water table adjacent to wellpoints.

Wellpoints may be installed at any desired spacing, usually varying from 2 to 5 ft, along the header. The maximum height that water can be lifted is about 18 to 20 ft. If it is necessary to lower the water table to a greater depth, one or more additional stages should be installed, each stage at a lower depth within the excavation. Figure 16-11 shows a typical single-stage wellpoint installation.

Installing a wellpoint system. If the soil conditions are suitable, a wellpoint is jetted into position by forcing water through an opening at the bottom of the point. After each point is jetted into position, it is connected through a pipe or a rubber hose to a header pipe. Header pipes are usually 6 to 10 in. in diameter. A valve is installed between each wellpoint and the header to regulate the flow of water. The header is connected to a self-priming centrifugal pump, which is equipped with an auxiliary air pump to remove any air from the water before it enters the pump proper.

Capacity of a wellpoint system. The capacity of a wellpoint system depends on the number of points installed, the permeability of the soil, and the amount of water present. An engineer who is experienced in this kind of work can make tests which will enable him to estimate with reasonable accuracy the capacity necessary to lower the water to the desired depth. The flow per wellpoint may vary from 3 or 4 gpm to as much as 30 or more gpm on some installations.

When excavating 45 to 50 ft below the surface of the water in the Colorado River for the cutoff wall for the Morelos Dam, the contractor installed three main stages, with a supplemental fourth stage of wellpoints to enclose an area of 15 acres. A total of 2,750 wellpoints were serviced by 49 pumps. The maximum pumping rate was 17,400 gpm, with 2,150 wellpoints in operation. This gave an average yield of 8.1 gpm per point and 528 gpm per pump.

FIGURE 16-11
Single-stage wellpoint installation. (*Moretrench-American Corporation.*)

Prior to designing the wellpoint system for the Davis Dam on the Colorado River, a 45- by 58-ft test area was enclosed with 66 wellpoints, spaced $3\frac{1}{2}$ ft apart, each 21 ft long. The test, which was run for 172 hours, using two 8-in. pumps, gave an average yield of 13 gpm per wellpoint.

PROBLEMS

16-1. A two-cylinder duplex double-acting pump, size 6×12 in., is driven by a crankshaft which makes 120 rpm. If the water slippage is 7%, how many gallons of water will the pump deliver per minute? If the total head is 100 ft and the efficiency of the pump is 60%, what is the minimum horsepower required to operate the pump?

16-2. The centrifugal pump whose performance curves are given in Fig. 16-5 will be used to pump water against a total head of 50 ft. The dynamic suction lift will be 10 ft. Determine the capacity and efficiency of the pump and the horsepower required to operate the pump.

16-3. A centrifugal pump is to be used to pump all the water from a cofferdam whose dimensions are 70 ft long, 50 ft wide, and 12 ft deep. The water must be pumped against an average total head of 45 ft. The average height of the pump above the water will be 12 ft. If the cofferdam must be emptied in 15 hours, determine the minimum model self-priming pump class M to be used based on the ratings of the Contractors Pump Bureau.

16-4. Use Table 16-2 to select a centrifugal pump to handle 300 gpm of water. The water will be pumped from a pond through 460 ft of 6-in. pipe to a point 30 ft above the level of the pond, where it will be discharged into the air. The pump will be set 10 ft above the surface of the water in the pond. What is the designation of the pump selected?

16-5. Select a self-priming centrifugal pump to handle 600 gpm of water for the project illustrated in Fig. 16-7. Increase the height of the vertical pipe from 54 to 60 ft. All other conditions will be as shown in the figure.

16-6. Select a self-priming centrifugal pump to handle 300 gpm of water for the project illustrated in Fig. 16-7. Change the size of the pipe, fittings, and valves to 5 in.

REFERENCE

1. *Selection Guidebook for Portable Dewatering Pumps,* Contractors Pump Bureau, P.O. Box 5858, Rockville, MD 20855.

THE PRODUCTION OF CRUSHED-STONE AGGREGATE

INTRODUCTION

The production of crushed-stone aggregate involves drilling, blasting, loading, transporting, *crushing, screening,* and *product handling* and *storage.* As the first four operations have already been discussed, this chapter deals with studies of the last three operations.

In operating a quarry and crushing plant, the drilling pattern, the amount of explosives, the size shovel or loader used to load the stone, and the size of the primary crusher should be coordinated to assure that all stone from the quarry can be economically utilized. It is desirable for the loading capacity of the shovel or loader in the pit and the capacity of the crushing plant to be approximately equal. Table 17-1 gives the recommended minimum sizes of jaw and gyratory crushers required to handle the stone being loaded with buckets of the specified capacities.

TYPES OF CRUSHERS

GENERAL INFORMATION

Crushers are sometimes classified according to the stage of crushing which they accomplish, such as primary, secondary, tertiary, etc. A primary crusher receives the stone directly from a quarry after blasting, and produces the first reduction in size. The output of the primary crusher is fed to a secondary crusher, which further reduces the stone size. Some of the stone may pass through four or more crushers before it is reduced to the desired size.

TABLE 17-1
Recommended minimum sizes of primary crushers for use with shovel buckets of the indicated capacities

Capacity of bucket [cu yd (cu m)]		Jaw crusher [in. (mm)][†]		Gyratory crusher, size of openings [in. (mm)][‡]	
$\frac{3}{4}$	(0.575)	28 × 36	(712 × 913)	16	(406)
1	(0.765)	28 × 36	(712 × 913)	16	(406)
$1\frac{1}{2}$	(1.145)	36 × 42	(913 × 1,065)	20	(508)
$1\frac{3}{4}$	(1.340)	42 × 48	(1,065 × 1,200)	26	(660)
2	(1.530)	42 × 48	(1,065 × 1,200)	30	(760)
$2\frac{1}{2}$	(1.910)	48 × 60	(1,260 × 1,525)	36	(915)
3	(2.295)	48 × 60	(1,260 × 1,525)	42	(1,066)
$3\frac{1}{2}$	(2.668)	48 × 60	(1,260 × 1,525)	42	(1,066)
4	(3.060)	56 × 72	(1,420 × 1,830)	48	(1,220)
5	(3.820)	66 × 86	(1,675 × 2,182)	60	(1,520)

[†] The first two digits are the width of the opening at the top of the crusher, measured perpendicular to the jaw plates. The second two digits are the width of the opening, measured across the jaw plates.

[‡] The recommended sizes are for gyratory crushers equipped with straight concaves.

Crushing plants utilize step reduction because the amount of size reduction accomplished is directly related to the energy applied. When there is a large difference between the size of the feed material and the size of the crushed product, a large amount of energy is required. If there is a concentration of this energy in a single-step process, excessive fines will be generated and normally there is only a limited market for fines. At many plants fines are a nonrevenue-producing waste material. Therefore, the degree of breakage is spread over several stages as a means of closely controlling product size and limiting waste material.

As stone passes through a crusher, the reduction in size may be expressed as a reduction ratio: the ratio of crusher feed size to product size. The sizes are usually defined as the 80% passing size of the cumulative size distribution. For a jaw crusher the ratio can be estimated by the gape, which is the distance between the fixed and moving faces at the top, divided by the distance of the open-side setting at the bottom. Thus, if the gape distance between the two faces at the top is 16 in. and at the bottom the open-side setting is 4 in., the reduction ratio is 4.

The reduction ratio of a roller crusher can be estimated as the ratio of the dimension of the largest stone that can be nipped by the rolls, divided by the setting of the rolls, which is the smallest distance between the faces of the rolls.

A more accurate measurement of the reduction ratio is to use the ratio of size corresponding to 80% passing for both the feed and the product.

Crushers are also classified by their method of mechanically transmitted fracturing energy to the rock. Jaw, gyratory, and roll crushers work by applying compressive force. Impact crushers apply, as the name implies, high-speed impact force to accomplish fracturing. By using units of differing size, crushing chamber configuration, and

TABLE 17-2
The major types of crushers

Crusher type	Reduction ratio range
Jaw	
a. Double toggle	
(1) Blake	4:1–9:1
(2) Overhead pivot	4:1–9:1
b. Single toggle: Overhead eccentric	4:1–9:1
Gyratory	
a. True	3:1–10:1
b. Cone	
(1) Standard	4:1–6:1
(2) Attrition	2:1–5:1
Roll	
a. Compression	
(1) Single roll	Maximum 7:1
(2) Double roll	Maximum 3:1
Impact	
a. Single rotor	to 15:1
b. Double rotor	to 15:1
c. Hammer mill	to 20:1
Specialty crushers	
a. Rod mill	
b. Ball mill	

speed, the same mechanical-type crusher can be employed at different stages in the crushing operation.

Jaw crushers, however, are typically used as primary units because of their large energy-storing flywheels and high mechanical advantage. True gyratories are the other crusher type employed as primary units. A *true* gyratory is a good primary crusher because it provides continuous crushing and can handle slabby material. Jaw crushers do not handle slabby material well. Models of gyratory, roll, and impact crushers can be found in both secondary and tertiary applications.

Table 17-2 lists the major types of crushers and presents data on attainable material reduction ratios.

JAW CRUSHERS

These machines operate by allowing stone to flow into the space between two jaws, one of which is stationary while the other is movable. The distance between the jaws diminishes as the stone travels downward under the effect of gravity and the motion of the movable jaw, until the stone ultimately passes through the lower opening. The movable jaw is capable of exerting a pressure that is sufficiently high to crush the hardest rock. Jaw crushers are usually designed with the toggle as the weakest part. The toggle will break if the machine encounters an uncrushable object or is subjected to overload. This limits damage to the crusher.

In selecting a jaw crusher, consideration must be given to the size of the feed stone. The top opening of the jaw should be at least 2 in. wider than the largest stones that will be fed to it.

Double toggle. The *Blake* type, illustrated in Fig. 17-1, is a double-toggle crusher. The movable jaw is suspended from a shaft mounted on bearings on the crusher frame. The crushing action is produced by rotating an eccentric shaft, which raises and lowers the pitman, which actuates the two toggles. As the two toggles are raised by the pitman, a high pressure is exerted near the bottom of the swing jaw, which partially closes the opening at the bottom of the two jaws. This operation is repeated as the eccentric shaft is rotated.

The jaw plates, which are made of manganese steel, may be removed, replaced, or, in some cases, reversed. The jaws may be smooth, or, in the event the stone tends to break into slabs, corrugated jaws may be used to reduce the slabbing. The swing jaw may be straight, or it may be curved to reduce the danger of choking.

The movable jaw operates at a fairly slow speed but has a large stroke at its bottom. This large stroke and a conservative nip angle allow Blake-type crushers to handle hard, tough, abrasive rock and still have good capacity.

Table 17-3 gives representative capacities for various sizes of Blake-type jaw crushers. Capacity tables can be based on the open or closed position of the bottom of the swing jaw; therefore, the table should specify which setting applies. The closed position is commonly used for most crushers and is the basis for the values given in Table 17-3. However, Blake-type jaw crushers are often rated based on the open-side setting. The capacity is given in tons per hour based on a standard material unit weight of 100 lb per cu ft when crushed.

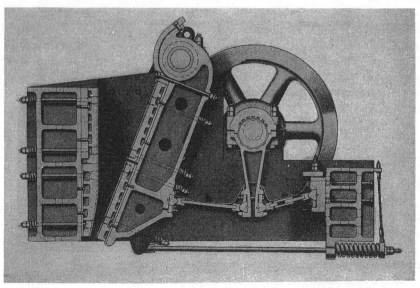

FIGURE 17-1
Blake-type jaw crusher. (*Fiat-Allis Construction Machinery, Inc.*)

TABLE 17-3
Representative capacities of Blake-type jaw crushers, in tons per hour (metric tons per hour) of stone[†]

Size crusher [in. (mm)][‡]	Maximum rpm	Maximum hp (kW)	Closed setting of discharge opening [in. (mm)]										
			1 (25.4)	1½ (38.1)	2 (50.8)	2½ (63.5)	3 (76.2)	4 (102)	5 (137)	6 (152)	7 (178)	8 (203)	9 (229)
10 × 6 (254 × 406)	300	15 (11.2)	11 (10)	16 (14)	20 (18)								
10 × 20 (254 × 508)	300	20 (14.9)	14 (13)	20 (18)	25 (23)	34 (31)							
15 × 24 (381 × 610)	275	30 (22.4)		27 (24)	34 (31)	42 (38)	50 (45)						
15 × 30 (381 × 762)	275	40 (29.8)		33 (30)	43 (39)	53 (48)	62 (56)						
18 × 36 (458 × 916)	250	60 (44.8)		46 (42)	61 (55)	77 (69)	93 (84)	125 (113)					
24 × 36 (610 × 916)	250	75 (56.0)			77 (69)	95 (86)	114 (103)	150 (136)					
30 × 42 (762 × 1,068)	200	100 (74.6)				125 (113)	150 (136)	200 (181)	250 (226)	300 (272)			
36 × 42 (916 × 1,068)	175	115 (85.5)				140 (127)	160 (145)	200 (181)	250 (226)	300 (272)			
36 × 48 (916 × 1,220)	160	125 (93.2)				150 (136)	175 (158)	225 (202)	275 (249)	325 (294)	375 (339)		
42 × 48 (1,068 × 1,220)	150	150 (111.9)				165 (149)	190 (172)	250 (226)	300 (272)	350 (318)	400 (364)	450 (408)	
48 × 60 (1,220 × 1,542)	120	180 (134.7)					220 (200)	280 (254)	340 (309)	400 (364)	450 (408)	500 (454)	550 (500)
56 × 72 (1,422 × 1,832)	95	250 (186.3)						315 (286)	380 (345)	450 (408)	515 (468)	580 (527)	640 (580)

[†] Based on the closed position of the bottom swing jaw and stone weighing 100 lb per cu ft when crushed.

[‡] The first number indicates the width of the feed opening, whereas the second number indicates the width of the jaw plates.

An *overhead pivot* jaw crusher is similar to the Blake type, but by placing the swing jaw's pivot over the centerline of the crushing chamber, there is more stroke at the feed opening. Additionally, this causes the motion to be more in a perpendicular direction to the stationary jaw. By having a higher operating speed, this type of crusher will have capacities similar to the Blake design.

Single toggle. When the eccentric shaft of the single-toggle crusher, illustrated in Fig. 17-2, is rotated, it gives the movable jaw both a vertical and a horizontal motion. This type of crusher is used quite frequently in portable rock-crushing plants because of its compact size, lighter weight, and reasonably sturdy construction. The capacity of a single-toggle crusher is usually rated at the closed-side setting and is less than that of a Blake-type unit.

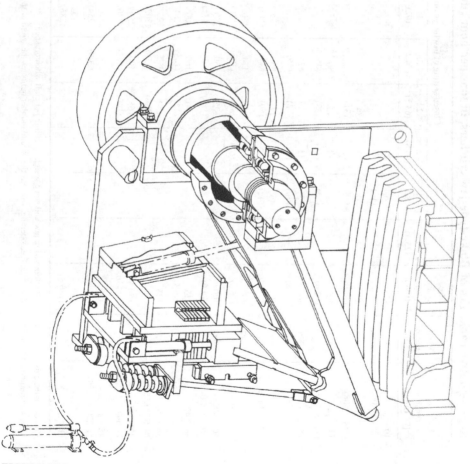

FIGURE 17-2
Single toggle type jaw crusher. (*Cedarapids Inc., A Raytheon Company.*)

Sizes of stone produced by jaw and roll crushers. While the setting of the discharge opening of a crusher will determine the maximum-size stone produced, the aggregate sizes will range from slightly greater than the crusher setting to fine dust. Experience gained in the crushing industry indicates that for any given setting for a jaw or roll crusher approximately 15% of the total amount of stone passing through the crusher will be larger than the setting. If the openings of a screen which receives the output from such a crusher are the same size as the crusher setting, 15% of the output will not pass through the screen. Figure 17-3 gives the percent of material passing or retained on screens having the size openings indicated. The chart can be applied to both jaw- and roll-type crushers. To read the chart, select the vertical line corresponding to the crusher setting. Then go down this line to the number which indicates the size of the screen opening. From the size of the screen opening proceed horizontally to the left to determine the percent of material passing through the screen or to the right to determine the percent of material retained on the screen.

Example 17-1. A jaw crusher, with a closed setting of 3 in., produces 50 tons per hour of crushed stone. Determine the amount of stone produced in tons per hour within the following size ranges: in excess of 2 in.; between 2 and 1 in.; between 1 and $\frac{1}{4}$ in.

From Fig. 17-3 the amount retained on a 2-in. screen is 42% of 50, which is 21 tons per hour. The amount in each of the size ranges is determined as follows:

Size range (in.)	Percent passing screens	Percent in size range	Total output of crusher (ton/hr)	Amount produced in size range, (ton/hr)
Over 2	100–58	42	50	21.0
2–1	58–33	25	50	12.5
1–$\frac{1}{4}$	33–11	22	50	11.0
$\frac{1}{4}$–0	11–0	11	50	5.5
Total		100%		50.0 tph

GYRATORY CRUSHERS

These crushers are characterized by a gyrating mantle mounted within a deep bowl. They provide continuous crushing action and are used for both primary and secondary crushing of hard, tough, abrasive rock. To protect the crusher from uncrushable objects and overload, the outer crushing surface may be spring-loaded or the mantle height may be hydraulically adjustable.

True gyratory. A section through a gyratory crusher is illustrated in Fig. 17-4. The crusher unit consists of heavy cast-iron or steel frame, with an eccentric shaft setting and driving gears in the lower part of the unit. In the upper part there is a cone-shaped crushing chamber, lined with hard-steel or manganese-steel plates called the "concaves." The crushing member includes a hard-steel crushing head mounted on a vertical steel shaft. This shaft and head are suspended from the spider at the top of the frame, which is so

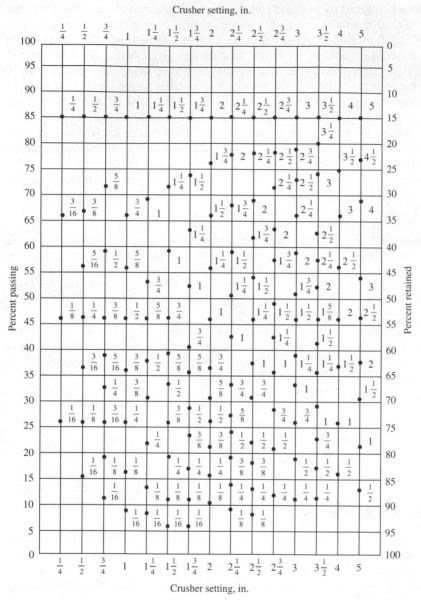

FIGURE 17-3
Analysis of the size of aggregate produced by jaw and roll crushers. (*Universal Engineering Company.*)

constructed that some vertical adjustment of the shaft is possible. The eccentric support at the bottom causes the shaft and the crushing head to gyrate as the shaft rotates, thereby varying the width of the space between the concaves and the head. As the rock which is fed in at the top of the crushing chamber moves downward, it undergoes a reduction in size until it finally passes through the opening at the bottom of the chamber.

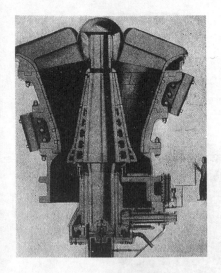

FIGURE 17-4
Section through a Hydroset gyratory crusher. (*Fiat-Allis Construction Machinery, Inc.*)

The size of a gyratory crusher is the width of the receiving opening, measured between the concaves and the crusher head. The setting is the width of the bottom opening and may be the open or closed dimension. When a setting is given, it should be specified whether it is the open or closed dimension. Normally, the capacity of a *true* gyratory crusher is based on an open-side setting. The ratio of reduction for *true* gyratory crushers usually ranges from about 3:1 to 10:1, with an average value around 8:1. A gyratory crusher receiving stone in an aggregate plant is shown in Fig. 17-5.

If a gyratory crusher is used as a primary crusher, the size selected may be dictated by the size of the rock from the quarry or by a desired capacity. When this machine is used as a secondary crusher, the capacity of a gyratory crusher may be increased by increasing the speed of the machine within reasonable limits.

Table 17-4 gives representative capacities of gyratory crushers, in tons per hour, based on a continuous feed of stone having a unit weight of 100 lb per cu ft when crushed. The crushers with straight concaves are commonly used as primary crushers, whereas those with nonchoking concaves are commonly used as secondary crushers.

Cone crushers. Cone crushers are used as secondary or tertiary crushers. They are capable of producing large quantities of uniformly fine crushed stone. A cone crusher differs from a *true* gyratory crusher in the following respects:

1. It has a shorter cone.
2. It has a smaller receiving opening.
3. It rotates at a higher speed, about twice that of a *true* gyratory.
4. It produces a more uniformly sized stone.

Standard models have large feed openings for secondary crushing and produce stone in the 1 to 4 in. range. The capacity of the *standard* model is usually rated at the closed-side setting.

FIGURE 17-5
Gyrosphere crusher in an aggregate plant. (*Telesmith Division, Barber-Greene Company.*)

Attrition models are for producing stone having a maximum size of about $\frac{1}{4}$ in. The capacity of an *attrition* model gyratory crusher may not be related to the closed-side setting.

Figure 17-6 shows a section through a *standard* cone crusher. The conical head, usually made of manganese steel and mounted on the vertical shaft, serves as one of the crushing surfaces. The other surface is the concave, which is attached to the upper part of the crusher frame. The bottom of the shaft is set in an eccentric bushing to produce the gyratory effect as the shaft rotates.

Whereas the maximum diameter of the crusher head may be used to designate the size of a cone crusher, the size of the feed opening, which limits the size of the rocks that may be fed to the crusher, is the width of the opening at the entrance to the crushing chamber. The magnitude of the eccentric throw and the setting of the discharge opening may be varied within reasonable limits. Because of the high speed of rotation, all particles passing through a crusher will be reduced to sizes no larger than the closed-size setting, which should be used to designate the size of the discharge opening.

TABLE 17-4

Representative capacities of gyratory crushers, in tons per hour (metric tons per hour) of stone[†]

Size of crusher [in. (cm)]	Approximate power required [hp (kW)]	Open-side setting of crusher, [in. (mm)]											
		1½ (38)	1¾ (44)	2 (51)	2¼ (57)	2½ (63)	3 (76)	3½ (89)	4 (102)	4½ (114)	5 (127)	5½ (140)	6 (152)
Straight concaves													
8 (20.0)	15–25 (11–19)	30 (27)	36 (33)	41 (37)	47 (42)								
10 (25.4)	25–40 (19–30)		40 (36)	50 (45)	60 (54)								
13 (33.1)	50–75 (37–56)				85 (77)	100 (90)	133 (120)						
16 (40.7)	60–100 (45–75)						160 (145)	185 (167)	210 (190)				
20 (50.8)	75–125 (56–93)							200 (180)	230 (208)	255 (231)			
30 (76.2)	125–175 (93–130)								310 (281)	350 (317)	390 (353)		
42 (106.7)	200–275 (150–205)										500 (452)	570 (515)	630 (569)
Modified straight concaves													
8 (20.0)	15–25 (11–19)	35 (32)	40 (36)	45 (41)									
10 (25.4)	25–40 (19–30)		54 (49)	60 (54)	65 (59)								
13 (33.1)	50–75 (37–56)					95 (86)	130 (117)						
16 (40.7)	60–100 (45–75)						150 (135)	172 (155)	195 (176)				
20 (50.8)	75–125 (56–93)							182 (165)	200 (180)	220 (199)			
30 (76.2)	125–175 (93–130)								340 (308)	370 (335)	400 (362)		
42 (106.7)	200–275 (150–205)										607 (550)	650 (589)	690 (625)
Nonchoking concaves													
8 (20.0)	15–25 (11–19)	42 (38)	46 (42)										
10 (25.4)	25–40 (19–30)	51 (46)	57 (52)	63 (57)	69 (62)								
13 (33.1)	50–75 (37–56)	79 (71)	87 (79)	95 (86)	103 (93)	111 (100)							
16 (40.7)	60–100 (45–75)			107 (96)	118 (106)	128 (115)	150 (135)						
20 (50.8)	75–125 (56–93)				155 (140)	169 (152)	198 (178)	220 (198)	258 (233)	285 (257)	310 (279)		

[†]Based on continuous feed and stone weighing 100 lb per cu ft when crushed.

FIGURE 17-6
Rollercone crusher. (*Cedarapids Inc., A Raytheon Company.*)

Table 17-5 gives representative capacities for the Symons standard cone crusher, expressed in tons of stone per hour for material having a unit weight of 100 lb per cu ft when crushed.

ROLL CRUSHERS

Roll crushers are used for producing additional reductions in the sizes of stone after the output of a quarry has been subjected to one or more stages of prior crushing. A *roll crusher* consists of a heavy cast-iron frame equipped with either one or more hard-steel rolls, each mounted on a separate horizontal shaft.

Single roll. With a single roll crusher, the material is forced between a large diameter roller having knoblike teeth and an adjustable liner (see Fig. 17-7). Because the

TABLE 17-5

Representative capacities of Symons standard cone crushers, in tons per hour (metric tons per hour) of stone†

Size of crusher [ft(m)]	Size of feed opening [in. (mm)]	Minimum discharge settings [in. (mm)]	Discharge setting, [in. (mm)]										
			$\frac{1}{4}$ (6.3)	$\frac{3}{8}$ (9.5)	$\frac{1}{2}$ (12.7)	$\frac{5}{8}$ (15.9)	$\frac{3}{4}$ (19.1)	$\frac{7}{8}$ (22.3)	1 (25.4)	$1\frac{1}{4}$ (31.8)	$1\frac{1}{2}$ (38.0)	2 (50.8)	$2\frac{1}{2}$ (63.5)
2	$2\frac{1}{4}$	$\frac{1}{4}$	15	20	25	30	35						
(0.61)	(57)	(5.6)	(14)	(18)	(23)	(27)	(32)						
2	$3\frac{1}{4}$	$\frac{3}{8}$		20	25	30	35	40	45	50	60		
(0.61)	(82)	(9.5)		(18)	(23)	(27)	(32)	(36)	(41)	(45)	(54)		
3	$3\frac{7}{8}$	$\frac{3}{8}$		35	40	55	70	75					
(0.91)	(96)	(9.5)		(32)	(36)	(50)	(63)	(68)					
3	$5\frac{1}{8}$	$\frac{1}{2}$			40	55	70	75	80	85	90	95	
(0.91)	(130)	(12.7)			(36)	(50)	(63)	(68)	(72)	(77)	(81)	(86)	
4	5	$\frac{3}{8}$		60	80	100	120	135	150				
(1.22)	(127)	(9.5)		(54)	(72)	(90)	(109)	(122)	(136)				
4	$7\frac{3}{8}$	$\frac{3}{4}$					120	135	150	170	177	185	
(1.22)	(187)	(19.0)					(109)	(122)	(136)	(154)	(160)	(167)	
$4\frac{1}{4}$	$4\frac{1}{2}$	$\frac{1}{2}$			100	125	140	150					
(1.29)	(114)	(12.7)			(90)	(113)	(126)	(136)					
$4\frac{1}{4}$	$7\frac{3}{8}$	$\frac{5}{8}$				125	140	150	160	175			
(1.29)	(187)	(15.8)				(113)	(126)	(136)	(145)	(158)			
$4\frac{1}{4}$	$9\frac{1}{2}$	$\frac{3}{4}$					140	150	160	175	185	190	
(1.29)	(241)	(19.0)					(126)	(136)	(145)	(158)	(167)	(172)	
$5\frac{1}{2}$	$7\frac{1}{8}$	$\frac{5}{8}$				160	200	235	275				
(1.67)	(181)	(15.8)				(145)	(181)	(213)	(249)				
$5\frac{1}{2}$	$8\frac{5}{8}$	$\frac{7}{8}$						235	275	300	340	375	450
(1.67)	(219)	(22.2)						(213)	(249)	(272)	(304)	(340)	(407)
$5\frac{1}{2}$	$9\frac{7}{8}$	1							275	300	340	375	450
(1.67)	(248)	(25.4)							(249)	(272)	(304)	(340)	(407)
7	10	$\frac{3}{4}$					330	390	450	560	600		
(2.30)	(254)	(19.0)					(300)	(353)	(407)	(507)	(543)		
7	$11\frac{1}{2}$	1							450	560	600	800	
(2.30)	(292)	(25.4)							(407)	(507)	(543)	(725)	
7	$13\frac{1}{2}$	$1\frac{1}{4}$								560	600	800	900
(2.30)	(343)	(31.7)								(507)	(543)	(725)	(815)

† Based on stone weighing 100 lb per cu ft when crushed.

Courtesy Nordberg Manufacturing Company.

material is dragged against the liner, these crushers are not economical for crushing highly abrasive materials. But they can handle sticky materials.

Double roll. Roll crushers with two rollers are so constructed that each roll is driven independently by a flat-belt pull or a V-belt sheave. One of the rolls is mounted on a slide frame to permit an adjustment in the width of the discharge opening between the two rolls. The movable roll is spring-loaded to provide safety against damage to the rolls when trap iron or other noncrushable material passes through the machine.

FIGURE 17-7
Cutaway of single roll crusher showing deep-ribbed pitman and segment-type rotor. Breaker plate with ribs provides concentrated crushing action between teeth and ribs and acts as a sizing anvil for close control of product size. (*Grundler Crusher & Pulverizer Company.*)

Feed size. The maximum size of material that may be fed to a roll crusher is directly proportional to the diameter of the rolls. If the feed contains stones that are too large, the rolls will not grip the material and pull it through the crusher. The angle of nip, B in Fig. 17-8, which is constant for smooth rolls, has been found to be $16°54'$.

The maximum-size particles that can be crushed is determined as follows. Let

R = radius of rolls
B = angle of nip

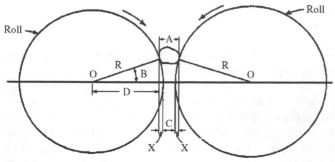

FIGURE 17-8
Crushing rock between two rolls.

$$D = R\cos B = 0.9575R$$

A = maximum-size feed

C = roll setting = size of finished product

Then

$$
\begin{aligned}
X &= R - D \\
&= R - 0.9575R = 0.0425R \\
A &= 2X + C \\
&= 0.085R + C
\end{aligned}
$$

(17-1)

Example 17-2. Determine the maximum-size stone that may be fed to a smooth-roll crusher whose rolls are 40 in. in diameter, when the roller setting is 1 in.

$$
\begin{aligned}
A &= (0.085 \times 20) + 1 \\
&= 2.7 \text{ in.}
\end{aligned}
$$

Capacity. The capacity of a roll crusher will vary with the kind of stone, the size of feed, the size of the finished product, the width of rolls, the speed at which the rolls rotate, and the extent to which the stone is fed uniformly into the crusher. Referring to Fig. 17-8, the theoretical volume of a solid ribbon of material passing between the two rolls in 1 min will be the product of the width of the opening times the width of the rolls times the speed of the surface of the rolls. The volume may be expressed in cubic inches per minute or in cubic feet per minute (cfm). In actual practice, the ribbon of crushed stone will never be solid. A more realistic volume should approximate one-fourth to one-third the theoretical volume. An equation which may be used as a guide in estimating the capacity is derived as follows. Let

C = distance between rolls, in.

W = width of rolls, in.

S = peripheral speed of rolls, in. per min

N = speed of rolls, rpm

R = radius of rolls, in.

V_1 = theoretical volume, cu in. or cfm

V_2 = actual volume, cu in. or cfm

Q = probable capacity, tons per hour

Then

$$V_1 = CWS$$

Assume $V_2 = V_1/3$.

$$V_2 = \frac{CWS}{3} \text{ cu in. per min}$$

Divide by 1,728 cu in. per cu ft.

$$V_2 = \frac{CWS}{5,184} \text{ cfm}$$

Assume the crushed stone has a unit weight of 100 lb per cu ft.

$$Q = \frac{100 \times 60V_2}{2,000} = 3V_2$$

$$= \frac{CWS}{1,728} \text{ tons per hr}$$

(17-2)

S may be expressed in terms of the diameter of the roll and the speed in rpm.

$$S = 2\pi RN$$

Substituting this value of S into Eq. (17-2) gives

$$Q = \frac{CW\pi RN}{864}$$

(17-3)

Table 17-6 gives representative capacities for smooth-roll crushers, expressed in tons of stone per hour for material having a unit weight of 100 lb per cu ft when crushed. These capacities should be used as a guide only in estimating the probable output of a crusher. The actual capacity may be more or less than the given values.

If a roll crusher is producing a finished aggregate, the reduction ratio should not be greater than 4:1. However, if a roll crusher is used to prepare feed for a fine grinder, the reduction may be as high as 7:1.

IMPACT CRUSHERS

In impact crushers stones are broken by the application of high-speed impact forces. Advantage is also taken of the rebound between the individual stones and against the machine surfaces to utilize fully the initial impact energy. The design of some units additionally seeks to shear and compress the stones between the revolving and stationary parts. Speed of rotation is important to the effective operations of these crushers as the energy available for impact varies as the square of the rotational speed.

Single rotor. The single rotor-type impact crusher breaks the stone both by the impact action of the impellers striking the feed material and by the impact which results when the impeller-driven material strikes against the aprons within the crusher unit. These units produce a cubical product but are economical only for low abrasion feeds. The unit's production rate is affected by the rotor speed; however, speed also affects the reduction ratio. Therefore, any speed adjustment should only be done after consideration is given to both elements, the production rate and the final product size.

Double rotor. Figure 17-9 is a cutaway view of a double rotor impact crusher. These units are similar to the single rotor models and accomplish aggregate-size reduction by the same mechanical mechanisms. They will produce a somewhat higher proportion of fines. With both single and double rotor crushers, the impacted material flows freely to the bottom of the units without any further size reduction.

TABLE 17-6
Representative capacities of smooth-roll crushers, in ton/hr (metric ton/hr) of stone*

Size of crusher [in. (mm)]†	Speed (rpm)	Power required [hp (kW)]	Width of opening between rolls [in. (mm)]						
			$\frac{1}{4}$ (6.3)	$\frac{1}{2}$ (12.7)	$\frac{3}{4}$ (19.1)	1 (25.4)	$1\frac{1}{2}$ (38.1)	2 (50.8)	$2\frac{1}{2}$ (63.5)
16 × 16 (414 × 416)	120	15–30 (11–22)	15.0 (13.6)	30.0 (27.2)	40.0 (36.2)	55.0 (49.7)	85.0 (77.0)	115.0 (104.0)	140.0 (127.0)
24 × 16 (610 × 416)	80	20–35 (15–26)	15.0 (13.6)	30.0 (27.2)	40.0 (36.2)	55.0 (49.7)	85.0 (77.0)	115.0 (104.0)	140.0 (127.0)
30 × 18 (763 × 456)	60	50–70 (37–52)	15.0 (13.6)	30.0 (27.2)	45.0 (40.7)	65.0 (59.0)	95.0 (86.0)	125.0 (113.1)	155.0 (140.0)
30 × 22 (763 × 558)	60	60–100 (45–75)	20.0 (18.1)	40.0 (36.2)	55.0 (49.7)	75.0 (67.9)	115.0 (104.0)	155.0 (140.0)	190.0 (172.0)
40 × 20 (1,016 × 508)	50	60–100 (45–75)	20.0 (18.1)	35.0 (31.7)	50.0 (45.2)	70.0 (63.4)	105.0 (95.0)	135.0 (122.0)	175.0 (158.5)
40 × 24 (1,016 × 610)	50	60–100 (45–75)	20.0 (18.1)	40.0 (36.2)	60.0 (54.3)	85.0 (77.0)	125.0 (113.1)	165.0 (149.5)	210.0 (190.0)
54 × 24 (1,374 × 610)	41	125–150 (93–112)	24.0 (21.7)	48.0 (43.5)	71.0 (64.3)	95.0 (86.0)	144.0 (130.0)	192.0 (173.8)	240.0 (217.5)

Courtesy Iowa Manufacturing Company.

*Based on stone weighing 100 lb per cu ft when crushed.

†The first number indicates the diameter of the rolls, and the second indicates the width of the rolls.

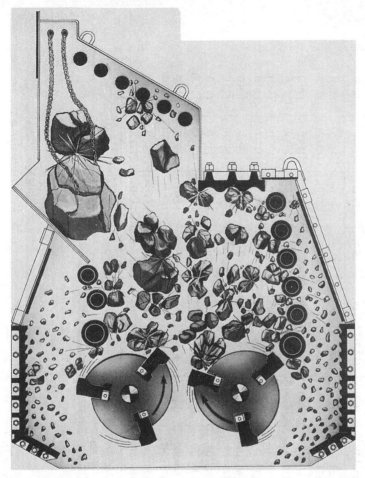

FIGURE 17-9
Cutaway showing double rotor impact breaker. (*Iowa Manufacturing Company.*)

Hammer mills. The hammer mill, which is the most widely used impact crusher, may be used for primary or secondary crushing. The basic parts of a unit include a housing frame, a horizontal shaft extending through the housing, a number of arms and hammers attached to a spool which is mounted on the shaft, one or more manganese-steel or other hard-steel breaker plates, and a series of grate bars whose spacing may be adjusted to regulate the width of openings through which the crushed stone flows. These parts are illustrated in the section through the crusher shown in Fig. 17-10.

As the stone to be crushed is fed to the mill, the hammers, which travel at a high speed, strike the particles, breaking them and driving them against the breaker plates, which further reduces their sizes. Final size reduction is accomplished by grinding the material against the bottom grate bars.

The size of a hammer mill may be designated by the size of the feed opening. The capacity will vary with the size of the unit, the kind of stone crushed, the size of the material fed to the mill, and the speed of the shaft. Hammer mills will produce a high proportion of fines and cannot handle wet or sticky feed material. Table 17-7 gives representative capacities of hammer mills expressed in tons of stone per hour for material having a unit weight of 100 lb per cu ft when crushed.

FIGURE 17-10
Cutaway of hammer mill rock crusher showing breaking action. (*Cedarapids Inc., A Raytheon Company.*)

TABLE 17-7
Representative capacities for hammer mills, in ton/hr (metric ton/hr) of stone[†]

Size feed opening [in. (mm)]	Size feed [in. (mm)]	Power required [hp (kW)]	Width of openings between grate bars [in. (mm)]						
			$\frac{1}{8}$ (3.2)	$\frac{3}{16}$ (4.7)	$\frac{1}{4}$ (6.4)	$\frac{3}{8}$ (9.5)	$\frac{1}{2}$ (12.7)	1 (25.4)	$1\frac{1}{4}$ (31.8)
$6\frac{1}{4} \times 9$ (159 × 229)	3 (76.2)	15–20 (11–15)	2.5 (2.3)	3.5 (3.2)	5.0 (4.5)	8.0 (7.2)	10.0 (9.1)		
12 × 15 (304 × 380)	3 (76.2)	50–60 (37–45)	9.0 (8.2)	13.0 (11.8)	17.0 (15.4)	23.0 (20.8)	29.0 (26.2)	36.0 (32.6)	39.0 (35.2)
15 × 25 (380 × 635)	6 (152.4)	100–125 (75–93)	18.0 (16.4)	25.0 (22.6)	31.0 (28.1)	40.0 (36.3)	47.0 (42.6)	65.0 (59.0)	70.0 (63.5)
15 × 37 (380 × 940)	6 (152.4)	150–200 (112–149)	27.0 (24.5)	37.0 (33.6)	47.0 (42.6)	60.0 (54.5)	71.0 (64.4)	97.0 (88.0)	105.0 (95.4)
15 × 49 (380 × 1,245)	6 (152.4)	200–250 (149–187)	36.0 (32.6)	50.0 (45.4)	63.0 (57.0)	80.0 (72.5)	95.0 (85.9)	130.0 (117.5)	140.0 (126.8)

[†] Based on stone weighing 100 lb per cu ft when crushed.

Courtesy Fiat-Allis Construction Machinery, Inc.

SPECIAL AGGREGATE PROCESSING UNITS

Rod mills. To produce fine aggregate, such as sand, from stone that has been crushed to suitable sizes by other crushing equipment, rod or ball mills are frequently used. It is not uncommon for concrete specifications to require the use of a homogeneous aggregate regardless of size. If crushed stone is used for coarse aggregate, sand manufactured from the same stone can satisfy the specifications.

A *rod mill* is a circular steel shell that is lined on the inside with a hard wearing surface. The mill is equipped with a suitable support or trunnion arrangement at each end and a driving gear at one end. It is operated with its axis in a horizontal position. The rod mill is charged with steel rods, whose lengths are slightly less than the length of the mill. Crushed stone, which is fed through the trunnion at one end of the mill, flows to the discharge at the other end. As the mill rotates slowly, the stone is constantly subjected to the impact of the tumbling rods, which produce the desired grinding. A mill may be operated wet or dry, with or without water added. The size of a rod mill is specified by the diameter and the length of the shell, such as 8×12 ft, respectively. Figure 17-11 shows a section through a rod mill.

Ball mill. A *ball mill* is similar to a rod mill but it uses steel balls instead of rods to supply the impact necessary to grind the stone. Ball mills will produce fine material with smaller grain sizes than those produced by a rod mill. Figure 17-12 shows a section through a ball mill.

Log washers. When natural deposits of aggregate, such as sand and gravel, or individual pieces of crushed stone contain deleterious material as a part of the matrix or as deposits on the surface of the aggregate, it will be necessary to remove these materials before using the aggregate. One method of removing the material is to pass the aggregate through a machine called a "log washer," which is illustrated in Fig. 17-13. This unit consists of a steel tank with two electric-motor-driven shafts, to which numerous replaceable paddles are attached. When the washer is placed in operation, the end of the tank on which the motor is mounted is raised above the opposite end. The aggregate to be processed is fed into the unit at the lower end, while a constant supply of water flows into the upper end. As the shafts are rotated in opposite directions, the paddles move the aggregate toward the upper end of the tank, while producing a continuing scrubbing

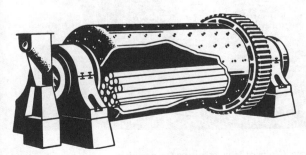

FIGURE 17-11
Section through a rod mill.

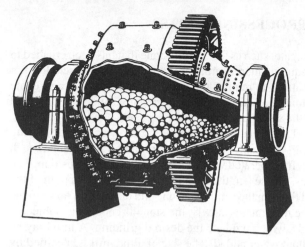

FIGURE 17-12
Section through a conical ball mill.

action between the particles. The stream of water will remove the undesirable material and discharge it from the tank at the lower end, whereas the processed aggregate will be discharged at the upper end.

Sand preparation and classification machines. When the specifications for sand and other fine aggregates require the materials to meet size gradations, it is frequently necessary to produce the gradations by mechanical equipment. Several types of equipment are available for this purpose. Figure 17-14 shows a plan and two sections of a machine

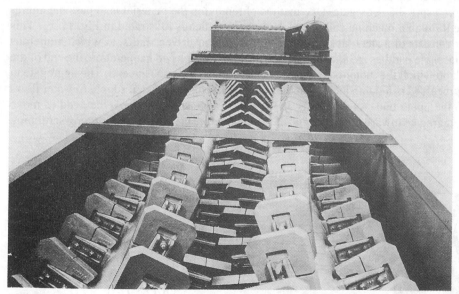

FIGURE 17-13
Log washer for scrubbing coarse aggregate. (*Kolberg Manufacturing Corporation.*)

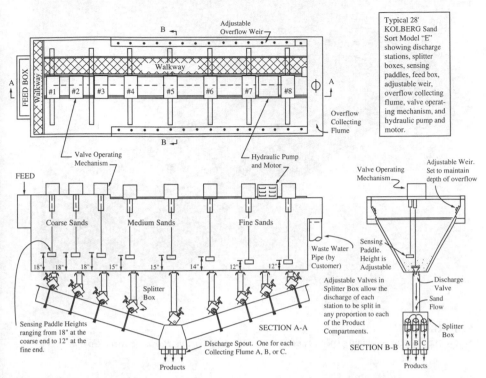

FIGURE 17-14
Details of a sand preparation and classification machine. (*Kolberg Manufacturing Corporation.*)

that is used to classify sand into eight sizes. Sand and water are fed to the classifier as indicated at the left end of the unit. As the water flows to the outlet end of the tank, the sand particles settle to the bottom of the tank, the coarse ones first and the fine ones last. When the depth of a given size reaches a predetermined level, a sensing paddle will actuate a discharge valve at the bottom of the compartment to permit that material to flow into the splitter box, from which it can be removed and used.

Figure 17-15 illustrates a screw-type classifier which may be used to produce specification sand. When the machine is placed in operation, the discharge end, where the electric motor is mounted, is elevated above the opposite end. Sand and water are fed into the hopper. As the spiral screws rotate, the sand is moved up the tank to the discharge outlet under the motor. Undesirable material is flushed out of the tank by the overflowing water.

Figure 17-16 illustrates the product of a classification machine arranged by the size of the grains.

SELECTING CRUSHING EQUIPMENT

In selecting crushing and screening equipment, it is essential that certain information be known prior to making the selection. The information needed should include, but will not necessarily be limited to, the following items:

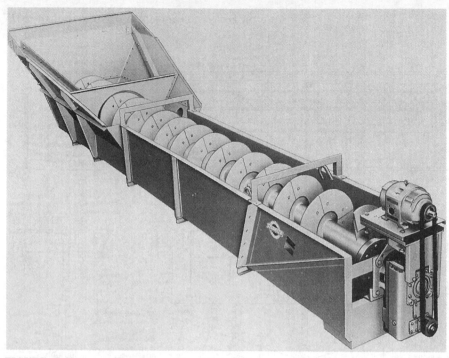

FIGURE 17-15
Screw classifier for producing specification sand. (*Telsmith Division, Barber-Greene Company.*)

FIGURE 17-16
Various sizes of sand produced by a preparation and classification machine. (*Kolberg Manufacturing Corporation.*)

1. The kind of stone to be crushed.
2. The maximum individual size of the feed stones and perhaps the size ranges of the feed to the plant.
3. The method of feeding the crushers.
4. The required capacity of the plant.
5. The percent of material falling within specified size ranges.

The following example illustrates a method which may be used to select crushing equipment.

Example 17-3. Select a primary and a secondary crusher to produce 100 tons per hour of crushed limestone. The maximum-size stones from the quarry will be 16 in. The quarry stone will be hauled by truck, dumped into a surge bin, and fed to the primary crusher by an apron feeder, which will maintain a reasonably uniform rate of feed. The aggregate will be used on a project whose specifications require the following size distributions:

Size screen opening (in.)		
Passing	Retained on	Percent
$1\frac{1}{2}$		100
$1\frac{1}{2}$	$\frac{3}{4}$	42–48
$\frac{3}{4}$	$\frac{1}{4}$	30–36
$\frac{1}{4}$	0	20–26

Consider a jaw crusher for the primary crushing and a roll crusher for the secondary crushing. The output of the jaw crusher will be screened to remove specification sizes before the oversize material is fed to the roll crusher.

Assume a setting of 3 in. for the jaw crusher. This will give a ratio of reduction of approximately 5:1, which is satisfactory. Table 17-3 indicates a size 24- by 36-in. crusher with a probable capacity of 114 tons per hour. Figure 17-3 indicates that the product of the jaw crusher will be distributed by sizes as follows:

Size range (in.)	Percent passing screens	Percent in size range	Total output of crusher (ton/hr)	Amount produced in size range (ton/hr)
Over $1\frac{1}{2}$	100–46	54	100	54.0
$1\frac{1}{2}-\frac{3}{4}$	46–26	20	100	20.0
$\frac{3}{4}-\frac{1}{4}$	26–11	15	100	15.0
$\frac{1}{4}-0$	11– 0	11	100	11.0
Total		100%		100.0 tph

As the roll crusher will receive the output from the jaw crusher, the rolls must be large enough to handle 3-in. stone. Assume a setting of $1\frac{1}{2}$ in. From Eq. (17-1) the minimum radius will be 17.7 in. Try a 40- by 20-in. (Table 17-6) crusher with a capacity of approximately 105 tons per hour for a $1\frac{1}{2}$-in. setting.

For any given setting the crusher will produce about 15% stone having at least one dimension larger than the setting. Thus, for a given setting 15% of the stone that passes through the roll crusher will be returned for recrushing. The total amount of stone passing through the crusher, including the returned stone, is determined as follows:

Let

$$Q = \text{total amount of stone through the crusher}$$

Then

$$0.15Q = \text{amount of returned stone}$$
$$0.85Q = \text{amount of new stone}$$
$$Q = \frac{\text{amount of new stone}}{0.85}$$
$$= \frac{54}{0.85} = 63.5 \text{ ton/hr}$$

The 40- by 20-in. roll crusher will handle this amount of stone easily. The distribution of the output of this crusher by size range will be as follows:

Size range (in.)	Percent passing screens	Percent in size range	Total output of crusher (ton/hr)	Amount produced in size range (ton/hr)
$1\frac{1}{2}-\frac{3}{4}$	85–46	39	63.5	24.8
$\frac{3}{4}-\frac{1}{4}$	46–18	28	63.5	17.8
$\frac{1}{4}-0$	18– 0	18	63.5	11.4
Total		85%		54.0 tph

Now combine the output of each crusher by specified sizes.

Size range (in.)	From jaw crusher (ton/hr)	From roll crusher (ton/hr)	Total amount (ton/hr)	Percent in size range
$1\frac{1}{2}-\frac{3}{4}$	20.0	24.8	44.8	44.8
$\frac{3}{4}-\frac{1}{4}$	15.0	17.8	32.8	32.8
$\frac{1}{4}-0$	11.0	11.4	22.4	22.4
Total	46.0 tph	54.0 tph	100.0 tph	100.0%

SCALPING CRUSHED STONE

The term *scalping,* as used in this chapter, refers to a screening operation. Scalping removes, from the main mass of stone to be processed, that stone which is too large for the crusher opening or is small enough to be used without further crushing. Scalping

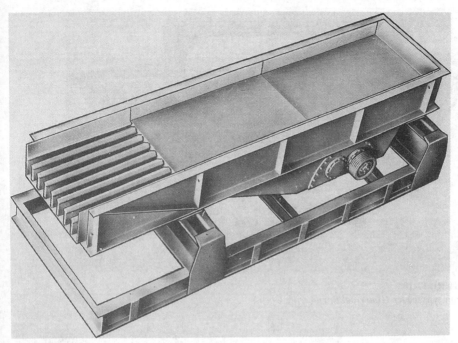

FIGURE 17-17
Vibrating grizzly feeder. (*Iowa Manufacturing Company.*)

may be performed ahead of a primary crusher, and it represents good crushing practice to scalp all crushed stone following each successive stage of reduction.

Scalping ahead of a primary crusher serves two purposes. The use of a grizzly, which consists of a number of widely spaced parallel bars, will prevent oversize stones from entering the crusher and blocking the opening. If the product of the quarry contains such stones, it is desirable to remove them ahead of the crusher. The product of the quarry may contain dirt, mud, or other debris which is not acceptable in the finished product, and therefore it must be removed from the stone. Scalping should accomplish this removal.

Also, the product of the quarry may contain an appreciable amount of stone which was reduced by the blasting operation to specification sizes. In this event it may be good economy to remove such stone ahead of the primary crusher, thereby reducing the total load on the crusher and increasing the overall capacity of the plant.

It is usually economical to install a scalper after each stage of reduction in order to remove specification sizes. This stone may be transported to grading screens, where it can be sized and placed in appropriate storage. Figure 17-17 illustrates a commercial bar grizzly.

FEEDERS

Crushing equipment is designed to utilize particle interaction in the crushing process. An underfed compression crusher produces a larger percentage of oversize material,

FIGURE 17-18
Apron-type feeder. (*Universal Engineering Corp.*)

as the necessary material is not present to fully develop interparticle crushing. In an impact crusher efficient use of interparticle collisions is not possible with an underfed machine.

The capacity of a crusher will be increased if the stone is fed to it at a uniform rate. Surge feeding tends to overload a crusher, and then the surge is followed by an insufficient supply of stone. This type of feeding, which reduces the capacity of a crusher, may be eliminated by using a mechanical feeder ahead of a crusher. The installation of such a feeder may increase the capacity of a jaw crusher as much as 15%. An apron-type feeder, as illustrated in Fig. 17-18, is suitable for use ahead of a primary crusher.

SURGE PILES

A stationary stone-crushing plant may include several types and sizes of crushers, each probably followed with a set of screens and a belt conveyor to transport the stone to the next crushing operation or to storage. A plant may be designed to provide temporary storage for stone between the successive stages of crushing. This plan has the advantage of eliminating or reducing the surge effect that frequently exists when the crushing, screening, and handling operations are conducted on a straight-line basis.

The stone in temporary storage ahead of a crusher, which is referred to as a "surge pile," may be used to keep at least a portion of a plant in operation at all times. Within reasonable limits, the use of a surge pile ahead of a crusher permits the crusher to be fed uniformly at the most satisfactory rate regardless of variations in the output of other equipment ahead of the crusher. The use of surge piles has enabled some plants to increase their final output production by as much as 10 to 20%.

Arguments against the use of surge piles include the following:

1. They require additional storage area.
2. They require the construction of storage bins or reclaiming tunnels.
3. They increase the amount of stone handling.

The decision to use or not to use surge piles should be based on an analysis of the advantages and disadvantages for each plant.

SCREENING AGGREGATE

Screening of crushed stone is necessary in order to separate the aggregate by size ranges. Most specifications covering the use of aggregate stipulate that the different sizes shall be combined to produce a blend having a given size distribution. Persons who are responsible for preparing the specifications for the use of aggregate realize that crushing and screening cannot be done with complete precision, and accordingly they allow some tolerance in the size distribution. The extent of tolerance may be indicated by a statement such as: The quantity of aggregate passing a 1-in. screen and retained on a $\frac{1}{4}$-in. screen shall not be less than 30% or more than 40% of the total quantity of aggregate.

Revolving screens. Revolving screens have several advantages over other types of screens, especially when they are used to wash and screen sand and gravel. The operating action is slow and simple, and the maintenance and repair costs are low. If the aggregate to be washed contains silt and clay, a scrubber can be installed near the entrance of a screen in order to agitate the material in water. At the same time streams of water may be sprayed on the aggregate as it moves through the screen. Figure 17-19 shows a revolving screen in operation. The aggregate, which is separated by size, is stored temporarily in the bins below the screen.

Vibrating screens. The vibrating screen is the most widely used screen for aggregate production. Figures 17-20 and 17-21 show multiple-deck screen units of the vibrating type. The steel frame may be designed to permit the installation of one or more screens, one above the other. Each screen is referred to as a "deck." The vibration is obtained by means of an eccentric shaft, a counterweight shaft, or electromagnets attached to the frame or to the screens.

A unit is installed with a slight slope from the receiving to the discharge end, which combined with the vibrations causes the aggregate to flow over the surface of the screen. Most of the particles that are smaller than the openings in a screen will drop through the screen, while the oversize particles will flow off the screen at the discharge end. For a multiple-deck unit the sizes of the openings will be progressively smaller for each lower deck.

A screen will not pass all material whose sizes are equal to or less than the dimensions of the openings in the screen. Some of this material may be retained on and carried over the discharge end of a screen. The efficiency of a screen may be defined as the ratio of the amount of material passing through a screen divided by the total amount

FIGURE 17-19
Revolving screen in an aggregate processing plant.

that is small enough to pass through, with the ratio expressed as a percent. The highest efficiency is obtained with a single-deck screen, usually amounting to 90–95%. As additional decks are installed, the efficiencies of these decks will decrease, being about 85% for the second deck and 75% for the third deck.

The capacity of a screen is the number of tons of material that 1 sq ft will pass per hour. The capacity will vary with the size of the openings, the kind of material screened, the material moisture content, and other factors. Because of the factors that affect the capacity of a screen, it will seldom if ever be possible to calculate in advance the exact capacity of a screen. If a given number of tons of material must be passed per hour, it is good practice to select a screen whose total calculated capacity is 10 to 25% greater than the required capacity.

The chart in Fig. 17-22 gives capacities for dry screening which may be used as a guide in selecting the correct size screen for a given flow of material. The capacities given in the chart should be modified by the application of appropriate correction factors. Representative values of these factors are given hereafter.

Efficiency factors. If a low screening efficiency is permissible, the capacity of a screen may be higher than the values given in Fig. 17-22. Table 17-8 gives the factors by which

FIGURE 17-20
Flat vibrating screen. (*Cedarapids Inc., A Raytheon Company.*)

FIGURE 17-21
Triple-deck screen with bars for washing aggregate. (*Iowa Manufacturing Company.*)

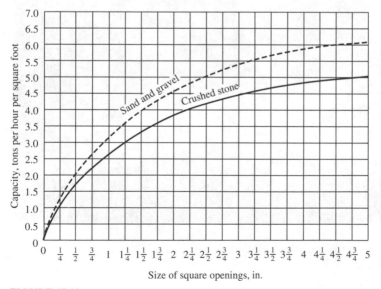

FIGURE 17-22
Screen-capacity chart.

TABLE 17-8
Efficiency factors for aggregate screening

Permissible screen efficiency (%)	Efficiency factor
95	1.00
90	1.25
85	1.50
80	1.75
75	2.00

TABLE 17-9
Deck factors for aggregate screening

For deck number	Deck factor
1	1.00
2	0.90
3	0.75
4	0.60

the chart values of capacities may be multiplied to obtain corrected capacities for given efficiencies.

Deck factors. This is a factor whose value will vary with the particular deck position for multiple-deck screens. The values are given in Table 17-9.

Aggregate-size factors. The capacities of screens given in Fig. 17-22 are based on screening dry material which contains particle sizes such as those found in the output of a representative crusher. If the material to be screened contains a surplus of small sizes, the capacity of the screen will be increased, whereas if the material contains a surplus of large sizes, the capacity of the screen will be reduced. Table 17-10 gives representative factors which may be applied to the capacity of a screen to correct for the effect of fine or coarse particles.

Determining the screen size required. Figure 17-22 gives the theoretical capacity of a screen in tons per hour per square foot based on material weighing 100 lb per cu ft when crushed. The corrected capacity of a screen is given by the equation

TABLE 17-10
Aggregate-size factors for screening

Percent of aggregate less than $\frac{1}{2}$ the size of screen opening	Aggregate-size factor
10	0.55
20	0.70
30	0.80
40	1.00
50	1.20
60	1.40
70	1.80
80	2.20
90	3.00

$$Q = ACEDG \qquad (17\text{-}4)$$

where Q = capacity of screen, tons per hour

A = area of screen, sq ft

C = theoretical capacity of screen, tons per hour per sq ft

E = efficiency factor

D = deck factor

G = aggregate-size factor

The minimum area of a screen to provide a given capacity is determined from the equation

$$A = \frac{Q}{CEDG} \qquad (17\text{-}5)$$

Example 17-4. Determine the minimum-size single-deck screen, having $1\frac{1}{2}$-in.-sq. openings, for screening 120 tons per hour of dry crushed stone, weighing 100 lb per cu ft when crushed. A screening efficiency of 90% is satisfactory. An analysis of the aggregate indicates that approximately 30% of it will be less than $\frac{3}{4}$ in. in size. The values of the factors to be used in Eq. (17-5) are

$$
\begin{aligned}
Q &= 120 \text{ ton/hr} \\
C &= 3.3 \text{ ton/hr per sq ft} & \text{(Fig. 17-22)} \\
E &= 1.25 & \text{(Table 17-8)} \\
D &= 1.0 & \text{(Table 17-9)} \\
G &= 0.8 & \text{(Table 17-10)}
\end{aligned}
$$

Substituting these values in Eq. (17-5), we get

$$A = \frac{120}{3.3 \times 1.25 \times 1.0 \times 0.8} = 36.4 \text{ sq ft}$$

In view of the possibility of variations in the factors used, and to provide a margin of safety, it is recommended that a 4- by 10-ft (40-sq ft) screen be selected.

Portable crushing and screening plants. Many types and sizes of portable crushing and screening plants are used in the construction industry. When there is a satisfactory deposit of stone near a project that requires aggregate, it frequently will be more economical to set up a portable plant and to produce the crushed stone instead of purchasing it from a commercial source. Larger commercial aggregate plants are, however, the major source of crushed stone for the construction industry in metropolitan areas. Figure 17-23 is a mobile track primary jaw crusher at a commercial aggregate-processing operation.

Typical portable crushing and screening plants are illustrated in Figs. 17-24 and 17-25. In Fig. 17-25 the stone from the quarry is fed to the plant by a belt conveyor at

FIGURE 17-23
Mobile track primary jaw crusher. (*Cedarapids Inc., A Raytheon Company.*)

the right. This particular machine is designed to permit the quarry product to pass over a bottom-deck screen, which removes the material smaller than the screen, thereby reducing the load on the primary crusher. The oversize stone from this screen is fed to a jaw crusher, then to a belt conveyor, which returns it to a top-deck screen, where the specification sizes are removed. The oversize stone is fed to a roll crusher. Portable plants commonly use a jaw crusher for primary crushing and a roll crusher for secondary crushing. Changes in the specification sizes may be met, over a reasonably wide range, by adjusting the crusher settings and changing the sizes of the screens.

FLOW DIAGRAMS OF AGGREGATE-PROCESSING PLANTS

Figure 17-26 illustrates the flow diagram for a portable aggregate-processing plant. By passing the stone for the quarry over a screen before it goes to the primary crusher, any stone within the specification sizes will be removed prior to crushing. This arrangement should increase the output of the plant.

FIGURE 17-24
Portable aggregate plant in operation. (*Cedarapids Inc., A Raytheon Company.*)

FIGURE 17-25
Cutaway of portable rock-crushing plant. (*Protec, Inc., Pioneer Division.*)

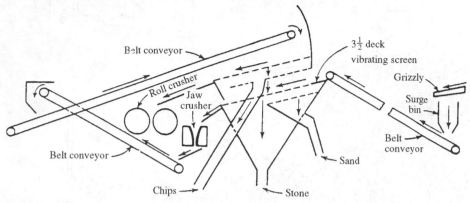

FIGURE 17-26
Portable aggregate-processing plant flow diagram.

Representative sizes of crushers and other equipment for this plant are as follows:

Jaw crusher, 10×36 in.
Roll crusher, 40×22 in.
Vibrator screen, 4×12 ft, $3\frac{1}{2}$ decks
Feeder, 4-ft hopper
Feeder conveyor, 30 in. wide, 50 ft long
Return conveyor, 24 in. wide

Figure 17-27 illustrates the flow diagram of the aggregate-processing plant for the Philpott Dam in Virginia. This plant was located near the quarry, and trucks were used to haul the finished aggregate to the concrete mixing plant at the dam.

Example 17-5. When constructing the Perris Dam in California, the contractor opened a rock quarry to drill, blast, crush, and deliver 50,000 tons per week of aggregate to the project [4].

He drilled 4-in.-diameter holes to depths of 40 ft, loaded them with Du Pont Pourvex slurry, then blasted 300 to 400 holes at a time to produce 40,000 to 50,000 tons of rock. All the rock in excess of 48 in. in size was removed for riprap before sending the smaller-size material to a crusher plant.

Because the project required more than 2,500,000 cu yd of crushed rock, the crushing plant was designed to provide the quantities and sizes of material needed for the job. As illustrated in Fig. 17-28, the plant produced aggregate in three size ranges.

HANDLING CRUSHED-STONE AGGREGATE

After stone is crushed and screened to provide the desired size ranges, it is necessary to handle the stone carefully or the large and small particles may separate, thereby destroying the blend in sizes which is essential to meeting graduation requirements. If

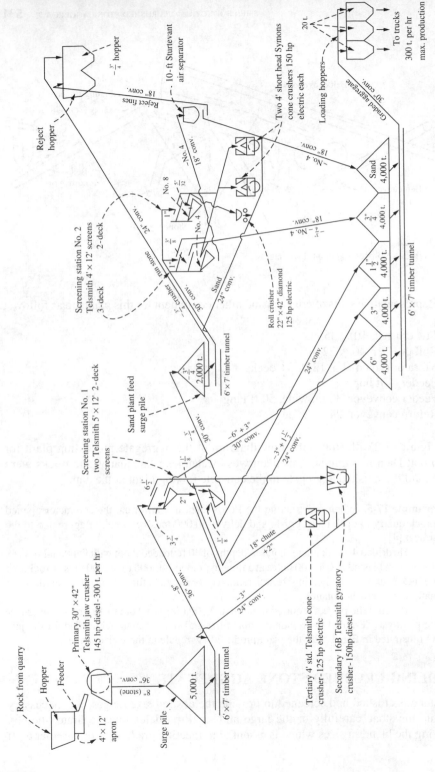

FIGURE 17-27
Flow diagram for the aggregate-processing plant at the Philpott Dam.

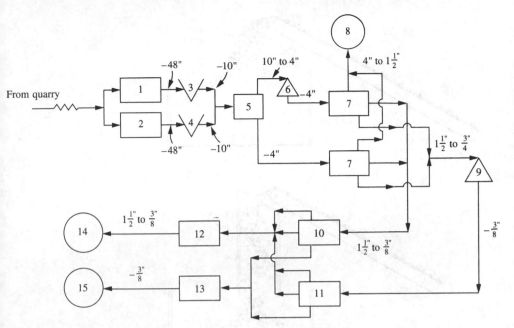

FIGURE 17-28
Flow diagram for the aggregate production plant at the Perris Dam: (1) $5 \times 20'$ grizzly feeder; (2) $5 \times 16'$ vibrating feeder; (3) $48 \times 48''$ jaw crusher; (4) $42 \times 48''$ jaw crusher; (5) $6 \times 16'$ scalping screen; (6) $7'$ standard cone crusher; (7) $6 \times 16'$ doubledeck screens; (8) stockpile for 4 to $1\frac{1}{2}''$ aggregate; (9) $5\frac{1}{2}'$ shorthead cone crusher; (10) $8 \times 20'$ doubledeck screen; (11) $8 \times 20'$ doubledeck screen; (12) double screw classifier; (13) double screw classifier; (14) stockpile for $1\frac{1}{2}$ to $\frac{3}{8}''$ aggregate; (15) stockpile $\frac{3}{8}''$ minus aggregate.

aggregate is permitted to flow freely off the end of a belt conveyor, especially at some height above the storage pile, the material will be segregated by sizes, as illustrated in Fig. 17-29. A strong cross wind tends to separate the smaller sizes from the larger ones.

Specifications covering the production of aggregate frequently stipulate that the aggregate transported by a belt conveyor shall not be permitted to fall freely from the discharge end of a belt. The end of the belt should be kept as low as possible, and the aggregate should be discharged through a rock ladder, containing baffles, to prevent segregation.

Figure 17-30 shows a rock ladder used to reduce segregation.

PROBLEMS

17-1. A jaw crusher, with a closed setting of 3 in., produces 200 tons per hour of crushed stone. Determine the number of tons per hour produced in each of the following size ranges: in excess of $2\frac{1}{2}$ in.; between $2\frac{1}{2}$ and $1\frac{1}{2}$ in.; between $1\frac{1}{2}$ and $\frac{1}{4}$ in.; less than $\frac{1}{4}$ in.

17-2. A roll crusher, set at 2 in., produces 120 tons per hour of crushed stone. Determine the number of tons per hour produced in each of the following size ranges: in excess of $1\frac{1}{2}$ in.; between $1\frac{1}{2}$ in. and $\frac{3}{4}$ in.; between $\frac{3}{4}$ and $\frac{1}{4}$ in.

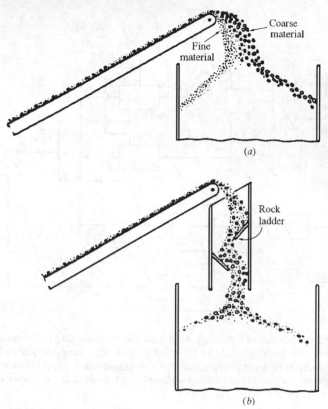

FIGURE 17-29
Method of preventing the segregation of aggregate discharge from a conveyor belt.

17-3. Select a jaw crusher for primary crushing and a roll crusher for secondary crushing to produce 200 tons per hour of limestone rock. The maximum-size stone from the quarry will be 12 in. The stone is to be crushed to the following specifications:

Size screen opening (in.)		
Passing	Retained on	Percent
$2\frac{1}{2}$		100
$2\frac{1}{2}$	$1\frac{1}{4}$	30–40
$1\frac{1}{4}$	$\frac{3}{4}$	22–30
$\frac{3}{4}$	$\frac{1}{4}$	20–30
$\frac{1}{4}$	0	15–25

Specify the size and setting for each crusher selected.

FIGURE 17-30
A rock ladder used to reduce the segregation of aggregate.

17-4. A jaw crusher and a roll crusher are used in an attempt to crush 140 tons per hour of stone to the following specifications:

Size screen opening (in.)		
Passing	Retained on	Percent
$2\frac{1}{2}$		100
$2\frac{1}{2}$	$1\frac{1}{2}$	40–48
$1\frac{1}{2}$	$\frac{3}{4}$	30–36
$\frac{3}{4}$	$\frac{1}{4}$	20–25
$\frac{1}{4}$	0	10–20

Select crushers to produce this aggregate. Is it possible to produce aggregate to meet these specifications with the indicated crushers without surpluses in any of the size ranges? Can the product of these crushers be processed to provide the desired sizes in the specified percentages? If so, tell how.

17-5. A 30- by 42-in. jaw crusher is set to operate with a $2\frac{1}{2}$-in. opening. The output from the crusher is discharged onto a screen with $1\frac{1}{2}$-in. openings, whose efficiency is 90%. The aggregate that does not pass through the screen goes to a 40- by 20-in. roll crusher, set at $1\frac{1}{4}$ in. The output from the roll crusher is fed back over the screen.

Determine the maximum output of the plant in tons per hour.

Determine the output of the plant in tons per hour in each of the two sizes 1 in. to $\frac{1}{2}$ in., and less than $\frac{1}{2}$ in.

17-6. A portable crushing plant is equipped with the following units:

One jaw crusher, size 15×30 in.
One roll crusher, size 30×22 in.
One set of horizontal vibrating screen, two decks, with $1\frac{1}{2}$- and $\frac{3}{4}$-in. openings

The specifications require that 100% of the aggregate should pass a $1\frac{1}{2}$-in. screen and 50% should pass a $\frac{3}{4}$-in. screen.

Assume that 10% of the stone from the quarry will be smaller than $1\frac{1}{2}$ in. and that this aggregate will be removed by passing the quarry product over the screen before sending it to the jaw crusher. The aggregate will weigh 110 lb per cu ft.

Determine the maximum output of the plant, in tons per hour. Include the aggregate removed by the screens prior to sending it to the crushers.

17-7. The output from a 36- by 42-in. crusher, with a closed opening of $2\frac{1}{2}$ in., is passed over a single horizontal vibrating screen with $1\frac{1}{4}$ in. openings. If the permissible screen efficiency is 90%, use the information in this book to determine the minimum-size screen, in square feet, required to handle the output of the crusher.

17-8. The output from a 36- by 42-in. jaw crusher, with a closed setting of 4 in., is to be screened into the following sizes: $2\frac{1}{2}$ to $1\frac{1}{2}$ in.; $1\frac{1}{2}$ to $\frac{3}{4}$ in.; less than $\frac{3}{4}$ in. A three-deck horizontal vibrating screen will be used to separate the three sizes. The stone weighs 115 lb per cu ft. If the permissible screen efficiency is 90%, determine the minimum-size screen for each deck, in square feet, required to handle the output of the crusher.

REFERENCES

1. Barksdale, Richard D. (ed): *The Aggregate Handbook,* National Stone Association, Washington, DC, 1991.
2. *Aggregate Reference Guide,* 1976, Kolberg Manufacturing Corporation, 20 West 21st Street, Yankton, SD 57078.
3. *Cedarapids Pocket Reference Book,* 13th Pocket Ed., Cedarapids Inc., 916 16th Street NE, Cedar Rapids, IA 52402.
4. "Contractor-Planned Crushing Plant Keeps Dam on Schedule," *Roads & Streets,* vol. 115, pp. 46–48, August 1972.
5. Higgins, Lindley R.: "Aggregates Today; Breakthrough in Methodology, Advances in Automation and Movement," *Construction Methods & Equipment,* vol. 54, pp. 72–75, January 1972.
6. Kelly, Errol G., and Spottiswood, David J.: *Introduction to Mineral Processing,* Wiley, New York, NY 10016, 1982.
7. Newman, Donald: "Mathematical Method for Blending Aggregates," *Journal of the Construction Division,* in *Proceedings of the ASCE,* vol. 90, pp. 1–13, September 1964.
8. *Telsmith Mineral Processing Handbook,* 1976, Telsmith Division, Barber-Greene Company, 532 East Capitol Drive, Milwaukee, WI 53212.

CHAPTER
18

CONCRETE

INTRODUCTION

Portland cement concrete is unquestionably the most widely used structural material in the world for civil works projects. Its versatility, economy, adaptability, and worldwide availability, and especially its low maintenance requirements, make it very useful. The term "concrete" is applicable for many products but is most generally used with portland cement concrete. It consists of portland cement, water, and aggregate which have been mixed together, placed, consolidated, and allowed to solidify and harden. The portland cement and water form a paste, which acts as the glue, or binder. When fine aggregate is added (aggregate whose size range lies between the No. 200 mesh sieve and the No. 4 sieve), the resulting mixture is termed mortar. Then when coarse aggregate is included (aggregate sizes larger than the No. 4 sieve), concrete is produced. Normal concrete consists of about three-fourths aggregate and one-fourth paste, by volume. The paste usually consists of water–cement ratios between 0.4 and 0.7 by weight. Admixtures are sometimes added for specific purposes, such as to entrain numerous microscopic air bubbles, to impart color, to retard the initial set of the concrete, to waterproof the concrete, etc.

The operations involved in the production of concrete will vary with the type of end use for the concrete, but, in general, the operations include (see Fig. 18-1):

1. Batching the materials
2. Mixing
3. Transporting
4. Placing
5. Consolidating
6. Finishing
7. Curing

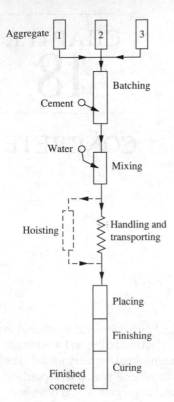

FIGURE 18-1
Flow diagram showing the operations performed in constructing a concrete project.

HISTORY OF CONCRETE

Concrete, as we know it today, had its beginning in 1824 when Joseph Aspdin took out a patent in England on "Portland" cement. This product, which consists of limestone and clay burned at temperatures in excess of 2,700°F, is termed hydraulic in that it will react with water and harden under water. Concrete became widely used in Europe during the late 1800s and was brought to the United States late in that century. Its use continued to spread rapidly as knowledge about it and experience with it grew.

PROPORTIONING CONCRETE MIXTURES

For successful concrete utilization the mixture must be properly proportioned. The American Concrete Institute (ACI) has a number of excellent recommended practices, including one on proportioning concrete mixtures [1]. While it is beyond the scope of this text to cover the specific details of proportioning, a few observations are in order. First, although it takes water to initiate the hydraulic reaction, the higher the water–cement ratio, the lower the resulting strength and durability. Second, the more water that is used (which is not to be confused with the water–cement ratio), the higher will be the slump. Third, the more aggregate that is used, the lower the cost of the concrete. Fourth, the larger the maximum size of coarse aggregate, the less the amount of cement paste that will be needed to coat all the particles and to provide necessary workability. Fifth, the more the fresh concrete is consolidated, the stronger and more durable it becomes. Sixth, the use of properly entrained air enhances almost all concrete properties with little, or no, decrease in strength if the mix proportions are adjusted for the air. And seventh, the surface abrasion resistance of the concrete is almost entirely a function of the properties of the fine aggregate.

FRESH CONCRETE

To the designer, fresh concrete is of little importance. To the constructor, fresh concrete is *all-important,* because it is the fresh concrete that must be mixed, transported, placed, consolidated, finished, and cured. To satisfy both the designer and the constructor, the concrete should [2]:

1. Be easily mixed and transported
2. Be uniform throughout, both within a given batch and between batches
3. Be of proper workability so that it can be consolidated, will completely fill the forms, will not segregate, and will finish properly

The major property of importance to the constructor is the workability which is difficult to define in precise terms. Like the terms "warm" and "cold," workability depends on the situation. One measure of workability is slump, which is a measurable value based on an American Society for Testing and Materials standard test (ASTM C143) [3]. The test is very simple to perform. Fresh concrete is placed into a hollow frustrum of a cone, 4 in. in diameter at the top, 8 in. in diameter at the bottom, and 12 in. high. After filling according to a prescribed procedure, the cone is raised from the concrete, allowing the fresh concrete to "slump" down. The amount of slump is measured in inches (or millimeters) from its original height of 12 in., with the stiffest concrete having zero slump and the most fluid concrete having slumps in excess of 8 in. Although the slump only measures one attribute of workability, the flowability of fresh concrete, it is the most widely used measure. Table 18-1 gives the recommended slumps for various types of concrete construction [4].

TABLE 18-1
Recommended slumps for various types of construction (ACI 211.1) [4]

Types of Construction	Slump (in.)	
	Maximum	Minimum
Reinforced foundation walls and footings	3	1
Plain footings, caissons, and substructure walls	3	1
Beams and reinforced walls	4	1
Building columns	4	1
Pavements and slabs	3	1
Mass concrete	2	1

HANDLING AND BATCHING CONCRETE MATERIALS

Most concrete batches, although designed on the basis of absolute volumes of the ingredients, are ultimately controlled in the batching process on the basis of weight. Therefore, it is necessary to know the weight–volume relationships of all the ingredients. Then each ingredient must be accurately weighed if the resulting mixture is to have the desired properties. It is the function of the batching equipment to perform this weighing measurement.

Handling cement.   Cement may be supplied to the project in paper bags, each containing 1 cu ft loose measure and weighing 94 lb net. However, for most large projects, the cement is supplied in bulk quantities from cement transport trucks, each holding 25 tons or more, or from railroad cars.

Bag cement must be stored in a dry place on pallets and should be left in the original bags until used for concrete. If the batching of concrete requires one or more whole bags of cement, the use of bag cement simplifies the batching operation.

Bulk cement usually is unloaded by air pressure from rail cars or special truck trailers and stored in overhead silos or bins.

Batching and concrete.   Usually, concrete specifications require the concrete to be batched with aggregate having at least two size ranges (coarse and fine) and up to six ranges. Figure 18-2 illustrates the proper and improper methods of batching. Aggregate from each size range must be accurately measured. The aggregate, water, cement, and admixtures (if used) are introduced into a concrete mixer and mixed for a suitable period of time until all the ingredients are adequately blended together. ASTM C94 [5] recommends, where no mixer performance tests are available, a minimum mixing time of 1 min for mixers of 1 cu yd or less, with an increase in mixing time of $\frac{1}{4}$ min for each additional cubic yard of concrete. Thus, an 8-cu-yd mixer should mix the concrete a minimum of $1 + 7 \times \frac{1}{4} = 3\frac{3}{4}$ min.

Interestingly, most modern plants have performance data on their mixers to show that they can adequately mix the concrete in less time than that specified by ASTM [3]. Quite often, modern plants completely mix up to 8 cu yd of concrete in 1 min.

Batch plants and mixers.   There are two types of concrete-mixing operations in use, job-batched concrete and central-batched concrete. Today, unless the project is in a remote location or is relatively large, more and more of the concrete is batched in a central batch plant and transported to the job site in ready-mixed concrete trucks. This type of concrete is controlled by ASTM specification C94 [5], and there is a national organization promoting its use (National Ready Mixed Concrete Association [6]). Figure 18-3 shows the layout of the central batch plant for the Phillpot Dam. Note that a concrete batch required four different sizes of coarse aggregate, plus sand, two types of cement, flaked ice, and water. The water and liquid admixtures are normally measured by volume, whereas the cement and aggregates are measured by weight. To control the batching, close tolerances are maintained. Table 18-2 gives the permissible tolerances in accordance with ACI 304 [2]. Batch plants are available in three categories: manual, semiautomatic, and fully automatic. Manual batching is generally used for small jobs

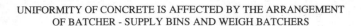

UNIFORMITY OF CONCRETE IS AFFECTED BY THE ARRANGEMENT OF BATCHER - SUPPLY BINS AND WEIGH BATCHERS

(a)

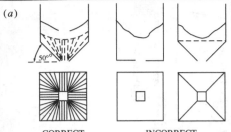

CORRECT	INCORRECT
FULL BOTTOM SLOPING 50° FROM HORIZONTAL IN ALL DIRECTIONS TO OUTLET WITH CORNERS OF BIN PROPERLY ROUNDED SO THAT ALL MATERIAL MOVES TOWARD THE OUTLET.	FLAT BOTTOM BINS OR THOSE WITH ANY ARRANGEMENT OF SLOPES HAVING CORNERS OR AREAS SUCH THAT ALL MATERIAL IN BINS WILL NOT FLOW READILY THROUGH OUTLET WITHOUT SHOVELING.

SLOPE OF AGGREGATE BIN BOTTOMS

(b)

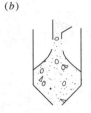

CORRECT	INCORRECT
MATERIAL DROPS VERTICALLY INTO BIN DIRECTLY OVER THE DISCHARGE OPENING PERMITTING DISCHARGE OF MORE GENERALLY UNIFORM MATERIAL.	CHUTING MATERIAL INTO BIN ON AN ANGLE. MATERIAL FALLING OTHER THAN DIRECTLY OVER OPENING NOT ALWAYS UNIFORM AS DISCHARGED.

AGGREGATE BIN FILLING

(c) GRAVEL BINS ARRANGED CONCENTRICALLY AROUND CEMENT BINS.

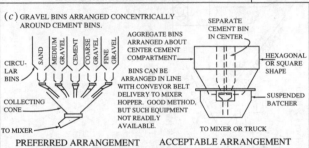

SEPARATE CEMENT BIN IN CENTER

AGGREGATE BINS ARRANGED ABOUT CENTER CEMENT COMPARTMENT

HEXAGONAL OR SQUARE SHAPE

BINS CAN BE ARRANGED IN LINE WITH CONVEYOR BELT DELIVERY TO MIXER HOPPER. GOOD METHOD, BUT SUCH EQUIPMENT NOT READILY AVAILABLE.

SUSPENDED BATCHER

TO MIXER OR TRUCK

(d) SIDE OPENINGS

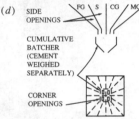

CUMULATIVE BATCHER (CEMENT WEIGHED SEPARATELY)

CORNER OPENINGS

PREFERRED ARRANGEMENT	ACCEPTABLE ARRANGEMENT	POOR ARRANGEMENTS
AUTOMATIC WEIGHING OF EACH INGREDIENT IN INDIVIDUAL WEIGH BATCHERS, DISCHARGING THROUGH COLLECTING CONE DIRECTLY INTO MIXER. DISCHARGE OF CEMENT BATCHER CONTROLLED SO THAT CEMENT IS FLOWING WHILE AGGREGATE IS BEING DELIVERED. BATCHERS INSULATED FROM PLANT VIBRATION WILL PERMIT OVERLOAD CORRECTION.	AGGREGATE AUTOMATICALLY WEIGHED SEPARATELY OR CUMULATIVELY. CEMENT WEIGHED SEPARATELY. BATCHERS INSULATED FROM PLANT VIBRATION. WEIGHT RECORDING EQUIPMENT PLAINLY VISIBLE TO OPERATOR. PROPER SEQUENCE OF DUMPING MATERIALS NECESSARY. AVOID AGGREGATE CONSTANTLY FLOWING OVER TOP OF MATERIAL IN BINS. WILL NOT PERMIT CORRECTING OVERLOADS.	EITHER OF ABOVE CLOSE GROUPINGS OF BIN DISCHARGES THAT CAUSE LONG SLOPES OF MATERIAL IN BINS RESULTS IN SEPARATION AND IMPAIRED UNIFORMITY.

(e)

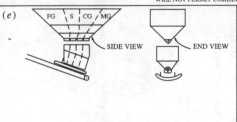

SIDE VIEW   END VIEW

(f)

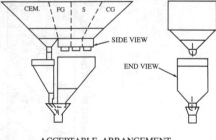

SIDE VIEW   END VIEW

PREFERRED ARRANGEMENT	ACCEPTABLE ARRANGEMENT
AGGREGATE AUTOMATICALLY WEIGHED CUMULATIVELY, AND CARRIED TO MIXER ON CONVEYOR BELT. CEMENT WEIGHED SEPARATELY AND DISCHARGE IS CONTROLLED SO THAT CEMENT IS FLOWING WHILE AGGREGATE IS BEING DELIVERED.	AGGREGATE AUTOMATICALLY WEIGHED CUMULATIVELY. CEMENT WEIGHED SEPARATELY AND DISCHARGE CONTROLLED SO THAT CEMENT IS FLOWING WHILE AGGREGATE IS BEING DELIVERED.

FIGURE 18-2
Proper and improper methods of concrete batching (from ACI 304) [1].

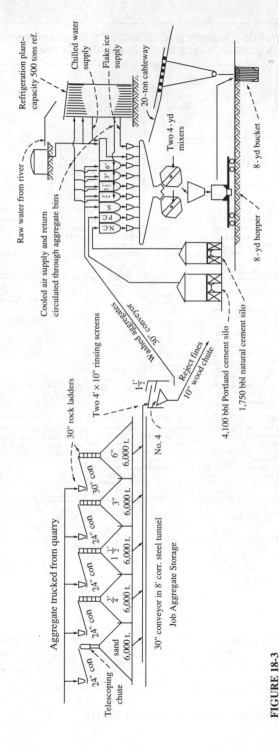

FIGURE 18-3

Flow-diagram for the concrete-mixing plant at Philpott Dam.

TABLE 18-2
Typical batching tolerances (ACI 304R) [2]

Ingredient	Batch weights greater than 30% of scale capacity		Batch weights less than 30% of scale capacity	
	Individual batching	.Cumulative batching	Individual batching	Cumulative batching
Cement and other cementitious materials	±1% of ±0.3% of scale capacity, whichever is greater		Not less than required weight or 4% more than required weight	
Water (by volume or weight) (%)	±1	Not recommended	±1	Not recommended
Aggregates (%)	±2	±1	±3	±0.3% of scale capacity or ±3% of required cumulative weight, whichever is less
Admixtures (by volume or weight) (%)	±3	Not recommended	±3	Not recommended

or low output values (less than about 500 cu yd total or around 20 cu yd per hour). In semiautomatic plants the charging and discharging of the batchers are activated manually but are automatically terminated. In a fully automatic batch plant a single starter switch activates the batching sequence, the weights and volumes of which have been previously programmed into the system.

Present-day plants usually have mixers capable of mixing up to 8 cu yd of concrete in each batch (although plants have been built with mixers capable of mixing 15 cu yd of concrete in each batch) and can produce more than 200 cu yd of concrete per hour. The mixer either tilts to discharge the concrete into a truck or a chute is inserted into the mixer to catch and discharge the concrete. To increase efficiency, many large plants contain two mixers connected in series. The back mixer premixes the aggregates and cement, which reduces the time necessary for the front mixer to mix the batch completely. Although the discussion presented here covers drum mixing of concrete, there are two other types of mixers in use—the pan mixer and the continuous mixer. These latter two will not be covered, as their use is limited to special situations.

In determining the quantities needed and the output for a given plant, one should include any delays in productivity resulting from reduced operating factors. The following example illustrates the method of calculating quantities and output.

Example 18-1. Determine the quantities of materials required per batch and the probable output for an 8-cu-yd central-mix plant. The quantities of materials per cubic yard are:

Cement, 5.6 bags
Sand, 1,438 lb
Gravel, 1,699 lb
Water, 39 gal

If the batch is 8.0 cu yd, the required amount of (1) cement will be $8 \times 5.6 \times 94 = 4,211$ lb, (2) sand will be $8 \times 1,438 = 11,504$ lb, (3) gravel will be $8 \times 1,699 = 13,592$ lb, and (4) water will be $8 \times 39 = 312$ gal. The calculated fresh unit weight of the concrete will be (in lb per cu yd):

Cement, 5.6×94 =	526.4	lb
Sand	1,438	lb
Gravel	1,699	lb
Water, 39×7.48 =	291.7	lb
Total	3,955.1	lb

The fresh unit weight = $3,955.1/27 = 146.5$ lb per cu ft.

If the mixer discharges the entire load into one truck, the time per cycle can be about:

Charging mixer	= 0.50 min	
Mixing concrete	= 2.25 min	
Discharging mixer	= 0.50 min	
Lost time	= 0.25 min	(average of minor mechanical problems)
Total time	= 3.50 min	
No. of batches per hour	= 60/3.5 = 17.1	
Output	= 17.1×8 = 136.8 cu yd per hour	

If the lost time can be eliminated, then the production can be raised to 147.7 cu yd per hour. Furthermore, if the mixing time can be reduced to 1 min, the production can be raised to 240 cu yd per hour. However, even the best plants do not operate a full 60-min hour.

READY-MIXED CONCRETE

Increasingly, concrete is proportioned in a central location and transported to the purchaser in a fresh state, mixed at the plant or en route. This type of concrete is termed "ready-mixed concrete" and is governed by ASTM C94 [5]. Because of its economy and quality, and through the efforts of the National Ready Mixed Concrete Association [6], concrete purchased in this manner enjoys wide acceptance. Obviously, to be useful, ready-mixed concrete must be available within a reasonable distance from the project. At remote locations and locations requiring large quantities of concrete, generally concrete batch plants are set up on site.

Concrete purchased from a ready-mixed concrete plant can be provided in several ways. These include:

1. *Central-mixed concrete.* This is concrete which is mixed completely in a stationary mixer and transported to the project in either a truck agitator, a truck mixer operating at agitating speed, or a nonagitating truck.
2. *Shrink-mixed concrete.* This is concrete which is partially mixed in a stationary mixer and then mixed completely in a truck mixer (usually en route to the project).
3. *Truck-mixed concrete.* This is concrete that is completely mixed in a truck mixer, with 70 to 100 revolutions at a speed sufficient to mix the concrete completely. This

type of concrete is usually termed "transit-mixed concrete" because it is mixed en route.

The specifications for the batch plant and the transport trucks, to include the transit mixers, are covered in detail in ASTM C94 [5]. Of particular importance is the elapsed time from the introduction of water to the placement of the concrete into the forms. ASTM C94 allows a maximum of $1\frac{1}{2}$ hour, or before the drum has revolved 300 revolutions, whichever comes first.

Transit mixers are available in several sizes up to about 14 cu yd, but the most popular size is 8 cu yd. They are capable of thoroughly mixing the concrete with about 100 revolutions of the mixing drum (see Fig. 18-4). Mixing speed is generally 8 to 12 rpm. This mixing during transit usually results in stiffening the mixture, and ASTM C94 allows the addition of water at the job site to restore the slump, followed by remixing. This has caused problems and raised questions concerning the uniformity of ready-mixed concrete. ACI 304 [1] recommends that some of the water be withheld until the mixer arrives at the project site (especially in hot weather), then the remaining water be added and an additional 30 revolutions of mixing be required. To offset any stiffening, small amounts of additional water are permitted, *provided the design water–cement ratio is not exceeded.* The uniformity requirements of ready-mixed concrete are given in Table 18-3.

FIGURE 18-4
Sectional view through the drum of a transit mixer.

TABLE 18-3
Uniformity requirements for ready-mixed concrete (ASTM C94) [5]

Test	Requirement, expressed as maximum permissible difference in results of tests of samples taken from two locations in the concrete batch
Weight per cu ft calculated to an air-free basis	1.0 lb/cu ft
Air content, volume percent of concrete	1.0%
Slump:	
If average slump is 4 in. or less	1.0 in.
If average slump is 4 to 6 in.	1.5 in.
Coarse aggregate content, portion by weight retained on No. 4 sieve	6.0%
Unit weight of air-free mortar based on average for all comparative samples tested	1.6%
Average compressive strength at 7 days for each sample, based on average strength of all comparative test specimens	7.5%

Ready-mixed concrete may be ordered in several ways. They are:

1. *Recipe batch.* The purchaser assumes responsibility for proportioning the concrete mixture, to include specifying the cement content, the maximum allowable water content, and the admixtures required. The purchaser may also specify the amounts and type of coarse and fine aggregate. Under this approach the purchaser assumes full responsibility for the resulting strength and durability of the mixture, provided that the stipulated amounts are furnished as specified.
2. *Performance batch.* The purchaser specifies the requirements for the strength of the concrete, and the manufacturer assumes full responsibility for the proportions of the various ingredients that go into the batch.
3. *Part performance and part recipe.* The purchaser generally specifies a minimum cement content, the required admixtures, and the strength requirements, allowing the manufacturer to proportion the concrete mixture within the constraints imposed.

Today most purchasers of concrete use the third approach, part performance and part recipe, as it ensures a minimum durability while still allowing the ready-mixed concrete supplier some flexibility to supply the most economical mixture.

MOVING AND PLACING CONCRETE

Once the concrete arrives at the project site, it must be moved to its final position without segregation and before it has achieved an initial set. This movement may be accomplished in several ways, depending on the distance, elevation, and other constraints imposed. These methods include buckets or hoppers, chutes and drop pipes, belt conveyors, and concrete pumps.

Buckets or hoppers. Normally, properly designed bottom-dump buckets permit concrete placement at the lowest practical slump. Care should be exercised to prevent the concrete from segregating as a result of discharging from too high above the surface or allowing the fresh concrete to fall past obstructions. Gates should be designed so that they can be opened and closed at any time during the discharge of the concrete.

Manual or motor propelled buggies. Hand buggies and wheelbarrows are usually capable of carrying from 4 to 9 cu ft of concrete, and thus are suitable on many projects, provided there are smooth and rigid runways upon which to operate. Hand buggies are safer than wheelbarrows because they have two wheels rather than one. Hand buggies and wheelbarrows are recommended for distances less than 200 ft, whereas power-driven or motor-driven buggies—with capacities up to around 14 cu ft—can traverse up to 1,000 ft economically.

Chutes and drop pipes. Chutes are often used to transfer concrete from a higher elevation to a lower elevation. They should have a round bottom, and the slope should be steep enough for the concrete to flow continuously without segregation. Drop pipes are used to transfer the concrete vertically down. The pipe should have a diameter at least 8 times the maximum aggregate size at the top 6 to 8 ft, and may be tapered so that the lower end is approximately 6 times the maximum aggregate size [1]. Drop pipes are used when concrete is placed in a wall or column to avoid segregation from allowing

FIGURE 18-5
56 ft long portable conveyor transporting fresh concrete. (*Morgan Manufacturing Company.*)

the concrete to free-fall through the reinforcement. In such areas pipes should always be used (see Fig. 18-5).

Belt conveyors. Belt conveyors can be classified into three types: (1) portable or self-contained conveyors, (2) feeders or series conveyors, and (3) side-discharge or spreader conveyors. All types provide for the rapid movement of fresh concrete but must have proper belt size and speed to achieve the desired rate of transportation. Particular attention must be given to points where the concrete leaves one conveyor and either continues on another conveyor or is discharged, as segregation can occur. The optimum concrete slump for conveyed concrete is from $2\frac{1}{2}$ to 3 in. [4]. Figure 18-5 shows a 56-ft portable conveyor transporting concrete to a drop pipe into a column form. Figure 18-6 shows the use of several portable conveyors to transport fresh concrete over a 252-ft-long bridge being built in Sioux Falls, South Dakota. As the job progressed, the conveyors retracted on the double rail system. Excess conveyors were removed from the charging end. Figure 18-7 shows a side-discharge conveyor with 20-in. belts transporting and placing concrete on deck slabs of 80- to 90-ft widths.

Concrete pumps. The placement of concrete through rigid or flexible lines is not new. In fact, a patent for this method of moving concrete was issued in 1913 [7]. Pumping was not used extensively until the 1930s when German pumping equipment was intro-

FIGURE 18-6
String of portable conveyors transporting fresh concrete over a bridge. (*Morgan Manufacturing Company.*)

FIGURE 18-7
Side-discharge conveyor transporting and placing fresh concrete on a bridge deck. (*Morgan Manufacturing Company.*)

duced in this country. The pump is an extremely simple machine. By applying pressure to a column of fresh concrete in a pipe, the concrete can be moved through the pipe if a lubricating outer layer is provided and if the mixture is properly proportioned for pumping. In order to work properly, the pump must be fed concrete of uniform workability and consistency. Today concrete pumping is one of the fastest growing specialty contracting fields in the United States, as perhaps one-fourth of all concrete is placed by pumping. Pumps are available in a variety of sizes, capable of delivering concrete at sustained rates of 10 to 150 cu yd per hour. Effective pumping range varies from 300 to 1,000 ft horizontally, or 100 to 300 ft vertically [8], although occasionally pumps have moved concrete more than 5,000 ft horizontally and 1,000 ft vertically [9].

Pumps require a steady supply of *pumpable* concrete to be effective. Today there are three types of pumps being manufactured: piston pumps, pneumatic pumps, and squeeze pressure pumps. They are shown diagrammatically in Figs. 18-8(*a*), (*b*), and (*c*), respectively. Most piston pumps currently contain two pistons, with one retracting during the forward stroke of the other to give a more continuous flow of concrete. The pneumatic pumps normally use a reblending discharge box at the discharge end to bleed off the air and to prevent segregation and spraying. In squeeze pressure pumps hydraulically powered rollers rotate on the flexible hose within the drum and squeeze

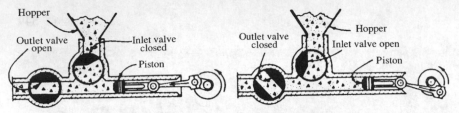

Inlet valve opens while outlet valve is closed and concrete is drawn into cylinder by gravity and piston suction. As piston moves forward inlet valve closes, outlet valve opens, and concrete is pushed into pump line.

(a)

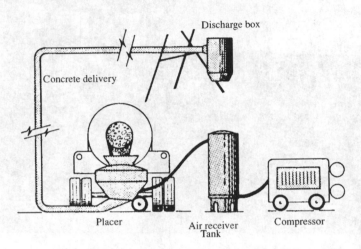

Compressor builds up air pressure in tank, which forces concrete in placer through the line.

(b)

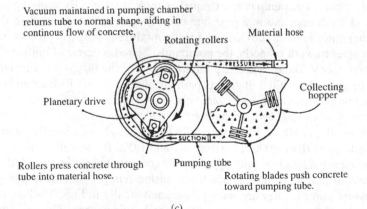

Rollers press concrete through tube into material hose.

Rotating blades push concrete toward pumping tube.

(c)

FIGURE 18-8
(a) Schematic drawing of piston-type concrete pump (from ACI 304.2R) [8]. (b) Schematic drawing of pneumatic-type concrete pump (from ACI 304.2R) [8]. (c) Schematic drawing of squeeze pressure-type concrete pump (from ACI 304.2R) [8].

the concrete out at the top. The vacuum keeps a steady supply of concrete in the tube from the receiving hopper.

Pumps may be mounted on trucks, trailers, or skids. The truck-mounted pump and boom combination is particularly efficient and cost-effective in saving labor and eliminating the need for pipelines to carry the concrete. Hydraulically operated and articulated, booms come in lengths up to 100 ft and more.

Successful pumping of concrete is no accident. A common fallacy is to assume that any good placeable concrete will pump successfully. The basic principle of pumping is that the concrete moves as a cylinder through a lubricated line, with the lubrication continually being replenished by the cylinder of concrete. To pump concrete successfully, a number of rules should be carefully followed. They are:

1. Use a minimum cement factor of 517 lb of cement per cubic yard of concrete ($5\frac{1}{2}$ sacks per cu yd).
2. Use a combined gradation of coarse and fine aggregate that ensures *no* gaps in sizes that will allow paste to be squeezed through the coarser particles under the pressures induced in the line. In particular, it is important for the fine aggregate to have at least 5% passing the No. 100 sieve and about 3% passing the No. 200 sieve (see gradations given in reference [8]). Line pressures of 300 psi are common, and they can reach as high as 1,000 psi. This is the most often overlooked aspect of good pumping!
3. Use a minimum pipe diameter of 5 in.
4. Always lubricate the line with cement paste or mortar before beginning the pumping operation.
5. Ensure a steady, uniform supply of concrete, with a slump of between 2 and 5 in. as it enters the pump.
6. Always presoak the aggregates before mixing them in the concrete to prevent their soaking up mix water under the imposed pressure. This is especially important when aggregates are used which have a high absorption (such as structural lightweight aggregate).
7. Avoid the use of reducers in the conduit line. One common problem is the use of a 5 to 4-in. reducer at the discharge end so that workers will have only a 4-in. flexible hose to move around. This creates a constriction and significantly raises the pressure necessary to pump the concrete.
8. Never use aluminum lines. Aluminum particles will be scraped from the inside of the pipe as the concrete moves through and will become part of the concrete. Aluminum and portland cement react, liberating hydrogen gas, which can rupture the concrete—with disastrous results.

CONSOLIDATING CONCRETE

Concrete, a heterogeneous mixture of water and solid particles in a stiff condition, will normally contain a large quantity of voids when placed into the forms. The purpose of consolidation is to remove these entrapped air voids. The importance of proper consolidation cannot be overemphasized, as entrapped air can render the concrete totally unsatisfactory. Entrapped air can be reduced two ways—use more water or consolidate the concrete. Figure 18-9 shows qualitatively the benefits of consolidation, especially on low-water-content concrete.

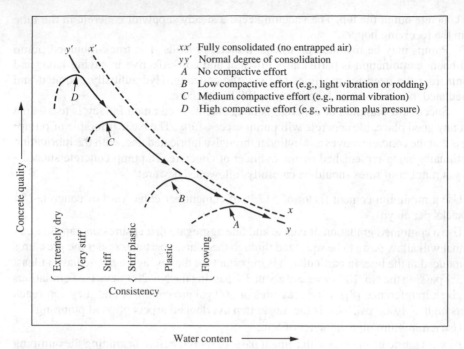

FIGURE 18-9
Effect of compactive effort on concrete quality (from ACI 309R) [10].

Consolidation is normally achieved through the use of mechanical vibrators. There are three general types [10]: internal, surface, and form vibrators. Internal, or spud vibrators as they are often called, have a vibrating casing or head which is immersed into the concrete and vibrates at a high frequency (often as high as 10,000 to 15,000 vibrations per minute) against the concrete. Currently these vibrators are the rotary type and come in sizes from $\frac{3}{4}$ in. to 7 in., each with an effective radius of action [10]. They are powered by electric motors or compressed air. Manufacturers have extensive data on their vibrators.

Surface vibrators exert their effects at the top surface of the concrete and consolidate the concrete from the top down. They are used mainly in slab construction, and there are four general types: the vibrating screed, the pan-type vibrator, the plate or grid vibratory tamper, and the vibratory rolling screed. These surface vibrators operate in the range from 3,000 to 6,000 vibrations per minute.

Form vibrators are external vibrators attached to outside the form or mold. They vibrate the form, which in turn vibrates the concrete. These types of vibrators are generally used in large precast concrete plants.

Recommended vibration practices. Internal vibration is generally best suited for ordinary construction provided the section is large enough for the vibrator to be manipulated. As each vibrator has an effective radius of action, vibrator insertions should be vertical at about $1\frac{1}{2}$ times the radius of action. The vibrator should never be used to move concrete laterally, as segregation can easily occur. The vibrator should be rapidly inserted to the bottom of the layer (usually 12 to 18-in.-maximum-lift thickness) and at least 6 in. into the previous layer. It should then be held stationary for about 5 to 15 sec until the consolidation is considered adequate. The vibrator should then be withdrawn slowly. Where several layers are being placed, each layer should be placed while the preceding layer is still plastic.

Vibration accomplishes two actions. First, it "slumps" the concrete, removing a large portion of air that is entrapped when the concrete is deposited. Then continued vibration consolidates the concrete, removing most of the remaining entrapped air. Generally, it will not remove entrained air. The question concerning overvibration is often raised: When does it occur and how harmful is it? The fact is that on low-slump concrete (concrete with less than a 3-in. slump) it is almost impossible to overvibrate the concrete with internal vibrators! When in doubt as to how much vibration to impart to low-slump concrete, vibrate it some more. The same cannot be said of concrete whose slump is 3 in. or more. This concrete can be overvibrated, which results in segregation as a result of coarse aggregate moving away from the vibrating head. Here the operator should note the presence of air bubbles escaping to the concrete surface as the vibrator is inserted. When these bubbles cease, vibration is generally complete and the vibrator should be withdrawn. Another point of caution concerns surface vibrators. They too can overvibrate the concrete at the surface, significantly weakening it if they remain in one place too long.

Another concern is the vibration of reinforcing steel. Such vibration *improves* the bond between the reinforcing steel and the concrete, and thus is desirable. The undesirable side effects include damage to the vibrator and possible movement of the steel from its intended position.

Finally, *revibration* is the process whereby the concrete is vibrated again after it has been allowed to remain undisturbed for some time. Such revibration can be accomplished at any time the running vibrator will sink of its own weight into the concrete and liquefy it momentarily [10]. Such revibration will improve the concrete through increased consolidation.

FINISHING AND CURING CONCRETE

It cannot be stated too strongly that *any* work done to a concrete surface after it has been consolidated will weaken the surface. All too often, concrete technicians overlook this fact and manipulate the surface of the concrete to produce a smooth, attractive surface. On walls and columns an attractive surface may be desirable and the surface strength may not be too important, but on a floor slab, sidewalk, or pavement the surface strength is very important. On the latter types of surfaces only the absolute minimum finishing necessary to impart the desired texture should be permitted, and the use of "jitterbugging" (the forcing of coarse aggregate down into the concrete with a steel grate tool) should not be permitted, as the surface can be weakened significantly. Furthermore, each step in the finishing operation, from first floating to the final floating or troweling, should be delayed as long as possible and still permit the desired grade and surface smoothness to be obtained. In no case should finishing commence if any free bleed water has not been blotted up, nor should neat cement or mixtures of sand and cement be worked into such surfaces to dry them up.

Along with placement and consolidation, proper curing of the concrete is extremely important. Curing may be considered as the method whereby the concrete is assured of adequate time, temperature, and supply of water for the cement to continue to hydrate. The time normally required is 3 days, and optimum temperatures are between 40 and 80°F. As most concrete is batched with sufficient water for hydration, the only problem is to ensure that the concrete does not become dried out. This may be accomplished by ponding with water (for slabs), covering with burlap or polyethylene sheets, or spraying with an approved curing compound. Curing is one of the least costly operations in the production of quality concrete, and one that is all too frequently overlooked. Concrete, if allowed to dry out during the curing stage, will attempt to shrink. The developing bonds from the cementitious reaction will attempt to restrain the shrinkage from taking place. But the end result is *always* the same: The shrinkage wins out and a crack forms, as the shrinkage stresses are always higher than the tensile strength of the concrete. Proper curing does reduce the detrimental effects of cracking and develops the intended strength of the concrete.

SHOTCRETING

Shotcreting is mortar or concrete conveyed through a hose and pneumatically projected at high velocity onto a surface [11]. The force of the jet impacting on the surface compacts the mixture. Usually, a relatively dry mixture is used, and thus it is able to support itself without sagging or sloughing, even for vertical and overhead applications. Shotcrete, or gunite, as it is more commonly known, is used most often in special applications involving repair work, thin layers, or fiber-reinforced layers. Figure 18-10

FIGURE 18-10
Using the shotcrete method to place concrete lining for a canal. (*Challenge-Cook Bros., Inc.*)

FIGURE 18-11
Equipment used to produce shotcrete concrete. (*Challenge-Cook Bros., Inc.*)

illustrates the use of shotcrete to line a pond. Figure 18-11 shows the equipment used to produce shotcrete. There are two methods of producing shotcrete: the dry-mix process and the wet-mix process. The dry-mix process, in which the cement and damp sand are thoroughly mixed and carried to the nozzle, where water is introduced under pressure and intimately mixed with the cement and sand before being jetted onto the surface, has been used successfully for more than 50 years. The wet-mix process is newer (around 20 years old) and involves mixing all the ingredients including water before being delivered through a hose under pressure to the desired surface. Using the wet-mix process, aggregates up to $\frac{3}{4}$ in. in size have been shotcreted. With either process there is some rebound of the mortar or concrete, resulting in some loss (usually held to 5–10%).

FLY ASH

Fly ash is produced as a by-product in the production of electricity from the burning of coal. It is the fine residue which would "fly" out of the stack of a modern power plant if it were not captured. With the ever-increasing drive to wring every possible Btu out of the coal, modern power plants pulverize it before burning so that almost 100% will pass the No. 200 sieve. In the furnace the coal is heated to in excess of 2,700°F, melting all the incombustibles. Because of the strong induced air currents in the furnace, the molten residue from the coal becomes spherical in shape and the majority is carried out at the top of the furnace. Captured in massive electrostatic precipitators or bag houses, the fly ash is extremely fine (often finer than portland cement). Fly ash has been found to be an excellent mineral admixture in portland cement concrete, improving almost all properties of the concrete [12]. Recently the Environmental Protection Agency ruled that fly ash must be allowed in all concrete construction involving federal funds [13], so the use of fly ash will become the rule rather than the exception.

There are basically two types of fly ash: class F from bituminous coal and class C from subbituminous and lignitic coal. Their quality is governed by ASTM C618 [14]. Portland cement, when it combines with water, releases calcium hydroxide (the white streaks noticeable adjacent to exposed concrete around cracks). This calcium hydroxide does not contribute to strength or durability. By introducing fly ash, the calcium hydroxide and fly ash chemically combine in a process called pozzolanic action. It takes a relatively long time (compared with the cementitious action involved between cement and water), but the resulting concrete is stronger, less permeable, and more durable than before. And if the designer can wait for the strength development, fly ash may be used to replace part of the portland cement, resulting in a lower cost product.

In addition to strength and durability improvements, fly ash also improves the workability of concrete, primarily because of its spherical shape. It has been used to improve the pumpability of concrete mixes, and finishers report that fly ash concrete is easier to finish.

The previous discussion applies to both class F and class C fly ashes. However, *some* class C fly ashes possess significant cementitious properties themselves, probably because of their relatively high calcium contents [14]. Thus, when used as an admixture, extremely high strengths can be obtained, as illustrated by the use of class C fly ash to achieve 7,500 psi concrete in the Texas Commerce Tower in Houston [15]. These fly ashes can replace significant portions of portland cement with no detrimental effects, as demonstrated with 25% replacement percentages on several concrete pavements in Texas [16].

Fly ash poses two problems to the concrete designer and constructor. One is that while it has been shown to be a valuable addition to concrete and can result in significant cost savings, it is a by-product in the production of electric power. This means that it can vary in its properties from day to day, and thus a good quality management program is needed to ensure that only high-quality fly ash is used. Furthermore, because fly ash produced by different plants will vary in quality, it is mandatory that each fly ash be tested prior to its use to assure that it has the desired quality. Second, adding fly ash means that the concrete batch has five major ingredients rather than four. The chances for a mistake being made in the batching are increased, making it desirable to increase the quality control efforts.

BLENDED CEMENTS

Blended cements are cements that have been made by intergrinding portland cement and fly ash at the plant. These cements are governed by ASTM C595 [15] and can be used anywhere type 1 portland cement can be used. Because of the energy savings resulting through the use of fly ash, the use of this type of cement will increase as more and more cement plants start producing it.

PLACING CONCRETE IN COLD WEATHER

When concrete is placed in cold weather, some provision must be made to keep the concrete above freezing during the first few days after it has been placed. Specifications generally require that the concrete be kept at not less than 70°F for 3 days or not less than 50°F for 5 days after placement. ACI 306R contains guidelines for concreting in cold weather [18]. Preheating the water is generally the most effective method of providing the necessary temperature for placement.

When the temperatures of the ingredients are known, the chart in Fig. 18-12 may be used to determine the temperature of concrete. A straight line across all three scales, passing through any two known temperatures, will permit the determination of the third temperature. If the sand is surface-dry, the solid lines of the scales giving the

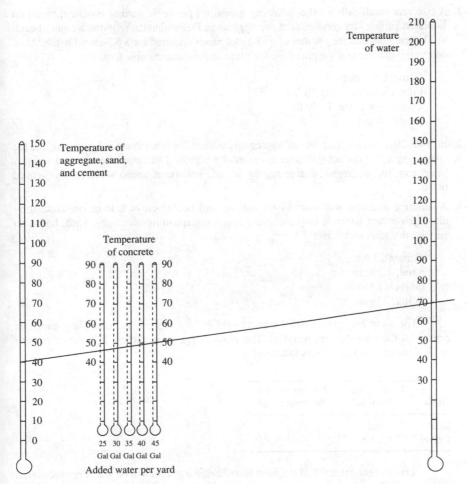

FIGURE 18-12
Chart for determining the temperature of concrete.

temperature of concrete should be used. However, if the sand contains about 3% moisture, the dotted lines should be used.

PLACING CONCRETE IN HOT WEATHER

When the temperature of fresh concrete exceeds around 85 to 90°F, the resulting strength and durability of the concrete can be reduced. Therefore, most specifications require the concrete to be placed at a temperature less than 90°F. When concrete is placed in hot weather, the ingredients should be cooled before mixing. ACI 305R contains guidelines for mixing and placing concrete in hot weather [19]. Methods of cooling include using ice instead of water in the mix and cooling the aggregate with liquid nitrogen.

PROBLEMS

18-1. A concrete batch calls for the following quantities per cubic yard of concrete, based on saturated surface-dry conditions of the aggregate. Determine the required weight of each solid ingredient and the number of gallons of water required for a 6.5-cu-yd batch. Also, determine the wet unit weight of the concrete in pounds per cubic foot.

> Cement, 6.0 bags
> Fine aggregate, 1,420 lb
> Coarse aggregate, 1,840 lb
> Water, 34 gal

18-2. In Prob. 20-1, assume that the fine aggregate contains 7% free moisture, by weight, and the coarse aggregate contains 3% free moisture, by weight. Determine the required weights of cement, fine aggregate, coarse aggregate, and volume of added water for an 8-cu-yd batch.

18-3. A concrete retaining wall whose total volume will be 245 cu yd is to be constructed by using job-mixed concrete containing the following quantities per cubic yard, based on surface-dry sand and gravel:

> Cement, 5.6 bags
> Sand, 1,340 lb
> Gravel, 1,864 lb
> Water, 33 gal

The sand and gravel will be purchased by ton weight, including any moisture present at the time they are weighed. The gross weights, including the moisture present at the time of weighing, are as follows:

Item	Gross weight (lb/cu yd)	Percent moisture by gross weight
Sand	2,918	5
Gravel	2,968	3

It is estimated that 8% of the sand and 6% of the gravel will be lost or not recovered in the stockpile at the job.

Determine the total number of tons each of sand and gravel required for the project.

18-4. The aggregate, sand, and cement used in a concrete have an initial temperature of 76°F. The sand contains 4% moisture. If 35 gal of water, at a temperature of 46°F, is used per cubic yard of concrete, determine the temperature of the concrete.

18-5. The aggregate, sand, and cement used in a concrete have an initial temperature of 44°F. The sand contains 4% moisture. If 30 gal of water is used per cubic yard of concrete, what should be the temperature of the water to produce a concrete having a temperature of 72°F?

REFERENCES

1. ACI Committee 304, "Recommended Practice for Measuring, Mixing, Transporting, and Placing Concrete," ACI 304R, *ACI Manual of Concrete Practice, Part 2*, American Concrete Institute, Detroit, MI, published annually.
2. Mindess, Sidney, and J. Francis Young: "Concrete," Prentice-Hall, Englewood Cliffs, NJ, 1981.
3. ASTM Committee C9, "Test for Slump of Portland Cement Concrete," *Annual Book of ASTM Standards*, vol. 04.02, published annually.
4. ACI Committee 211, "Standard Practice for Selecting Proportions for Normal, Heavyweight, and Mass Concrete," ACI 211.2, *ACI Manual of Concrete Practice, Part 1*, American Concrete Institute, Detroit, MI, published annually.
5. ATSM Committee C94, "Standard Specification for Ready-Mixed Concrete," *Annual Book of ASTM Standards*, vol. 04.02, published annually.
6. National Ready Mixed Concrete Association, 900 Spring Street, Silver Spring, MD 20910.
7. Ledbetter, Bonnie S., W. B. Ledbetter, and Eugene H. Boeke: "Mixing, Moving, and Mashing Concrete—75 Years of Progress," *Concrete International*, pp. 69–76, November 1980.
8. ACI Committee 304, "Placing Concrete by Pumping Methods," ACI 304.2R, *ACI Manual of Concrete Practice, Part 2*, American Concrete Institute, Detroit, MI, published annually.
9. ACI Committee 304, "Pumped Concrete Climbs 75 Flights," *Engineering News Record*, pp. 28–29, March 5, 1981.
10. ACI Committee 309, "Standard Practice for Consolidation of Concrete," ACI 309R, *ACI Manual of Concrete Practice, Part 2*, American Concrete Institute, Detroit, MI, published annually.
11. ACI Committee 506, "Recommended Practice for Shotcreting," ACI 506R, *ACI Manual of Concrete Practice, Part 5*, American Concrete Institute, Detroit, MI, published annually.
12. Berry, E. E., and V. M. Malhotra: "Fly Ash for Use in Concrete—A Critical Review," *Journal of the ACI*, pp. 59–73, March–April 1980.
13. EPA, "Guidelines for Federal Procurement of Cement and Concrete Containing Fly Ash," *Federal Register*, vol. 48, no. 20, pp. 4230–4253, January 28, 1983.
14. McKerall, W. C., and W. B. Ledbetter: "Variability and Control of Class C Fly Ash," *Cement, Concrete, and Aggregates*, CCAGOP, vol. 14, no. 2, pp. 87–93. Winter 1982, American Society for Testing and Materials, Philadelphia, PA.
15. Cook, James E.: "Research and Application of High Strength Concrete Using Class C Fly Ash," *Concrete International*, July 1982.
16. Ledbetter, W. B., D. J. Teague, R. L. Long, and B. N. Banister: "Construction of Fly Ash Test Sites and Guidelines for Construction," *Research Report* 240-2, Texas Transportation Institute, Texas A&M University, College Station, TX, October 1981, 111 p.
17. ASTM C9, "Specification for Blended Hydraulic Cements," *Annual Book of ASTM Standards*, vol. 04.02, published annually.
18. ACI Committee 306, "Cold Weather Concreting," ACI 306R, *ACI Manual of Concrete Practice, Part 2*, American Concrete Institute, Detroit, MI, published annually.
19. ACI Committee 305, "Hot Weather Concreting," ACI 305R, *ACI Manual of Concrete Practice, Part 2*, American Concrete Institute, Detroit, MI, published annually.
20. Morgen Manufacturing Company, P.O. Box 160, Yankton, SD 57078-0160.
21. Allentown Pneumatic Gun, Master Builders, Inc., 421 Schantz Road, Allentown, PA 18104.

CHAPTER

19

ASPHALT MIX PRODUCTION AND PLACEMENT

INTRODUCTION

This chapter deals with the equipment and methods used for the production and placement of asphalt paving materials. Although the same or similar equipment may in some instances be used for other purposes, such as rollers for compaction of other materials, they will be treated separately in this chapter in relation to asphalt operations.

Most asphalt paving materials are produced for the construction of highway and airfield pavements. The ability to easily accommodate a pavement section to stage construction and to recycle old pavements, and the fact that mix designs can be adjusted to utilize local materials are three critical factors favoring the use of asphalt paving materials. When appraising asphalt production and paving equipment, consideration must be given to the types of projects anticipated. Some asphalt mixing plants are operated primarily as producers of multiple mixes for FOB (free on board) plant sales or to serve multiple paving spreads on small jobs. These plants must be able to easily and quickly change their production mix in order to meet the requirements of multiple customers. Other plants are high-volume producers serving a single paving spread; this is particularly true of portable plants which are moved from project to project. There is equipment available that is specifically designed to meet the needs of both these situations. A constructor must select the equipment and methods which allow the service flexibility best suited to the specific project types that are expected to be undertaken.

GLOSSARY OF TERMS

The following glossary defines the important terms that are used in describing asphalt equipment and procedures.

Alligator cracks. Interconnected cracks in an asphalt pavement that form a pattern similar to an alligator's skin.

Asphalt. The binder commonly used in asphalt paving materials.

Asphalt cement (AC). A heavy binder used in the preparation of hot asphalt paving materials.

Asphalt paver. A machine designed to receive and spread asphalt materials to the desired width and thickness, and to provide initial finish and compaction.

Asphalt paving material. A mixture of asphalt and aggregate to form a strong, flexible, weather-resistant paving layer in a pavement structure.

Asphalt plant. A plant used to proportion and mix asphalt paving materials.

Asphaltic concrete. A high-type asphalt paving material used for construction of highway or airfield pavements having high traffic volumes and axle loads.

Automatic feeder control. A device on an asphalt paver that controls the level of mix in the screw chamber ahead of the screed.

Automatic screed controls. A system that overrides the self-leveling action of the asphalt paver screed and permits it to pave to a predetermined grade and slope, using either a rigid- or mobile-type reference.

Baghouse. An asphalt plant component for capturing, by the use of special fabric filter bags, the fine material particles contained in either the dryer or drum mixer exhaust gases. The captured dust is normally returned to the mix.

Base course. That part of the pavement structure placed directly on the subbase.

Batch plant. An asphalt mixing plant that proportions and mixes liquid asphalt and aggregates in individual batches.

Binder. The material in a paving mix used to bind the aggregate particles together, to prevent the entrance of moisture, and to act as a cushioning agent.

Binder course. A layer of mix placed between the base and the surface course.

Black base. An economical asphalt paving material composed of asphalt-stabilized aggregates, ranging from coarse stone to sand mixes, and from road mix to high-type plant mixes.

Blade mixing. The mixing of materials in-place with a motor grader blade.

Bleeding. The formation of a film of asphalt on a pavement surface due to the upward movement of liquid asphalt in the mix.

Breakdown. The initial compaction behind the paver that is intended to achieve maximum density in the shortest time frame.

California bearing ratio. A testing method used to determine the required pavement structural thickness.

Cold feed system. The equipment used in an asphalt mixing plant to proportion and feed the aggregates prior to drying.

Cold planer (milling machine). A machine used to remove old roadway material, without adding heat, by a rotating drum with cutting teeth.

Combination screed. A type of asphalt paver screed which utilizes both a tamper bar and vibration to achieve compaction of the mix.

Continuous mix plant.   An asphalt plant that continuously proportions and mixes aggregates and liquid asphalt utilizing interlocking feeding systems and a separate mixing pugmill.

Cracking and seating.   The process of cracking portland cement concrete pavements into small pieces, rolling the pieces to seat them on the base or subgrade, and overlaying with asphaltic concrete to produce a new pavement structure.

Cutoff shoe.   A device used to reduce, in small increments, the paving width of an asphalt paving machine.

Drum mix plant.   An asphalt mixing plant which combines both the aggregate drying and the mixing function in a single drum.

Dwell time.   The time required for material to pass through a dryer or mixer.

EAL (equivalent axle loading).   A means of calculating loads imposed on a pavement structure that takes into account both traffic density and the weight imposed by each axle.

Echelon paving.   Using two or more asphalt pavers operating one ahead of another to obtain a hot joint between the mats.

Edge cracks.   Longitudinal cracks near the edge of the pavement, sometimes branching toward the shoulder, usually caused by insufficient shoulder support.

Flash point.   A test of the volatility of asphalts based on the temperature at which a small flame drawn across the surface produces a flash at any point on the surface, AASHTO T48 for asphalt cements.

Flights.   Metal plates of various shapes placed longitudinally inside the shell of a drum dryer or mixer. As the material moves through the drum, the flights serve to first lift the aggregate and then to drop it through the flame and hot gases.

Friction course.   A layer of asphalt paving material usually less than 1 in. thick placed on a structurally sound pavement to improve skid resistance and smoothness.

Grade or string line.   A wire or string erected at a specified grade and alinement which is used as a reference for an automatic control system of a paver, cold planer, or fine-grade machine.

Grade reference.   An erected string line, curb, gutter, adjacent mat, or mobile averaging device used to provide reference to an automatic control system of a paver, cold planer, or fine-grade machine.

Hot bins.   Bins used to store dried aggregates in an asphalt plant prior to proportioning and mixing.

Hot elevator.   A bucket elevator used to carry hot, dried aggregate from the dryer to the gradation unit or weigh hopper of an asphalt plant.

Hot mix asphalt.   An asphalt paving material produced in a central mixing plant in which the aggregates have been heated and dried for placement at high temperatures.

Hot oil heater.   A heater for increasing the temperature of heat transfer oil which in turn is used as the means to provide temperature control for plant process operations and for increasing or maintaining the temperature of liquid asphalt stored at an asphalt plant.

Hveem.   A method of asphalt mix design based on the cohesion and friction of a compacted specimen.

Leveling arms.   Two long arms extending forward from each side of the asphalt paver screed and attached to tow points on the tractor. This mechanical connection allows the screed to float on the mix during placement.

Leveling course.   A new layer of asphalt paving material placed over a distressed roadway to improve its geometry prior to resurfacing.

Leveling wedges.   Patches of asphalt paving material used to level sags and depressions in an old pavement prior to resurfacing.

Lift (mat).   A layer of asphalt paving material separately placed and compacted.

Live zone.   The volume of a pugmill in cubic feet below a line extending across the top of the paddle arc with the volume of the shafts, liners, arms, and tips deducted.

Longitudinal crack.   A pavement crack that is roughly parallel to the centerline.

Los Angeles abrasion test.   A widely used means of determining the resistance of an aggregate to wear and abrasion.

Lute.   A type of rake used to smooth out minor surface irregularities in the hot asphalt paving material behind the paver.

Marshall stability.   The maximum load resistance that an asphalt paving material test specimen will develop at 140°F (60°C) under carefully controlled conditions.

Porosity.   The relative volume of voids in a solid or mixture of solids. Porosity is used to indicate the ability of the solid or the mixture to absorb a liquid such as asphalt.

Prime coat.   An application of liquid asphalt material over an untreated base to coat and bond the loose aggregate particles, to waterproof the surface, and to promote adhesion between the base and the overlying course.

Pugmill.   A mechanical device for mixing materials, usually with paddles attached to rotating shafts.

RAP (reclaimed asphalt pavement).   The asphalt paving material removed from an old existing roadway by cold planing or ripping.

Raveling.   The loosening and loss of aggregate particles from a pavement surface during use.

Recycling.   The reuse of reclaimed asphalt pavement (RAP) with virgin asphalt paving materials to produce asphaltic concrete for new roadways.

Reflective cracking.   Fissures in an asphalt overlay that exhibit the crack pattern in the underlying pavement structure.

Rejuvenating agent (softening agent).   An organic material with chemical and physical attributes which restore desired properties to aged asphalt.

Road widener.   A special machine used to place asphalt paving material, aggregate, or stabilized materials adjacent to a roadway structure.

Rubberized asphalt.   An asphalt paving material containing powered or shredded rubber which is introduced to produce a more resilient pavement.

Ruts.   Channels which develop in a pavement as a result of wheel loads being repetitively applied in the same locations.

Sand seal coat. A single application of liquid asphalt to an existing pavement with a light covering of fine aggregate.

Screed. That part of an asphalt paver which smooths and compacts the asphalt paving materials.

Self-leveling. The action of a floating asphalt paver screed which permits it to reduce humps and to fill in low spots while paving.

Slope. The transverse inclination of a roadway or other surface.

Surface course. The top or riding surface of a pavement structure.

Surge bin. A storage bin, usually cylindrical, used to hold hot asphalt paving materials at the plant in order to allow continuous plant operation and for faster load-out of trucks.

Tack coat. A light application of liquid asphalt, usually emulsified with water. Used to help ensure a bond between the surface being paved and the mat which is being placed.

Tamping screed. A type of asphalt paver screed which utilizes a tamper bar mounted in front of the screed plate to achieve compaction of the mix.

Thickness controls. Manually operated controls usually located at the ends of the main asphalt paver screed by which the screed operator can raise or lower the angle of attack of the screed plate to increase or decrease the mat thickness.

Total moisture. The total of both the surface and internal moisture present in an aggregate. Generally expressed as a percentage of the aggregate weight.

Transverse crack. A pavement crack that is roughly perpendicular to the roadway centerline.

Washboarding. Ripples formed transversely across the width of a pavement, or road section.

Weigh hopper. A batch plant component usually located under the hot bins in which the aggregates and asphalt are weighed prior to discharge into the mixing pugmill.

Wet collector. An asphalt plant dust collection system utilizing water and a high-pressure venturi to capture dust particles from the exhaust gas of a dryer or drum mixer. Wet collected dust cannot be returned to the mix.

Windrow. A continuous pile of material placed on a grade or previously placed mat for later pickup or spreading.

Windrow elevator. A device that travels ahead of an asphalt paver and is usually attached to the paver which picks up windrowed mix and feeds it into the paver hopper. This allows for more continuous paver operation to be achieved.

ASPHALT PAVING MATERIALS

The objectives which drive the design and construction of a road or airfield pavement section are:

1. Support the axle loads imposed by the traffic.
2. Protect the base and subbase from moisture.

3. Provide a stable-smooth and skid-resistant riding surface.

4. Resist weathering.

The aggregate and asphalt binder, which make up the asphalt paving material (often termed "asphalt mix"), must provide a stable structure capable of supporting the repetitive vertical wheel loads imposed and of resisting the kneading mechanism that wheel rotation and movement transmits to the structure. Drainage is the first, second, third, fourth, etc. rule of highway construction. This is because of the influence of moisture on the strength of soils. Therefore, the pavement structure must protect the underlying and supporting materials from water. The pavement surface will be subjected to abrasive wear, while the entire section will have to resist structural movement. Fuel efficiency, comfort, and safety are affected by surface texture. Besides moisture effects, the action of heat and cold can be very destructive to pavements. These objectives fix the performance criteria of a pavement section. The purpose of blending aggregates and asphalt binder is to achieve a final product which satisfies these objectives.

Aggregates. The load applied to an asphalt pavement is primarily carried by the aggregates in the mix. The aggregate portion of a mix accounts for 90 to 95% of the material by weight. Good aggregates and proper gradation of those aggregates are critical to the mix's performance. Ideally, an aggregate gradation should be provided which permits the minimum amount of expensive binder (asphalt) to be used. The binder fills most of the voids between the aggregate particles as well as the voids *in* the particles. The larger-size aggregate, greater than a No. 8 sieve, used in an asphalt mix can be gravel, crushed stone, or slag. Slag is structurally a good paving mix material, but it can be very porous. This porosity can significantly increase the amount of binder used in the mix. Both sand and a small portion of some very fine material less than a No. 200 sieve, referred to as mineral filler, will also be incorporated into most mixes. The asphalt plant provides the mechanism to achieve a controlled blend of these aggregates.

The blending of different size aggregates to obtain a desired mix gradation is vital to successful pavement performance. A pavement mix which fails to fall within certain gradation limits may exhibit problems such as segregation, lack of stability, or lack of tensile strength. Besides gradation, the aggregate properties of cleanliness, resistance to wear and abrasion, texture, porosity, and resistance to stripping (debonding between the asphalt and the aggregate) are important.

The amount of foreign matter, whether soil or organic material, which is present with the aggregate will reduce the load-carrying ability of a pavement. Visual inspection can often identify an aggregate cleanness problem, and washing, wet screening, or other methods as discussed in the aggregate production chapter can be employed to correct the situation.

The effects of aggregate surface texture are manifested in the strength of the pavement structure and in the workability of the mix. Strength is influenced by the ability of the individual aggregate particles to "lock" together under load. This ability to lock is enhanced by angular rough textured particles. Smooth aggregates, such as "river run" gravels and sands, produce a pavement which exhibits a reduced strength compared to one constructed from aggregates having rough surfaces. When necessary rounded gravels can be crushed to create more angular surfaces. A mix using aggregates having a rough surface will require slightly more asphalt binder.

The porosity of an aggregate affects the amount of asphalt required in a mix. More asphalt must be added to a mix containing porous aggregates to make up for that which is absorbed by the aggregates and is not available to serve as a binder. Slag and other manufactured aggregates can be highly porous, which will increase the asphalt cost proportion of a mix. However, because of the ability of these materials to resist wear, often their use can be justified based on total lifetime project economics.

Some aggregates exhibit stripping of the asphalt film from the individual particles when water is present. Such separation will manifest itself in disintegration of the pavement structure. These aggregates should be avoided. When they cannot be avoided, antistrip additives can be added to the mix and steps should be taken to reduce pavement voids, as it is important to seal out water.

Asphalts. There are both natural asphalts and commercially refined asphalts. Most asphalts used in the United States are obtained by the distillation of crude petroleum. Natural asphalts can be found in Trinidad and Venezuela. Both refined and natural asphalts are the result of driving off the lighter oils of the crude, one by the action of induced distillation using steam or air, and the other as a natural process of sunlight and wind across crude exposed on the ground surface. The properties of the crude will define the properties of the resulting asphalt. Therefore, two asphalts may have the same viscosity or penetration classification, yet they will exhibit decidedly different characteristics.

Asphalt cements (AC) are usually classified by penetration, AASHTO M20, although some western states use a viscosity grade system, AASHTO M226. The penetration test, AASHTO T49, as the name indicates, is a measure of the depth of penetration into a 77°F asphalt cement sample by a standard 100 gram (g) weighted needle in a 5-sec time duration. Asphalt cements are used as the binder in paving mixes. The AC usually represents less than 10% of the mix by weight. However, it serves the very important functions of bonding the aggregate particles together, preventing the entrance of moisture, and acting as a cushioning medium. The AC penetration grades are 40–50, 60–70, 85–100, 120–150, and 200–300 pen.

The other four asphalt classifications are:

1. Slow-curing (SC) liquid asphalts
2. Cutback asphalts:
   a. Medium-curing (MC) liquid asphalts
   b. Rapid-curing (RC) liquid asphalts
3. Emulsified asphalts
4. Powdered asphalts

Slow-curing liquid asphalts, SC-70, 250, 800, and 3000, contain little or no volatile portions. A higher number indicates a greater asphalt content. Cutbacks are produced by adding volatile products to asphalt cement. Medium-curing products are a kerosene blend and are workable at relatively low temperatures. The medium-curing grades are MC-30, 70, 250, 800, and 3000. Rapid-curing cutbacks are a naphtha or gasoline-type distillate blend of lower penetration asphalt cements. The grades begin with RC-70 and go to 3000.

Emulsified asphalts are a mixture of asphalt cement and water using an emulsifying agent to control separation. To prevent premature separation, "breaking," care must be exercised in handling emulsions. Emulsions offer the advantage of eliminating fire and toxic hazards associated with cutbacks and are adaptable with wet aggregates.

Powdered asphalts are used in cold mix applications with a fluxing medium such as higher SC grades. They are solid materials which have been granulated down to a minus No. 10 sieve gradation.

Asphalt mix design. There are numerous methods of asphalt mix design, all of which seek to satisfy the following pavement performance criteria:

- Stability
- Durability
- Impermeability
- Flexibility

- Skid resistance
- Fatigue resistance
- Workability

Stability refers to the ability of a pavement to resist shoving and rutting. The internal friction and cohesion of a mix determine stability. The shape of the aggregate particles affects internal friction (see Fig. 19-1), and the binder affects the cohesion. Resistance to oxidation of the asphalt, to disintegration of the aggregate, and to stripping of the asphalt binder from the aggregates is termed *durability*. The amount of asphalt content in the mix and the aggregate gradation and impermeability of the mix govern its durability (see Fig. 19-1). *Impermeability* is the resistance to the movement of water and air through the mix. Compaction and the resulting final void content of the mix define its permeability. Most mixes which perform satisfactorily have less than 8% air voids in the final compacted pavement (see Fig. 19-1).

The ability to adjust to minor movements which take place over long time durations is *flexibility*.

The final surface of the pavement must minimize the *skidding* of vehicle tires. To reduce skidding, a tire must be able to contact with the pavement even under wet conditions. Some aggregates are easily polished under traffic and should be avoided in surface mixes (see Fig. 19-2). Pavements are distressed not only by the magnitude of an individual load, but also by the multiple repetitions of minor loads to which they are subjected every day. *Resistance to fatigue* from bending under repeated loading is influenced by both air voids and asphalt binder viscosity (see Fig. 19-2).

A mix can be satisfactory in terms of all the preceding factors, but if it cannot be placed and compacted, it has little value. It must be *workable*. It should not segregate during handling or be gummy during compaction (see Fig. 19-2).

Mix design procedures seek to quantify the proportions of aggregate and asphalt to satisfy these criteria. The two procedures having the widest use are the Marshall and the Hveem methods [7]. The Marshall method, AASHTO T245, seeks to determine the optimum amount of asphalt for a particular gradation of aggregate through tests of compacted test specimens. It also provides an optimum density and void content that can

Low Stability	
Causes	**Effects**
Excess asphalt in mix	Washboarding, rutting, and flushing and bleeding
Excess medium size sand in mix	Tenderness during rolling and for period after construction, difficulty in compacting
Rounded aggregate, little or no crushed surfaces	Rutting and channeling

Poor Durability	
Causes	**Effects**
Low asphalt content	Dryness or raveling
High void content through design or lack of compaction	Early hardening of asphalt followed by cracking or disintegration
Water susceptible aggregate	Films of asphalt strip from aggregate leaving an abraded, raveled, or mushy pavement

Mix Too Permeable	
Causes	**Effects**
Low asphalt content	Thin asphalt films will cause early aging and raveling
High voids content	Water and air can easily enter pavement causing oxidation and disintegration
Inadequate compaction	Will result in high voids in pavement leading to water infiltration and low stength

FIGURE 19-1
Asphalt mix—stability, durability, and permeability cause and effect relationships. (Courtesy *The Asphalt Institute*)

be used for quality control during construction. The Hveem method uses a stabilometer test, AASHTO T246 and T247 (a triaxial-type test), to make the same determinations, optimum amount of asphalt for a given aggregate gradation, optimum density, and void content.

ASPHALT PLANTS

GENERAL INFORMATION

An *asphalt plant* is a high-tech group of equipment which is capable of uniformly blending, heating, and mixing the aggregates and asphalt cement of asphalt concrete, while at the same time meeting strict environmental regulations, particularly in the area of

Poor Skip Resistance	
Causes	Effects
Excess asphalt	Bleeding, low skid resistance
Poorly textured or graded aggragate	Smooth pavement, potential for hydroplaning
Polishing of aggregate in mixture	Low skid resistance

Poor Fatigue Resistance	
Causes	Effects
Low asphalt content	Fatigue cracking
High design voids	Early aging of asphalt followed by fatigue cracking
Lack of compaction	Early aging of asphalt followed by fatigue cracking
Inadequate pavement thickness	Excessive bending followed by fatigue cracking

Poor Workability	
Causes	Effects
Large maximum-sized particles	Rough surface, difficult to place
Excessive coarse aggregate	May be hard to compact
Too low a mix temperature	Uncoated aggregate, not durable, rough surface, hard to compact
Too much medium-sized sand	Mix shoves under roller, remains tender
Low mineral filler content	Tender mix, highly permeable
High mineral filler content	Mix may be dry or gummy, hard to handle, not durable

FIGURE 19-2
Asphalt mix—skid resistance, fatigue resistance, and workability cause and effect relationships. (Courtesy *The Asphalt Institute*)

emissions. The drum mix plant and the batch plant are the two most common plant types. Drum mix plants are leading the industry because they have fewer wear parts, their capability to handle mixes having high percentages of RAP, and availability in highly portable models. Batch plants are still economical for operations where there is a requirement to produce several different mixes during a single production time frame. Batch plants are efficient in such situations, as they can rapidly change the production mix with little wasted material.

BATCH PLANTS

Batch plants date from the beginning of the asphalt industry. Their primary components in the order of material flow are:

- Cold feed system
- Drum dryer
- Hot elevator
- Screens
- Hot bins
- Pugmill mixer

Cold feed systems. Both drum mix and batch-type plants use cold feed bins to provide aggregate surge storage and a uniform flow of properly sized material for mixing. The cold feed is much more critical to a drum plant, as such plants have no other mechanism for controlling the blend of materials. In a batch plant the materials will pass through a screening and weighing process before being mixed.

Cold feed systems usually consist of three or four open top bins mounted together as a single unit (see Fig. 19-3). The individual bins have steep sidewalls to promote material flow. In the case of sticky material it may be necessary to have wall vibrators. The individual bins can be fed from sized aggregate stockpiles by a front-end loader,

FIGURE 19-3
Asphalt plant three-bin cold feed system. (ASTEC Inc.)

a clamshell, or a conveyor. At the bottom of each bin there is a gate for controlling material flow and a feeder unit for metering the flow. Belt feeders are most common but vibratory and apron feeds can be found. Cold feeds for drum plants will, additionally, require a scalping screen to ensure that no oversize material contaminates the mix. The size of the bins must correspond to the operating capacity of the plant.

Drum dryer. The purposes of a drum dryer are to heat and dry the aggregates of the mix. Aggregate temperature controls the resulting temperature of the mix. If the aggregate has been heated excessively, the asphalt will harden during mixing. If the aggregates have not been heated adequately, it is difficult to coat them completely with asphalt. Therefore, the aggregate must be heated sufficiently at this step in the process in order to produce a final mix at the desired temperature (further discussion is given under "Mixing").

Aggregates are introduced at the end of the drum dryer opposite the burner and travel through the drum counter to the gas flow. The drum is inclined downward from the aggregate feed end to the burner end. This slope causes the aggregate to move through the drum by gravity. The drum rotates and steel angles, "flights," mounted on the inside lift the aggregate and dump it through the hot gas and burner flame. Finally, the heated aggregate is discharged into the hot (bucket) elevator, which carries it to the screens at the top of the batch plant tower.

Screening. The batch plant vibrating screen unit is usually a $3\frac{1}{2}$-deck arrangement. This allows graduation control of four aggregate sizes into four different hot bins. The screen unit rejects oversized material out of the production cycle. While the screens provide gradation control, they will not function properly unless the proportioning from the cold feed is correct. If the screens are overloaded, material which should be passing through a screen and into a bin is carried instead into the bin of the next larger aggregate size. Such a situation destroys the mix formulation and must be avoided.

Mixing. Aggregate from the hot bins is dropped into a weight hopper situated below the bins and above the pugmill. The plant is structured so that the mixer is sufficiently high to allow truck passage directly below for loading (see Fig. 19-4). The aggregates are weighed cumulatively in the hopper, with the mineral filler added last. Once the correct proportions of aggregate are measured, the material is dropped into the pugmill. The liquid asphalt for the batch is either weighed or metered volumetrically, and then is pumped through spray bars into the pugmill. Most plants use a twinshaft pugmill for mixing the batch.

To achieve uniform mixing, a pugmill's live zone should be completely filled with mix. The live zone (see Fig. 19-5) is from the bottom of the box to the top of the paddle arc.

Because of the influence of temperature on the quality of the mix, the mixing temperature is usually specified. The specified temperature is that of the mix immediately after discharge from the pugmill. The specification range will vary with the type and grade of the asphalt cement used. In the case of dense-graded mixes the range across all asphalt cements is from 225 to 350°F. The range for open-graded mixes is from 180 to

FIGURE 19-4
Batch plant with truck below pugmill mixer. *(Barber-Greene, A Division of Caterpillar Paving Products Inc.)*

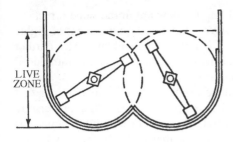

FIGURE 19-5
The live zone of a pugmill. *(Caterpillar Paving Products Inc.)*

250°F. Mixing should be at the lowest temperature which will achieve complete asphalt coating of the aggregates and still allow for satisfactory workability.

DRUM MIX PLANTS

The primary unit in a drum mix plant both dries the aggregate and performs the mixing function. As with a batch plant, the cold feed system is the critical aggregate proportioning unit. It feeds the virgin aggregates into the inclined rotating drum mixer (see Fig. 19-6). Usually the burner and the aggregate feed are both located at the upper end

FIGURE 19-6
Drum-mix asphalt plant with three storage silos. (ASTEC Inc.)

of the drum, which means the aggregates and hot gas flow are in the same direction. There are some counter flow plants, however. A very extensive arrangement of flights within the drum dumps the virgin aggregate through the flame and hot gases. Farther down the length of the drum beyond the direct flame the liquid asphalt is introduced and the drum flights provide the mixing mechanism.

The drum for a drum mix plant has a slope in the range of $\frac{1}{2}$ to 1 in. per foot of drum length. Rotation speeds are normally 5 to 10 rpm and common diameters are from 3 to 12 ft, with lengths between 15 and 60 ft. The ratio of length to diameter is from 4 to 6. Longer drums are found in recycling applications. Dwell time— which is controlled by the drum slope, length, rotation speed and flights, and the nature of the material—will range from 2 to 6 min.

DUST COLLECTORS

Because of air pollution requirements, asphalt plants are equipped with dust control systems. The two most commonly utilized systems are the water venturi approach and the cloth filtration "baghouse" system. The wet approach does require the availability of adequate water supplies. This approach introduces water at the point where dust laden gas moves through the narrow throat of a venturi-shaped chamber. The dust becomes entrapped in the water and is thereby separated from the exhaust gas. A disadvantage of the wet approach is that the collected material cannot be reclaimed for use in the mix.

The dry baghouse systems allow mechanical collection and recycling of fines. The system works by forcing the dust laden gas through fabric filter bags which hang in a baghouse. By using a reverse pulse of air or by mechanically shaking the bags, the collected dust is removed from the filter. The dust falls into hoppers in the bottom of the baghouse and is moved by augers to a discharge vane feeder. The vane feeder is necessary to keep the baghouse airtight.

Filter bags are made of fabrics which can withstand temperatures up to 450°F. But care must be exercised when using a baghouse system, as excessive temperatures can melt the bags and/or cause a fire.

LIQUID ASPHALT STORAGE AND HEATING

When liquid asphalt is combined with the aggregate for mixing, the temperature of the asphalt should be in the range of 300°F. Therefore, both drum mix and batch plants have heating systems to keep the liquid asphalt at the required temperature. If asphalt is delivered at a cooler temperature, the systems must be capable of raising the temperature. The two methods commonly used for heating liquid asphalt are the direct fire and the hot oil process.

A direct fire heater consists of a burner which fires into a tube in the asphalt storage tank. With such systems, sufficient asphalt must be kept in the tank so that the burner tube is always submerged. The direct fire systems will have a high thermal efficiency.

The hot oil system is a two-stage approach. First, heat transfer oil is heated and then the heated oil is circulated through piping within the asphalt tank.

STORAGE SILOS

To keep a batch plant running continuously or to allow a drum plant to handle multiple mixes economically requires the availability of surge or storage facilities. Upright cylindrical structures, "silos," fed at the top by a drag flight conveyor provide such a capacity. A silo allows a batch plant to continue production even when trucks are not available to receive the batch from the mixer. Trucking cost is reduced, as trucks do not have to queue at the plant waiting for batches to be mixed. They can be loaded directly from the bottom of the storage silo.

Silos are sealed to prevent the hardening and the aging of the mix which results from oxidation. They use drop control methods to avoid segregation problems as the mix is introduced at the top, and steep cone side slopes ensure the first material in is the first out.

RECYCLING

Existing asphalt pavements represent a large investment in aggregates and asphalt. By reclaiming these materials, using either cold milling or ripping methods, much of that investment can be recaptured. Additionally, cold milling allows restoration of the pavement section without the need to change the grade, thereby eliminating the problems associated with raising curbs and drainage structures.

The reclaimed asphalt paving materials (RAP) are combined with virgin aggregates, additional asphalt, and/or recycling agents in a hot mix plant to produce new paving mixes. In those cases where the pavement sections were ripped up instead of milled it may be necessary to crush the reclaimed materials in order to reduce the particle size. The new mix design will have to account for both the graduation of the aggregate in the RAP and the asphalt content of the RAP.

The mixing of virgin material and RAP to produce a new mix is performed by heat transfer methods. This approach is used because the asphalt contained in the RAP can cause significant emission problems if exposed to direct flame. In some plants the virgin aggregates are introduced first and superheated, farther downstream in the drum the RAP enters and the two are blended together. The virgin material must have sufficient heat both to heat the RAP and to drive off moisture from the RAP. Other plants use a double drum system to protect the RAP from the flame (see Fig. 19-7).

PAVING EQUIPMENT

ASPHALT DISTRIBUTORS

When applying an asphalt prime, tack, or seal coat, a specially designed distributor truck is utilized. These trucks must be able to apply the liquid asphalt to a surface at uniform rates. The factors which affect uniform application are:

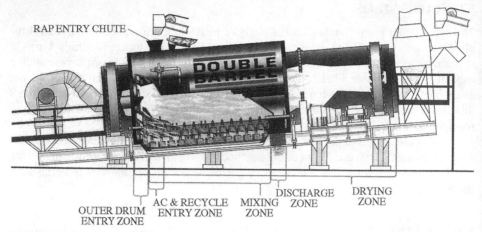

FIGURE 19-7
Heating Reclaimed Asphalt Paving (RAP) materials in a double barrel drum-mix plant. (ASTEC Inc.)

The asphalt spraying temperature

The liquid pressure across the spray bar length

The angle of the spray nozzles

The nozzle height above the surface

The distributor speed

Asphalt distributors have insulated tanks for maintaining material temperature and are equipped with burners for heating the asphalt material to the proper application temperature. Either independently powered or PTO-driven discharge pumps are used to maintain continuous and uniform pressure for the full length of the spray bar. The nozzle angle must be set properly, usually 15–30° from the horizontal axis of the spray bar so that the individual spray fans do not interfere or intermix with one another. The height of the nozzle above the surface determines the width of an individual fan. To ensure the proper lap of the fans, the nozzle (spray bar) height must be set and maintained. The relationship between the application rate (gallons per square yard) and the truck speed is obvious; truck speed must be held constant during the spraying to achieve a uniform application.

The relationship between the application rate, the truck configuration, and the surface area to be covered is given by Eq. (19-1).

$$L = \frac{9 \times T}{W \times R} \tag{19-1}$$

where L = length of covered surface

T = total gallons to be applied

W = spray bar coverage width, ft

R = rate of the application, gal per sq yd

Prior to the placement of an asphalt mix on a new base a prime coat is applied to the base. Normal rates of application for prime vary between 0.20 and 0.60 gal per sq yd. The prime promotes adhesion between the base and the overlying asphalt mix course by coating the absorbent base material, whether it is gravel, crushed stone, a stabilized material, or an earthen grade.

Tack coats are designed to create a bond between old existing pavements and new overlays. A tack coat acts as an adhesive to prevent the slippage of the two mats. The tack coat is a very thin uniform blanket of asphalt, usually 0.05 to 0.15 gal per sq yd of diluted emulsion. An application that is too heavy will defeat the purpose by causing the layers to creep, for the asphalt serves as a lubricant rather than as a tack.

Seal coats consist of an application of asphalt followed by a light covering of fine aggregate, which is rolled in with pneumatic rollers. Application rates are normally from 0.10 to 0.20 gal per sq yd.

ASPHALT PAVERS

An asphalt paver consists of a tractor, either track or rubber-tired, and a screed (see Fig. 19-8). The tractor power unit has a receiving hopper in the front and a system of

FIGURE 19-8
Track-type asphalt paver. *(Barber-Greene, A Division of Caterpillar Paving Products Inc.)*

slat conveyors and augers to spread the asphalt evenly across the front of the screed. Two tow arms, pin-connected to the tractor unit, draw the screed behind the tractor. The screed controls the asphalt placement width and depth and imparts the initial finish and compaction to the material.

Pavers can receive mix directly into their hoppers from rear dump or flow bottom trucks. In such situations push rollers mounted on the front frame of the paver and extending beyond the hopper contact the rear wheels of the truck. The paver pushes the truck forward during the unloading process. Pavers can be equipped with windrow elevators mounted in front of the hopper. This gives the paver the capacity to pick up material which has been dumped in windrows on the grade or on the previously placed mat. In such cases bottom-dump trailer trucks are used to haul the mix.

Screed. The "floating" screed is free to pivot about its pin connections. This pin-connected tow arm arrangement allows the screed to be self-leveling and gives it the ability to compensate for base surface irregularities. The paver's ability to level out irregularities is controlled by the tractor's wheel base length and by the length of the screed towing arms. Greater lengths of these two components mean smooth transitions across irregularities and therefore a smooth riding surface.

Mat thickness can be maintained by using grade sensors tracing an external reference with a shoe or ski to control the screed. Or the screed can be tied to a specified grade by the use of sensors tracing a stringline. When all the forces acting on the screed are constant, it will ride at a constant elevation above the grade or follow the stringline. However, there are factors which can cause the sensor regulated screed height to vary:

- The screed *angle of attack*
- The *head of asphalt* in front of the screed
- The *paver speed*

The angle created by the plane of the surface upon which the asphalt is being placed and the plane of the screed bottom is known as the "screed angle of attack" (see Fig. 19-9). This angle is the principal mechanical factor affecting variations in mat thickness. It regulates the amount of material passing under the screed in a given

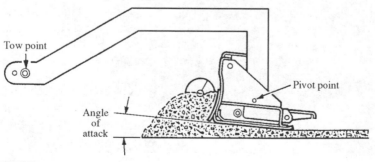

FIGURE 19-9
Screed angle of attack. *(Caterpillar Paving Products Inc.)*

distance. When either the screed or the tow points are vertically displaced, the angle of attack is changed. The screed will immediately begin to move, restoring the original angle, but this correction requires about three tow arm lengths to be accomplished.

The asphalt material directly in front and across the length of the screed is referred to as the head of material. When this material is not held constant by the hopper drag conveyor and the auger feed, the screed angle of attack will be affected and in turn the mat thickness will change. If the head of material becomes too high, the mat thickness will increase as the screed rides up on the excess material with the paver's forward progress. If the volume decreases, the screed moves down, resulting in reduced mat thickness.

Paver speed is linked to the rate at which asphalt mix is delivered from the plant. To produce a smooth mat, forward travel speed should be held constant. Changes in paver speed will affect the screed's angle of attack. Increasing the speed causes the screed to ride down, whereas decreasing the speed has the opposite effect. Additionally, when the paver is stopped, the screed tends to settle into the mat.

Initial mix compaction is achieved by the vibration of the screed. Vibrators mounted on the screed are used to impart compaction force to the mat. On many pavers vibrator speed can be adjusted to match paver speed and mat thickness. Other factors which influence compaction are mix design and placement temperature.

The width of a screed can be changed by stopping the paver and adding fixed width extensions on one or both sides of the basic screed. Some screeds are hydraulically extendable, allowing the paving width to be varied without stopping the paver. Auger additions may be required as screed width is increased in order to spread material evenly across the entire screed and screed extension. Most screeds can also be adjusted to create a crown or superelevation.

To prevent material from sticking to the screed at the beginning of a paving operation, it is necessary to heat the screed. Built-in diesel burner heaters are used to heat the bottom screed plates. Required burner heating time will vary with air temperature and the type of mix being placed. About 10 min of heating is normal, but care must be exercised as overheating can warp the screed.

WINDROW ELEVATORS

A paving operation being served by trucks means that there must be paver/truck load transfers and times when the paver must operate between truck loads or even stop if deliveries are delayed. These transfers and stops can cause undulations and imperfections in the mat. Windrow elevators (see Fig. 19-10), were developed to address transfer and truck queuing effects on mat quality. Elevators can also improve production by loosening the paver/truck link. If two trucks arrive at the paver at the same time, they can both unload by spacing their windrows down the grade.

Pavers with integral windrow pickup elevators are beginning to be introduced, but a separate elevator unit attachable to the front of a regular paver is the most common approach. By using an attachment, there is the flexibility of employing the paver in both direct load and windrow situations.

The flight system of the elevator continuously lifts the mix into the hopper from the windrow. For efficient operation the amount of material in the windrow cross section

FIGURE 19-10
Windrow elevator for loading an asphalt paver. *(Barber-Greene, A Division of Caterpillar Paving Products Inc.)*

must equal the amount required for the mat cross section. Minor quantity variations are accommodated by the surge capacity of the paver hopper. Conventional windrow machines have limited width and can only handle fairly narrow rows of material. This can limit hauling unit selection to only bottom-dump-type trucks. New elevator designs are being introduced having the capacity to handle wider windrow cross sections. These machines will open windrow operations to smaller, limited area projects and will allow the use of regular dump trucks for hauling.

Continuous paving operations depend on balancing paver production with plant production. The critical choke points in the operation which must be analyzed and managed are the *plant-load haul unit* and the *haul unit-feed-paver* links.

Example 19-1. An asphalt plant can produce 324 tons per hour (tph). A project requires paving individual 12-ft lanes with a 2-in. lift averaging 112 lb per sq yd-in. What average paver speed will match the plant production? How many 20-ton-bottom-dump trucks will be required if the total hauling cycle time is 55 min?

$$\frac{324 \text{ tph}}{60 \text{ min/hr}} = 5.4 \text{ ton/min average laydown production}$$

$$\frac{2 \text{ in. (thick)} \times 12 \text{ ft(wide)} \times 1 \text{ ft (length)}}{9 \text{ sq ft/sq yd}} = 2.66 \text{ sq yd-in per ft of paving length}$$

$$\frac{2.66 \text{ sq yd-in} \times 112 \text{ lb/sq yd-in}}{2000 \text{ lb/ton}} = 0.149 \text{ ton per ft of paving length}$$

$$\frac{5.4 \text{ ton/min}}{0.149 \text{ ton/ft}} = 36.2 \text{ ft/min, average paver speed}$$

$$20 \text{ tons per truck} \times \frac{60 \text{ min/hr}}{55 \text{ min cycle}} = 21.8 \text{ tph per truck}$$

$$\frac{324 \text{ tph}}{21.8 \text{ tph per truck}} = 14.9$$

therefore, 15 trucks are required.
Another way to analyze the situation would be to consider time. The paver requires a truck every

$$\frac{20 \text{ tons per truck}}{5.4 \text{ ton/min, required for paver}} = 3.7 \text{ min}$$

$$\frac{55 \text{ min (total truck cycle time)}}{3.7 \text{ min (paver requirement)}} = 14.9 \quad \text{or 15 trucks are required}$$

With a windrow machine, if queuing delays individual trucks, the effect to paving speed is limited or nonexistent because the windrow storage allows the paver to continue moving. This is an advantage that windrowing brings to asphalt laydown operations. However, there is a limit to windrow stockpiling dictated by specification placement temperature or the necessary mix laydown temperature. Project management must recognize these temperature restrictions and ensure that windrows are not overextended ahead of the paver laydown operation.

COMPACTION EQUIPMENT

Because of the relationships between pavement air voids and mechanical stability, durability and water permeability, asphalt pavements are designed based on the mix being placed at a specified density. Three basic roller types are used to compact asphalt paving mixes: smooth drum steel wheel, pneumatic tire, and smooth drum steel wheel vibratory rollers.

In the case of a steel wheel roller the contact surface area is an arc of the cylindrical wheel surface and the roller width (see Fig. 19-11). This contact area will decrease as the rolling progresses and the contact pressure will approach a maximum value. As discussed in Chap. 10, the contact area of a pneumatic tire is an ellipse, influenced by wheel load, tire inflation pressure, and tire sidewall flexure (see Fig. 19-12). With a pneumatic roller, the change in contact area as compaction progresses is less dramatic than in the case of a steel wheel roller. This last fact is significant when considering roller selection and utilization.

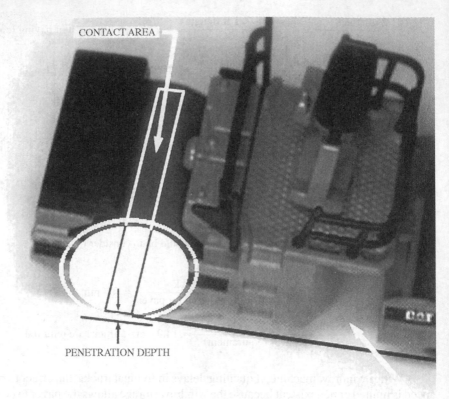

CONTACT AREA

PENETRATION DEPTH

COMPACTED MATERIAL

FIGURE 19-11
Contact surface area for a steel wheel roller.

Both the pneumatic roller, by variable tire inflation pressure, and the vibratory roller, by changing the vibrator frequency, have the ability to adjust their compaction pressure. These capabilities enhance the operational flexibility of both roller types.

Rolling temperature. To compact a mix properly, the asphalt binder must be fluid enough to allow the aggregate portion to assume a new configuration. At temperatures below 185°F the asphalt begins to bind the aggregates, making compaction extremely difficult. The temperature at which the mix was produced is the important factor in determining the time duration that is available for hauling, placing, and compaction. To extend the available time, it may be necessary to use trucks having insulated bodies.

Rolling should begin at the maximum temperature possible. This maximum temperature is that point at which the mix will support the roller without moving horizontally.

Rolling steps. Compaction of an asphalt mat is usually viewed in terms of three distinct steps:

FIGURE 19-12
Contact surface area for a pneumatic roller.

- Breakdown
- Intermediate
- Finish

The breakdown step seeks to achieve a required density within a time frame defined by temperature constraints and consistent with paver speed. There is an optimum mix temperature range for achieving proper compaction. If the mix is too hot, the mat will tear and become scarred. If the mix is too cold, the energy requirement for compaction becomes impractical because of viscous resistance. These physical limits define the practical time duration available for the rolling operation.

Sometimes density cannot be achieved by a single roller within the time duration available. In that case an intermediate rolling step is required to supplement the breakdown step in reaching the required density. Finally, there is a finish rolling step to remove any surface marks left by the previous rolling or the paver.

Steel wheel rollers are used for finish rolling. Pneumatic rollers are multipurpose and can be used for breakdown and intermediate rolling. The vibratory steel wheel-type rollers are usually the roller of choice for breakdown and intermediate rolling because of their adaptability to a range of mixes and differences in mat thickness. With the vibrator turned off, they can also be used for finish rolling.

Roller capacity. Paver speed and production is set by the asphalt plant capability. Net roller speed is influenced by:

The gross roller speed
The number of passes
The number of laps
The overlap between adjacent laps to cover the mat width
The extension overedge
The extra passes for joints
The nonproductive travel (overrun for lap change)

Roller capability for a project must match the net roller speed with the average paver speed. It must be remembered that increased roller speed simply reduces compactive effort, so speed alone cannot be used to compensate for increased production. Typical acceptable roller speeds are 2 to $3\frac{1}{2}$ mph for breakdown, $2\frac{1}{2}$ to 4 mph for intermediate, and 3 to 7 mph for finish rolling.

Example 19-2. A plant will produce 260 tph for a project. The mat will be 12 ft wide and 2 in. thick, and will have a density of 110 lb/sq yd-in. A vibratory roller with a 66-in. wide drum will be used for compaction. Assume a 50-min hour efficiency factor for the roller. The overlap between adjacent laps and overedges will be a minimum of 6 in. It is estimated that nonproductive travel will add about 15% to total travel. From a test mat it was found that three passes with the roller are required to achieve density. To account for acceleration and deceleration when changing directions, add 10% to the average roller speed to calculate a running speed. How many rollers should be used on this project?

$$\frac{12 \text{ ft (wide)} \times 2 \text{ in.} \times 110 \text{ lb/sq yd-in}}{9 \text{ sq ft/sq yd} \times 2000 \text{ lb/ton}} = 0.147 \text{ ton per ft of paving length}$$

$$\frac{260 \text{ tph}}{60 \text{ min/hr}} = 4.3 \text{ ton/min}$$

Average paving speed,

$$\frac{4.3 \text{ ton/min}}{0.147 \text{ ton/ft}} = 29 \text{ ft/min}$$

Rolling width, 12 ft × 12 in./ft + 2 (6 in. each edge) = 156 in.

Effective roller width, 66 in. − 6 in. (overlap) = 60 in.

Number of laps: First lap 66 in.; 156 − 66 = 90 in. remaining

Additional laps,

$$\frac{90 \text{ in.}}{60 \text{ in.}} = 1.5$$

Therefore, three laps will be necessary.

Total number of roller passes, 3 laps × 3 passes per lap = 9 passes

Each pass must cover:

29 ft per min, rolling + 29 ft per min, return + maneuver distance

Total roller distance required to match paver speed,

9×58 ft/min $\times 1.15$ (nonprod) $\times 60$ min/hr $= 36,018$ ft/hr

Average roller speed,

$$\frac{36,018 \text{ ft/hr}}{50 \text{ min}} = 720 \text{ ft/min} \quad \text{or } 8.2 \text{ mph}$$

Running speed, $8.2 \times 1.1 = 9$ mph

Roller speed is very important during breakdown and intermediate rolling. As speed decreases, compactive effort is improved and the tendency of the mix to displace is reduced. Therefore, in this case it is necessary to consider alternatives which will reduce the required roller speed.

One possible solution is to use three rollers. This will yield a running speed of 3 mph. Another solution will be to use a roller having a drum width equal to or greater than 84 in. The use of such a roller will reduce the number of laps to 2, and therefore the number of passes to 6.

Effective roller width, 84 in. $-$ 6 in. (overlap) $= 78$ in.

Number of laps: First lap 84 in. $156 - 84 = 72$ in. remaining

Additional laps,

$$\frac{72 \text{ in.}}{78 \text{ in.}} = 0.9$$

The required running speed will then be 6 mph and the project will require only two such rollers.

Safety. Personnel working around asphalt plants must be trained to be safety conscious [8]. The potential for a serious fire results from the presence of burner fuel for the dryer, liquid asphalt, and hot oil of the heat transfer system. No open flames or smoking should be permitted in the plant area. All fuel, asphalt, and oil lines should have control valves which can be activated from a safe distance. Both asphalt and hot oil lines should be checked regularly for leaks.

Besides the fire potential, many of the mechanical parts are very hot. These will cause severe burns if personnel come into contact with them. The mechanical system for moving the aggregates with its belts, sprockets, and chain drives presents a hazard to personnel if they become entangled in the system's moving parts. All these parts should be covered or protected, but they do require maintenance. Maintenance should only be performed when the plant has been completely shut down. The plant operator must be informed that personnel are working on the plant and the lockout switch should be tagged.

Even at the paving spread, the mix is still very hot and direct contact will result in severe burns. Additionally, trucks backing to the paver have limited rear visibility. Personnel must be made aware of these hazards on a regular basis and necessary safety equipment must be provided.

PROBLEMS

19-1. An asphalt plant can produce 300 tph. A project requires paving individual 10-ft lanes with a $1\frac{1}{2}$-in. lift averaging 115 lb per sq yd-in. What average paver speed will match the plant production? How many 14-ton dump trucks will be required if the total hauling cycle time is 40 min?

19-2. A plant will produce 440 tph for a project. The mat will be 12 ft wide and 1 in. thick, and will have a density of 112 lb per sq yd-in. A vibratory roller with a 60-in. wide drum will be used for compaction. Assume a 50-min hour efficiency factor for the roller. The overlap between adjacent laps and overedges will be a 6-in. minimum. It is estimated that nonproductive travel will add about 15% to total travel. From a test mat it was found that three passes with the roller are required to achieve density. To account for acceleration and deceleration when changing directions, add 10% to the average roller speed to calculate a running speed. What is the required roller speed if only one roller is available?

19-3. An asphalt distributor having an 8-ft-long spray bar will be used to apply a prime coat at a rate of 0.3 gal per sq yd. The road being paved is 16 ft wide and 2,200 ft in length. How many gallons of prime will be required?

19-4. An asphalt plant will produce 180 tph for a highway project. The mat will be 12 ft wide and $1\frac{1}{2}$-in. thick, and will have a density of 115 lb per sq yd-in. A vibratory roller with a 66-in. wide drum will be used for compaction. Assume a 50-min hour efficiency factor for the roller. The overlap between adjacent laps and overedges will be a 6-in. minimum. It is estimated that nonproductive travel will add about 15% to total travel. From a test mat it was found that three passes with the roller are required to achieve density. To account for acceleration and deceleration when changing directions, add 10% to the average roller speed to calculate a running speed. If it is desired to keep the rolling speed under 3 mph, how many rollers are required for the project?

REFERENCES

1. *Asphalt Construction Handbook*, Barber-Greene, DeKalb, IL, 1992.
2. *Asphalt Hot-Mix Recycling (MS-20)*, The Asphalt Institute, Lexington, KY.
3. *Asphalt Paving Manual for Rubber-Tired Pavers*, Caterpillar Inc., Peoria, IL, 1987.
4. *Asphalt Plant Manual (MS-3)*, The Asphalt Institute, Lexington, KY.
5. "Asphalt Recycling and Reclaiming '87, Special Report Roads & Bridges," *Roads & Bridges*, October 1987.
6. *Hot-Mix Asphalt Paving Handbook*, U.S. Army Corps of Engineers, UN-13(CEMP-ET), July 1991.
7. *Mix Design Methods for Asphalt Concrete and Other Hot-Mix Types (MS-2)*, The Asphalt Institute, Lexington, KY.
8. *OSHA Compliance Manual for Hot Mix Plants*, National Asphalt Pavement Association, Riverdale, MD.
9. *Principles of Construction of Hot-Mix Asphalt Pavements (MS-22)*, The Asphalt Institute, Lexington, KY.

APPENDIX

A

INTEREST TABLES

			$i = 0.5\%$			
n	P/F	P/A	A/F	A/P	F/P	F/A
1	0.9950249	0.9950249	1.0000000	1.0050000	1.005000	1.000000
2	0.9900745	1.9850990	0.4987531	0.5037531	1.010025	2.005000
3	0.9851488	2.9702480	0.3316722	0.3366722	1.015075	3.015025
4	0.9802475	3.9504960	0.2481328	0.2531328	1.020151	4.030100
5	0.9753707	4.9258660	0.1980100	0.2030100	1.025251	5.050251
6	0.9705181	5.8963850	0.1645955	0.1695955	1.030378	6.075502
7	0.9656896	6.8620740	0.1407285	0.1457285	1.035529	7.105880
8	0.9608852	7.8229590	0.1228289	0.1278289	1.040707	8.141409
9	0.9561047	8.7790640	0.1089074	0.1139074	1.045911	9.182116
10	0.9513479	9.7304120	0.0977706	0.1027706	1.051140	10.228030
11	0.9466149	10.6770300	0.0886590	0.0936590	1.056396	11.279170
12	0.9419053	11.6189300	0.8106640	0.0860664	1.061678	12.335560
13	0.9372192	12.5561500	0.0746422	0.0796422	1.066986	13.397240
14	0.9325565	13.4887100	0.0691361	0.0741361	1.072321	14.464230
15	0.9279169	14.4166200	0.0643644	0.0693644	1.077683	15.536550
16	0.9233004	15.3399300	0.0601894	0.0651894	1.083071	16.614230
17	0.9187068	16.2586300	0.0565058	0.0615058	1.088487	17.697300
18	0.9141362	17.1727700	0.0532317	0.0582317	1.093929	18.785790
19	0.9095882	18.0823600	0.0503025	0.0553025	1.099399	19.879720
20	0.9050629	18.9874200	0.0476665	0.0526665	1.104896	20.979120
21	0.9005601	19.8879800	0.0452816	0.0502816	1.110420	22.084010
22	0.8960797	20.7840600	0.0431138	0.0481138	1.115972	23.194430
23	0.8916216	21.6756800	0.0411347	0.0461347	1.121552	24.310400
24	0.8871857	22.5628700	0.0393206	0.0443206	1.127160	25.431960
25	0.8827718	23.4456400	0.0376519	0.0426519	1.132796	26.559120

			$i = 0.5\%$			
n	P/F	P/A	A/F	A/P	F/P	F/A
26	0.8783799	24.3240200	0.0361116	0.0411116	1.138460	27.691910
27	0.8740099	25.1980300	0.0346856	0.0396856	1.144152	28.830370
28	0.8696616	26.0676900	0.0333617	0.0383617	1.149873	29.974520
29	0.8653349	26.9330200	0.0321291	0.0371291	1.155622	31.124400
30	0.8610297	27.7940500	0.0309789	0.0359789	1.161400	32.280020
32	0.8524836	29.5032800	0.0288945	0.0338945	1.173043	34.608620
34	0.8440223	31.1955500	0.0270559	0.0320559	1.184803	36.960580
36	0.8356449	32.8710200	0.0254219	0.0304219	1.196681	39.336110
38	0.8273507	34.5298600	0.0239604	0.0289604	1.208677	41.735450
40	0.8191389	36.1722300	0.0226455	0.0276455	1.220794	44.158850
48	0.7870984	42.5803200	0.0184850	0.0234850	1.270489	54.097830
60	0.7413722	51.7255600	0.0143328	0.0193328	1.348850	69.770030
72	0.6983024	60.3395100	0.0115729	0.0165729	1.432044	86.408860
80	0.6709885	65.8023100	0.0101970	0.0151970	1.490339	98.067720
100	0.6072868	78.5426500	0.0077319	0.0127319	1.646669	129.333700
120	0.5496327	90.0734500	0.0061021	0.0111021	1.819397	163.879400
180	0.4074824	118.5035000	0.0034386	0.0084386	2.454094	290.818700
240	0.3020961	139.5808000	0.0021643	0.0071643	3.310205	462.040900

			$i = 0.75\%$			
n	P/F	P/A	A/F	A/P	F/P	F/A
1	0.9925558	0.992558	1.0000000	1.0075000	1.007500	1.000000
2	0.9851671	1.977723	0.4981320	0.5056320	1.015056	2.007500
3	0.9778333	2.955556	0.3308458	0.3383458	1.022669	3.022556
4	0.9705542	3.926110	0.2472050	0.2547050	1.030339	4.045225
5	0.9633292	4.889440	0.1970224	0.2045224	1.038067	5.075565
6	0.9561580	5.845598	0.1635689	0.1710689	1.045852	6.113631
7	0.9490402	6.794638	0.1396749	0.1471749	1.053696	7.159484
8	0.9419754	7.736613	0.1217555	0.1292555	1.061599	8.213180
9	0.9349632	8.671576	0.1078193	0.1153193	1.069561	9.274779
10	0.9280032	9.599580	0.0966712	0.1041712	1.077583	10.344340
11	0.9210949	10.520670	0.0875509	0.0950509	1.085664	11.421920
12	0.9142382	11.434910	0.0799515	0.0874515	1.093807	12.507590
13	0.9074324	12.342350	0.0735219	0.0810219	1.102010	13.601390
14	0.9006773	13.243020	0.0680115	0.0755115	1.110276	14.703400
15	0.8939725	14.136990	0.0632364	0.0707364	1.118603	15.813680
16	0.8873177	15.024310	0.0590588	0.0665588	1.126992	16.932280
17	0.8807123	15.905020	0.0553732	0.0628732	1.135445	18.059270
18	0.8741561	16.779180	0.0520977	0.0595977	1.143960	19.194720

			$i = 0.75\%$			
n	P/F	P/A	A/F	A/P	F/P	F/A
19	0.8676488	17.646830	0.0491674	0.0566674	1.152540	20.338680
20	0.8611899	18.508020	0.0465306	0.0540306	1.161184	21.491220
21	0.8547790	19.362800	0.0441454	0.0516454	1.169893	22.652400
22	0.8484159	20.211210	0.0419775	0.0494775	1.178667	23.822300
23	0.8421001	21.053310	0.0399985	0.0474985	1.187507	25.000960
24	0.8358314	21.889150	0.0381847	0.0456847	1.196414	26.188470
25	0.8296093	22.718760	0.0365165	0.0440165	1.205387	27.384880
26	0.8234336	23.542190	0.0349769	0.0424769	1.214427	28.590270
27	0.8173038	24.359490	0.0335518	0.0410518	1.223535	29.804700
28	0.8112197	25.170710	0.0322287	0.0397287	1.232712	31.028230
29	0.8051808	25.975890	0.0309972	0.0384972	1.241957	32.260940
30	0.7991869	26.775080	0.0298482	0.0373482	1.251272	33.502900
32	0.7873326	28.355650	0.0277663	0.0352663	1.270111	36.014830
34	0.7756542	29.912780	0.0259305	0.0334305	1.289234	38.564580
36	0.7641490	31.446810	0.0242997	0.0317997	1.308645	41.152720
38	0.7528144	32.958080	0.0228416	0.0303416	1.328349	43.779820
40	0.7416480	34.446940	0.0215302	0.0290302	1.348349	46.446480
48	0.6986141	40.184780	0.0173850	0.0248850	1.431405	57.520710
60	0.6386997	48.173370	0.0132584	0.0207584	1.565681	75.424140
72	0.5839236	55.476850	0.0105255	0.0180255	1.712553	95.007000
80	0.5500417	59.994440	0.0091682	0.0166682	1.818044	109.072500
100	0.4736903	70.174620	0.0067502	0.0142502	2.111084	148.144500
120	0.4079373	78.941690	0.0051676	0.0126676	2.451357	193.514300
180	0.2605494	98.593410	0.0026427	0.0101427	3.838043	378.405800
240	0.1664128	111.145000	0.0014973	0.0089973	6.009151	667.886900

			$i = 1\%$			
n	P/F	P/A	A/F	A/P	F/P	F/A
1	0.9900990	0.990099	1.0000000	1.0100000	1.010000	1.000000
2	0.9802960	1.970395	0.4975125	0.5075125	1.020100	2.010000
3	0.9705901	2.940985	0.3300221	0.3400221	1.030301	3.030100
4	0.9609803	3.901965	0.2462811	0.2562811	1.040604	4.060401
5	0.9514657	4.853431	0.1960398	0.2060398	1.051010	5.101005
6	0.9420452	5.795476	0.1625484	0.1725484	1.061520	6.152015
7	0.9327181	6.728194	0.1386283	0.1486283	1.072135	7.213535
8	0.9234832	7.651678	0.1206903	0.1306903	1.082857	8.285670
9	0.9143398	8.566017	0.1067404	0.1167404	1.093685	9.368527
10	0.9052870	9.471304	0.0955821	0.1055821	1.104622	10.462210

			$i = 1\%$			
n	P/F	P/A	A/F	A/P	F/P	F/A
11	0.8963237	10.367630	0.0864541	0.0964541	1.115668	11.566830
12	0.8874492	11.255080	0.0788488	0.0888488	1.126825	12.682500
13	0.8786626	12.133740	0.0724148	0.0824148	1.138093	13.809330
14	0.8699630	13.003700	0.0669012	0.0769012	1.149474	14.947420
15	0.8613495	13.865050	0.0621238	0.0721238	1.160969	16.096900
16	0.8528213	14.717870	0.0579446	0.0679446	1.172579	17.257860
17	0.8443775	15.562250	0.0542581	0.0642581	1.184304	18.430440
18	0.8360173	16.398270	0.0509820	0.0609820	1.196147	19.614750
19	0.8277399	17.226010	0.0480518	0.0580518	1.208109	20.810890
20	0.8195445	18.045550	0.4541530	0.0554153	1.220190	22.019000
21	0.8114302	18.856980	0.0430308	0.0530308	1.232392	23.239190
22	0.8033962	19.660380	0.0408637	0.0508637	1.244716	24.471590
23	0.7954418	20.455820	0.0388858	0.0488858	1.257163	25.716300
24	0.7875661	21.243390	0.0370735	0.0470735	1.269735	26.973460
25	0.7797684	22.023160	0.0354068	0.0454068	1.282432	28.243200
26	0.7720480	22.795200	0.0338689	0.0438689	1.295256	29.525630
27	0.7644039	23.559610	0.0324455	0.0424455	1.308209	30.820890
28	0.7568356	24.316440	0.0311244	0.0411244	1.321291	32.129100
29	0.7493422	25.065780	0.0298950	0.0398950	1.334504	33.450390
30	0.7419229	25.807710	0.0287481	0.0387481	1.347849	34.784890
32	0.7273041	27.269590	0.0266709	0.0366709	1.374941	37.494070
34	0.7129733	28.702670	0.0248400	0.0348400	1.402577	40.257700
36	0.6989250	30.107500	0.0232143	0.0332143	1.430769	43.076880
38	0.6851534	31.484660	0.0217615	0.0317615	1.459527	45.952720
40	0.6716310	32.834690	0.0204556	0.3045560	1.488864	48.886370
48	0.6202604	37.973960	0.0163338	0.0263338	1.612226	61.222610
60	0.5504496	44.955040	0.0122444	0.0222444	1.816697	81.669670
72	0.4884961	51.150390	0.0095502	0.0195502	2.047099	104.709900
80	0.4511179	54.888210	0.0082189	0.0182189	2.216715	121.671500
100	0.3697112	63.028880	0.0058657	0.0158657	2.704814	170.481400
120	0.3029948	69.700520	0.0043471	0.0143471	3.300387	230.038700
180	0.1667834	83.321660	0.0020017	0.0120017	5.995802	499.580200
240	0.0918058	90.819420	0.0010109	0.0110109	10.892550	989.255300

			$i = 1.25\%$			
n	P/F	P/A	A/F	A/P	F/P	F/A
1	0.9876543	0.9876543	1.0000000	1.0125000	1.012500	1.000000
2	0.9754611	1.963115	0.4968944	0.5093944	1.025156	2.012500

			$i = 1.25\%$			
n	P/F	P/A	A/F	A/P	F/P	F/A
3	0.9634183	2.926534	0.3292012	0.3417012	1.037971	3.037656
4	0.9515243	3.878058	0.2453610	0.2578610	1.050945	4.075627
5	0.9397771	4.817835	0.1950621	0.2075621	1.064082	5.126572
6	0.9281749	5.7460100	0.1615338	0.1740338	1.077383	6.190654
7	0.9167159	6.6627260	0.1375887	0.1500887	1.090850	7.268037
8	0.9053984	7.5681240	0.1196331	0.1321331	1.104486	8.358888
9	0.8942207	8.4623450	0.1056706	0.1181706	1.118292	9.463374
10	0.8831809	9.3455260	0.0945031	0.1070031	1.132271	10.581670
11	0.8722775	10.2178000	0.0853684	0.0978684	1.146424	11.713940
12	0.8615086	11.0793100	0.0777583	0.0902583	1.160755	12.860360
13	0.8508727	11.9301800	0.0713210	0.0838210	1.175264	14.021120
14	0.8403681	12.7705500	0.0658051	0.0783051	1.189955	15.196380
15	0.8299932	13.6005500	0.0610265	0.0735265	1.204829	16.386330
16	0.8197463	14.4202900	0.0568467	0.0693467	1.219890	17.591160
17	0.8096260	15.2299200	0.0531602	0.0656602	1.235138	18.811050
18	0.7996306	16.0295500	0.0498848	0.0623848	1.250577	20.046190
19	0.7897587	16.8193100	0.0469555	0.0594555	1.266210	21.296770
20	0.7800086	17.5993200	0.0443204	0.0568204	1.282037	22.562980
21	0.7703788	18.3696900	0.0419375	0.0544375	1.298063	23.845020
22	0.7608680	19.1305600	0.0397724	0.0522724	1.314288	25.143080
23	0.7514745	19.8820400	0.0377967	0.0502967	1.330717	26.457370
24	0.7421971	20.6242300	0.0359866	0.0484866	1.347351	27.788080
25	0.7330341	21.3572700	0.0343225	0.0468225	1.364193	29.135430
26	0.7239843	22.0812500	0.0327873	0.0452873	1.381245	30.499630
27	0.7150463	22.7963000	0.0313668	0.0438668	1.398511	31.880870
28	0.7062185	23.5025200	0.0300486	0.0425486	1.415992	33.279380
29	0.6974998	24.2000200	0.0288223	0.0413223	1.433692	34.695380
30	0.6888887	24.8889100	0.0276785	0.0401785	1.451613	36.129070
32	0.6719841	26.2412700	0.0256079	0.0381079	1.488130	39.050440
34	0.6554943	27.5604600	0.0237839	0.0362839	1.525566	42.045300
36	0.6394092	28.8472700	0.0221653	0.0346653	1.563944	45.115500
38	0.6237187	30.1025000	0.0207198	0.0332198	1.603287	48.262940
40	0.6084133	31.3269300	0.0194214	0.0319214	1.643619	51.489560
48	0.5508565	35.9314800	0.0153307	0.0278307	1.815355	65.228390
60	0.4745676	42.0345900	0.0112899	0.0237899	2.107181	88.574510
72	0.4088441	47.2924700	0.0086450	0.0211450	2.445920	115.673600
80	0.3701668	50.3866600	0.0073465	0.0198465	2.701485	136.118800
100	0.2887333	56.9013400	0.0050743	0.0175743	3.463404	197.072300
120	0.2252144	61.9828500	0.0036335	0.0161335	4.440213	275.217000
180	0.1068795	71.4496400	0.0014959	0.0139959	9.356334	668.506700
240	0.0507215	75.9422800	6.679E-40	0.0131679	19.715490	1,497.239000

			$i = 1.5\%$			
n	P/F	P/A	A/F	A/P	F/P	F/A
1	0.9852217	0.9852217	1.0000000	1.0150000	1.000000	1.000000
2	0.9706617	1.9558830	0.4962779	0.5112779	1.030225	2.015000
3	0.9563170	2.9122000	0.3283830	0.3433830	1.045678	3.045225
4	0.9421842	3.8543850	0.2444448	0.2594448	1.061364	4.090903
5	0.9282603	4.7826450	0.1940893	0.2090893	1.077284	5.152267
6	0.9145422	5.6971870	0.1605252	0.1755252	1.093443	6.229551
7	0.9010268	6.5982140	0.1365562	0.1515562	1.109845	7.322994
8	0.8877111	7.4859250	0.1185840	0.1335840	1.126493	8.432839
9	0.8745922	8.3605170	0.1046098	0.1196098	1.143390	9.559332
10	0.8616672	9.2221850	0.0934342	0.1084342	1.160541	10.702720
11	0.8489332	10.0711200	0.0842938	0.0992938	1.177949	11.863260
12	0.8363874	10.9075100	0.0766800	0.0916800	1.195618	13.041210
13	0.8240270	11.7315300	0.0702404	0.0852404	1.213552	14.236830
14	0.8118493	12.5433800	0.0647233	0.0797233	1.231756	15.450380
15	0.7998515	13.3432300	0.0599444	0.0749444	1.250232	16.682140
16	0.7880310	14.1312600	0.0557651	0.0707651	1.268986	17.932370
17	0.7763853	14.9076500	0.0520797	0.0670797	1.288020	19.201360
18	0.7649116	15.6725600	0.0488058	0.0638058	1.307341	20.489380
19	0.7536075	16.4261700	0.0458785	0.0608785	1.326951	21.796720
20	0.7424740	17.1686400	0.0432457	0.0582457	1.346855	23.123670
21	0.7314979	17.9001400	0.0408655	0.0558655	1.367058	24.470520
22	0.7206876	18.6208200	0.0387033	0.0537033	1.387564	25.837580
23	0.7100371	19.3308600	0.0367308	0.0517308	1.408377	27.225140
24	0.6995439	20.0304100	0.0349241	0.0499241	1.429503	28.633520
25	0.6892058	20.7196100	0.0332635	0.0482635	1.450945	30.063020
26	0.6790205	21.3986300	0.0317320	0.0467320	1.472710	31.513970
27	0.6689857	22.0676200	0.0303153	0.0453153	1.494800	32.986680
28	0.6590992	22.7267200	0.0290011	0.0440011	1.517222	34.481480
29	0.6493589	23.3760800	0.0277788	0.0427788	1.539981	35.998700
30	0.6397624	24.0158400	0.0266392	0.0416392	1.563080	37.538680
32	0.6209929	25.2671400	0.0245771	0.0395771	1.610324	40.688290
34	0.6027741	26.4817300	0.0227619	0.0377619	1.658996	43.933090
36	0.5850897	27.6606800	0.0211524	0.0361524	1.709140	47.275970
38	0.5679242	28.8050500	0.0197161	0.0347161	1.760798	50.719890
40	0.5512623	29.9158500	0.0184271	0.0334271	1.814018	54.267890
48	0.4893617	34.0425500	0.0143750	0.0293750	2.043478	69.565220
60	0.4092960	39.3802700	0.0103934	0.0253934	2.443220	96.214650
72	0.3423300	43.8446700	0.0078078	0.0228078	2.921158	128.077200
80	0.3038901	46.4073200	0.0065483	0.0215483	3.290663	152.710900
100	0.2256294	51.6247000	0.0043706	0.0193706	4.432046	228.803000
120	0.1675232	55.4984500	0.0030185	0.0180185	5.969323	331.288200

			$i = 1.5\%$			
n	P/F	P/A	A/F	A/P	F/P	F/A
180	0.0685666	62.0955600	0.0011042	0.0161042	14.584370	905.624500
240	0.0280640	64.7957300	4.331E-40	0.0154331	35.632820	2,308.854000

			$i = 1.75\%$			
n	P/F	P/A	A/F	A/P	F/P	F/A
1	0.9828010	0.982801	1.0000000	1.0175000	1.017500	1.000000
2	0.9658978	1.948699	0.4956630	0.5131630	1.035306	2.017500
3	0.9492853	2.897984	0.3275675	0.3450675	1.053424	3.052806
4	0.9329585	3.830943	0.2435324	0.2610324	1.071859	4.106230
5	0.9169125	4.747855	0.1931214	0.2106214	1.090617	5.178089
6	0.9011425	5.648998	0.1595226	0.1770226	1.109702	6.268706
7	0.8856438	6.534641	0.1355306	0.1530306	1.129122	7.378408
8	0.8704116	7.405053	0.1175429	0.1350429	1.148882	8.507530
9	0.8554413	8.260494	0.1035581	0.1210581	1.168987	9.656412
10	0.8407286	9.101223	0.0923753	0.1098753	1.189444	10.825400
11	0.8262689	9.927492	0.0832304	0.1007304	1.210260	12.014840
12	0.8120579	10.739550	0.0756138	0.0931138	1.231439	13.225100
13	0.7980913	11.537640	0.0691728	0.0866728	1.252990	14.456540
14	0.7843649	12.322010	0.0636556	0.0811556	1.274917	15.709530
15	0.7708746	13.092880	0.0588774	0.0763774	1.297228	16.984450
16	0.7576163	13.850500	0.5469960	0.0721996	1.319929	18.281680
17	0.7445861	14.595080	0.0510162	0.0685162	1.343028	19.601610
18	0.7317799	15.326860	0.0477449	0.0652449	1.366531	20.944630
19	0.7191940	16.046060	0.0448206	0.0623206	1.390445	22.311170
20	0.7068246	16.752880	0.0421912	0.0596912	1.414778	23.701610
21	0.6946679	17.447550	0.0398146	0.0573146	1.439537	25.116390
22	0.6827203	18.130270	0.0376564	0.0551564	1.464729	26.555930
23	0.6709782	18.801250	0.0356880	0.0531880	1.490361	28.020650
24	0.6594380	19.460690	0.0338857	0.0513857	1.516443	29.511020
25	0.6480963	20.108780	0.0322295	0.0497295	1.542981	31.027460
26	0.6369497	20.745730	0.0307027	0.0482027	1.569983	32.570440
27	0.6259948	21.371730	0.0292908	0.0467908	1.597457	34.140420
28	0.6152283	21.986950	0.0279815	0.0454815	1.625413	35.737880
29	0.6046470	22.591600	0.0267642	0.0442642	1.653858	37.363290
30	0.5942476	23.185850	0.0256298	0.0431298	1.682800	39.017150
32	0.5739825	24.343860	0.0235781	0.0410781	1.742213	42.412200
34	0.5544084	25.462380	0.0217736	0.0392736	1.803725	45.927120
36	0.5355018	26.542750	0.0201751	0.0376751	1.867407	49.566130
38	0.5172400	27.586280	0.0187499	0.0362499	1.933338	53.333620

$i = 1.75\%$

n	P/F	P/A	A/F	A/P	F/P	F/A
40	0.4996010	28.594230	0.0174721	0.0349721	2.001597	57.234130
48	0.4348585	32.293800	0.0134657	0.0309657	2.299599	74.262780
60	0.3531303	36.963990	0.0095534	0.0270534	2.831816	104.675200
72	0.2867622	40.756450	0.0070360	0.0245360	3.487210	142.126300
80	0.2496011	42.879930	0.0058209	0.0233209	4.006392	171.793800
100	0.1764242	47.061470	0.0037488	0.0212488	5.668156	266.751800
120	0.1247010	50.017090	0.0024932	0.0199932	8.019183	401.096200
180	0.0440357	54.626530	8.061E-40	0.0183061	22.70885	1,240.506000
240	0.0155503	56.254270	2.764E-40	0.0177764	64.30730	3,617.560000

$i = 2\%$

n	P/F	P/A	A/F	A/P	F/P	F/A
1	0.9803922	0.9803922	1.0000000	1.0200000	1.020000	1.000000
2	0.9611688	1.9415610	0.4950495	0.5150495	1.040400	2.020000
3	0.9423223	2.8838830	0.3267547	0.3467547	1.061208	3.060400
4	0.9238454	3.8077290	0.2426238	0.2626238	1.082432	4.121608
5	0.9057308	4.7134600	0.1921584	0.2121584	1.104081	5.204040
6	0.8879714	5.6014310	0.1585258	0.1785258	1.126162	6.308121
7	0.8705602	6.4719910	0.1345120	0.1545120	1.148686	7.434283
8	0.8534904	7.3254810	0.1165098	0.1365098	1.171659	8.582969
9	0.8367553	8.1622370	0.1025154	0.1225154	1.195093	9.754628
10	0.8203483	8.9825850	0.0913265	0.1113265	1.218994	10.949720
11	0.8042630	9.7868400	0.0821779	0.1021779	1.243374	12.168720
12	0.7884932	10.5753400	0.0745596	0.0945596	1.268242	13.412090
13	0.7730325	11.3483700	0.0681184	0.0881184	1.293607	14.680330
14	0.7578750	12.1062500	0.0626020	0.0826020	1.319479	15.973940
15	0.7430147	12.8492600	0.0578255	0.0778255	1.345868	17.293420
16	0.7284458	13.5777100	0.0536501	0.0736501	1.372786	18.639290
17	0.7141626	14.2918700	0.0499698	0.0699698	1.400241	20.012070
18	0.7001594	14.9920300	0.0467021	0.0667021	1.428246	21.412310
19	0.6864308	15.6784600	0.0437818	0.0637818	1.456811	22.840560
20	0.6729713	16.3514300	0.0411567	0.0611567	1.485947	24.297370
21	0.6597758	17.0112100	0.0387848	0.0587848	1.515666	25.783320
22	0.6468390	17.6580500	0.0366314	0.0566314	1.545980	27.298980
23	0.6341559	18.2922000	0.0346681	0.0546681	1.576899	28.844960
24	0.6217215	18.9139300	0.0328711	0.0528711	1.608437	30.421860
25	0.6095309	19.5234600	0.0312204	0.0512204	1.640606	32.030300
26	0.5975793	20.1210400	0.0296992	0.0496992	1.673418	33.670910
27	0.5858620	20.7069000	0.0282931	0.0482931	1.706886	35.344320

$i = 2\%$

n	P/F	P/A	A/F	A/P	F/P	F/A
28	0.5743746	21.2812700	0.0269897	0.0469897	1.741024	37.051210
29	0.5631123	21.8443800	0.0257784	0.0457784	1.775845	38.792230
30	0.5520709	22.3964600	0.0246499	0.0446499	1.811362	40.568080
32	0.5306333	23.4683300	0.0226106	0.0426106	1.884541	44.227030
34	0.5100282	24.4985900	0.0208187	0.0408187	1.960676	48.033800
36	0.4902231	25.4888400	0.0192329	0.0392329	2.039887	51.994370
38	0.4711872	26.4406400	0.0178206	0.0378206	2.122299	56.114940
40	0.4528904	27.3554800	0.0165557	0.0365557	2.208040	60.401980
48	0.3865376	30.6731200	0.0126018	0.0326018	2.587070	79.353520
60	0.3047823	34.7608900	0.0087680	0.0287680	3.281031	114.051500
72	0.2403187	37.9840600	0.0063268	0.0263268	4.161140	158.057000
80	0.2051097	39.7445100	0.0051607	0.0251607	4.875439	193.772000
100	0.1380330	43.0983500	0.0032027	0.0232027	7.244646	312.232300
120	0.0928922	45.3553900	0.0020481	0.0220481	10.765160	488.258200
180	0.0283119	48.5844000	5.827E-40	0.0205827	35.320830	1,716.042000
240	0.0086290	49.5685500	1.741E-40	0.0201741	115.888700	5,744.437000

$i = 2.5\%$

n	P/F	P/A	A/F	A/P	F/P	F/A
1	0.9756098	0.9756097	1.0000000	1.0250000	1.025000	1.000000
2	0.9518144	1.9274240	0.4938272	0.5188272	1.050625	2.025000
3	0.9285994	2.8560240	0.3251372	0.3501372	1.076891	3.075625
4	0.9059506	3.7619740	0.2408179	0.2658179	1.103813	4.152516
5	0.8838543	4.6458280	0.1902469	0.2152469	1.131408	5.256328
6	0.8622969	5.5081250	0.1565500	0.1815500	1.159693	6.387737
7	0.8412652	6.3493910	0.1324954	0.1574954	1.188686	7.547430
8	0.8207466	7.1701370	0.1144673	0.1394673	1.218403	8.736116
9	0.8007284	7.9708650	0.1004569	0.1254569	1.248863	9.954519
10	0.7811984	8.7520640	0.0892588	0.1142588	1.280085	11.203380
11	0.7621448	9.5142090	0.0801060	0.1051060	1.312087	12.483470
12	0.7435559	10.2577600	0.0724871	0.0974871	1.344889	13.795550
13	0.7254204	10.9831800	0.0660483	0.0910483	1.378511	15.140440
14	0.7077272	11.6909100	0.0605365	0.0855365	1.412974	16.518950
15	0.6904656	12.3813800	0.0557665	0.0807665	1.448298	17.931930
16	0.6736249	13.0550000	0.0515990	0.0765990	1.484506	19.380220
17	0.6571951	13.7122000	0.0479278	0.0729278	1.521618	20.864730
18	0.6411659	14.3533600	0.0446701	0.0696701	1.559659	22.386350
19	0.6255277	14.9788900	0.0417606	0.0667606	1.598650	23.946010
20	0.6102709	15.5891600	0.0391471	0.0641471	1.638616	25.544660

$i = 2.5\%$

n	P/F	P/A	A/F	A/P	F/P	F/A
21	0.5953863	16.1845500	0.0367873	0.0617873	1.679582	27.183270
22	0.5808647	16.7654100	0.0346466	0.0596466	1.721571	28.862860
23	0.5666972	17.3321100	0.0326964	0.0576964	1.764611	30.584430
24	0.5528754	17.8849900	0.0309128	0.0559128	1.808726	32.349040
25	0.5393906	18.4243800	0.0292759	0.0542759	1.853944	34.157760
26	0.5262347	18.9506100	0.0277687	0.0527687	1.900293	36.011710
27	0.5133997	19.4640100	0.0263769	0.0513769	1.947800	37.912000
28	0.5008778	19.9648900	0.0250879	0.0500879	1.996495	39.859800
29	0.4886613	20.4535500	0.0238913	0.0488913	2.046407	41.856300
30	0.4767427	20.9302900	0.0227776	0.0477776	2.097568	43.902700
32	0.4537706	21.8491800	0.0207683	0.0457683	2.203757	48.150280
34	0.4319053	22.7237900	0.0190068	0.0440068	2.315322	52.612880
36	0.4110937	23.5562500	0.0174516	0.0424516	2.432535	57.301410
38	0.3912849	24.3486000	0.0160701	0.0410701	2.555682	62.227300
40	0.3724306	25.1027700	0.0148362	0.0398362	2.685064	67.402550
48	0.3056712	27.7731500	0.0110060	0.0360060	3.271490	90.859580
60	0.2272836	30.9086600	0.0073534	0.0323534	4.399790	135.991600
72	0.1689981	33.2400800	0.0050842	0.0300842	5.917228	196.689100
80	0.1387046	34.4518200	0.0040260	0.0290260	7.209568	248.382700
100	0.0846474	36.6141100	0.0023119	0.0273119	11.813720	432.548600
120	0.0516578	37.9336900	0.0013618	0.0263618	19.358150	734.326000
180	0.0117410	39.5303600	2.970E-40	0.0252970	85.171790	3,366.871000
240	0.0026685	39.8932600	6.689E-50	0.0250669	374.737900	14,949.520000

$i = 3\%$

n	P/F	P/A	A/F	A/P	F/P	F/A
1	0.9708738	0.9708738	1.0000000	1.0300000	1.030000	1.000000
2	0.9425959	1.9134700	0.4926108	0.5226108	1.060900	2.030000
3	0.9151417	2.8286110	0.3235304	0.3535304	1.092727	3.090900
4	0.8884870	3.7170980	0.2390270	0.2690270	1.125509	4.183627
5	0.8626088	4.5797070	0.1883546	0.2183546	1.159274	5.309136
6	0.8374843	5.4171910	0.1545975	0.1845975	1.194052	6.468410
7	0.8130915	6.2302830	0.1305064	0.1605064	1.229874	7.662462
8	0.7894092	7.0196920	0.1124564	0.1424564	1.266770	8.892336
9	0.7664167	7.7861090	0.0984339	0.1284339	1.304773	10.159110
10	0.7440939	8.5302030	0.0872305	0.1172305	1.343916	11.463880
11	0.7224213	9.2526240	0.0780774	0.1080774	1.384234	12.807800
12	0.7013799	9.9540040	0.0704621	0.1004621	1.425761	14.192030

			$i = 3\%$			
n	P/F	P/A	A/F	A/P	F/P	F/A
13	0.6809513	10.6349600	0.0640295	0.0940295	1.468534	15.617790
14	0.6611178	11.2960700	0.0585263	0.0885263	1.512590	17.086320
15	0.6418619	11.9379400	0.0537666	0.0837666	1.557967	18.598910
16	0.6231669	12.5611000	0.0496108	0.0796108	1.604706	20.156880
17	0.6050164	13.1661200	0.0459525	0.0759525	1.652848	21.761590
18	0.5873946	13.7535100	0.0427087	0.0727087	1.702433	23.414440
19	0.5702860	14.3238000	0.0398139	0.0698139	1.753506	25.116870
20	0.5536758	14.8774700	0.0372157	0.0672157	1.806111	26.870370
21	0.5375493	15.4150200	0.0348718	0.0648718	1.860295	28.676490
22	0.5218925	15.9369200	0.0327474	0.0627474	1.916103	30.536780
23	0.5066917	16.4436100	0.0308139	0.0608139	1.973587	32.452880
24	0.4919337	16.9355400	0.0290474	0.0590474	2.032794	34.426470
25	0.4776056	17.4131500	0.0274279	0.0574279	2.093778	36.459260
26	0.4636947	17.8768400	0.0259383	0.0559383	2.156591	38.553040
27	0.4501891	18.3270300	0.0245642	0.0545642	2.221289	40.709630
28	0.4370768	18.7641100	0.0232932	0.0532932	2.287928	42.930920
29	0.4243464	19.1884500	0.0221147	0.0521147	2.356566	45.218850
30	0.4119868	19.6004400	0.0210193	0.0510193	2.427262	47.575420
32	0.3883370	20.3887700	0.0190466	0.0490466	2.575083	52.502760
34	0.3660449	21.1318400	0.0173220	0.0473220	2.731905	57.730180
36	0.3450324	21.8322500	0.0158038	0.0458038	2.898278	63.275950
38	0.3252261	22.4924600	0.0144593	0.0444593	3.074784	69.159450
40	0.3065568	23.1147700	0.0132624	0.0432624	3.262038	75.401260
48	0.2419988	25.2667100	0.0095778	0.0395778	4.132252	104.408400
60	0.1697331	27.6755600	0.0061330	0.0361330	5.891603	163.053400
72	0.1190474	29.3650900	0.0040540	0.0340540	8.400017	246.667200
80	0.0939771	30.2007600	0.0031117	0.0331117	10.640890	321.363000
100	0.0520328	31.5989100	0.0016467	0.0316467	19.218630	607.287700
120	0.0288093	32.3730200	8.899E-40	0.0308899	34.710990	1,123.700000
180	0.0048899	33.1703400	1.474E-40	0.0301474	204.503400	6,783.446000
240	8.300E-40	33.3056700	2.492E-50	0.0300249	1,204.853000	40,128,420.000

			$i = 4\%$			
n	P/F	P/A	A/F	A/P	F/P	F/A
1	0.9615385	0.9615385	1.0000000	1.0400000	1.040000	1.000000
2	0.9245562	1.8860950	0.4901961	0.5301961	1.081600	2.040000
3	0.8889964	2.7750910	0.3203485	0.3603485	1.124864	3.121600
4	0.8548042	3.6298950	0.2354900	0.2754900	1.169859	4.246464
5	0.8219271	4.4518220	0.1846271	0.2246271	1.216653	5.416323

			$i = 4\%$			
n	*P/F*	*P/A*	*A/F*	*A/P*	*F/P*	*F/A*
6	0.7903145	5.2421370	0.1507619	0.1907619	1.265319	6.632975
7	0.7599178	6.0020550	0.1266096	0.1666096	1.315932	7.898294
8	0.7306902	6.7327450	0.1085278	0.1485278	1.368569	9.214226
9	0.7025867	7.4353320	0.0944930	0.1344930	1.423312	10.582800
10	0.6755642	8.1108960	0.0832909	0.1232909	1.480244	12.006110
11	0.6495809	8.7604770	0.0741490	0.1141490	1.539454	13.486350
12	0.6245970	9.3850740	0.0665522	0.1065522	1.601032	15.025810
13	0.6005741	9.9856480	0.0601437	0.1001437	1.665074	16.626840
14	0.5774751	10.5631200	0.0546690	0.0946690	1.731676	18.291910
15	0.5552645	11.1183900	0.0499411	0.0899411	1.800944	20.023590
16	0.5339082	11.6523000	0.0458200	0.0858200	1.872981	21.824530
17	0.5133732	12.1656700	0.0421985	0.0821985	1.947900	23.697510
18	0.4936281	12.6593000	0.0389933	0.0789933	2.025817	25.645410
19	0.4746424	13.1339400	0.0361386	0.0761386	2.106849	27.671230
20	0.4563869	13.5903300	0.0335818	0.0735818	2.191123	29.778080
21	0.4388336	14.0291600	0.0312801	0.0712801	2.278768	31.969200
22	0.4219554	14.4511200	0.0291988	0.0691988	2.369919	34.247970
23	0.4057263	14.8568400	0.0273091	0.0673091	2.464716	36.617890
24	0.3901215	15.2469600	0.0255868	0.0655868	2.563304	39.082600
25	0.3751168	15.6220800	0.0240120	0.0640120	2.665836	41.645910
26	0.3606892	15.9827700	0.0225674	0.0625674	2.772470	44.311740
27	0.3468166	16.3295900	0.0212385	0.0612385	2.883369	47.084210
28	0.3334775	16.6630600	0.0200130	0.0600130	2.998703	49.967580
29	0.3206514	16.9837100	0.0188799	0.0588799	3.118651	52.966290
30	0.3083187	17.2920300	0.0178301	0.0578301	3.243398	56.084940
35	0.2534155	18.6646100	0.0135773	0.0535773	3.946089	73.652220
40	0.2082890	19.7927700	0.0105235	0.0505235	4.801021	95.025520
45	0.1711984	20.7200400	0.0082625	0.0482625	5.841176	121.029400
50	0.1407126	21.4821800	0.0065502	0.0465502	7.106683	152.667100
60	0.0950604	22.6234900	0.0042018	0.0442018	10.519630	237.990700
70	0.0642194	23.3945100	0.0027451	0.0427451	15.571620	364.290500
80	0.0433843	23.9153900	0.0018141	0.0418141	23.049800	551.245000
90	0.0293089	24.2672800	0.0012078	0.0412078	34.119330	827.983300
100	0.0198000	24.5050000	8.080E-40	0.0408080	50.504950	1,237.624000

				$i = 5\%$		
n	P/F	P/A	A/F	A/P	F/P	F/A
1	0.9523810	0.9523810	1.0000000	1.0500000	1.050000	1.000000
2	0.9070295	1.8594100	0.4878049	0.5378049	1.102500	2.050000
3	0.8638376	2.7232480	0.3172086	0.3672086	1.157625	3.152500
4	0.8227025	3.5459510	0.2320118	0.2820118	1.215506	4.310125
5	0.7835262	4.3294770	0.1809748	0.2309748	1.276282	5.525631
6	0.7462154	5.0756920	0.1470175	0.1970175	1.340096	6.801913
7	0.7106813	5.7863730	0.1228198	0.1728198	1.407100	8.142008
8	0.6768394	6.4632130	0.1047218	0.1547218	1.477455	9.549109
9	0.6446089	7.1078220	0.0906901	0.1406901	1.551328	11.026560
10	0.6139133	7.7217350	0.0795046	0.1295046	1.628895	12.577890
11	0.5846793	8.3064140	0.0703889	0.1203889	1.710339	14.206790
12	0.5568374	8.8632520	0.0628254	0.1128254	1.795856	15.917130
13	0.5303214	9.3935730	0.0564558	0.1064558	1.885649	17.712980
14	0.5050680	9.8986410	0.0510240	0.1010240	1.979932	19.598630
15	0.4810171	10.3796600	0.0463423	0.0963423	2.078928	21.578656
16	0.4581115	10.8377700	0.0422699	0.0922699	2.182875	23.657490
17	0.4362967	11.2740700	0.0386991	0.0886991	2.292018	25.840370
18	0.4155207	11.6895900	0.0355462	0.0855462	2.406619	28.132380
19	0.3957340	12.0853200	0.0327450	0.0827450	2.526950	30.539000
20	0.3768895	12.4622100	0.0302426	0.0802426	2.653298	33.065950
21	0.3589424	12.8211500	0.0279961	0.0779961	2.785963	35.719250
22	0.3418499	13.1630000	0.0259705	0.0759705	2.925261	38.505210
23	0.3255713	13.4885700	0.0241368	0.0741368	3.071524	41.430480
24	0.3100679	13.7986400	0.0224709	0.0724709	3.225100	44.502000
25	0.2953028	14.0939400	0.0209525	0.0709525	3.386355	47.727100
26	0.2812407	14.3751900	0.0195643	0.0695643	3.555673	51.113450
27	0.2678483	14.6430300	0.0182919	0.0682919	3.733456	54.669130
28	0.2550936	14.8981300	0.0171225	0.0671225	3.920129	58.402580
29	0.2429463	15.1410700	0.0160455	0.0660455	4.116136	62.322710
30	0.2313774	15.3724500	0.0150514	0.0650514	4.321942	66.438850
35	0.1812903	16.3741900	0.0110717	0.0610717	5.516015	90.320310
40	0.1420457	17.1590900	0.0082782	0.0582782	7.039989	120.799800
45	0.1112965	17.7740700	0.0062617	0.0562617	8.985008	159.700200
50	0.0872037	18.2559300	0.0047767	0.5477670	11.467400	209.348000
60	0.0535355	18.9292900	0.0028282	0.0528282	18.679190	353.583700
70	0.0328662	19.3426800	0.0016992	0.0516992	30.426430	588.528500
80	0.0201770	19.5964600	0.0010296	0.0510296	49.561440	971.228800
90	0.0123869	19.7522600	6.271E-40	0.0506271	80.730370	1,594.607000
100	0.0076045	19.8479100	3.831E-40	0.0503831	131.501300	2,610.025000

			$i = 6\%$			
n	P/F	P/A	A/F	A/P	F/P	F/A
1	0.9433962	0.9433962	1.0000000	1.0600000	1.060000	1.000000
2	0.8899964	1.8333930	0.4854369	0.5454369	1.123600	2.060000
3	0.8396193	2.6730120	0.3141098	0.3741098	1.191016	3.183600
4	0.7920937	3.4651060	0.2285915	0.2885915	1.262477	4.374616
5	0.7472582	4.2123640	0.1773964	0.2373964	1.338226	5.637093
6	0.7049605	4.9173240	0.1433626	0.2033626	1.418519	6.975319
7	0.6650571	5.5823810	0.1191350	0.1791350	1.503630	8.393838
8	0.6274124	6.2097940	0.1010359	0.1610359	1.593848	9.897468
9	0.5918985	6.8016920	0.0870222	0.1470222	1.689479	11.491320
10	0.5583948	7.3600870	0.0758680	0.1358680	1.790848	13.180790
11	0.5267875	7.8868750	0.0667929	0.1267929	1.898299	14.971640
12	0.4969694	8.3838440	0.0592770	0.1192770	2.012196	16.869940
13	0.4688390	8.8526830	0.0529601	0.1129601	2.132928	18.882140
14	0.4423010	9.2949840	0.0475849	0.1075849	2.260904	21.015070
15	0.4172651	9.7122490	0.0429628	0.1029628	2.396558	23.275970
16	0.3936463	10.1059000	0.0389521	0.0989521	2.540352	25.672530
17	0.3713644	10.4772600	0.0354448	0.0954448	2.692773	28.212880
18	0.3503438	10.8276000	0.0323565	0.0923565	2.854339	30.905650
19	0.3305130	11.1581200	0.0296209	0.0896209	3.025599	33.759990
20	0.3118047	11.4699200	0.0271846	0.0871846	3.207135	36.785590
21	0.2941554	11.7640800	0.0250045	0.0850045	3.399564	39.992730
22	0.2775051	12.0415800	0.0230456	0.0830456	3.603537	43.392290
23	0.2617973	12.3033800	0.0212785	0.0812785	3.819750	46.995830
24	0.2469785	12.5503600	0.0196790	0.0796790	4.048935	50.815580
25	0.2329986	12.7833600	0.0182267	0.0782267	4.291871	54.864510
26	0.2198100	13.0031700	0.0169043	0.0769043	4.549383	59.156380
27	0.2073680	13.2105300	0.0156972	0.0756972	4.822346	63.705770
28	0.1956301	13.4061600	0.0145926	0.0745926	5.111687	68.528110
29	0.1845567	13.5907200	0.0135796	0.0735796	5.418388	73.639800
30	0.1741101	13.7648300	0.0126489	0.0726489	5.743491	79.058190
35	0.1301052	14.4982500	0.0089739	0.0689739	7.686087	111.434800
40	0.0972222	15.0463000	0.0064615	0.0664615	10.285720	154.762000
45	0.0726501	15.4558300	0.0047005	0.0647005	13.764610	212.743500
50	0.0542884	15.7618600	0.0034443	0.0634443	18.420150	290.335900
60	0.0303143	16.1614300	0.0018757	0.0618757	32.987690	533.128200
70	0.0169274	16.3845400	0.0010331	0.0610331	59.075930	967.932200
80	0.0094522	16.5091300	5.725E-40	0.0605725	105.796000	1,746.600000
90	0.0052780	16.5787000	3.184E-40	0.0603184	189.464500	3,141.075000
100	0.0029472	16.6175500	1.774E-40	0.0601774	339.302100	5,638.368000

				$i = 7\%$		
n	P/F	P/A	A/F	A/P	F/P	F/A
1	0.9345794	0.9345794	1.0000000	1.0700000	1.070000	1.000000
2	0.8734387	1.8080180	0.4830918	0.5530918	1.144900	2.070000
3	0.8162979	2.6243160	0.3110517	0.3810517	1.225043	3.124900
4	0.7628952	3.3872110	0.2252281	0.2952281	1.310796	4.439943
5	0.7129862	4.1001970	0.1738907	0.2438907	1.402552	5.750739
6	0.6663422	4.7665400	0.1397958	0.2097958	1.500730	7.153291
7	0.6227497	5.3892890	0.1155532	0.1855532	1.605781	8.654021
8	0.5820091	5.9712990	0.0974678	0.1674678	1.718186	10.259800
9	0.5439337	6.5152320	0.0834865	0.1534865	1.838459	11.977990
10	0.5083493	7.0235820	0.0723775	0.1423775	1.967151	13.816450
11	0.4750928	7.4986740	0.0633569	0.1333569	2.104852	15.783600
12	0.4440120	7.9426860	0.0559020	0.1259020	2.252192	17.888450
13	0.4149644	8.3576510	0.0496508	0.1196508	2.409845	20.140640
14	0.3878172	8.7454680	0.0443449	0.1143449	2.578534	22.550490
15	0.3624460	9.1079140	0.0397946	0.1097946	2.759032	25.129020
16	0.3387346	9.4466490	0.0358576	0.1058576	2.952164	27.888050
17	0.3165744	9.7632230	0.0324252	0.1024252	3.158815	30.840220
18	0.2958639	10.0590900	0.0294126	0.0994126	3.379932	33.999030
19	0.2765083	10.3356000	0.0267530	0.0967530	3.616528	37.378960
20	0.2584190	10.5940100	0.0243929	0.0943929	3.869684	40.995490
21	0.2415131	10.8355300	0.0222890	0.0922890	4.140562	44.865180
22	0.2257132	11.0612400	0.0204058	0.0904058	4.430402	49.005740
23	0.2109469	11.2721900	0.0187139	0.0887139	4.740530	53.436140
24	0.1971466	11.4693300	0.0171890	0.0871890	5.072367	58.176670
25	0.1842492	11.6535800	0.0158105	0.0858105	5.427433	63.249040
26	0.1721955	11.8257800	0.0145610	0.0845610	5.807353	68.676470
27	0.1609304	11.9867100	0.0134257	0.0834257	6.213868	74.483820
28	0.1504022	12.1371100	0.0123919	0.0823919	6.648838	80.697690
29	0.1405628	12.2776700	0.0114487	0.0814487	7.114257	87.346530
30	0.1313671	12.4090400	0.0105864	0.0805864	7.612255	94.460790
35	0.0936629	12.9476700	0.0072340	0.0772340	10.676580	138.236900
40	0.0667804	13.3317100	0.0050091	0.0750091	14.974460	199.635100
45	0.0476135	13.6055200	0.0034996	0.0734996	21.002450	285.749300
50	0.0339478	13.8007500	0.0024598	0.0724598	29.457030	406.528900
60	0.0172573	14.0391800	0.0012292	0.0712292	57.946430	813.520400
70	0.0087727	14.1603900	6.195E-40	0.0706195	113.989400	1,614.134000
80	0.0044596	14.2220100	3.136E-40	0.0703136	224.234400	3,189.063000
90	0.0022670	14.2533300	1.591E-40	0.0701591	441.103000	6,287.185000
100	0.0011525	14.2692500	8.076E-50	0.0700808	867.716300	12,381.660000

				$i = 8\%$		
n	P/F	P/A	A/F	A/P	F/P	F/A
1	0.9259259	0.9259259	1.0000000	1.0800000	1.080000	1.000000
2	0.8573388	1.7832650	0.4807692	0.5607692	1.166400	2.080000
3	0.7938322	2.5770970	0.3080335	0.3880335	1.259712	3.246400
4	0.7350299	3.3121270	0.2219208	0.3019208	1.360489	4.506112
5	0.6805832	3.9927100	0.1704565	0.2504565	1.469328	5.866601
6	0.6301696	4.6228800	0.1363154	0.2163154	1.586874	7.335929
7	0.5834904	5.2063700	0.1120724	0.1920724	1.713824	8.922803
8	0.5402689	5.7466390	0.0940148	0.1740148	1.850930	10.636630
9	0.5002490	6.2468880	0.0800797	0.1600797	1.999005	12.487560
10	0.4631935	6.7100810	0.0690295	0.1490295	2.158925	14.486560
11	0.4288829	7.1389640	0.0600763	0.1400763	2.331639	16.645490
12	0.3971138	7.5360780	0.0526950	0.1326950	2.518170	18.977130
13	0.3676979	7.9037760	0.0465218	0.1265218	2.719624	21.495300
14	0.3404610	8.2442370	0.0412969	0.1212969	2.937194	24.214920
15	0.3152417	8.5594790	0.0368295	0.1168295	3.172169	27.152110
16	0.2918905	8.8513690	0.0329769	0.1129769	3.425943	30.324280
17	0.2702690	9.1216380	0.0296294	0.1096294	3.700018	33.750230
18	0.2502490	9.3718870	0.0267021	0.1067021	3.996020	37.450240
19	0.2317121	9.6035990	0.0241276	0.1041276	4.315701	41.446260
20	0.2145482	9.8181470	0.0218522	0.1018522	4.660957	45.761960
21	0.1986557	10.0168000	0.0198323	0.0998323	5.033834	50.422920
22	0.1839405	10.2007400	0.0180321	0.0980321	5.436540	55.456760
23	0.1703153	10.3710600	0.0164222	0.0964222	5.871464	60.893300
24	0.1576993	10.5287600	0.0149780	0.0949780	6.341181	66.764760
25	0.1460179	10.6747800	0.0136788	0.0936788	6.848475	73.105940
26	0.1352018	10.8099800	0.0125071	0.0925071	7.396353	79.954420
27	0.1251868	10.9351600	0.0114481	0.0914481	7.988061	87.350770
28	0.1159137	11.0510800	0.0104889	0.0904889	8.627106	95.338830
29	0.1073275	11.1584100	0.0096185	0.0896185	9.317275	103.965900
30	0.0993773	11.2577800	0.0088274	0.0888274	10.062660	113.283200
35	0.0676345	11.6545700	0.0058033	0.0858033	14.785340	172.316800
40	0.0460309	11.9246100	0.0038602	0.0838602	21.724520	259.056500
45	0.0313279	12.1084000	0.0025873	0.0825873	31.920450	386.505600
50	0.0213212	12.2334800	0.0017429	0.0817429	46.901610	573.770200
60	0.0098759	12.3765500	7.979E-40	0.0807979	101.257100	1,253.213000
70	0.0045744	12.4428200	3.676E-40	0.0803676	218.606400	2,720.080000
80	0.0021188	12.4735100	1.699E-40	0.0801699	471.954800	5,886.935000
90	9.814E-40	12.4877300	7.859E-50	0.0800786	1,018.915000	12,723.940000
100	4.546E-40	12.4943200	3.638E-50	0.0800364	2,199.761000	27,484.520000

			$i = 9\%$			
n	P/F	P/A	A/F	A/P	F/P	F/A
1	0.9174312	0.9174312	1.0000000	1.0900000	1.090000	1.000000
2	0.8416800	1.7591110	0.4786890	0.5684689	1.188100	2.090000
3	0.7721835	2.5312950	0.3050548	0.3950548	1.295029	3.278100
4	0.7084252	3.2397200	0.2186687	0.3086687	1.411582	4.573129
5	0.6499314	3.8896510	0.1670925	0.2570925	1.538624	5.984711
6	0.5962673	4.4859190	0.1329198	0.2229198	1.677100	7.523335
7	0.5470342	5.0329530	0.1086905	0.1986905	1.828039	9.200435
8	0.5018663	5.5348190	0.0906744	0.1806744	1.992563	11.028470
9	0.4604278	5.9952470	0.0767988	0.1667988	2.171893	13.021040
10	0.4224108	6.4176580	0.0658201	0.1558201	2.367364	15.192930
11	0.3875329	6.8051910	0.0569467	0.1469467	2.580426	17.560290
12	0.3555347	7.1607250	0.0496507	0.1396507	2.812665	20.140720
13	0.3261786	7.4869040	0.0435666	0.1335666	3.065805	22.953380
14	0.2992465	7.7861500	0.0384332	0.1284332	3.341727	26.019190
15	0.2745380	8.0606880	0.0340589	0.1240589	3.642482	29.360920
16	0.2518698	8.3125580	0.0302999	0.1202999	3.970306	33.003400
17	0.2310732	8.5436310	0.0270462	0.1170462	4.327633	36.973700
18	0.2119937	8.7556250	0.0242123	0.1142123	4.717120	41.301340
19	0.1944897	8.9501150	0.0217304	0.1117304	5.141661	46.018460
20	0.1784309	9.1285460	0.0195465	0.1095465	5.604411	51.160120
21	0.1636981	9.2922440	0.0176166	0.1076166	6.108808	56.764530
22	0.1501817	9.4424250	0.0159050	0.1059050	6.658600	62.873340
23	0.1377814	9.5802070	0.0143819	0.1043819	7.257874	69.531940
24	0.1264049	9.7066120	0.0130226	0.1030226	7.911083	76.789810
25	0.1159678	9.8225800	0.0118063	0.1018063	8.623081	84.700900
26	0.1063925	9.9289720	0.0107154	0.1007154	9.399158	93.323980
27	0.0976078	10.0265800	0.0097349	0.0997349	10.245080	102.723100
28	0.0895484	10.1161300	0.0088520	0.0988520	11.167140	112.968200
29	0.0821545	10.1982800	0.0080557	0.0980557	12.172180	124.135400
30	0.0753711	10.2736500	0.0073364	0.0973364	13.267680	136.307500
35	0.0489861	10.5668200	0.0046358	0.0946358	20.413970	215.710800
40	0.0318376	10.7573600	0.0029596	0.0929596	31.409420	337.882400
45	0.0206922	10.8812000	0.0019017	0.0919017	48.327290	525.858700
50	0.0134485	10.9616800	0.0012269	0.0122690	74.357520	815.083600
60	0.0056808	11.0479900	5.142E-40	0.0905142	176.031300	1,944.792000
70	0.0023996	11.0844500	2.165E-40	0.0902165	416.730100	4,619.223000
80	0.0010136	11.0998500	9.132E-50	0.0900913	986.551700	10,950.570000
90	4.282E-40	11.1063500	3.855E-50	0.0900386	2,335.527000	25,939.180000
100	1.809E-40	11.1091000	1.628E-50	0.0900163	5,529.041000	61,422.670000

				$i = 10\%$		
n	P/F	P/A	A/F	A/P	F/P	F/A
1	0.9090909	0.9090909	1.0000000	1.1000000	1.100000	1.000000
2	0.8264463	1.735537	0.4761905	0.5761905	1.210000	2.100000
3	0.7513148	2.486852	0.3021148	0.4021148	1.331000	3.310000
4	0.6830135	3.169865	0.2154708	0.3154708	1.464100	4.641000
5	0.6209213	3.790787	0.1637975	0.2637975	1.610510	6.105100
6	0.5644739	4.355261	0.1296074	0.2296074	1.771561	7.715610
7	0.5131581	4.868419	0.1054055	0.2054055	1.948717	9.487171
8	0.4665074	5.334926	0.0874440	0.1874440	2.143589	11.435890
9	0.4240976	5.759024	0.0736405	0.1736405	2.357948	13.579480
10	0.3855433	6.144567	0.0627454	0.1627454	2.593742	15.937420
11	0.3504939	6.495061	0.0539631	0.1539631	2.853117	18.531170
12	0.3186308	6.813692	0.0467633	0.1467633	3.138428	21.384280
13	0.2896644	7.103356	0.0407785	0.1407785	3.452271	24.522710
14	0.2633313	7.366687	0.0357462	0.1357462	3.797498	27.974980
15	0.2393920	7.606080	0.0314738	0.1314738	4.177248	31.772480
16	0.2176291	7.823709	0.0278166	0.1278166	4.594973	35.949730
17	0.1978447	8.021553	0.0246641	0.1246641	5.054470	40.544700
18	0.1798588	8.201412	0.0219302	0.1219302	5.559917	45.599170
19	0.1635080	8.364920	0.0195469	0.1195469	6.115909	51.159090
20	0.1486436	8.513564	0.0174596	0.1174596	6.727500	57.275000
21	0.1351306	8.648694	0.0156244	0.1156244	7.400250	64.002500
22	0.1228460	8.771540	0.0140051	0.1140051	8.140275	71.402750
23	0.1116782	8.883218	0.0125718	0.1125718	8.954302	79.543020
24	0.1015256	8.984744	0.0112998	0.1112998	9.849733	88.497330
25	0.0922960	9.077040	0.0101681	0.1101681	10.834710	98.347060
26	0.0839055	9.160945	0.0091590	0.1091590	11.91818	109.181800
27	0.0762777	9.237223	0.0082576	0.1082576	13.10999	121.099900
28	0.0693433	9.306567	0.0074510	0.1074510	14.42099	134.209900
29	0.0630394	9.369606	0.0067281	0.1067281	15.86309	148.630900
30	0.0573086	9.426914	0.0060792	0.1060792	17.44940	164.494000
35	0.0355841	9.644159	0.0036897	0.1036897	28.10244	271.024400
40	0.0220949	9.779051	0.0022594	0.1022594	45.25926	442.592600
45	0.0137192	9.862808	0.0013910	0.1013910	72.89048	718.904800
50	0.0085186	9.914814	8.592E-40	0.1008592	117.39090	1,163.909000
60	0.0032843	9.967157	3.295E-40	0.1003295	304.4816	3,034.816
70	0.0012662	9.987338	1.268E-40	0.1001268	789.7470	7,887.470
80	4.882E-40	9.9951180	4.884E-50	0.1000488	2,048.400	20,474.00
90	1.882E-40	9.998118	1.883E-50	0.1000188	5,313.023	53,120.23
100	7.257E-50	9.999274	7.257E-60	0.1000073	13,780.61	137,796.1

			$i = 11\%$			
n	P/F	P/A	A/F	A/P	F/P	F/A
1	0.9009009	0.9009009	1.0000000	1.1100000	1.110000	1.000000
2	0.8116224	1.7125230	0.4739337	0.5839337	1.232100	2.110000
3	0.7311914	2.4437150	0.2992131	0.4092131	1.367631	3.342100
4	0.6587310	3.1024460	0.2123264	0.3223264	1.518070	4.709731
5	0.5934513	3.6958970	0.1605703	0.2705703	1.685058	6.227801
6	0.5346408	4.2305380	0.1263766	0.2363766	1.870415	7.912860
7	0.4816584	4.7121960	0.1022153	0.2122153	2.076160	9.783274
8	0.4339265	5.1461230	0.0843211	0.1943211	2.304538	11.859430
9	0.3909248	5.5370480	0.0706017	0.1806017	2.558037	14.163970
10	0.3521845	5.8892320	0.0598014	0.1698014	2.839421	16.722010
11	0.3172833	6.2065150	0.0511210	0.1611210	3.151757	19.561430
12	0.2858408	6.4923560	0.0440273	0.1540273	3.498451	22.713190
13	0.2575143	6.7498700	0.0381510	0.1481510	3.883280	26.211640
14	0.2319948	6.9818650	0.0332282	0.1432282	4.310441	30.094920
15	0.2090043	7.1908700	0.0290652	0.1390652	4.784589	34.405360
16	0.1882922	7.3791620	0.0255167	0.1355167	5.310894	39.189950
17	0.1696326	7.5487940	0.0224715	0.1324715	5.895093	44.500840
18	0.1528222	7.7016170	0.0198429	0.1298429	6.543553	50.395940
19	0.1376776	7.8392940	0.0175625	0.1275625	7.263344	56.939490
20	0.1240339	7.9633280	0.0155756	0.1255756	8.062311	64.202830
21	0.1117423	8.0750700	0.0138379	0.1238379	8.949166	72.265140
22	0.1006687	8.1757390	0.0123131	0.1223131	9.933574	81.214310
23	0.0906925	8.2664320	0.0109712	0.1209712	11.026270	91.147880
24	0.0817050	8.3481370	0.0097872	0.1197872	12.239160	102.174200
25	0.0736081	8.4217450	0.0087402	0.1187402	13.585460	114.413300
26	0.0663136	8.4880580	0.0078126	0.1178126	15.079860	127.998800
27	0.0597420	8.5478000	0.0069892	0.1169892	16.738650	143.078600
28	0.0538216	8.6016220	0.0062571	0.1162571	18.579900	159.817300
29	0.0484879	8.6501100	0.0056055	0.1156055	20.623690	178.397200
30	0.0436828	8.6937930	0.0050246	0.1150246	22.892300	199.020900
35	0.0259236	8.8552400	0.0029275	0.1129275	38.574850	341.589600
40	0.0153844	8.9510510	0.0017187	0.1117187	65.000870	581.826100
45	0.0091299	9.0079100	0.0010135	0.1110135	109.530200	986.638600
50	0.0054182	9.0416530	5.992E-40	0.1105992	184.564800	1,668.771000
60	0.0019082	9.0735620	2.103E-40	0.1102103	524.0572	4,755.066
70	6.720E-40	9.0848000	7.397E-50	0.1100740	1,488.019	13,518.36
80	2.367E-40	9.0887570	2.604E-50	0.1100260	4,225.113	38,401.02
90	8.336E-50	9.0901510	9.170E-60	0.1100092	11,996.87	109,053.4
100	2.936E-50	9.0906420	3.229E-60	0.1100032	34,064.17	309,665.2

				$i = 12\%$		
n	P/F	P/A	A/F	A/P	F/P	F/A
1	0.8928571	0.8928571	1.0000000	1.1200000	1.120000	1.000000
2	0.7971939	1.6900510	0.4716981	0.5916981	1.254400	2.120000
3	0.7117802	2.4018310	0.2963490	0.4163490	1.404928	3.374400
4	0.6355181	3.0373490	0.2092344	0.3292344	1.573519	4.779328
5	0.5674269	3.6047760	0.1574097	0.2774097	1.762342	6.352847
6	0.5066311	4.1114070	0.1232257	0.2432257	1.973823	8.115189
7	0.4523492	4.5637570	0.0991177	0.2191177	2.210681	10.089010
8	0.4038832	4.9676400	0.0813028	0.2013028	2.475963	12.299690
9	0.3606100	5.3282500	0.0676789	0.1876789	2.773079	14.775660
10	0.3219732	5.6502230	0.0569842	0.1769842	3.105848	17.548740
11	0.2874761	5.9376990	0.0484154	0.1684154	3.478550	20.654580
12	0.2566751	6.1943740	0.0414368	0.1614368	3.895976	24.133130
13	0.2291742	6.4235480	0.0356772	0.1556772	4.363493	28.029110
14	0.2046198	6.6281680	0.0308712	0.1508712	4.887112	32.392600
15	0.1826963	6.8108640	0.0268242	0.1468242	5.473566	37.279710
16	0.1631217	6.9739860	0.0233900	0.1433900	6.130394	42.753280
17	0.1456443	7.1196300	0.0204567	0.1404567	6.866041	48.883670
18	0.1300396	7.2496700	0.0179373	0.1379373	7.689966	55.749710
19	0.1161068	7.3657770	0.0157630	0.1357630	8.612762	63.439680
20	0.1036668	7.4694440	0.0138788	0.1338788	9.646293	72.052440
21	0.0925596	7.5620030	0.0122401	0.1322401	10.803850	81.698740
22	0.0826425	7.6446460	0.0108105	0.1308105	12.100310	92.502580
23	0.0737880	7.7184340	0.0095600	0.1295600	13.552350	104.602900
24	0.0658821	7.7843160	0.0084634	0.1284634	15.178630	118.155200
25	0.0588233	7.8431390	0.0075000	0.1275000	17.000060	133.333900
26	0.0525208	7.8956600	0.0066519	0.1266519	19.040070	150.333900
27	0.0468936	7.9425540	0.0059041	0.1259041	21.324880	169.374000
28	0.0418693	7.9844230	0.0052439	0.1252439	23.883870	190.698900
29	0.0373833	8.0218060	0.0046602	0.1246602	26.749930	214.582800
30	0.0333779	8.0551840	0.0041437	0.1241437	29.959920	241.332700
35	0.0189395	8.1755040	0.0023166	0.1223166	52.799620	431.663500
40	0.0107468	8.2437770	0.0013036	0.1213036	93.050970	767.091400
45	0.0060980	8.2825160	7.363E-40	0.1207363	163.987600	1,358.230000
50	0.0034602	8.3044980	4.167E-40	0.1204167	289.002200	2,400.018000
60	0.0011141	8.3240490	1.338E-40	0.1201338	897.5969	7,471.641
70	3.587E-40	8.3303440	4.306E-50	0.1200431	2,787.800	23,223.33
80	1.155E-40	8.3323710	1.386E-50	0.1200139	8,658.483	72,145.69
90	3.719E-50	8.3330230	4.462E-60	0.1200045	26,891.93	224,091.1
100	1.197E-50	8.3332340	1.437E-60	0.1200014	83,522.27	696,010.6

				$i = 13\%$		
n	P/F	P/A	A/F	A/P	F/P	F/A
1	0.8849558	0.8849558	1.0000000	1.1300000	1.130000	1.000000
2	0.7831467	1.6681020	0.4694836	0.5994836	1.276900	2.130000
3	0.6930502	2.3611530	0.2935220	0.4235220	1.442897	3.406900
4	0.6133187	2.9744710	0.2061942	0.3361942	1.630474	4.849797
5	0.5427599	3.5172310	0.1543145	0.2843145	1.842435	6.480271
6	0.4803185	3.9975500	0.1201532	0.2501532	2.081952	8.322706
7	0.4250606	4.4226100	0.0961108	0.2261108	2.352605	10.404660
8	0.3761599	4.7987700	0.0783867	0.2083867	2.658444	12.757260
9	0.3328848	5.1316550	0.0648689	0.1948689	3.004042	15.415710
10	0.2945883	5.4262430	0.0542896	0.1842896	3.394567	18.419750
11	0.2606977	5.6869410	0.0458415	0.1758415	3.835861	21.814320
12	0.2307059	5.9176470	0.0389861	0.1689861	4.334523	25.650180
13	0.2041645	6.1218120	0.0333503	0.1633503	4.898011	29.984700
14	0.1806766	6.3024880	0.0286675	0.1586675	5.534753	34.882710
15	0.1598908	6.4623790	0.0247418	0.1547418	6.254270	40.417460
16	0.1414962	6.6038750	0.0214262	0.1514262	7.067326	46.671730
17	0.1252179	6.7290930	0.0186084	0.1486084	7.986078	53.739060
18	0.1108123	6.8399050	0.0162009	0.1462009	9.024268	61.725140
19	0.0980640	6.9379690	0.0141344	0.1441344	10.197420	70.749410
20	0.0867823	7.0247520	0.0123538	0.1423538	11.523090	80.946830
21	0.0767985	7.1015500	0.0108143	0.1408143	13.021090	92.469920
22	0.0679633	7.1695130	0.0094795	0.1394795	14.713830	105.491000
23	0.0601445	7.2296580	0.0083191	0.1383191	16.626630	120.204800
24	0.0532252	7.2828830	0.0073083	0.1373083	18.788090	136.831500
25	0.0471020	7.3299850	0.0064259	0.1364259	21.230540	155.619600
26	0.0416831	7.3716680	0.0056545	0.1356545	23.990510	176.850100
27	0.0368877	7.4085560	0.0049791	0.1349791	27.109280	200.840600
28	0.0326440	7.4412000	0.0043869	0.1343869	30.633490	227.949900
29	0.0288885	7.4700880	0.0038672	0.1338672	34.615840	258.583400
30	0.0255651	7.4956530	0.0034107	0.1334107	39.115900	293.199200
35	0.0138757	7.5855720	0.0018292	0.1318292	72.068510	546.680800
40	0.0075312	7.6343760	9.865E-40	0.1309865	132.781600	1,013.704000
45	0.0040876	7.6608640	5.336E-40	0.1305336	244.641400	1,874.165000
50	0.0022186	7.6752420	2.891E-40	0.1302891	450.735900	3,459.507000
60	6.536E-40	7.6872800	8.502E-50	0.1300850	1,530.053	11,761.95
70	1.925E-40	7.6908270	2.503E-50	0.1300250	5,193.870	39,945.15
80	5.672E-50	7.6918710	7.374E-60	0.1300074	17,630.94	135,614.9
90	1.671E-50	7.6921790	2.172E-60	0.1300022	59,849.42	460,372.4
100	4.922E-60	7.6922700	6.399E-70	0.1300006	203,162.9	1,562,784.0

				$i = 14\%$		
n	P/F	P/A	A/F	A/P	F/P	F/A
1	0.8771930	0.8771930	1.0000000	1.1400000	1.140000	1.000000
2	0.7694675	1.646661	0.4672897	0.6072897	1.299600	2.140000
3	0.6749715	2.321632	0.2907315	0.4307315	1.481544	3.439600
4	0.5920803	2.913712	0.2032048	0.3432048	1.688960	4.921144
5	0.5193687	3.433081	0.1512835	0.2912835	1.925415	6.610104
6	0.4555865	3.888668	0.1171575	0.2571575	2.194973	8.535519
7	0.3996373	4.288305	0.0931924	0.2331924	2.502269	10.730490
8	0.3505591	4.638864	0.0755700	0.2155700	2.852586	13.232760
9	0.3075079	4.946372	0.0621684	0.2021684	3.251949	16.085350
10	0.2697438	5.216116	0.0517135	0.1917135	3.707221	19.337300
11	0.2366174	5.452733	0.0433943	0.1833943	4.226232	23.044520
12	0.2075591	5.660292	0.0366693	0.1766693	4.817905	27.270750
13	0.1820694	5.842362	0.0311637	0.1711637	5.492411	32.088650
14	0.1597100	6.002072	0.0266091	0.1666091	6.261349	37.581060
15	0.1400965	6.142168	0.0228090	0.1628090	7.137938	43.842410
16	0.1228917	6.265060	0.0196154	0.1596154	8.137249	50.980350
17	0.1077997	6.372859	0.0169154	0.1569154	9.276464	59.117600
18	0.0945611	6.467420	0.0146212	0.1546212	10.575170	68.394070
19	0.0829484	6.550369	0.0126632	0.1526632	12.055690	78.969230
20	0.0727617	6.623131	0.0109860	0.1509860	13.743490	91.024930
21	0.0638261	6.686957	0.0095449	0.1495449	15.667580	104.768400
22	0.0559878	6.742944	0.0083032	0.1483032	17.861040	120.436000
23	0.0491121	6.792056	0.0072308	0.1472308	20.361580	138.297000
24	0.0430808	6.835137	0.0063028	0.1463028	23.212210	158.658600
25	0.0377902	6.872927	0.0054984	0.1454984	26.461920	181.870800
26	0.0331493	6.906077	0.0048000	0.1448000	30.166580	208.332700
27	0.0290783	6.935155	0.0041929	0.1441929	34.389910	238.499300
28	0.0255073	6.960662	0.0036645	0.1436645	39.204490	272.889200
29	0.0223748	6.983037	0.0032042	0.1432042	44.693120	312.093700
30	0.0196270	7.002664	0.0028028	0.1428028	50.950160	356.786800
35	0.0101937	7.070045	0.0014418	0.1414418	98.100180	693.572700
40	0.0052943	7.105041	7.451E-40	0.1407451	188.883500	1,342.025000
45	0.0027497	7.123217	3.860E-40	0.1403860	363.679100	2,590.565000
50	0.0014281	7.132656	2.002E-40	0.1402002	700.233000	4,994.521000
60	3.852E-40	7.140106	5.395E-50	0.1400540	2,595.919	18,535.13
70	1.039E-40	7.142115	1.455E-50	0.1400145	9,623.645	68,733.18
80	2.803E-50	7.142657	3.924E-60	0.1400039	35,676.98	254,828.4
90	7.561E-60	7.142803	1.059E-60	0.1400011	132,262.5	944,724.8
100	2.039E-60	7.142843	2.855E-70	0.1400003	490,326.2	3,502,323.0

				$i = 15\%$		
n	P/F	P/A	A/F	A/P	F/P	F/A
1	0.8695652	0.8695652	1.0000000	1.1500000	1.150000	1.000000
2	0.7561437	1.6257090	0.4651163	0.6151163	1.322500	2.150000
3	0.6575162	2.2832250	0.2879770	0.4379770	1.520875	3.472500
4	0.5717532	2.8549780	0.2002654	0.3502654	1.749006	4.993375
5	0.4971767	3.3521550	0.1483156	0.2983156	2.011357	6.742381
6	0.4323276	3.7844830	0.1142369	0.2642369	2.313061	8.753738
7	0.3759370	4.1604200	0.0903604	0.2403604	2.660020	11.066800
8	0.3269018	4.4873220	0.0728501	0.2228501	3.059023	13.726820
9	0.2842624	4.7715840	0.0595740	0.2095740	3.517876	16.785840
10	0.2471847	5.0187690	0.0492521	0.1992521	4.045558	20.303720
11	0.2149432	5.2337120	0.0410690	0.1910690	4.652391	24.349280
12	0.1869072	5.4206190	0.0344808	0.1844808	5.350250	29.001670
13	0.1625280	5.5831470	0.0291105	0.1791105	6.152788	34.351920
14	0.1413287	5.7244760	0.0246885	0.1746885	7.075706	40.504710
15	0.1228945	5.8473700	0.0210171	0.1710171	8.137062	47.580410
16	0.1068648	5.9542350	0.0179477	0.1679477	9.357621	55.717470
17	0.0929259	6.0471610	0.0153669	0.1653669	10.761260	65.075090
18	0.0808051	6.1279660	0.0131863	0.1631863	12.375450	75.836360
19	0.0702653	6.1982310	0.0113364	0.1613364	14.231770	88.211810
20	0.0611003	6.2593310	0.0097615	0.1597615	16.366540	102.443600
21	0.0531307	6.3124620	0.0084168	0.1584186	18.821520	118.810100
22	0.0462006	6.3586630	0.0072658	0.1572658	21.644750	137.631600
23	0.0401744	6.3988370	0.0062784	0.1562784	24.891460	159.276400
24	0.0349343	6.4337710	0.0054298	0.1554298	28.625180	184.167800
25	0.0303776	6.4641490	0.0046994	0.1546994	32.918950	212.793000
26	0.0264153	6.4905640	0.0040698	0.1540698	37.856800	245.712000
27	0.0229699	6.5135340	0.0035265	0.1535265	43.535310	283.568800
28	0.0199738	6.5335080	0.0030571	0.1530571	50.065610	327.104100
29	0.0173685	6.5508770	0.0026513	0.1526513	57.575450	377.169700
30	0.0151031	6.5659800	0.0023002	0.1523002	66.211770	434.745100
35	0.0075089	6.6166070	0.0011349	0.1511349	133.17550	881.170200
40	0.0037332	6.6417780	5.621E-40	0.1505621	267.86350	1,779.090000
45	0.0018561	6.6542930	2.789E-40	0.1502789	538.76930	3,585.128000
50	9.228E-40	6.6605150	1.385E-40	0.1501385	1,083.65700	7,217.716000
60	2.281E-40	6.6651460	3.422E-50	0.1500342	4,383.999	29,219.99
70	5.638E-50	6.6662910	8.458E-60	0.1500085	17,735.72	118,231.5
80	1.394E-50	6.6665740	2.091E-60	0.1500021	71,750.88	478,332.5
90	3.445E-60	6.6666440	5.168E-70	0.1500005	290,272.3	1,935,142.0
100	8.516E-70	6.6666610	1.277E-70	0.1500001	1,174,313.0	7,828,750.0

$i = 20\%$

n	P/F	P/A	A/F	A/P	F/P	F/A
1	0.8333333	0.8333333	1.0000000	1.2000000	1.200000	1.000000
2	0.6944444	1.5277780	0.4545455	0.6545455	1.440000	2.200000
3	0.5787037	2.1064810	0.2747253	0.4747253	1.728000	3.640000
4	0.4822531	2.5887350	0.1862891	0.3862891	2.073600	5.368000
5	0.4018776	2.9906120	0.1343797	0.3343797	2.488320	7.441600
6	0.3348980	3.3255100	0.1007057	0.3007057	2.985984	9.929920
7	0.2790816	3.6045920	0.0774239	0.2774239	3.583181	12.915900
8	0.2325680	3.8371600	0.0606094	0.2606094	4.299817	16.499080
9	0.1938067	4.0309670	0.0480795	0.2480795	5.159780	20.798900
10	0.1615056	4.1924720	0.0385228	0.2385228	6.191736	25.958680
11	0.1345880	4.3270600	0.0311038	0.2311038	7.430084	32.150420
12	0.1121567	4.4392170	0.0252650	0.2252650	8.916100	39.580500
13	0.0934639	4.5326810	0.0206200	0.2206200	10.699320	48.496600
14	0.0778866	4.6105670	0.0168931	0.2168931	12.839180	59.195920
15	0.0649055	4.6754730	0.0138821	0.2138821	15.407020	72.035110
16	0.0540879	4.7295610	0.0114361	0.2114361	18.488430	87.442130
17	0.0450732	4.7746340	0.0094401	0.2094401	22.186110	105.930600
18	0.0375610	4.8121950	0.0078054	0.2078054	26.623330	128.167000
19	0.0313009	4.8434960	0.0064625	0.2064625	31.948000	154.740000
20	0.0260841	4.8695800	0.0053565	0.2053565	38.337600	186.688000
21	0.0217367	4.8913160	0.0044439	0.2044439	46.005120	225.025600
22	0.0181139	4.9094300	0.0036896	0.2036896	55.206140	271.030700
23	0.0150949	4.9245250	0.0030653	0.2030653	66.247370	326.236900
24	0.0125791	4.9371040	0.0025479	0.2025479	79.496850	392.484200
25	0.0104826	4.9475870	0.0021187	0.2021187	95.396220	471.981100
26	0.0087355	4.9563230	0.0017625	0.2017625	114.475500	567.377300
27	0.0072796	4.9636020	0.0014666	0.2014666	137.370600	681.852800
28	0.0060663	4.9696680	0.0012207	0.2012207	164.844700	819.223300
29	0.0050553	4.9747240	0.0010162	0.2010162	197.813600	984.068000
30	0.0042127	4.9789360	8.461E-40	0.2008461	237.376300	1,181.882000
35	0.0016930	4.9915350	3.392E-40	0.2003392	590.668200	2,948.341000
40	6.804E-40	4.9965980	1.362E-40	0.2001362	1,469.772	7,343.858000
45	2.734E-40	4.9986330	5.470E-50	0.2000547	3,657.262	18,281.310000
50	1.099E-40	4.9994510	2.198E-50	0.2000220	9,100.438	45,497.190000
60	1.775E-50	5.9999110	3.529E-60	0.2000035	56,347.51	281,732.6
70	2.866E-60	4.9999860	5.732E-70	0.2000006	348,889.0	1,744,440.0
80	4.629E-70	4.9999980	9.258E-80	0.2000001	2,160,228.0	10,801,137.0
90	7.476E-80	5.0000000	1.495E-80	0.2000000	13,375,565	66,877,822
100	1.207E-80	5.0000000	2.145E-90	0.2000000	82,817,975	4.1409E8

				$i = 25\%$			
n	P/F	P/A	A/F	A/P	F/P		F/A
1	0.8000000	0.800000	1.0000000	1.2500000	1.250000		1.000000
2	0.6400000	1.440000	0.4444444	0.6944444	1.562500		2.250000
3	0.5120000	1.952000	0.2622951	0.5122951	1.953125		3.812500
4	0.4096000	2.361600	0.1734417	0.4234417	2.441406		5.765625
5	0.3276800	2.689280	0.1218467	0.3718467	3.051758		8.207031
6	0.2621440	2.951424	0.0888195	0.3388195	3.814697		11.258790
7	0.2097152	3.161139	0.0663417	0.3163417	4.768372		15.073490
8	0.1677722	3.328911	0.0503985	0.3003985	5.960464		19.841860
9	0.1342177	3.463129	0.0387562	0.2887562	7.450581		25.802320
10	0.1073742	3.570503	0.0300726	0.2800726	9.313226		33.252900
11	0.0858993	3.656403	0.0234929	0.2734929	11.64153		42.566130
12	0.0687195	3.725122	0.0184476	0.2684476	14.55192		54.207660
13	0.0549756	3.780098	0.0145434	0.2645434	18.18989		68.759580
14	0.0439805	3.824078	0.0115009	0.2615009	22.73737		86.949470
15	0.0351844	3.859263	0.0091169	0.2591169	28.42171		109.686800
16	0.0281475	3.887410	0.0072407	0.2572407	35.52714		138.108500
17	0.0225180	3.909928	0.0057592	0.2557592	44.40892		173.635700
18	0.0180144	3.927942	0.0045862	0.2545862	55.51115		218.044600
19	0.0144115	3.942354	0.0036556	0.2536556	69.38894		273.555800
20	0.0115292	3.953883	0.0029159	0.2529159	86.73617		342.944700
21	0.0092234	3.963107	0.0023273	0.2523273	108.42020		429.680900
22	0.0073787	3.970485	0.0018584	0.2518584	135.52530		538.101100
23	0.0059030	3.976388	0.0014845	0.2514845	169.40660		673.626400
24	0.0047224	3.981111	0.0011862	0.2511862	211.75820		843.032900
25	0.0037779	3.984888	9.481E-40	0.2509481	264.69780		1,054.791000
26	0.0030223	3.987911	7.579E-40	0.2507579	330.87220		1,319.489000
27	0.0024179	3.990329	6.059E-40	0.2506059	413.59030		1,650.361000
28	0.0019343	3.992263	4.845E-40	0.2504845	516.98790		2,063.952000
29	0.0015474	3.993810	3.875E-40	0.2503875	646.23490		2,580.939000
30	0.0012379	3.995048	3.099E-40	0.2503099	807.79360		3,227.174000
35	4.056E-40	3.998377	1.015E-40	0.2501015	2,465.19000		9,856.76100
40	1.329E-40	3.999468	3.324E-50	0.2500332	7,523.16400		30,088.660000
45	4.356E-50	3.999826	1.089E-50	0.2500109	22,958.87000		91,831.500000
50	1.427E-50	3.999943	3.568E-60	0.2500036	70,064.92000		280,255.700000
60	1.532E-60	3.999994	3.831E-70	0.2500004	652,530.4		2,610,118.0
70	1.646E-70	3.999999	4.114E-80	0.2500000	6,077,163.0		24,308,649
80	1.767E-80	4.000000	4.417E-90	0.2500000	56,597,994		2.2639E8
90	1.897E-90	4.000000	4.74E-100	0.2500000	5.2711E8		2.1084E9
100	2.04E-100	4.000000	5.09E-110	0.2500000	4.9091E9		1.964E10

				$i = 30\%$		
n	P/F	P/A	A/F	A/P	F/P	F/A
1	0.7692308	0.7692308	1.0000000	1.3000000	1.300000	1.000000
2	0.5917160	1.3609470	0.4347826	0.7347826	1.690000	2.300000
3	0.4551661	1.8161130	0.2506266	0.5506266	2.197000	3.990000
4	0.3501278	2.1662410	0.1616292	0.4616292	2.856100	6.187000
5	0.2693291	2.4355700	0.1105815	0.4105815	3.712930	9.043100
6	0.2071762	2.6427460	0.0783943	0.3783943	4.826809	12.756030
7	0.1593663	2.8021120	0.0568736	0.3568736	6.274852	17.582840
8	0.1225895	2.9247020	0.0419152	0.3419152	8.157307	23.857690
9	0.0942996	3.0190010	0.0312354	0.3312354	10.604500	32.015000
10	0.0725382	3.0915390	0.0234634	0.3234634	13.785850	42.619500
11	0.0557986	3.1473380	0.0177288	0.3177288	17.921600	56.405350
12	0.0429220	3.1902600	0.0134541	0.3134541	23.298090	74.326950
13	0.0330169	3.2232770	0.0102433	0.3102433	30.287510	97.625040
14	0.0253976	3.2486750	0.0078178	0.3078178	39.373760	127.912500
15	0.0195366	3.2682110	0.0059778	0.3059778	51.185890	167.286300
16	0.0150282	3.2832390	0.0045772	0.3045772	66.541660	218.472200
17	0.0115601	3.2948000	0.0035086	0.3035086	86.504160	285.013900
18	0.0088924	3.3036920	0.0026917	0.3026917	112.455400	371.518000
19	0.0068403	3.3105320	0.0020662	0.3020662	146.192000	483.973400
20	0.0052618	3.3157940	0.0015869	0.3015869	190.049600	630.165500
21	0.0040475	3.3198420	0.0012192	0.3012192	247.064500	820.215100
22	0.0031135	3.3229550	9.370E-40	0.3009370	321.183900	1,067.280000
23	0.0023950	3.3253500	7.202E-40	0.3007202	417.539100	1,388.464000
24	0.0018423	3.3271920	5.537E-40	0.3005537	542.800800	1,806.003000
25	0.0014172	3.3286090	4.257E-40	0.3004257	705.641000	2,348.803000
26	0.0010901	3.3297000	3.274E-40	0.3003274	917.333300	3,054.444000
27	8.386E-40	3.3305380	2.518E-40	0.3002518	1,192.533000	3,971.778000
28	6.450E-40	3.3311830	1.936E-40	0.3001936	1,550.293000	5,164.311000
29	4.962E-40	3.3316790	1.489E-40	0.3001489	2,015.381000	6,714.604000
30	3.817E-40	3.3320610	1.145E-40	0.3001145	2,619.996000	8,729.985000
35	1.028E-40	3.3329910	3.084E-50	0.3000308	9,727.860	32,422.870000
40	2.769E-50	3.3332410	8.306E-60	0.3000083	36,118.86	120,393.900000
45	7.457E-60	3.3333080	2.237E-60	0.3000022	134,106.8	447,019.400000
50	2.008E-60	3.3333270	6.025E-70	0.3000006	497,929.2	1,659,761.000000
60	1.457E-70	3.3333330	4.370E-80	0.3000000	6,864,377.0	22,881,254
70	1.057E-80	3.3333330	3.170E-90	0.3000000	94,631,268	3.1544E8
80	7.67E-100	3.3333330	2.30E-100	0.3000000	1.3046E9	4.3486E9
90	5.56E-110	3.3333330	1.67E-110	0.3000000	1.798E10	5.995E10
100	4.03E-120	3.3333330	1.21E-120	0.3000000	2.479E11	8.264E11

				$i = 35\%$		
n	P/F	P/A	A/F	A/P	F/P	F/A
1	0.7407407	0.7407407	1.000000	1.3500000	1.350000	1.000000
2	0.5486968	1.2894380	0.4255319	0.7755319	1.822500	2.350000
3	0.4064421	1.6958800	0.2396645	0.5896645	2.460375	4.172500
4	0.3010682	1.9969480	0.1507642	0.5007642	3.321506	6.632875
5	0.2230135	2.2199610	0.1004583	0.4504583	4.484033	9.954381
6	0.1651952	2.3851570	0.0692597	0.4192597	6.053445	14.438410
7	0.1223668	2.5075230	0.0487999	0.3987999	8.172151	20.491860
8	0.0906421	2.5981650	0.0348870	0.3848870	11.03240	28.664010
9	0.0671423	2.6653080	0.0251912	0.3751912	14.89375	39.696410
10	0.0497350	2.7150430	0.0183183	0.3683183	20.10656	54.590160
11	0.0368408	2.7518840	0.0133875	0.3633875	27.14385	74.696720
12	0.0272894	2.7791730	0.0098193	0.3598193	36.64420	101.840600
13	0.0202144	2.7993870	0.0072210	0.3572210	49.46967	138.484800
14	0.0149736	2.8143610	0.0053204	0.3553204	66.78405	187.954400
15	0.0110916	2.8254530	0.0039256	0.3539256	90.15847	254.738500
16	0.0082160	2.8336690	0.0028994	0.3528994	121.7139	344.897000
17	0.0060859	2.8397550	0.0021431	0.3521431	164.3138	466.610900
18	0.0045081	2.8442630	0.0015850	0.3515850	221.8236	630.924700
19	0.0033393	2.8476020	0.0011727	0.3511727	299.4619	852.748300
20	0.0024736	2.8500760	8.679E-40	0.3508679	404.2736	1,152.210000
21	0.0018323	2.8519080	6.425E-40	0.3506425	545.7693	1,556.484000
22	0.0013572	2.8532650	4.757E-40	0.3504757	736.7886	2,102.253000
23	0.0010054	2.8542700	3.522E-40	0.3503522	994.6646	2,839.042000
24	7.447E-40	2.8550150	2.608E-40	0.3502608	1,342.7970	3,833.706000
25	5.516E-40	2.8555670	1.932E-40	0.3501932	1,812.7760	5,176.504000
26	4.086E-40	2.8559750	1.431E-40	0.3501431	2,447.2480	6,989.280000
27	3,027E-40	2.8562780	1.060E-40	0.3501060	3,303.7850	9,436.528000
28	2.242E-40	2.8565020	7.849E-50	0.3500785	4,460.1090	12,740.310000
29	1.661E-40	2.8566680	5.814E-50	0.3500581	6,021.1480	17,200.4200000
30	1.230E-40	2.8567910	4.306E-50	0.3500431	8,128.5490	23,221.5700000
35	2.744E-50	2.8570640	9.603E-60	0.3500096	36,448.69	104,136.3000000
40	6.119E-60	2.8571250	2.142E-60	0.3500021	163,437.10	466,960.4000000
45	1.365E-60	2.8571390	4.776E-70	0.3500005	732,857.6	2,093,876.0000000
50	3.043E-70	2.8571420	1.065E-70	0.3500001	3,286,158.0	9,389,020.0000000
60	1.513E-80	2.8571430	5.297E-90	0.3500000	66,073,317	1.8878E8
70	7.53E-100	2.8571430	2.63E-100	0.3500000	1.3285E9	3.7957E9
80	3.74E-110	2.8571430	1.31E-110	0.3500000	2.671E10	7.632E10
90	1.86E-120	2.8571430	6.52E-130	0.3500000	5.371E11	1.535E12
100	9.26E-140	2.8571430	3.24E-140	0.3500000	1.080E13	3.085E13

				$i = 40\%$		
n	P/F	P/A	A/F	A/P	F/P	F/A
1	0.7142857	0.7142857	1.0000000	1.4000000	1.400000	1.000000
2	0.5102041	1.2244900	0.4166667	0.8166667	1.960000	2.400000
3	0.3644315	1.5889210	0.2293578	0.6293578	2.744000	4.360000
4	0.2603082	1.8492290	0.1407658	0.5407658	3.841600	7.104000
5	0.1859344	2.0351640	0.0913609	0.4913609	5.378240	10.945600
6	0.1328103	2.1679740	0.0612601	0.4612601	7.529536	16.323840
7	0.0948645	2.2628390	0.0419228	0.4419228	10.541350	23.853380
8	0.0677604	2.3305990	0.0290742	0.4290742	14.757890	34.394730
9	0.0484003	2.3789990	0.0203448	0.4203448	20.661050	49.152620
10	0.0345716	2.4135710	0.0143238	0.4143238	28.925470	69.813660
11	0.0246940	2.4382650	0.0101277	0.4101277	40.49565	98.739130
12	0.0176286	2.4559040	0.0071821	0.4071821	56.69391	139.234800
13	0.0125990	2.4685030	0.0051039	0.4051039	79.37148	195.928700
14	0.0089993	2.4775020	0.0036324	0.4036324	111.12010	275.300200
15	0.0064281	2.4839300	0.0025879	0.4025879	155.56810	386.420200
16	0.0045915	2.4885210	0.0018451	0.4018451	217.7953	541.988300
17	0.0032796	2.4918010	0.0013162	0.4013162	304.9135	759.783700
18	0.0023426	2.4941440	9.392E-40	0.4009392	426.8789	1,064.697000
19	0.0016733	2.4958170	6.704E-40	0.4006704	597.6304	1,491.576000
20	0.0011952	2.4970120	4.787E-40	0.4004787	836.6826	2,089.206000
21	8.537E-40	2.4978660	3.418E-40	0.4003418	1,171.356	2,925.889000
22	6.098E-40	2.4984760	2.441E-40	0.4002441	1,639.898	4,097.245000
23	4.356E-40	2.4989110	1.743E-40	0.4001743	2,295.857	5,737.142000
24	3.111E-40	2.4992220	1.245E-40	0.4001245	3,214.200	8,032.999000
25	2.222E-40	2.4994440	8.891E-50	0.4000889	4,499.880	11,247.200000
26	1.587E-40	2.4996030	6.350E-50	0.4000635	6,299.831	15,747.080000
27	1.134E-40	2.4997170	4.536E-50	0.4000454	8,819.764	22,046.910000
28	8.099E-50	2.4997980	3.240E-50	0.4000324	12,347.670	30,866.670000
29	5.785E-50	2.4998550	2.314E-50	0.4000231	17,286.740	43,214.340000
30	4.132E-50	2.4998970	1.653E-50	0.4000165	24,201.430	60,510.080000
35	7.683E-60	2.4999810	3.073E-60	0.4000031	130,161.100	325,400.300000
40	1.428E-60	2.4999960	5.714E-70	0.4000006	700,037.700	1,750,092.000000
45	2.656E-70	2.4999990	1.062E-70	0.4000001	3,764,971.000	9,412,424.000000
50	4.939E-80	2.5000000	1.975E-80	0.4000000	20,248,916.000	50,622,288.000000
60	1.707E-90	2.5000000	6.83E-100	0.4000000	5.8571E8	1.4643E9
70	5.90E-110	2.5000000	2.36E-110	0.4000000	1.694E10	4.235E10
80	2.04E-120	2.5000000	8.16E-130	0.4000000	4.901E11	1.225E12
90	7.05E-140	2.5000000	2.82E-140	0.4000000	1.418E13	3.544E13
100	2.44E-150	2.5000000	9.76E-160	0.4000000	4.100E14	1.025E15

					$i = 45\%$		
n	P/F	P/A	A/F	A/P	F/P		F/A
1	0.6896552	0.6896552	1.000000	1.4500000	1.450000		1.000000
2	0.4756243	1.1652790	0.4081633	0.8581633	2.102500		2.450000
3	0.3280167	1.4932960	0.2196595	0.6696595	3.048625		4.552500
4	0.2262184	1.7195150	0.1315595	0.5815595	4.420506		7.601125
5	0.1560127	1.8755270	0.0831834	0.5331834	6.409734		12.021630
6	0.1075950	1.9831220	0.0542553	0.5042553	9.294114		18.431370
7	0.0742034	2.0573260	0.0360679	0.4860679	13.476470		27.725480
8	0.0511748	2.1085000	0.0242707	0.4742707	19.540880		41.201950
9	0.0352930	2.1437930	0.0164629	0.4664629	28.334270		60.742820
10	0.0243400	2.1681330	0.0112262	0.4612262	41.084690		89.077090
11	0.167862	2.1849200	0.0076827	0.4576827	59.572800		130.161800
12	0.115767	2.1964960	0.0052705	0.4552705	86.380560		189.734600
13	0.0079839	2.2044800	0.0036217	0.4536217	125.251800		276.115100
14	0.0055061	2.2099860	0.0024915	0.4524915	181.615100		401.367000
15	0.0037973	2.2137840	0.0017153	0.4517153	263.341900		582.982100
16	0.0026189	2.2164030	0.0011816	0.4511816	381.845800		846.324000
17	0.0018061	2.2182090	8.142E-40	0.4508142	553.676400		1,228.170000
18	0.0012456	2.2194540	5.612E-40	0.4505612	802.830800		1,781.846000
19	8.590E-40	2.2203130	3.869E-40	0.4503869	1,164.105000		2,584.677000
20	5.924E-40	2.2209060	2.668E-40	0.4502668	1,687.952000		3,748.782000
21	4.086E-40	2.2213140	1.839E-40	0.4501839	2,447.530000		5,436.734000
22	2.818E-40	2.2215960	1.268E-40	0.4501268	3,548.919000		7,884.264000
23	1.943E-40	2.2217900	8.746E-50	0.4500875	5,145.932000		11,433.180000
24	1.340E-40	2.2219240	6.032E-50	0.4500603	7,461.602000		16,579.110000
25	9.243E-50	2.2220170	4.160E-50	0.4500416	10,819.320000		24,040.720000
26	6.374E-50	2.2220810	2.869E-50	0.4500287	15,688.0200		34,860.040000
27	4.396E-50	2.2221250	1.978E-50	0.4500198	22,747.6300		50,548.060000
28	3.032E-50	2.2221550	1.364E-50	0.4500136	32,984.0600		73,295.680000
29	2.091E-50	2.2221760	9.409E-60	0.4500094	47,826.8800		106,279.700000
30	1.442E-50	2.2221900	6.489E-60	0.4500065	69,348.9800		154,106.600000
35	2.250E-60	2.2222170	1.012E-60	0.4500010	444,508.5		987,794.500000
40	3.510E-70	2.2222210	1.579E-70	0.4500002	2,849,181.0		6,331,512.000000
45	5.476E-80	2.2222220	2.464E-80	0.4500000	18,262,495		40,583,319.000000
50	8.543E-90	2.2222220	3.844E-90	0.4500000	1.1706E8		2.6013E8000000
60	2.08E-100	2.2222220	9.36E-110	0.4500000	4.8093E9		1.069E10000000
70	5.06E-120	2.2222220	2.28E-120	0.4500000	1.976E11		4.391E11000000
80	1.23E-130	2.2222220	5.54E-140	0.4500000	8.118E12		1.804E13000000
90	3.00E-150	2.2222220	1.35E-150	0.4500000	3.335E14		7.412E14000000
100	7.30E-170	2.2222220	3.28E-170	0.4500000	1.370E16		3.045E16000000

			$i = 50\%$			
n	*P/F*	*P/A*	*A/F*	*A/P*	*F/P*	*F/A*
1	0.6666667	0.6666667	1.0000000	1.5000000	1.500000	1.000000
2	0.4444444	1.111111	0.4000000	0.9000000	2.250000	2.500000
3	0.2962963	1.407407	0.2105263	0.7105263	3.375000	4.750000
4	0.1975309	1.604938	0.1230769	0.6230769	5.062500	8.125000
5	0.1316872	1.736626	0.0758294	0.5758294	7.593750	13.187500
6	0.0877915	1.824417	0.0481203	0.5481203	11.390630	20.78125
7	0.0585277	1.882945	0.0310831	0.5310831	17.085940	32.17188
8	0.0390184	1.921963	0.0203013	0.5203013	25.628910	49.25781
9	0.0260123	1.947975	0.0133535	0.5133535	38.443360	74.88672
10	0.0173415	1.965317	0.0088238	0.5088238	57.665040	113.33010
11	0.0115610	1.976878	0.0058481	0.5058481	86.497560	170.99510
12	0.0077073	1.984585	0.0038836	0.5038836	129.746300	257.49270
13	0.0051382	1.989724	0.0025824	0.5025824	194.619500	387.23900
14	0.0034255	1.993149	0.0017186	0.5017186	291.929300	581.85850
15	0.0022837	1.995433	0.0011444	0.5011444	437.893900	873.78780
16	0.0015224	1.996955	7.624E-40	0.5007624	656.840800	1,311.68200
17	0.0010150	1.997970	5.080E-40	0.5005080	985.261200	1,968.52200
18	6.766E-40	1.998647	3.385E-40	0.5003385	1,477.892000	2,953.78400
19	4.511E-40	1.999098	2.256E-40	0.5002256	2,216.838000	4,431.67600
20	3.007E-40	1.999399	1.504E-40	0.5001504	3,325.257000	6,648.51300
21	2.005E-40	1.999599	1.003E-40	0.5001003	4,987.885	9,973.77000
22	1.337E-40	1.999733	6.684E-50	0.5000668	7,481.828	14,961.6600
23	8.910E-50	1.999822	4.456E-50	0.5000446	11,222.740	22,443.4800
24	5.940E-50	1.999881	2.970E-50	0.5000297	16,834.110	33,666.22
25	3.960E-50	1.999921	1.980E-50	0.5000198	25,251.170	50,500.34
26	2.640E-50	1.999947	1.320E-50	0.5000132	37,876.75	75,751.51
27	1.760E-50	1.999965	8.801E-60	0.5000088	56,815.13	113,628.3
28	1.173E-50	1.999977	5.867E-60	0.5000059	85,222.69	170,443.4
29	7.823E-60	1.999984	3.911E-60	0.5000039	127,834.00	255,666.1
30	5.215E-60	1.999990	2.608E-60	0.5000026	191,751.10	383,500.1
35	6.868E-70	1.999999	3.434E-70	0.5000003	1,456,110.0	2,912,217.0
40	9.044E-80	2.000000	4.522E-80	0.5000000	11,057,332	22,114,663
45	1.191E-80	2.000000	5.955E-90	0.5000000	83,966,617	1.6793E8
50	1.568E-90	2.000000	7.84E-100	0.5000000	6.3762E8	1.2752E9
60	2.72E-110	2,000000	1.36E-110	0.5000000	3.677E10	7.354E10
70	4.72E-130	2,000000	2.36E-130	0.5000000	2.120E12	4.241E12
80	8.18E-150	2.000000	4.09E-150	0.5000000	1.223E14	2.445E14
90	1.42E-160	2,000000	7.09E-170	0.5000000	7.050E15	1.410E16
100	2.46E-180	2,000000	1.23E-180	0.5000000	4.066E17	8.131E17

DEFINITIONS
OF SELECTED
SI UNITS

Name	Unit	Definition
Energy	joule	The joule is the work done when the point of application of a force of one newton is displaced a distance of one meter in the direction of the force.
Force	newton	The newton is that force which, when applied to a body having a mass of one kilogram, gives it an acceleration of one meter per second squared.
Frequency	hertz	The hertz is the frequency of a periodic phenomenon of which the period is one second.
Power	watt	The watt is the power which gives rise to the production of energy at the rate of one joule per second.
Pressure or stress	pascal	The pascal is the pressure or stress of one newton per square meter.
Temperature (thermodynamic)	kelvin	The kelvin is the unit of thermodynamic temperature measured from absolute zero; it is the same size as the degree Celsius.
Temperature (practical)	degree Celsius	The degree Celsius is the temperature in kelvins minus 273.15. The Celsius scale was formerly called centigrade.

Source: Standard for Metric Practice, ASTM E 380-76, IEEE 268-1976, American Society for Testing and Materials, 1916 Race Street, Philadelphia, PA 19103.

APPENDIX C

ALPHABETICAL LIST OF UNITS WITH THEIR SI NAMES AND CONVERSION FACTORS

To convert from	to	Symbol	Multiply by
Acre (U.S. survey)	square meter	m²	4.047×10^3
Acre-foot	cubic meter	m³	1.233×10^3
Atmosphere (standard)	pascal	Pa	1.013×10^5
Board foot	cubic meter	m³	$2.359 \div 10^3$
Degrees Celsius	kelvin	K	$t_K = t_{°C} + 273.15$
Degree Fahrenheit	Celsius degree	°C	$t_{°C} = (t_{°F} - 32)/1.8$
Degree Fahrenheit	kelvin	K	$t_K = (t_{°F} + 459.67)/1.8$
(Degree) Kelvin	Celsius degree	°C	$t_{°C} = t_K - 273.15$
Foot	meter	m	$3.048 \div 10$
Foot, square	square meter	m²	$9.290 \div 10^2$
Foot, cubic	cubic meter	m³	$2.831 \div 10^2$
Feet, cubic, per minute	cubic meters per second	m³/s	$4.917 \div 10^4$
Feet per second	meters per second	m/s	$3.048 \div 10$
Foot-pound force	joule	J	1.355×1
Foot-pounds per minute	watt	W	$2.259 \div 10^2$
Foot-pounds per second	watt	W	1.355×1
Gallon (U.S. liquid)	cubic meter	m³	$3.785 \div 10^3$
Gallons per minute	cubic meters per second	m³/s	$6.309 \div 10^5$

To convert from	to	Symbol	Multiply by
Horsepower (550 ft-lb/sec)	watt	W	7.457×10^2
Horsepower	kilowatt	kW	$7.457 \div 10$
Inch	meter	m	$2.540 \div 10^2$
Inch, square	square meter	m^2	$6.452 \div 10^4$
Inch, cubic	cubic meter	m^3	$1.639 \div 10^5$
Inch	millimeter	mm	2.540×10
Kelvin	degree Celsius	°C	$t_{°C} = t_K - 273.15$
Mile	meter	m	1.609×10^3
Mile	kilometer	km	1.609×1
Miles per hour	kilometers per hour	km/h	1.609×1
Miles per minute	meters per second	m/s	2.682×10
Pound	kilogram	kg	$4.534 \div 10$
Pounds per cubic yard	kilograms per cubic meter	kg/m^3	$5.933 \div 10$
Pounds per cubic foot	kilograms per cubic meter	kg/m^3	1.602×10
Pounds per gallon (U.S.)	kilograms per cubic meter	kg/m^3	1.198×10^2
Pounds per square foot	kilograms per square meter	kg/m^2	4.882×1
Pounds per square inch (psi)	pascal	Pa	6.895×10^3
Ton (2,000 lb)	kilogram	kg	9.072×10^2
Ton (2,240 lb)	kilogram	kg	1.016×10^3
Ton (metric)	kilogram	kg	1.000×10^3
Tons (2,000 lb) per hour	kilograms per second	kg/s	$2.520 \div 10$
Yard, cubic	cubic meter	m^3	$7.646 \div 10$
Yards, cubic, per hour	cubic meter per hour	m^3/h	$7.646 \div 10$

Note: All SI symbols are expressed in lowercase letters except those that are used to designate a person, which are capitalized.

Sources: Standard for Metric Practice, ASTM E 380-76, IEEE 268-1976, American Society for Testing and Materials, 1916 Race Street, Philadelphia, PA 19103.

National Standard of Canada Metric Practice Guide, CAN-3-001-02-73/CSA Z 234.1-1973, Canadian Standards Association, 178 Rexdale Boulevard, Rexdale, Ontario, Canada M94 IRS.

APPENDIX
D

SELECTED ENGLISH TO SI CONVERSION FACTORS

In general, the units appearing in this list do not appear in the list of SI units but they are used frequently, and it is probable that they will continue to be used by the construction industry. The units meter and liter may be spelled metre and litre. Both spellings are acceptable.

Multiply USC (English) unit	by	To obtain metric unit
Acre	0.4047	Hectare
Cubic foot	0.0283	Cubic meter
Foot-pound	0.1383	Kilogram-meter
Gallon (U.S.)	0.833	Imperial gallon
Gallon (U.S.)	3.785	Liters
Horsepower	1.014	Metric horsepower
Cubic inch	0.016	Liter
Square inch	6.452	Square centimeter
Miles per hour	1.610	Kilometers per hour
Ounce	28.350	Grams
Pounds per square inch	0.0689	Bars
Pounds per square inch	0.0703	Kilograms per square centimeter

SELECTED U.S. CUSTOMARY (ENGLISH) UNIT EQUIVALENTS

Unit	Equivalent
1 acre	43,560 square feet
1 atmosphere	14.7 lb per square inch
1 Btu	788 foot-pounds
1 Btu	0.000393 horsepower-hour
1 foot	12 inches
1 cubic foot	7.48 gallons liquid
1 square foot	144 square inches
1 gallon	231 cubic inches
1 gallon	4 quarts liquid
1 horsepower	550 foot-pounds per second
1 mile	5,280 feet
1 mile	1,760 yards
1 square mile	640 acres
1 pound	16 ounces avoirdupois
1 quart	32 fluid ounces
1 long ton	2,240 pounds
1 short ton	2,000 pounds

APPENDIX
F

SELECTED METRIC UNIT EQUIVALENTS

Unit	Equivalent
1 centimeter	10 millimeters
1 square centimeter	100 square millimeters
1 hectare	10,000 square meters
1 kilogram	1,000 grams
1 liter	1,000 cubic centimeters
1 meter	100 centimeters
1 kilometer	1,000 meters
1 cubic meter	1,000 liters
1 square meter	10,000 square centimeters
1 square kilometer	100 hectares
1 kilogram per square meter	0.97 atmosphere
1 metric ton	1,000 kilograms

INDEX